Global politics in the 7

Objective, critical, optimistic, and with a global focus, this textbook combines international relations theory, history, up-to-date research, and current affairs to give students a comprehensive, unbiased understanding of international politics. It integrates theory and traditional approaches with globalization and research on newer topics such as terrorism, the rise of new economic superpowers, and the impact of global communications and social networking to offer the ideal breadth and depth of coverage for a one-semester undergraduate course. Student learning is supported and enhanced by box features and "Close Up" sections with context and further information; "Critical Case Studies" that highlight controversial and complex current affairs topics and show how the world works in practice; and questions to stimulate discussion, review key concepts, and encourage further study. It brilliantly demonstrates the significance and interconnectedness of globalization and new security challenges in the 21st century and illuminates the role of leadership in transnational crises.

Dr. Robert J. Jackson is the Fletcher Jones Professor of Government at the University of Redlands in California. He is a Senior Associate at St. Antony's College and Visiting Fellow at the Changing Character of War Programme at the University of Oxford. He also holds the positions of Distinguished Research Professor of Political Science at Carleton University in Ottawa, Canada, and Life Member and Visiting Fellow at Clare Hall and the Centre of International Studies, University of Cambridge, England. He is an Associate Fellow in International Security at Chatham House (Royal Institute of International Affairs), London.

Global politics in the 21st century

ROBERT J. JACKSON

University of Redlands, California

CAMBRIDGE
UNIVERSITY PRESS

CAMBRIDGE
UNIVERSITY PRESS

32 Avenue of the Americas, New York, NY 10013-2473, USA

Cambridge University Press is part of the University of Cambridge.

It furthers the University's mission by disseminating knowledge in the pursuit of education, learning, and research at the highest international levels of excellence.

www.cambridge.org
Information on this title: www.cambridge.org/9780521756532

First published 2013

Printed in the United States of America

A catalog record for this publication is available from the British Library.

Library of Congress Cataloging in Publication Data
Jackson, Robert J.
Global politics in the 21st century / Robert J. Jackson, University of Redlands.
  pages cm
Includes bibliographical references and index.
ISBN 978-0-521-76745-3 – ISBN 978-0-521-75653-2 (pbk.)
1. International relations – History – 21st century.   2. World politics – 21st century.
I. Title.
JZ1318.J333   2013
327–dc23   2012036734

ISBN 978-0-521-76745-3 Hardback
ISBN 978-0-521-75653-2 Paperback

For Doreen – Love from the beginning to the end

Brief contents

Contents

Preface

With the advent of modern mass communications, readers are bombarded with colorful images of the world's political events. They can ascertain quickly from international news the changing realities around them. However, to make sense of these ad hoc, seemingly disparate events, students need conceptual clarifications, interpretative tools, and a basic understanding of the world and how their own country fits into it. They need to understand global politics as a whole.

Individuals today are no longer isolated but are active participants connected to the world through Internet and social networking technologies. The vocabulary has changed. Words such as *Facebook*, *Twitter*, *Apps*, and *Cloud* have meanings today that differ entirely from those less than a decade ago. In other words, at a low level students are already engaged, and to some extent knowledgeable, when they begin to study global politics. They need, however, to be encouraged to understand that making good choices requires being informed and reflective. To do this, they need to read, inquire, debate, and consider; not push facts and ideas into convenient boxes if they do not belong there. As well, the study of global politics is not simply moralizing. Political affairs certainly have an ethical dimension, but they are not solely about morality. And keeping thoughts clear and straightforward and avoiding jargon is vital. As one wag put it, "What did you have for breakfast – the upper part of a hog's hind leg with two ovals encased in a shell laid by a female bird?" Or bacon and eggs?

With the new world situation in view, *Global Politics in the 21st Century* has two goals. The first is to introduce students in universities and colleges to the field of global politics. To do this, by stock taking and analysis, the book maps how the world works, making an effort to be objective and dispassionate about the systems of politics – inclusive not exclusive, critical not sensational, optimistic not pessimistic. The second goal is to introduce theories and methods. With the world as a laboratory, the challenge is to understand the basic concepts, themes, and ideas about global politics and apply them to the world's diverse problems.

This volume does not set out to teach readers *what* to think about the push and pull of conflicting ideas about global politics but *how* to think. As they encounter new ideas, individuals need to learn to be averse to absolutes and understand that there are no "right" or "wrong" answers to questions of global politics. This approach was appreciated by the great French writer Voltaire, who said that he honored the man who seeks truth but despised the many who claimed to have found it! It is in this vein that the book tries to avoid political correctness, to be fair in commenting on the reigning orthodoxies that compete for attention, and to look fairly at the assumptions and biases of both questions and answers. Students need to openly ponder questions even when they cannot resolve them. They may find that the disagreements are actually often over definitions and forms of framing questions.

If, as this author believes, the purpose of a liberal education is to unsettle assumptions and reveal what is going on behind appearances, students need to learn about key historical events and processes of global politics. They also need to learn alternative approaches and theories of the discipline and world issues, engaging facts and theories with critical and challenging thinking. Not all students will take up the "question-driven" life of academics, but an eclectic understanding of theory will enable them to examine the strengths and weaknesses of claims about the world in which they live. Perhaps, following Winston Churchill, they will at least appreciate that fanatics are those who cannot change their minds and will not change the topic.

Since the approach of this text is not dominated by any single paradigm that would force the analysis into a straitjacket, it does not attempt to fit each theory to every case and problem. Applying ideas from international relations theory into problems they cannot appropriately address is akin to using constitutional law principles to discuss parties and electoral behavior. Even in physics there is not an agreement on *one* fundamental theory of reality, so it is not surprising that political scientists have disagreements and jousting matches about interpretations, theories, and judgments. In this book, therefore, theories are employed when they are pertinent. As one French scholar mockingly questioned, "I know this works in practice, but does it work in theory?"

University students sometimes complain that professors too often shunt aside the "real world" in a quest for certainty about theory. Conceptual rigor is valuable, but academic authors often do talk to and about one another rather than engaging students' concerns. Writers and political theorists, on the whole, tend to be contrarians, comfortable sorting out and balancing opposing principles and conflicting theories. Their debates sometimes leave students nonplussed because they do not pose concrete problems to solve. Have political scientists been relinquishing the role of intelligent commentator on global affairs too much to journalists and others? Have academics relegated themselves to scholarly infighting rather than competing in the public world of ideas and clashes of opinion over policy? These are fair questions and implied criticisms.

In this regard, throughout the book, up-to-date graphs, tables, photos, and contemporary "Close-Ups" and "Critical Case Studies" are used to illustrate concepts, theories, and events. Carefully chosen and stimulating examples are in every chapter; for example, the Iranian nuclear problem is used to illustrate the importance of applying various levels of analysis to study issues and the Afghanistan war is analyzed from the point of view of different theories in international relations. A great number of timely and significant issues are examined, including the role of social networking; the nuclear crisis in Fukushima, Japan; the Arab Awakening in the Middle East and North Africa; the internal wars in Somalia, Sudan, and Congo; and the use of children in armed conflict. The section on war provides a deep analysis of the U.S. wars in Iraq and Afghanistan. This is only a small sample of the relevant and dramatic use of examples to illustrate general principles and significant arguments about global politics.

The book invites students to explore the exciting world of global politics, to pursue areas of interest, and to expand their knowledge while building their understanding of world events on a historical and theoretical foundation. Those who take up the challenge will be rewarded by a deep understanding of the complexity of global issues, driven as they are by the forces of globalization and the changing nature of security.

Organization of the book

This book is organized into five parts and sixteen chapters. Part I covers the foundations of global politics. It comprises three chapters that outline important fundamentals. Chapter 1 provides an overview of three significant issues that interact to create a pattern of world politics: the perpetual quest for security, the march of globalization, and the ongoing role of states and identities on the world stage. To learn how we ended up with six major power centers today, Chapter 2 traces the rise and fall of the world's most important powers and extended empires from the earliest recorded history in Babylon until the end of the Cold War. Chapter 3 discusses levels of analysis and methods and outlines the best-known theories of international relations and their offshoots – realism, liberalism, political economy (Marxism and public choice), social constructivism, feminism, and critical approaches.

Part II on institutions and actors in global politics consists of five chapters. It outlines the role of states, their leaders, and their challengers in international affairs. The first two chapters in this part describe political authority, global power, and the importance of the six major powers, placing them in the context of contemporary international discussions. Chapter 4 outlines the role of states and their leaders, assessing them in terms of their power, capabilities, and decision making. Chapter 5 maps the distribution of power and influence in the modern world, paying particular attention to the United States, China, Russia, India, Japan, and the European Union. Chapter 6 focuses on important aspects of global governance in our interdependent but disordered world. Chapters 7 and 8 depart from discussing states, concentrating instead on the role of other actors, social movements, the media and social networking, and forces such as identity and religion in global politics.

Part III on global conflict and war examines violent conflict in global politics. The character of war has changed dramatically over the centuries not only in terms of technology and strategy but also in terms of the security dilemmas posed as states try to protect themselves and their citizens. Chapter 9 focuses on international war and its causes, conduct, and consequences. The advent of the nuclear era changed the basic concepts of national security and brought new issues of arms control to the fore and the establishment of new security organizations. With the end of the Cold War, the nature of war began to change again; civil war became more typical, and international terrorism erupted with a new intensity. The chapter examines issues such as weapons of mass destruction, alliance formation, and the ethics of war. Chapter 10 changes the focus to internal or civil wars and insurgencies, in particular the wars in Afghanistan, Iraq, Libya, and Syria. It deals with the failing states of Somalia, Sudan, and South Sudan and the 2011–13 Arab uprisings in the Middle East and North Africa. Private armies and new technologies such as robots and drones are also examined in the context of the changing nature of war, in particular targeted killing. Chapter 11 focuses on terrorism and counterterrorism, including nuclear terrorism and al-Qaeda.

Part IV on the politics of global economics introduces the reader to the international aspects of economics. Chapter 12 outlines and assesses the various concepts and theories essential to understanding this field. It considers the importance of liberal internationalism, economic nationalism, neo-Marxism, and state capitalism. Problems of global economic governance are discussed in terms of the benefits and criticisms of such organizations as the World Bank, the International Monetary Fund, and the World Trade Organization. The chapter concludes with a discussion of the recent global economic downturn, the European financial crisis, and current issues of government debt and economic reform. Chapter 13 deals with global inequalities. It assesses the winners and losers among states and peoples in the global economy and discusses the issues of poverty and how they are being addressed by the UN Millennium Development Goals.

Part V on global challenges and prospects examines how, as globalization continues, more and more issues have both domestic and international ramifications and implications. Many of the major issues of the 21st century are "intermestic" in nature and cannot be solved by single states, no matter how powerful. Chapter 14 addresses human rights concerns such as ethnic group persecution, genocide, and the abuses of women and children in war situations. It debates the role of international institutions in providing human security for all. Chapter 15 focuses on threats related to the global environment, population, and health. The degradation of the earth's air, soil, and water, as well as the reliance on dirty, nonrenewable energy to power our economies, combined with demographic issues such as aging, massive international migration, and world health issues such as pandemics are pressing and critical issues that involve the entire globe. Chapter 16 draws our study of global politics together with a discussion of crises and ethics based on the issues that have been presented throughout the book and points us toward the future.

Acknowledgments

Few scholars can have been blessed with the support received for this project. Many institutions and individuals have helped with various aspects of my research and deserve particular mention and genuine thanks for their outstanding contributions and encouragement. The Fletcher Jones Foundation in Pasadena, California, has provided vital support by sponsoring my endowed chair at the University of Redlands in California. I have been allowed the leisure and good fortune to work and study as a member of the vibrant Department of Government. My colleagues have been generous with their time and patience – led by our chair, Renee van Vechen, and the indefatigable Graeme Auton, I have been aided by many colleagues, including Michael N'Quinn, Art Svenson, Greg Thorson, and Steve Wuhs.

Many other fine scholars at the university have contributed to this book. Jack Osborn in the Department of Global Business has been a friend and consultant on many occasions. Our talented administrator, Starla Strain, has been a joy to work with for several years. Students in my Advanced Seminar on International Relations and Comparative Politics have taught me much about what American students need to learn about the world in which they one day will hold responsible positions – as our alumni already do in Washington, Sacramento, and elsewhere. Of course, much credit must also be given for the stimulating questions from thousands of undergraduate and graduate students of global politics over decades of teaching at Canadian, British, and American universities.

Abroad, in the outposts (sic) of tradition, learning, and eccentricities in the Universities of Oxford and Cambridge, I have been aided as well by outstanding colleagues and scholars. At Cambridge special mention must be made of Clare Hall, a college devoted to advanced studies, and the Centre of International Studies, which hosted me over several years. The prominent Peterhouse historian Brendan Simms has been helpful on many topics, as has the astute Stefan Halper of Magdalene College on U.S.–China relations. My former coauthor and wise friend Philip Towle has been extremely helpful and generous on countless opportunities in many countries and continents.

At Oxford I have had the privilege of dining at High Table at St. Antony's College with such luminaries as Sir Adam Roberts, Dr. Rosemary Foot, and the delightful and wise warden Margaret Macmillan. My work on war and peace has been stimulated by being a continuing visiting Fellow at the Changing Character of War program, under the direction of Sir Hew Strachan, Chichele Professor of the History of War. Pembroke College, with its inspirational literary figures such as Dr. Samuel Johnson and legal authority William Blackstone, was my first home in Oxford. The late master of the college R. B. McCallum first introduced me to university politics – and fine wine – while David Butler tutored me about psephology and sherry. In London, as an associate Fellow in international security at Chatham House, I have learned a great deal about policy research from Paul Cornish (now professor at Bath University), and I have benefited from the friendship of the new director, Patricia Lewis, Claire Yorke, and others. The Oxford and Cambridge Club remains my home away from home.

In the dominions, I retain my long-term and wonderful association with Carleton University in Ottawa, where I hold the title of distinguished professor and teach courses on international security. There, my friend and chair of the Department of Political Science and political economy expert, Randall Germain, has instructed me through his writings on global political economy. Long-standing friends and scholars Scott E. Bennett, Piotr Dutkiewicz, Ken Hart, Glen Williams, and Conrad Winn have informed me throughout the years. Also in Ottawa, my dear friend Michael Behiels, at the University of Ottawa, has been a beacon of light about world history and the need to adhere rigorously to the canons of research strategy. In Canberra at the European Centre at the Australian National University and in Brisbane with the Centre of Excellence in Policing and Security at Griffith University, my friend, director Simon Bronitt, has given excellent advice and has hosted me on numerous occasions. My friend and best-selling author Professor Patrick Weller continues to instruct me about the importance of institutions in politics.

The book has benefited from the constructive and brilliant comments of six anonymous reviewers who can now be revealed as Yoram Z. Haftel, University of Illinois at Chicago; Patrick James, University of Southern California; Karen T. Litfin, University of Washington; Kristina Mani, Oberlin College; Richard Nolan, University of Florida; and Alexander Thompson, The Ohio State University.

It is widely agreed that Cambridge University Press is the best publisher of books on topics such as history, political science, and international relations. I can attest to the extremely high quality of its staff. In New York, they include Robert Dreesen, who gave exemplary advice and guidance throughout the project; James Dunn, who skillfully managed the whole process; and senior editorial assistant Abigail Zorbaugh. In Cambridge, the team is led by the sage Catherine Flack with Raihana Begum and Charles Howell. Peggy Rote, of Aptara, Inc., who directed the copyediting, was a tower of strength.

Dr. Nicole Jackson, of the School of International Studies at Simon Fraser University, has been an excellent source of ideas and commentary throughout the project on theory and ideas about global politics generally and about Russia and Central Asia specifically. I also thank Professor Carl Hodge of the University of British Columbia, who read every word of the text. He may not have agreed with everything he read, but his comments were invaluable. My debt to him is beyond comment – well, OK, thanks a million, Carl.

Last, I want to thank my wife and coauthor of many books throughout the years. The book is dedicated to Doreen. Without her analysis and assiduous academic work and brilliant judgment on the whole manuscript, it would never have been completed. She is the beginning and the end of my life, my alpha and omega.

While acknowledging my debt to all these individuals, I accept full responsibility for any errors, omissions, and interpretations in the book. If you have comments, suggestions, or questions about this book, or simply want to carry on a dialogue about global politics, contact the author at Robert_Jackson@redlands.edu.

Part I

Foundations of global politics

We cannot always build the future for our youth but we can build our youth for the future.

FRANKLIN D. ROOSEVELT, 32ND PRESIDENT OF THE UNITED STATES

The three chapters that comprise Part I of this book outline important fundamentals for the study of contemporary global politics. They take a pragmatic approach, highlighting the complexities of the subject and recognizing the contributions of historians and modern theorists. They show the need for a question-driven approach by stressing the significance of history and theory to an understanding of how our disordered world works.

Chapter 1 discusses three significant topics that profoundly influence the patterns of world politics today: the perpetual quest for security, the march of globalization, and the complex role of states and identities. Together they help us understand the continuities and changes in global politics.

Chapter 2 shows that the study of global politics requires an understanding of history that is not limited to Europe and North America. It traces the rise and fall of the world's extended empires and great powers from the earliest recorded history to the end of the Cold War. For many centuries it was not clear whether Asia, Europe, or the Middle East would dominate the world. The rise of the modern state and the economic progress that followed the industrial revolution tipped the scale in favor of Europe and, later, the United States. The chapter traces the historical patterns of interaction of the world's great powers over time, concluding with the six areas that dominate global politics today: the United States, China, Japan, India, Russia, and the European Union. In Part II we focus on these great powers today and ask whether the balance of power is about to shift again.

Chapter 3 highlights a broad set of ideas and universal themes about global politics that provide analytical frameworks for the study. It discusses how to approach the subject through levels of analysis and methods and then outlines the best-known and most useful theories that help make sense of our world – realism, liberalism, political economy (Marxism and public choice), social constructivism, feminism, and critical approaches. These theories help guide our enquiry throughout the book and enable us to understand events and behavior in global politics.

Introduction to global politics

The world faces many threats to human security and prosperity in the 21st century. Many of them are from people; others are products of the economic and physical environment. Recently, the U.S. Commission on the Prevention of Weapons of Mass Destruction Proliferation and Terrorism produced a slim, powerful volume on future world risks.[1] It concluded that we know the threats we face, we know that our margin of safety is shrinking, and we also know what must be done to counter the risks. With similar concern, the Secretary-General of the United Nations, Ban Ki-moon, declared that rising temperatures due to climate change would "increase pressure on water, food, and land; reverse years of development gains; exacerbate poverty; destabilize fragile states; and topple governments."[2]

This book describes and explains the factors behind these and other global issues and invites readers to consider whether the conclusions and warnings of the U.S. president's advisors and the leader of the world organization were well founded. It challenges readers to study, understand, and evaluate power and responsibility in global politics. The most serious threats today include the proliferation of weapons of mass destruction, worldwide terrorist networks, the tenuous end to the wars in Afghanistan and Iraq, armed conflict in the Middle East and North and Central Africa, world financial

crises, global climate change, global reliance on oil, global poverty, global infectious diseases, and the rising power of hostile actors on the world stage. These and other issues are, or should be, of deep concern to everyone in all parts of our evermore connected world.

Global politics is a dynamic, messy, constantly evolving phenomenon. It is a stimulating, inspiring, even transformational field of study. But it is also ambiguous and puzzling. Students engage with global politics constantly – when friends or family members join the military; when foreign terrorists attack major cities like New York, Washington, London, Madrid, or Mumbai; and when they travel abroad and have trouble obtaining clean water, health care, proper sanitation, and personal security.

A student can easily relate to the three following hypothetical scenarios, the first of which takes place in Spain:

American undergraduates are wandering through the gardens and antechambers of the Alhambra Palace in Granada. They gawk at the intricate lacework decorating the ceiling of the Hall of Diplomats. Having been deprived of all but U.S. history, they are truly amazed when t heir guide tells them that the same year the Spanish Queen sent Christopher Columbus to find the Americas in 1492 she also expelled the Muslims from Spain, forcing them back to Africa and the Middle East, laying the base for the geographical divisions between Christians and Muslims that we experience today. Later that day, the students learn from the International Herald Tribune that the United States and its allies have attacked Baghdad, Iraq, a city in a leading Muslim country, in response to the 9/11 terrorist attacks on the United States.

---

[1] Bob Graham, et al., *The World at Risk: The Report of the Commission on the Prevention of Weapons of Mass Destruction, Proliferation and Terrorism* (New York: Random House, 2008).

[2] Quoted in *The New Yorker*, October 5, 2009, p.23.

The second scenario takes place in Eastern Europe:

A Canadian student is enjoying a coffee at a Starbucks in Poti, Georgia. She and her two friends are surprised that the brew is exactly the same as the one they drink in their home towns of Vancouver, Los Angeles, and New York. Why is Starbucks always the same, they wonder. Where did they get the coffee? How did it get here? As they contemplate these questions of political economy another event consumes their attention. The television, tuned to CNN in London, announces that Russia has just attacked Georgia, not far from where they are in Poti. They grab their cell phones in anticipation of sending texts and pictures of tanks and soldiers to their friends and parents back home. Only yesterday at the same café, they had listened to results of a girl's swim meet at the Olympics in Beijing. Perhaps tomorrow there would be news about the winter Olympics in Vancouver or about genocide in Darfur, Sudan.

The third scenario takes place in Iran:

Iranian students are sipping tea outside Teheran University. They glance up at the television to see Leon Panetta, former director of the dreaded CIA, describing how no film had been taken of the actual killing of Osama bin Laden by U.S. special forces. "These damned Americans," they muse, "who do they think they are!" Then, they turn to complaining about the lack of civil liberties in their own country and the dictatorial President Ahmadinejad before resuming their ongoing discussions about how the only way Iran can protect itself is by getting nuclear weapons.

Traveling, like education, can be humbling. How do the students interpret these snippets of world news? Daily, they receive disjointed images of violence, pain, death, and chaos, along with more hopeful stories and information that provide continuity and meaning to their life experiences. They form strong perspectives about what can be done about the problems of world conflict and violence. There are many ways to think about global politics, and there is more than one side to each story, but unfortunately, as the students quickly find out, the media rarely provide context for the news they report. As the old adage goes, if a plane takes off and lands, it is not news. If it crashes, it is. If it crashes because a terrorist bomb was aboard, it is headline news. But is it accurate bad news, or is it exaggerated and distorted?

The daily news is little more than a series of video clips so slowed down that we get to view only one issue at a time. It is as if events are not connected through history and society. We never get to see the complete story, just fragments – or, in the cases described previously, disjointed events. In democracies, we continually hope that the media will lead discussions of public affairs, but they rarely do. Its superficiality is illustrated by the vulgarity and sensationalism of its output. We are fed a steady diet of scandals, secrets, outrages, conflicts, quarrels, sex, celebrities, and gossip. The media is less concerned with what is in the public interest than with what interests the public!

In *A Passage to India*, the great English novelist E. M. Forster advises us to "connect, only connect." But connection is difficult even with television, radio, cell phones, the Internet, Facebook, and Twitter. We want to link our inner moral worlds to the reality outside ourselves – but it is difficult. Our perceptions are distorted by emotions – fear, empathy, helplessness, love of country – and yet our knowledge base is often too slim to meaningfully integrate events from foreign countries. In recent years, the international news has been dominated by such issues as terrorism and civil wars in the Middle East, genocide and poverty in Central Africa, earthquakes in South America and Asia, a global economic depression, and the possibility of Iran obtaining nuclear weapons. These issues are constantly changing, and new ones are considered just as vital. To understand them, comprehend how they are shaping the global agenda, and assess how policymakers are approaching them, students need a background understanding of global politics. If students want to help end hatred, alleviate poverty, reduce the likelihood of war, and prevent global environmental degradation, they need to understand the factors underlying world issues and how actors in the international environment approach them.

In the chapters of this book, we cover the foundations of the discipline of international relations from a global perspective. We attempt to provide a degree of unity to a disorganized, somewhat shapeless body of information about world politics. The world is a complicated, interrelated, and violent place and the media generally do little to clarify the patterns and make the connections that transform information into knowledge. It is difficult, maybe impossible, to comprehend, let alone judge, the blurbs, bits, and bytes of current news as the broad brush of global politics covers a massive amount of material in which fact competes with opinion.

Apart from specific topics in the news, there are many large, emerging issues and challenges in our changing world. Is the power of the United States diminishing? Is its hegemony on the decline? Is the globalization of trade and finance a force for good or bad? Can it be halted? Is the process weakening sovereign states? Is it increasing the power of societal, international, and transnational actors? What are the sources of and solutions to international terrorism? What are the causes and consequences of global economic inequality? Why is there an Arab Awakening in much of North Africa and the Middle East?

It is hard to be an informed citizen and not study global politics. Close Up 1.1 considers some practical reasons for wanting to do so.

Close Up 1.1 **Why study global politics?**

Global politics provides a broad understanding of the world that makes one a more informed and discriminating member of society. In doing so it opens a vast number of career options. A few students will become so fascinated with the subject that they will choose to stay in the field, teaching in a school, college, or university where they can continue to do research and explore with their students the vital issues of our disordered world. The various levels of government also employ millions of people, and employment possibilities span branches dealing with a wide range of international issues and social concerns. Politicians also require the services of consultants and other aides.

Many other professions deal with domestic and foreign governments on a regular basis and they, too, require people who understand how governments work. They need people with the political knowledge, exploratory skills, and methods of analysis that come from studying global politics. Many graduates will therefore find that their courses have given them an extremely useful background for careers in fields such as journalism, law, business, government, interest groups, political activism, social work, and nongovernmental organization (NGO) administration.

Even those who do not wish to specialize in global politics will find that training in this field provides a useful background for many other career choices – sometimes directly following a BA, sometimes later. It can be a stepping stone to law school, journalism school, or some other specialty. But perhaps most importantly, global politics provides an understanding of how the world works, and that is a necessary ingredient for informed citizenship.

Global politics

To understand global politics, students need to get beyond Cold War paradigms about how to conceptualize about the world. They also need to study global politics less in terms of their own country's interests and more in terms of the global concerns of others. They need to widen their horizons beyond their comfortable, familiar environment, and relate to the wider world in which they find themselves. For most people around the world, the immediate issues are not nuclear warfare or international terrorism but rather those that involve meeting basic human needs such as safe drinking water, the elimination of hunger and malnutrition, and the lack of fuel. Students need to experience the world in all its complexity – to challenge the idea that the world can be understood from a single viewpoint. A distinguishing characteristic of new studies of global politics is the concern to expand beyond the U.S.- or Euro-centric view of the world to include the concerns of all seven billion people who share this globe.

Globalization, security, and the global system

International relations has traditionally been studied as the relations among states, while global politics has been defined as the basic patterns of international beliefs and behavior that help define and condition states and other actors. The chapters of this book examine the themes of global politics and illustrate them with important contemporary events. They contextualize the past to illuminate the present, straightforwardly presenting the historical and theoretical perspectives required to fully understand the contemporary world. They discuss the bracing effects that globalization and the search for security have on global affairs, including how to manage the differences that are emerging because of the new global configurations of power and responsibilities.

The domestic politics of individual states are not independent of the relations among countries, and international relations are interwoven with the realities of a variety of different governments throughout the world. As the world grows more interdependent, global politics wields a growing influence on the domestic decision making of political leaders. No country, however powerful, is totally self-sufficient or independent because the actions of each state have repercussions for the others. A great many issues today are intermestic, that is, they are simultaneously domestic and transnational or global. Some pundits even use the coined word

glocal, meaning global and local at the same time, to characterize this reality.

The global system refers to the broad network of relations among states and the activities of their citizens and nonstate institutions in the world. It patterns the behavior of states and nongovernmental actors. The foreign policy of countries, on the other hand, is narrower. It depicts state or government behavior that has external ramifications, including diplomatic and military relations among states. Foreign policy is at the forefront of the study of global politics, but understanding foreign policy requires one to look beyond his or her own state borders to consider the world as a whole. It necessitates thinking and caring about global politics as well as one's personal cultural, economic, technological, and, increasingly, ecological interests. In other words, to comprehend foreign policy and global politics it is necessary to interpret the changing world.

In order to provide a map for examining the world, this book introduces students to the *old* and *new* security issues and dilemmas that characterize the contemporary world. The old security issues refer basically to state security and how states maintain their vitality in the world. The new security issues and dilemmas are about how both states and societies are affected, and perhaps afflicted by, nonstate actors such as networks of terrorists and others who would harm people around the world. They include issues of human security that are posed by economic inequalities, illness, and environmental degradation. The old concept of security is well established in the study of international relations. The new security issues are not as developed and do not constitute uniform concepts or theories in the discipline. Nevertheless, they are central to an understanding of global politics today and vital for achieving a secure future for all of us.

Pablo Picasso's awesome painting *Guernica* expresses the universal horror of war (Figure 1.1). There is nothing accidental or by chance in his work. The painting graphically describes in painful detail the deaths and injuries that resulted on April 26, 1937, when General Franco's allies in the

Spanish Civil War, the German Luftwaffe and Italian air force, bombed the city of Guernica, killing 1,654 civilians. It was the first major event of modern warfare, a horrific expression of what would become known as the importance of *air power* – the use of bombardment not to kill enemy soldiers but to put pummel civilians into submission. This sickening new form of winning wars proved emblematic of the Spanish Civil War and the brutality toward noncombatants that would escalate over the rest of the 20th century to include Nazi death camps, atomic bombs on Hiroshima and Nagasaki, the use of Agent Orange in Vietnam, and other brutal, indiscriminate assaults on civilians.

Picasso's *Guernica* raises timeless issues of war and security. Before people can lead healthy and productive lives they must have security. It is the most important requirement for human societies and it is the primary function of states and international organizations to provide it. Until the end of World War II, wars between empires and states were a common form of mass violence, but since then internal or civil wars have become more customary. Since 9/11, terrorism against states and individuals has joined civil war as the subject most in the news. Terrorists do not negotiate or play the democratic game of politics. Instead, they vent their anger in suicide bombings and target civilians with improvised explosive devices. They have no desire for dialogue, preferring to become martyrs or cut off heads and display carcasses on the Internet. Certainly, if there is another event on the scale of 9/11, people will be taking off more than their shoes at the airport.

Another factor that distinguishes traditional international relations courses from new studies is the concern for global issues. Proponents of new studies do not wish to stray from the conceptual and theoretical aspects of the standard problems, but they also want to address global problems. Isolating trends and analyzing the changing nature of the disordered world has become of primary importance because of urgent problems in the global economy, global health, and the global environment. We need to understand the world's mutual interests and develop shared solutions to common risks.

At one time in ancient Greece the human condition was attributed to the gods, who people believed created the forces of history and caused societal failures and successes. As the Greeks were jealous of the various deities for their lifestyle and longevity, they created the idea of the Olympics so that man could aspire to a status somewhere between gods and humans. Those who won athletic contests were accorded divine-like characteristics, much as well-known sport figures are today. Today we attribute the human condition to forces that are greater than individuals – forces such as the social, economic, climatic, and political conditions that drive human history.

In our study of global politics we expect to make some progress in analysis and explanation – to achieve some tying up of the threads. These are unusual times; no other period is really comparable. And yet we still need to try to understand the forces that drive the human condition. Emblematic of the present situation is how big events such as the 2008–09 worldwide financial meltdown affect everyone from adults in New York to children in Darfur and how small events like the hijacking of ships by pirates off the east coast of Africa or the occurrence of swine flu in Mexico disrupt lives elsewhere. The broadest term used when discussing these diverse phenomena is globalization, the integration of states and people through increasing contact, communication, and trade that binds the world together.

The globalization issue haunts contemporary analysis of world politics. The widespread financial crisis of 2008–09 affected not only the abstract economy but the lives of millions of people, perhaps even the international order. Although poverty has always been with us, globalization and the recent economic meltdown have exacerbated the inequalities of wealth inside states and around the world. Indeed, today the international systems for monitoring the global economy, health, and conflict are now so sensitive that, on occasion,

Figure 1.1 Picasso's graphic painting captures the horrors of war. The indiscriminate killing of noncombatants from the air in the town of Guernica during the Spanish Civil War was a premonition of wars to follow. *Source:* DACS and Bridgman.

they provide forewarnings that are overly sensitive and scare people more than they help avert catastrophes.

Globalization and global politics

The idea that the world has become more interdependent is commonplace today. Indeed, Jules Verne's book *Around the World in Eighty Days*, published in 1873, suggested that the world was shrinking in size. In it, Phileas Fogg circumnavigated the globe with unprecedented speed to prove to his wagerers in the Reform Club that "the world has grown smaller." In recent years, academics and policymakers have adopted the term *globalization* as if it were something completely novel. But as we see in Chapter 2, the process has deep historical roots. Patterns of trade, finance, migration, intercultural influence, and even international systems have

Figure 1.1 (*continued*)

been developing and undergoing constant change from the beginning of history.

But there is something novel in today's globalization. It is connecting more people and connecting them more closely. Current issues concern not only the existence of globalization as a process but also its rapid development and its impact on state power. This new form of globalization has both critics and supporters. Some theorists believe that globalization has taken on a life of its own – that it creates new institutions and problems – while others, more optimistically, think that globalization is a positive force for good, creating "a world society and culture." Many issues that in the past mobilized individuals, groups, and states now possess an international dimension. However, globalization and the march toward one global system do not mean that all states and people are affected in a similar manner. The process has, and will continue to have, divergent effects – both good and bad – in different countries and also on peace and war. Despite important and sometimes bitter differences over its normative importance, however, there is no denying the extensive impact of the march of what goes on under the loose rubric of globalization (Figure 1.2).

Globalization means that business, politics, and even the media are becoming more closely intertwined. It means that the world is growing increasingly integrated in terms of economics, communications, and politics. Globalization has significantly increased the volume and velocity of just about everything from goods and services and people to email, drugs, weapons, and even greenhouse gases and viruses. Asian artists can now sell their work in Europe, and Afghan terrorists can communicate easily with their North American followers. Everyone can have an opinion on the wars in Mali and Syria, the use of drones, or the killing of Osama bin Laden. Over time, this process is having an important impact on sovereignty. Today, no country, including the United States, can be a gated community. There is a maze of facts and opinions about globalization, but the important thing to note is that its acceleration is without precedent. Even

when private investment and credit slowed during the 2008–09 economic downturn, the international movement of public funds continued to boom. Keeping abreast of these developments and their implications is imperative in the struggle to maintain social order and provide social justice on a worldwide basis.

Technological advances in communications and transportation have reduced the size of the world in real terms and revolutionized the patterns of interaction between countries and individuals. They have eliminated some social and political problems while creating others. The revolutions in science and technology have also dramatically changed the world. Scientific knowledge more than doubled in each of the decades following World War II and the pace of technological change has accelerated at a comparable rate since then. In short, the consequence of this enhanced technology speeds up and augments globalization.

The speed of change is best illustrated by a few examples. In 1900 the world was still dominated by colonial empires; today those empires no longer

Figure 1.2 Huge cruise ships in the tiny harbor of St. Kitts and Nevis illustrate both positive and negative aspects of economic globalization. Comparatively wealthy tourists often outnumber their foreign hosts – contributing to the host economy, but often causing resentment because of their cultural intrusion.

exist. Of the powerful monoliths that replaced them as world powers – the former Soviet Union and the United States – one has disintegrated, leaving a relatively economically impoverished Russia. The United States stands alone as a superpower. In 1900 the only way to circle the globe – either for travel or for communication – was by ship. Today, sea travel has been eclipsed by vast aviation networks. Communications systems have entered the space age, making use of fiber optics, microwaves, and satellites for instant global communication. It is hard to imagine daily life without cars, radios, televisions, household appliances, computers, fax machines, the Internet, and other modern conveniences, all of which were only science-fiction dreams in 1900. Students live in a world of easily accessible data with Wikipedia, social connections with Facebook, instant messaging with Twitter, and many more possibilites.

Technology has also brought new and enormous challenges to world peace. In 1900, rifles and cannons were the most dangerous weapons of war. Today there are atomic bombs, computerized fighter jets, heat-seeking missiles, chemical and biological warheads, nuclear submarines, and automated weapons of every description. Pilotless Predator aircraft, used in much of the Middle East and South Asia, are directed and controlled by operators in Nevada, in the United States. They have killed Afghanis, Pakistanis, Yemenis, and Libyians. Plans for even more sophisticated and futuristic weapons are on the drawing board.

Economic and technological developments have shifted the focus of politics to some extent from the national, regional, and international levels to the global level. The global economy has melded all the elements of wealth creation – finance, investment, production, distribution, and marketing. World trade today accounts for approximately one-fifth of the gross world product (GWP), which is the total value of goods and services produced in the world. The increasing interdependence of states through contact, communication, and trade is impinging on the domestic affairs of states, their government,

and politics.[3] The world is shrinking in the face of new electronic technologies and the extremely rapid movement of people, goods, capital, information, and ideas.

Business corporations and intercorporate networks are increasingly transnational. In terms of global activities, ownership, and control, many companies are becoming "stateless," without dominant links to any specific country. Because of this, a state's competitive advantage may not be identified with its own particular group of companies as much as it was in 1900 or earlier. Many multinational corporations even exceed the economic strength of most states. Today, very few of the world's 193 states in the United Nations have a higher gross domestic product (GDP) than the three largest global companies.

Finally, another factor promoting interdependence and globalization is that many noneconomic cross-border problems are now being resolved internationally. Many world issues such as health, the environment, and human rights cannot be handled by single states alone and are increasingly being treated as transnational challenges. Problems such as terrorism, environmental pollution, drug trafficking, and so on require concerted international action. As countries have become increasingly interlinked and interdependent it has become imperative to study them in a broad international context.

As Table 1.1 shows, there are also criticisms of the globalization phenomenon. State sovereignty still prevails in many domestic areas but, as international variables impinge on the priorities of governments, global forces are quickly affecting how governments act in all fields. Developing countries, particularly the economically weakest, are especially vulnerable and are being undermined. Environmental degradation and health issues affect all states. Human rights that are blatantly ignored in some states become the focus of attention in others. The frontiers of knowledge and development – in

[3] F. Gerard Adams, *Globalization, Today and Tomorrow* (Abingdon, Oxon: Routledge, 2011).

Table 1.1 Globalization: components, causes, and criticisms

Components:

1. development of a single global market for most widely used products and financial services
2. huge-scale migrations and diasporas
3. globally organized media
4. state interests are increasingly global

Causes:

1. reduced barriers to cross-border trade and investment
2. similarity in state regulations and laws
3. technological changes in telecommunications, microprocessors, the Internet, transportation
4. emergence of global institutions

Criticisms:

1. uneven distribution of trade benefits – countries representing a small proportion of the world's population account for most of world trade and income prosperity
2. increasing environmental degradation, demographic and health issues
3. human rights concerns

weapons systems, communications, economics, and so on – are now on a global scale.

Along with this global togetherness there is another trend toward smaller groupings, sometimes called a downward drift. Many countries currently on the map owe their existence and shape to the collapse of larger empires – the Ottoman, French, and British empires, for example. Recently some of the largest states have broken up again, particularly because of the rise of nationalism and religious fundamentalism. Examples include the 1991 breakup of the Soviet Union and the 1993 collapse of Yugoslavia into several states and warring factions. Regional and ethnic challenges to contemporary states exist on every continent and are growing significantly in many areas, especially Central Asia and North and Central Africa. This has created a growing concern for security everywhere.

Security and global politics

During the Cold War, security was interpreted as being essentially about the East-West conflict, and Western policy was based on protecting interests without aggravating relations with the Soviet Union. The bipolar configuration of the Cold War period reflected the principle that states attempt to increase their security by enhancing their power and military strength and in so doing they make other states feel less secure. As we see in Chapter 3, realists believe each state looks out for itself in terms of survival and security, and this may frighten others. Each state is encouraged to strengthen its own military. As power cannot be shared, and is in essence zero sum in nature, each state's security is defined by, and rests on, other states' insecurity. The security dilemma means that each state faces the dilemma of whether to increase its military strength and provoke the others or not to arm and leave itself vulnerable to attack.

Today, security also includes how states can protect themselves against transnational challenges. It is about how to aid those states that are weak, failing, and underdeveloped, because dangers generally arise not from strong states but from those that are divided and disintegrating. Almost all of the violent conflicts in the post-Cold War period have been internal, not international. It was a weak state that harbored Osama bin Laden, the mastermind of the 9/11 attacks, not a strong one. A new security dilemma therefore arises from the fact that an increase in a country's military strength may not provide a corresponding increase in its security. Moreover, the stronger a state becomes the more it opens itself up to increased challenges from globalization forces. The state is under challenge and, although it is not obsolete and will not disappear, its security can no longer be based entirely on weapons and soldiers. At a minimum, strategic and military planning is extraordinarily difficult in a world with no single clear enemy and many dangers. The new security issues arise from the implications of ubiquitous insecurity – violent threats coming from a number of places and nonstate sources all at the same time. The idea of a 'new' security dilemma to enhance the traditional concept of security dilemma as a framework for understanding international relations is discussed in several chapters, especially 9, 10, 11, 14, 15, and 16. The advent of the new security issues indicates that even the most powerful countries cannot deal with their problems alone. Table 1.2 outlines some characteristics of the "traditional" and "new" aspects of contemporary security issues.

The current difficult and unstable situation is due to the *simultaneous* existence of both traditional state challenges, such as the ones recently posed by China, Iran, and North Korea, and the new security threats emerging from subnational actors, particularly from parts of the Muslim world. It is the multiplicity and interconnectedness of threats that is the new challenge. Understanding this changing nature of security is crucial. The issue is not just about UN legitimacy or U.S. actions. Those who argue that the United States is now so powerful that its government is tempted to act alone in international affairs are obviously correct. Where many err is in assuming that because America possesses this power it knows how to use it wisely. Moreover, some countries that are much weaker militarily than the United States are almost equally powerful in economic and social fields. The U.S. margin of overall superiority is not unassailable, and American political leaders realize that, in a turbulent and violent world, collective action will be more effective in the long run.

As we think about global security we should bear in mind that its modern conception entails not only security of persons and property but also human rights, democratic government, and possession of the basic necessities of life. Security has become tied to wide concepts of democratization – free societies, free elections, and free markets. Security is seen as a public or collective good and democratic leaders have a necessary and ethical role to play in seeking such goods for their peoples.[4] Understand-

ing the new world pattern, based on human security and basic rights, requires novel concepts and theories. Our discussion of global politics and international relations in this text is therefore based on an adjusted vocabulary and an approach appropriate for contemporary circumstances.

The advent of the new security issues indicates that even the most powerful country in the world cannot deal with its problems alone. The new transnational threats include climate change, energy security, disease and poverty, population and demographic distortions, food and water safety, failing states, and organized crime and cybersecurity, to mention only a few outstanding ones.

Table 1.2 **Some characteristics of security issues and dilemmas**

Traditional and Ongoing	Novel and Contemporary
States	Failed States, Stateless, Rootless Individuals and Groups
State-based: territory, borders, resources, values	Identity-based interests: ideological and ideational (nations, ethnicity, religion); global causes (human security, child soldiers, climate change)
State militaries and police (hierarchical)	Movements, rebels, networks, individuals, (horizontal)
Security dilemma, military confrontation	Ubiquitous insecurity, asymmetrical warfare, terrorism
Minimize collateral damage (people and property). International rules of war.	Violent radicalism, revenge, suicide terrorism
Victories and defeats	Noble struggles, fanaticism

[4] Ian Loader and Neil Walker, *Civilizing Security* (Cambridge: Cambridge University Press, 2007).

States and global poltics

States remain the basic unit of global politics. In this book the word state refers to the political unit of an entire territory. Considerably less than 1 percent of the world's geographical land mass remains outside the state system. In everyday language, the word "state" is synonymous with "country." Many of today's states were established after World War II, when the decolonization process was at its height. In recent years the number of states has continued to increase, though more slowly. In 1945 there were only 65 states; today 193 are represented in the United Nations.

State sovereignty is an important concept that refers to a number of characteristics, such as territory, authority, and recognition. It conveys a sense of legitimacy, and describes and justifies the notion that states should not intervene in the internal affairs of other states (Chapter 4 discusses this topic in detail). In practice, formal equality among states and the concomitant notion of autonomy has always been to some extent a fiction. States rely on the concept of sovereignty to defend their legitimacy and role in the international system, but weak states have always been at the mercy of more powerful ones. They have never been inviolable as their borders have always been penetrable and penetrated. The concept of statehood, however, continues to be accepted as a doctrine because it establishes formal equality for any governmental organization that achieves it and thereby the concept provides the necessary foundation for international law and order.

What is unique today is that the world's state-dominated system is being undermined by increasing globalization and also by enhanced concern for diversity within and across states. Stable states have not only shared interests but also shared identities. While there are 193 states, there are about 10,000 nations or societies spread out around the globe. The "state" and "nation" and "people" do not coincide in most countries. There are many millions of overseas Chinese, Russians, Hungarians, Romanians, and Turks in other peoples' countries; millions of Kurds, Palestinians, Tamils, Ibos, Zulus, and Tibetans are without a state; millions of Muslims, Hindus, and Sikhs are living in each other's laps in Asia. Many do not acknowledge as their nation the state in which they find themselves. Such diversity also haunts North America and Europe; with the exception of a very few countries, most of the states of Europe have sizable ethnic minorities, and inside many of them there are even what we would call nations, that is, culturally linked groupings of people (see the discussion of identity in Chapter 8).

There is a major difference between the newly emerging states of recent years and those of earlier times. The latter, the colonial territories, were granted recognition of their right to self-determination. International law recognized their right to self-determination, allowing them to escape external domination by a "mother country" that might have been reluctant to let them go. Today, many substate groups agitate for self-determination up to and including secession. They want the right to break away from *existing* states – the Québec separatist movement, the Basque separatist movement, and the former Sri Lanka Tamil Tigers are well-known examples. Such substate groups want to emulate nations that historically were forced into states by war but then successfully claimed the right to regain their independence. Lithuania, Latvia, and Estonia were all forced into the Soviet Union for many years but then regained their status as independent states when the Soviet Union collapsed. Especially in the poorer countries of the world, ethnically diverse groups are increasingly coming into conflict and even collision with state authorities and elites. The clashes make it mandatory to consider the paradox of how to make the world safe for such diversity and diversity safe for the world.

The post-Cold War revival of ethnicity threatens the state system in many parts of the world. Globalization and the Western policies of democratization and economic liberalization are exacerbating problems for weak states. Modern technology and the process of globalization are to some extent devolving power away from state institutions. In

some cases this is helping to cause states to collapse, while in others it is giving rise to transnational or transovereign problems of refugees, disease, ethnic conflict, drug smuggling, violence, and
civil war. There is also a growing belief that states
should not be able to do anything they please with
their citizens. Former Secretary-General of the UN
Boutros Boutros-Ghali put it starkly: "Sovereignty
is no longer absolute. ... Sovereignty must be kept
in its place." Indeed, the growing acceptance of international intervention in the affairs of sovereign
states, albeit for humanitarian purposes, may have
reduced the significance of statehood and sovereignty as foundational concepts in international
relations.

There are many questions about the modern
state, but perhaps the most salient one is whether
it is being diminished in importance because of
globalization and new security concerns. As individuals we experience the importance of the state
when we pay our taxes and line up for security
checks at airports. It is by far the most powerful
force in our lives, but it certainly is changing with
the times. Many new problems related to health,
the environment, terrorists, and even piracy cannot
be handled by individual states, but this does not
mean that the state is now insignificant. In fact, one
could argue that modern forms of surveillance, data
processing, and information control are actually
increasing the power of individual states. Some of
the strongest states in the world are members of
the European Union, where the formal surrender
of some aspects of sovereignty is a requirement of
membership, and yet the capacity of the individual
states to govern their populations has in many ways
been enhanced. The idea that the state is in demise
is premature and tied to an idealized and abstract
notion of the state which never existed in history.

Many of the new problems the world faces are
difficult to address because they are inside the protective shells of extant states or are transnational
in nature and also because existing concepts and

institutions based on them are structured on earlier
state-to-state relations and the East-West conflict
in general. As the world becomes more united –
with global economics, global technology, global
communications, and global weapons – what will
remain of the notion of sovereignty and its notion of a hard-shelled state? Sovereignty is being
reduced in importance. Belief in a kind of "limited
sovereignty" is developing, leading large numbers
of people to believe it is acceptable for them or for
international organizations to interfere in someone
else's state.

The destiny of the world may well be tied to an
inevitable march toward the interdependence of
peoples, nations, and states. Some globalization theorists even argue that individual states and governments have lost control over their own policies and
are being dictated to by the global marketplace. It is
true that while states hold on to most functions in
the military and security sectors, they are, to some
extent, losing out to markets and nonstate organizations in other fields. But at this time in the 21st
century the most important politics continue to be
within and *among* sovereign states, despite that fact
that security and prosperity increasingly depend on
international cooperation. The state is clearly under
challenge but it is not obsolete and will not disappear. There are no alternatives with which to replace
it. It is adapting.

States are required to provide security for their
people. Security is arguably the most important public good as there is no higher form of political organization that is accountable to the public it governs.
Societies may function adequately if some public
goods are produced privately, but security is not one
of them – transportation or electricity may be run by
private entities, states, or international bodies, but if
government does not provide security there will be
none. Collective action is required at the state level,
and security needs to be supplied as an international
public good at the global level as well. (For detailed
discussions see Chapters 13, 14, 15, and 16.)

Conclusion: Patterns of contemporary global politics

The study of global politics helps us understand how the world works, identify patterns, and make generalizations about global affairs. Good political science is based on disinterested observation; it is not nationalistic, polemical, shrill, harsh, or black and white. It stresses the role of knowledge, doubt, and learning to recognize prejudices and preconceived ideas. Debate and argumentation in political science are not mere quarrels. They are about reasoned judgment, not emotional, unsupported outbursts of opinion. In a complex and value-laden field this can be difficult. There are no right or wrong answers to most of the questions posed, only a range of possibilities. It is important to help stimulate rigorous thinking among students, create informed citizens, and produce future politicians or policymakers. As informed citizens we need to catalyze intellectual discourse and pragmatic policy discussions on global politics. We want leaders to have a solid understanding of global politics, make informed evaluations and judgments, and perhaps even be involved in public debates on the topic.

Students of international relations and global politics have a daunting task in the early 21st century. The world is in a novel and crucial phase of its history. In 2013 there are about seven billion people on earth – a figure that is projected to reach more than eight billion by 2025. Every second, the world population grows by more than two human beings. Shock waves from the dramatic finale of the Cold War are still reverberating and political issues have been overtaken by a global economic crisis. The sudden disintegration of the Soviet Union and the collapse of communism in the former Soviet territory and Eastern Europe destroyed the infamous Iron Curtain and ended the rigid alignment of the world's states into two confrontational camps. The initial euphoria that followed those transitional events has evaporated and the new reality that followed has created uncertainties, problems, and opportunities around the world.

The world is adjusting to having the United States as the lone military superpower and "policeman" of the world. Global politics pivots around the United States, but countries everywhere are jockeying for increased economic power and influence on the world stage. They are also coping with economic uncertainty and global terrorism. New regional, economic, and military powers are aspiring to shape world events. Political actors are forming new alliances to meet the economic, security, and social challenges of a new era. The North Atlantic Treaty Organization (NATO) is restructuring and redefining its goals, especially with an intervention on behalf of rebels overthrowing a dictatorship in Libya, and along with a handful of like-minded states is trying to get its troops out of Afghanistan. As a sign of future change, a relatively new organization, the Shanghai Cooperation Organization, links China and Russia with central Asian states in a relatively weak pact.

In Europe, France, the United Kingdom, and a united Germany are the foremost players in the powerful European Union. In North America, Canada, the United States, and Mexico are working to expand free trade throughout the Americas. In Central and South America, all countries except Cuba have embraced democracy. Across Africa as well, dictators and military regimes have given way to experiments with democracy. Nearly three-quarters of sub-Saharan African countries now offer their citizens some form of political choice. Authoritarian governments are being overthrown in North Africa. Religion is once more becoming a powerful force for change in parts of the world. In parts of North Africa, the Middle East, and Central Asia, Islamic extremists are gaining social and political strength. Violence and genocide are taking place throughout much of Central Africa as Christian fundamentalists march north and Muslim adherents move south. In the southern states of the former Soviet Union, Islamic fundamentalists are competing with Orthodox Christians to replace the discredited dogma of Marxism.

Ideologies such as communism that were used to suppress ethnic and nationalist assertiveness for most of the last century are now dead or in rapid decline in almost all parts of the world, and demands for political rights, independence, and autonomy are rising. The end of the Cold War also triggered a rise in ethnic and nationalist conflicts inside large countries, such as the former USSR, and within relatively smaller, multiethnic countries, such as Ethiopia, Nigeria, Sudan, and the former Yugoslavia. Darfur replaced Rwanda as a scene of ethnic cleansing and Zimbabwe became a one-party black state. Even when issues seem far away, their repercussions reverberate around the world. Refugees from Congo, Ethiopia, Haiti, Myanmar, Rwanda, Somalia, Syria, and Sudan are desperately searching for homes in more peaceful and secure areas. And industrialized countries are finding it relatively easy to get sucked into the vortex of armed conflicts half a world away.

The number of wars fought each year remains fairly constant. International wars have decreased, but regional and civil wars rage unabated. Old fires burn brightly in Afghanistan, Ethiopia, Iraq, the Middle East, North Africa, Somalia, the two Sudans, and corners of the Caucasus. Embers smolder dangerously in Colombia, both Congos, Iraq, Kosovo, and Macedonia. Pirates off the east coast of Somalia hijack ships and wreak havoc with international shipping routes and cargo. The world's foremost international body, the United Nations, is rarely more than a bystander to the turmoil, carnage, and terror. Sophisticated weaponry has allowed conflicts such as civil wars to continue and escalate. India and Pakistan are engaged in an open nuclear rivalry. North Korea has developed nuclear weapons and Iran is close to acquiring them. Terrorists have sporadically attacked the United States, Britain, India, Spain, and other countries, and Washington has responded by attacking terrorist havens in Afghanistan, Iraq, and Yemen and setting up new governments in war-torn countries.

Globalization has affected countries everywhere to the extent that many states can no longer govern their own economies independently. The tension between globalization and democracy is profound with widening gaps between what electorates are demanding of their governments and what those governments can deliver.[5] These changing patterns of global politics are vitally important, fascinating to observe, and sometimes difficult to understand but impossible to avoid. Some individual states have lost their self-sufficiency: economic, social, and political interdependence have become the most salient features of modern life. The flow of goods, services, technology, capital, and even terrorism around the world has changed how we live. The interdependence of states is affecting levels of investment, economic prosperity, and even unemployment levels.

Despite the 2008–09 world economic collapse and its continuing impact on slowing globalization, Brazil, China, and India continue to flourish as centers of economic strength, helping to change traditional patterns of trade and the distribution of wealth in the world. The United States remains the only superpower but it is heavily indebted to other countries, particularly powerful communist China, which owns much of America's debt and continues to increase the significance of its military forces. India, too, is on the march with a new-found optimism. Some people believe that the terrorist events of 9/11 "changed everything" while others believe the events represent a return to the type of state relationships encountered before World War II and the Cold War. There is no doubt, however, that radical jihad terrorism has expanded from a base in South Asia and is now found in some 60 countries around the world.

Contemporary thought about world politics is framed by two global events: 9/11 and the responses to it and the financial collapse of 2008–09. While bearing in mind the difficulty of having a complete sense of perspective – because we are immersed in our own times – several interwoven trends or strands in global politics characterize the new world pattern:

- The rise of the United States as a hegemon (or empire) and the growing opposition to this in the rest of the world, symbolized by the rise of powerful states such as China and India and the alienation of large parts of the Muslim community.
- Civil wars in Afghanistan, Iraq, Mali, Sudan, Yemen, and elsewhere in North and Central Africa; instability throughout the Middle East with a clash of democratic, authoritarian, and religious values throughout the region.
- The impact of globalization on world politics, leading to the rapid emergence of India and China as major powers. The Elephant and Dragon are changing how the peoples of the world interact in new and unexpected ways. The political significance of the European Union and Japan continues alongside newly emerging countries such as Brazil.
- The rise of militant Islamist groups and others with virulent anti-Western, particularly anti-U.S., prejudices and actions, and a concomitant growth in terrorist

---

[5] Charles Kupchan, *No One's World: The West, The Rising Rest, and the Coming Global Turn* (Oxford: Oxford University Press, 2012).

organizations intent on using asymmetrical warfare as a tool of international politics.

- The rise of global concern for human security and all the ideas associated with this concept, from clean water to reduction of poverty and sustainable development. Accompanying this is a growth in acceptance of the idea that foreign intervention in the affairs of weak countries is sometimes justifiable and sovereignty is considered by some to be expendable.
- Shifting and competing pressures, with states challenged from below by secessionist and subnational groups, sideways by private actors such as corporations and nongovernmental organizations and even civil society movements, and from above by regional and supranational bodies.

Today, political events and crises within states can quickly escalate to the regional and global levels. Security is a shared issue, not just the concern of individual states. In the final chapter of this book we will look back through the various types of crises that we have encountered in the first fifteen chapters and consider how they can be managed for a safer, just, and more peaceful world.

Select bibliography

Brzezinski, Zbigniew, *Strategic Vision: America and the Crisis of Global Power* (New York: Basic Books, 2012).

Clark, I., *The Post-Cold War Order: The Spoils of Peace* (Oxford: Oxford University Press, 2001).

Diamond, Jared, *Collapse: How Societies Choose to Fail or Succeed* (New York: Viking, 2005).

Frieden, Jeffry A., *Global Capitalism: Its Fall and Rise in the Twentieth Century* (New York: Norton, 2006).

Friedman, George, *The Next Decade* (New York: Doubleday, 2011).

Friedman, Thomas, *The World Is Flat: A Brief History of the Twenty-First Century* (New York: Farrar, Straus, and Giroux, 2005).

Fukuyama, Francis, *The End of History and the Last Man* (New York: Free Press, 1992).

_____, *The Origins of Political Order: From Prehuman Times to the French Revolution* (New York: Farrar, Straus, and Giroux, 2011).

Grande, Edgar and Louis W. Pauly, eds., *Complex Sovereignty: Reconstituting Political Authority in the Twenty-First Century* (Toronto: University of Toronto Press, 2007).

Ikenberry, G. John, *After Victory: Institutions, Strategic Restraint and the Rebuilding of Order after Major Wars* (Princeton, NJ: Princeton University Press, 2000).

Jackson, Robert and Philip Towle, *Temptations of Power: The United States in Global Politics Since 9/11* (London: Palgrave, 2007).

Jones, Bruce, Carlos Pascual, and Stephen J. Stedman, *Power and Responsibility: Building International Order in an Era of Transnational Threats* (Washington DC: Brookings, 2008).

Kagan, Robert, *The World America Made* (New York: Knopf, 2012).

King, Gary, ed., *The Future of Political Science: 100 Perspectives* (London: Routlege, 2009).

May, Ernest R., Richard Rosecrance, and Zara Steiner, eds., *History and Neorealism* (Cambridge: Cambridge University Press, 2010.

Nye, Joseph S. Jr., and John D. Donahue, eds., *Governance in a Globalizing World* (Washington DC: Brookings, 2000).

Prewitt, Kenneth, "Political Ideas and a Political Science for Policy." *Annals of the American Academy of Political and Social Sciences* (2005), vol. 600, no. 1, pp. 14–29.

Sil, Rudra and Peter Katzenstein, *Beyond Paradigm: Analytic Eclecticism in the Study of World Politics* (Basingstoke: Palgrave Macmillan, 2010).

Wolf, Martin, *Why Globalization Works* (New Haven, CT: Yale University Press, 2006).

2 Global history

The making of the 21st century

The Greek historian Thucydides once said that history is philosophy teaching by examples. A recent scholar commented that perhaps Thucydides should have said "*trying* to teach by examples," because often we do not use history well. We miss the real point of its lessons or we follow the wrong precedents. Just think of early prognosticators who thought that because triplanes flew better than biplanes future aircraft would end up with twelve wings![1] Or think of Thomas Watson, head of IBM, who is alleged to have predicted in 1943 that "I think there is a world market for about five computers"! Prediction is an unpredictable business!

One thing that history does do well is deepen our understanding of current global problems. It can inform us about the world in which we live, not just the country we inhabit, and in doing so provides an essential foundation for the study of global politics. History tells us not only who we are but who others are (and were) and helps explain our similarities and differences. Everything happens in a historical context. Contemporary events are constrained by the past but they are not determined by it. They reflect continuity with the past but can also break from it. Although history cannot be used to predict the future it can elucidate why relations between countries and peoples take the shape they do and provide clues to what they might be in the future. It can reveal the changing configurations of authority and power over time and the diversity of systems, institutions, actors, and ideas that have dominated global politics.

In this chapter we survey the historical evolution of international politics from the ancient world to the fall of communism and the period after the end of the Cold War in 1989. This synthesis provides a broad overview of our global political heritage that goes far beyond a eurocentric/North American bias. The standard approach teaches that Europe emerged as an advanced civilization by 1500, launched an age of exploration and discovery, created the modern state system in 1648, then physically and culturally dominated the globe and paved the way for globalization that matured after 1945. While important, this approach is too narrow a perspective for a comprehensive understanding of contemporary global politics. There is a strong argument that this framework, although accurate, is misleading because it turns world history into a moral success story of the rise and triumph of the West. International history is interpreted through European eyes "as if nothing could happen without a European being present, or at his instigation."[2]

[1] An observation made by A. C. Grayling, *The Heart of Things: Applying Philosophy to the 21st Century* (London: Phoenix, 2005), p. 169.
[2] Dutch historian J. C. Van Leur (1908–42) was one of the first to denounce the trend of interpreting history through European eyes in *Indonesian Trade and Society: Essays in Asian Social and Economic History* (The Hague, W. van Hoeve, 1955), p. 261.

In the recent past a new global history has emerged in the search for linkages between different parts of the world. Europe's assumed centrality has come under attack.

Europe should no longer be seen as the pivot of change, or as the agent acting on passive civilizations of the non-Western world ... the European path to the modern world should no longer be treated as natural or "normal."[3]

Indeed, a broader sweep of history reveals that Eastern civilizations (including Persians, Arabs, Africans, Indians, and Chinese) had created a widespread economy and communications network as early as the year 500. Their ideas, institutions, and technologies were diffused to the West, contributions that greatly assisted the rise of the West about a thousand years later. In many respects, Europeans were, in fact, latecomers. Today's ever-shrinking globe makes it important to understand the historical backgrounds of countries and regions beyond Europe and America, particularly where ideas and relationships are rooted in significantly different historical experiences.

Until the 17th century, the world was dominated by rulers who brought large geographical territories together under the absolute control of centralized governments. The most advanced centers of power were outside of Europe, especially in the Middle East and Asia, where powerful political entities flourished well before modern states began to form in Europe. According to one scholar, the "leading Western powers were all inferior economically and politically to the leading Asian powers" until about 1840.[4] Two centuries ago, China produced about one-third of the world's wealth and India not much less. In the Middle East, Arab Muslims built on prior achievements of Babylonian and Persian civilizations to create a great Islamic regional empire that lasted until World War I. For the most part, Europe and Asia were relatively isolated by distance and natural obstacles and had only sporadic contact. Not until the 18th century did European countries become significant global powers as sea routes began to link the world. European colonization of the world then began to develop a truly global economy and eventually a single global system of states.

The emphasis of this chapter is on how and where great powers began and how they evolved over the centuries. It examines how and when modern states achieved legitimacy and authority and how, since then, the world has evolved from regional patterns of state interaction to a truly global system. The world today is more than the sum of its countries and other actors. Over time even the most extensive empires dissolved, paving the way for the great powers that exist today. To varying degrees the new powers share some of the characteristics of former empires. As we discuss in Chapter 5, the current major powers include China, India, Japan, Russia, the United States, and the European Union.

In this historical overview we are particularly concerned with the big picture, a comprehensive approach that affords a view of how global patterns of interaction developed and changed over time. Our approach is necessarily selective as we trace patterns of historical events to create a broad timeline that is crucial to an understanding of the major forces and events that shaped the modern world. Many critical flashpoints or hotspots in international relations today include long-standing fault lines that have never been resolved.[5]

---

[3] John Darwin, *After Tamerlane: The Rise and Fall of Global Empires 1400–2000* (London: Bloomsbury Press, 2008), p. 14.

[4] John M. Hobson, *The Eastern Origins of Western Civilization* (Cambridge: Cambridge University Press, 2004), p. 20.

[5] Ibid. See Chapter 8, especially the section on Samuel Huntington.

From prehistory to five regional powers (10,000 BCE–476 CE)

We begin our survey of global history with five of its greatest early civilizations – Persia, China, India, Greece, and Rome. These were arguably the most extensive and powerful civilizations of their times. Tracing the history and development of these regional powers from ancient times through to the beginning of modern European states and their global expansion with colonial empires, we end with the paramount players in the turbulent World Wars and the Cold War powers that dominated 20th-century global politics.[6] In their early histories we find the beginnings of the Middle East, China, India, and Europe as we know them today.

Table 2.1 provides an overview of the chapter. Each historical section that follows begins with an overview and summary box before a more detailed discussion. The summary boxes include "enduring concepts" in international relations as well as "highlights" from the time frame under discussion that remain an important part of political discourse on global politics.

By 10,000 BCE, during the last of a series of Ice Ages, humans had colonized almost all of the habitable areas of the world as nomadic hunters and gatherers.[7] Civilizations began to develop based on agriculture, which allowed permanent settlement as well as the development of writing. Around the globe, populations gradually settled where irrigation made it possible to sustain agriculture and where proximity to rivers, lakes, and oceans enabled trade to develop. Evidence of early permanent settlements, dating to about 9000 BCE, have been found in the Near East, North Africa, and the southern tip of South America. Agriculture made possible a massive growth in human population and gave rise to relatively stable village communities with increasingly complex societies and, eventually, to what we would call urban life.[8]

The Asian and European landmasses of the ancient world were populated by increasingly sophisticated civilizations. The largest of them were ruled by emperors who extended their territories to the limits that their military abilities, economies, and geography permitted. Like the political systems that followed, *territory* defined their political entity. A ruler conquered and "owned" territory, and the people on that territory belonged to him and his clan. We also see ever more sophisticated patterns of warfare as military technology developed, making wars over larger swaths of territory endemic.

Many societies in ancient times were interconnected in spite of great distances, uncertain geographical knowledge, competition between clans and empires, and slow and difficult communications. By water and land, far-flung webs of trade allowed disparate cultures to reach and influence each other. Trade laid the foundation for the exchange of ideas, and commerce and finance interacted with politics and strategy.[9] There is considerable archeological evidence of interactions between the ancient Near Eastern and Mediterranean regions as early as the Bronze Age (roughly 2200–800 BCE). Exchanges included not only raw materials but manufactured goods and intellectual and aesthetic influences.[10] However, these early patterns of interaction were sporadic and restricted to specific regions of the globe as there was as yet no means of transportation across oceans.

The first civilizations to leave written records were in the fertile areas of Mesopotamia and

---

[6] As preparation for this journey we highly recommend Neil MacGregor, *A History of the World in 100 Objects* (London: Allen Lane, 2010), which presents a fascinating tour of human history from Africa two million years ago to the dawn of the 21st century.

[7] Throughout the text we use the BCE (before common era) and CE (common era) rather than BC and AD. The dates remain the same as in previous usage.

[8] Richard Overy, ed., *The Times Complete History of the World* (London; Harper Collins, 2007), p. 36.

[9] William J. Bernstein, *A Splendid Exchange: How Trade Shaped the World* (New York: Grove Press, 2008).

[10] In 1984 the oldest surviving example of a cargo ship was discovered off the coast of Turkey, having sunk about 1300 BCE packed with cargo from sites between Nubia in Egypt and the Balkans.

Table 2.1 World history overview: From extensive early empires to contemporary global powers

The Ancient World: Evolution to Five Extensive Regional Powers (10,000 BCE–476 CE)
Persia: Achaemenid, Sassanid
China: Qin, Han,
India: Mauryan
Greek city states;[a] Alexander the Great's Hellenistic Empire
Rome

A Period of Transition: The Middle Ages to Westphalia (476–1648)
Europe: European monarchies, Holy Roman Empire, Byzantium
Middle East: Arab (2 caliphates), Ottoman
Asia: China – Tang, Sung, Mongols, Ming, Qing
Indian subcontinent: Mughals

Origin, Development and Expansion of the Modern State (1648–1800)
Europe: European powers and colonial empires,[b] Britain, France, Prussia (Germany), Dutch United Provinces,
Portugal, Russia, Austria, Spain
Middle East: Ottoman
Asia: China, Japan

The 19th Century, Enhancement of the Global System
Europe: Colonial empires, Britain, France, Russia, Austria, Prussia
Asia: China (divided: invaded by Japan), Japan (invaded China)
Indian subcontinent: India (a British colony; mutiny)
Middle East: Ottoman Empire (declining)
North America: United States (consolidating; expanding)

The 20th Century: Two Bloody World Wars and Two Great Powers[c]
Europe: Britain, France, Germany, Italy
Eurasia: Soviet Union
North America: United States
Asia: China, Japan

A New Age of Superpowers (1949–89)
Soviet Union, United States

Coming Full Circle?: Current Great or Global Powers[d]
United States, China, India, Japan, Russia, European Union

---

[a] The Greek city states were not an empire but independent city states joined in a mini international system and are included here because of their major influence on European politics and philosophy. The Hellenistic Empire which followed was short lived but extensive.

[b] Mercantilist.

[c] Some of these states were active globally and, thus, aspired to global significance, while others were paramount in their regions. What links them is two world wars.

[d] Controversially, some are, or could be, classified as empires.

Figure 2.1 The pyramids and archaeological treasures of ancient Egypt are vulnerable today as the "Arab Awakening" plays out. Tourism has diminished, the economy has collapsed, and security is often inadequate or absent. *Source:* Shutterstock.

Egypt from about 3000 BCE.[11] In Mesopotamia (modern-day Iraq), Hammurabi, king of Babylon, produced a code of law inscribed in stone – the first known written laws. Interwoven with the history of Babylon, Assyria, and Sumeria was that of the Semitic Hebrew people who had settled in Judea. In the 4th and 5th centuries BCE they produced written literature, history, and the Hebrew bible. Their capital city was Jerusalem. Further along the Mediterranean, in Egypt, the prosperous "old" kingdom in the Nile valley thrived, leaving a legacy of pyramids as symbols of their kings' divine power. Egypt's golden age was from 1550–1070 BCE when the pharaohs created the most powerful empire of its day (Figure 2.1).

Throughout the remainder of the ancient period until about 476 AD, five powers, much more extensive than Egypt and Mesopotamia, set the stage for developments through the Middle Ages and on to the contemporary world. It is here we begin our study of a number of extensive powers (Box 2.1). Any selection of powerful governments and empires undoubtedly leaves some entities out of the discussion and may drive experts to complain, but such a summary is needed to show the broad linkages

---

Box 2.1 **The ancient world: Extensive regional powers, enduring concepts, and highlights**

Extensive Powers:

Middle East:	Persian Empire
Europe:	Greek city states; Roman Empire
Indian subcontinent:	Mauryan Empire
China:	Qin, Han dynasties

Enduring Concepts and Highlights:
satrapies; regional international system; spheres of influence; balance of power; hegemony; democracy; political participation; Hinduism; Buddhism; free trade zone; monotheism; Confucianism

---

[11] For an excellent history of early Europe from its geographical foundations, including the prehistory period before written records, see Barry Cunliffe, *Europe Between the Oceans: 9000 BC–AD 1000* (Worldprint, China: Yale University Press, 2008).

between early political systems and today's global picture. In the Middle East, Persia dominated; in Europe, the Greek city states and then the Roman Empire were extensive and influential; the Indian subcontinent was united for a time by the Mauryan Empire, and China was unified first under the Qin and later the Han dynasties.

Persia By the 2nd and 1st centuries BCE, Persia dominated the Mediterranean. Its Achaemenid ruling family brought together several million people under one administration centered in the area later known as Iran. This empire included a patchwork of kingdoms that extended west to Libya in north Africa, and included many Greek cities in Asia Minor, northeast into modern-day Afghanistan, Uzbekistan, and eastern Europe, and directly east as far as the Indian subcontinent. The Persians divided their immense domains into geographical parts called satrapies ruled by kings called *satraps* under the control of the emperor. The satraps then appointed lower level governors to manage smaller districts. Later empires used the same model of geographically divided rule. The Persian Empire co-existed for much of its existence with a rival Greek civilization to its northwest.

Greek city states to the Hellenic Empire A period often known as "classical antiquity" began around 1000 BCE. It included various civilizations in the area of the Mediterranean Sea. During this period, the Greeks created an extensive network of power relations. Their 154 city states constituted a mini regional international system that is still examined by scholars for parallels and understandings about interstate relations today. Their influence on the Western world was and remains immense, from politics and history to culture and ideas (Close Up 2.1). The city states each centered on a single large city that shared a common identity, but they had different internal organizations, with some ruled by aristocracy, others by oligarchy, tyranny, and even democracy. The states varied in wealth and power but all aspired to be independent. During the 5th

century BCE two city states – Sparta and Athens – became dominant in the area.

The ancient Greek historian Thucydides (460–401 BCE), distinguishing between the underlying and the immediate causes of war, concluded that what made war between the Greek cities inevitable was the growth of Athenian power. He documented how, as Athens' power grew, its main rival, Sparta, became progressively more insecure and this led to the destructive Peloponnesian Wars.[12] After the first war, he says, Sparta and Athens created geographical spheres of influence and established an equilibrium or balance of power between themselves. However, in the second Peloponnesian War, Sparta defeated Athens.[13] When Sparta tried to assert hegemony (military and political preponderance) over the other city states, shifting coalitions formed, creating new balances of power that were designed to thwart the growing power of a single state and avoid another war.

As Sparta declined, Macedonia, to the north of Greece, rose. Philip of Macedon gained control of Greece, and he and his son Alexander the Great (who succeeded him in 336 BCE) extended their relatively short-lived Hellenistic Empire as far as the Indian subcontinent, Persia, and Egypt. Only thirty-five years later, Alexander was dead and what was left of ancient Greece was wracked by bigotry, ethnic division, and wars that left it vulnerable. Power and glory in the Mediterranean region passed to Rome.

---

[12] Thucydides, *History of the Peloponnesian War*, written in 431 BCE, is translated by Richard Crawley, available online at: http://classics.mit.edu/Thucydides/pelopwar.htm. Recent historians note that Thucydides interpreted the wars with respect to human politics and power struggles, rather than referring to quarrels of the gods, and this was revolutionary in his day. However, the contorted language of the writing has often left interpretation of his thoughts in the hands of the translators. See, for example, Simon Hornblower, *A Commentary on Thucydides, Vol. III, Books 5.25–8.109* (Oxford: Oxford University Press, 2010).

[13] Donald Kagan argues that Athens was not aggressive enough and that is why it lost to the Spartans. *Thucydides: The Reinvention of History* (New York: Viking, 2010).

Close Up 2.1 **Aristotle**

The Greek philosopher Aristotle (384–322 BCE) introduced the concept that the political unit of the city-state (polis) was the highest legitimate authority, above rulers or religions. Each polis had its own laws and system of government. The city state an individual belonged to became a significant focus of political identity, an early precursor of modern *nationalism*. The idea of **democracy** took root as people saw themselves as citizens who could participate in government and not as mere subjects of a ruler. Athenian democracy was primitive and limited in who could participate, but it was a landmark beginning of the concept and practice of widespread **political participation** in public life.

Close Up 2.2 **Kautilya**

Kautilya (350–283 BCE aproximately) was a Hindu statesman and philosopher. His book *Arthashastra* (authoritative instruction in the art of material possession) describes the independent state system and provides a systematic exploration of statecraft. It outlines the international relations and war strategies that made him the man behind the throne – the architect of the empire of Chandragupta Maurya. The work has been likened to the writings of Plato and Aristotle, who were near contemporaries in the Greek city states. Much later the book won Kautilya the reputation of the "Indian Machiavelli" for his advice and harsh pragmatism on topics such as the duties of a king, recovery of debts, and execution with or without torture. However, his writings also demonstrate his compassion for the weakest in society. His maxims include "Learn from the mistakes of others...you can't live long enough to make them all yourself."

The Indian subcontinent   Even before Athens and Sparta were engaged in the Peloponnesian Wars, the relatively geographically isolated Indian subcontinent also contained an international system of independent political units. These primitive governments were based on city units linked by a common culture and shared identity based on the values of Brahmanism, an ancient religion that came to be known as Hinduism. By the 6th century BCE, Hindu ideas competed with those set forth by Buddha, a Nepalese aristocrat whose ideas spread from northern India to Tibet, China, Southeast Asia, and Japan. Alexander the Great ruled the western portion of the subcontinent (present-day Pakistan) for a short time, and after he died, Chandragupta Maurya, aided by his adviser, Kautilya, transformed the multiple-state system into a large, centralized Mauryan Empire. Chandragupta Maurya's grandson was the last leader of the united territory. When he died, the Mauryan Empire collapsed and India reverted to small, independent, warring states. Smaller kingdoms flourished in different parts of the subcontinent over the following centuries.[14]

[14] See John Keay, *India: A History* (New York: Grove/Atlantic, 2000).

The Roman Empire   The Roman Empire began as a city state on the traditional Greek model, but by 264 BCE the city of Rome controlled the entire Italian peninsula. Within decades Rome defeated Carthage in the third Punic War (149–146 BCE) and gained control of the entire western and central Mediterranean. Following the internal struggle between Gaius Julius Caesar and the Senate, which triggered two civil wars, Rome emerged under Augustus as an empire in 27 BCE. From 98 to 180, the empire enjoyed its golden age, incorporating at its height about 45 million people (Figure 2.2). Roman culture and organization blanketed Europe from Hadrian's Wall in the north of England to the natural frontier of the Rhine and Danube, and on to the Arab territories of the Middle East and the entire the Mediterranean. Expansion was often motivated by the need for grain

Figure 2.2 The ruins of the ancient Roman forum are preserved in the heart of Rome. The forum was the focal point for elections, market life, public speeches, criminal trials, and gladiatorial matches. Its decay depicts the passage of time and illustrates how empires rise but also fall.

and olives, which had the value of petroleum in today's commerce.[15]

The empire had no challengers. Power and authority were centralized in the emperor in Rome, but local rulers were allowed considerable local autonomy. During its golden years the Roman Empire presided over an enormous free trade zone with few barriers to the movement of goods from Britain to Cyprus and beyond. Officials in the vast area used Latin and Greek languages, governed with Roman law, used Rome's bronze coins as common currency, and shaped ideas about international law and the state.[16] Roman merchants traveled the Asian Silk Road to bring back silk and other exotic wares from Asia for the empire's large centers of Alexandria, Rome, and London. Rome even had links with contemporary empires in India and China.

Although it began and endured for several centuries as a relatively tolerant political power, by the end Rome was tyrannical. Over time, walls and fortifications could not prevent waves of "barbarians" from Europe's poor and rebellious northeastern regions from migrating into Roman territory. Subjects far from the capital grew restive. About 28 BCE in Galilee, Roman administrators executed Jesus of Nazareth, whose life and crucifixion inspired the monotheistic (belief in one God) Christian Church. Christians quickly became a powerful force that helped hasten the empire's decline by spreading its truth of one God throughout the empire. By 395 the once great Roman Empire was permanently split in two between a Latin-speaking west and a Greek-speaking east. Within less than a century there was little left but an assortment of warring kingdoms in the west and north, while in the east, the Byzantine Empire, based in Constantinople, grew in significance and grandeur. The Mediterranean would never again play such a major role in international politics as it did in the ancient world, but Greece and Rome had already shaped much of the intellectual and organizational entity that would become Europe.

China　During the early years of the Roman Empire, prior to 221 BCE, what is China today was

---

[15] For a description of the Roman Empire at its peak see Thorsten Opper, *Hadrian: Empire and Conflict* (London: The British Museum Press, 2008).

[16] Anthony Pagden, *Peoples and Empires* (London: Weidenfeld & Nicolson, 2001) p. 42.

divided into quarrelsome kingdoms and tribes that existed in constant strife for half a millennium. The periods known as the "Spring and Autumn" (770–476 BCE) and "Warring States" (475–221 BCE) eras were, however, extremely productive in terms of intellectual achievements. All of China's major schools of philosophy, including Confucianism, Taoism, and Legalism, originated in this early period. Confucius, a near contemporary of Buddha in India, was one of many itinerant philosophers who traveled widely seeking to advise rulers on statecraft and provide moral instructions for managing society. His teachings became orthodox doctrine and dominated Chinese ethical and political thought, especially in the north, until about the 20th century. South China was more Taoist, following the teachings of Lao Tse, thereby setting

a contrast between the upright, conservative north and a more skeptical, artistic, and lax south that endured for centuries. In the same period, historian Sun Tzu became famous for his book, *The Art of War,* which provided the ruling Chou dynasty with rules for war and peace.

The first emperor of the Qin (pronounced "chin," from which the word China is derived) unified China politically in 221 BC. China was the world's first large, centralized empire.[18] To unify the kingdom, Emperor Qin suppressed diversity and philosophical debate, setting a pattern of intolerance and isolationism (Figure 2.3). This unity set the stage for a highly literate, urbanized, and advanced society, both technologically and culturally. Although the territory experienced periodic division and anarchy many times in its history, the Qin principle that authority stems from a single source of power took root. An emperor, with an unquestioned right to issue commands and laws, was accepted as the norm in China throughout the succeeding centuries.[19] Some skeptics would even say it laid the cultural foundation for contemporary communist China.

Civil war followed the death of Emperor Qin until a new Han Dynasty was established in 206 BCE. The Han rulers developed what historians have called the best organized and most civilized political system in the world – far superior in area and population to the Roman Empire at its zenith.[20] The Han supported Confucianism with its emphasis on good statesmanship and benevolent rule. They expanded their territory south as far as present-day Vietnam

---

Close Up 2.3 **Sun Tzu**

As an adviser of the Chou Dynasty, Sun Tzu (500 BCE–?) wrote the earliest known work on military strategy. His emphasis on surprise and deception, among other principles, brought him some fame in 18th century Europe and his work is still discussed by military strategists today. His principal advice was to adapt to circumstances and recognize opportunities, not to stick to a preconceived plan. He counseled that the *threat* of force is as important as the *use* of force for gaining concessions and warned that when a war is protracted, the resources of the state may not be equal to the strain. He also pointed to the usefulness of diplomacy: a skillful leader subdues the enemy's troops without any fighting; he captures their cities without laying siege to them. One of his best known maxims for gaining advantage is "when capable, feign incapacity."[17]

---

[17] See Sun Tzu, *The Art of War: The Modern Interpretation* (New York: Sterling, 2000).

[18] Today Emperor Qin Shi Huang is remembered particularly for the continuous 1,500-mile-long Great Wall he constructed to secure his advanced civilization from invasions and for his magnificent tomb that is still guarded by echelons of life-size terracotta warriors, horses, and chariots. Many walls already existed, and the emperor joined them together. Mark Edward Lewis, *The Early Chinese Empires Qin and Han* (Cambridge MA: Harvard University Press, 2007).

[19] Jane Portal, ed., *The First Emperor* (London: The British Museum, 2008), p. 79.

[20] H. G. Wells, *A Short History of the World* (London: Penguin, 2000), p. 153. For population see Joseph M. Colomer, *Great Empires, Small Nations* (London: Routledge, 2007), p. 7.

Figure 2.3 Protection from barbarian hordes was the prime motive for the Qin Dynasty's 1,500 mile long Great Wall, constructed from 220 to 206 BCE. Many shorter walls had existed from about 700 BCE, but Emperor Qin was the first to join them together. Such walls represent early attempts at providing state security. *Source:* Shutterstock.

and started a large export trade west along the Silk Road stretching as far as the Roman Empire. However, given the huge distance and poor communications, the two empires remained quite ignorant of each other and did not clash militarily. China was technologically advanced in many areas. Early Chinese discoveries included the magnetic compass, silk, and paper.[21] Silk was one of the first exports from Asia to astound the Romans, who thought it must grow on trees or bushes like cotton. The Chinese, conversely, were impressed with Western cotton and thought it must come from an animal.[22] With some interruptions, the Han dynasty lasted until 220 CE, when, weakened by a virulent plague, the empire was divided into three independent kingdoms. There followed a long period of territorial fragmentation during which China's contact with the outside world diminished.

By the end of the ancient period, in Europe the advanced civilizations and great powers of Greece and Rome had all but vanished. In Asia, China had fragmented but was still the most advanced economic power. The Indian subcontinent also had fragmented, and the rulers struggled with invasions. The Persian Empire centered in present-day Iran was soon to become part of a great Islamic civilization. The United States was not even on the horizon.

A period of transition: The Middle Ages to Westphalia (476–1648)

During this period, governmental institutions relating to authority and order in society continued to evolve unevenly around the globe with many surges and sags. Borders and boundaries were fluid as aggression and wars flourished. The concept of law was limited and applied primarily to buttress state control and security. There was not yet any concept of citizenship or consent of the governed. Authoritarian leadership, war, religion, and economic domination were more important than transformative ideas about the rule of the people. The democratic ideal put forward by Aristotle in ancient Greece was dormant. The irreversible transition to modern states would not come for some time.

[21] The Han were the first to make wood-derived paper, about 3,000 years after the Egyptians used papyrus. Block printing was used by the Chinese by the 7th century. The magnetic compass was probably invented under the Qin in 221–226 BC.

[22] See Colin Thurbron, *Shadow of the Silk Road* (New York: Harper Collins, 2007).

After classical Greece had disintegrated and the glories of Rome had faded, Europe receded into backward, fragmented fiefdoms. These were the Middle Ages, lasting until about 1500. For Europe they were relatively dark ages in which learning and societal progress stagnated until the Renaissance in the 14th century. In both Europe and the Middle East political empires gave way to religious ones. Two religious orthodox powers, Christianity and Islam, initially provided rigid, dogmatic organization to much of society. The transition to modern states and institutions stalled. In Europe, authority was centralized in the church but disputed by kings. The Roman Catholic Church eventually lost its battle with civil political authorities after a long and tortuous struggle climaxing in the Protestant Reformation, the Eighty Years' War (1586–1648), and the Thirty Years' War (1618–48). Islam never ceded to the concept of separation of church and state; therefore, many of today's Islamic states are still strongly influenced by religious authorities.

In the early Middle Ages these two monotheistic religions controlled territory and people and wielded a universalistic authority that bred intolerance, schisms, and wars. Yet the Islamic world for a time was exceedingly tolerant and progressive. Arabic was the world's common language of scholarship as Islam brought together different systems of thought, including the learning of ancient India, Persia, Babylonia, and Greece, and passed that knowledge on to medieval Europe.[23] Arab Muslims from the Middle East built upon the earlier achievements of the Persians and created a vast regional economy reaching across the Afro-Eurasian landmass and sea lanes from Western Europe to China.

For the Chinese, the Middle Ages began relatively much brighter than for the Europeans. While Europe engaged in religious wars, China enjoyed the fruits of an "industrial miracle" that had begun as early as 600 BC. Under the Tang Dynasty, then under the Mongols under Kublai Khan and the Ming,

> ## Box 2.2 The Middle Ages to Westphalia: Great powers, enduring concepts, and highlights
>
> **Great Powers:**
>
> | | |
> |---|---|
> | *Middle East*: | Imayyad and Abbasid caliphates; Ottoman Empire (Suleyman) |
> | *Europe*: | Christian Byzantine Empire; Holy Roman Empire; Spain; France; England |
> | *China*: | Tang Dynasty; Sung Dynasty; Mongol empires (Genghis Khan; Kublai Khan); Ming Dynasty; Qing Dynasty |
> | *Indian subcontinent*: | Mughal Empire (Akbar) |
>
> **Enduring Concepts and Highlights:**
> Islam; Christianity; crusades; feudalism; Renaissance; Protestant Reformation; Divine Right of Kings; pandemic; China's "industrial miracle"

Qing, and Sung dynasties, China was superior to Europe militarily and technologically and far more advanced in terms of culture and trade. "For more than a millennium China was the dominant power in Asia, the only advanced civilization in a world of barbarians, the centre of its own universe."[24]

For thousands of years China had used the steppes of Central Asia to access the Mediterranean and create a corridor for trade and migration.[25] For centuries as well, the Chinese had also been a great sea power. But, astonishingly, by 1600, with expensive wars on its land frontiers, China withdrew and left the oceans to the Europeans. India during the latter part of this period was dominated by the

[23] See Jonathan Lyons, *The House of Wisdom: How the Arabs Transformed Western Civilization* (London: Bloomsbury Press, 2009).

[24] Robert Kagan, *The Return of History and the End of Dreams* (London: Atlantic Books, 2008), p. 27.

[25] See, for example, Barry Cunliffe, *Europe Between the Oceans* (Yale: Yale University Press, 2008).

Mughal Empire, from which it acquired a strong Muslim population that competed with the Hindus and Buddhists of the ancient era. Europe in the Middle Ages was, in many ways, both geographically and culturally merely the western fringe of the highly progressive continent of Asia.

The Middle East: The origin and development of Islam as a political power

Mohammad (570–632) was the founder of Islam,[26] a religion that, apart from its spiritual guidance, provides a comprehensive system of law and instructions for good government. After Mohammad's death, divisions about succession consolidated two rival groups, Sunnis and Shias, and many smaller sects. The Umayyad Dynasty founded a caliphate (system of government) in Damascus and created a culturally advanced Arabic empire that conquered all of Persia and the Christian Byzantine lands in north Africa and the Middle East.[27] The empire even spread to southern Spain (al-Andalus) and northeast India and took their religious and commercial influence into Africa. Their people were significant middlemen in trade between China and the Mediterranean. However, doctrinal differences undermined their unity. Nearly the entire ruling Umayyad family (Sunni) was massacred in 750 by rival Abbasids (aided by Shiites), who moved the caliphate to Baghdad. Persia (Iran) later became the main home of the Shiites and remains so today.[28]

Islamic civilization thrived. It learned from the Chinese how to manufacture paper, and created magnificent libraries, buildings, and centers of learning, absorbing scientific Greek literature, Jewish intellectual traditions, and Indian mathematics and philosophy. Islamic scholars discovered algebra, charted the constellations, and became adept at astronomy and navigation. While Europeans wallowed in relative ignorance, Islamic scholars made maps, accurately told time, and advanced medicine and physical science. They replaced clumsy Roman numerals with the Arabic figures that we use today. Ibn Sina's *The Canon of Medicine*, an advanced Arab medical text, was required reading for European medical students well into the 17th century. The Arabs were also adept warriors. They fought the Christians in the crusades in the 11th century and held back regular incursions by the Mongols from Central Asia. The Islamic world became "the Bridge of the World," across which trade and resources passed through to the West from about 650 to 1800.[29]

By the 13th century, however, Christian armies had reconquered most of Spain. In 1492, the same year that Columbus set sail for America, Spanish rulers expelled the Muslim caliphate from Granada, the last Muslim foothold in Europe (Figure 2.4). By the early 1600s the Moors, who had lived for centuries in Spain and contributed much to its culture, had all been rounded up and put on ships for North Africa.[30] Routed from Europe, Islam nonetheless continued to spread around the globe. By the 16th century, its missionaries were established in Indonesia and the Philippines where they remain in large numbers today.

Meanwhile, in the 11th century, the Seljuk Turks in Constantinople converted to Sunni Islam and laid the foundation of the powerful Ottoman Empire. Straddling Asia and Europe, it was the largest and longest-lasting Islamic empire and had perhaps the best chance to become the world's first dominant Islamic power. In the 12th century it invaded the Indian subcontinent. It was a constant threat to the Christian world and ended European supremacy in the Mediterranean. Islamic trading hegemony over Europe endured while the Ottomans maintained

---

[26] Islam means "submission to the will of God."

[27] The caliph is the head of state. In theory, the caliph and other officials are representatives of the people and govern according to established law. Sunnis claim the caliph is to be elected by Muslims or their representatives. Shias believe the caliph has to be a descendent of a particular branch of the family of Mohammad.

[28] Iran has been a Shiite state since the 16th century, beginning with the Safavid Dynasty.

[29] Hobson, *The Eastern Origins of Western Civilization*, p. 38.

[30] The story is documented by Matthew Carr in *Blood and Faith: The Purging of Muslim Spain* (New York: The New Press, 2010).

Figure 2.4 The Alhambra is a Moorish complex of magnificent fortresses and palaces in Granada that was the home base of the Muslim Nasrid dynasty before Catholic Queen Isabella began the expulsion of Muslims from Spain in 1492 – the same year she sent Columbus to discover the Americas. *Source:* Shutterstock.

their hold over the Indian Ocean. At the empire's zenith, under Suleyman the Magnificent (1520–66), it reached from Vienna to the Red Sea and from Gibraltar in North Africa to the Balkans. It occupied all the historic and holy cities of Islam in the Middle East. Its leaders tolerated the political independence of the Shiite Persians provided they did not threaten Ottoman interests.[31] The Ottoman Empire prospered economically and culturally with Islam as the supreme law and central authority. After Suleyman, however, the schism between Sunnis and Shiites intensified. Islamic thought became less tolerant, and economic and technological innovation, trade, and commerce were suppressed, allowing Western European powers to gain economic and technological superiority, and setting the stage for later conflicts.[32]

Christian Europe as a political power

Like Islam, Christianity also originated in the Middle East. In the Middle Ages it became a predominantly European religion closely entwined with political power. As we saw in the previous section, it was the religion of the Roman Empire before the empire broke apart. In the eastern portion, the Christian Byzantine Empire was based in Constantinople until it was overtaken by the Ottoman Empire in 1453. In the west, late in the 8th century the Pope made Charlemagne (742–814) emperor of a new Holy Roman Empire that was much smaller (essentially central Europe), less powerful, and less centralized than the earlier Roman Empire. He gave Charlemagne authority to unite fragmented Western Europe, and in return Charlemagne was to provide protection for the Pope. The arrangement unleashed centuries of religious wars and a struggle between secular and religious authority in Europe. By the 11th century the papacy organized the crusades in an attempt to wrest the Holy Land from Islam.

The Roman Catholic religion at this time, like Islam, was a source of universalistic authority. Papal authority was supreme. However, the Christian message was fragmented by many different political actors. Territory was disaggregated into feudal principalities in which power and authority overlapped. God and the Pope blessed monarchs and gave them the right to rule certain territories, and the monarchs divided their subjects among subordinates.

[31] Malise Ruthven, *Islam: A Very Short Introduction* (Oxford: Oxford University Press, 1997), p. 70.
[32] Justin McCarthy, *The Ottoman Turks: An Introductory History to 1923* (London: Longman, 1997).

Feudalism represented a kind of "chain of being" with God and monarchs at the top and commoners, no more than serfs or pawns, at the bottom. All were part of a hierarchically organized system of rights and obligations.

The early 14th century saw a great famine in northern Europe, followed by a horrific plague pandemic that lasted until 1363 and killed about 40 percent of the population.[33] Europe then slowly emerged from its backward condition. A movement known as the Renaissance, meaning "rebirth," spread across the continent until about 1650. This period was characterized by a new appreciation of the ideas and arts of Greek antiquity and advances in science. In some ways, a unified Spain led Europe in the 15th century. However, under Roman Christian influence it became obsessed with enforcing religious conformity. In 1478 the Spanish Inquisition was founded with an announcement calling on Christians to purify the country of heretics; Muslims and Jews were expelled. The Spanish took on the role of defender of the faith not just in Spain but throughout Europe and even South America.

By 1500, Europe was a wholly Christian civilization, but challenges to papal authority multiplied, with protests against its wealth, depravity, and some of its teachings. Revolts culminated in the Protestant Reformation, a 16th-century movement that undermined the authority of the Roman Catholic Church. When a priest, Martin Luther, rejected the idea that the Roman Catholic Church was the necessary intermediary between individuals and God, he set off a wave of desertions from Catholicism, as well as political/religious struggles across Europe. When Luther had the Bible translated into German, making it more accessible to the public and undermining the monopoly of the church in the interpretation of scripture, it was a direct challenge to the use of Latin and the authority of the Holy Roman Empire. In England, Henry VIII rejected papal authority and established the Anglican Church

in its place, with himself as its head. By about 1550 about two-thirds of Europe had broken loose from the Catholic authority. The power of the Roman Catholic Church plummeted.

By the end of the Middle Ages, in spite of religious divisions, persecution, and warfare, communications and technology had gradually advanced and modern economies were established throughout Europe. European explorers had begun to draw the map of the world. Monarchs became stronger, and in France, England, and Spain they ruled as the personification of law, and by the grace of God, providing coherent, centralized power based on the Divine Right of Kings. It took 100 years of religious wars, including the Thirty Years' War (1618–48), to bring about the early manifestations of modern sovereign states.[34]

China leads the world

While Europe was in disarray in the early Middle Ages, China for a time enjoyed a golden age under strong, centralized governments. The Tang Dynasty (AD 618–907) lasted for about three centuries and became a massive, sophisticated empire. The first Tang Emperor, Taizong, assumed the titles Son of Heaven and Heavenly Khan and set out to establish an empire that would encompass all known territory. He and his successors extended control throughout central Asia as far as modern-day Afghanistan and Iran. Going east, he engulfed Manchuria, much of the Korean peninsula, and Vietnam. He renovated the Silk Road, making it safe and encouraging trade between East and West. The city of Changan (the first capital of a unified China in 221 BC and once the greatest city in the world; today it is known as Xian) became the eastern terminus of the Silk Road, attracting commerce and embassies with diplomatic envoys from as far as Byzantium and Persia. Inventions that percolated west along the ancient road now included not only silk but also gunpowder, lock-gates, drive-belts, the mechanical clock,

---

[33] Darwin, *After Tamerlane*, p. 31.

[34] See Bruce D. Porter, *War and the Rise of the State: The Military Foundations of Modern Politics* (New York: Free Press, 1994).

the spinning wheel, iron-chain suspension bridges, printing, and deep-drilling techniques. The Chinese made gunpowder as early as the 9th century.

The Tang began to lose control when they had to rely on powerful military governors with foreign armies. Non-Chinese groups like the Uighurs and Tibetans, in particular, became aggressive threats. The last boy-emperor of the house of Tang was murdered and China fell into a variety of local kingdoms and short-lived dynasties before the Sung Dynasty came to power in 960. China's "industrial miracle" that had begun about 600 BC culminated during the Sung Dynasty – about six centuries before Britain entered its industrialization phase. Iron and steel production and breakthroughs in smelting to produce cast iron fueled economic growth. There were also significant achievements in textile manufacturing, with the widespread adoption of water-powered spinning machine for hemp and silk.[35] The years 907–1276 were characterized by wars and coups, political control deteriorated from centralization to fragmentation, but the south prospered economically, reaching new heights in science and technology.

The Mongol Empire of Genghis Khan extends to China   The power vacuum in central Asia and China that began with the fall of the Tang Dynasty eventually was filled by a relatively small band of Mongols under Genghis Khan (1162–1227). Genghis Khan (born Temujin) conquered more territory than any other person in world history before or since. He and his successors (including Tamerlane) tried to bring "the whole of Eurasia – the 'world island' – under the rule of a single vast empire."[36] For 150 years they governed an empire that stretched over half the known world from Vienna to the Sea of Japan and from Russia to Iran and Iraq. When Genghis Khan died his Mongol Empire was split into four large parts. His grandson Kublai (1260–94) ruled a reunited China, the most populous society in the world. He adopted a Chinese title and established a Chinese dynasty. The Mongol Empire became the most expansive contiguous empire in world history and conquered more advanced peoples largely by virtue of the military superiority of its mounted archers and mobility (Figure 2.5). Their people were largely nomadic.

Kublai Khan's attempt to create a one-world system centered in China has been seen by some scholars as the first serious attempt at worldwide free trade.[37] Of course, the extent of the known world at that time was essentially the Eurasian land mass, so the result was still more regional than global. But the concept was certainly on a grand scale. Kublai Kahn used Arab, Chinese, and Greek expertise to create a huge area of free trade in products, culture, and people by land and by sea. He also tried to establish a universal alphabet and calendar that would encompass and unify the entire world. On his watch, Europe, the Middle East, northern India, and the Far East were linked not just by trade routes but also by a new method of communications, the Yam, "a network of relay stations, roughly thirty miles apart that stretched from one end of the empire to the other."[38]

Mongol rule in China ended in 1368 when the ethnic Chinese Ming rulers succeeded in taking back China's territory. Genghis Khan's descendents continued their conquests elsewhere, eventually founding the Mughal Empire that ruled India until the British arrived in the 19th century. Tamerlane was the last to try to reinstate a great Eurasian empire, but he died before he reached China's border. (Figure 2.6). His death in 1405 marked the end of a long quest to unite Europe, Islamic Middle Eurasia, and Confucian East Asia into a single empire.[39]

[37] Amy Chua, *Day of Empire: How Hyperpowers Rise to Global Dominance – And Why They Fail* (New York: Doubleday, 2007), chapter 4.

[38] Ibid., p. 120. Messages were relayed between the stations by horse riders who were so obsessed by speed that they were reputed to run down anyone or anything in their path.

[39] Darwin, *After Tamerlane*, p. 6.

[35] Hobson, *The Eastern Origins of Western Civilization*, chapter 3.

[36] Darwin, *After Tamerlane*, p. x.

Figure 2.5 Historically, the peoples of Central Asia were largely nomadic, living in portable yurts. Modernization has changed this, but these dwellings made of sheep wool felt have become a national symbol illustrating the passing traditions of many Central Asian countries.

Figure 2.6 Tamerlane (Timur the Lame) is celebrated throughout Central Asia as one of the most successful and ferocious Muslim leaders in history but also a great patron of the arts. In Persia and India, however, he is despised for his vicious atrocities. He envisioned restoring the empire of Genghis Khan but died before he could succeed.

China turns inward: The Ming Dynasty   The Ming Dynasty (1368–1644) that ousted the Mongols had a navy, military power, and a sophisticated culture. Under their rule, China was the most populous and technologically advanced state in the world, governing more people than in all of Europe put together. Its naval might was far greater than any other power. While other parts of the world were torn apart by religious conflicts, different creeds coexisted in China with comparatively little conflict.

Virtually all the nautical and navigational technologies and techniques that later made it possible for European explorers to navigate and colonize the globe were invented either in China or the Islamic Middle East during this period and transmitted later to Europe.[40] China's superior navy explored and traded extensively. For about two decades it explored the oceans "to exact tribute, and to demonstrate to the world the unsurpassed power and splendor of Ming China."[41]

By 1636 much of the country was in rebellion and the Ming emperors, plagued by corruption and external attacks, turned inward, scrapping their navy and outlawing foreign trade and ideas. In 1644 the Ming were toppled and a new Qing dynasty from Manchuria took over, bringing peace and prosperity

[40] Hobson, *The Eastern Origins of Western Civilization*, p. 21.
[41] Ibid., p. 180.

for more than a century. Historians debate what actually appened to China in the next century and a half. Some argue that by 1600 "the Chinese had fallen far behind Europe technologically, militarily and commercially."[42] However, records show that it continued to dominate the world in manufacturing and trade. "As of 1750 China's lead was clear, enjoying 33 per cent of the world manufacturing output" and "over 1600 per cent that of Britain's...." Only as late as 1860 did the British share of the world economy finally equal that of the Chinese.[43]

As the Middle Ages drew to a close, Asia remained the most densely populated and richest continent in the world. However, as the European countries began to control the seas and extend their influence in the New World, China became relatively inward looking, along with the Islamic Middle East and India. The Silk Road deteriorated, and Europe began to challenge Asia's dominant position in the world.

The Indian subcontinent

After the Mongols were forced from China, a branch that included the Ottoman Turks and Afghans founded a new Mughul empire that eventually extended over much of the Indian subcontinent (1550s to 1650s), bringing parts of what today is northern and central India, much of Afghanistan, and almost all of Pakistan under the same Muslim government. (Mughal is Persian for Mongol.[44]) Because of invasions during its earlier history the population of the Indian subcontinent was already very diverse. About 85 percent were non-Muslims – mainly Hindus, with a lesser numbers of Sikhs, Jains, and Christians.

The Mughal Empire's golden age was under Akbar (1556–1605), who united all but the extreme south of the Indian subcontinent with a central government. Muslim control linked the area closely to central and western Asia. Many Indians, particu-

larly in the north, converted to Islam. One-third of the world's Muslims still live in India today, though they remain only one of many religious groupings and are vastly fewer in number to Hindus.

Other great powers around the globe

By now, strong governments were springing up in Asia and elsewhere. Japan emerged in 1185 under the rule of military leaders called *shogun*, but the country was highly unstable during this early period. Japanese raids along the coast of China helped destroy the Ming Dynasty. In Africa, between the 5th and 13th centuries, the Ancient Kingdom of Ghana consolidated power and territory. The Kingdom of Zimbabwe was a center for trade in gold and ivory from the 12th to the 15th centuries and its reach extended as far as China. Its monumental stone walls and buildings known as the Great Zimbabwe are some of the oldest and largest structures in Africa. In the 13th and 14th centuries the Kingdom of Mali also became a powerful political and economic territory, and the great trading city of Timbuktu reflected the spread of Islam in Africa.

In South America a great Mayan civilization flourished from AD 250 to 900 in what is today Mexico, Guatemala, and northern Honduras. The Aztecs followed in Mexico in 1300–1521. From 1200 the Incas established an authoritarian empire in the Andes with complex governmental structures and cities. They included the Quechuas, the part of their empire that is now Bolivia, Peru, and Ecuador. As great as they were these civilizations were geographically isolated, so their influence and extent were comparatively restricted. To a large extent Africa and South America were not part of the developing global political power or influence.

Origin, development, and expansion of the modern state (1648–1800)

In the century and a half following the Middle Ages, events happened that dramatically changed the face of world politics. Until 1648, empires,

---

[42] Chua, *Day of Empire*, p. 179.

[43] Hobson, *The Eastern Origins of Western Civilization*, pp. 61 and 76.

[44] Babur, the first Mughal emperor, was a descendent of Tamerlane and Ghenghis Khan. *The Baburnama: Memoirs of Babur, Prince and Emperor*, translated and edited by Wheeler M. Thackston (New York: Modern Library, 2002).

states, religious authorities, and simply tyrants had organized and governed the most powerful political units. They exercised authority over people within their reach, but their leadership was rarely based on public consent and therefore lacked legitimacy. Wars kept boundaries fluid and in Europe states that had cast off the restrictions of religious domination became increasingly powerful.

It was within Western Europe that the most crucial changes took place. The breakdown of feudalism in Europe during this period allowed for the development of modernization – a process by which societies became developed or modern, bringing a new organization of political and social life. When the Thirty Years' War was brought to a close in 1648, the Treaty of Westphalia recognized the new, *modern state system.* A self-regulating balance of power system began to prevail among the states. This combination of events changed the relationship between rulers and ruled and set the stage for a period of relative peace in which imperial expansion flourished. In Europe the French Revolution thrust new ideas about freedom, justice, and equality into political debates. Colonies proliferated. In the Americas, colonists demanded their freedom and the United States won its independence.

In Asia, meanwhile, less changed politically. China, still a strong entity economically, continued peacefully under Manchu rule. Japan developed into a significant power. In neither state were rulers hampered by the need for public consent. In India the disintegrating Mughal Empire left a vacuum that was filled by the British East India Company, setting the stage for it to become the "star" colony of the British Empire. In the Middle East, the Ottoman Empire began a long, slow decline.

Two events during the late Middle Ages had paved the way for the European transition to a new system of territorially defined sovereign states. First, rulers gradually consolidated control over larger territorial units, as had occurred in England, the Netherlands, and French- and Spanish-speaking areas in the late 13th and 14th centuries (it took several more centuries for German- and Italian-speaking

---

Box 2.3 Origin of the modern state era, 1648–1800: Great powers, enduring concepts, and highlights

Great Powers:

Europe:	Portugal; Spain; France; the Dutch United Provinces; Britain; Prussia; Russia; Austria
Middle East:	Ottoman Empire
India:	East India Company; British colony
Asia:	China (Manchu rule); Japan
America:	United States becomes independent

Enduring Concepts and Highlights:
Treaty of Westphalia; modern state system; sovereign state; legitimacy; modern nationalism; popular sovereignty, serf; citizen; state; nation; law; legalism; alliances; classic balance of power system; mercantilism; slavery; colonial empires; global system; industrial revolution; imperialism; American Revolution; French Revolution

---

areas to unify). Second, as noted in the previous section, the Protestant Reformation undermined the authority of the Roman Catholic Church.

The 1648 Treaty of Westphalia ended the Thirty Years' War, the culmination of a hideous century of wars of religion in Europe, and brought the final break between church and secular authorities. This treaty ended the Holy Roman Empire as the linchpin of European solidarity and legitimized several legally equal states, each controlling a specific population and territory. In this modern state system states were no longer subject to higher secular or religious authority but were sovereign entities with defined rights. Under the doctrine of *cuius regio, eius religio*, each ruler had complete political authority over his territory and could determine the religion of its inhabitants. No external state had the right to interfere. Very importantly, states recognized the authority of other states. The new states were able to meet the growing desire for prosperity and security by forming a strategic and economic unit, the shell or boundaries of which helped make it secure from foreign penetration. At the same time agrarian societies were being transformed into industrial ones, making the state the major locus of economic activity and the guarantor of economic autonomy.

When the Bible was translated from Latin into many European languages, it paved the way for new, linguistic identities. For the first time, Europeans began to define themselves as English-, French-, or German-speaking, as well as by their religion. By 1648, rulers and statesmen were finding it increasingly difficult to trade territories at will for strategic or economic reasons. People had begun to take pride in, and wanted to be part of, certain specific states. The concept of legitimacy, meaning a requirement for those who govern to have the consent of the governed, gained prominence. Modern nationalism – the idea that the nation is the primary unit of political allegiance, and that boundaries of nations and states should coincide, emerged and flourished along with the concept of popular sovereignty, which holds that people are not serfs (persons attached to the soil as property) or mere subjects but rather citizens with rights who have a stake in their state. Leaders found that populations with nationalistic sentiments made it much easier to institute conscription and build citizen armies, as France would do in 1791, thereby enabling Napoleon to conquer much of Europe.

Gradually, the notion grew that the boundaries of the state (a defined territory and government) and nation (a group of people who share historical experiences and cultural characteristics) should coincide, encompassing, in effect, nation-states. States like England and France tried to incorporate inside their borders other territories in which people spoke their language. In Italian- and German-speaking areas, movements rose to unite small units into single national territories. Over time, in multiethnic, multilingual empires such as Austria-Hungary,

the Russian Empire, and the Ottoman Empire, the movement was to smaller rather than larger units. The many small nations that had been subsumed by such large empires created nationalist revolutions and tried to form separate countries.

The essential difference between the new European states and those entities in other parts of the world at that time was that the relationship between the government and the individual were increasingly being based on law. The individual possessed certain inherent rights and could be deprived of them only by due process. This concept of legalism meant that law developed a paramount sanctity. Individuals were no longer merely *subjects*, but citizens with certain inherent rights to life, liberty, and property; penalties for crimes were restricted to those who perpetrated them; private property was respected by governments; and means existed to sue government officials for alleged wrongdoing.[45]

As the new European states developed in the 15th and 16th centuries, they did so as competing, territorially defined, sovereign political units. In other parts of the world multiple territorially based states did not arise until much later. In the Islamic world this development was hampered by religious beliefs that did not allow for concepts such as the separation of church and state, and that impeded the transfer of popular loyalty to the state. In China it was impeded by a firm dynastic domination of one vast territory with a dominant philosophy of social cohesion and hierarchy. In the Indian subcontinent it was delayed largely by the power and beliefs of the Muslim minority. It was the West, then, that began to shape and dominate the international system after 1648. Yet China remained the power to beat. China held its striking lead in the share of world manufacturing output until about 1870. And China and the Middle East supplied many of the ideas and technological inventions that enabled Europe to compete. European ships were "drastically inferior to

---

[45] See Samuel Finer, "Problems of the Liberal-Democratic State: An Historical Overview." *Government and Opposition* 25(3), p. 358.

Chinese ships in every respect imaginable" even as late as 1800.[46]

The post-1648 era did not have a comprehensive, authoritative system for resolving conflicts among the new, sovereign actors. Instead, it relied on *self-restraint*. If a state was becoming too powerful or aggressive, the others forged temporary antihegemonic alliances to create a classic balance of power among themselves. Wars and territorial exchanges were limited. No single state was sufficiently powerful to defeat the others. Britain often took a leadership role in helping to keep the continental powers in equilibrium. On the continent, Austria remained a significant power, while Prussia (a forerunner of modern Germany) and Russia both strengthened and expanded.

European powers go global: Colonization and imperialism

From the late 15th century European colonial empires became increasingly global. Portugal and Spain launched an era of discovery abroad and began a competition to establish sea routes that became the arteries and nerves of great maritime empires that spanned the globe. Christopher Columbus discovered America in 1492.[47] Spain quickly became the most far-reaching empire the world had ever known. It directed huge amounts of money to naval expeditions and warfare and pursued aggressive imperial expansion, especially in the Americas, where Jesuit priests founded missions to spread Catholicism.

Following the doctrine of mercantilism (a philosophy in which government regulates all of its country's commercial interests and trade by encouraging exports and discouraging imports in order to increase the country's financial wealth and power) economic activity served the interests of the state. Governments used their military power to establish lucrative trade monopolies with their colonies, exploiting and incorporating undeveloped territories into their domestic economies and building an international capitalist system. International trade flourished and stimulated the European economies. States that bordered on the Atlantic built new trade routes. Competition among the Dutch, French, and British, particularly in the Caribbean, was intense. By the mid-17th century the Dutch Republic was the greatest trading nation in existence, with outposts around the world and unsurpassed maritime and commercial supremacy.[48] The new European states followed up their exploratory discoveries with large colonial empires covering most of the globe. In this way the rest of the world was forcibly integrated into Europe's new *global system* – first as colonies and eventually as sovereign states.

In the latter part of the 17th century Britain rose as a world power.[49] The London Stock Exchange was established and within a short time was able to finance Britain's explosion of maritime and commercial expansion. At the same time, inventions, such as the steam engine and the modern blast furnace, revolutionized economic life there. The industrial revolution, a transformation from an agricultural to an industrial economy, produced a need for more raw materials, and this stimulated a new global economy based on the colonies. Advances in weaponry and other technologies stimulated a need for resources and new markets to fuel and fund their economies. European states gained economic and military control over most of the nonindustrialized areas of the world. They engaged in what came to be known pejoratively as imperialism, in which one country controls another country or territory against its interests or desires. This dominance principle structured world order into conquerors and conquered peoples, and its after-effects are still felt today in global North-South disparities. This subject is discussed fully in Chapter 13 on global inequalities.

[46] Robert Tempke, *The Genius of China* (London: Prion Books, 1999), p. 186.

[47] In 1507 the name "America" was placed on a map to honour Amerigo Vespucci, a Florentine who was the first to believe that Columbus had discovered a continent separate from Asia.

[48] Jonathan Israel, *The Dutch Republic: Its Rise, Greatness, and Fall 1477–1806* (New York: Oxford University Press, 1995).

[49] See Niall Ferguson, *Empire: How Britain Made the Modern World* (London: Allen Lane, 2002).

European countries governed their colonies from the imperial center, exploiting the resources and native peoples. Africans were transported to do hard labor in the colonies. In the 18th and 19th centuries about 12 million people were forcibly taken as human chattels, mainly from West Africa.[50] Triangular trade flourished in which rum, cloth, guns, and metal products were shipped from Europe to Africa; slaves (persons who are the legal property of another and are bound to obedience) from Africa were transported to the New World to work in the sugar industry; then sugar, tobacco, and bullion from the New World were brought to Europe.[51] With money, ships, and a need for raw materials, British colonies expanded at an astounding rate, marking the beginning of the British Empire.[52]

Wars within Europe in the 18th century had a great impact on colonies abroad. The War of Spanish Succession that ended in 1713 with the Treaty of Utrecht effectively ended the great colonial power of Spain. France ceded its North American colonies to Britain by 1760. The American War of Independence ended with the Treaty of Versailles in 1783, which granted the colonies independence as the United States of America. The American Revolution had a significant impact on Europe, encouraging new social forces to challenge the old royal regimes and traditional privileges. It was followed in 1789 by the French Revolution that overthrew the most powerful monarchy in Europe but initially failed to produce a democratic state and instead launched itself into twenty years of war under the Jacobin regime and then Napoleon Bonaparte, ending with Bonaparte's final defeat at Waterloo in 1815 by the British Duke of Wellington.

[50] See Khalid Koser, "Why Migration Matters." *Current History* (April 2009), pp. 147–49.
[51] Slavery was far from a new concept. Africans had been exploited as slaves by the Islamic Empire for both domestic and hard labor for centuries. Of the 11 million African slaves transported to the Americas about 40 percent were taken to Brazil. Brazil was the last country to end slavery in 1888.
[52] P. J. Cain and A. G. Hopkins, *British Imperialism 1688–2000* (Harlow: Pearson Education, 1993).

The two revolutions confirmed the democratic principle that monarchs or other rulers derive their legitimacy from the consent of the governed. English philosopher John Locke argued that rebellion is permissible when a government subverts the ends for which it is established, and those ends are based on popular consent (discussed in Chapter 4). The revolutions further consolidated the principle of *nationalism*, recognizing an emotional bond between the masses and the state, and advanced the doctrine of popular sovereignty. Initially, nationalism was seen by many as a threat, and nationalist agitators were punished. However, nationalism continued to be a powerful force. The ideas of nationalism and popular sovereignty spread around the globe, inspiring independence movements in Europe and in the colonies. In 1793, with France weakened and Britain preoccupied outside of Europe, Prussia, Russia, and Austria expanded their territories. Russia became a significant power early in the 18th century under Tsar Peter the Great.

The 19th century: Enhancement of the global system

The transformation from regional systems to a global system was completed during the 19th century. Europe dominated the world. In France, Napoleon broke the balance of power that had been established after Westphalia and tried to create another extensive empire. After his defeat, the great powers made another attempt to prevent war. Germany and Italy unified their territories and Austria expanded. The British Empire was at its peak, but India was already chafing under the bonds of its foreign ruler. China was pulled unwillingly into the European sphere of influence. It was forced to cede powers to Britain, several other European states, and, eventually, Japan. In the Middle East, meanwhile, the once powerful Ottoman Empire continued its long, slow decline.

Box 2.4 19th century: Great powers, enduring concepts, and highlights

Great Powers:

Europe:	British Empire and other great colonial empires; France (Napoleon); Russia; Austria; Prussia (Germany) (expands and unifies)
China:	divided; invaded by Japan
Japan:	invades China
India:	a British colony (mutiny)
Middle East:	Ottoman Empire (declining)
United States:	consolidating; expanding

Enduring Concepts and Highlights:

sphere of influence; Congress of Vienna; Concert of Europe; collective hegemony; capitalism; nationalism; competing alliance systems, Triple Alliance; Dual Alliance; Triple Entente

---

Europe: Napoleon, the Concert of Europe, and collective hegemony

In Europe, the classic balance of power that followed Westphalia was unable to maintain peace for long. It worked relatively well until after the 1789 French Revolution when Napoleon's military buildup in France became a threat to the established European order, but then it failed completely. The idea that state sovereignty and a classic balance of power could maintain peace proved an illusion. The history of Europe from 1792 to 1815 is basically the history of revolutionary and Napoleonic conquests as France overthrew the balance of power, dismissed the new state system, and extended France's power throughout continental Europe against seven successive coalitions of allies. Napoleon's exploits were engraved in history by Peter Tchaikovsky in the *1812 Overture* and by Leo Tolstoy in his novel *War and Peace*.

In 1815, Napoleon's forces were crushed at the Battle of Waterloo, and peace was established by the Congress of Vienna, in which the great powers of Europe attempted to establish a more regulated system that would avoid another major war. The five dominant powers – Austria, Britain, France, Prussia, and Russia – pledged to cooperate to maintain peace and stability on the continent. This agreement, known as the Concert of Europe, was the first of its kind in modern history. Its purpose was to hold the powers of Europe in balance and prevent any further attempt to turn a state into an empire, as Napoleon had done. The key, they agreed, was to maintain an *explicit* balance of power among the great powers. However, since peace clearly could not be preserved by self-interested states acting independently, they tried to develop a way to provide *collective oversight* to maintain the balance. They set rules for their collective hegemony: (1) the great powers shared collective responsibility for the territorial decisions of the Congress of Vienna; (2) changes to the Vienna settlement could not be made unilaterally, only by great-power consensus; and (3) no changes could be made that would upset the balance of power.[53]

The era that followed the Concert was the most peaceful century in Europe's history, although there is disagreement about whether credit should be given to the rules of the Concert agreement or the explicit balance of power and effective diplomacy. The core five states, along with the Dutch United Provinces, prospered and dominated the world until the beginning of the 20th century. The most western of them followed the path of capitalism, encouraging private enterprise and commerce and developing large trading companies and banks. By 1815 the world's financial system was centered in London.[54] Russia and Prussia, however, clung to feudal practices, stifling economic change. The European

---

[53] See Kalevi J. Holsti, *Peace and War: Armed Conflicts and International Order 1648–1989* (Cambridge: Cambridge University Press, 1991), p. 167.

[54] See William J. Bernstein, *The Birth of Plenty: How the Prosperity of the Modern World Was Created* (New York: McGraw-Hill, 2004), pp. 146–49; 154–60.

Figure 2.7 Castel Sant'Angelo, next to St. Peter's Basilica in Rome, was commissioned by Emperor Hadrian as a mausoleum for himself and his family. In the 6th century, it was used as a fortress, and in the Middle Ages as a castle home (where Tosca in Puccini's opera leapt to her death). Later it was used as a prison by the pope and came to symbolize the contest between secular and religious power.

states shifted alliances within Europe, while abroad they continued to vie for power and glory in their colonies around the world.

Consolidation and imperialism Within Europe, power was shifting. Russia expanded into Asia taking over the largely Muslim areas of central Asia and territory along the Pacific coast and penetrating Manchuria and Korea, but it remained in domestic turmoil. In 1861, Tsar Alexander emancipated the serfs, overhauled the legal system, and reformed the army, but he refused political concessions that would detract from royal autocracy or allow widespread industrialization. Civil unrest grew. In Western Europe, Italy and Prussia were preoccupied with internal battles concerning unification. Prussian chancellor Otto von Bismarck was the architect of Germany's unification in 1871. To unify German-speaking areas he broke the cooperative system of the Concert of Europe by initiating separate wars against Denmark, Austria, and France. The result was a larger and increasingly powerful united Germany in the heart of Europe that *changed the*

balance of power. Italian unification was accomplished at roughly the same time.[55] There, the Holy See refused to become part of the Kingdom of Italy. Deprived of all temporal power, the Pope remained a spiritual sovereign only, based in the Vatican (Figure 2.7).

As European states pursued territorial expansion abroad they exported their rivalries to the Middle East, Africa, and Asia. In 1885 the major powers divvied up Africa, giving Germany a sphere of influence in the east, west, and south. Germany thus was able to satisfy its territorial aspirations without endangering its European neigbors. By the end of the 19th century, 85 percent of Africa was colonized by British, Dutch, French, German, Italian, Portugese, Belgian, and Spanish powers. Creating colonies often involved the expropriation, and sometimes the extirpation, of indigenous inhabitants – in the name of progress, of course. The Spanish and Portugese colonies in South and Central America won their

[55] See Christopher Duggan, *The Force of Destiny: A History of Italy Since 1796* (London: Houghton Mifflin, 2008).

independence by 1830. Canada became an independent country in 1867, and Australia in 1901.

The British Empire reached its peak between 1815 and 1865, even though by then it had lost the United States.[56] During those fifty years it grew by 100,000 square miles on average every year, stretching around the globe, becoming the most extensive empire since Genghis Khan and his successors. No other state (or alliance of states) came close to challenging Britain's control of the seas.[57] By 1900 it contained about 25 percent of the world's land surface (about 70 percent if oceans are included) and approximately a quarter of the world's population. However, the British economy eventually experienced a downward slide that became irreversible.[58] In 1857 a horrific mutiny raged in India for two years and India's nationalist movement gained strength, propelling the country toward independence.

China: Opium wars and humiliation

In Asia, only Japan and Thailand never came under direct European or U.S. control. China was never a colony, but it came close to it. In the early 1800s the Chinese, who had been accustomed to being the dominant power in Asia, if not the world, found themselves cast out to the margins of a suddenly eurocentric world.[59] Europeans, mainly British, began a lucrative operation smuggling opium from there, draining China's wealth. When the emperor tried to stop it, the First Opium War broke out (1839–42). Britain defeated China, divided it into spheres of influence and forced it to cede political and territorial rights to foreign powers, including Britain and,

eventually, Japan. These foreign powers claimed exclusive trading rights in various regions and opened the country to missionaries and traders.

Empress Ci Xi, an oppressive tyrant, ruled China for about half a century. She was infamous for "disappearing" her opponents, filling mass graves, torturing, and starting wars. Imperial authority weakened and rebellions broke out all over China. Aggression by invaders who thought China was going to collapse increased, and rivalry between Japan and China intensified. In 1895 the Japanese invaded and occupied northern China and Taiwan, a defeat that Chinese scholars still regard as the greatest humiliation of China's long history.[60]

Whereas in Europe people had come together to form independent states, many colonies had been put together without a national consensus at each colony's core. Around the globe, nationalism and resentment against colonial status spread. African and Asian colonies fought wars to gain independence from their European colonial masters. The United States, meanwhile, was becoming an imperial power. It captured Hawaii and Samoa in the 1890s, and in 1898 it won the Spanish-American War, thereby pushing the Spanish out of Cuba, the Philippines, Puerto Rico, and Guam. It took no colonies in South America, but it continued to intervene there frequently in the following decades, constructed a first-class navy, and built the Panama Canal connecting the Atlantic and Pacific Oceans for both commercial and strategic interests.

Competing European alliance systems

As the struggle for global economic power became destabilizing, European states formed rigid, competing alliance systems for security. In 1877 Russia invaded Turkey, and the balance of power that had held under the Concert of Europe began to fray. It was gradually replaced by a series of alliances. Two camps buttressed by opposing alliances emerged. One was the Triple Alliance of Germany, Austria,

[56] Chua, *Day of Empire*, provides convincing evidence for this; see p. 203. Conversely, Piers Brendon in *The Decline and Fall of the British Empire 1781–1997* (New York: Alfred A. Knopf, 2007) follows the British Empire from 1781, when Lord Cornwallis surrendered to George Washington, to the hauling down of the Union Jack in Hong Kong in 1997. He considers the apogee of the empire to be in 1918 at the end of World War I.

[57] Chua, *Day of Empire*, p. 205.

[58] Fareed Zakaria, "The Future of American Power." *Foreign Affairs* (May/June 2008), vol. 87, no. 3, p. 19.

[59] Kagan, *The Return of History*, p. 27.

[60] Ibid., p. 39. Immanuel C. Y. Hsu, *The Rise of Modern China* (New York: Oxford University Press, 2000), pp. 313–31.

and Italy (1882), in which each pledged to come to the other's aid if one were attacked by France or Russia; the other was the Dual Alliance of France and Tsarist Russia in 1894. Apart from an informal Triple Entente with France and Russia to counter the Triple Alliance, Britain remained neutral until 1902 when it joined a naval alliance with Japan – the first alliance between a European and an Asian power.

By the end of the 19th century, the rise of nationalism and the colonial system abroad became destabilizing for Europe. The Concert system that had helped maintain peace among the new European states had broken down. India was chafing under colonial rule, as were other colonies in Africa and Asia. China was humiliated. The Ottoman Empire in the Middle East was still crumbling, but the United States was prospering and expanding in North America.

The 20th century: Two bloody world wars and two great powers

By 1914, Europeans controlled about four-fifths of the world. The European state system had spread around the globe, disseminating Western values, economic practices, commercial standards, and international law and creating a web of interdependence among states in most geographical regions. There were some major democratic states such as the United States, Britain, and France, but many were authoritarian, including Germany, Russia, and Japan. Technological inventions and scientific discoveries brought momentous change in many areas in the 20th century. The globe was becoming increasingly interconnected.

When the 20th century began, monarchs still ruled most countries. By its end, government by elected politicians was the norm. Global organizations like the United Nations and the World Bank had sprung up and the world population had quadrupled to more than 6 billion people. Imperialism fell into disfavor. India gained its independence as part

of the general dismemberment of the British Empire after World War II, but Britain also partitioned the territory so that the western, Muslim portion became the independent state of Pakistan.

This was a century of two world wars linked by a global depression. The continent of Europe began the 20th century with relatively ethnically homogeneous states, but by the end many contained a jumbled mosaic of peoples because of events such as wars, revolution, changed boundaries, and policies such as deportation, racial discrimination, and genocide. In the Middle East the Ottoman Empire was permanently dismantled and new states were carved out, eventually making room for Israel. In China the century began in turmoil, which led to a "people's" revolution and communism under Mao Zedong. Russia endured a revolution early in the century, became a superpower as the Soviet Union, and then crumbled near the end of the century. Japan emerged as a major world player, but surrendered unconditionally to the Allies at the end of the World War II and eventually reemerged as an economic, but not a military, power. For nearly fifty years the globe was dominated by two superpowers, the United States and the Soviet Union. It ended with the disintegration of the latter and what some critics have called the new American empire or hegemony.

Europe: World War I, the Treaty of Versailles, and the Russian Revolution

As the new century began in Europe the remaining Ottoman and Austro-Hungarian empires were weak and eroding. Germany was unified and had become more powerful and ambitious, seeking to supplant Britain as Europe's dominant power. Weakness in the rigid European alliance system of the previous century, based on the Triple Alliance and Dual Alliance, was becoming evident. According to its principles, if a state from one alliance provoked a war with a state from the other alliance, all of the states in the alliances would be dragged into war. In 1914 it happened when the allied forces entered into a "war to end all wars." This war was the first

Box 2.5 20th century: The clash of great powers, enduring concepts, and highlights

Great Powers:

Europe: World Wars I and II: Allies defeat Germany; Russian Revolution; rise of communism; USSR emerges as superpower; European Union formed; USSR disbanded

Middle East: Ottoman Empire disbanded (after WWI); new states formed

China: revolution; communist state

Japan: imperialist; defeated and occupied in WWII

India: partitioned; gains independence

United States: key to allied victories in both World Wars; shares superpower status with the Soviet Union; becomes world's only superpower

Enduring Concepts and Highlights:
Treaty of Versailles; collective security; League of Nations; Russian Revolution; isolationism; appeasement; Peace of Paris; atomic bomb; Yalta; NATO; Warsaw Pact; Iron Curtain; United Nations; global collective security; Bretton Woods System; Marshall Plan; Jewish homeland; Cold War; superpowers; containment

example of total war, meaning that domestic populations were more directly affected than in earlier wars, and it became a world war in that the empires of Europe became recruiting grounds for the armies.

A quarrel between Serbia and Austria-Hungary was the spark that brought war to the entire continent and beyond. Archduke Franz Ferdinand, heir to the Austro-Hungarian throne, was assassinated in Sarajevo. Austria-Hungary immediately declared war on Serbia, an ally of Russia, France, and Great Britain. Like falling dominoes, one country after the other, the entire continent was dragged into war, along with their colonies abroad. The United States joined in 1917. The war, fought with new technologies, including tanks, the machine gun, poisoned gas, barbed wire, and even aircraft, left more than 8.5 million soldiers and 1.5 million civilians dead. There was stalemate until 1917 when the United States threw its weight behind the allies and helped bring the war to an end in November 1918, formalized in the Treaty of Versailles in June 1919.

The war had major repercussions within Europe and internationally. The British Empire had lost its uncontested global supremacy by the close of the war and the United States had demonstrated its military, industrial, and financial power. The end of the war hastened the creation of a number of new states within Europe. The German, Austrian, and Ottoman empires were dismantled. In Africa, the Middle East, and Asia, colonies of the defeated powers were taken over by the victors.

For all concerned, World War I suggested that the *balance of power*, even one governed by rules about responsibility, could not prevent war. That failure instigated a drive for collective security based on the idea that organizations of states had a legal right to enforce international law by taking collective action to stop a country if it committed aggression against another state. According to that principle, states agreed to band together against any aggressor. The League of Nations, based on this idea of collective security, was the conception of U.S. President Woodrow Wilson. Collective security differs from balance of power in two important ways:

1. Collective security is based on the idea that there should be one grand association of peace-loving states, not many competitive alliances.
2. Collective security creates an organization of states with the right, obligation, and power to monitor the behavior of individual states within the organization and to impose order and prevent war by punishing aggressors.

The United States never joined the League and that is one of the prominent reasons why the League ultimately failed and the ideal of collective security was tarnished.

Perhaps the most significant repercussion of World War I was that the peace agreement at the end of the war carried within it the seeds of yet another war. Germany was bloodied and beaten. The Treaty of Versailles forced it to take sole responsibility for the cost of the war – not least because Germany's wartime allies, Austria-Hungary and the Ottoman Empire, were completely dismembered – and, as a consequence, Germany was saddled with staggering war reparations. Its humiliating punishment included the confiscation of its colonial empire, the loss of part of its territory to France and Poland, and the reduction of its army to a small volunteer force. When the Great Depression developed, German aggression and Hitler were the result.

In the Middle East, the League of Nations took responsibility for distributing former Ottoman and German dependencies as "mandates" among the victorious powers. The Ottomans lost the Middle East (Syria, Palestine, Arabia, and Mesopotamia) and was reduced to only Turkey. In 1922, the empire officially ended when Turkey was declared a republic. Britain gained trusteeship of Palestine, Mesopotamia (Iraq), and Transjordan, a region that became increasingly volatile over the years and continues to be so today. Iraq became independent in 1932.

The war also hastened the Russian Revolution. In 1917, the Bolsheviks fomented a civil war inside the new Russian state, based on ideological divisions between communists and anticommunists. Nearly a million Russians fled the country. Radical communists under Vladimir Lenin seized power in the heartland of Russia, but the rest of the empire broke into many smaller states. Civil war continued. In March 1918, Russia withdrew from World War I. Russia did not participate in the Treaty of Versailles. In May 1919, a period of terror was unleashed in which the Tsar, his wife, and children, among many others, were slaughtered. The socialist ideas of Karl Marx had a great influence on Lenin and the development of Russian communism. Civil war lasted until a communist regime was set up. In 1922, the

new state of the USSR was established as the world's first communist state with Joseph Stalin as general secretary. Its power extended over the Ukraine, the far eastern territories, and the Caucasus as a federation of Bolshevik-dominated socialist republics.

World War II

Within a generation of the "war to end all wars" a second world war broke out. At the time it was the globe's longest military confrontation with estimates of war dead, including civilians, up to 60 million.

By 1932 the German Nazi Party had established itself as a broad-based, violent movement, enabling Adolf Hitler to become chancellor. Japan was ruled by an emperor. Germany and Japan both began to pursue expansion based on military conquest. With authoritarianism and racial hatred, Hitler led the German people in search of "Lebensraum" – living space, which necessitated expelling and exterminating unwanted people from other lands – initially Poland, Ukraine, and Russia but eventually the whole of Europe. Hitler's envisioned new world order entailed a "Greater Germany" surrounded by satellite states that he would exploit economically and cleanse of Jews, handicapped people, homosexuals, and Romani people.

Between 1935 and 1939, Germany, allied with Italy under Benito Mussolini, began a course of territorial expansion. The League of Nations and its collective security system proved inadequate. If a state committed aggression against another one, all the other states were supposed to join together to redress the wrongs. But World War I had been so horrific and taken such a toll that no European country had an appetite for war and, as we have seen, the United States did not join the League and became isolationist.

Japan used the war in Europe to pursue political and economic expansion in China. It invaded Manchuria in 1931 and got away with it. The next year Japanese forces landed in Shanghai, China. Italy occupied Albania and took Ethiopia in 1935.

In 1936, Germany flouted the Versailles settlement, taking back the Saar, remilitarizing the Rhineland, incorporating, first, Austria and then the Czech Sudetenland and then occupying Bohemia and Moravia. When Germany demanded to occupy part of Czechoslovakia in 1938 it created the Munich Crisis during which British Prime Minister Neville Chamberlain advocated appeasement – making concessions in order to avoid war. He thought by acceding to Hitler's demands he could secure "peace in our time." The strategy failed miserably.

It was Hitler's invasion of Poland that finally provoked France and Britain to declare war in 1939. By late 1941, Germany had conquered much of continental Europe. It had taken the Netherlands, Luxembourg, Belgium, and France in Western Europe, Denmark and Norway in the north, expelled British forces from the continent, and attacked the Soviet Union. Italy, meanwhile, invaded France, Egypt, and Greece. Hitler initially succeeded, largely because his strategy of *divide and conquer* kept his main adversaries – the United States, Britain, and France to the west and the Soviet Union in the east – from attacking in unison. His armies began to lose only when they overreached and took on both fronts simultaneously.

By late 1942 the Soviet Red Army had worn down the German army in the east while Britain and the British Commonwealth countries, joined by the United States, kept up major assaults on the west and south. Italy surrendered, and the allies invaded France in June 1944 – D-day. Germany surrendered in May 1945. By then more than 55 million people had lost their lives, including an estimated 6 million European Jews. Millions more people were displaced, and Europe lay in ruins.

Japan, too, had aggressively challenged the status quo. In 1894–95 it took Formosa (Taiwan) from China; in 1904–05 it defeated Russia on land and sea, taking more territory along the coast and eventually annexing Korea in 1910. The 1919 Peace of Paris confirmed many of Japan's territorial gains and gave it mandates to German colonies in the Pacific. By the 1920s, Japan was a great world power.

Two factors spurred Japan's continuing aggressive behavior. The first was economic. To industrialize, Japan needed raw materials and it had few of its own. The Great Depression in the 1930s made this problem particularly acute because Japan had begun to industrialize later than the United States and Europe, and the deep world depression limited its ability to catch up. Also, like Nazi Germany, some Japanese believed they were the "master race" with the moral right and duty to lead. "Japanese wartime cartographers showed both Europe and Africa as part of the Asian continent, and Japanese officials described America as Asia's 'eastern wing.'"[61]

Japan launched a full-scale invasion of China in 1937, but did not enter World War II until December 1941, when it attacked Pearl Harbor. That act brought the United States into the war. A year later, Japan was gaining ground and had added to its conquests Indonesia, Malaysia, Singapore, Thailand, parts of Burma, most of North and Central China, including the main costal ports and centers of modern industry, the Philippines, and many South Pacific islands. They were brutal occupiers. The turning point of the war came at the Battle of Midway in 1942 when Japan lost four of its aircraft carriers in combat with the U.S. Navy and was thereafter thrown on the defensive for the remainder of the war. In August 1945 the United States dropped atomic bombs on Hiroshima and Nagasaki, immediately killing over 200,00 people. Japan was in ruins. It surrendered unconditionally to the Allies and was occupied by foreign forces for the first time since Kublai Khan's brief, unsuccessful invasion in the 13th century. It regained its independence in 1952 under a new, democratic constitution written under U.S. tutelage.[62]

India: Independence and partition

In World War II, hundreds of thousands of Indian troops fought around the world for the British

---

[61] Chua, *Day of Empire*, p. 275.

[62] Historian Tony Judt analyzes how democracy and peace were consolidated after the war in *Postwar: A History of Europe Since 1945* (New York: Penguin, 2005).

Empire, raising expectations in India that the colony would earn self-government as Canada and Britain's other "white" colonies had done. In the end, however, as in Rhodesia, Kenya, Iraq, Egypt, Burma, and other imperial holdings, the transition to statehood was much more difficult and violent than for the "white" colonies. In India, it was Gandhi's call for nonviolent noncooperation with the British government that precipitated independence.

After World War II, Muslims in northern India campaigned for a separate state. In 1947, after much violence, the British partitioned the territory into two independent states, India and Pakistan, to accommodate the Muslims. Fifteen million people found themselves on the wrong side of the border and were uprooted. Law and order broke down, and more than 500,000 were killed in the chaos. More than 150 million Muslims remain in India today – and the India-Pakistan border is highly militarized. There were also 600 princely states that had existed under British rule and their situation had to be resolved. Kashmir was one such state where a disputed Muslim-majority territory was assigned to India but claimed by Pakistan. The region constitutes an ongoing, and dangerous, problem. (See Chapter 8.)

China: The death of the imperial system, the rise of Mao Zedong, and the communist takeover

As the 20th century began in China, the former great power was in free fall. The Boxer Uprising against foreigners with its siege of foreign legations took place in Peking from 1899–1901.[63] Foreign armies suppressed the rebellion, further humiliating the Chinese. In 1911, the 2,000-year-old imperial system fell,[64] and Sun Yat-sen, leader of the revolutionary alliance, and a Westernized intellectual, became provisional president. His party became the Nationalist Party (KMT). China entered World War I on the side of the Allies, believing the war would end imperialism. When it did not, radicalized Chinese students began to identify with the Soviet struggle against imperialism.

In 1921, young intellectuals founded a peasant-based Communist Party (CCP) that quickly fell under Soviet control. A period of internal anarchy followed as warlords, Nationalists, and Communists vied for control of the weak Chinese state. In 1925, Chiang Kai-shek took over the Nationalists. Conflicts escalated and the CCP and Nationalist troops fought in Shanghi. In 1927, Mao Zedong, one of the founders of the Communist Party, came to dominate it and in 1934 led it on a Long March to northern China that lasted almost a year, fighting Nationalists, local warlords, and the Japanese who had invaded Manchuria and northern China.[65] It was a great success for the CCP, as it made allies among the peasants and got credit for resisting the Japanese occupation.

When Japan was defeated in World War II, Chinese communists obtained control of much of the north of China and Manchuria. Civil war broke out, ending with a communist revolution. In 1949, The People's Republic of China was united under a strong, centralized, communist government with Mao Zedong as Chairman of the Republic (1949–59) and party chairman until his death in 1976. The Nationalist government fled to Taiwan. This was a turning point in China's history. China's transition to Marxist socialism meant redistribution of the resources of a poor, abject society. The Communist Party emphasized rural development, culture, and ideology and enforced ideological conformity with draconian zeal. Mao used the People's Liberation Army to initiate the vicious Cultural Revolution in 1966 when intellectuals and prominent political figures were sent to the countryside for "re-education."[66] Many millions of Chinese died during the difficult years of these purges, the Great Leap Forward, and the Cultural Revolution. The exact

---

[63] The Boxers were one of several groups that believed that martial training ("fists") would make them invulnerable to attack.

[64] There were twenty-five dynasties over about 2,000 years.

[65] See Patricia Buckley Ebrey, *The Cambridge Illustrated History of China* (Cambridge: Cambridge University Press, 2010).

[66] See Jonathan D. Spence, *The Search for Modern China* (London: W. W. Norton, 1990), chapter 16.

number of deaths is disputed, but estimates range from some forty-four million to seventy million.

The country remained mired in poverty. After Mao died in 1976, China began to pursue economic liberalization with considerable success and normalized relations with the outside world after years of isolation. Internal politics in China remained repressive with a communist system firmly in place, but a capitalist economy began to flourish.

Global consequences of World War II

When the war ended, Europe was in ruins, there was a new superpower – the United States – and the Soviet Union was beginning to assert itself as another one. Since extreme nationalist and nondemocratic regimes in Germany, Italy, and Japan had instigated the war, many observers concluded that democracy was a vital key to keeping aggression in check and preventing war. They also believed that economic pressures had contributed to the war and that more effective governance of the global economy would help maintain peace in the future.

The Allied victory ensured that both Germany and Japan were demilitarized and democratized so that they would not become aggressive again. Germany's new frontiers were established at Yalta in February 1945. Berlin was surrounded by communist East Germany and divided into sectors under joint control of the Soviet Union, the United Kingdom, France, and the United States, and eventually the communists constructed a massive wall to prevent passage between the East and West zones of the country and city. Territorially, the Soviet Union was the major victor, shifting its borders dramatically to the west and politically dominating Eastern Europe. The Soviets absorbed most of the territories of the former Tsarist Empire, including eastern Poland, the Baltic States, Bessarabia (largely Moldova and Ukraine today), and, eventually, Czechoslovakia. Only Yugoslavia, under Tito's communists, retained independence from Moscow. Germany became two states in 1949.

At the end of the war, to prevent the USSR from further aggression in Europe, a new Western alliance, the North Atlantic Treaty Organization (NATO), was established to bind democratic states together. Soviet leaders brought much of Eastern Europe under their communist control and in 1955 formed the Warsaw Pact as a protective alliance. Winston Churchill called this division of Europe between the forces of democracy and communism the Iron Curtain. The largely invisible but very strong curtain divided the two great powers for roughly four decades, in a standoff that created a fairly stable, but generally tense, peace in Europe. NATO and the Warsaw Pact are covered extensively in Chapters 5 and 9.

In an effort to create a credible international constitutional order, allied nations negotiated what became known as the Bretton Woods System in 1944. This general agreement led to a series of cooperative economic arrangements dedicated to lowering barriers to international trade and investment. Among them, the International Bank for Reconstruction and Development was set up to pump billions of dollars from the United States into the European economy (see Chapters 11 and 12 for a discussion of contemporary international economic institutions).

The victors created the United Nations in 1945 in an effort to provide stability and institutionalize global collective security. This time, unlike with the League that preceded it, the United States joined the new international organization. The dream of ending war seemed ever more distant. World War I had shown that diplomatic means should be exhausted before going to war. World War II had shown that expansionist powers should be confronted. But would following those rules prevent another conflagration – this time with nuclear weapons?

A new age of superpowers

The United States had been a sleeping giant when the Japanese attacked its base at Pearl Harbor in December 1941. Enraged, it brought its full military might – warships, submarines, bombers, and even the atomic bomb – into the war and turned the tide in favor of the Allies. At the war's end it was the United States that came to the aid of Japan and the crippled European economies with the Marshall Plan, providing them with billions of dollars and assistance to rebuild their countries. The war had created an economic boom in the United States. U.S. industry between 1940 and 1944 "exploded, expanding at a higher rate than ever before or since."[67] "By the war's end, the United States was the world's greatest exporter of goods and accounted for more than half of the world's total manufacturing output."[68] It had also become the West's preeminent military power (see Chapters 4, 5, and 9).

Europe began the long road to recovery. In 1952, France, Germany, Italy, and the Benelux countries set up the European Coal and Steel Community to coordinate their industries, and in 1957 they developed the European Economic Community (EEC), a full customs union. Western Europe's economy boomed. The EEC made the possibility of another war between Germany and France very remote, and over time it developed into the European Union (EU), one of the great power centers of today. (See Chapters 4, 5, and 6.)

When World War II began, European colonial powers still controlled much of Asia, the Pacific, the Caribbean, and almost all of Africa. Between 1945 and 1960, the remaining colonial empires vanished. The colonies, buttressed by nationalist ideas and democratic ideals, all gradually gained political and economic independence, some peacefully, some, like India and French Indochina (later Vietnam), violently. All of these new states were integrated into the new international system. Their borders were demarcated and they were recognized as members of the United Nations. The Westphalian state system of government and global institutions now covered most of the world but was overlaid with an array of multilateral institutions and international organizations tasked with administering specific aspects of international relations.

As new states proliferated, the modern-day political map of the world was created. Borders

[67] Chua, *Day of Empire*, p. 253.
[68] Ibid., p. 253.

were disputed; old issues were not always resolved by the changes, and some indeed worsened. In the Middle East, where Britain was in charge of the mandated territory of Palestine after World War I, the British encouraged Arab aspirations, including independence for Palestine. However, Britain also later committed support for the creation of a Jewish homeland in biblical Israel. The situation developed into a bitter, triangular conflict of Jews, Arabs, and the British. Britain finally turned the issue over to the United Nations and, in 1947, the UN divided the area into separate Jewish and Arab sections; Britain withdrew and Israel was proclaimed in 1948. The hostility between Jews and Arabs continues to be a serious focal point of instability within the Middle East and one of the most difficult and vital issues today. (See Chapters 4 and 8.)

The Cold War, Russia, and the United States

The world that emerged in 1945 after World War II was no longer centered in Western Europe. The United States and the former Soviet Union together dominated the international system until the breakup of the communist regime at the end of the 20th century. The ideological differences between the two powers produced a polarization between the capitalist West and the communist bloc. The United States was the first to build a nuclear bomb, and used it twice in 1945 against Japan, but the Soviet Union broke that monopoly in 1949. Both sides went on to develop vast arsenals of nuclear weapons, intercontinental ballistic missiles, and submarine-launched missiles. The consequences of a possible future war were so devastating that war was unthinkable. The period was termed the Cold War, a confrontation short of armed conflict because, although the two superpowers constantly prepared for war, no hot war ever developed between them. (See Chapter 5.)

The United States adopted a policy of global containment of the Soviet Union. Both sides sought to bring allies onto their side. Brutal military interventions, conflicts, and violence erupted periodically throughout the globe. In the Middle East, for example, Jews (backed by the United States) and Arabs (backed by the Soviet Union) clashed over territory and sovereignty of ancient lands. In parts of Asia, peasant communists competed with feudal systems of government. And in many developing countries in Africa, Asia, and Latin America violent clashes took place over forms of government, economic advantage, the location of territorial boundaries, and even food supplies. Both superpowers countered the slightest aggression by the other. (See Chapters 5 and 9.)

The Cuban Missile Crisis in 1962 was the most dangerous event of the Cold War. The Soviets were installing medium-range missiles in Cuba, less than 100 miles from the U.S. coast when the United States blockaded Cuba and threatened retaliation. The standoff brought the world to the brink of nuclear disaster and was averted only when the Soviets agreed to withdraw the missiles. Both sides looked back to the lessons of World War I and put more emphasis on diplomacy and communications, installing a "hotline," and working toward *arms control*. Both built up their nuclear weapons arsenals until it was clear that neither side could win a war that would result in mutual assured destruction (MAD) and that neither could get away with a surprise attack on the other.

As the Cold War progressed, the USSR stagnated economically. The United States, meanwhile, attracted massive numbers of immigrants, flourished economically and militarily, and consolidated its leadership role of the West. The Cold War finally ended with the tearing down of the Berlin Wall in 1989, followed by the formal breakup of the Soviet Union and the dismantlement of the Warsaw Pact in 1991. The demise of the Soviet Union left the United States as the only superpower on the global scene.

Has the United States become yet another empire? It has been the most powerful country in the world since the end of World War I, and since World War II it has assumed much of the responsibility for maintaining the global economic and political system. It has had an impact on the world's culture, technology, politics, and even religion perhaps equal to that of ancient Egypt, Persia, Greece, Rome, China, or Arabia – or Spain, Italy, or Great Britain in the 18th and 19th centuries.

Some argue that the United States differs markedly from its predecessors because its influence is almost entirely indirect and economic, and it refuses to rule colonies directly like the Romans or British did. However, this argument does not take into account that the United States has about one thousand military bases and installations on the sovereign land of other nations. Chalmers Johnson calls this a "base world."[69] It includes places like Guantanamo Bay in Cuba and isolated islands such as the Bikini Atoll, which was used for nuclear tests before it was turned over to the Republic of the Marshall Islands in 1979, and Diego Garcia, where the United States had native inhabitants expelled to make way for a military base that would help control the Indian Ocean. Some argue that these outposts exist through voluntary, bilateral agreements. Others call it expropriation of land and dispossession of some of the world's weakest people.[70]

We examine the role of the United States in the world today, along with other global powers, throughout the rest of the text, but especially in Chapter 5. The Cold War and East-West relations in particular are discussed in detail in Chapters 5 and 9.

Coming full circle?

Our survey of global history has traced the fall of extensive empires around the world as well as the development of the modern state. There are many definitions of empire but, for our initial purposes, they consist essentially of a single political unit that rules other groups and states directly or through intermediaries. Early empires absorbed only contiguous territory but later, as technology permitted,

[69] Chalmers Johnson, *Blowback: The Costs and Consequences of American Empire* (London: Little Brown, 2000).
[70] See David Vine, *Island of Shame: The Secret History of the US Military Base on Diego Garcia* (Princeton: Princeton University Press, 2009).

colonial empires extended around the globe, far from their center of power and authority.[71] Empire has been the "default mode" of political organization throughout history.[72]

Proponents of the long-cycle theory of history note that political power is fluid and ever changing and inevitably leads to war.[73] Cyclical periods of war by great powers and empires have been followed by institution building and national rulemaking. Each major war was like a political earthquake, shattering one equilibrium and imposing another as it brought about one major state's relative loss of power and the advent of a new country with unrivaled power. Then, within a few decades, or as much as a century, circumstances led to another war and the cycle repeated itself. There is disagreement about what factors produce these cycles – is it economics, military, or domestic factors – or perhaps a combination of them? Are great powers predetermined to fail?

Power cycle theory provides a contrasting explanation to the long-cycle theory. It explains structural change and the cycles of war in terms of the cyclical pattern of a state's rise, maturation, and decline in relative power – its *power cycle*.[74] Charles Doran argues that, throughout history, a single dynamic of structural change contours the power cycles of all the great powers. Differing growth rates among the great powers set power cycles in motion, and this competitive dynamic puts "bounds" on the extent to which any great power can rise above others. All great powers eventually reach an upper limit and are ultimately pulled into a declining path

as smaller states sustain growth at higher rates. If "failure" is the impossibility of retaining unrivaled power, then empires and great powers are destined to fail. But everything is emergent, and no behaviors are deterministic; the collapse into major war is not determined. Such competing theories of the causes of war are discussed in Chapter 9.

There are many other competing arguments about why empires collapse. Timothy Parsons believes that they always fail eventually because they are structures of conquest.[75] Paul Kennedy claims that great powers and megastates "overextend" themselves and then decay because of internal economic pressures.[76] Similarly, Jane Burbank and Frederick Cooper argue that protracted boundary conflicts undermine imperial structures.[77] Amy Chua proffers that empires decline because they grow increasingly intolerant and corrupt.[78] Finally, Niall Ferguson argues that great powers are complex systems with many interacting components that "function in apparent equilibrium for some unknowable period. And then, quite abruptly, they collapse." He associates empire decline with fiscal crises.[79] Successful empires preserve differences among the peoples they bring under their control. They also unite them with a "big idea" such as cultural unity, law, economic development, or religion.[80]

Today the world has one relatively dominant global power, the United States, that leads the world economically, militarily, and culturally. However, particularly since the global recession of 2008, the United States has had stiff competition. It is highly

[71] Historian Timothy Parsons argues that Empire has never been more than naked self-interest masquerading as virtue. Timothy Parsons, *The Rule of Empires: Those Who Built Them, Those Who Endured Them, and Why They Always Fail* (Oxford: Oxford University Press, 2010).

[72] John Darwin, *After Tamerlane*, p. 22.

[73] George Modelski, "The Long Cycle of Global Politics and the Nation-State." *Comparative Studies in Society and History* 20(2), pp. 214–35.

[74] Charles F. Doran, "Economics, Philosophy of History, and the 'Single Dynamic' of Power Cycle Theory: Expectations, Competition, and Statecraft." *International Political Science Review* 24(1) (special issue Power Cycle Theory and Global Politics), pp. 13–49.

[75] Parsons, *The Rule of Empires.*

[76] Paul Kennedy, *The Rise and Fall of the Great Powers: Economic Change and Military Conflict from 1500 to 2000* (New York: Vintage Books, 1989).

[77] Jane Burbank and Frederick Cooper, *Empires in World History: Power and the Politics of Difference* (Princeton: Princeton University Press, 2010).

[78] Amy Chua, *Day of Empire: How Hyperpowers Rise to Global Dominance – and Why They Fail* (New York: Doubleday, 2007).

[79] Niall Ferguson, "Complexity and Collapse." *Foreign Affairs*, 2010 (March/April), pp. 18–32. Also see, by the same author "The Fragile Empire." *Los Angeles Times*, Feb. 28, 2010, p. A26.

[80] Charles S. Maier, "Empire Without End: Imperial Achievements and Ideologies." *Foreign Affairs*, 2010 (July/August), pp. 153–59.

indebted to China. The Chinese are reasserting themselves in the world more than one and a half millenia after the eclipse of the Qin Dynasty that first united the country. They have opened their formerly closed economy and are making major advances militarily and economically.

China is gradually purchasing modern ships, submarines, guided missile destroyers, and aircraft and, for the first time in centuries, it is beginning to think of itself as a sea power. Chinese are now taught to think of sea as "territory," that their sovereignty includes "three million square kilometers of oceans and seas."[81] Is this a sign that the world has come full circle and resumed a new conflict cycle with diminishing and rising empires or global powers? Is the West in decline? Is it threatened by the rise of Asia?[82]

Japan and Russia, like the United States, came relatively late to the great power game. Japan was defeated in World War II but is now the world's third-largest economy. The rivalry between Japan and China that began centuries ago endures, and Japan's rise in the late 19th century was in large part at China's expense. Russia is recovering from the collapse of the former Soviet Union in 1991 but was in fact a major power before the Bolshevik Revolution and remains a major power today. Its weak economy was stifled by communism, but it is recovering and is still among the world's great military powers.

India is another rising Asian power. Conquered by the British and kept as a colony until after World War II, it appears to be headed for great power status in spite of serious issues of poverty, corruption, and lack of modernization.[83] In the late 20th century, after two world wars that devastated the continent, many European states joined together to form what today is the European Union, a prosperous and powerful bloc that is gradually consolidating a fragmented Europe as a political unit.

---

[81] David Shambaugh, *Modernizing China's Military: Progress, Problems, Prospects* (Berkeley CA: University of California Press, 2004) p. 67.

[82] Niall Ferguson argues this point in *Civilization: The West and the Rest* (London: Allen Lane, 2010).

[83] See C. Raja Mohan, "India and the Balance of Power." *Foreign Affairs*, 2006 (July/Aug.) vol. 85, no. 4, pp. 17–32.

Conclusion: Is global history destiny?

History is composed of an enormous body of facts, many of them disputed. What we have covered in this chapter is a bare outline of world history but one that provides essential context for the study of contemporary global politics. It explains how and why intransigent issues persist and discourages parochial conclusions. It also shows that the transition from local to regional to global history was a slow, uneven trajectory of surges and sags between fragmentation and globalization. We provide more historical background about specific modern events as required throughout the book, but this chapter presents the "big picture," a necessary frame of reference. It is not possible to grasp the importance of topics such as war, terrorism, arms control, or international institutions or to comprehend hot-spot issues such as those in Israel and Palestine, Kashmir and India, or Iran and the United States without historical background. Understanding other peoples' perspectives is crucial. It is not possible to understand, for example, the aspirations of China as an international actor without knowing what a great power it was historically. All countries have histories and perspectives that provide their people with a concept of self and expectations that they hope others share.

History gives us some answers about how the world developed and became what it is today, but it poses many more questions. Do the ideas or actions of certain individuals determine the unfolding of events in the world? Would global history have been different if, say, Hitler had been born in the middle class; or Josef Djugashvili (Stalin) had never have been born; or the Archduke of Austria-Hungary had not been murdered in Sarajevo? Or are there larger forces at work that would have produced the same general trajectory? The answers to these questions are generally complicated by the fact that governments are willing to cherry-pick and co-opt history to support their own agendas and control the narrative of history.[84]

Was the United States destined to be a world superpower? Are certain concepts so basic that every generation and every people search to master them? For example, security is a very significant concept today – but also as far back as antiquity. We have followed the evolution of the search for security throughout the centuries, as states after Westphalia tried one form of relationship after another – balance of power, informal alliances, formal alliances, collective security, and containment – to hold back enemies and end the specter of war. Even walls represent a search for security. Great walls such as the Great Wall of China, Hadrian's Wall, the Berlin Wall, and countless others have been constructed to keep people out of or in a certain territory. Even the 19th-century British navy could be seen as a massive wooden wall to protect its island kingdom. These structures all provide enduring testimony to the priority people give to defense and security. As far as we have come, walls are still being reverted to in places like Israel and Palestine. Yet none has ever succeeded in keeping anyone out or in. As one scholar noted, physical fences often rise when mental fences have already been built.[85]

There are two opposing views of history. One extreme position argues that history can neither teach us anything about the future nor can it help us avoid past mistakes. The other argues that it teaches a great deal because the future is nothing but a reflection of the past. Perhaps both views are too extreme. History gives us knowledge of what has happened before and therefore of what could happen in the future given the right conditions. In predicting where a society is headed it is helpful to know where it has been. It shows how bad decisions can have repercussions that impact on world peace and prosperity for decades or even centuries. For those who listen, it teaches humility, skepticism, and an awareness of our own place in history.[86]

History is easily abused. It should not be written to justify governments or make present generations feel good. Rather, at its best it makes one face how and when past generations pursued paths that now may seem wrong or even disgraceful, such as slavery. There are plenty of atrocities to go around. We can trace the decisions

---

[84] This is effectively argued by John W. Dower in *Cultures of War: Pearl Harbor/Hiroshima/9–11/Iraq* (New York: W. W. Norton & Co., 2011).

[85] A. C. Grayling, *The Heart of Things*, pp. 106–07.

[86] See Margaret MacMillan, *Dangerous Games, the Uses and Abuses of History* (London: The Modern Library, 2009).

and events that helped create the modern world with all its accomplishments and problems, its rising and falling powers, its increasing globalization, and its flashpoints of conflict and war. Looking back reminds us where we have been and may make it easier to identify potential problems before they happen. "We create history by our observations rather than history creating us."[87]

[87] Stephen Hawking and Leonard Mlodinow, *The Grand Design* (New York: Bantam Books, 2010).

Selected bibliography

Akbar, M. J., *The Shade of Swords: Jihad and the Conflict between Islam and Christianity* (London: Routledge, 2002).

Almond, Ian, *Two Faiths One Banner: When Muslims Marched with Christians across Europe's Battlegrounds* (Harvard: Harvard University Press, 2009).

Bayley, C. A., *The Birth of the Modern World: Global Connections and Comparisons, 1780–1914* (Oxford: Blackwell Publishing, 2004).

Boot, Max, *War Made New: Technology, Warfare, and the Course of History, 1500 to Today* (New York: Penguin, 2006).

Brendon, Piers, *The Decline and Fall of the British Empire 1781–1997* (New York: Alfred A. Knopf, 2007).

Burbank, Jane and Frederick Cooper, *Empires in World History: Power and the Politics of Difference* (Princeton: Princeton University Press, 2010).

Christian, David, *Maps of Time: An Introduction to Big History* (Los Angeles: University of California Press, 2005).

Chua, Amy, *Day of Empire: How Hyperpowers Rise to Global Dominance – And Why They Fail* (New York: Doubleday, 2007).

Evans, Richard J., *The Third Reich at War* (New York: Penguin, 2009).

Ferguson, Niall, *Civilization: The West and the Rest* (London: Allen Lane, 2010).

Gaddis, Lewis, *Surprise, Security, and the American Experience* (Harvard: Harvard University Press, 2005).

Herring, George C., *From Colony to Superpower: US Foreign Relations since 1776* (Oxford: Oxford University Press, 2008).

Hobson, John M., *The Eastern Origins of Western Civilization* (Cambridge: Cambridge University Press, 2004).

Judt, Tony, *Postwar: A History of Europe Since 1945* (New York: Penguin, 2005).

Kagan, Robert, *Dangerous Nation* (New York: Random House, 2006).

Luttwak, Edward N., *The Grand Strategy of the Byzantine Empire* (Cambridge MA: Belknap Press, 2009).

MacMillan, Margaret, *Dangerous Games: The Uses and Abuses of History* (London: The Modern Library, 2009).

Menzies, Gavin, *1421, The Year China Discovered the World* (New York: Phantom, 2002).

Morris, Ian, *Why the West Rules – For Now* (New York: Farrar, Straus and Giroux, 2010).

Pagden, Anthony, *Peoples and Empires* (London: Weidenfeld and Nicolson, 2001).

Parson, Timothy, *The Rule of Empires: Those Who Built Them, Those Who Endured Them and Why They Always Fail* (Oxford: Oxford University Press, 2010).

Renfrew, Colin, *Prehistory: The Making of the Human Mind* (London: Weidenfeld and Nicolson, 2007).

Rowe, William T. and Timothy Brook, *China's Last Empire: The Great Qing* (Cambridge MA: Belknap Press, 2009).

Roberts, Andrew, *The Storm of War: A New History of the Second World War* (London: Allen Lane, 2009).

Sarotte, Mary Elise, *The Struggle to Create Post-Cold War Europe* (Princeton: Princeton University Press, 2009).

Sebestyen, Victor, *Revolution 1989: The Fall of the Soviet Empire* (New York: Pantheon, 2009).

3 Competing theories, methods, and intellectual debates about global politics

Before beginning a study of global politics there are important ground rules to be mastered. Scholars and practitioners possess different world views about the nature of politics. These views are based on diverse schools of thought, each of which has a cluster of ideas that guide their questions and explanations about how the world works and should work. This chapter will lead you through the sometimes daunting maze of competing theories and issues that dominate the study of global politics.

There is a pertinent analogy in an old Indian story about four blind men who meet an elephant for the first time. They grope about, seeking to understand the beast. One grasps the trunk and concludes it is a snake. Another explores a leg and describes it as a tree. A third finds the tail and envisages it as a rope. Yet another of them touches the elephant's huge side and concludes it is a wall. None can imagine the whole animal. Similarly, scholars and practitioners disagree about which worldview best explains global politics – they describe various aspects of the whole in different ways. Although none has discovered the complete truth, all are communicating vital information about it.

The grand debates or arguments in global studies that need to be mastered revolve around three basic approaches to issues. The first concerns the *level* at which research ought to be carried out. There are three *levels of analysis* for understanding global politics: the individual, the state, and the international system. Most studies need to consider evidence at more than one level. We will use the case of Iran's alleged nuclear weapons program in Close Up 3.1 to illustrate how the various levels can be helpful in discussing global politics.

The second issue concerns what *theoretical perspectives* should be used to study global politics. What grand or general theories will best answer general questions and explain how power is obtained and the purpose to which it is put?[1] There are five basic theories that currently dominate this endeavor – realism, liberalism, political economy (Marxism and public choice), social constructivism, and feminism – as well as myriad revisions and new approaches. Each represents a world view and has proponents who attempt to use their preferred perspective to shape public discussion and debate about public policy in foreign affairs.

The third issue is concerned with *how to test* or confirm the validity of claims and theories about global politics. Two main groups dominate: *behavioralists*, who believe there are objective, scientific laws that govern international relations, and *traditionalists*, who do not. We examine each of these three basic

[1] Peter Burger and Thomas Luckman, *The Social Construction of Reality: A Treatise in the Sociology of Knowledge* (Garden City, NY: Doubleday, 1966).

issues in turn before considering the global role of the state, power, leadership, and decision making in Chapter 4.

The purpose of theory is to provide explanations and evaluations of real events, so at the conclusion of this chapter we choose a practical question: what do these approaches and theories tell us about the causes and continuation of the Afghanistan War that began in 2001? We ask how each might enlighten our understanding of this crisis situation: (1) what would studies at the different levels of analysis tell us? (2) what would the various theories explain? and (3) how can we test the validity of what we have concluded about the war?

Levels of analysis

When we choose a research question in global politics what evidence should be marshaled to answer it? First, one needs to determine the level at which to aim the analysis. This endeavor, known as the levels of analysis issue, ought to precede any research study (Table 3.1). The framework used should help to systematically organize understanding and avoid simplistic and superficial answers. A standard approach is to break the investigation into three parts: the *individual level*, the *state level*, and the *global level*.[2]

If, for example, one wished to understand a subject, such as the cause of a particular war or the origin of an international institution, we might study it at more than one level of analysis. At the individual level, we might examine the role of key individuals and their psychologies or personalities, analyzing their beliefs, values, and ideologies about politics. What motivates them in their preferences and choices? For example, we could debate what impact Hitler's behavior had in causing World War II or what impact Winston Churchill's character had on the war's outcome. Was Churchill's personality a vital factor or only a minor one in bringing about the defeat of Nazi Germany? Or, if war is not instigated by particular individuals, is it caused by human nature or by individual characteristics such as aggressiveness and deterred by personalities dominated by

[2] The original use of this approach is found in Kenneth Waltz, *Man, the State and War: A Theoretical Analysis* (New York: Columbia University Press, 1959).

Table 3.1 **Levels of analysis in global politics**

Individual	personalities; perceptions; choices
State	government; economy; interest groups; military institutions
International system	international organizations; multinational corporations; alliances; international rules/norms

modesty and humility? What personality characteristics described and animated the terrorist Osama bin Laden, former Libyan president Muammar Gaddafi, or the Indian pacifist Mohandas Gandhi? Are these traits pertinent to the study of global politics?

At the second or state level we could study the actions of single or multiple states to determine their key characteristics and examine how they make and implement foreign policy. This internal or domestic level of analysis points the analyst to the structure of the state's authority and its military and economic capabilities. Is the country democratic or authoritarian? Does it have primitive or advanced weapons? The study might also include topics such as examinations of government, bureaucracies, public opinion, parties, pressure groups, religious and secular groupings, and gender. Do these internal attributes and capabilities influence foreign policy? Do they influence decisions about peace or war?

The third or global level of analysis refers to examination of the interactions among states, noting the effect they may have on each other and the impact that global conditions or factors have on them. This level includes such variables as the nature of the international system and the distribution of military and economic capabilities among the major, middle, and less powerful states and would assess laws, treaties, diplomacy, global institutions and nonstate actors on the international stage. But it would also need to include broad system-wide concepts such as globalization, global terrorism, the North-South divide over wealth and poverty, and the technological and information revolutions. How do such worldwide forces impact on foreign policy choices? Can one analyze the causes of war or the rise of new

institutions with such broad system-wide characteristics?

Close Up 3.1 indicates how an analyst can separate an issue into discrete subjects for examination. Of course, actions at one level may affect behavior at another level. Robert Putnam, for example, has shown how foreign policy making can be understood in terms of a "two-level game" between domestic political calculations and international interests.[3] To become a sophisticated analyst of global politics we will need to understand the three levels and the relations among them. An important point to remember is that as long as you are asking a good question about levels of analysis in a rigorous way, nothing is off limits. (For a detailed discussion of the controversial Iranian nuclear issue and international action about it see Chapter 4.)

Theories and perspectives

The second important topic in global studies concerns theoretical issues. The concept *theory* derives from the Greek word *theoria*, meaning "contemplation." Theory is used in global studies to make sense of events by explaining how or why they are interconnected. It distinguishes the significant from the irrelevant by examining commonalities and elucidating the most convincing explanations. Like doctrines and "isms," theories provide principles for understanding global politics. Theories are human inventions – bold conjectures – about operations in the real world. We might describe them as intellectual "nets" used to catch or explain the world. They direct attention to specific features of politics – like different lenses through which the world may be observed. They are as indispensable to political analysis as a map is to a traveler crossing unknown terrain.

Each generation brings to the study of politics its own interests, values, and theories, often carrying over ideas from other disciplines such as

Close Up 3.1 **Applying levels of analysis: Iran**

The contemporary Iranian issue is an excellent case to help understand the importance of the use of these three levels of analysis. In order to study Iran's alleged development of nuclear weapons, a scholar might examine the situation at one or several levels. At the *individual* level one could, for example, study the importance of Iran's leaders in the decision to develop nuclear technology and its possible application to nuclear weapons. To what extent are the personal characteristics and power of President Ahmadinejad or those of Supreme Religious Guide Ayatollah Ali Khamenei important? At the *state* level we might study the structure of Iranian theocracy and concentrate on institutions such as the Revolutionary Guards that enforce Islamic law using intimidation and sometimes murder. At the *global* level we might wish to consider Iran's role as a major oil exporter, as a leader of Shiite Muslims in the Middle East, as a potential nuclear power, and perhaps as a people that fears U.S. imperialism in the Middle East.

[3] Robert Putnam, "Diplomacy and Domestic Politics: The Logic of Two-Level Games." *International Organization* 42(3), pp. 427–60.

history, law, philosophy, sociology, economics, or anthropology. In this sense, global studies includes multiple approaches and is a multidisciplinary subject. The inconsistencies caused by this diversity are reduced by the accepted principle that political scientists should be self-consciously analytical and avoid basing generalizations on casual observation. At their best, theories help us to understand the shape of global politics and to assess explicitly our own assumptions and biases about the subject.

The frame of reference used by a researcher may be implicit or explicit, but it should be identifiable because it determines the questions, procedures, and methods that the researcher uses. Different generations of scholars have developed approaches based on their unique interests, values, and methodologies, with notions about which ones are best, shifting according to what is needed or sometimes what is fashionable. Mostly, however, they focus on similar vital questions such as who exercises power and influence in political decision making and how leaders and states seek and maintain power.

There are basic disagreements about theory. Some modern approaches are based on the belief that studies of global politics should employ a *scientific theory*, that is, they should *identify* the critical structures and processes of international relations, *explain* their interrelationships, and *predict* a wide array of outcomes. Such a theory, its proponents argue, would allow scholars to arrive at scientific, lawlike generalizations that would enable the researchers to describe, explain, and predict political outcomes. Other scholars are more elastic or inclusive in their definition of theory, simply using it to mean interwoven generalizations about a topic. Others use it even more broadly to encompass normative positions, as in the contention that theory can provide correct prescriptions about how to change the world to conform to particular goals and ideologies.

Two analogies summarize the core of this debate. One is that politics is amorphous, like the shifting formlessness of clouds; the other is that it is based on precise, mechanical causation, like a watch.

After careful analysis, Gabriel Almond and Stephen Genco concluded that the quandary in political science can, to a large extent, "be explained by the fact that, by themselves, clock-model assumptions are inappropriate for dealing with the substance of political phenomena." Their conclusion comes from the belief that all theories must necessarily include transient and fleeting phenomena. Politics is not totally predictable, Almond and Genco maintain, because human behavior is involved – political reality "has distinctive properties which make it unamenable to the forms of explanation used in the natural sciences." Therefore, the science of politics should not be seen as a set of methods with a predetermined theory but instead as a "commitment to explore and attempt to understand a given segment of empirical reality."[4]

Bearing these laudatory yet cautionary remarks in mind, we outline and analyze the most important theories in international relations and their most important derivatives. While we cannot mention all of the authors associated with each topic, we attempt to provide enough understanding of the theories' central characteristics to make them meaningful and useful in studying global politics. Moreover, it would be a mistake to assume that these theories are mutually exclusive. Some focus on national interests and others on general values, but all influence foreign policy making and the study of it.

Theories of global politics

Two theoretical perspectives dominate the study of modern global politics: realism and liberalism. They are the central lenses or filters through which the global system is viewed by many observers. The two approaches are usually contrasted somewhat simplistically as being pessimistic or optimistic about human nature. Realists claim that liberal idealists are naïve in their assertions about hope for progress in

---

[4] Gabriel A. Almond and Stephen J. Genco, "Clouds, Clocks and the Study of Politics." *World Politics* 29(4) (July 1977), p. 505.

overcoming the natural drive for power in politics. Liberals claim that the realists are conservatives with no comprehensive understanding of politics, especially not of the roles that values and beliefs play in it. Both arguments are used to explain international relations, but perhaps realism has been more acceptable to political elites as a justification for *realpolitik* – especially during periods of global tension and wars – while liberalism has drawn more attention to the normative (is/ought distinction) themes of politics. Contemporary neorealism and neoliberalism have amended both of these theories, and both broad schools of thought are contested by a variety of critical and alternative theories. The theories can be confusing because their advocates often do not use mutually exclusive terms and writers often adopt more than one approach. Thus, the perspectives of authors and their theories often merge or overlap.[5]

Realism

The dominant historical force in modern international relations studies has been realism. Throughout the Cold War period it was used both to explain relations between states and to justify their foreign policies. Classical realism begins with the assumption that individuals are primarily selfish and power seeking. States, as human contrivances, are also considered to act in their own *interests*, and national interest is viewed in terms of power. (For elaboration on the concept of power see Chapter 4.) Realists claim that individuals should be practical and represent the world as it is. They stress that the values of self-interest, prudence, and expediency should and do count more than other more ethically disposed ideas. They are interested in examining how society shapes peoples' lives, even if the results break hallowed notions of what are considered appropriate or ethical explanations of politics. In

global studies realists focus on the distribution of power among states. They accept as fact that, since states exist in an anarchic international system, they will and must create security for themselves by such methods as increasing their economic and military power and seeking to create a balance of power with other states.

Exponents of realism and its central concept of *power* have come from all the continents and throughout all history. More than two millennia ago Asian philosopher Sun Tzu (500 BCE–?) outlined the need for Chinese leaders to use power to protect their interests. Later, Shang Yang (390–338 BCE) wrote that power was achieved by full granaries and large armies, and another Chinese scholar, Han Fei (280–233 BCE), showed how power could be used to support an autocratic government. In another part of the world in about 300 BCE, Kautilya, an adviser to the Maurya emperor of India, advised in his work *Arthashastra* that a leader should always aspire to more power and that only power characterized a king. Greek historian Thucydides (431–404 BCE) examined the use of power in the violent conflict between Athens and Sparta. He saw the state as the principal actor in war and politics and argued that rational decision making by a state would further the pursuit of its national interests. He concluded that the Peloponnesian War showed that states are motivated to fight when they fear a rival is growing too strong.

Among better known exponents of the roots of realism in the West are Niccolo Machiavelli (1469–1527; Figure 3.1), whose book *The Prince* advised Italian leaders how to use power prudently, and Thomas Hobbes (1588–1679), who, in the *Leviathan*, described the origin of the state in terms of power and who believed that states, like individuals, have the responsibility and the right to preserve themselves. The classic realist position was put by Machiavelli, who claimed, "It is necessary for a prince who wishes to maintain his position to learn how not to be good, and to use this knowledge or not use it according to necessity." In a similar vein, U.S. President Abraham Lincoln is claimed to

---

[5] See, for example, Robert S. Snyder, "Bridging the Realist/Constructivist Divide: The Case of the Counter-revolution in Soviet Foreign Policy at the End of the Cold War." *Foreign Policy Analysis* 1(1) (March 2005), pp. 55–71; J. Samuel Barkin, "Realist Constructivism." *International Studies Review* 5(3) (September 2003), pp. 325–42.

Figure 3.1 Niccolo Machiavelli (1469–1627), thought by many to be the most important political scientist ever, highlighted the importance of power in politics and the techniques leaders could exercise to retain it.
Source: Alamy.

have said, "I hope to have God on my side, but I must have Kentucky." Well-known modern American scholars of the realist tradition include Hans Morgenthau (1904–80), whose book *Politics among Nations* was the realist bible for decades following World War II. Like his realist, predecessors he viewed international politics as a constant struggle for power and put national interests ahead of moral issues. Henry Kissinger, secretary of state to U.S. presidents Richard Nixon and Gerald Ford, based his policy recommendations on realist theory. A good example was his 1970s advice to the American government to support weaker powers such as Pakistan in order to offset India's growing power as an ally

of the Soviets.[6] Historian George Kennan, another influential realist, advocated the U.S. follow a policy of containment during the Cold War to prevent the Soviets from extending their sphere of influence and power in Europe.

For "hard core" realists, the state is the most important actor in global politics, and conflicts among states are inevitable. For this reason they argue that statesmen should strive to increase their state's power. The possibility that good will and cooperation will replace conflict is thought to be extremely low. This realist argument is most persuasive during times of conflict, war, and terrorism as it focuses debate on pragmatism and military strength. Contrary to popular opinion, however, realists do not always advocate the use of force and often support joining alliances and signing arms control agreements if they consider it prudent to do so. U.S. realists were vociferously divided over the wisdom of the U.S. intervention in Vietnam and the 2003 attack on Iraq. In the first case, many of them disputed whether Vietnam really represented a communist domino, the fall of which would lead to more expansion of this detested philosophy. In the second case, pragmatic realists proposed the adoption of many prudent policies short of war with Saddam Hussein.

Essentially, realist theory has five core principles:

1. Individuals and states seek power, particularly military power, in order to ensure their security and preferences. Early classical realists were pessimistic about human nature and the possibility of change. They found the idea of eliminating power from politics naïve and utopian. Later realists dropped concern for the roots of human nature and concentrated instead on the concept of anarchy in the international system. In the anarchical world of international politics, the features that matter most are thought to be power, national security, and material interests rather than altruistic issues.

---

[6] See Henry Kissinger, *A World Restored: Metternich, Castlereagh and the Problems of Peace, 1812–1822* (London: Weidenfeld & Nicolson, 1957).

2. International politics is about states and their relationships. Countries strive for power and position naturally, and each one competes for its own national interests in an anarchical world. National interests are defined as those goals (including security, military and economic power, and influence in global politics) that states pursue to maximize their country's selfish interests. What matters from a realist perspective is not ethics, identity, ideology, or leadership; rather, it is the capability of state leaders to carry out their intentions and to do what they must to retain power for themselves and their country.

3. Global politics is about the shifting distribution of power among states. Military strength plays a central role in this calculation as realists do not accept the idea that morality, international institutions, and law can preserve peace even in an era of interdependence. Balance of power, deterrence, and a strong military are required because the world is a dangerous place. Even rudimentary international governance will work only if it is grounded on the essential principle of the global distribution of power.

4. In their search for power and security, states are guided by amoral, rather than moral, calculations about national interests. Realists are skeptical of claims to universal goodwill and advise that leaders should not engage in moral crusades but devote themselves to preserving their own state's national interests. They believe that liberal idealists and others accept arguments about how the world *should* act rather than how it really *does* act.

5. Since the global arena is basically an anarchy, with each state fending for itself, there is a constant *security dilemma*. As one state becomes more secure, it automatically diminishes the security of others.

Several assumptions about realism have been challenged over the years. Since states are by far the most important actors in this theory, how do they account for the importance of nonstate actors such as powerful multinational corporations and/ or nonterritorial-based terrorist groupings or networks? This argument is generally countered by stating that not only states are involved in politics and that realist assumptions can include powerful statelike institutions. A second and perhaps more fundamental attack on realism is that it cannot adequately define and explain power or of what it consists. Does power include only military and economic capabilities or does a country's power also include its culture, history, ideas, and ideology? Are variables such as public commitment important in providing cohesion and, if so, are shared values not also a vital ingredient of state power? Can a country be powerful if its people do not support their leaders? These questions have proven difficult to answer.

In the past two decades, realism has been updated as neorealism or structural realism. These revisions discard the classical notion that human nature is inherently pessimistic and shift the focus from the domestic level to the anarchical international system with its unequal distribution of power. While all realists accept the idea that states act in a fundamentally anarchical world, neorealists believe that the structure of the international system is *the* most important factor influencing the states within it. Professor Kenneth N. Waltz's classic book, *Theory of International Politics*, for example, focuses on how anarchy and the structure of global politics shape the behavior of states within the system.[7] The absence of a world government compels states to consider their own security and their relative power compared to others and is the primary factor in global politics. It therefore becomes important to rank-order states based on their relative power capabilities.

Another updated version of the neorealist approach is provided by John Mearsheimer, who argues that the degree of uncertainty about how states will act in the international arena compels states to

---

[7] Kenneth N. Waltz, *Theory of International Politics* (Reading MA: Addison-Wesley, 1979).

maximize their power capabilities.[8] Mearsheimer's views are sometimes called offensive realism as he considers that states are entirely driven by power maximization, making cooperation limited and tenuous. Conversely, some theorists are tagged as defensive realists because they argue that because states achieve security by maintaining their position in the international system they constantly will try to maintain an appropriate or adequate degree of power in relation to other states. In each of these cases global politics is seen to be mostly about the great powers' contest for power on the international stage.[9] By ignoring human nature and domestic politics as explanations, realism and neorealism may have lost some of the explanatory richness of global politics that can be gleaned from history, geography, identity, ethics, and idiosyncratic state attributes. It may also mean that, for realists, power has perhaps become too closely aligned with specific military power capabilities rather than difficult psychological variables such as societal cohesion and the will to engage in warfare.

Realism is sometimes portrayed as a simplistic world view. However, it is far from that. It encourages a pragmatic assessment of the role of power and warns states about wasting power by over-reaching their capabilities or the misuse of energy on moral crusades that can never be successful. In that sense, realism is not an immoral theory but an amoral one in that its advocates believe adherence to its premises will lead to a peaceful world. For realists, power is not an end in itself, nor does it guide one to the ends to which it should be put. But for them ideals without power cannot achieve anything. Realists, and neorealists in particular, also concede

---

Box 3.1 **Key to realism in global politics**

Major actors:	states as unitary actors
Significant concepts:	national interests; power
International system:	anarchic
Beliefs:	only slow structural change

---

the importance of economic vitality when determining the military potential of a state. It is, after all, mostly self-described realists who keep warning that China is an emergent military power, and they do so on the grounds that China is becoming wealthy and starting to throw its weight around in global politics.

Liberalism

Liberalism comes in many forms. Unlike early realism, classical liberalism views human nature as basically good and holds that people are capable of improving their moral and material conditions, thereby making societal progress possible. Liberal theory focuses on changing norms about the state, sovereignty, human rights, and international justice. Injustice, aggression and war are not inevitable in the liberal view and can be moderated or eliminated by institutions of collective action. In its modern mode, liberalism often highlights the changing nature and distribution of democracies (which are thought to best expand human freedom) and the importance of international institutions and market capitalism.

Liberal theory has gone through several transitions from its classical origins in the 17th century to idealism in the pre-Second World War period and finally to the liberal institutionalism of today.[10] Among the foremost exponents of

---

[8] John J. Mearsheimer, "The False Promise of International Institutions." *International Security* 19(3) (winter 1994–95), pp. 5–49.

[9] There are many important debates and controversies in this field. See, for example, Robert Keohane, ed., *Neorealism and its Critics* (New York: Columbia University Press, 1986); Scott Burchill, *The National Interest in International Relations Theory* (New York: Palgrave, 2005); John Mearsheimer, *The Tragedy of Great Power Politics* (New York: W. W. Norton, 2001); Chris Brown and Kirsten Ainsley, *Understanding International Relations*, 3rd ed. (New York: Palgrave, 2005).

[10] For a detailed history and analysis of liberalism see M. Doyle, *Ways of War and Peace: Realism, Liberalism, and Socialism* (New York: W. W. Norton, 1997).

Figure 3.2 John Locke (1632–1704) is known as a "father" of classical liberalism. His arguments concerning liberty influenced the founding fathers of the United States. Scholars trace the phrase "life, liberty, and the pursuit of happiness" in the American Declaration of Independence to Locke's theory of rights. *Source:* Alamy.

liberalism historically were John Locke (1632–1704; Figure 3.3) and Immanuel Kant (1724–1804), who believed that lasting peace among states was possible. Kant argued that people should be treated as ends and not means and that the spread of human rights, liberal democracy, and the horror of war could convince people to find peaceful ways of resolving their disputes. The Scottish economist Adam Smith (1723–90) added the liberal notion that individuals pursuing their own self-interest would provide the most efficient, and hence the most productive, economies. In the 19th century, British liberals such as Richard Cobden stressed the role of free trade in creating a peaceful world. The best-known liberal proponent of the 20th century was U.S. president Woodrow Wilson, who backed

concepts such as self-determination and supranational institutions such as the League of Nations. Unfortunately, his noble quest to make collective security the touchstone of global politics failed when the American Senate declined to ratify the treaty after World War I. Today, all liberals coalesce around the task of building a more perfect international system of laws and institutions.

Essentially, liberalism has five core principles:

1. The global system is not a simple anarchy but rather an "ordered" one. Individuals, commercial actors, international institutions and transnational networks, as well as states, can all play important roles in global politics.
2. Global politics is shaped by ideas, values, culture, and social identities as well as by power. Liberals stress the need to obtain a consensus on ethics and values in global politics in order to avoid wars and other disasters. In their view, acceptance of cooperative beliefs can lead to a peaceful and just world.
3. Liberalism focuses on the impact that ideas have on political behavior. It tends to define politics not in terms of power relationships but rather in terms of a struggle for consensus. In a search for agreements that will make the world more orderly, just, and cooperative, liberalism highlights issues such as human rights and international justice. At their most idealistic, liberals assert that the physical world is less important than intangibles such as ideas or values. Conversely, they are prepared to use military force in some situations such as defense of their values or country or even in UN-sponsored humanitarian ventures such as stopping genocide in the former Yugoslavia, Rwanda, and Darfur.
4. Cooperative rather than conflictual behavior or pure power relations explains how states act together, conducting themselves peacefully in diplomacy, free trade, and financial transactions. To the realist claim that military power is required in an anarchical and conflictual world, liberals contend that the world is dangerous

precisely because so many states possess powerful militaries. The concept of national interest, therefore, needs to include the interests of others in order to contruct a peaceful world. Liberals also stress the role of nonstate actors and even individuals in promoting greater interdependence and hence enhancing the probability of world peace.

5. The goal of liberal thought is to obtain collaborative security and institutionalize peace by the actions of supranational organizations and the development of international law. This is based on a belief that international organizations should coordinate states through collective security, arms control, and disarmament agreements. Democratic values should also be protected throughout the world. In fact, for many liberals, research that indicates the importance of democracy for peace enhancement has provided one of the most persuasive conclusions of international relations studies. (This hypothesis is examined in detail in Chapter 9.) Many liberals, especially those who are more progressive, also believe that conflict and war emerge from the poor and wretched conditions that most people live in; therefore, these scholars tend to favor international aid development projects and humanitarian ventures.

Liberals believe that the global system is an *ordered anarchy* because cooperation best describes the pattern of much global interaction. They forecast a sluggish but optimistic movement toward a more peaceful and desirable world as democratic norms and practices spread and trade and finance globalize. Liberals believe that the "real" or "overlooked" national interest is found in the search for a more orderly and just world. International norms, or the shared expectations that people hold about global relations and their appropriateness, can develop over time and be manifest in cooperative behavior. Even those liberals who are less optimistic about continual progress stress moderation and oppose realist hard-line views about world politics.

They tend to promote humanitarian intervention by the United Nations, for example, and place considerable faith in multilateral institutions because such institutions foster habits of cooperative behavior. Liberals contend that even when states act against the accepted norms of cooperative behavior their leaders find it necessary to spend considerable effort explaining why they do so.

The modern neoliberal school accepts many of the assumptions of realism, in particular the role of states in an anarchical framework, but it contests its pessimism about the lack of a world government preventing cooperation. Neorealists are structuralists in that they claim that states' behavior is primarily shaped by changes in the properties of the global system such as shifts in the balance of power. Neoliberals, on the other hand, argue that norms and rules across states can develop into "international regimes," providing cooperative institutions and making peace and security possible.

Neoliberal institutionalists such as Robert Axelrod and Robert O. Keohane accept the realist assumption of world anarchy as a prevalent characteristic of global politics but also hold the view that the interactions among the states can be positive if there is a spirit of cooperation.[11] In other words, they do not accept the realists' essentially negative idea that state interaction will always produce selfish actions. States may conclude that their future is dependent on the states they interact with and therefore accept norms – shared expectations about what behavior is considered proper – and set rules that benefit all. Therefore, neoliberals consider a state's intentions, interests, and ideals may be more important criteria in foreign policy making than its power capabilities.

There are many other varieties of the liberal approach. Liberal theorists today are increasingly interested to determine why democracies do not go to war with each other. Their explanations include the idea that shared democratic norms and culture

[11] Robert Axelrod and Robert O. Keohane, "Achieving Cooperation under Anarchy, Strategies and Institutions." In Kenneth Oye, ed., *Cooperation under Anarchy* (Princeton NJ: Princeton University Press, 1986), pp. 226–54.

inhibit aggression, democracies have voters that restrain their behavior, and international institutions and agreements bind democracies together.[12] The breakup of the Soviet Union in 1991 was a particularly dramatic and hopeful event for such theorists. Many saw it as a victory for international liberalism because there was a sudden absence of any viable theoretical alternatives to democracy. Francis Fukuyama even asked whether the world was witnessing "the end of history" with the victory of liberal democracy supplanting all other ideologies and the end of large-scale conflict.[13]

The English School of international relations (sometimes referred to as liberal realism) is a form of liberal and realist interpretation. For its advocates, the globe consists of separate states, but those states exist in much more than pure anarchy. For Hedley Bull and his followers, states exist in a kind of *international society* because they recognize common interests and consent to rules such as international law and join institutions such as the UN.[14] For advocates of the English School, ideas and rules, rather than just power, shape international relations and should be given their proper due. Like constructivists these theorists pay considerable attention to the normative structure of global politics and, therefore, to the importance of cooperation and the norms, rules, and institutions.[15]

A further point of clarification is required about liberalism because the term is used differently in scholarly and public policy fields. Today in academia the term refers broadly to liberal institutionalism and ways to study it. In politics it includes

---

Box 3.2 **Key to liberalism in global politics**

Major actors:	states; nonstate actors; individuals; international organizations
Significant concepts:	values; cooperation; interdependence
International system:	ordered anarchy; international society; international institutions
Beliefs:	change is desirable and probable

---

the promotion of specific policies such as free trade and democratic values and institutions. Although he was a Republican, President George W. Bush believed his administration should impose democratic values and institutions and free trade – classic liberal policies – in the Middle East and Iraq. His presidency was dominated by neoconservatives (neocons), discussed in the following section. The neocons also have a great deal in common with liberal thought, including a belief in moral leadership and the individual. They are, however, distrustful of international institutions.

Neoconservatives   American Republicans blend different schools of political thought, including realist, neoconservative, and nationalist, and under President George W. Bush's administration there was a conjunction of values and events in and around the government in which the neoconservative agenda was more influential than the other two traditions. The earliest neoconservatives were not Republicans but rather Democrats who, during the 1970s, argued that the United States was not conducting its Cold War diplomacy aggressively enough and who then rallied to the Republican Party during the presidency of Ronald Reagan.

As we have seen, realists are mainly characterized by their concern for the realities of power, but

---

[12] Bruce Russett, *Grasping the Democratic Peace* (Princeton NJ: Princeton University Press, 1993); Edward D. Mansfield and Jack Snyder, *Electing to Fight: Why Emerging Democracies Go to War* (Cambridge MA: MIT Press, 2005).

[13] Francis Fukuyama, "The End of History?" *National Interest* 16 (summer 1989), p. 4.

[14] H. Bull, *The Anarchical Society: A Study of Order in World Politics* (London: Macmillan, 1977).

[15] Barry Buzan and Richard Little, *International Society in World History* (Oxford: Oxford University Press, 2000), A. James, *Sovereign Statehood: The Basis of International Society* (London: Allen and Unwin, 1986), and A. Linklater, *Men and Citizens in the Theory of International Relations*, 2nd ed. (London: Macmillan, 1990).

neocons are perhaps more concerned with the art of the desirable than the possible. Realists treat global power relations as given; neocons believe that the United States should enlighten the world with its values of democracy, freedom, and the goodness of American life. Nationalists favor an inward-looking America-first agenda.[16] Neoconservatism represents a much younger school of thought than either realism or liberalism and in no way constitutes an established school of international relations analysis. It is a specifically American policy-advocacy faction, blending realism (the application of power) with Wilsonian liberalism (the spread of democracy). Historically, all three Republican groups focused on opposing international communism but later the neocons stressed an aggressive ideological agenda, particularly about politics in the Middle East. They advocated using state power to transform global politics rather than conserving older traditions and alliances, supporting the concept of the United States as empire and policeman of the world.

Over time the neoconservative camp included thinkers such as Irving Kristol and Norman Podhoretz, policymakers such as Paul Wolfowitz, David Frum, and Richard Perle, and public intellectuals such as Donald Kagan, William Kristol, Robert Kagan, Fouad Ajami, and Francis Fukuyama. They maintained that America's national interests and moral purposes were the same.[17] Irving Kristol defined a neoconservative as "a liberal who had been mugged by reality."[18] They fostered the intellectual climate that gave sustenance to a new American militarism,[19] calling for a revolution in military affairs that would take advantage of technological changes to give the United States overwhelming military dominance. Although there have been serious divisions within the group its values and ideas live on.

Neocons share five viewpoints:

1. *Leadership*: men and values, not impersonal forces, determine the course of history.
2. *Realism*: military power is the primary determinant in global affairs; indeed, it is the first and perhaps the only option of power politics.
3. *Unilateralism*: suspicion of internationalism and international organization.
4. *Moralism*: a view of the world expressed in absolutes and with a conviction that there is a need to reassert traditional American values.
5. *Focus*: concentration on the Middle East and Islam perhaps more than other areas of the world.

Political economy perspectives: Neo-Marxism and public choice

Political economy as a theory is concerned with the relationships between government and economics. Politics and economics are never entirely separate phenomena: the way people earn their living as professionals, businesspeople, or laborers always influences politics and international relations. Economics involves conflict over scarce resources; politics generally involves government decisions about power and who will pay and who will benefit from the production and distribution of items ranging from health care to armaments. States influence the extent to which resources are placed in the hands of the poorest and richest segments of society, and richer states affect the well-being and even the power of weaker states.

The political economy approach has been of particular importance in the study of public policy – or the study of what states or governments do. Ideologies and political beliefs differ over what the role of government should be, and especially over how large it should be. Underlying this dispute is the question: what ought to be the role of government concerning regulation and intervention in economic and social affairs? Those who accept values such

---

16 See Stephan Halper and Jonathan Clarke, *America Alone: The Neo-Conservatives and the Global Order* (Cambridge MA: Cambridge University Press, 2004).

17 See, for example, Robert Kagan and William Kristol, "Towards a Neo-Reaganite Foreign Policy." *Foreign Affairs* (July/August 1996), pp. 22–23.

18 Quoted in *The New York Times*, Sept. 19, 2009, p. A15.

19 Andrew J. Bacevich, *The New American Militarism, How Americans are Seduced by War* (Oxford: Oxford University Press, 2005), p. 71.

as private enterprise, freedom, and individualism answer the question one way; those who believe that social and political relations are largely predetermined and constrained by the economic basis of society answer it quite differently.

These opposing views are reflected in starkly contrasting studies of political economy found in neo-Marxism and public choice theories. Neo-Marxism is based on Karl Marx's ideas about the relationship among economic, social, and political structures. For Marx and his followers, economics provides the most important explanations for virtually all phenomena, including international relations. Neo-Marxism contrasts with a relatively new public choice school, which is sometimes referred to as "liberal political economy" because it tends to follow the logic of classical economic reasoning and advocates statistical studies of economics. In public choice theory the key idea begins with man as a rational actor; in Marxism it develops from the concept of class. In this book we give more attention to the traditional approach of neo-Marxism because of its significance in the historical study and practice of global politics, especially in communist states and less economically developed parts of the world.

Karl Marx (1818–83; Figure 3.3) was the first to theorize about the evolution of capitalism on the basis of economic change and class conflict, and his writing underpins a wide variety of subsequent radical thought. British economist John A. Hobson (1858–1940) later focused on the relationship between Marxist economics and the global system, which he viewed as hierarchical and largely the by-product of imperialism. The domination and suppression of states arises, he said, from the uneven development inherent in the capitalist system, and imperialism leads to rivalry among developed countries and efforts to balance power.[20] Russian leader Vladimir Ilyich Lenin (1870–1924) called this imperialism and argued that imperialism leads to war.[21]

[20] John A. Hobson, *Imperialism: A Study* (Ann Arbor: University of Michigan Press, 1965).
[21] V. I. Lenin, *Imperialism: The Highest Stage of Capitalism* (New York: International Publishers, 1939).

KARL MARX

Figure 3.3 Karl Marx (1818–1883) was without a doubt the most influential socialist thinker to emerge in the 19th century. His *Communist Manifesto*, written with Friedrich Engels, was a radical critique of capitalism used as a rallying cry and a core text by Bolsheviks in their overthrow of the Russian monarchy in 1917. *Source:* Photos.com.

The neo-Marxist approach is a radical, political economy approach to public policy. At its basic conceptual level, *materialism* underpins Marxism. It assumes that a person's social, intellectual, and even religious life is molded by his/her economic environment. Neo-Marxism is, thus, a generic label for theories and propositions that seek to develop a systematic and radical understanding of the relations between economics and politics, in particular the role of the state in capitalist societies.

The essence of the Marxist argument is that all stages of historical development are determined by the economic basis of society. The unequal relations between classes are based on the mode of production that exists at any given time. In the present era (the capitalist mode of production) the two main social classes are differentiated by their respective economic roles: the "capitalist class," or "bourgeoisie," owns and controls the means of production (factories, financial capital, and so on) and the "working class," or "proletariat," sells its labor to the capitalists. According to Marx's economic theory, the dynamics of capitalism require entrepreneurs to extract "surplus value" from labor – effectively exploiting the working class – because this is the only mechanism by which capitalists can make profits for the accumulation of capital and further investment. This exploitative economic relationship between capital and labor forms the basis of conflictual class relations in social and political life.

Marxists argue that the primary function of the modern state is to serve the interests of capitalists. The state creates and maintains conditions favorable to capital accumulation by concentrating wealth in a few hands and, thus, societies are stratified into groups with uneven resources. The resultant unequal relations among economic classes shape both domestic and global politics. However, in order to reduce the inherent conflict between classes and forestall the possibility of revolution by the exploited working class, the modern state must also create and maintain conditions for social harmony by providing policies that legitimize capitalism. The dominant ideology of capitalist countries therefore includes beliefs and justifications about private property, the possibility of upward socio-economic mobility, and the importance of markets, all of which buttress the role of the state and make it difficult for the vast majority of individuals to understand that they are being exploited. However, Karl Marx argued that, in the long run, capitalism cannot withstand the desires of workers, who will eventually gain control of the means of production and power in a future collectivist society.

If one accepts the premises on which their arguments are based, neo-Marxist analyses can be used to account for the expanding activities of capitalist states over time and also the broad patterns of economic, foreign, and defense policies in different societies, such as the promotion of free trade by the most prosperous and powerful. For example, because Marxist economics predicts that the rate of return on capital investment tends to fall as capitalism progresses, it becomes increasingly necessary for governments to underwrite some of the costs of production. Thus, all states eventually have to become directly involved in the economy. Neo-Marxism also addresses issues of external constraints on foreign policymaking, especially in a time of extensive multinational corporations and the interdependence of capitalist economies. Indeed, the 2008–9 financial crisis and its exposure of the deep interconnectedness of advanced market states produced a new generation of neo-Marxist analysis of international economic relations.

Despite attempts by some scholars to get inside the policy process and develop a neo-Marxist approach to foreign policy analysis, neo-Marxist scholars on the whole remain unclear about exactly how the state makes specific policy choices or decisions. However, it is certainly true that it is harder for the poor and the working classes to become politically organized than it is for the rich and for business interests. At the global level the issues are even more complex but the existence of high levels of poverty at the same time as there is globalization of the world in terms of trade, transportation, and communications makes it important to understand Marxist analysis of world politics.

Essentially, Marxism has five core principles:

1. People are stratified into unequal social classes or groups of rich and poor. The concept of class is essential to the understanding of domestic and global politics. Individuals act as agents of their own economic class – the *bourgeoisie* that owns the means of production and the *proletariat* that provides its labor engage in a class struggle. Indeed, history *is the history of class struggle.*
2. Domestic politics is a contest between richer and poorer people in a class struggle for advantage and distribution of wealth. Communists, following the economic reasoning of Marxist theory,

spread these concepts around the world and used the ideas to help revolutionaries capture several states, especially Russia and China. Less revolutionary socialists, who follow Marxist theory and yet accept democratic principles, advocate the redistribution of wealth from the rich to the poor domestically and internationally. Socialist parties that are based on these principles have blossomed in many parts of the world, especially in Europe.

3. States are agents of the bourgeoisie and their capitalist leaders. In their search for international power, states are guided by their calculations about the "interests" of their own powerful elites.

4. Global politics is essentially a struggle among self-interested states for power and wealth, and its study should focus on the uneven distribution of economic power among states. Global politics is dominated by the structure of capitalism, trade, and the role of elites and multinational corporations. The rich Northern states dominate those of the poorer South.

5. The global arena consists of a stratification of "core" or wealthy states that control the destiny of the poorer states on the "periphery." Early Marxists such as Lenin called this stage of world economic development *imperialism.* The rich states invested in colonies and then exploited the indigenous people for the economic advantage of the colonialists. They then used the surplus capital to keep their own proletariats in their place. Later a new language of *dependency theory* was added. At the international level, a "dependency" relationship is said to exist when the core states control the capital in the world and exploit the poorer countries on the periphery. Much of the poverty in the periphery states of Asia, Africa, and Latin America comes from this exploitative capitalist world economy. Class relations, then, are seen as significant both within states and around the world.

Since the end of the Cold War, Marxism has become less important in the academic study of

> ### Box 3.3 Key to Neo-Marxism in global politics
>
> | | |
> |---|---|
> | *Major actors*: | states; elites; multinational corporations |
> | *Significant concepts*: | class |
> | *International system*: | dominated by international capitalism |
> | *Beliefs*: | radical change to achieve equality is necessary and inevitable |

politics. Fewer than half a dozen states claim to be Marxist today and the most powerful of them, China, claims that it blends communism and capitalism. A few states, such as Brazil and Venezuela, are influenced by leftish ideology (see Chapter 5). In universities, Marxist critical theory has often evolved into studies of imperialism and postcolonialism. Recent academic scholarship in this field tends to carve up the literature into a debate between liberal international political economy (IPE) and neo-Marxist approaches. Some critical theorists adopt a world system approach that regards the entire globe as one capitalist world economy with all the attributes of a single-state economy. Neo-Marxist theorists like Immanuel Wallerstein focus on the system-wide phenomenon of capitalism.[22] They believe that a world system is defined in terms of economic processes and links rather than any other criteria. We discuss these hypotheses and other economic issues such as colonialism and poverty in Chapters 12 and 13.

The public choice approach is the study of economic nonmarket decision making or, more broadly, the application of economics to political science. According to public choice theory, each individual is essentially a self-interested, rational actor. Their individual desires are constrained by

---

[22] Immanuel Wallerstein, *The Modern World System, vol. 2, Mercantilism and the Consolidation of the European World Economy, 1600–1750* (New York: Academic Press, 1980).

scarcity and by competition with others who want the same things. When people engage in collective nonmarket decision making in the political arena (making "public" choices), they behave exactly as classical economists believe individuals do when making market-oriented choices in the economic sphere. They act in a rational and calculating way to maximize their own interests, causing rules and institutions to change in order to maximize their desires. For example, voters provide electoral support for the party that offers the programs most likely to maximize their individual well-being, and interest groups lobby governments for policies that will maximize their needs or desires. It is not surprising, therefore, that politicians and bureaucrats formulate policies largely to satisfy their own narrow interests – just like everyone else – with the difference that politicians are required to broker the influence of voting blocks and interest groups into a manageable coalition of interests that will get them elected.

In the public choice model, individuals do not have equal opportunities to realize their respective interests. Ordinary citizens have little impact except through elections and these are rarely very significant. According to the public choice model, therefore, powerful interest groups, bureaucrats, and politicians – especially leaders of the governing parties – are the central actors in the policy-making process, even though the primary unit of political action is the individual, not the group. Individuals may join forces in pursuit of their interests, but they do so only when collective action promises greater rewards than acting alone. It may also be rational for the individual to abstain from participation in collective action.

Essentially, the public choice approach has five core principles:

1. Both individuals and states seek power in order to enhance their economic opportunities.
2. International politics is about states and their relationships but also individuals, especially elites, and their quest for dominance.

Box 3.4 **Key to public choice in global politics**

Major actors:	individuals; states
Significant concepts:	self-interest; competition
International system:	quest for dominance
Beliefs:	value-free; scientific analysis

---

3. In their search for economic dominance, individuals and elites are guided by amoral calculations about "personal interests."
4. The global arena is basically an *anarchy* with each individual or corporation fending for itself. As each person or state searches for dominance in the global anarchical system, it automatically diminishes the well-being of others.
5. Global politics entails a struggle among self-interested states and individuals for power and economic well-being, and its study concerns the shifting of economic and political power among states and people.

Scholars of public choice theory have made major contributions to the study of world politics in such fields as collective goods, alliances, and models of strategic interaction.[23] However, public choice is still a relatively underdeveloped art as an approach to politics and public policy analysis. Its assumptions about "rationality" have been savagely attacked by many students of politics. Although its application has produced some very interesting insights into the policy-making process, its focus remains rather restrictive. It is at best a partial aid for understanding how and why public policies are developed and global politics takes its contemporary shape.

Postmodernism and critical theory

A short discussion on the history of ideas is required at this point, as new and alternative criticisms of

[23] Dennis Mueller, *Public Choice* (Cambridge: Cambridge University Press, 2003).

realism, liberalism, and Marxism emerged in the late 20th century. Together these alternative ideas have had a major impact on thinking about theory in international relations. Although postmodernists disagree profoundly with traditional social science approaches, this scholarly tradition, launched in the field of literary criticism in France, is now part of intellectual and divisive ideological debates in European and North American universities. Postmodernist arguments are based on philosophical deconstructionism and the premise that comprehensive and satisfactory descriptions and explanations about global politics are impossible and should be replaced by efforts to uncover the hidden motives of practitioners. They ridicule the academic ideal of disinterested, objective research on the grounds that outsiders can never understand or interpret thought from the experiences of groups to which they do not belong. The idea of social function is central to their reasoning and a belief in the importance of studying *texts* and *discourses* is essential in their approach. For them there is no objective reality: it is merely an illusion.[24]

Postmodernists demand new ways to think and organize institutions and politics in international relations. For example, states and power as envisioned by social science scholars are fictions, as are other social science constructs that attempt to categorize or generalize about the diversity of experiences that constitute global politics. Postmodernists argue that "national interests," as envisioned in traditional international relations theory, do not exist independently of social thought and are merely social constructs that need to be deconstructed and understood as instruments of social and political control.

The basic assumption of postmodernism is an acceptance of relativity because it advocates that no society or culture is more important than any other and that scholars should help to undermine the way society constructs and imposes its hierarchy of cultural values and meaning on everyone. Postmodernists explore the power underlying political, social, and economic institutions and attempt to explain how these social forces exert their power by shaping the identities of individuals and societies. Postmodernists are, therefore, often accused of negativity because of their attacks on what they regard as the repressive orthodoxy of international relations. They are also criticized as being pessimistic and failing to provide a positive vision or theory of what they attack.

Postmodernists do not believe there is any compelling standard for judging facts or, for that matter, for determining what a fact is. Following the precepts of the late French intellectual Michel Foucault (Figure 3.4), they maintain that knowledge about other people always involves exercising power over them.[25] For them one narrative account of the world has as much validity as any other: "The task of the scholar is not to discover ultimate truth, but rather to construct a convincing explanation of selected aspects of human behavior."[26] Postmodernists argue that political actions are determined by the way individuals and states "construct" their images of reality. They agree that peoples' conceptions of domestic and global politics, for example, are conditioned by their personal understandings and that there is no objective theory or approach that is separate from one's own personal point of view.

Many strands of social theory could be discussed here, especially those concerning the idea that the world should not be seen as a set of "objective" facts. The work of the so-called Frankfurt School, which included such scholars as Herbert Marcuse

---

[24] This debate is ongoing and cannot be solved in this text. Some philosophers claim that *reality* cannot be accessed without human mediation although others claim that such ideas generate relativism that denies that there are universal norms such as truth, evidence, consistency, rationality, and coherence. See John R. Searle, *Mind, Language, and Society: Philosophy in the Real World* (New York: Basic Books, 2000). Paul A. Boghossian, *Fear of Knowledge: Against Relativism and Constructivism* (Oxford: Oxford University Press, 2009), and Burger and Luckman, *The Social Construction of Reality*.

[25] M. Foucault, *The Foucault Reader* (New York: Pantheon Books, 1984).

[26] John Kankford, historian at Kansas State University, quoted in *The New York Times*, July 9, 1995, p. 15.

Figure 3.4 Michel Foucault (1926–1984) was a leading French critical philosopher associated with structuralist and poststructuralist movements. His ideas helped to construct the postmodernist critique of social science. *Source:* Corbis.

and Jürgen Habermas, gave rise to the ideas of emancipation and critical theory. Both ideas have had a significant impact on aspects of international relations today. Emancipation is a highly contested concept in international relations that is usually associated with an idealistic belief in the positive transformation of the world. Critical theory focuses on how existing political relationships can be changed so that people can be freed from social, economic, or political constraints.[27]

---

[27] For advanced studies of newer theories on these topics, see Richard Wyn Jones, ed., *Critical Theory and World Politics* (Boulder CO: Lynne Rienner, 2000), C. Brown, *International Relations Theory: New Normative Approaches* (Hemel Hempstead: Harvester Wheatsheaf, 1992), and Tim Dunne, Milja Kurki, and Steve Smith, eds., *International Relations Theories: Discipline and Diversity*, 2nd ed. (Oxford: Oxford University Press, 2010).

Social constructivism

Social constructivism can be considered an important offshoot of postmodernism and critical theory that encompasses many, but not all, of their concepts and approaches. It has now essentially replaced postmodernism and its offshoots in the study of politics in most North American universities. A major proponent has been Alexander Wendt, whose book, *A Social Theory of International Politics*, was important in the early development of the discipline. Other distinguished scholars in this tradition include Martha Finnemore, Peter Katzenstein, and John G. Ruggie.

Constructivism is a reaction to the domination of realism and liberalism as mainstream theories of international relations. It is a theoretical "broad church" encompassing many authors and approaches that deal with how we should think about politics and relationships. Although it emerged from the philosophical school of postmodernism and critical theory, it differs from them in that it accepts the reality of many parts of global architecture and is more concerned with researching issues in international relations than with rehashing old arguments about what constitutes reality and truth. Constructivism does not attempt to offer hypotheses about all of the enduring regularities in global politics. It does, however, highlight the importance of ideas and shared understandings rather than power and explores how ideas shape what count as legitimate or illegitimate beliefs and action. In their analyses of language and symbols in politics, constructivists maintain that other schools, especially realism, privilege decision making over agenda and outcomes over process. Constructivists make humanity the primary focus of analysis and, therefore, stress how ideas impart meaning and value to politics.

Constructivists, unlike realists, argue that states will act on their identities in ways not necessarily predicted by "rational" calculations.[28] They

---

[28] Stephanie R. Golob, "North America Beyond NAFTA? Sovereignty, Identity and Security in Canada-US Relations." *Canadian-American Public Policy* Issue 52 (December 2002), pp. 1–50.

emphasize the role of ideas, discourse, social interaction, and purpose. For these scholars, foreign policy is basically a product of identity and cultural values stimulated by the discourses that shape a country's self-perception. Interests are not innate or "objective" facts but constructed through history and social interaction. Institutions therefore are not fixed but can be changed by actors according to their interests or identities. This means that constructivists are fundamentally interested in how change comes about and some, as idealists, attempt to shame those who deviate from what they regard as norms of appropriate standards in politics. Constructivism provides a helpful way to think critically about other theories and approaches. However, in its most radical perspective it perhaps approaches a negation of shared conceptions of science and social science as disciplines.

Essentially, social constructivism has five core principles:

1. The state, its national interests, and global politics do not stand alone outside human consciousness. Individuals, groups, and social structures (including states) construct their own identities and the state and sovereignty are social constructs. These social structures shape the culture, identities, interests, and foreign policies of states. People can have novel understandings of their interests and identities. They can change these constructs and the causes of change or transformation are vital to this construction, as are understandings of what is proper in human and political behavior. Constructivists find significance in the purpose of politics and international relations and stress the role of shared purpose in developing and influencing action. They are less concerned with how power or resources are achieved and used than are realists, political economists, liberals, and perhaps even feminists.

2. Individuals, groups (especially elites), and non-governmental institutions, as well as states, can be powerful if they can persuade people to adopt their concerns, ideas, discourses, and policies.

Constructivists emphasize the importance of the meaning and images of groups as well as identities and ideologies in the study of international relations to the extent that such things as treaties, laws, and international organizations can be created and amended by human agents with cooperative or conflictual consequences.

3. Power and institutions are based on people's values and beliefs. There is nothing intrinsic in their nature. Power is important but can come in the form of ideas and contested concepts. Power is not only the ability to get one's way but also something that emerges from the interests and identities that *shape* and/or *limit* the ability of actors to get their way. In idealist versions of the theory there is a claim that foreign policy can, and should, be guided by judgments based on ethical or moral standards. The "world can be changed" or "alternative pathways can be found" might constitute mottos for this theory.

4. Global politics is essentially a struggle among self-interested elites to control the shaping of norms and values. These ideas influence patterns of global politics and can enhance or constrain certain actions. Even what states are regarded as friends or enemies is determined by shared norms and values that emerge from history and relationships. Some countries, such as the Nordic states, approach global politics with a cooperative spirit based on their judgments about the appropriateness or inappropriateness of certain kinds of actions. Of course, countries may change their behavior over time. At one time Britain and Canada were enemies of the United States. Today the United States does not arm itself militarily against Britain or Canada but it does so against other countries. After World War II the United States thought it was appropriate to provide Marshall Plan funding for its former European enemies so they could revive economically and rebuild their countries. However, many would say that the United States did not follow such norms of peaceful behavior with its attack on Iraq in 2003.

5. The global arena is basically "up for grabs." There is a kind of intellectual *anarchy* of ideas, values, and identities. Reality is in the eye of the beholder. All the trappings of realism, such as military strength, state power, arms races, and the security dilemma, can be surmounted, as they were in the breakup of the USSR and in the rise of the European Union. Military capability therefore can be less significant than other factors, such as values and beliefs, in the global area. It is not surprising, therefore, that such nonstate actors as nongovernmental organizations (NGOs), transnational networks, and other institutions involved in reorienting goals and policies are given considerable attention in constructivist research.

Constructivists make a valiant effort to explain changes in norms and practices in international politics. They make a dramatic pitch for the need for scholars to recall that they, too, are part of the global system they are examining – that is, that a *constitutive* approach (in which the theorist sees oneself in the system rather than outside of it looking in) is required. They argue that culture and its values and norms give meaning to political action and change. Their major attack is on realists who they believe have a misperceived "concreteness" in their fundamental concepts. Although such expressions as the "state," "anarchy," "security," and "sovereignty" are habitually discussed in realist literature as having an objective existence, they are in reality dependent on the dynamics of consciousness, discourse, and interpretation for their meaning.

The international arena is a mixture of anarchy and society – one does not exclude the other. Security, for example, is regarded in realist thought as "synonymous with the security of the state against external dangers, which was to be achieved by increasing military capabilities."[29] Some critics of realism, therefore, seek to *widen* the concept of security to include nonmilitary issues such as the economy, environment, human rights, and so on while others seek to *deepen* the concept by shifting the focus from the security of the state to the security of people, or *human security*. Again, neither realism nor neorealism excludes the economy from the calculation of a state's power. They merely assume it as a given that only states with a significant economic capacity can afford to be militarily powerful.

Where constructivist theory is strong is in asserting that security issues and foreign policy are not *mere* expressions of a rationally deduced national interest but rather shaped by cultural norms and conceptions of identity.[30] Where the theory may be weaker is in explaining how such ideas lead to change. The USSR may have fallen apart because of the rise of new ideas such as *glasnost* and *perestroika*, but why did these new ideas or norms appear? Why did they become persuasive? European states may have learned that cooperation in the European Union is more beneficial than hostility and that this is a step forward. But why now? Why not in 1919? Or 1939? That is the conundrum. After all, if international system change is understood to be caused by innovations in ideas, how do these changes in ideas come about? Could it be in the material conditions of the world, as realists and Marxists might say? This desire to resolve the ancient issue of what constitutes the fundamental cause of human action is unlikely to be achieved in the study of global politics. Indeed, it may be the case, as some would argue, that in explaining the collective predispositions of states, constructivist language is more

[29] J. Ann Tickner, "Re-Visioning Security." In Ken Booth and Steve Smith, eds., *International Relations Theory Today* (Cambridge: Polity Press, 1995), p. 176.

[30] There is an extensive literature on this debate. See, for example, Bill McSweeney, *Security, Identity and Interests: A Sociology of International Relations* (New York: Columbia University Press, 1999); Peter Katzenstein, ed., *Culture of National Security: Norms and Identity in World Politics* (New York: Columbia University Press, 1996); David Rousseau, *Identifying Threats and Threatening Identities* (Stanford CA: Stanford University Press, 2006); Sean Lynn-Jones and Steven Miller, *Global Dangers: Changing Dimensions of International Security* (Cambridge MA: MIT Press, 1995); Jessica Tuchman Mathews, "Redefining Security." *Foreign Affairs* 68(2) (1989), pp. 162–77.

VANITY FAIR. March 29, 1873.

No. 230. STATESMEN, No. 141.
" A Feminine Philosopher."

Figure 3.5 John Stuart Mill (1806–1873) was the most influential English philosopher of the 19th century. He fought for women's rights, women's suffrage, and women's equal access to education. His work *The Subjection of Women* is an enduring defense of gender equality. *Source:* Alamy.

helpful in understanding the political rhetoric about decision making than in understanding the making of the decisions themselves.

Gender and feminist theory

A major attack on mainstream theories in global studies has come from feminists who believe that women have been improperly excluded from discussions of world politics. Historically, feminists campaigned to remove barriers to the political equality of men and women. Today feminism is also regarded as a partial theory of global affairs in that it may be used to explain large segments of political institutions and behavior. Like other new ways of understanding politics and challenges to political science, feminism has influenced the discipline – as well as socialist and liberal thought – and has raised a counterreaction among theorists of other traditions.

Feminism is a system of beliefs with a vision, perspective, and program. It has a rich history. In his play *Lysistrata*, the Greek author Aristophanes (448–380 BCE) wrote how women could end war by depriving their men of sex. Even before

Machiavelli's classic realism in his 15th century *The Prince*, another Italian, Christine de Pisan (1365–1434), outlined women's strengths for making peace rather than war. Feminism emerged in its modern garb with the writings of John Stuart Mill (Figure 3.5) at the end of the 19th century, with the British suffragettes in the early 20th century who sought and won voting rights for women, and later, throughout Europe and North America, with the women who fought for pacifist goals. Their initial goals were intensified and expanded to include increasing opportunities for women within the existing social structure and opposition to discrimination and active oppression of women.

Currently, proponents seek more active representation by women in all aspects of life, including politics, and they have forced a range of new policies onto the public agenda, especially in Western democracies. These policies stress gender equality with equal pay for work of equal value, wider employment opportunities, child-care facilities, and the like. On the whole, feminist theory has been concerned with attempting to find cooperative solutions to problems concerning women, sometimes stressing equality and at other times differences.

Feminism as a concept and partial theory has challenged, and to a large extent reformed, political science – and to a lesser extent the study of international relations. Leading scholars in the field include Cynthia Enloe, whose volume *Bananas, Beaches and Bases: Making Feminist Sense of International Relations* charted the initial American steps in the field, and J. Ann Tickner, whose work seeks to redescribe the basic principles of international politics from a female viewpoint.[31] Ann E. Towns and others explore the role of women in the history of political reforms.[32]

Following social constructivism, the theory considers gender to be socially constructed. It begins by clearly distinguishing gender from sex. Feminists define gender as an unequal structural relationship of power that defines what is meant by masculinity and femininity. Feminism's most convincing contribution has been to show that orthodox political science ignored gender issues and that gender matters greatly in both domestic politics and international relations. Feminists have uncovered assumptions and biases about gender in the discipline of political science. They have articulated arguments about which topics should be in the "public" sphere and which in the "private" and thereby changed public policy. For example, they have pointed out simple facts such as that housework and daily chores (primarily carried out by women in most countries) are not registered in the gross domestic product (GDP) of a country, and they have found and examined gross inequalities between men and women in both freedom and income. As a radical theory, therefore, feminism has a quarrel even with orthodox Marxist political economy because gender competes with class to explain economic and political outcomes.

There are various schools of feminism. Liberal feminists support policies aimed at opening up equal competition between the sexes and claim that this requires government support for such amenities as day care, as well as policies to encourage equal representation in male-dominated professions. Radical, second-wave feminists argue that a social revolution is needed to restructure society. They maintain that gender is a more important social cleavage than class or race. Women, they say, are subjugated because of their biological function of having babies. Some radical feminists have condemned liberal feminists for trying merely to involve more women in the extant corrupt state and international system rather than helping to tear down the structures of masculine hierarchy. At their most graphic, some radical feminists have described state capabilities in weapons such as canons and missiles as phallic and male. Some have gone so far as to advocate more test-tube babies and child rearing by social institutions to break the patriarchal social pattern.

In short, feminism describes and explains the inequalities in income and freedom of women around the world. This critical approach serves to sensitize one to the fact that, for a variety of reasons, some interests, in this case those of women, are less easily organized than others and that some groups have *greater* influence on policy making than others. Like postmodernism and constructivism, this theory draws our attention to problems in the assumptions of realist and liberal thought and proposes new approaches to resolving the issues including challenging the concepts of gender itself.

[31] J. Ann Tickner, *Gender in International Relations: Feminist Perspectives on Achieving Global Security* (New York: Columbia University Press, 1992).

[32] Ann E. Towns, *Women and States: Norms and Hierarchies in International Society* (Cambridge: Cambridge University Press, 2010).

Essentially, feminism has five core principles:

1. Gender is an important component of analysis that has been left out of mainstream political science and international relations, especially in regard to power in domestic politics and war in international relations.
2. Feminism is both a partial theory of global politics and a movement with a program for the promotion of equality. As a theory it is concerned with how gender affects politics and is affected by politics. In other words it is concerned with how gender inequality is created and sustained.
3. To a large extent, contemporary feminists have moved away from early arguments about the need to improve women's roles in society to emphasize the proposition that gender shapes definitions of political realties, shapes foreign policy, and reinforces inequalities between men and women. In other words, they have adopted much of the language and approaches of constructivists. But the theory remains debatable because feminists themselves argue over its very meaning and approaches. Like other theorists they are divided *within* their own group.
4. In many parts of the world women still do not have basic human rights and this needs to be changed. In these areas they are still treated as the property of their husbands, and in circumstances of war they are often treated abysmally, with rape sometimes used as a political weapon.
5. Global politics may be essentially a struggle for power among self-interested states but it should be for the enhancement of all citizens regardless of gender.

Integrating theoretical insights

For a variety of reasons, it is unlikely that any of the approaches outlined above will emerge as a universally accepted theory of global politics. They each explain some issues very well and ignore others. While the traditional approaches offer insights about power, conflict, and survival, they simply cannot explain the history of change in

---

Box 3.6 **Key to feminism in global politics**

Major actors: gender roles
Significant concepts: gender, power
International system: gender shapes definitions of political realities
Beliefs: gender equality; gender difference, struggle for the enhancement of all citizens regardless of gender

---

international relations. Neither realism nor liberalism predicted the breakup of the USSR or the rise of transnational terrorism in the 21st century. But these two basic theories still represent the dominant frameworks of analysis found in the current literature in political science. Each approach has its strengths and weaknesses and students of global politics must be conversant with them and be able to apply them to political questions and policy decisions. Marxism explains how some classes dominate in politics and makes some sense of international capitalism, poverty, and dominant belief systems but it does not offer much insight into questions of global power and security. To a large extent, the development of the distinct field of IPE has brought major advancements in this field. Social constructivism is excellent at describing change, and enlightens us on the role of culture and identity politics. Feminism brings the formerly ignored issue of gender into the foreground.

New ideas about global politics continually impinge on the subject and restructure the aspects scholars believe to be important. A student must be aware of these various approaches and their advantages and disadvantages. Students should work with these theories and research conclusions and test which are the most comprehensive and persuasive. All have continued validity in specific areas and should be regarded as tools in argumentation about political reality. The "form of arguments" used for and against the theories and specific public policies will often tell us if the author or speaker is a realist, liberal, marxist, or constructivist, but this does not mean that there will not be differences among supporters, because they assess the various assumptions and weigh the conclusions about political reality differently. Thus, we need the theories to understand global politics but we should not be restricted to or by any one of them. All of the theories continue to influence the academic discipline of international relations and analytic eclecticism is warranted.

Methodology and social science

Besides levels of analysis and theory, the third basic issue in global studies concerns how to test or confirm claims of validity in the discipline. Like all social sciences, the study of global politics confronts epistemological issues. In other words, researchers ask "what is knowledge", "how can it be acquired", and "what are the acceptable analytical principles for research in the field?" Because there is no overall agreement on a theory of global politics this issue continues to haunt debates in global studies. Because they run through all the social sciences the intellectual issues transcend the study of global politics. But perhaps they are more pronounced in the study of politics because of the large number of contested concepts and interests involved.

Much of the study of global politics relates to questions of power and to what purpose it is, or ought to be, dedicated. The foundational concepts and theories of international relations all relate in one way or another to this topic. The field is diverse and controversial and is covered in this chapter and Chapter 4 and less directly throughout the text. The classic ideas about power and its use concern five basic theoretical perspectives – realism, liberalism, political economy (Marxism and public choice), social constructivism, and feminism – along with mutations and other more specific approaches. This book is based on the premise that the field is best understood through a juxtaposition of the various

arguments about global politics. The discipline is also concerned with both empirical theory (which deals with the observable world and how it can be understood) and normative theory (which involves value judgments about the correct goals and behavior of politics). Different perspectives emphasize one or other of these approaches. Empirical theory asks *how* the world works, while normative theory asks how it *should* work. This "is or ought" question is central to the discipline of international relations and, indeed, to much of social science and modern philosophy. A scientific and objective approach brings a technical vocabulary to the study of politics and international relations, while questions about how norms or normative positions inform and instruct in politics require a different approach. In studying the role of shared purposes many scholars link normative and empirical issues.

Students will find that although all these theories contribute to various aspects of our understanding of global politics, none of them is complete or universally accepted. In order to give each its due, some authors merely line up one theory after another about each topic they discuss and then force the theories into boxes to make artificial distinctions. It is reminiscent of the comedian Groucho Marx's aphorism, "These are my principles; if you don't like them, I have others." We need to examine carefully the assumptions that underpin the theories and the claims they make. General theories provide only partial explanations of reality and in this book whenever clear and sharp distinctions can be made about how one of the theories explains an issue better than another one we will be declaring it.

Every process of selection requires exclusion and that can, in the final analysis, entail distortion. But in this book we do not force a straightjacket on the arguments so that one school of thought looks extreme, naïve, or foolish. We write about the theories, not the individuals associated with them. We discuss the ideas of realism or liberalism, for example, but not name or criticize specific individuals as if they personally cleave totally and naively to any one doctrine or "ism." The theoretical debates are often important and fascinating but they are not all there is to know about global politics, and an obsession with theory inevitably robs us of an appreciation of the richness of political affairs.

Finally, we all use theories whether we know it or not – claims to the contrary are naïve. Every time we make an argument about global politics we are using some general explanation. To use theory in global studies means to make sense of events by explaining how or why they are interconnected, and that means making an effort at generalization – that is, using theories. Theories enable us to clarify concepts and ideas and distinguish among dissimilar elements that may be confused or entangled. Of course, ideas have consequences, so it is important to be open-minded – but as one wag put it, "not so open-minded that one's brains fall out." In many cases you may find that disagreements arise not just over the conclusions reached but also over the framing of the questions themselves. Much of the field is full of righteous anger. While such emotions can add to our motivations in studying global politics, they can also be a barrier to progress.

Whatever the disagreements about the relative importance of empirical versus normative theory, and over which major theory contributes more to the study of global politics, all practitioners agree that the primary goal is to make arguments about politics as explicit as possible and to approach global politics from a spirit of inquiry. In order to understand politics and discuss it intelligently, we have to be clear about what is meant by several basic terms. In political science, words are often used in very specific ways that differ from common usage. It is important to clarify what is meant by them in order to provide the basis for intelligent agreement or disagreement about the substance of what is being communicated. This is not as easy as it might seem because words are richly textured and can have many meanings. We therefore clarify concepts carefully as we proceed throughout the book because if one neglects to employ key terms with a consistent meaning it is not possible to hold an intelligent debate on global politics or any topic.

Methodology is the manner of gathering, measuring, and explaining information. For example, all political scientists use terms such as a *necessary* cause versus a *sufficient* cause of an event or condition. A necessary cause means that the conditions cannot occur without that cause being present, but other causes are also involved, whereas a sufficient cause means that it alone can cause the effect or condition. But although all political scientists rely on such logical reasoning, some aspire to rigorous methodology and objectivity, building evidence through experiments or observations. Some claim their research is based on the so-called exact sciences. Such positivists believe that the accumulation of knowledge requires (1) similarities in the methodologies of the scientific and social science world, (2) a stark distinction between normative and empirical research with claims that the is/ought distinction should not be bridged, and (3) that there are observable regularities in the social and political worlds that can be understood by such methods.

In the early 20th century, American political scientists increasingly studied observable human political behavior in the light of theories borrowed from other social sciences. Because the social sciences had often developed from biological models the concept of the political system as a political organism became popular, especially in the study of subjects such as systems analysis and international systems. Later, political scientists relied increasingly on the fields of mathematics and statistics to help analyze political data, making political science even more quantitative and interdisciplinary. In this so-called *behavioral* period (discussed below), the discipline focused primarily on the problem of measurable issues in world politics.

But the discipline did not break away completely from the humanities. Studies of philosophy and history continued. There was, as Lucien Pye noted, a sense that as a discipline modern political science wanted to have its cake and eat it too – to be simultaneously humanistic and scientific.[33] The search by positivists for universal and enduring laws about global politics similar to Newton's laws of physics has been frustrated because "human behavior is too sensitive to the fluctuations of culture and the circumstances of history to yield permanently enduring findings."[34] It is not surprising that today there is no agreed-on "essential scientific core" for the discipline as a whole – neither in content nor in method. It is both the strength and the weakness of political science that it is a composite of other social sciences and the humanities.

The traditional-historical method

The traditional-historical approach predominated in the early years of political science when studies of politics concentrated on an essentially legal-formal description of governments. Most political scientists make some use of history, but traditionalists in international relations concentrate almost exclusively in this area, emphasizing the development of foreign-policy making structures and international institutions. But this traditional approach was attacked for being parochial (biased toward Western thought and ideas), formal-legal, and unscientific (concepts, models, and theories were rudimentary or even nonexistent). Furthermore, the approach was said to exclude informal politics and therefore ignored a large and important source of relevant information. Although many of these charges were vastly exaggerated, they did point to the simple fact that there were shortcomings in the formal-legal approach.

The behavioralist method

Behavioralists are concerned mainly with *empirical theory* (which deals with the observable world)

rather than *normative theory* (which involves value judgments) used by political philosophers or traditional political theorists. With the behavioral approach, political scientists strive to use scientific methods to explain or predict political phenomena by discovering uniformities in political behavior. They make hypotheses about politics that they then verify or disprove with empirical data. The tools of their craft include statistics and computers.

The scientific approach of behavioralists brought a new, technical vocabulary to the study of politics and international relations, a vocabulary that must be learned in order to understand much of contemporary political science. Behavioralists have made many rules of the discipline more explicit through their methodology. As in the physical sciences, these researchers begin with curiosity about some "variable" or "variables" – that is, some changeable phenomena that they are trying to understand. A variable is a feature of a social situation or institution that may appear in different degrees or forms in various situations and institutions. Disciplines within the social sciences select different variables for examination. Psychologists concentrate primarily on individual behavior; economists on scarcity. For political scientists the variable is generally state power and authority – how it is obtained and used.

Political science today is a science in that it aims to provide plausible explanations for phenomena. Political scientists develop "hypotheses" that offer explanations of political phenomena and then test them against empirical evidence. A hypothesis is a statement or generalization presented in tentative and conjectural terms. It is used to speculate about causes or effects by linking one or several variables to others. One might, for example, hypothesize that the level of political stability increases or decreases depending on the possible threat of external attack on a state and then conduct a study to see if this explanation is valid over time and in various settings. In global studies we might hypothesize that democracies do not go to war with each other. If these concepts can be operationalized and measured

---

[33] Lucien W. Pye, "Political Science and the Crisis of Authoritarianism." *APSR* 84(1) (March 1990), p. 16.
[34] Ibid., p. 4.

properly, relationships (or correlations) may be found that confirm or refute the hypothesis.

A scientific theory involves three elements: generalizations, new observations, and testability. Albert Einstein, the physicist, put it like this: theories involve positing problems, applying a tentative theory, eliminating error, and proceeding on to a new problem. In summary, the scientific enterprise encompasses:

1. identifying a significant issue or problem;
2. devising a plausible hypothesis to explore the phenomena;
3. finding reliable evidence with which to test the hypothesis;
4. exploring the findings; and
5. exploring how the results may be combined with other explanations to form a theory.

The main criticism of the behavioralist approach is that it ignores history, values, and context and offers compelling explanations only for comparatively trivial political phenomena and by concentrating on methods and statistics it often ends up with precise answers to trivial questions. Furthermore, because political science studies human beings rather than inanimate objects, it is rarely able to achieve replicable rules of political behavior that are equivalent to those in the exact sciences. In general, political science cannot predict future events based on past behavior, and, given the immense number of contested variables that have to be considered, it is doubtful that this will ever be achieved to the degree possible in the exact sciences. Although some of the problems are conceptual, others are caused by the nature of evidence about humans and data collection and methods of analysis. As David Easton noted, natural sciences have the advantage of dealing with inanimate matter. "Atoms ... do not have feelings or intentions that, by their very nature, are unpredictable or inaccessible to observation or prediction."[35] However even in the exact sciences there is extraordinary and unavoidable unpredictability. In fact, modern physicists refer to "chaos theory" as a way of studying how incredibly minute uncertainties in the initial state of a system can lead to total uncertainty in even the best conceivable predictions of the futures of those systems.

Postbehavioralism

Most political scientists now rely on a combination of methods of inquiry derived from both the traditional and behavioral schools. Single approaches are rarely able to capture the complexities of politics. By their very nature different topics of inquiry require different approaches, and both schools have made important contributions to the study of politics. Efforts are often made to combine aspects of both approaches and reconcile them, retaining a deep concern for history and values and using whatever techniques seem best suited for answering particular questions. To a large extent it has become widely accepted that normative assumptions are either explicit or implicit in all theories of international relations. However, even advocates of traditional approaches to the study of politics rarely recommend discarding scientific methods. This modified approach is sometimes labeled postbehavioralism. This moderate approach has been extremely important in modern studies of global politics as it favors neither purely scientific nor traditional approaches to the discipline. It adopts both. To a large extent, international relations scholarship has moved away from the adoption of single theories or approaches. Sil and Katzenstein have shown how a mix of theories and approaches can provide strong explanations and policy-relevant scholarship in the study of international relations.[36]

[35] David Easton, "Political Science in the United States: Past and Present." *IPSR* 6(1) (January 1985), p. 142.

[36] Rudra Sil and Peter Katzenstein, *Beyond Paradigms: Analytical Eclecticism in the Study of World Politics* (Basingstoke: Palgrave Macmillan, 2010).

Critical Case Study 3.1 **Applying the approaches and theories to the current Afghanistan war**

The three complex approaches in global studies help us to identify and understand the causes and perpetuation of the war in Afghanistan (Figure 3.6). We are all familiar with the basic facts about this ongoing war (the details are discussed in Chapter 10). Here we are concerned only with an initial discussion using the material developed in this chapter – levels of analysis, theories, and methods.

The events of 9/11 generated extreme rhetoric about the world order, the place of the United States in it, and the superiority of American ideals of democracy and freedom. The unprecedented terrorist attack led President George W. Bush and his advisers to focus on fundamental ideas about state security. President Bush, who had described himself as a "uniter, not a divider," committed the United States to war in Afghanistan, a weak state that had harbored terrorists and terrorist training camps for the 9/11 attacks. Only weeks after 9/11, U.S. and British aircraft and special forces were actively seeking out al-Qaeda in Afghanistan. Later, with UN agreement, the United States and its allies launched an attack on the territory and government of Afghanistan. Eventually NATO, Australia, Japan, New Zealand, and other states sent troops to the region. Many remain there today.

What can we learn about this event by examining it at the three different levels of analysis? At the individual level, we would study the personality, perceptions, ideologies, choices, and decisions of key individuals such as President Bush, Vice President Dick Cheney, and Secretary of Defense Donald Rumsfeld in the United States and Osama bin Laden and Mullah Omar in Afghanistan.

At the state level we would find that the United States had the most powerful military in the world. It had the best-trained men and equipment, whereas Afghanistan was a weak, failing state that allowed terrorists to train on its territory. Afghanistan had an insignificant military and the country was divided

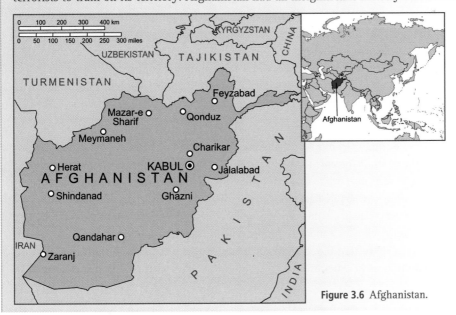

Figure 3.6 Afghanistan.

into fiefdoms run by mujahedeen fighters. Major institutions such as Congress did not resist the impetus to war, and public sentiment in the United States was very strongly in favor of retribution because of the horrific terrorist attacks, whereas Afghanistan was divided into conflicting groups and tribes all contesting for power. A powerful hegemonic democracy stared down a weak, poor state that was under the authoritarian rule of the Taliban.

At the international system level a new world order had emerged when the Cold War ended, with the United States as the only superpower. Militant Islamist groups with virulent anti-Western prejudices had become more open, engaging in terrorist rhetoric and actions. After 9/11, world sentiment swung behind the United States in the war and supported an invasion. The United Nations Security Council passed a resolution condemning the attack on the United States and sanctioned an attack on Afghanistan. NATO declared "Article 5" and agreed to support the United States. Internationally, there was a growing accept-ance of the idea that foreign intervention in the affairs of certain weak countries was justifiable.

What can the five theories tell us about the causes and aftermath of the Afghanistan war? The facts remain the same no matter which theory we use to answer the question. But in each case the focus differs, as do the consequent explanations. Whenever an author adopts a single element and declares this as the only ex-planation we know he or she is probably wrong. As we turn the kaleidoscope to reveal the five theories that we outlined in this chapter we find different explanations for the causes of this war and its conduct.

Realists and their critics explain the causes and conduct of the war in dramatically different ways. As we have seen, for realists the central concern is with the consequences of an anarchical world and how this impacts on the need to bolster state security to the extent that states are constantly preparing to defend themselves. As the world's major power the United States naturally relies on its military to de-fend its national interests and assert its power in the international system. Realists argue that America's military strength gives its leaders not just the capability, but also the responsibility, to act forcefully in the world. The terrorists, who were trained in a weak state, Afghanistan, harmed the national interests of the United States by their attack on 9/11, and they were able to do so because there was no interna-tional institution or world government to stop them. After the events of 9/11, Afghanistan's sovereignty was seen as expendable. The UN provided the consent of the "international community" to an act of self-defense – an attack on the terrorist bases in Afghanistan. The U.S. military and its allies responded by attacking the terrorist bases and the state that harbored them.

Support for military force is always available in realist thought but that does not mean it is always chosen. Many realists argued during the Cold War that American hegemony was vital for global order. These realist theorists see the central concepts for understanding the Afghanistan war as anarchy, state, and power. Some hard-core realists also argue that the United States had to protect its interests and those of its friends by stabilizing the Middle East and safeguarding oil imports from that part of the world. On the Iraq war, however, realists divided. Some supported the neocon position although others said the war was not a prudent choice for American foreign policy. One realist critic of the war, Stephen M. Walt, denied that realists believed that U.S. democratic ideals should be spread by warfare if it meant sacrificing other important interests in order to do so.[37] Of all the theories discussed in this chapter only

---

[37] Stephen M. Walt explains why a realist could believe the United States should tread lightly abroad in his *Taming American Power* (New York: W. W. Norton, 2005).

realism is not the child of an emancipationist tradition, so the conflict between neoconservatives and realists over regime change in Iraq touched upon a critical faultline between them.

The critics of realism tend to look beyond the actual terrorist events of 9/11 and theorize about the root causes of war. Liberal internationalists, for example, stress the role of individuals and international institutions more than states. They theorize that there ought to have been more viable international regimes and norms in place to prevent an attack such as 9/11. Moreover, even after 9/11 international institutions played a major role – the UN justified the attack on Afghanistan and NATO allies assisted in the conduct of the war. This support led to aid from most states and individuals who were horrified at the scale of the terrorist attacks. Once the UN sanctioned the attack on Afghanistan, the United States and its allies, indeed most countries of the UN, contributed to the war or at least the reconstruction efforts.

Liberal internationalists argue that if the world had built better collective security structures in the UN, then the anarchy that produced 9/11 would not have occurred or that if the United States had acted differently in world affairs before 9/11 there might not have been a terrorist attack. Some liberals also see value in promoting freedom and democracy abroad, spreading democratic institutions to a failing South Asian state. The central concepts for liberals would be states, international organizations, international community, and the values associated with democracy and freedom.

Marxists would perhaps be most critical of the war. They believe that the imperialist, capitalist system puts the economic motivations of capitalist states above all other considerations. Dependency theorists, for example, claim that American domination of the world increasingly leads to "haves and have nots" and that the United States will never stop defending its selfish economic interests around the world. The war in Afghanistan simply proves Marxist ideas about domination. The central concepts would be capitalism, dependency, and power.

Constructivists might argue that American values and actions were the root causes of the development of Muslim hatred of the West (keeping Western military bases on foreign soil, defending authoritarian governments such as those in Saudi Arabia and Egypt, controlling the oil resources of the Middle East, and generally acting like "ugly Americans" everywhere). Without such U.S. behavior, Muslims and Christians would not be clashing, and the terrorist events might not have taken place. In other words, the values motivating the two sides might differ and conflict might have been avoided. On this topic, constructivists and liberal internationalists would find common cause.

Feminists would probably not be engaged in arguments about the cause of the war but they would likely want to address how women were, and are, treated in Afghanistan and criticize the lack of opportunity for them to receive education and be treated as equal citizens in society. Their focus, therefore, would likely be on the conditions for Afghan women before the war and the consequences for them after the war. Radical feminists might blame the world patriarchal system for both the terrorist attacks and the reprisals.

In terms of the third main issue in global studies, the methodology with which to test or confirm the validity of claims about global politics, behavioralists might make their most significant contribution by scientifically studying the causes of terrorism or attitudes about going to war or about the conduct of the war. Traditionalists would be more likely to study the background history, perhaps concluding that eventually the United States, NATO, and others will fail to tame the Afghan people – like all the invaders of the past.

Conclusion: Analytic eclecticism

There is no one theory that can explain all global affairs. Usually only some theories or different parts of some theories apply. Students do not need to memorize approaches but rather to use levels of analysis, theory, and methods to learn to think critically about global politics. Sometimes the tit-for-tat arguments among schools or divisions of political scientists seem more about the authors themselves than about global politics, but we do need theories to see world politics in its complexity and from multiple points of view. Enduring approaches help scholars to be creative in understanding global politics and perhaps to reach their own judgments about foreign policies. Theories or perspectives are not just the result of academic hand-wringing. The debates and ideas simmer below the surface of all politics and to various degrees, provide theoretical and normative justifications for groups that wish to challenge the status quo as well as for those who wish to maintain it.

Select bibliography

Burger, Peter and Thomas Luckman, *The Social Construction of Reality: A Treatise in the Sociology of Knowledge* (Garden City NY: Doubleday, 1966).

Burns, Nancy, Kay Lehman Scholzman, and Sidney Verba, *The Private Roots of Public Action: Gender, Equality, and Political Participation* (Cambridge MA: Harvard University Press, 2001).

Doyle, Michael W., *Ways of War and Peace: Realism, Liberalism, and Socialism* (New York: W. W. Norton, 1997).

Enloe, Cynthia, *Bananas, Beaches and Bases: Making Feminist Sense of International Politics*, 2nd ed. (Berkeley: University of California Press, 2000).

Finnemore, Martha, *The Purpose of Intervention: Changing Beliefs about the Use of Force* (Ithaca NY: Cornell University Press, 2005).

Gilpin, Robert, *Global Political Economy: Understanding the International Economic Order* (Princeton: Princeton University Press, 2001).

Inkenberry, G. John, *After Victory: Institutions, Strategic Restraint, and the Rebuilding Order after Major Wars* (Princeton: Princeton University Press, 2001).

Katzenstein, Peter J., ed., *The Culture of National Security: Norms and Identity in World Politics* (New York: Columbia University Press, 1996).

Keohane, Robert O., ed., *Neorealism and its Critics* (New York: Columbia University Press, 1986).

Mearsheimer, John J., *The Tragedy of Great Power Politics* (New York: W. W. Norton, 2001).

Peterson, V. Spike, ed., *Gendered States: Feminist (Re) Visions of International Relations Theory* (Boulder CO: Lynne Rienner, 1992).

Pettman, Jan Jindy, *Worlding Women: A Feminist International Politics* (London: Routledge, 1996).

Sil, Rudra and Peter Katzenstein, *Beyond Paradigms: Analytical Eclecticism in the Study of World Politics* (Basingstoke: Palgrave Macmillan, 2010).

Steans, Jill, *Gender and International Relations: Issues, Debates, and Future Directions* (Malden MA: Polity Press, 2006).

Sylvester, Christine, *Feminist Theory and International Relations in a Postmodern Era* (Cambridge: Cambridge University Press, 1994).

Tickner, J. Ann, *Gender in International Relations: Feminist Perspective on Achieving Global Security* (New York: Columbia University Press, 1992).

Wallerstein, Immanuel, *The Capitalist World-Economy* (Cambridge: Cambridge University Press, 1977).

Waltz, Kenneth N., *Theory of International Politics* (Reading MA: Addison-Wesley 1979).

Wendt Alexander, *Social Theory of International Politics* (New York: Cambridge, 1999).

Part II Institutions and actors in global politics

Everyone is entitled to his own opinion. He is not entitled to his own facts.

DANIEL PATRICK MOYNIHAN, U.S. SENATOR

The five chapters of Part II outline the role and the relative powers of states, their leaders, and their challengers in international affairs, providing an overview of the numerous actors in global politics.

The first two chapters describe political authority and global power, placing the six major powers – the United States, China, Russia, India, Japan, and the European Union – in the context of contemporary international debates and controversies. Chapter 4 assesses all states and their leaders in terms of their power, capabilities, and decision-making processes. Chapter 5 maps the shifting distribution of state power and influence in the modern world, particularly among the six major powers. Chapters 4 and 5 both confront the issues of comparative advantage and international action.

Chapter 6 focuses on important aspects of global governance in our interdependent but disordered world – the growth and role of international law and supranational courts, institutions such as the United Nations and the European Union, and functions such as peacekeeping and peace enforcement. Together with other institutions such as the International Criminal Court, these institutions create a landscape of creeping global governance that affects state sovereignty and people everywhere. Realists may downplay the importance of such institutions, and liberals may conclude that these institutions are desirable but not perfect, but both recognize them as increasingly significant and resilient.

The themes of Chapters 7 and 8 change the focus to nonstate actors and identity in global politics. Most of the issues that have historically mobilized individuals and groups in domestic politics now have an international dimension, supported by an equivalent advocacy group or movement. These two chapters include such diverse and vital topics as nongovernmental organizations, international business corporations, mass communications, nationalism, ethnicity, religion, and transnational criminal and terrorist groups.

4 Modern states: Power, leaders, and decisions in global politics

It is impossible to conceive of a world without states. But as we witnessed in Chapter 2, the modern form of the state is only a few centuries old. At various times in history tribes, bands, city-states, empires, and religious or other authorities performed many of the functions of governing people. Unlike the modern state, **government**, the organization of people for the resolution of dispute and conflict, has always been present in some form. Government first appeared about one hundred centuries ago in the early civilizations of Asia Minor, Egypt, and northern Mesopotamia (today's Iraq) well before modern states were formed.

The *modern* state, with its emphasis on legitimacy and consent of the people, as well as authority and order, is today the paramount actor in global affairs. The world is conditioned and constrained by the governments of states because they provide and regulate most aspects of public affairs both domestically and internationally and influence (directly or indirectly) the choices made by citizens in conducting their private lives. Modern states are defined not by cultural, ethnic, or language homogeneity but by sovereignty and power. States may or may not coincide with nations. Often they do not. For example, is Palestine a state, a nation, or something else? Just how much power do states have? The answers are neither simple nor static. A few countries – those with larger economies and extensive technologically advanced militaries – have dramatically more significance than others, but most states are relatively weak and have to rely on the more powerful militaries of other states or international organizations for political leverage. Some states, even though their sovereignty is officially recognized by other states, barely exercise meaningful authority over their own territory.

This chapter assesses how states acquire and use power in global politics in their pursuit of their interests and values. State power is observable in decisions, diplomatic maneuvers, and other choices about how to confront other countries and nonstate actors. The **national interests** of a state are multifaceted but essentially refer to a state's goals and ambitions. The term has been used to justify both interventionist and isolationist policies. Examining the concept of national interests and how to measure state power leads to a discussion of the major components of power: economies, resources, technologies, militaries, and even the geographies of the major world states. At the extreme of military power, nuclear weapons are held by only a select few countries. Those like Iran that want to join the club have to engage in subterfuge to build their capacity without being subject to severe international sanctions. To illustrate the power of states and their various approaches toward foreign policy strategy, we analyze the international reaction to Iran's movement to develop nuclear weapons.

State leaders play a significant role in directing foreign policy. How they exercise their state's power on the world stage is fascinating. They have a range of possibilities at their disposal, including diplomacy, sanctions, military actions, and a variety of "soft" power options. We examine these, as well as the impact of personalities, idiosyncrasies, and psychological attributes, for insights into how external policy is made. What are the tools that leaders use to get their way in global politics? What are the characteristics of strong and weak leaders? How do their perceptions and biases influence their decision making?

Many theories about individuals and groups are helpful in understanding how foreign policy is made, as well as various approaches to organizational decision making and even game theory. We evaluate three basic models of the foreign policy process – rational actor, organizational processes, and government or bureaucratic – before considering the contribution of game theory – with the games Chicken, Prisoner's Dilemma, and Stag Hunt – to understanding decision making in international relations.

Chapters 5 and 6 return our focus to states in the international system. They compare the leading six major powers and show how states organize global governance. The role of nonstate actors and others in global politics is considered in Chapters 7 and 8. But first we tackle the traditional difficult issues concerning states, nations, and sovereignty in order to clarify definitions and set the groundwork for later chapters.

States and sovereignty

In Chapter 2 we saw how the state as we know it today originated in Europe in the 17th century, and how Europeans carried the model with them when they colonized most of the globe. In far-off lands new states formed either for self-defense or in emulation of European states – or both. The number of states increased very gradually until after World War II, when the dissolution of European colonial empires led to a sudden flurry of new states being created. The most recent surge came with the emergence of postcommunist regimes in Eastern Europe after the collapse of the Soviet Union in 1991.

When we use the word state, we refer to the political unit of an entire territory. A state has three components – a territory, a population, and a government. In everyday language the word *state* is synonymous with *country*. Actions may be carried

out in the name of the state, as when laws are enforced or countries go to war. The word *state* is also an abstraction, in that it depicts many institutions and rules – but it is much more than an abstraction. States require loyalty, allegiance, and patriotism as part of their legitimacy. They also possess symbols such as unique flags and anthems to distinguish their citizens from others and to promote national identity. The German sociologist Max Weber defined the state as a "human community" that, through a set of institutions, "successfully uphold[s] a claim to the monopoly of the legitimate use of physical force in the enforcement of its order ... within a given territorial area."[1] This definition highlights a state's authority and indicates that it is able to use coercive force, to issue rules that are binding on all people within its territory, and to act in their name

[1] Max Weber, *The Theory of Social and Economic Organization* (Oxford: Oxford University Press, 1947), chapter 3.

in global affairs. In international politics, the result may be cooperation, competition, or even warfare among countries.

Thus, a state is defined by its power, both internally and externally. It is normally considered sovereign when final authority rests in a national government, so that domestically it possesses the ability to tax and coerce its citizens, and externally it is able to conduct relations with the international community free from outside interference by other states. Sovereignty, therefore, includes a bundle of characteristics, including territory, authority, and recognition. It conveys a sense of legitimacy, and it describes and justifies the notion that states should not intervene in the internal affairs of other states.[2]

Domestically, sovereignty grants a government the sole authority to issue decisions and obligatory commands, whereas externally it confers autonomy and independence. Under international law, people are identified by the state of which they are citizens, carrying national identity with them in the form of a passport, and sovereignty is a vital part of the official language of international affairs. States recognized as sovereign have the legal right to govern their people and territory, and they are equal to all other states in this regard. Recognition as a state is a sign to its people that they have the right to be free and in control of their own destiny.

In actuality, sovereign states may or may not be totally independent of other states. Some satellite countries possess all the formal ingredients of sovereignty but remain highly dependent on another country in some respects, often in the field of security. For example, many Canadians know that their country is sovereign but also believe that it is economically and militarily dependent on the United States. While this may be an ideological exaggeration, there are states such as Andorra (dependent on both Spain and France) and San Marino (inside Italy) that clearly could not exist without the

agreement of their powerful neighbors. Sovereignty, in other words, is not the same thing as independence, and it may not translate into full-blown autonomy.

Sovereignty under attack?

The concept and reality of sovereignty has always been central to the study of international relations. There is nothing new about controversial debates concerning its definition, its import in the world of states, the tension it brings to questions about the international legal order, or the inherent contradictions it creates in the search for effective international action. Since the 17th-century Treaty of Westphalia, sovereignty has meant control over peoples and territory and a necessary one-to-one correspondence between authority and territory. Currently, however, this important concept is eroding. It is under attack from economic and trade liberalization, globalization forces, new security issues, evolving concepts of the role of the state, and even humanitarian intervention by the United Nations and other international organizations.

Definitions of sovereignty abound. The concept and its lineage with the state arose from the Latin word *status*, which referred to the position or standing of the rulers of European territories after the Wars of Religion. In abstract terms, the word came to mean that no authority existed that could order the state how to act. The 1648 Treaty of Westphalia confirmed the notion of loyalty to the authority of the ruler, king, or prince and the concomitant principle that monarchs did not have to answer to any external authority such as the Holy Roman Empire. All authority and legitimacy resided in the state and its leaders. In other words, domestically, the doctrine came to mean a single authority had the legitimate right to issue decisions and obligatory commands. Externally, it conferred autonomy and independence.

Traditionally, therefore, sovereignty conveyed a sense of legitimacy or moral right to rule, as well as the empirical properties of *de jure* (legal) and

[2] Stephen D. Krasner, *Sovereignty: Organized Hypocrisy* (Princeton, NJ: Princeton University Press, 1999).

de facto (actual or practical) power. But the fundamental point is that sovereignty described and justified the idea that states should not intervene in the internal affairs of other states. However, this idea of *indivisible* sovereignty has always been controversial. The existence of such organizational patterns as "collective security" with the League of Nations and later the United Nations, regional security organizations such as the North Atlantic Treaty Organization (NATO), international organizations such as the International Court of Justice (ICJ), and even powerful nonstate actors such as major multinational corporations all militate against the principle of absolute state sovereignty. Moreover, many federal constitutions agree to some limitations on central state authority. Novel and modern trade arrangements such as the North American Free Trade Agreement (NAFTA) go so far as to provide binational panels that can make decisions binding on Canada, the United States, and Mexico – even against the wishes of their governments. The European Union (EU) goes further still. Its European Court of Justice (ECJ) asserts supremacy over national courts in the interpretation of the treaties signed by the member states and has been largely successful in making its decisions stick. Some states are able to exercise domestic and international authority without external recognition of their sovereignty: witness Taiwan, which, in the 1970s, lost recognition of its sovereignty and membership in the United Nations and yet remains a viable state.

Dealing with this historical and conceptual issue may appear to be flogging a dead horse, but if sovereignty is not the foundation of modern international life, what is? Stephen D. Krasner calls sovereignty nothing but "organized hypocrisy" and concludes that it has always enjoyed more prestige in principle than adherence in practice.[3] However, the fact is that sovereign states remain the most legitimate and accepted form of governmental institution. The concept of sovereignty is a necessary

part of the nature and legality of the international system. The conundrum is clear. The concept was and is accepted as a doctrine because it gives states formal equality and provides a necessary foundation to international order and law. Weaker states especially have a vested interest in the vitality of the concept and reality of sovereignty.

States and nations

States share few characteristics other than sovereignty. There are military giants like the United States and Russia, and there are other countries like Costa Rica, Haiti, Iceland, Liechtenstein, Panama, and Samoa that do not even have formal armies. There are populous states like China and India that each have more than a billion people, and microstates like Nauru and Tuvalu that have fewer than ten thousand inhabitants. The Vatican City's population is less than one thousand. There are geographically large states such as Canada and Australia and very small ones such as Andorra, Monaco, and San Marino. The United States ranks between these large and small populous states with more than 300 million people, and territorially, it is the third-largest country on Earth, following Russia and Canada.

Almost all states in the world belong to the United Nations (UN). A state is normally admitted to that institution when it has satisfied the member states that it is sovereign both internally and externally. There are some interesting anomalies, however. Recognized states sometimes expand in territorial size, and sometimes they contract. Sometimes even officially recognized states may lack an effective government. Failed states (those without a functioning government) sometimes continue to be considered sovereign and even retain membership in the UN during intense internal conflicts over sovereignty. For example, while recent wars were proceeding in Afghanistan, Congo, Rwanda, Sierra Leone, Somalia, and Uganda, their governments continued to function in the General Assembly of the UN.

Conversely, official recognition of sovereignty sometimes is not achieved, even though a

[3] Krasner, *Sovereignty.*

government has clearly established control over its people and territory. For example, the United States and several other countries would not recognize the communist government of Mao Zedong in China (People's Republic of China, PRC), even after it had decisively won a bloody revolution in 1949. When the communists took power, the losers, led by Chiang Kai-shek, fled to the island of Taiwan but continued to hold on to China's UN seat. It was not until 1979 that the United States and most other states supported communist China's claim to membership in the United Nations, with the result that the Taiwanese government was expelled. While the PRC is now a member of the UN and the Security Council, Taiwan remains a sovereign state with a territory, population, and government. It does not, however, claim independence from China, and China continues to assert that Taiwan is an integral part of the PRC.

A nation, as opposed to a state, is a cultural entity. It is essentially subjective, a sense of social belonging and ultimate loyalty based on a feeling of commonality. A nation is not the same as the citizenry of a state but usually encompasses people who possess a common language, ancestry, or cultural heritage, although not all these components are necessarily present. It may or may not be a politically conscious collectivity of people that aspires to self-government or independent statehood. In this sense, most states contain one or more nations. Nations exist inside states and, therefore, there are dramatically more of them than there are states. In fact, in today's world, virtually all states have persons within their borders that have identities and interests that overlap with persons and organizations in other states.

Most nations and states are an ethnic mismatch: millions of Hungarians reside outside Hungary, Chinese outside China, Russians outside Russia, and so on. Kurds live in Iraq, Iran, Syria, and Turkey. Somalis live in Djibouti, Kenya, Ethiopia, and Somalia. Settler states like Australia, Canada and the United States are especially heterogeneous. Moreover, a nation may be dispersed in more than one state, as was the case with the German nation, which until recently was divided between East and West Germany.[4] Some nations, like the Palestinians, may not even have a state despite their known aspirations for one (see Critical Case Study 4.1 below).

Another related concept widely used in political science is nation-state. Its usage has become highly

---

[4] Robert Jackson and Doreen Jackson, *Introduction to Political Science: Comparative and World Politics*, 5th ed. (Toronto: Prentice Hall, 2008), chapter 5.

Critical Case Study 4.1 **Territory and states: Israel and Palestine**

After World War I, the Ottoman Empire collapsed and Palestine became a mandated territory of Britain. After World War II, European Jews flooded into Palestine, and Britain asked the UN to help administer the territory. The United Nations partitioned Palestine into Arab and Jewish areas, an arrangement vehemently rejected by the Arabs. In 1948 the state of Israel was established, and shortly thereafter a UN vote gave Israel full statehood in the General Assembly. Neighboring Arabs immediately invaded, and war ensued. Arab-Israeli wars broke out again in the 1950s, 1960s, and 1970s, with Israel winning every time. In 1979 the Israelis signed a peace treaty with Egypt. Israel annexed the Golan Heights in 1981 but in 1982 withdrew from the Sinai pursuant to the Israel-Egypt Peace Treaty. Israel eventually evacuated its settlers and military while retaining control over border crossings to the Gaza.

In 1993, the Oslo accords between Israelis and Palestinians gave the Palestinians limited autonomy over the Gaza Strip and the town of Jericho, but conflict over Israel's occupation of the Gaza Strip and West Bank has continued. Today, Israel occupies much of the historical region of Palestine. More than four million Palestinians inhabit the West Bank and Gaza, land on which they have long dreamed of creating an independent Palestinian state. Palestine is not recognized as a state but has its own legislative assembly, is given nonmember observer status in international bodies such as the United Nations, and its residents come under the jurisdiction of its own Palestine National Authority.

In 1996, Palestinians made what many called a major step toward achieving their own state. Approximately three-quarters of the voters in the Palestinian-ruled areas voted to elect a president and a transitional self-governing council, thus providing for Palestine's first freely elected leadership. The Palestine Liberation Organization (PLO) chief Yasser Arafat won the presidency with a landslide victory. But in November 2004 Arafat died, and in the ensuing elections support for leadership of the Palestinians in the West Bank and Gaza divided. Hamas (a reputed terrorist group based in Gaza) won a large majority (76 of 132 seats) in the new Palestinian parliament. President Mahmoud Abbas appointed a member of the losing party, Fatah, prime minister of the Palestinian National Authority. In reality, this meant that the Palestinian government controlled only the West Bank while Hamas ran Gaza.

Negotiations continued, but the situation remained violent. Since 2002, Israel has been building a physical barrier between the peoples of the region. Israelis claim that they need a wall to protect their people from Palestinian attacks. In Hebrew, Israelis call the wall a "separation fence." In Arabic, Palestinians call it a "racial segregation wall." The barrier originally was to extend 486 miles, the entire length of Israeli's eastern border. So far it is almost all on West Bank territory, as it coils in various directions – sometimes to protect Israeli settlements and sometimes to divide Palestinians from one another. In 2004, the International Court of Justice declared the wall "contrary to international law."[5]

In 2008, after being constantly bombarded by rockets from Gaza, Israeli military forces once again attacked the region. In June 2009, newly elected Israeli prime minister Benjamin Netanyahu endorsed the idea of a Palestinian state on condition that it would be demilitarized and that Palestinians would recognize Israel as the state of the Jewish people. He also said the new Palestine would have no control over borders or airspace, that Jerusalem would remain under Israeli control, and that Palestinian refugees would not be allowed back into Israel. He rejected U.S. demands for a complete freeze on Israeli settlements in the West Bank. President Obama congratulated the Israeli prime minister for accepting a "two-state solution," but the Palestinian authorities immediately rejected Netanyahu's offer because of its attached caveats. Direct talks between the two sides collapsed in 2010 (Figure 4.1).

In September 2011, President Abbas asked the UN Security Council to admit Palestine as a full member of the United Nations. The request would have been denied if put to a final vote (only eight of the nine needed Security Council votes were achieved on a ritual vote and the United States was certain to use its veto), so Abbas withdrew the request. In 2012, he made the same request of the General Assembly, and it voted overwhelmingly to recognize Palestine as a nonmember observer state even though the United States and Israel were strongly opposed.

[5] David Hare, "Wall: A Monologue." *New York Review of Books*, April 30, 2009, p. 8.

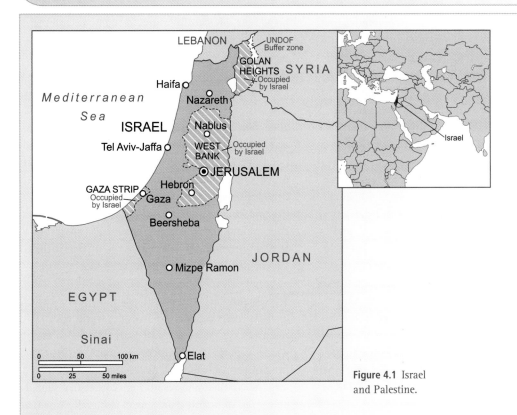

Figure 4.1 Israel and Palestine.

The peace process between Palestine and Israel remains frozen, with neither side ready to provide a compromise that is satisfactory to the other. For many observers, the Palestine issue is unlikely to be resolved as long as Hamas controls Gaza and a conservative Likud-led government is in place in Tel Aviv. Despite a tentative agreement between Fatah and Hamas over future elections, the two Palestinian authorities remain divided on fundamentals. Israel refuses to deal with Hamas because it is a terrorist group, and Israel cannot agree on an acceptable compromise about what security guarantees it would need from a new state of Palestine. The issue is complicated further by Iran, which supports Hamas and appears determined to become a nuclear power.

Since Egypt's Arab Awakening in 2011, Israel can no longer count on Egypt for support. Even the Egypt-Israeli Peace Treaty is now in jeopardy. A rocket attack from Gaza in November 2012 once again forced the Israeli government to retaliate with its military. The population of Palestine and neighboring Arab states is growing fast and putting considerable pressure on Israel. Israel needs to find compromises and get along in the region, but given its turbulent history, it insists that it must be able to defend itself without depending on others.

Is Palestine a state? A nation? Is the so-called two-state solution an answer to the need for compromise or only a smoke screen to hide concrete differences between the two sides? Is the United Nations likely to admit Palestine to full membership?

problematic in the discipline. The term implies that each state consists of only one nation, yet there are very few such states. The term is an artifact of the development of the modern state in Europe, where one nation typically dominated others in the creation of the state, as the English over the Irish, Scots, and Welsh in Great Britain or the Prussians over the Saxons and Bavarians in the unification of Germany. Japan has essentially one state and one nation because 99 percent of Japan's population is ethnically Japanese, speaks Japanese, and belongs to the Japanese culture. The remaining 1 percent consists of transplanted Koreans, foreigners, and a tiny leftover feudal class known as *burakumin*. But such homogeneity is rare. Most states of the world encompass many different peoples, cultures, and languages. With the addition of South Sudan in 2011, there are 193 states represented in the United Nations, but they contain some ten thousand cultural groupings. In fact, much of the instability and conflict in global politics occurs precisely where states and nations do not coincide. We examine nations and nationalism in Chapter 8.

Power and capabilities

There are recurring debates about which countries have the most political power and whether the balance of power is shifting in some fashion or other.[6] Analysis of what constitutes power is complicated by the fact that power is an abstract commodity that changes in response to the dynamic political and social environment. As resources, issues, problems, and personalities change, so do sources and types of power. The concept is, therefore, difficult to define and measure. Nevertheless, it is the core concept for realists and an important one in all international relations theories.

The word *power* comes from the Latin *potere*, meaning "to be able." In its broadest sense, power is

being able, physically or intellectually, or both, to achieve what one wants. Power can be implicit or manifest. In implicit power, A wants B to do something, and B does it simply because he or she realizes that A wants it done and, for whatever reasons, B wants to accommodate those wishes. Conversely, when power is manifest, it is directly observable: A acts to make B do what A wants despite B's objections. We define power, then, as the ability to cause others to do what one desires using means ranging from influence to coercion. Power permeates politics and, thus, global affairs. But it is a relational concept and not an absolute one. What matters in a state getting its way is its having more power than adversaries, not any particular amount of power.

Despite all its complexity, global politics provides a fascinating array of power relationships to dissect, analyze, and evaluate. We live in a world where resources are scarce and unevenly distributed and where disputes and conflicts constantly arise and need to be resolved. This never-ending chain of dispute, conflict, and resolution ensures that global politics is an ongoing process. It is literally true that politics never stops. It takes place at the individual, societal, state, and global levels as part of a struggle for goals such as equality, liberty, justice, economic well-being, and even power itself.

Power and national interest

In global affairs, power involves a network of relationships among states and other actors. The *national interests* of states change over time depending on the relative power of different political actors inside and outside the state. But there is no doubt that leaders claim to act on behalf of their respective country's national interests regardless of their own ideas, party affiliation, or ideology. While power can be thought of as multidimensional, and realists stress the role of military power, all theorists understand that state power is important and can be achieved in different ways. Military, economics, and even ideas and culture all play a role in determining the relative ability of a country to get its way in global politics.

---

[6] A good introduction to this topic is found in Joseph S. Nye, "The Future of American Power," *Foreign Affairs* 89, no. 6 (2010), pp. 2–12.

Ever-changing norms about power and its components do not diminish the essential quest of state leaders to define, compete, and use power in the international arena. Iran's nuclear program and its quest for nuclear weapons represents a search for power in the Middle East and world politics. The use of persuasion, economic embargoes, and threats of military force by the United States, Israel, and other Western states to counter Iran's ambitions are also forms of power. In the Iraq wars of 1991 and 2003 the United States had significantly more power than Iraq, but it was weakened in 2003 because it lacked the support of large parts of its own population and especially of other countries – even allies. This points to the fact that power is difficult to measure, because it includes both tangible and intangible ingredients. Political scientists, therefore, tend to write about the capacity of states to *use* power. Potential power includes military force, economic strength, technological superiority, and even leadership. Theorists may differ over which of these capabilities supplies the most power, but they all agree that each component can help a state, and, in theory, the more power capabilities a state possesses, the greater the likelihood that it will be able to get its way in international politics.

In this chapter we isolate a number of these power capabilities and show how they can be employed. Leaders may, of course, choose different strategies about what capabilities to develop and how to use them to maximize their international influence. In later chapters we assess the ingredients or conditions for their successful use. What must be clear is that power comes in many forms and that policymakers use it to pursue their state's interests when bargaining with other actors.

Sources of state power and capabilities

Economy

The overall potency of a country can be estimated by the strength of its economy. The stronger the economy, the greater is the capacity for the development of military power and potentially even the number

---

> ### Box 4.1 **Sources of state power and capability**
>
> Economy
> Geography
> Population
> Natural resources
> Technical and scientific abilities
> Military
> Soft power

---

of friends and allies that can be influenced. Several indicators of the strength of an economy are useful for understanding the power of individual states. The gross domestic product (GDP) is often employed, as it measures the total goods and services of each country. When the statistic is adjusted to measure how much a country can actually buy with its money, it is called purchasing-power parity (PPP). This figure adjusts for the relative price differences among countries. These data are useful but, like all such data, should be handled cautiously. Data cannot distinguish precisely, or perhaps fairly, among countries that possess vastly different types of currencies, levels of economic development, and types of economic or political systems such as capitalist and communist.

Nevertheless, according to comparative GDP statistics, the United States possesses the largest economy in the world (Table 4.1). In 2010, its GDP was measured at well more than US$14 trillion. The term *great powers* is often used to depict the most economically powerful countries. According to this criterion, following the United States in rank order are China, Japan, and then several individual EU countries. If the countries of the European Union are considered as one unit, they have the largest world economy (see Chapter 5).

Geography and population

Geopolitics refers to the role that territory and location play in global politics. Countries with extensive territories have both advantages and disadvantages

Table 4.1 **Top 15 economies by gross domestic product, 2010**

Ranking economy	Country	Billions of International dollars
1	United States	14,586.7
2	China	5,926.6
3	Japan	5,458.8
4	Germany	3,280.5
5	France	2,560.0
6	United Kingdom	2,261.7
7	Brazil	2,087.9
8	Italy	2,061.0
9	India	1,727.1
10	Canada	1,577.0
11	Russian Federation	1,479.8
12	Spain	1,407.4
13	Australia	1,131.6
14	Mexico	1,035.9
15	Korea, Rep.	1,014.5

Source: Adapted from *World Development Indicators Database*, May 3, 2012.

in terms of power. A large state is likely to have the advantage of a sizable population and natural resources. But it probably also will have to defend a large landmass, long shorelines, and long borders. Russia, the United States and China are respectively the first-, third-, and fourth-largest countries in the world, and they are two of the most powerful. Canada, the second-largest country, and Australia and Brazil, which also control huge territories, are not nearly as significant in geopolitical terms. Australia and Canada have low population densities and dramatically smaller populations. The United

States has more than 305 million people. Brazil has 188 million and Russia only 141 million, but no one yet thinks that Brazil is as powerful as Russia.

China, with a population of 1.3 billion, and India, with 1.15 billion, are growing in significance, but their populations are both an advantage and a handicap. Each of these countries needs to use much of its economic wealth to house, feed, and educate the large numbers of babies being born and to allay the massive poverty that already exists in its territories. They have only modest resources left to spend on security requirements. If population were all that mattered in the power equation, China, India, the United States, Indonesia, Pakistan, Nigeria, and Brazil would be the most powerful states in the coming few years, because they will have the largest populations. Population aging, a related issue, is discussed in Chapter 15.

Geographical location, too, is significant. In some historical periods geopolitics may have been the paramount factor in determining power. Civilizations and political power first developed in fertile areas along waterways. Urban centers grew where water and water transportation were readily available, and during the 18th and 19th centuries, Britain's control of the seas allowed it to develop a massive colonial empire through-out the world, yet obliged it to devote enormous resources to maintaining a large navy (partly from the savings from having only a comparatively small army). Even today lack of access to the sea can be a hindrance to trade, since shipping goods by water is normally much less expensive than by land or air. Forty-three states, including Afghani-stan, are landlocked, and most of them are very poor. There are a few exceptions, with Austria and Switzerland as two prime examples of landlocked countries that are also rich. Moreover, the ability to control important and dangerous passageways, such as the Gulf of Aden, the Persian Gulf, the Suez and Panama Canals, the Strait of Gibraltar, the Dardanelles, and the Straits of Malacca and Hormuz, is also vital for powerful states. Without control of these waterways international shipping could be severely damaged.[7] Piracy off the east coast of Africa (in the area of the Persian Gulf) and south of Malaysia and Singapore is currently playing havoc with shipping and is already a major security issue (see Chapter 11).

Natural resources and technical and scientific capabilities

Energy supplies are crucial for all states. Oil in particular plays a major part in the economies of all industrialized states and is essential for national security. Commerce cannot operate competitively without it. Industrialized states need to ensure a secure supply to keep their economies growing and to retain their status as global actors. Dependence on foreign resources can be a serious handicap, however, especially when they are limited and nonrenewable. Many relatively small countries derive considerable economic power from their exports of oil. Saudi Arabia, Kuwait, Qatar, and the United Arab Emirates are all relatively small Middle East countries made very rich by their petroleum resources. These resources need to be moved by pipelines and tankers through peaceful and hostile areas of the world, and these areas therefore can become significant parts of the geopolitical landscape of world politics.

A large population and ample natural resources may or may not translate into an industrial or postindustrial power base, however. A country's educational, scientific, and technological bases are also important, as they may enable a country to develop advanced military equipment and even nuclear weapons. Israel and Pakistan possess nuclear arsenals, but neither of them is among the world's wealthiest countries, nor do they have significant natural resources (Figure 4.2). Israel, nonetheless, has a very advanced scientific community and devotes a comparatively large portion of its economy to research and development as a

Figure 4.2 The buildup of armaments and even nuclear weapons in India and Pakistan illustrates the belief that states must arm themselves to be secure against their enemies. The security dilemma is a consequence of such beliefs. *Source:* Press Association.

deterrent against hostile interests in the Middle East. Pakistan devotes a considerable portion of its rather weak economy to nuclear weapons because of its fear of confrontation with India.

Military capabilities

The size, composition, and equipment of military forces are very significant elements in a country's ability to project power. If a state is to achieve its goals it may have to use or threaten to use military force. Although some theorists contest how important

---

[7] The navies refer to these waterways as choke points, which include the Straits of Dover, Hormuz, Bab el Mandeb, Malacca, and Gibraltar.

military power is or should be, none disputes its central role in global politics. Clearly, it is useful in the competition for advantage. If one component of state power can be converted to another form – for example, if extra funds from a strong economy can be used to purchase military strength – that asset is called *fungible*. Not all capabilities are fungible in the short term, and this raises the question of how large a military a state should keep in the form of a standing army during peacetime.

Because the United States has by far the largest economy of any single state in the world, it is not surprising that it spends more than any other country on its military. It has the largest supply of the most powerful conventional weapons as well as the greatest arsenal of nuclear weapons. In 2011, world military expenditure topped US$1,738 billion, with the United States alone spending almost half of it (Table 4.2). The top ten countries towered over the rest, accounting for three-quarters of total military expenditures. That means that the vast majority of countries do not even register on a scale of military capability. The huge outlay by the United States ensures that it remains the most powerful country in the world militarily, with enough of a margin to ensure that it is the only superpower. However, such massive expenditures are a heavy burden, and the financial costs of increasing the "base" military budget and paying for wars in Iraq and Afghanistan have aggravated the country's problems of deficits and long-term debt. Following far behind the United States in terms of military expenditure in 2011 are China, Russia, the United Kingdom, France, and Japan. China has increased its military expenditure threefold in the past decade. Europe has had relatively slow growth, but Russia, indeed all of Eastern Europe, has made huge increases in military expenditure during the past ten years.[8]

Realists in particular consider military capabilities essential, but even their critics agree that military budgets are a significant factor in amassing power (Table 4.2). However, there is no direct causal

[8] *SIPRI Yearbook*, 2008, available online at http://www.sipri.org.

Table 4.2 Top ten militaries by budgets, 2011

Rank	Country	Spending (US$ billions)
1	United States	711
2	China[a]	143[a]
3	Russia[a]	71.9[a]
4	United Kingdom	62.7
5	France	62.5
6	Japan	59.3
7	India	48.9
8	Saudi Arabia	48.5
9	Germany	46.7[a]
10	Brazil	35.4
	World	1,738

Source: Adapted from data at www.sipri.org. Assessed May 2, 2011.
[a] Estimated.

relationship between the amount of military power a country has and its success in fighting wars. In spite of the fact that the United States and its allies had huge military budgets, they were unable to either end the wars in Afghanistan and Iraq quickly or stop global terrorism. The wars in Iraq and Afghanistan lasted longer than either World War I or World War II. Countries with more powerful militaries have not always triumphed over weaker enemies. Russia was driven out of Afghanistan in 1989 by hostile groups that had far fewer financial resources and weaker militaries but considerably more commitment and willpower. It is clear, as evidenced by the events of September 11, 2001, in the United States and by the ensuing bombings in London, Madrid, and elsewhere, that terrorists with relatively primitive weapons such as boxcutters and home-made bombs can do great harm to rich and powerful countries. Indeed, enemies of the United States may have increased their use of terrorist strategies precisely because the United States is so powerful in terms of conventional weapons and weapons of mass destruction (WMD). Perhaps a combination of expenditures that included different types of weapons or personnel, or perhaps spending more money on "soft power," might have produced better results, but such speculation is debatable and controversial.

Soft power

Soft power refers to the means or attributes a country may use to ensure that it gets what it wants without resorting to coercion. This capability is likely to consist of an attractive culture and values, as well as policies that are seen as inclusive, respectful, and legitimate. These characteristics enable diplomacy to be persuasive and attractive. Public support can also be an important component of soft power. Leaders who are able to mobilize their own people to commitment and action may enhance their countries' power to influence other states. Appealing to the attributes of a country's culture or to certain ideals may give leaders the ability to obtain cohesion and solidarity among their populations in the face of threats or enemy action. Ideas or shared values may aid in shaping public opinion in a state or in mobilizing a state to action or even to war. Reciprocity, or rewarding other countries for supporting a state's policy positions, may also prove a significant aspect of soft power.

Appeals to nationalism, ideology, or religion may convince people to fight for a cause, boost morale, and contribute to a state's power. Leadership is also important. Winston Churchill, Franklin Roosevelt, and Joseph Stalin all played major leadership roles in defeating Adolf Hitler. Lyndon Johnson's decision to conscript troops to fight in Vietnam in the 1960s was legal, but over time many Americans came to believe that it was unacceptable, and this undermined his war planning. Eventually, public support grew so weak that the American government had to pull all of its troops out of Vietnam. A country's image abroad can also be an important component of its power. After the invasion of Iraq, U.S. president George W. Bush's personal popularity and the image of the United States around the world fell to such an extent that it was very difficult for the world's only superpower to find friends, partners, or allies to fight in Iraq or help with other international problems such as Iran's buildup of nuclear power facilities.

In short, soft power may prove significant in some circumstances. This realization has given rise to the newly minted concept of smart power, which refers to strategies that create the right balance among military, economic, and soft power approaches. Joseph S. Nye developed this concept to counter the argument that soft power alone could produce effective foreign policy.[9] In many cases the appeal of democracy and human rights may be better conveyed by soft power than military power. The Berlin Wall was destroyed by people who had lost faith in communism, not by military force. But in other cases perhaps only military power will suffice. In 2009, Hillary Rodham Clinton referred to smart power when she was confirmed as secretary of state: "We must use what has been called 'smart power,' the full range of tools at our disposal."[10] Students of global politics must be wary of new and seductive terms, however. Soft power and smart power are enticing concepts, but it remains a challenge to *measure* the significance of either of them. The Berlin Wall fell at a time of reduced tension between the United States and the Soviet Union, when significant mutual reductions in their nuclear arsenals were being negotiated. Change in Berlin was part of a larger change in the strategic confrontation of the Cold War superpowers.

Implementing foreign policy

There are three ways to employ the power capabilities of a state in the global arena: diplomacy, economic strategy, and military force. These three approaches are not necessarily mutually exclusive, and strategies usually include all forms of power and

[9] Joseph S. Nye, "Get Smart: Combining Hard and Soft Power," *Foreign Affairs* 88, no. 4, pp. 160–63.
[10] *Los Angeles Times*, January 21, 2009.

Box 4.2 **Ways to implement foreign policy**

Diplomacy
Economic strategy
Military force

---

influence. Sometimes the components of power are combined, and sometimes they are used sequentially, advancing in order from negotiation to sanctions and eventually to war. We shall have an opportunity to judge these various techniques of statecraft – the art of managing state affairs by strategizing, negotiating, and bargaining with other states – throughout the book, but in this section we consider the main diplomatic approaches and then apply them to a case study of U.S.-Iranian relations. A country's foreign policy needs to match its ends with its means – policies need to be achievable.

Diplomacy

Diplomacy is one of the oldest arts in the exercise of state power, with a history as far back as the earliest civilization in Babylon. It entails a state pursu-

ing objectives, goals, and demands it wants others to accept and conducting discussions or negotiations to achieve these objectives. States use diplomacy, or complex games of maneuvering, to influence other states by (1) developing accommodative policies on specific subjects; (2) negotiating with them to get their support; (3) chastising them for not following their direction or not joining others in handling a problem; or (4) if a state cannot achieve its aims by negotiation and diplomacy, it may try to convince, influence, induce, manipulate, and even coerce other states to its point of view by reducing aid, severing diplomatic ties, or implying that it will punish them in some manner for their actions or inactions (Figure 4.3).

In negotiations, the experience and skills of professional diplomats can be very helpful; the ability to craft arguments that support their governments' policies and interests can be vital. In settling the finer points of a broad agreement diplomats are usually indispensable. Simply persuading other countries that what your country wants is in *their* best interest is an age-old strategy in international relations. As professional diplomats are not bound by strictly political (electoral) calculations, they

Figure 4.3 The United Nations' effort to bring peace to the world through diplomacy and collective security is a primary illustration of the principle that "jaw jaw is better than war war."

may be better able than politicians to bear in mind both domestic and international factors. However, the context of diplomacy has changed in recent decades. The speed of travel and communications now means that there are more, and quicker, channels for direct government-to-government decisions than there used to be, and this has, to some extent, reduced the crucial role of diplomats in day-to-day relations among countries and their leaders.

Mass media have increased public awareness and the ability of ordinary people to see events happening around the world. For this reason, politicians and diplomats have become very cognizant of the need for public diplomacy – the need to communicate a state's views for public consumption in the media of television, radio, and the press. Reporters and commentators depend on governments and their agencies for information but risk being manipulated by their sources because public promotion of the official government position on important issues may end up being little more than propaganda.

All states employ propaganda, usually understood as deliberate distortions of the truth, in their attempt to influence people that their point of view is superior to that of their opponents. During the height of the Cold War, the former Soviet Union used its propaganda agencies to try to convert the world to communism, and the United States employed positive propaganda about democracy to achieve the same for democracy. Both the United States and the former Soviet Union also engaged in espionage (spying) and subversion (defined as support for the rebellious activity of disaffected groups in foreign countries). They used secret, or covert, actions, including diplomacy, or more coercive means up to and including war to overthrow governments or influence foreign and even domestic policies. Novelist John le Carré conveys this atmosphere perfectly in his books, in particular *A Spy Who Came in from the Cold* and *Smiley's People*. All states employ propaganda in one form or another, but not all states have the capacity to employ full-time intelligence services.

At the highest level, a state may give or withhold recognition from another state to try to get its way. The United States withheld recognition from the victorious 1949 communist government of Mao Zedong in China until 1979. We examine this question more fully in Chapter 6, but here we need to recognize that questions of recognition (either de facto or de jure) may have a major impact on negotiating strategies. Even today the United States does not accord diplomatic recognition to Cuba, and this affects trade, travel, and other issues in the Southern Hemisphere.

Economic strategies

Wealthier states are able to employ economic strategies – both positive and negative – to get their way in foreign affairs. Those with spare cash (the Chinese), extensive finances (the United States), and resources such as petroleum (the Organization of the Petroleum Exporting Countries or OPEC) are more likely to be able to exercise this kind of power. Use of economic sanctions by the Commonwealth and other countries including the United States was remarkably successful in ending apartheid in South Africa in 1992. However, the use of economic sanctions can have negative effects. The 1919 Versailles Treaty imposed harsh sanctions on Germany after World War I, and many historians deem this action at least partially responsible for World War II. The success of the UN sanctions against Syria that began in 2011 will be determined only when the civil war ends (see Chapter 10).

States may use positive inducements, or use or threaten to use negative economic sanctions, to try to influence other countries to act in compliance with their views.[11] Both positive and negative forms of coercion can be productive. Boycotting the products of a state or freezing the assets or bank accounts of foreign states or individuals may get the desired results. Threatening to take away advantages or standing in the way of diplomatic initiatives also may be effective. Today, for example, many Arab states refuse to do business with companies

[11] For skeptical work about economic sanctions, see Steve Chan and A. Cooper Drury, *Sanctions as Economic Strategies* (Basingstoke, UK: Palgrave Macmillan, 2000).

that cooperate with Israel and will not even allow people to cross their borders if their passport indicates that they have traveled to Israel. As another example: the United Nations placed broad sanctions on Libya and allowed NATO to assist the rebels with air strikes in an effort to force President Muammar Gaddafi from office in 2011 (see Chapter 10).

Military and coercive strategies

The use or threat of military or other coercive force is central to foreign policy strategy. Prussian strategist Carl von Clausewitz (1780–1831) argued in *On War* that aggression is merely an extension of politics or diplomacy by other means.[12] Certainly, wars persist in global politics despite the personal and collective horrors they impose. States defend their borders with force and try to influence neighbors with their strength. Even today there are numerous disputes over borders, often, but not always, in defense of sovereignty. States use deterrence to keep adversaries from doing something they do not want, such as making incursions into their territory or attacking their allies. They use compellence to get another state to do what they want by using, or threatening to punish them with, force. The relative power of one state over another determines whether diplomacy backed up by force is sufficient or whether going to war might be more effective despite the risks inherent in any resort to force.

States make choices when they use deterrence or compellence. While a strategy (overall goal) may remain constant, leaders may employ different approaches before engaging in war. They may, for example, supply arms or advisers to other governments, rebel forces, or mercenaries or use covert forces such as special military personnel or intelligence agencies to carry out clandestine activities. Direct warfare may be tried, but even in that case an escalation ladder is possible depending on whether, for example, a state wishes to merely harass or intimidate the enemy or defeat the enemy outright. A state may escalate or de-escalate tensions and

---

[12] Carl von Clausewitz, *On War* (London: Penguin, 1982).

may or may not use all of its country's resources. Conscription (forced enlistment) may be considered necessary by the military leadership to prosecute a large-scale conventional conflict, but the elected leadership might balk at the political costs involved. It is an open question whether opposition to the Vietnam War in the United States would have been so strong if the war had not been fought by a conscript army. A state may employ its forces one after another sequentially as a kind of escalation ladder, or it may use them all concurrently. It can change the type of weapons employed from small arms to artillery or from conventional to nuclear.

Even while military force is being employed, state leaders may continue to use diplomacy and economic strategies. The major problem with escalation of assertive diplomacy is that it may lead both sides to increase weapons procurement to the point that they create an arms race – that is, a reciprocal process that may make war more likely. The historical record here is very unclear. An international arms race certainly played a central role in the tensions that led to World War I, but the lack of rearmament on the part of the Western democracies and the aggressive arming by Germany and Japan may have contributed to the level of risk that each side was willing to take going into World War II. In the Cold War, the competitive buildup of thousands of nuclear missiles (discussed in detail in Chapter 9) created the largest arms race in world history, but it ended peacefully.

Contemporary U.S.-Iranian relations provide an excellent illustration of the choice of foreign policy instruments and the complications and interlaced nature of such choices (Critical Case Study 4.2).

Leaders and leadership

History is replete with individuals whose roles, power, and thinking helped direct world events. Think of leaders such as Napoleon, Lenin, Stalin, Hitler, and Mao Zedong. Sometimes their individual impact on foreign policy decisions was significant because decision-making institutions around them were weak.

Critical Case Study 4.2 **Levels of foreign policy analysis and the Iranian nuclear issue: A march to war?**

The 1979 Iranian Revolution set off a series of events that are still reverberating in international affairs. After years of excellent relations between the United States and Iran under Shah Mohammad Reza Pahlavi, leaders of the revolution blamed the United States for interfering in their country. Revolutionary guards took over the government, and militant Iranian students seized the United States embassy, holding its diplomats hostage for more than a year. Since then, for more than thirty years, formal relations between the two countries have been virtually nonexistent.

Recent conflict with Iran has centered on the country's decision to build nuclear power plants, missiles, and, potentially, nuclear weapons. Iran would like to assert its leadership in the Middle East, and a nuclear capability would help to accomplish that goal. Iran has reasons to be fearful. Its sworn enemy, Israel, and regional competitor, Pakistan, both have nuclear weapons. Former U.S. president George W. Bush branded Iran a member of the "axis of evil" along with Iraq and North Korea. In 2003, the United States, Britain, and others attacked Iraq. The Iranian leadership, therefore, has good reason to believe that it could be the next target of foreign military action.

As of 2012, Iran is continuing its potentially dual-use fuel-cycle activities.[13] It has eight thousand centrifuges for producing low-enriched uranium at its main nuclear site in Natanz (Figure 4.4). This site is not suitable for building nuclear weapons, nor is another similar site at Bushehr. But Iran has a heavy water reactor at Arak that could be used to produce plutonium for military purposes, and in late 2009

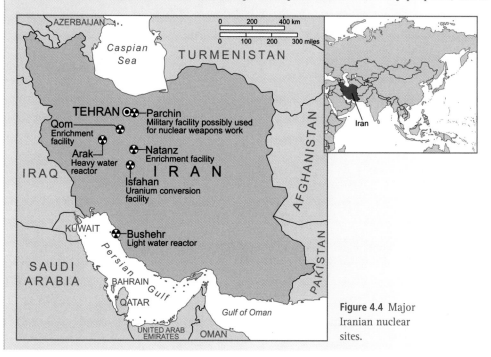

Figure 4.4 Major Iranian nuclear sites.

---

[13] Detailed analysis, timelines, statistics, and predictions can be found online at: http://www.criticalthreats.org.

it was discovered that it also had a secret uranium enrichment plant at Qum. Iran maintains that its development of nuclear energy is absolutely necessary because it must replace its diminishing natural gas and petroleum with other energies, including nuclear.[14]

While Iran's leaders continue to assert that they have no intention of producing nuclear weapons, the Institute for Science and International Security (ISIS) estimates that Iran is close to producing a nuclear weapon. The International Atomic Energy Agency (IAEA) announced in February 2009 that Iran had produced enough low-grade enriched uranium to begin building one nuclear bomb. The uranium needed to be further enriched to be weapons grade, and a missile would be needed to deliver the nuclear weapon. In early 2012 the IAEA concluded that Iran had conducted advanced research on a miniaturized warhead that could be delivered by medium-range missiles and that it had conducted computer simulations of nuclear detonations. Israeli prime minister Benjamin Netanyahu declared that Iran was on track to build an atomic bomb by the summer of 2013 and that he was prepared to attack the Iranian nuclear facilities without support from the United States or elsewhere.[15]

Led by the West, most countries, including members of the UN Security Council, believe that every effort should be made to prevent Iran from obtaining nuclear weapons. The reasoning is based not only on the possibility that an Iranian bomb would threaten Israel or other countries in the region but also, and more important, that it could lead to a regional nuclear arms race and further weaken the nonproliferation regime (discussed in Chapter 9). Given this situation, the three principle options for the West to pursue include diplomacy, economic sanctions, and military force.

Diplomacy is the first option. Under the international Non-Proliferation Treaty (NPT), to which it is a party, Iran can develop and use nuclear technology but only for peaceful purposes – not to produce nuclear weapons. As all treaty members have the "inalienable right" to research, produce, and use nuclear energy for peaceful purposes, it is not surprising that Iran rejects demands to cease its nuclear enrichment program. However, the P5 plus One (the five permanent members of the Security Council plus Germany) reject Iran's right to continue fuel-cycle activities unless appropriate safeguards are put in place to ensure that Iran will not build a nuclear bomb. Extra safeguards, offshore enrichment, and a time-limited suspension of uranium enrichment at the 20 percent level (which is higher than that required for nuclear power generation) have all been suggested as possible options by the six negotiating states, but so far no binding agreement has been reached. Negotiations began again in mid-2012, when Iran signaled that it might be prepared to come to a compromise and agreed that diplomacy needed to be given another chance.[16]

Sanctions are a second option. The UN Security Council has put in place several rounds of sanctions against Iran. So far they have not forced Iran to halt its nuclear program. Many experts believe, however, that adopting harsher economic sanctions could achieve that result.[17] As of 2012, the sanctions

[14] Richard Dalton, *Iran: Breaking the Nuclear Deadlock* (London: Chatham House, 2008), p. 25.
[15] *The New York Times*, November 6, 2012.
[16] *International Herald Tribune*, April 30, 2012.
[17] For an understanding of European fears about the Iranian nuclear ambitions, see Emanuele Ottolenghi, *Under a Mushroom Cloud: Europe, Iran and the Bomb* (London: Profile, 2009).

had begun to weaken the Iranian economy. The rial had fallen by 40 percent and domestic protests were taking place in the capital, Tehran.

It is unlikely, however, that sufficiently harsh United Nations–inspired sanctions will be forthcoming, because Russia and China are likely to veto any Security Council resolutions that include stiffer new sanctions. The president of Russia has hinted that Russia might change its position on this topic,[18] but energy-starved China is unlikely to accept a system of harsher sanctions. Further dire IAEA assessments of Iran's lack of compliance, and perhaps proof that a bomb actually has been produced, may be needed to induce the Security Council to act more forcefully.

The third and least appealing option is *military force.* Short of overt military action, the United States and Israel have engaged in cyberwarfare with Iran. Beginning in the Bush era and accelerating under President Obama, the two countries used the stuxnet computer worm to infect Iran's nuclear operations. However, this did not halt the nuclear program, as in 2010, Iran modified its computer programs and put the nuclear centrifuges back to work. Use of direct military force to replace the Islamic Republic of Iran with a democratic regime would require a land invasion and occupation of the country. The United States has increased its naval strength in the Persian Gulf and is adding antimissile systems in the region. On occasion, the United States has seemed to be headed toward a kind of nuclear "containment policy" (as was used with success against the Soviet Union) as a backup in case Iran does obtain nuclear weapons.

The central dispute is between states which think Iran can be prevented from ever obtaining a bomb and those which believe that it can be "contained" if it does get one. Currently, the United States backs Israel's position that Iran must not be allowed to have a bomb and says all options are on the table. Israel, however, wants the United States to set clear "red lines" to indicate what actions by Iran would trigger an attack. Former U.S. national security adviser Zbigniew Brzezinski thinks that a containment strategy would work. He argues that only if Iran attacks another country should the United States and its allies automatically counterattack – but Iran will not begin a war, he argues, because it is not "suicidal."[19]

Could Israel or the United States attack Iranian nuclear facilities before a nuclear bomb is produced? Yes, it is possible. Israel claims that it needs to protect its security and the United States demands that there must be no further proliferation of nuclear weapons. But no one can be certain what Iran's response would be to such an action. Over time, it could rebuild its destroyed facilities and claim that it would not have been attacked if it had actually possessed nuclear arms. In other words, such action would provide Iran and other states with a potent argument for producing nuclear weapons. Iran might also react by encouraging violent, explosive reactions inside Syria, Iraq, and Afghanistan or perhaps even block the Strait of Hormuz. Such actions would certainly harm its interests, but it might also do catastrophic damage to regional and global interests.

---

[18] Medvedev's response was nuanced or ambiguous, as he actually said, "Sanctions rarely lead to productive results. But in some cases sanctions are inevitable." *The New York Times*, September 24, 2009.

[19] See *The Wall Street Journal*, March 5, 2010.

At what point might Israel, the United States, and others decide to launch a military strike on Iran? For some commentators, the mere possession of nuclear weapons is not in itself a legitimate reason for a preventive attack, but if Iran developed a nuclear capability based on a declared intent to attack Israel, a preemptive use of military force might be acceptable to wide parts of the international community. If Israel thought it were about to be attacked with nuclear weapons, would it care about international approval for its preemptive strike? At what point would an imminent Iranian attack call for a preemptive strike by Israel, the United States, or even the UN Security Council? The normal test has been that international force should be used only when a delay would result in the inability to defend one's own country.[20] But the issue of whether Iran would ever attack – with or without warning – is a dilemma hanging over international institutions. There are even realist scholars who argue that the best possible outcome would be Iran actually obtaining nuclear weapons because this would create a durable balance of power in the Middle East.[21]

Which strategies are most likely to succeed in resolving the Iran issue? Whereas it has been more than thirty years since the Iranian Revolution, Iran's leaders remain mistrustful of outsiders and obsessed with the possibility of foreign intervention. Iran strives to be both an ordinary state but also to defend its revolutionary regime with rhetoric and perhaps nuclear weapons. Should the United States and NATO back Israel if it uses military force? Or should they limit their support to diplomacy and impose further economic sanctions? Would a policy of containment work? Would threats persuade Iran that the consequences of nuclear development are too high, or would that only increase Iran's determination to build nuclear weapons? No one can be certain what will induce the Iranian government to comply with international regulations, and Ayatollah Ali Khamenei flatly rejects direct talks with the United States. Has the replacement of Ahmadinejad by the cleric Hassan Rowhani as president in June 2013 made a difference?

Which of the options in your opinion has the best possibility for success – diplomacy, economic sanctions, or military force?

But even when institutional restraints are strong, there is often room for significant independent leadership decisions, as evidenced, for example, by the contributions of British prime minister Winston Churchill and U.S. presidents Roosevelt and Truman during World War II.

Today, top executive leaders dominate the process of making foreign policy, sometimes as individuals and sometimes as members of political elites. They conduct leader-to-leader diplomacy and hold summits and forums. Leadership in foreign affairs also comes from heads of international institutions such as the United Nations and even nonstate actors. Many state leaders, such as Barack Obama and Vladimir Putin, seem larger than life to their supporters, thanks to their charisma, strength of character, massive media exposure, and social and political circumstances. To a high degree, they are able to manipulate their public images by carefully managing photo ops, speeches, interviews, exposure of their families, and so on, and by media control – timing

---

[20] See T. V. Paul et al., *Complex Deterrence: Strategy in the Global Age* (Chicago: University of Chicago Press, 2009).
[21] Kenneth N. Waltz, "Why Iran Should Get the Bomb" *Foreign Affairs*, vol. 91, no. 4 (July/August 2012) pp. 2–5.

announcements, publishing autobiographies, releasing photos, and the like. We are all familiar with the tapes that al-Qaeda leader Osama bin Laden regularly released to marshal his friends and frighten his enemies. Because members of the public rarely get to meet their leaders directly, everything they know about them comes through the media from spin doctors and hearsay, which is often manipulated by governments to detract from problems and/or to reinforce a desirable image.

Although many leaders may be recognized as outstanding, there is significant disagreement not only about how they make decisions but also about how much leadership even matters in the foreign policy process. Much of what transpires in politics derives from factors beyond the control or influence of individual leaders. The debate between the "great man" theorists of history and those who put their faith in broad cultural, economic, technological, and political forces to explain what shapes our world continues unabated.

Liberals tend to believe that leaders matter a great deal and connect individuals and their values with historical events – for better or for worse. For example, they credit President Mikhail Gorbachev with initiating the broad economic reforms that brought about the breakup of the Soviet Union in 1991, or they discredit George W. Bush for extending the "war on terror" to the 2003 preventative war on Iraq. Constructivists, in particular, may look beyond the traditional political elite and focus on the stories of individuals and groups who are peripheral to the center of political action but whose contribution to the development of new norms may be significant on some important occasions. They might focus, for example, on the contributions of leaders of nonstate actors or international advocacy groups.

Realists, conversely, may dismiss the impact of individuals on decision making as negligible, because, as they would argue, no matter how weak or powerful individuals are, they cannot avoid making decisions based on their country's national interests. Chancellor Angela Merkel of Germany, an avowed friend of the United States, expressed it this way before meeting President Barack Obama in early 2009 on his first transatlantic trip as head of state: "International policy is, for all the friendship and commonality ... always also about representing the interests of one's own country."[22] That visit was marked not by the adulation that was so evident in Obama's earlier preelection trip but more by the differences between the two leaders and the divergences between U.S. and European political interests. As another example, Marxists, because of their theories about the predominance of the class struggle, may also discount the role of individuals, but Marx himself thought that people make history, though rarely as they please.

Individuals and groups in foreign policy decision making

Making foreign policy is a complicated process that is affected by individual psychological processes and group dynamics. Decision making is based on a blend of rational and irrational factors. Emotional and personality factors impede purely rational decision making. In spite of this, most foreign policy tends to be relatively coherent and to express the interests of the states concerned, regardless of the personalities and decision-making skills of their leaders.

If leaders were always completely rational and issues relatively simple and straightforward, it would be relatively easy to map the decision-making process and predict outcomes from it. But aside from the complexity of political problems, several psychological processes interfere with decision making, even for leaders whose personal interests coincide perfectly with those of their state. These include misperceptions, affective biases, and cognitive biases. All three of these individual psychological processes affect decision making.

Political leaders have different natural endowments and idiosyncrasies, including values, beliefs, intellectual capabilities, personalities, experiences,

---

[22] "Merkel Will Tell Obama Where Interests Diverge," *The New York Times*, March 30, 2009, A6.

and styles with which they approach decision making. Their perceptions act as "screens" that enable them to interpret and process information selectively. As they compile, reduce, and filter the information to make decisions, these personal idiosyncrasies may bring *misperceptions* or biases to the process. Emotions, too, can undermine the quality of decisions. Leaders may be angry, depressed, sad, or jealous, just like anyone else, and that can affect their decisions. President Bush was furious with the audacity of the 9/11 terrorists and swore to "kick their asses." Similarly, some critics thought his decision to attack Iraq in 2003 was colored by his desire to avenge his father, who had earlier stopped short of invading deep into Iraq after the liberation of Kuwait in 1991. Affective bias refers to feelings of liking or disliking someone or something. We all have a tendency to focus on information that substantiates our affective biases. Even when decision makers strive to be rational, their strong emotions for or against an individual or group or state may distort the process, and even the *facts* may get colored or shaped by their psychology.

Cognitive bias refers to limitations of the human brain in making choices. Even thought processes themselves can undermine rational calculations. People intuitively try to create models of the world that are logically consistent to create a cognitive balance as opposed to cognitive dissonance.[23] This means, for example, that when a leader decides on a certain course of action (e.g., a propaganda war against another state), he or she later finds it difficult to deviate from that course because of his or her integrated belief system. Enemies are branded as "bad" or "evil," and all their actions are interpreted accordingly to avoid cognitive dissonance. When political leaders in Washington and London believed, without concrete evidence, that Iraq's Saddam Hussein was hiding weapons of mass destruction and supporting Islamist terrorists, the false perceptions provided cognitive consistency with

their view of Saddam as a tyrant and "evildoer" and may have led to biased decision making or at least helped to legitimate a decision already taken. Former UK prime minister Tony Blair, after all, wanted to invade Iraq back in 1998, when Bill Clinton was in power. He and others may have seen 9/11 as an opportunity.

Opponents in a political conflict usually create mirror images of each other. They both see themselves in a positive light and view their adversaries negatively as "bad," "aggressive," or "untrustworthy." U.S. president Obama referred to this phenomenon when, in reference to the relations between Jews and Muslims, he said in a 2009 address in Egypt that "this cycle of suspicion and discord must end."[24] In the same vein, a leader may dismiss the idea that an event such as a terrorist attack will occur simply because the probability of it happening is low or does not fit an accepted historical pattern of expectations. This type of decision making is based on wishful thinking and comes from trying to maintain cognitive balance. For example, when there was originally some slight evidence that the 9/11 terrorist attacks were being planned, leaders in the Bush administration ignored it.[25]

Another way leaders create cognitive balance is to look to the past for occasions that have some similarity to the current one in order to find direction about how to act. The results can be deceiving, however, if important differences in the situations are ignored – and they often are! In the 1930s, the leaders of France and Britain appeased Hitler by allowing him to expand into Czechoslovakia, which led to World War II, and leaders since then have often referred to this incident to justify bold action rather than acquiescence to aggression. In the 20th century the word *appeasement* came to mean that compromise encourages dictators to be bolder, but for leaders earlier in the 19th century it meant granting concessions that might render rival powers

[23] Donald A. Sylvan, and James F. Voss, *Problem Representation in Foreign Policy Decision-Making* (Cambridge: Cambridge University Press, 1998).

[24] *The New York Times*, June 5, 2009, p. A8.

[25] Robert Jackson and Philip Towle, *Temptations of Power: The US in Global Politics since 9/11* (London: Palgrave, 2007).

more likely to accept the international status quo and avoid war. This problem of the use of analogies is well handled by Margaret Macmillan in *Dangerous Games: The Uses and Abuses of History.*[26]

Individual leaders tend to have more influence in foreign affairs in certain types of situations than in others. Where institutional constraints on a leader are weak, as in authoritarian governments, leaders are relatively freer to act. Particularly in times of crisis, or in unusual or unstable situations, when decisions are compressed into a short time frame, even democratic leaders are likely to have freedom to make policy choices. In times of crisis, decision making becomes urgent, and pressures change the normal patterns. Leaders and politicians believe that they must act, and citizens often feel they should support them. We saw this happen after 9/11 when Americans supported the president's attack on Iraq even though there was little evidence that such action would further the "global war on terrorism." In times of crisis, decisions are harder to predict than in normal foreign policy making because they are rushed, and psychological stress amplifies emotions, thus promoting anger, hatred, and fear.[27] To save time, options are restricted, and communication lines become shorter and actions more stereotyped (see Chapter 16 on crises).

Personality and leadership

Why do some leaders succeed more than others in foreign policy? There are several explanations. Key personality characteristics have been found to influence leaders' style and policy orientations.[28] Leaders with high conceptual abilities, who believe strongly in their own personal ability to control events, and who distrust others are more likely to be independent in their approach to foreign affairs. Those with the opposite characteristics are more likely to be consultative in reaching decisions. These personality characteristics can be expected to affect the leadership patterns of dictators much more than democratic leaders because they are relatively freer of institutional checks.

There have been many attempts to analyze U.S. presidential personalities to determine their suitability for the office. One of the earliest was by James David Barber, who classified presidents according to whether they were active or passive and whether their emotional attitude toward politics and the office of the presidency was positive or negative.[29] These two dimensions, he said, were good predictors of presidential performance. He considered the best suited for the presidency were those who were active-positive because they creatively shaped their environment and enjoyed doing it. He included Harry Truman, John F. Kennedy, and Jimmy Carter in this category. Conversely, negative-positive types were the worst suited for the job because their personalities were driven by personal frustrations. Lyndon Johnson and Richard Nixon were examples of this type. As might be expected, there are strong disagreements over where to place individual presidents on this schema. Where would one place Bill Clinton, George Bush, and Barack Obama? Bill Clinton clearly enjoyed politics and was very active. But the personality characteristic that perhaps most defined his presidency and nearly destroyed him politically may have been his personal behavior with respect to ethics.

Intriguing as these categories are in judgments of personality, character, and leadership success, they are still little more than broad indicators of a candidate's suitability for high office. It would be very difficult to apply the theory to choose among prime ministerial or presidential contenders. Abraham Lincoln, for example, was known to be moody and somewhat aloof. Should that have eliminated him as presidential material? Personality, including

---

[26] Margaret Macmillan, *Dangerous Games: The Uses and Abuses of History* (London: Modern Library, 2009).

[27] A. Boin, P. t'Hart, E. Stern, and B. Sundelius, *The Politics of Crisis Management: Public Leadership under Pressure* (Cambridge: Cambridge University Press, 2005); B. Canes-Wrone, *Who Leads When? Presidents, Policy and the Public* (Chicago: University of Chicago Press, 2006). See also Paul t'Hart and Karen Findoll, *Framing the Global Economic Downturn* (Canberra: Australian National University Press, 2009).

[28] Margaret G. Hermann, "Explaining Foreign Policy Behavior Using the Personal Characteristics of Political Leaders," *International Studies Quarterly* 24, no. 1 (March 1980), 7–46.

[29] James David Barber, *The Presidential Character*, 4th ed. (Englewood Cliffs, NJ: Prentice Hall, 1992).

character, integrity, and leadership style, is only one factor determining success or failure. Other factors include public opinion and economic, social, and political forces of the day. Barack Obama scores very high on personality traits, but it may well be how and whether serious economic conditions or overseas wars are resolved that finally determine the ultimate success or failure of his U.S. presidency. In summary, it is impossible to create a direct link between personality traits and political accomplishments. Leaders with divergent personalities have both succeeded and failed. Many personality factors are neither conducive to systematic study by social scientists nor conducive to being learned or adopted. Oliver Wendell Holmes once said of Franklin Roosevelt, possibly the most popular U.S. president ever, that he had a second-rate intellect but a first-rate temperament. What is clear is that leaders and elites prove their mettle by correctly gauging the opportune time to "catch the wave" of public opinion or political opportunity.[30]

The advisers a leader chooses may also be significant in assessing performance. Leaders create groups around them to advise and help formulate decisions. Selecting wise and competent advisers is obviously important, following the principle that broadening the decision-making process promotes rationality, widens perspectives, and helps remove individual biases. However, group affiliation presents problems, too, perhaps the worst of which is groupthink – the tendency for group members to be "yes men," to disregard contradictory information, and go along with, rather than stand up against, popular decisions. Acting as part of a group relieves individuals of accountability for their decisions. It may also allow individuals to escape the wrath of a leader who might have a tendency to "kill the messenger." Another problem for leaders who create groups around them to help formulate decisions is the tendency to engage in satisficing. This concept refers to the tendency of groups to seek conformity and solidarity and therefore search for a solution that is simply OK rather than the most effective one. Such an approach may not resolve the issue, however, because not all alternatives and possibilities can ever be canvassed (see Chapter 16).[31]

In today's world it is not just leaders of states who are able to influence international relations. Private individuals with certain skills and/or resources may also be very influential. Retired politicians such as Tony Blair, Bill Clinton, and Jimmy Carter are periodically called on to engage in two-track diplomacy, or conflict resolution outside of government. This can be extremely useful because it enables informal exploration of ways to resolve disputes. Another example is the contribution of Microsoft founder Bill Gates and his wife, Melinda, to global immunization and AIDS programs.

Even mass publics can, and sometimes do, influence foreign policy by pressuring elites and leaders to accept their opinions. Mass media create public awareness of issues and often lead or reinforce public attitudes about them. Public opinion polls are used as barometers by political leaders and are watched carefully by those who depend on public support for their legitimacy. Leaders in most democracies would be unlikely to go to war or take aggressive actions toward another country without a substantial degree of public approval. Very occasionally, publics actually get ahead of their leaders and push change. This happened in East Germany when the spontaneous exodus of people through Hungary and Austria led to the tearing down of the Berlin Wall in 1989, followed by the reunification of Germany and the fall of the Soviet Union.

---

[30] See Henry E. Brady, "Elite Tough Talk and the Tides of History," in Gary King et al., eds., *The Future of Political Science* (New York: Routledge, 2009), p. 20.

[31] There is an extensive literature on this topic. The classics include Y. Dror, *Public Policymaking Reexamined* (San Francisco: Chandler, 1968); David Braybrook and C. Lindblom, *A Strategy of Decision* (New York: Free Press, 1963). My own views are found in Chapter 16 and earlier in "Crisis Management and Policy-Making," in Richard Rose, ed., *Dynamics of Public Policy* (London: Sage, 1976), pp. 209–35.

Close Up 4.1 **Personality and leadership: Adolf Hitler**

Since Adolf Hitler's dramatic rise to power in Germany in the 1930s, studies in sociology, psychology, and cultural history have yielded clues to his character and how he formed his "worldview." They partly explain the distortion of culture that fueled his lust for power and informed his plans for world domination (Figure 4.5).

No absolute connection has been established between Hitler's personality and his success as a dictator or his choices in foreign policymaking, but studies of the books Hitler read have given insight into what informed his leadership. Even before World War II was over, American journalist Frederick Oechsner published *This Is the Enemy*[32], based on interviews with the Führer's associates and a survey of his library. It was perhaps the first attempt to explain Hitler's character based on his reading material. From it we learned that Hitler's extensive collection was broad in scope, including mainly military history but also works on the Catholic Church, architecture, the occult, and a great many books that were racist and nationalistic. For entertainment he absorbed books of popular fiction, including cowboy-and-Indian tales (which he sometimes recommended to his generals as manuals of strategy), romances, and Edgar Wallace thrillers.

A recent study by Timothy W. Ryback surveyed the collection again but paid particular attention to a few annotated books to which Hitler evidently attached particular significance.[33] Ryback portrays Hitler as an autodidact whose learning was defective and distorted because he read subversive ideas. Among Ryback's findings was that Munich publisher Julius Lehmann supplied Hitler with complimentary copies of all the Nazi materials he published, in the hope that Hitler would use them as

Figure 4.5 Adolf Hitler (1889–1945) was the founder and leader of the National Socialist or Nazi Party in Germany. He eliminated his parliamentary opposition, suspended the constitution, and achieved dictatorial power. In 1941, he bragged that in 15 years he had "achieved the unity of the German nation, and ... freed it from the death sentence of Versailles." However, in doing so he also set in motion the genocide of the Jewish people, slaughtered the handicapped and others, and started World War II. *Source:* Photos.com.

"building blocks" for Nazism. They included a wide range of material, from philosophical diatribes to a manual on sterilization and a study of "racial hygiene." Hitler's reading preferences also showed that he looked to astrology to

---

[32] Frederick Oechsner, *This Is the Enemy* (New York: William Heinemann, 1943).
[33] Timothy W. Ryback, *Hitler's Private Library: The Books That Shaped His Life* (New York: Vintage, 2012).

bolster his idea that he was a man of destiny and to writers of mysticism and the occult to feed his musings about possible linkages between the physical and spiritual worlds that could guide his exceptional leadership.

What aspects of Hitler's library might hold clues to his actions as leader of Germany?

Making foreign policy

We have examined the power that states exercise to try to get their way in international politics and how individual leaders may or may not matter in making decisions. A state's foreign policy consists of decisions its leaders make and the priorities they set to realize their country's international goals. Next we examine how leaders arrive at such decisions. Political scientists have developed a number of concepts, models, and theories of decision making relating to this process.

In political science, as in everyday language, the word *model* is sometimes used to refer to a normative ideal that all should seek to emulate, as in the statement, "That person is a model citizen." But model is also used more rigorously in the sense of a simplified version of reality that is designed to show how various components fit together and work, as in a working model of a car or steam engine. In international relations there are three standard models of the foreign policy process: (1) the rational actor model, (2) the organizational process model, and (3) the bureaucratic or government bargaining model.

The rational actor model describes the elements or stages in the decision-making process. According to this model, decision making follows six basic steps:

1. The rational decision maker is presented with a problem that can be distinguished from other problems or at least meaningfully compared with them.
2. The values, goals, and objectives that guide the decision maker are reviewed and ranked in order of priority.
3. A list of alternative means of achieving these goals is compiled.
4. The consequences (costs and benefits) that would ensue from each alternative are estimated.
5. Each alternative and its likely consequences are then compared with all other alternatives.
6. Finally, the rational decision maker selects the course of action (and its consequences) that offers maximum attainment of the values, goals, or objectives identified in step 2.

According to the proponents of this model, the end product of the process is a "rational" decision – that is, one that selects the most effective and efficient means of achieving the chosen goal or objective.

Critics maintain that the rational actor model neither describes reality nor represents an ideal to be emulated. No single leader makes decisions totally alone, and leaders cannot avoid making decisions until they have perfect knowledge of a subject. They have to choose and act in highly uncertain situations. Critics also argue that such a process would make totally unreasonable demands on decision makers with regard to the information needed and the time and resources necessary to evaluate the costs and benefits of all possible alternative courses of action. Only very few decisions may be made by people making rational choices among measurable options, and much of politics is about changing complicated established preferences. In short, the model oversimplifies the decision-making process and cannot accommodate the high degree of uncertainty inherent in it.

The organizational process or bureaucratic bargaining models are considered more descriptive of the way leaders actually make decisions. The organizational process model assumes that decision makers rely on standardized responses or operating codes to reach their policy conclusions, especially in crisis situations. The government or bureaucratic model assumes that decisions result from constant bargaining among various government actors and organizations that are likely to hold different views about the goals and utility of each course of action. Although the rational actor model assumes that one leader makes a decision for his or her organization, the other two models argue that governments are not composed of a single, hierarchically arranged organization, and, therefore, policy has to emerge from a complex web of relationships, with many people having input. Often this collective deliberation of a problem does not result in an optimum choice but rather results in a concerted effort to avoid a disastrous outcome or even personal blame. Moreover, the situation may be so complex that, as President John F. Kennedy put it about the Cuban Missile Crisis:

The essence of ultimate decision remains impenetrable to the observer – often, indeed, to the decider himself. ... There will always be dark and tangled stretches in the decision-making process – mysterious even to those who may be the most intimately involved.[34]

Both of these latter models are variants of the incrementalist model that assumes that most problems are complex and interrelated and that political decision makers operate in a climate of uncertainty and limited resources. In contrast to the rational approach, the point of departure for incremental decision-making theory is not some ideal goal to be attained in the most efficient manner. The theories postulate instead that the decision maker has a fairly simplified set of ideas about the world and acts only in relation to them. Only a limited number of policy alternatives are considered, and only a few foreseeable consequences are evaluated. Simply put, the decision maker makes only marginal adjustments to policies and programs so that they can easily be reversed or altered. The incremental approach offers senior politicians and bureaucrats endless opportunities for redefining goals and adjusting both the means (e.g., programs,

activities) and ends (e.g., values, priorities) of foreign policies – in other words, they muddle through.

The incrementalist approach also has weaknesses. Critics argue that, whether or not the model is empirically valid, it is simply not the way that decisions *should* be made. Given the preoccupation of advocates of rationalism with "improving" the decision-making process in the interests of technical efficiency, it is perhaps not surprising that they are appalled by the prospect of decision makers "muddling through" on most issues. The incrementalist model has been labeled a "conservative" recipe for maintaining the status quo because it provides an "ideological reinforcement of the pro-inertia and anti-innovation forces prevalent in all human organizations, administrative and policy-making."[35]

Another significant problem, in our view, is that, although the incrementalist model is supposed to provide a general description of how policy decisions are made by making marginal adjustments to the policies and programs already in place, it quite clearly cannot account for the occasional radical departures from existing patterns of activity or inactivity. Thus, it can neither explain the entry of governments into new areas of policy nor account for drastic alterations to, or innovations in, existing policy. Decision making is only one part of the overall process of public policy activity. Therefore, to the extent that any model can tell us how policy decisions are made, it still would not be able to provide guidance as to why governments pursue particular directions in public policy or to what effect (see Chapter 16).

Decisions and game theory

While the rational theory approach may be impractical for some purposes, aspects of it are important for understanding and improving decision making.

---

[34] Graham Allison, *Essence of Decision: Explaining the Cuban Missile Crisis* (New York: Little, Brown, 1971).

[35] Yehezkel Dror, "Muddling Through – 'Science' or Inertia?" (p. 155) and Charles E. Lindblom's response, "Contexts for Change and Strategy: A Reply." *Public Administration Review* 24, no. 3 (September 1964), pp. 153–57 and 157–58.

Critical Case Study 4.3 **The Cuban Missile Crisis**

The best-known and best-researched case study using these three decision-making models is the 1962 Cuban Missile Crisis, when saber rattling came close to causing a nuclear war between the United States and the Soviet Union (Figure 4.6). The Soviet Union had deployed nuclear-armed ballistic missiles and 100 tactical nuclear weapons in Cuba to deter a possible U.S. invasion of its communist ally and to counter the fact that the United States had put missiles in Europe, and especially in Turkey along the Soviet border. The crucial was in regard to what the United States should do about these Soviet missiles that were so close to American territory – should it attack or do nothing?

Following the rational actor model argument, the U.S. president (a single actor) would have coolly assessed all the alternatives and calculated his response accordingly. He did not. But how was the decision actually made? Soviet aircraft had been seen lined up in offensive positions on a Cuban airport tarmac. The military took this as a sign that the aircraft were preparing to attack U.S. territory. Therefore, following standard operating procedures, the military advised an early attack on Cuba to eliminate the missiles before they became operational. In other words, the organizational process model fit the decision-making pattern of the military.

In his classic book *The Essence of Decision*, Graham Allison shows that President John F. Kennedy was more cautious and nuanced than the military.[36] President Kennedy would neither accept the advice to

Figure 4.6 Cuba.

[36] Graham Allison, *The Essence of Decision: Explaining the Cuban Missile Crisis* (New York: Little, Brown, 1971), p. 48.

attack nor allow Soviet missiles to remain in Cuba. Instead, he appointed a group of advisers to work on the topic who were isolated from the Departments of Defense and State and even on occasion from his authority. In other words, he wanted to receive different, or *countervailing*, advice from various sets of advisers, as well as from the standard officials in departments such as State and Defense. His advisers flew over U.S. air bases and found that the American military also had aircraft in offensive formations on the tarmac, even though no U.S. government decision had been made to attack Cuba. In short, one could not deduce the *intentions* of a country from its placement of planes on airport tarmacs. Even on strictly military matters Kennedy did not listen to only Pentagon advisers about what to do; he actually bypassed the secretary of defense to make direct, personal contact with U.S. military officers in the geographical neighborhood of Cuba. Therefore, the policy was not made by a single actor following the advice of a hierarchical set of advisers.

This scenario indicates that, at least in this case, a government bargaining model fits the facts better than the rational single actor model or even a hierarchical organizational model and standard operating procedures. President Kennedy ordered a naval blockade around the island and confidentially informed the Soviet leadership that the United States would not invade Cuba if it removed the missiles. He also issued a private ultimatum threatening to attack Cuba within 24 hours unless Khruschev accepted the offer. In exchange for removing the missiles, President Kennedy offered to withdraw U.S. missiles from Turkey within six months. It was a reasonable decision, as some Soviet missiles were already operational and Russian commanders had been ordered to respond if there was a U.S. attack on Cuba. After a forceful pounding of his fist at the United Nations, Nikita Khrushchev removed the missiles. The safest conclusion had been reached.

Kennedy acted appropriately and resolved the crisis without war – but what if he had not? Would there have been a worldwide nuclear confrontation? Chapters 9–11 and especially Chapter 16 discuss other events during which policy outcomes were considered crucial and time frames were compressed.

During the Cold War, scholars trying to understand nuclear war contingencies developed game theory to elicit what decisions players might make given their respective preferences and to help clarify the options open to players. Various games and related mathematical models were employed. Game theory uses logic and mathematics to predict bargaining outcomes. It assumes that players choose their moves objectively so as to maximize positive payoffs and results.[37] In zero-sum games one player or team always wins and the other always loses (a player's gains are precisely equal to the other player's losses), but in non-zero-sum situations many players can participate, and all can win, draw, or lose.

Chicken, prisoner's dilemma, and the stag hunt

Chicken is a conflict game that applies to confrontational, crisis situations. The model is based on two male teenagers speeding toward each other in their automobiles with the possibility of a head-on collision. The first to swerve is called "chicken." The train of thought for each of them is, "If he swerves, I won't, but if he doesn't swerve, I must, or we'll both crash." The driver who holds out the longest and does not swerve wins. But the risk of both dying is high because each may assume that the other person is "chicken." Commitment, foolish or not, is important

[37] Thomas C. Shelling, *The Strategy of Conflict* (Cambridge, MA: Harvard University Press, 1981).

in determining how the game will play out and who the winner and loser will be.

Chicken is often used as a metaphor when thinking about nuclear crises. No state wants a nuclear disaster, but in a crisis confrontation each state might prefer that its opponent back down. The state that takes the greatest risk by continuing to stockpile nuclear weapons might win, but the danger of mutual destruction is high. In Chicken each state has only two possible choices, but there are four possible consequences, and only one of them absolutely abolishes nuclear weapons. At the time of the 1962 Cuban Missile Crisis, John F. Kennedy appeared to follow this model when he seemed ready to risk nuclear war if the Soviets did not remove their missiles from Cuba.

Prisoner's Dilemma is another conflict game that is particularly popular with international relations specialists, who generally agree with the assumption that decision makers should make reasoned choices in their policy decisions. Prisoner's Dilemma is based on the story of two prisoners who robbed a bank together. The prosecutor knows the truth, but he has only enough evidence to convict them of illegal possession of a gun – which would let both prisoners off with minimal sentences. The prosecutor therefore tells each prisoner *separately* that if he confesses to the bank robbery and provides evidence against his partner he will receive only a minor penalty. The prosecutor does not tell the prisoners that if they both confess, they both will get twenty years in prison.[38]

What will the prisoners decide given these possibilities? There is a clear distinction between their choices and the consequences. For both to get the maximum benefit, they should trust each other and cooperate, and neither should confess. Instead, however, each may privately reason that getting the lightest sentence is the best outcome, because it appears more certain, and therefore, each should con-

fess and hope that his partner will not. In Prisoner's Dilemma, therefore, the mutually cooperative choice is ranked second by each player – that is, each prisoner seeks to gain a *relative* advantage over the other. In the real world, people and states similarly may tend to choose the self-interest option more frequently than the cooperative one. They prefer a "free ride," or to gamble on getting the maximum for themselves at the other's expense. They therefore end up worse off than if they had cooperated.

Prisoner's Dilemma provides a disincentive for individuals to take a chance on the best positive testimony from their partner. In such situations the prisoners might, after similar *repeated (iterative) interactions*, learn that they would be better off cooperating. Various versions of this game have been used to gain insight into how states fail to cooperate for their own collective good but cooperate readily after repeated interactions – throughout which they may learn how to achieve the optimal outcome.

The metaphor of the Prisoner's Dilemma can be used in international relations to illustrate decisions in which mutual trust is involved. Say, for example, that two countries are working on nuclear bombs. The safest and best scenario would be for neither country to have one, but the worst scenario would be for one not to have one while the other did. In this example, however, it would be better for both to have bombs in order to create an equilibrium between them. Figure 4.7 shows the difference between choices and consequences in Prisoner's Dilemma when applied to the building of nuclear bombs. A and B will achieve mutual security if they both build bombs, but the best choice is for neither of them to build them. In other words, in Prisoner's Dilemma the prisoners who do not cooperate are worse off than if they trusted each other. In the nuclear bomb-building scenario, if the two countries do not trust each other, they, too, end up in a worse situation.

Stag Hunt is another game used as a metaphor to illustrate problems of coordination and trust in international relations. The scenario is based on a parable originally told by the 18th-century French philosopher Jean-Jacques Rousseau. Two hunters need to

---

[38] The assumptions of this game also include that the prisoners will trust the prosecutor, that each prisoner will care only about himself, and that only the immediate outcome matters, as neither prisoner will have a chance to retaliate later.

State A

State B		Continues to Build Bombs	Stops Building Bombs
	Continues to Build Bombs	Equilibrium; both build bombs	A is disadvantaged
	Stops Building Bombs	B is disadvantaged	Safest: neither builds bombs

Figure 4.7 Prisoner's Dilemma: Building nuclear bombs.

kill a stag to feed their hungry families. They can get a stag only by cooperating, one flushing the animal out into the open and the other shooting it. However, when a rabbit hops into view, each of the hunters must make a decision. The hunter can forget the stag and go for the sure catch of a rabbit. But if he does, he is abandoning the hope of getting the much more valuable stag, and he is leaving his fellow hunter with nothing. Letting the rabbit get away and mutual co-operation would be the superior choice. But given the opportunity, there is a temptation to go for the rabbit and abandon the stag. The worst option would be to let the rabbit go and then not get the stag. What each hunter chooses is based on what he expects the other will do. The dilemma highlights the point that if there is a lack of trust, both hunters lose out. There needs to be mutual trust to get the best outcome.

This game also illustrates the problem of collaboration in the provision of public goods. Take, for example, the issue of a polluted lake shared by two states. Figure 4.8 shows that the countries could collaborate and clean up the lake. Or A could clean up its share while B bluffs and does nothing, thereby reaping benefits at no cost. Or A could do nothing. If both

bluff, the pollution will get worse for everyone. The figure shows that a public good cannot be achieved when people act only in their own self-interest – there has to be coordination (government action and perhaps regulation) to obtain a clean lake.

Game theory helps clarify core dilemmas in strategic situations. It can simplify the difficult choices leaders and states have to make. It forces both analysts and policy makers to examine their assumptions and choices systematically as well as those of the other side. However, game theory has limitations as to how it can inform international relations. It assumes that states are unitary and act rationally, but that is not the case. It assumes that the actors know in advance what the "payoff" will be for their choices, but that may not be the case. Last, it also assumes that only one decisive game takes place, whereas in reality interaction between states and individuals is ongoing. International relations are, thus, generally better conceived as non-zero-sum games with multiple players and ongoing relations and issues that change over time. Choices are interdependent and complex rather than independent and simple.

State A

State B		Collaborates to Clean Environment	Bluffs and Does Nothing
	Collaborates to Clean Environment	Both A and B benefit from cleaner environment	A gets the advantage of a cleaner lake without spending anything
	Bluffs and Does Nothing	B gets the advantage of a cleaner lake without spending anything	Neither cleans the lake and both suffer the consequences

Figure 4.8 Stag Hunt: Shared environment.

Conclusion: Is the equality of states reality or fiction?

Sovereignty is a vital part of the nature and legality of the international system. It provides a level playing field in that all states are theoretically accorded the ability to conduct relations with other members of the international community free of outside interference from other states. All member states of the UN have seats in the General Assembly, regardless of their size or significance. However, the world is ruled by a few states with huge advantages and many others with great disadvantages. The inequality in state capabilities and how diplomacy, sanctions, and military power are threatened or used in the struggle for advantage in foreign policy were described earlier in the chapter and then applied in three critical case studies concerning the relations between Israel and Palestine, nuclear issues between Iran and the West, and the Cuban Missile Crisis of the Kennedy era.

What role do individual leaders play in foreign policy decisions? Leadership in foreign affairs is largely about choosing among diplomacy, economic sanctions, and military initiatives in different situations. Some leaders, even with the same resources at their command, make much better decisions than others in foreign affairs. Academics from many fields have studied individual leadership qualities to discover which are advantageous in the decision-making process. Psychological studies show that leaders try to maintain cognitive balance through an integrated belief system when they make decisions. Key personality factors have also been found to influence leaders' style and policy orientations, but they have proven to be only broad indicators of a leader's performance. Ideas based on rational actor, organizational process, and government and bureaucratic bargaining models represent significant attempts to describe how foreign policy decisions are made. They each have strengths but also weaknesses; they can tell how policy is made but not why or to what effect. Game theory also offers insights into decision making, but it, too, has limitations.

In the next chapter we examine how these factors of state interaction and leadership play out in global politics. What are the leading states in the world today? What roles are played by major powers, middle powers, and other institutions? Is the U.S. hegemony about to end with the relative rise of other countries, such as China?

Select bibliography

Allison, Graham, *Essence of Decision: Explaining the Cuban Missile Crisis* (New York: Little, Brown, 1971).

Brown, E., Owen R. Coté, Sean M. Lynn-Jones, and Steven E. Miller, eds., *Rational Choice and Security Studies* (Cambridge, MA.: MIT, 2000).

Bueno de Mesquita, Bruce, et al., *The Logic of Political Survival* (Cambridge, MA: MIT Press, 2003).

Finnemore, Martha, *National Interests in International Society* (Ithaca, NY: Cornell University Press, 1996).

Ignatieff, Michael, *Blood and Belonging: Journeys into the New Nationalism* (Toronto: Viking, 1993).

Keohane, Robert O., *After Hegemony: Cooperation and Discord in the World Political Economy* (Princeton, NJ: Princeton University Press, 1984).

Lake, David A., and Robert Powell, *Strategic Choice and International Relations* (Princeton, NJ: Princeton University Press, 1999).

Lehrer, Jonah, *How We Decide* (New York: Houghton Mifflin Harcourt, 2009).

Nye, Joseph S., *Soft Power: The Means to Success in World Politics* (New York: PublicAffairs, 2004).

_____, *The Powers to Lead* (Oxford: Oxford University Press, 2010).

_____, *The Future of Power* (New York: Public Affairs, 2011).

Powell, Robert, *In the Shadow of Power: States and Strategies in International Relations* (Princeton, NJ: Princeton University Press, 1999).

Rothgeb, John, *Defining Power: Influence and Force in the Contemporary International System* (New York: St. Martin's Press, 1993).

Simon, Herbert A., *Models of Bounded Rationality* (Cambridge, MA: MIT, 1982)

Watson, Joel, *Strategy: An Introduction to Game Theory*, 2nd ed. (New York: Norton, 2008).

Shelling, Thomas C., *The Strategy of Conflict* (Cambridge, MA.: Harvard University Press, 1981).

5

The global system

Major and middle powers

The previous chapter set the groundwork for our continuing examination of global politics by defining and examining the concepts of state and power. It also considered leaders and how they make vital foreign policy decisions for their states. We are now ready to map the contemporary distribution of power and influence in the modern world. Which states are the most powerful and why?

To answer this central question, the chapter focuses on key concepts concerning the global system and its changing nature. First, it clarifies terms such as *comparative power*, *polarity*, *hegemony*, and *imperialism*, along with their importance in contemporary politics. It then examines in detail the six major powers that currently dominate global politics and structure the global system – the United States, China, India, Japan, Russia, and the European Union (which brings together twenty-seven states that in many respects function as one unit) – and surveys the roles of emerging middle and regional powers. We then return to our themes of security and globalization. What are the implications of the new global system for security? What is its relationship with globalization? To answer these questions, we conclude the chapter with a "New Global Security Map" – a conceptual framework of contemporary global politics.

In 2013, 193 countries are sovereign members of the United Nations; the Republic of South Sudan became the newest member on July 14, 2011. Virtually all territory on Earth is officially under the auspices of states, if only imperfectly under their control. They relate to one another directly and also through intergovernmental organizations such as the United Nations, the International Monetary Fund, and the World Bank. A great number of actors other than states are also significant in global politics. How do they all interact in the global system? The newest paradigms of global politics bear in mind both the "billiard ball" type descriptions of an anarchic world in which individual states randomly interact with one another and newer arguments about the constant interconnectedness of states, nonstates, and societies. In the next chapter, we examine current institutions and processes of global governance. Chapters 7 and 8 introduce a number of other actors (including multinational corporations (MNCs) and nongovernmental organizations (NGOs), criminal and terrorist organizations, and mass media) that are enmeshed in a dense web of global relationships.

The global system

The global system consists of sets of relationships, rules, and patterns of action among states and other significant actors of the world. These patterns developed and changed many times through the centuries, as we saw in earlier chapters, but they have become more explicit and coherent during the past four hundred years, with the rise of the modern state. In the past half century in particular, the speed of change has quickened, with the rate of adoption and specificity of rules governing the global system escalating at a tremendous speed.

A system consists of parts or entities, but it must also be more than the sum of its parts. The galaxies with their planets and stars form a system because their interactions are related mathematically. A sports team may also operate as a system, and the best soccer, football, and basketball squads are usually considered to function as systems. Does Manchester United form a squad? Do the New York Giants or the Los Angeles Lakers form a system? Or do their individual stars spoil the system concept? The best-known use of systems language concerns human biological organisms in which the arteries, veins, and heart interact with one another and in which a change in one affects the others. A blockage in an artery headed to the heart, for example, may cause the whole system to break down in a heart attack. In the global political system, the parts interact within given boundaries in a manner analogous to the circulatory system.

As with any system, the global political system is more than the sum of its parts, and general patterns and rules govern the interaction among the parts. However, the idea that interaction takes place among the different entities that form the global whole has weaknesses. First, such a simplified model does not discern which parts of the system are essential or influential. Second, given current levels of knowledge, it is impossible to predict how or even whether a change in one part of the system will affect another part. Will changes in military weapons, technology, resources or capital make one state or some combination of states automatically more powerful than others? Or do states become more powerful or more dominant because of their ideas, norms, and culture? A third weakness concerns whether we can identify when a whole new system has emerged. This is a difficult historical question, and as we saw in Chapter 2, answers may change over time and from one circumstance to another.

Perhaps we should not take the system analogy too literally. Some international rules are explicit and others implicit. Some parts of the global system are well integrated – such as trade and commerce and the rules of diplomacy – but other parts, such as peace and war, are less so. The global system is not as closely interrelated as the model might make it appear, nor is it as static. But there are some regularities in the relations among states and other entities at the international level, and it is these regularities that make comparison and analysis possible. The term global structure is often used to describe the defining characteristics that shape the actions of actors such as states, intergovernmental organizations, and other institutions of the global system. It conveys ideas about the nature of the units of the system, their goals, and their relative capabilities. When any or all of these shift dramatically, one may argue that there is a *new* system of global politics. Of course, there is fluidity and also rigidity in the global system, and the global economic architecture and global security architecture are in constant flux.

The global system and power

There are many centers of power on the world stage today. Richard N. Haass makes a telling argument about the nature of the present global order when he says, "States are being challenged from above, by regional and global organizations; from below, by militias; from the side, by a variety of nongovernmental organizations (NGOs) and corporations."[1] But these challenges are not new. We have seen how power was possessed and exercised in much earlier eras by groups as diverse as Persians, Greeks, Romans, Mongols, Ottomans, and Chinese. All were powerful players in their extensive regional systems for a time before they were challenged and their power dissipated. We normally date the development of the modern state system from the Treaty of Westphalia in 1648 to the 20th century, by which time Europeans had "discovered" and "conquered" most of the globe and disseminated their ideas and technology. From the 15th to the 20th centuries, Britain, France, Prussia, Spain, Portugal, Turkey, Austria, and Russia, among others, all enjoyed periods of imperial power in the international system, but over time their power and influence relative to each other and the peoples they governed rose and fell. Conflict, crisis, and war ensued. Alliances were formed and broken. Empires were created and destroyed by internal upheaval, economic competition, and violence.

Much of global history concerns great powers – the most powerful countries in the world economically and militarily. Over time these major powers changed on the basis of characteristics such as size of population, strategic geographical location, superior resources, and greater economic and military might. Usually, no more than a half dozen great powers exercised influence over large swaths of the world, and perhaps only a dozen or so middle powers have exercised any significance outside their own borders or region.

Global system concepts: Polarity and balance

We saw in Chapter 2 that global power has been distributed in different ways over the centuries. Political scientists use the term polarity, an analogy with magnetic poles, to characterize a situation in which dominant states attract or repel

other countries in their diplomatic orbit to varying degrees according to their economic, military, and diplomatic capabilities. The leaders of the most powerful poles may be able to influence or even compel states to follow their dictates. If this does not work, they may also be able to forge alliances to confront rivals and restructure the power configuration, the overall pattern of power and influence, to enhance and improve their position. Over time, shifts in power may strengthen one pole and its coalitions to the detriment of others. Of course, we have seen in Chapter 4 that the concept power is difficult to measure, so there are no absolute or quantitative distinctions about when one type of polarity ends and another begins.

In Chapter 2 we noted that before the rise of the modern state various types of political rulers, including kings, emperors, emirs, sultans, popes, and caliphs, vied for power with religious or other societal institutions. One might argue that before and during the Middle Ages the concept of polarity was meaningless, but certainly some spheres of influence were more important than others – such as the Roman Catholic Church in Europe and the Islamic Caliphate in the Middle East. For much of modern history (from about 1648 to 1945), the international system was multipolar (i.e., there were several poles of attraction). After the Treaty of Westphalia, several states shared power on the international stage, and much of the world's wealth and military strength was concentrated in Europe. As the Roman Catholic Church slowly lost its political authority, power became widely dispersed among various states across Europe.

The European multipolar system experienced constantly shifting coalitions and alliances. By the mid-19th century, a kind of "balance" existed in Europe. In other words, the distribution of power kept the states in a rough balance or equilibrium. The balance of power among Austria, France, Great Britain, Prussia, and Russia in the 19th century is often taken as a classic case. If one state grew more assertive, the others joined forces to deter it from open aggression. Britain was the classic balancer, and its support of

[1] Richard N. Haass, "The Age of Nonpolarity: What Will Follow U.S. Dominance," *Foreign Affairs* 87, no. 3 (May–June 2008), p. 45.

Turkey in alliance with France to oppose Russia in the 1854–56 Crimean War is often cited as a case in point. Today, the term balance of power still means the same thing – a relatively equal distribution of power among states sufficient to maintain security and peace among rivals. It is often described as the process or tendency of states to form coalitions or take actions to prevent one state or coalition from controlling others. If one coalition or state attempts to assume enough power to dominate the system by obtaining more territory or resources or military strength, it is constrained by the others through negotiation, new alliances, or war.

World Wars I and II were fought mainly, but not exclusively, on European soil. In World War I (1914–18) multipolarity began to weaken, and the war was fought between two fairly rigid alliances. Alliances are agreements among states, usually formalized in treaties concerning the use of force, to advance common goals and secure interests. The end of World War I coincided with the end of colonialism in most of the world and with the rise of powerful non-European states such as Japan and the United States; following World War II (1939–45), most of Africa and Asia were freed of European colonialism. European dominance and the period of classic multipolarity were over. Weak multipolarity endured along with the alliances that structured World War II.

Bipolarity and the Cold War

During World War II, the United States and the Soviet Union allied against Hitler's Germany. In Europe, Germany was defeated and divided. Britain, France, and Italy were impoverished, and only the Soviet Union had augmented its military (with a huge conventional army) and an expanded industrial base as a result of the war. In Asia, Japan was occupied by the United States, and elsewhere, especially in China, there was a period of internal change and revolutionary confusion. By the end of the war, the Eurocentric international system had been restructured. For a short time, until about 1949, a kind of unipolarity existed in which the international system had only one dominant state. The United States possessed overwhelming economic and military power, including the atomic bomb. This period of U.S. hegemony was very brief, as the economy of the Soviet Union quickly improved and Soviet client governments were installed in most of the states of Eastern Europe. By 1949 it, too, had nuclear weapons. With the other major European and Asian powers devastated from war, the two new superpowers, the United States and the Soviet Union, dominated the international system. Their combined strength in international affairs was so pronounced that scholars refer to this as a period of bipolar politics; that is, the two poles were in competition with each other, and each attracted its allies and supporters.

To prevent what they regarded as "encirclement" by the West, Soviet leaders used the Red Army to bring most of Eastern Europe under their control. Europe was literally divided between the forces of democracy in the West and Soviet communism in the East, a division Winston Churchill called the "Iron Curtain." In 1947, U.S. president Harry Truman confirmed America's support for Western Europe in his announcement of a policy of containment to prevent the Soviet Union from further aggression in Europe. In the West, the North Atlantic Treaty Organization (NATO) was established in 1949 to bind democratic states together in an alliance. Its members pledged support to one another in the event of external aggression.

A bipolar balance of power is one in which two rival superpowers dominate allied states as they pursue their military, economic, political, and ideological goals; each protagonist perceives any gain for its opponent as a loss for itself. After World War II, the United States constituted one pole surrounded by its allies in NATO. At the other pole, the Soviet Union was supported by its Eastern European allies in the Warsaw Treaty Organization (WTO), formed in 1955 and known thereafter as the Warsaw Pact. At one time, thirty-six countries around the world adopted communism as their system of government, though not all were members of the WTO.

Box 5.1 **Highlights of the Cold War: From beginning to end**

March 1946	Former British prime minister Winston Churchill warns of Soviet expansion and declares that an "Iron Curtain" has descended over Europe.
July 1947	George F. Kennan's "X" article in the journal *Foreign Affairs* sets forth "containment" of communism as the major goal of U.S. foreign policy.
June 1948	The Soviet Union imposes a blockade on West Berlin. The Allies, led by the United States, mount a Berlin air lift, sending food and other supplies to West Berlin
June 1950	North Korea invades South Korea, setting off a three-year war. The United States and other pro-Western nations fight for South Korea; Chinese troops assist the North.
November 1956	Soviet troops crush a popular uprising in Hungary.
October 1957	American B-52 bombers begin flying on full-time alert; planes carrying nuclear weapons are airborne twenty-four hours a day.
October 1957	The Soviet Union announces its successful launch of the first human-made Earth satellite, Sputnik.
April 1961	CIA-trained Cuban exiles invade Cuba at the Bay of Pigs in a fruitless attempt to overthrow the government of Fidel Castro.
August 1961	East Germany erects the Berlin Wall.
November 1961	The Kennedy administration announces that the number of American military advisers in South Vietnam will increase from 685 to 16,000 by late 1963.
October 1962	President Kennedy orders an air and naval blockade to force Cuba to remove Soviet missiles from its territory.
August 1964	Congress passes a resolution authorizing President Johnson to pursue a military buildup in Vietnam.
August 1968	Soviet troops and tanks roll into Czechoslovakia and crush reformists' efforts to remodel the communist system.
May 1972	President Nixon and Soviet leader Leonid I. Brezhnev sign the first treaties setting limits on strategic nuclear arms.
March 1983	President Reagan calls the Soviet Union "an evil empire."
March 1985	Mikhail S. Gorbachev becomes Soviet leader and emphasizes the need to reshape the economy and reduce rigidity in the Soviet system, in a process known as *perestroika*.
November 1989	East Germany lifts restrictions on emigration and travel to the West; after twenty-eight years, the Berlin Wall comes down.
August 1991	The day before President Gorbachev plans to sign a union treaty intended to keep several republics together, hard-liners move to overthrow him. The coup fails.
September 1991	President Bush announces his decision to take B-52 bombers off alert status.

| December 1991 | The leaders of Russia, Ukraine, and Belorussia declare that the Soviet Union has ceased to exist and proclaim a new Commonwealth of Independent States open to all states of the former union. |
| January 1992 | U.S. president Bush and Russian president Yeltsin declare the Cold War over. |

The two superpowers competed for friends and allies, and each had forward bases on its allies' territories – the most obvious being the division of Germany into two halves with the Western portion supported by NATO and the Eastern portion by the Warsaw Pact. The international bipolarity created by superpower confrontation brought extreme insecurity and zero-sum thinking to all international negotiations and conflicts, as each side regarded any success by its enemy as a defeat for itself.

For four decades the Iron Curtain divided the two great powers and their allies in Europe. Mutual hostility and fear coincided with a fairly stable peace. This period was called the Cold War, because although the two sides were engaged in a seemingly unending confrontation and were in constant preparation for war, no actual "hot" hostilities ever developed in Europe. On occasion, such as in 1948 when the Soviet Union blocked access to Berlin, and in 1961 when it supported the government of East Germany in erecting a wall to divide the city, military clashes were only narrowly avoided. Violent proxy wars were carried out by surrogate armies throughout the developing world – in Angola, Afghanistan, Cuba, Nicaragua, and Zaire, to mention only a few. These conflicts became an integral part of the East-West struggle, even though the issues in some regions often had little to do with ideology.

The United States brought direct force to bear in both Korea and Vietnam. The Korean War (1950–53) was fought by the United States and its allies under a UN mandate (discussed in Chapter 6). The Vietnam War (1964–73) emerged partially from the U.S. containment policy, which declared that communism should not be allowed to grow and had to be opposed, militarily if necessary. Vietnam was

the second test of containment in Asia, as Korea had been the first. Ho Chi Minh had won Vietnam's independence by defeating French military forces in 1954, when the Geneva Accords ended French Indochina and divided Vietnam into two states along the seventeenth parallel. Ho's communist-nationalists controlled the north; a pro-West government held the south. War broke out between the two sides, and in 1964 the United States intervened in the name of containing communism in Asia. By 1968, however, the American public had become weary of the war. Violent demonstrations broke out across the country, draft dodgers fled across the border to Canada, and in 1973 the last U.S. ground forces left Vietnam in shame. By April 1975 the North Vietnamese forces had taken over South Vietnam and completed the country's unification as a communist state (see Chapter 10).

The closest the two superpowers ever came to direct warfare with each other was over communist Cuba, after the Soviet Union placed nuclear missiles there. President John F. Kennedy courageously faced down Russian leader Nikita Khrushchev and forced him to remove the weapons, but he also promised that the United States would not invade Cuba (see Chapters 2 and 4). Despite this division of the world into two hostile but fairly stable blocs, other disputes, conflicts, and violence erupted throughout the globe, sometimes without direct reference to the contest between democracy and communism. In the Middle East, Israel (backed by the United States) and the neighboring Arab states (backed by the Soviet Union) clashed over territory and the sovereignty of ancient lands. In parts of Asia, peasant communists competed with feudal systems of government, and in many developing

Figure 5.1 This massive complex of concrete walls, trenches, and watch towers built by the German Democratic Republic divided Berlin for 28 years. About 200 people were killed trying to escape to the West. In 1989, the hated wall was torn down by the German people, an event that foreshadowed the breakup of the Soviet Union and the end of the Cold War in 1991.

countries in Africa, Asia, and Latin America clashes erupted over forms of government, economic advantage, the location of territorial boundaries, and even food supplies. A good example was the 1979 overthrow of the U.S.-supported Shah of Iran, who had initially been brought to the throne by Britain in 1925 and was confirmed in power in 1953 by an Anglo-American coup against his prime minister, Mohammad Mossadegh, who U.S. leaders wrongly deemed to be a stooge for the Soviet Union.

Long before the end of the Cold War, China and the Soviet Union had become competitors rather than allies, and inside the Soviet empire cracks had begun to appear. In 1968 Russia and its Warsaw Pact allies used force to prevent Czechoslovakia from drifting away from communism toward "socialism with a human face." One by one, the other countries of Eastern Europe found ways to escape from Soviet control or to minimize its control – under Tito, Yugoslavia claimed its independence early; Poland, Czechoslovakia, Hungary, Bulgaria, and Romania had to wait until the late 1980s to emerge from Soviet domination. The final decisive event that ended the Cold War occurred when the Berlin Wall fell in 1989 and communist East Germany rejoined democratic West Germany (Figure 5.1).

Inside the Soviet Union, President Mikhail S. Gorbachev began to reduce repression in the country and to institute significant economic reforms. By 1990 the disintegration of the Soviet Union itself was in progress, so that on December 25, 1991, Gorbachev resigned and declared the end of the Soviet Union. Many analysts question what actually caused the Soviet Union's collapse – was it military competition from the West or a flaw inherent in communism itself? Whatever the final historical judgment on this topic, the number of communist countries in the world declined from a peak of thirty-six to only five today – Cuba, Laos, North Korea, Vietnam, and China.

The dismantling of the Warsaw Pact and the severe economic difficulties of the former Soviet Union following 1991 led many commentators to conclude that the bipolar situation had ended and the global system had once more become unipolar. A few commentators believed naively that the decline of East-West rivalry might mean the "end of history," in the sense that there would be no more clashes between ideologies.[2] Others hoped that it

[2] Francis Fukuyama, *The End of History and the Last Man* (London: Hamish Hamilton, 1992).

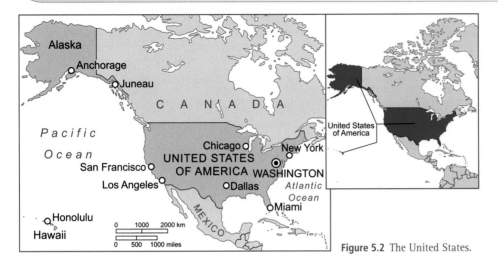

Figure 5.2 The United States.

might usher in a new world order – a new system of international relations built on the principle of collective security, perhaps embodied in a world government. All such views were short lived.

Geopolitics: The United States and unipolar politics

The United States is highly favored geographically, with great river systems, excellent farmland, natural resources, and much weaker states with which to share the continent (Figure 5.2). These built-in advantages and a strong spirit of entrepreneurship enabled the settlers of the original thirteen British colonies to thrive. From 1775 to 1783 they fought and won a war of independence and then proceeded to expand westward, consolidating control of much of the continent. The late 19th century saw a large influx of immigrants and its first overseas expeditionary wars. During World Wars I and II no battles were fought on the U.S. mainland, so that by 1945 when its competitors in Europe and Asia were massively devastated, the United States emerged as the single most powerful country on the globe.

After the collapse of the Soviet Union, the United States increased its power and influence around the world, and some observers began to call it a hegemon – a single state that, while not holding absolute power, remains far more powerful than all other countries and therefore can dominate the patterns of world politics and create rules for others to follow.[3] Others complain that the United States is so powerful that it decides on its own what is right in international affairs and acts on it. No doubt many countries resent this unipolarity and the perceived arrogance that accompanies it. Even its allies often express irritation that the United States seems to dominate not only in military matters but also in economics, currency, and even mass culture. Some critics even claim that the United States has become imperialistic – that is, that it imposes its power and influence over much of the world, as it did in the 19th century in Latin America with "Yankee imperialism." Today the term is mainly used as a buzzword to denigrate American policies and influence around the world with little regard for its political meaning of dominion of one people over others.

Many Americans also dislike the idea of the United States being called a hegemon and resent criticisms of their country as imperialistic. Some simply don't like paying taxes to support a huge military budget and overseas operations. They prefer

[3] *Hegemon* is used in some political theory circles to refer to ideas such as capitalism that hegemonic powers use to control the people of other countries. See Stephen Gill, ed., *Gramsci, Historical Materialism and International Relations* (Cambridge: Cambridge University Press, 1993).

Table 5.1 **Development of the global security system, 1648 to today**

1648–1914	World War I (1914–18) and interwar period	World War II (1939–45)	Post-1945 and Cold War	1991–2001	2001–Today
Classic multipolarity; European dominance modified by treaties and alliances	Classic multipolarity weakens; two rigid alliances form	Rigid alliances; weak multipolarity	Brief U.S. unipolarity changing to bipolar balance of power between United States and Soviet Union – two superpowers	U.S. unipolar	Modified U.S. unipolar system or mixed polarity (including nonstate actors and other actors)

that defense dollars are spent at home, perhaps diverted to domestic areas such as education and health care. Hegemony creates major and troublesome responsibilities for leaders who have to defend passing on the financial and military costs of maintaining authority over vast foreign territories to their constituents. Historically, American overseas policies have reflected this by shifting radically from interventionist internationalism to isolationism and then reversing. All hegemons have eventually overextended themselves and collapsed in war or crumbled domestically. Creating global order may have benefits, but it also has massive costs for the hegemon.

As Table 5.1 shows, only in the militarily sphere is the United States still without a peer. It shares the lead with Russia in terms of numbers of nuclear warheads and delivery systems, but it is vastly ahead of all other countries, including Russia, with regard to military expenditures, conventional armaments, and technology. However, even this may be changing. The 2008–09 economic crisis left the United States beleaguered, exposing an enormous gap between the government's domestic and overseas commitments and the financial resources made available by its stagnant economy.[4] Massive and ongoing economic troubles, budget deficits, and

national debt are causing it to lose the overwhelming advantages that allowed it to project unimpeded power worldwide. Some prominent scholars think that the world has already entered a new "Asian era," while others believe a shift is taking place but only very slowly.[5] However, the geopolitical reality is not that the United States has lost its dominance but that it is being challenged on several fronts at the same time. The latest study by the National Intelligence Council (NIC) concludes that the United States can no longer act on its own despite the fact that it remains the paramount power. *Global Trends 2025* suggests that within twenty years U.S. capabilities will be diminished by economic, financial, and domestic constraints.[6] Whereas Rome was a hegemon for five centuries, some cynics are asking whether the United States has reached its zenith in half a century.

There are two critical viewpoints that contest the idea that the United States is in decline. One claims that the United States is the only *satisfactory* hegemon available, and without it the world will succumb to rapidly increasing anarchy. As Colin Gray put it, such anarchy would produce

---

[4] Roger C. Altman, "The Great Credit Crash of 2008: A Geopolitical Setback for the West," *Foreign Affairs* 88, no.1 (January–February 2009), pp. 2–14.

[5] See Kishore Mahbubani, *The New Asian Hemisphere: The Irresistible Shift of Global Power to the East* (New York: PubliAffairs, 2008), and Fareed Zakaria, *The Post-American World* (New York: W. W. Norton, 2008).

[6] National Intelligence Council, *Global Trends 2025: A Transformed World* (Washington, DC: U.S. Government Printing Office, November 2008).

belligerency that could "erupt and bury guilty and innocent alike."[7] Some scholars, mainly American, claim that unipolarity is the most stable of all world systems. Hegemonic stability theorists, for example, posit that a unipolar concentration of power allows the hegemon to maintain global peace by use of their military and police. They can enforce rules and norms throughout the globe and thus put down aggression and prevent instability.[8]

The other school of thought simply denies that the United States is losing its place in the world. These advocates claim that the U.S. loss of American preeminence cannot take place for at least twenty years, thus giving it plenty of time to recoup its position of predominant power. Some, like Stephen G. Brooks and William C. Wohlforth, savagely criticize the "declinist" argument.[9] They contend that the world will remain unipolar for a long time and that it is not at all certain that the United States will lose its preeminence. For them, there is as yet no explicit balancing by other countries, and they calculate that within twenty years the United States can reshape "international institutions, standards of legitimacy, and economic globalization" to its own advantage. The flaw in their thesis may be that it does not account for the rapid change in world economics that seems to be taking place.

The ingredients of international power, including economic growth (measured by relative growth in gross domestic product, or GDP), use of advanced technology, and military expenditures, are growing much faster in some countries than in the United States. This combination of facts would seem to suggest that a realignment in the world's power configuration is under way. However, these trends do not guarantee that current American hegemony will give way to multipolarity. Measuring power is difficult, and future world configuration is hard to predict because of possibilities for upheaval and sudden changes. In a sea of predictions about the future, one should be very cautious. What next "big thing" is right around the corner? If the United States were to lead the way in climate-change technology or in the ability to engineer human cells, for example, what breakthroughs might those inventions produce in terms of the future of the United States and, thus, multipolarity? The overall question remains – how long can unipolarity endure? The answers so far are instructive but controversial. Perhaps the most objective conclusion is from *Global Trends 2025*. Using a futures model that measures GDP, defense spending, population, and technology, the report concludes that by 2025 the United States will be only one of a number of important actors on the world stage, albeit still the most powerful one.[10]

Could the United States overextend itself militarily and economically to the point that that it may no longer be able to influence global events? Paul Kennedy coined the term imperial overstretch to explain the rise and fall of great powers in the past, and some observers now believe that the United States is "overstretched."[11] If the size of the national debt and deficit are reliable measures, then perhaps the United States has taken on more tasks at home and abroad than its population is willing to cover with its taxes. However, despite the fact that there have been major changes, the United States remains the preeminent international power. When it wants to act, it can. In recent years, for example, it was able to use force in Lebanon, the Dominican Republic, Panama, Haiti, Libya, Afghanistan, and twice in Iraq. What is clear is that, despite the fact that the United States is still the most powerful state, its policies continue to shift radically between multilateral actions (cooperating with other countries or international institutions) and unilateralism, (going it alone and paying little attention to the

---

[7] Colin Gray, "Britain's National Security: Compulsion and Discretion," *RUSI* 153, no. 6 (December 2008), pp. 12–18.

[8] Of course, other theorists claim that bipolar and multipolar systems are more stable. The whole approach is contentious and inconclusive. See Robert Gilpin, *War and Change in World Politics* (Cambridge: Cambridge University Press, 1981), and Chapter 2 in this volume on long cycle and power cycle theory.

[9] Stephen G. Brooks and William C. Wohlforth, *World out of Balance: International Relations and the Challenge of American Primacy* (Princeton, NJ: Princeton University Press, 2008).

[10] National Intelligence Council, *Global Trends* 2025, p. 29.

[11] Paul Kennedy, *The Rise and Fall of Great Powers* (London: Unwin, 1988).

views of other states). Although the United States is reliant on other parts of the world to get its policies accepted, it angered many countries (especially France, Germany, and Russia) with its 2003 war against Iraq. It was unable to persuade a majority of states in the UN Security Council to vote for its policy of attacking Iraq, with even Angola, Mexico, and Pakistan refusing to support it.

Geopolitics: A modified U.S. unipolar system or mixed polarity?

In recent years there has been some implicit *balancing* against the United States by other countries. China and Russia have found new ways to cooperate and formalize their shared interests. For example, they joined with Central Asian countries to form the Shanghai Cooperation Organization and convened joint meetings with Brazil and India in what are called BRIC conferences.[12] The latter development has been particularly worrisome for some commentators because it is predicted that together the BRIC countries will reach the equivalent of the G-7 share of global gross national product (GNP) by 2040–50.[13] Russia and China also joined forces to block UN support for the U.S. attack on Iraq in 2003 and thwarted the application of rigid sanctions against Iran several times over the past decade. While they both supported the UN resolution to establish a no-fly zone over Libya in 2011, they voted against sanctions and UN intervention in Syria in 2012 (see Chapter 10).

For realists, the future of global politics depends on what happens in the distribution of power among states. The basic fact is that in the 21st century the United States has declined economically to some extent by comparison with China, India, and some emerging economies. This has led some commentators to conclude that the zenith of

American power (its unipolar moment) has passed.[14] Others believe that this argument is exaggerated but that the United States will become less dominant than it has been in the past. Both sides agree that the period of American predominance has ended and, therefore, that the global system is now better described as a limited or *modified unipolar system*. The system does appear to be gradually developing more multipolarity, and if we include the rising significance of nonstate actors, the global system perhaps ought to be described as mixed polarity. In situations where military strength matters most, the United States continues to enjoy an enormous advantage. In other circumstances, such as when critical issues require the attention and action of economic, media, or social elites, states may be less significant than nongovernmental actors. For example, multinational corporations may dominate in some economic crises and social elites may prove to be the most significant players in some environmental, humanitarian, and human rights issues. What is certain is that we are in a time of change, uncertainty, and increased geopolitical instability.

In short, power today is not concentrated only in one state or even only in states. Alternative power centers have created a decrease in the influence and ability of the United States or any other country to act unilaterally in global politics.[15] Some believe that a new world order is taking shape and that times of such dramatic shifts are dangerous, so they argue for the need to embrace the adjustments that will come with the rebalancing of global power. Others believe that analogies about the "decline" of the United States are misleading and even inaccurate.[16] They argue that there has not been an absolute, but only a relative, decline in U.S. power.

[12] When South Africa joined the group, it was referred to as the BRICS.

[13] National Intelligence Council, *Global Trends 2025*, p. vi. For an overview of this study, see Barry R. Posen, "Emerging Multipolarity: Why Should We Care?" *Current History* (November 2009), pp. 347–52.

[14] Charles Krauthammer, "The Unipolar Moment," *Foreign Affairs* 70, no.1 (1990–91), p. 25.

[15] Fareed Zakaria describes it in a different way. He says there has been no decline in the United States but a rise of "the Rest." Fareed Zakaria, *The Post-American World* (New York: W. W. Norton, 2008).

[16] Joseph S. Nye, "The Future of American Power: Dominance and Decline in Perspective," *Foreign Affairs* (November–December 2010), pp. 2–12.

Although the United States is only one of several great powers today, it remains by far the richest and most powerful country in the world. It has the largest economy of any single state, at some $14 trillion, and it spends more than all other major countries together on its military. Even if the chief rivals of the United States continue to be successful, they will need several more generations to approximate superpower status – and they may never do so. Two of the chief rivals to the United States, China and India, are burdened by large, and mostly poor, populations whose economic and social requirements will need to be satisfied before these countries can compete with the United States in military spending. A third rival, the European Union, does not intend to decrease its social spending in order to divert finances to foreign policy ventures. As for the World War II and Cold War enemies of the United States, Japan and Russia, they are plagued by aging, declining populations. Modern Japan is also hampered by a relative lack of interest in global affairs and Russia by internal factions and other difficulties. Overall, the United States possesses by far the most powerful military (discussed in detail in Chapters 4, 9, 10, and 11) and has the world's second-largest economy, with a gross domestic product (GDP) that is double that of any other single country but somewhat smaller than that of the combined European Union (discussed in detail in Chapters 4, 12, and 13).

A global shift in power has begun, and no one knows for certain where it will end. Will a new balance of power form, or will rivalries overwhelm the system and lead to increased competition and perhaps conflict or war? Whether the United States will significantly "reset" with Russia, "pivot" to Asia, or "tiptoe" to India remains the language of politicians and journalists, but none of these analogies completes our understanding of the nature of the international system and the role of the United States in it. Major shifts in the global balance have rarely led to peaceful conditions in the past, and we probably should not expect them to in the future. The peaceful termination of the Cold War represents

an exception, not the rule, in the history of international relations. There is also growing opposition to standard global politics from large, alienated parts of the Muslim and Arab communities around the world where militant Islamist groups and states with virulent anti-Western, particularly anti-U.S., prejudices have arisen. This issue is covered in depth in other chapters, but its existence indicates that even a hegemon's power can be diminished or shaken in a period of mixed polarity that includes the rise of newly powerful, often autocratic, states and powerful secondary institutions such as terrorist networks. The United States will need to adjust to the new global realities that it no longer controls and face the challenges that come from its relative decline.

Geopolitics: The competitors

Apart from the United States, the major states or centers of great power today are China, India, Japan, Russia, and the European Union (especially France, Germany, and Great Britain). These six power centers account for a massive percentage of global GDP and defense spending, as shown in Table 5.2. They possess almost all the world's nuclear weapons,[17] monopolize vetoes in the UN Security Council, and can decisively affect virtually every decision in most major global institutions.[18]

Few aspects of the changing character of global politics have greater implications than the rapid economic growth of China and India.[19] The transformative effects of the rise of these two countries

[17] Of the six, only Japan has no nuclear weapons. The EU does not possess nuclear weapons, but both France and the United Kingdom have nuclear arsenals. Nuclear weapon statistics are found in Chapter 9.

[18] Richard N. Haass, "The Age of Nonpolarity: What Will Follow U.S. Dominance," *Foreign Affairs* 87, no. 3 (May–June 2008), p. 45. G. John Ikenberry, Michael Mastanduno, and William C. Wohlforth, "Unipolarity, State Behavior, and Systemic Consequences," *World Politics* 61, no. 1 (January 2009); Christopher Layne, "The Waning of U.S. Hegemony – Myth or Reality," *International Security* 34, no. 1 (Summer 2009), pp. 147–72.

[19] Data in this section come from many sources, but particularly useful was National Intelligence Council, *Global Trends 2025*, http://www.dni.gov/nic/NIC_20025_project.html.

Table 5.2 Great-power capabilities indicators

	Economic indicator: GDP (US$ millions, 2010)[a]	Military expenditures (US$ billions, 2011)[b]	Size of population in 2010 (millions) (world share %)	Size of territory (millions km, approx.)[c] (world share %)
United States	14,586,736	711	308	9.6
China	5,926,612	143[d]	1,338.6	9.6
India	1,727,112	49	1,156.9	3.3
Japan	5,458,837	59	127	0.4
Russia	1,479,819	72[d]	140	17.1
European Union	9,509,750[e]	172[f]	491.9	4.2
Totals for the 6 great powers	38,688,866	1,206	3,562.4 (52%)	44.2 (8.6%)[g]

[a] From World Bank, World Development Indicators Database, May 3, 2012. [b] Data from http://www.sipri.org. [c] From Eurostat and World Bank. [d] Estimated. [e] Financial figures for the EU are obtained by adding the appropriate figures for only the largest countries, Britain, France, Germany, and Spain. [f] Includes only the largest military contributors in Europe – France, Germany, and the United Kingdom. [g] *World Facts*, 2009–10.

are unprecedented. With more than a third of the world's population, these two states are affecting the power distributions of the world in multiple ways. Even during the 2008 global economic turndown, China and India suffered less than other countries because their financial systems were more insulated from the financial markets than those of the United States and the European Union.[20] In two decades, there has been a massive transfer of economic activities from the richer countries to these two states. China has become the "workshop" of the world, and India the site of "outsourcing" services, from call centers to computer programming. These countries' rapid growth, which is the result of international rules and free trade (as exemplified in the World Trade Organization), has jolted the balance of economic power in the world. It illustrates the liberal idea that the growth and importance of intergovernmental organizations (IGOs) can have

a significant impact on world politics. It should be borne in mind, however, that while it is easy to declare that there has been a rise in the relative significance of India and China, it is much more difficult to measure the actual redistribution of power on a global basis.[21]

In this new pattern of politics, one should not overlook the vital significance of Japan, Russia, and the European Union. From northeastern Asia running west through to Central Asia and south to the Indian Ocean, Japan, India, China, and Russia compete with one another, as well as with the United States. In Europe, Russia and the European Union are contesting for influence, especially in Eastern Europe. Europe, Japan, and the United States are far ahead of India and China in per capita wealth, but the gap is slowly closing. Two of these countries – China and Russia – are not following the Western liberal economic model of liberal capitalism but instead are using state capitalism (in which the prominent economic role is

[20] Roger C. Altman, "Globalization in Retreat: Further Geopolitical Consequences of the Financial Crisis," *Foreign Affairs* 88, no. 4 (July–August 2009), pp. 2–7.

[21] Gregory F. Treverton and Seth G. Jones, *Measuring National Power* (Santa Monica, CA: RAND, 2005).

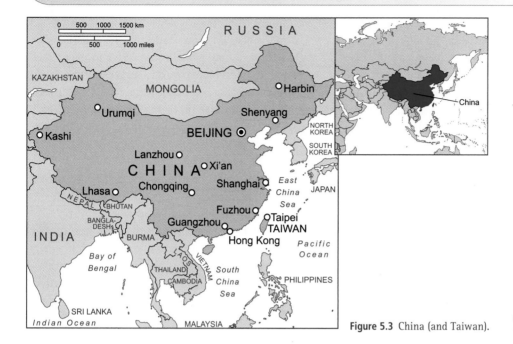

Figure 5.3 China (and Taiwan).

taken by the state rather than private enterprise) and are acting as models for other countries that wish to emulate them (see Chapter 12).

China

Although its territory extends to the Pacific Ocean, the Gobi Desert, the Himalayas, and the Tibetan Plateau, China has about the same land mass as the continental United States (Figure 5.3). Yet it houses the largest population in the world and has rapid economic growth, a large military, nuclear weapons, and cultural traditions that emphasize social order and harmony over individualism. China

has become a regional hegemon, much as it was centuries ago (see Chapter 2), and it is extending its power reach throughout Asia, the Indian Ocean, and parts of Africa.[22]

In 1989, China was on the brink of collapse, but then the Communist Party changed its strategy, putting in place the so-called Beijing Consensus.[23] The breakup of the Soviet Union had shown that economic success was critical to the survival of a one-party state, so the Chinese communist leaders opened their economy to outside markets and reduced social repression by extending economic and social freedoms while continuing to restrict political rights. Despite adopting capitalist practices, the government maintained control of the commanding parts of the economy and the careers of many white-collar workers. The details and debate about China's form and export of "state-directed capitalism" are discussed in Chapter 12.

---

[22] There is an extensive bibliography of new books on China and its growing global role in international relations. See, for example, Bill Emmott, *Rivals: How the Power Struggle between China, India and Japan Will Shape Our Next Decade* (Orlando, FL: Harcourt, 2008); James Kynge, *China Shakes the World: A Titan's Rise and Troubled Future – And the Challenge for America* (New York: Houghton Mifflin, 2006); William H. Overholt, *Asia, America, and the Transformation of Geopolitics* (New York: Cambridge University Press, 2007); Robert Ross and Zhu Feng, eds., *China's Ascent: Power, Security and the Future of International Politics* (Ithaca, NY: Cornell University Press, 2008); David Michael Lampton, *The Three Faces of Chinese Power: Might, Money and Minds* (Berkeley: University of California Press,

2008); Bates Gill, *Rising Star: China's New Security Diplomacy* (Washington, DC: Brookings, 2007); and Avery Goldstein, *Rising to the Challenge: China's Grand Strategy and International Security* (Stanford, CA: Stanford University Press, 2005).

[23] Referred to as the "Beijing Consensus" first in Joshua Ramos, *The Beijing Consensus* (London: Foreign Policy Center, 2004).

The market meltdown of 2008–09 (which began in New York and quickly spread around the globe) showed that the difficulties stemming from the Western form of free-market capitalism do not apply directly to the new economy of China. Although Chinese progress slowed following the meltdown, its insulated financial system protected the state from the dire consequences that overtook the United States, Europe, and Japan. Since opening the economy to foreign direct investment, China has maintained very high exports (especially to the United States) and a high savings rate, which gives it considerable foreign currency to invest abroad. In 2008 during the economic meltdown, China's surplus was more than US$800 billion, or about 10 percent of its overall GDP. China's currency is the yuan or renminbi (RMB), but it holds most of its foreign currency reserves in dollars, primarily in U.S. debt instruments. The Chinese have one of the lowest levels of personal consumption in the world, and their savings facilitate investments in the United States, which enable high personal consumption by Americans. A major reduction in the value of the U.S. dollar would reduce the worth of China's foreign exchange holdings, but China is unable to sell the dollars, as that action would further weaken the dollar and reduce the value of its holdings. So to some extent, China is caught in a "dollar trap" because its U.S. dollar holdings could be devalued. In 2009 some Chinese officials tentatively suggested, and then retracted, the idea that the U.S. dollar should be replaced by a new reserve currency.

Liberal democratic theory has long contended that authoritarian regimes cannot persist over time, and the 1991 fall of the Soviet Union seemed to confirm this argument. However, China appears to be disproving the thesis that authoritarian communism and capitalism cannot persist together. Its unique combination of communist political regime and capitalist economic system do not seem to be hindering development or political stability.[24] Internationally, China is becoming a role model for many countries. Its communist market economy model is attractive to many leaders in the developing world – especially those who wish to achieve significant economic growth without having to give up their authoritarian power. As well, China lends and spends money with few strings attached. In short, it is buying friends around the world.[25]

China is quickly becoming the first of the ancient empires to remerge as a great power.[26] In 2010, it officially overtook Japan to become the world's second-largest economy. It is expected to keep this status and by 2025 to have established itself as a leading military power.[27] So far, its strategy has been to avoid taking on the United States directly, focusing instead on peddling its successful hybrid model to countries around the globe. Within a few years, however, China and the United States may be in competition and perhaps conflict. But China has demonstrated a mania for stability, and its mutual dependence on the United States means that an economic breakdown between the two countries is unlikely.[28]

To maintain its success, China will have to manage several critical challenges in the future:

- Reliance on exports and too little domestic consumption
- High population growth (over the coming fifteen years the country is forecast to grow by three hundred million people or about the total population of the United States), with extreme migration to the largest cities
- Continual industrialization and foreign energy requirements

[24] See Joshua Ramos, *The Beijing Consensus* (London: Foreign Policy Center, 2004).

[25] Aaron L. Friedberg, *A Contest for Supremacy: China, America and the Struggle for Mastery in China* (New York: Norton, 2011).

[26] See David C. Kang, *China Rising: Peace, Power and Order in East Asia* (New York: Columbia University Press, 2009).

[27] *Global Trends 2025.*

[28] Thomas J. Christensen, "The Advantages of an Assertive China: Responding to Beijing's Abrasive Diplomacy," *Foreign Affairs* (March–April 2010), p. 52.

- Vast increases in nuclear power (China plans to build three times as many plants as the rest of the world combined in the coming decade)
- Environmental degradation and massive pollution, including a severe clean water shortage, especially in the north
- Poverty and growing income disparities that may lead to social unrest
- An inadequate social safety net, with poor availability of health care and education
- Political corruption[29]

Combined, these challenges indicate that continued economic growth is uncertain. Because their impact could be severe, some Western scholars believe that China will either weaken or democratize in the near future. American liberals in particular argue that "theory and history suggest that liberal democratic states and the liberal international order are best equipped to grapple with [these] issues and seize the opportunities ahead."[30] However, the basic fact is that China and the United States share major, ongoing, commercial and strategic interests. Today, the economy of not just the United States but also of the combined European Union countries is about three times that of China at market exchange rates, and most estimates conclude that the American economy will remain about twice that of China until at least 2025.[31]

China has many global commercial ties and is therefore dependent on world markets. It is the world's largest consumer of raw materials, from oil and natural gas to metals and wood. The U.S.-China trading relationship is vital to both countries, and they share similar nervousness about nuclear developments in Iran and North Korea, as well as geostrategic concerns in Central Asia, particularly over the possibility of instability in Pakistan. At the same time, China and the United States differ significantly in their approaches to resource countries – such as in Central Africa and Myanmar, where human rights abuses concern Washington but are ignored by Beijing.

China is concerned with its international position and honor. The Chinese government was badly humiliated by foreign reactions to several events and situations in recent decades – the brutal 1989 clamp-down on protestors in Tiananmen Square; the confrontation in the 1990s between the United States and China over Taiwan, in which the United States sent two aircraft carriers near the coastal waters of China; and the constant reality that the United States rules the seas and controls most of the naval choke points such as the Malacca Strait, which must remain open to supply China with resources and allow it to sell its exports. However, to a large extent China has overcome a sixty-year victimization narrative of being held down and coerced by foreign countries.[32] Under the leadership of President Hu Jintao (soon to be replaced by Xi Jinping) and Prime Minister Wen Jiabao, China became a world stakeholder and a major player in diplomatic and policy issues. It has a veto at the United Nations; great importance in regional organizations such as the East Asian Summit, the Association of Southeast Asian Nations (ASEAN), the Shanghai Cooperation Organization (SCO), and the China-Africa Cooperation Forum; weight in international economic institutions; and a good relationships with most important multinational corporations.

China's actions are sometimes sending mixed signals to the United States. Its increasingly assertive positions in the East China Sea, for example, are attracting nervous attention. It has been amending the doctrine of the People's Liberation Army (PLA) from the defense of homeland to include the protection of Chinese interests abroad. It has also been showing more interest in peace operations, protection of sea

---

[29] For details, see Susan Shirk, *China: Fragile Superpower: How China's Internal Politics Could Derail Its Peaceful Rise* (Oxford: Oxford University Press, 2008).

[30] Ibid., p. 157.

[31] Fareed Zakaria, "The Future of American Power," *Foreign Affairs* 87, no. 3 (May–June 2008), pp. 18–43, 27.

[32] See Wang Jisi, "China's Search for a Grand Strategy: A Rising Power Finds Its Way," *Foreign Affairs* (March–April 2011), pp. 68–69, and Even S. Medeiros, "Is Beijing Ready for Global Leadership?" *Current History* 108, no. 719 (September 2009), pp. 250–56.

lanes, and maritime interdiction. In this regard, for the first time, in 2009 China deployed naval vessels off Somalia's coast to participate in UN-sanctioned antipiracy operations. However, at the same time, it continued to increase spending on its military, with an annual growth rate in expenditures of about 15 percent during the past decade. While the United States still spends considerably more than any other state on defense, China is now second. The People's Liberation Army (PLA) has approximately 2.2 million active military personnel, the largest armed forces in the world. It is preparing to project power further from its shores and has built a large submarine base on the island of Hainan. It calls its new naval strategy "far sea defense." However, the PLA has very few overseas operating bases, and only a handful of PLA officers serve in UN peace-keeping operations.[33]

Close Up 5.1 China's relations with Hong Kong and Taiwan

On July 1, 1997, authority over six million people in Hong Kong suddenly changed hands. Britain, which had ruled Hong Kong and the New Territories as a democratically control-led colony for nearly a century, handed the territory over to the authoritarian, communist government of the People's Republic of China (PRC).

According to the negotiated agreement, Hong Kong's capitalist economic system would be retained for half a century. But China im-mediately disbanded the elected Hong Kong legislature and substituted a new legislature composed of pro-Beijing politicians.

Will China attempt to extend its authority to Taiwan as it did to Hong Kong? In 1949, when the communists won power in China,

the losers, led by Chiang Kai-shek, fled to the island of Taiwan. Although a majority of Tai-wanese had come from China in the 18th and 19th centuries, the new arrivals claimed Taipei as the provisional capital of the new Republic of China (RC). China continues to claim that Taiwan belongs to it, but only a minority of Taiwanese agree. The United States and most states support the claim of communist China but maintain that China should not employ military force to enforce its demands. Ten-sions remain high, but there has been some relaxation in the problems between China and Taiwan. In 2009, China dropped its objections to Taiwan's participation as an observer at the World Health Organization, a principle body of the UN, and proposed free-trade discussions with Taiwan.

Since most states of the world have rec-ognized the claims of continental China over Hong Kong, will its claims over Taiwan also prevail in the future? Would China be justified in using its power and military force to thwart Taiwan's claim to sovereignty? Is there a peace-ful solution? Should the United States intervene if China attempts a blockade or invasion?

India

India, located in South Asia, is the most populous democracy in the world, with a population of well over a billion people (Figure 5.4). Like China, India has prospered from globalization and its own internal economic reforms since the 1990s. Today, it provides services to the world through its call centers, and its high-technology industries are second to none.[34]

India has some major advantages over China. One is that it is democratic. The 2009 elections provided the Congress Party and second-term Prime Minister Manmohan Singh with a huge mandate and enhanced democratic stability. Besides an open

[33] English speakers who wish to keep up on current Chinese politics and economics should consult http://www.chinadigital-times.net and/or http://www.danwei.org.

[34] Arvind Panagariya, *India: The Emerging Giant* (Oxford: Oxford University Press, 2010).

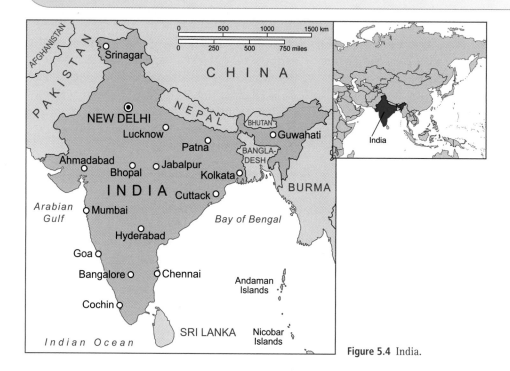

Figure 5.4 India.

and transparent democratic system, India has also benefited from a large English-speaking population, which has made it competitive in many fields. It is possibly the only country in the world where the number of daily newspapers is actually increasing. Moreover, although China has reduced the speed of its population growth – historically having limited family size to one child – India may actually profit from its high population growth in the long run. This factor cuts both ways, and some commentators even call it India's "demographic dividend." India's population has a median age of only twenty-five years, and it is falling, which indicates that it will have an advantage over countries with aging populations, which are costing more and producing less, as in Japan and many parts of Europe, for example.

There has been a recent change of mentality in India. Most Indians still live grim, poverty-stricken lives, but they are developing a new and more optimistic outlook. This positive and future-oriented view is shared by India's prime minister, Manmohan Singh, who said, "It is incumbent upon us to take all measures necessary to safeguard our country and keep pace with technological advancements worldwide."[35] India has begun to match its economic gains with diplomatic and military power, acting as a bridge between the United States and China, and it has been engaging in new organizations and partnerships to maximize its autonomy and significance as an international actor. A nuclear cooperation deal with the United States, for example, was a major benefit to the country.

India is wary of what it regards as hostile states in its region. Since 1947, it has had three wars with Pakistan, two of them over control of Kashmir, an issue that is still unresolved (see Chapter 8). It has one of the largest militaries in the world, with almost four million active and reserve troops, and it contributes actively to UN peacekeeping missions. India is a nuclear weapons state, possessing thirty to thirty-five nuclear warheads and enough weapons-grade plutonium to make up to ninety more warheads. In 2012 it successfully launched a long-range ballistic missile capable of carrying a

---

[35] Cited in *The Globe and Mail*, July 27, 2009.

nuclear warhead as far as Shanghai. This Agni 5 (*Agni* is Hindu for "god of fire") can carry a multiple independently targetable reentry vehicle (known as MIRV) warheads (see Chapter 9).

India's 2009 defense policy called for the expenditure of US$9 billion on 126 new fighter jets. It has been building up its submarine capacity, and in July 2009, it launched the first nuclear powered submarine built in India. In doing so, it became the sixth country able to produce such ships (until then only the United States, Russia, France, Britain, and China could do so). The new ship will not be operational for several years because India still has to develop its own cruise and ballistic missiles, as their sale is prohibited internationally. However, when complete, possession of a nuclear-powered submarine will allow India to claim the ability to deliver nuclear weapons from mobile platforms on both air and sea. It is also leasing a nuclear submarine from Russia and has sixteen other nonnuclear submarines, though these are aging.

India distrusts and fears China, and the acquisition of weapons such as nuclear submarines is part of its strategy to become a major power and, to some extent, counter China's growing significance in the region. It shares a long border with China that is the source of several ongoing disputes, and the Indian Ocean is becoming a central focus of their complex relations. To its east, India fears China's support for Myanmar's military and, to its west, it is nervous of China's construction of a deep-sea port on Pakistan's coast.[36] Indeed, the Indians are not alone in believing that they need to build up their military capability in the area. Robert D. Kaplan, a military analyst, has written that "the Indian Ocean is where global struggles will play out in the twenty-first century."[37] He maintains that the Indian Ocean will replace the Atlantic and Pacific Oceans as the center stage for international affairs. His argument is based on the growing

[36] Robert Kaplan, "Rivalry in the Indian Ocean," *Foreign Affairs* 88, no. 2 (March–April 2009), pp. 16–32.
[37] Ibid.

significance of the waters around India and a host of incidents – from piracy off the eastern coast of Africa to the terrorist attack on Mumbai in 2009 (see Chapter 11). India has also been forging diplomatic relations with Japan to help counter Chinese significance in Asia.

Despite its successes, India will have to manage several challenges in the future:

- A huge population within a relatively small geographical territory (India's population is four times that of the United States but the country has only one-third the terrain)
- A rapidly growing gap between the rich and poor, even though India has reduced the absolute number of people living in poverty in the past fifteen years (microcredit once seemed a partial solution, but over the past decade private companies have invaded the field, making enormous profits and leaving millions of people without the ability to repay their loans)
- A growing energy deficit
- A very low level of public health and inadequate policies to improve it
- Massive and worsening environmental problems (coal-fired emissions are the second greatest in the world – there are brown clouds, chemicals in rivers, and severe air pollution from increased automobile ownership)
- Unease over borders with China (Indians still remember their border war with China in 1962), unsettled disputes over Tibet and Kashmir, as well as other continuing regional issues with nuclear-armed Pakistan, and growing nervousness about future power configurations in the Indian Ocean

Russia

Russia is a massive country with rich mineral resources but severe geographic problems to overcome (Figure 5.5). Its severe climate, short growing seasons, and dry summers make agriculture risky. Under the Soviets the national government controlled the economy and the country was

Figure 5.5 Russia.

characterized by low productivity, chronic short-ages, and technological stagnation. After World War II it masked these problems behind a severe communist authoritarian system and became a world superpower.

Despite the 1991 breakup and humiliation of the Soviet Union, the Russian Federation remains the world's largest country and a significant global power. The country has one of the world's greatest reserves of natural resources and controls links to energy supplies from the Caucasus to Central Asia. It possesses the largest global petroleum reserves and nearly half the world's coal. Europe now de-pends more on Russia than the Middle East for its oil. Of course, the Russian-European relationship is reciprocal, as Russia needs the market as much as Europe needs the oil.

Vladimir V. Putin was president from 2000 to 2008 and then prime minister until 2012. The interim era has ironically been referred to as "from Putin to Putin" because he ran for and was reelected president a second time in 2012.[38] Since his first term as president, Putin has advocated the rapid development of natural resources and energy to help finance the country's economic rebirth.

Russia's economic, military, and diplomatic strengths are enormous. Putin has made it clear on many occasions that Russia aspires to traditional great-power status and actions, and he has become a leading voice in opposition to U.S. dominance at institutions such as the United Nations. Putin has adopted the vague phrase "Russian conservatism" to characterize his approach to politics, and although the country is more open than China, it has been moving slowly toward the Chinese model politi-cally and economically. Dmitri Kosyrev, a Russian political commentator, put it like this: "Everyone

[38] Philip Hanson, James Nixey, Lila Shevtsova, and Andrew Wood, *Putin Again: Implications for Russia and the West* (A Chatham House Report), February 2012.

here sees China as the model, because Russia is not the model."[39]

Despite the global economic difficulties of 2008–09, Russia continues to possess large trade and current account balances and holds significant currency reserves.[40] However, the country is likely to suffer from specific problems in the future, more than either India or China. The country accounts for less than 2 percent of world trade and uncertainty about future energy prices haunts the government. While it has the largest population of any single country in Europe, it is rapidly aging, and the social security system is in need of major restructuring.

Russia possesses the world's second-largest cache of nuclear weapons, has a military force of more than a million soldiers, and has the world's third-largest military budget. The leadership is intent on protecting its interests and maintains troops in the countries Georgia and Moldova. However, Russia is flanked by pro-Western governments in Europe, and further developments along its borders by either NATO or the European Union would threaten the regional dominance that Russia so desires. To a significant extent, an influence fault line over the Caucasus and Central Asia is developing in Eastern Europe between Russia and both the United States and the European Union. This is partly due to contests over oil and resources generally, but there is also a significant military component.[41]

Russia's powerful military, its stockpile of nuclear weapons, and established positions in international forums should allow it to maintain and perhaps even enhance its power over the coming decade. Like China, but unlike India, Russia retains considerable influence at the United Nations because of its veto in the Security Council. It has a major influence on many contemporary controversial issues, and its leadership reflects a Russian desire to be respected in the world. Russia defends its interests in energy issues in its "near abroad," including the Caucasus and Central Asia, as well as Eastern Europe, Iran, and the Shanghai Cooperation Organization. It has periodically cut off oil supplies to Lithuania, Latvia, and Belarus and gas to Ukraine and Moldova. While it supports Iran, it also shares the West's negative views on terrorism and Islamic fundamentalism.

Despite its successes, Russia will have to manage several challenges in the future:

- An aging population that will put severe strains on health care and housing
- Fluctuations in energy prices and heavy reliance on European sales will create economic uncertainty and the need to prepare for falling oil output in less than two decades
- Serious problems of decaying infrastructure
- Signs of growing authoritarianism and public discontent
- Political corruption
- Large-scale environmental problems

Japan

Since the 19th century Japan has been remarkably successful economically (Figure 5.6). Despite devastation caused by World War II, the country rebounded by the 1970s to become one of the world's most successful economies and democracies. At that time there were many predictions that Japan might even overtake the United States and become the world's economic leader. But severe financial difficulties curbed its rise, and for two decades it suffered from very low economic growth and three recessions.

In 1992, the Nikkei (Japan's stock market index) fell 69 percent from previous highs. As the economy began to improve again it was badly hit by the global 2008–09 financial crisis. The Japanese economic contraction was the worst among major economies and East Asian countries. Unlike the economies of China and India, Japan's economy is likely to

---

[39] *International Herald Tribune*, October 19, 2009.
[40] Mark Leonard and Nicu Popescu, "A Power Audit of EU-Russia Relations," *Report of European Council on Foreign Relations* (November 2007), and *World Bank Country Report, Russia* (2009).
[41] Bobo Lo, *Axis of Convenience: Moscow, Beijing, and the New Geopolitics* (Washington, DC: Brookings Institution Press, 2008).

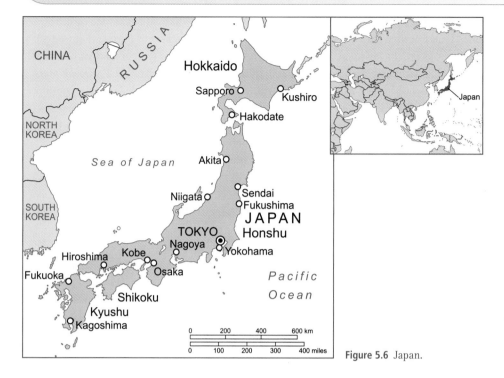

Figure 5.6 Japan.

continue to fall for some time, and there are deep economic insecurities in Tokyo. These were severely aggravated by the devastating earthquakes and tsunami in 2011 that severely damaged several nuclear reactors and forced Japan to reevaluate its nuclear industry (see Chapter 15 and 16). The country lacks adequate natural resources to meet its requirements and has continuing problems stemming from an aging population and heavy government debt. Despite these difficulties and its small territory, Japan still possesses the world's third-largest economy today.

In 2009 the defeat of the Liberal Democratic Party (LDP), which had dominated the country's electoral politics since 1955, suggested a new direction in Japanese domestic and foreign policies. However, the new government, led by Prime Minister Yukio Hatoyama and his Democratic Party of Japan (DPJ), was crippled by economic stagnation, stock market decline, bureaucratic mismanagement, and government scandals. There was little room for the new prime minister to maneuver in economic or foreign affairs, and in 2010 he resigned and Naoto Kan

took over as head of the DPJ and prime minister. In 2011, however, the country returned to its normal postwar pattern, and the LDP again returned to power, led by Yoshihiko Noda, who was replaced by Shinzo Abe on December 26, 2012.

Under article 9 of its constitution, Japan is restricted from preparing for war. However, it still spends about 1 percent of its GDP on "self-defense forces" and makes the world's fourth-largest total expenditure on armed forces. Japan does not possess nuclear weapons. Its major defense strategy is based on an agreement with the United States and security pacts with Australia and India. Under the treaty with the United States, both sides agree to develop their ability to resist aggression and assist each other in case of an armed attack *on Japanese territory*. Unlike common defense promises in other alliances, however, Japan cannot come to the defense of the United States because it is constitutionally forbidden from sending combat forces overseas. Japan did provide some noncombat troops and considerable nonmilitary support for the Iraq War, and it continues to support the war in Afghanistan.

Since 1945, Japan has been much closer politically to the United States than to China (there are about fifty thousand U.S. troops still in the area), but its close proximity to China will likely incline it toward much greater regional cooperation. In the midterm, Japan's relations with the mainland will determine its future relations with the United States, and to some extent this will depend on whether China continues its rapid economic growth. Although it is not a permanent member of the UN Security Council, Japan contributes substantially to UN finances and peacekeeping. It is also a leading contributor to international aid organizations.[42]

Despite its successes, Japan will have to manage several challenges in the future:

- An aging population that will strain health care and housing
- The need for costly agricultural imports will increase as Japan's highly limited land is expropriated for other purposes
- A lack of natural resources, which creates an extreme dependency on energy imports
- Reliance on growing trade with China (Japan's biggest trading partner), which will bring complications and perhaps difficulties in Japan's relations with the United States
- Displays of Japanese nationalism (it adopted a national anthem and flag only in 1999), which for historical reasons are met with disapproval in much of Asia. While troublesome, the 2012-13 clashes between Japan and China over tiny, uninhabited islands in the East China Sea are unlikely to lead to actual combat.

The European Union

European territory has often changed hands throughout history, so that European borders have never ceased shifting. Even today's European Union (EU), with its twenty-seven member states, does not cover all the territory that, at some time or other, has been "imagined" as part of Europe (Figure 5.7). However, its existence has gone a long way toward eliminating the possibility of future European wars. The EU is a complex and remarkable organization that stresses economic integration above geopolitics and military force.[43] It is a multinational body bound together by treaties and laws. One senior official called it "the best functioning organization in the world that attempts to deal with the fact that politics is local, and economics global."[44] It has the world's largest GDP, consumes half the world's foreign investment, has a large trade surplus, and is highly competitive in world markets.[45] Unlike China, India, Russia, and the United States, it has continued to cut back on defense expenditures while maintaining a high level of social services and for this reason has been tagged as a "Venus" not a "Mars."

The EU is not a sovereign power and can act only if its individual members want it to. Some authors, therefore, argue that Britain, France, and Germany should be studied separately, as they determine their own foreign and strategic policies. Indeed, the fact that these larger countries in the EU do have their own foreign and defense policies may make them less interested than other members in developing common EU policies. We discuss EU institutions in detail in Chapters 6 and 12, but as we determined earlier, there are good reasons to include this regional power in our list of challengers to the United States as a hegemon. On a large number of indicators of power, the EU belongs in the top six, even if this is not the common viewpoint.

The total population of the EU is considerably greater than that of the United States (see Table 5.1), but, like Russia and Japan, the population is aging rapidly. Counting its combined markets, the EU has the world's largest economy. Its overall combined military expenditure is relatively low – considerably

---

[42] Richard J. Samuels, *Securing Japan: Tokyo's Grand Strategy and the Future of East Asia* (Ithaca, NY: Cornell University Press, 2007).

[43] James A. Caporaso, *The European Union: Dilemmas of Regional Integration* (Cambridge, MA: Westview, 2000).

[44] *The Economist*, October 10, 2009, p. 25.

[45] Fareed Zakaria, "The Future of American Power," *Foreign Affairs* 87, no. 3 (May–June 2008), pp. 18–34.

Figure 5.7 European Union.

less than half that of the United States, but it still retains combat troops around the world and provides the bulk of non-U.S. troops in global operations.[46] While it does have considerable military power, its strength may be best illustrated in the field of soft power, where its combined members make the largest financial contribution to the UN system, including the general budget and peacekeeping operations. The EU, like its precursors, has

mostly looked inward – building a single market and institutions and trying to resolve monetary issues. Its economy flourished until the economic downturn of 2008–09, but it has been a relatively weak actor on the world political stage largely because individual countries maintain control of their own foreign policies. Since the implementation of the Lisbon Treaty in 2009, the EU has had a high representative for foreign policy, and some hope that it will take further steps toward a unified foreign and defense policy. This will not be easy, however, as unanimity remains the rule in security

[46] Andrew Moravcsik, "Europe, the Second Superpower," *Current History* 109, no. 729 (March 2010), pp. 91–98.

decision making (see Chapter 6), and the international interests of its individual member states do not always converge.

The gradual expansion of the European Union to twenty-seven members has increased the EU's size and economic clout while decreasing its ability to act (see Chapter 12). As well as being stymied by ongoing constitutional problems, decision making suffers from a lagging rapport between the EU leadership in Brussels and the citizens of the member states – providing a so-called democratic deficit. The issue of Turkey's eventual membership continues to be a test of the European desire to move further east and south and to include a population that is not Christian.

Difficulties in decision making have left the EU inadequately prepared to balance the new and aggressive Russia. Indeed, because of organizational flaws and Russian control of oil resources, the EU and its individual states are unable to engage in tough negotiations with Russia over the admission of new states such as Georgia or Ukraine to the EU or to NATO. Moreover, since the global economic crisis of 2008–09, Ireland, Greece, Portugal, and Spain have had serious debt crises that have shaken confidence in the EU and cast doubts on the viability of the euro (see Chapters 6 and 12).

Despite its successes, the EU has several challenges to manage in the future:

- Reliance on Russia and other parts of the world for a large percentage of its energy supplies, a dependency that is likely to increase
- A rapidly aging population will have negative effects on productivity, growth, and fiscal stability. Major trade-offs will be required in health, pension benefits, and military expenditures
- There is a need to reduce the so-called democratic deficit
- The admission of Turkey will be difficult, perhaps impossible, and indecision will exacerbate differences with Muslims inside and outside the EU
- The ongoing debt crises of several eurozone members have yet to be resolved satisfactorily

Middle powers and other rising powers

In particular areas of the globe, the six major power centers do not rule without challenge because middle powers exert considerable regional power, and some even have nuclear weapons or the ability to get them. Major regional powers include Argentina and Brazil in South America; Nigeria and South Africa in Africa; Saudi Arabia, Iran, and Israel in the Middle East; Pakistan in South Asia; and Australia and Indonesia in Asia. Other middle powers are Canada and Italy, as members of the G-8. This list raises many questions. For example, could a rapidly developing country such as Brazil, with its extensive resources and well-educated workforce, possibly become a long-term competitor of the United States, China, India, Russia, Japan, or the EU? How will weaker states survive in a world of six global major powers and numerous middle powers? Will they follow the richer, more powerful states or will they continue to develop their own regional alliances?

Brazil has established a solid economic and democratic foundation. Its diversified economy is buttressed by large offshore deep-sea oil deposits, which will soon fuel a rapid growth in its global significance. Brazil is enjoying a period of unprecedented prosperity, and while forecasts vary, many commentators believe that it may become the world's fifth-largest economy within a decade. Led by socialist-inclined President Lula de Silva (2003–10), the country began to establish a reputation as a regional leader in South America (Figure 5.8). Continuing his legacy, in January 2011, Dilma Rousseff became the country's first female president. In 2006 Brazil joined Russia, India, and China in discussing how they could influence world affairs. In 2009 the leaders of these four countries, known as the BRIC, met in Russia, calling for "a more democratic and just multipolar world order based on the rule of international law, equality, mutual respect, cooperation, co-ordinated action and collective decision-making of all

Figure 5.8 Brazil.

states."[47] China and Russia touted BRIC as a new forum for solving global problems and in 2010, South Africa joined as a new member so that the organization is now known as the BRICS.

Elsewhere, Iran is rich in natural gas and other resources, and it desires to be the regional hegemon of the Middle East. It wants to ensure this by possessing nuclear energy and perhaps nuclear weapons. But Iran (discussed earlier in Chapter 4) is not the only important Muslim country. Saudi Arabia and Turkey exert considerable influence among the Muslim and Arab countries. In fact, from Morocco to Indonesia no Muslim country can speak for all the others, or even for all Shiite or Sunni populations (see Chapter 8). Indonesia, the most populous Muslim state in the world, has mutated from an authoritarian to a democratic form of government and is destined to play a larger role in South Asia. (The issue of rebellions and

the so-called Arab Awakening are discussed in Chapter 8 on religion and Chapter 10 on civil wars).

The difficulty of ranking countries as middle powers is illustrated by the case of Canada. The Canadian government endorsed the notion of Canada as a middle power after the end of World War II, when it rallied with like-minded states to contest the domination of the United Nations by the "great powers." Officials and scholars alike began to use the phrase "middle power" somewhat indiscriminately. However, many on the intellectual left in Canada have never accepted that the term applies to Canada, believing instead that Canada is dominated by American economic interests and overwhelmingly depends on it for security as well as prosperity. For some, Canada went from being a colony of Britain to a puppet of the United States. While this argument has some merit, it is nevertheless true that Canada has frequently opposed U.S. policies and has not always acted as a satellite – Canada's continued opposition to the U.S. embargo of Cuba, to fighting

---

[47] Blake Hounshell, "BRICS," *Foreign Policy* (March–April 2011), p. 31.

in Vietnam, and to the second Iraq war are cases in point.[48] In the final analysis, whether people consider their country to be a major, middle, or dependent power may be irrelevant. What matters most is what leaders think about other countries' relative power and political resources in global competition.

The global system and security today

A new set of dynamics has dominated global relations since the fall of the Berlin Wall and the breakup of the Soviet Union. During the Cold War, the security dilemma was interpreted as essentially about the East-West conflict. Western policy was based on protecting the West's own interests without aggravating relations with the communist enemy. The bipolar configuration of the Cold War period reflected the principle that states attempt to increase their own security by enhancing their power, joining alliances, and building up their militaries. In pursuing their own security, however, they inherently make other states less secure. As realist theory puts it, states look out for themselves in terms of security and survival: their actions frighten others, encouraging them to strengthen their own militaries, as power cannot be shared, since it is essentially zero sum in nature. Each state's security is defined and rests on the insecurity of other states.[49]

We have seen that the bipolar world of the Cold War ended abruptly, giving way to a period of American predominance. But there is serious disagreement among scholars and practitioners about how to describe this new set of dynamics. At first, the period simply went by the term *post–Cold War*. However, when nineteen Arab terrorists attacked New York's World Trade Center and the Pentagon in Washington, DC, on September 11, 2001, the United States and its allies suddenly faced a new

and different security challenge that required new strategies and terminology. The United States was still the predominant power, but new security issues had arisen. Instead of confronting a powerful state and its allies, the West had to combat a hidden nonstate enemy capable of launching surprise terrorist attacks or targets in its homeland. It could not respond in routine or standard ways to the perpetrators of 9/11, bringing its massive military power to bear as it had done to avenge the attack on Pearl Harbor in 1941 or to deter the communist threat after World War II. It was the first manifestation of the new security dilemma, which will haunt all future presidents.

The security dilemma that characterized the Cold War years has not disappeared, but today it is complicated by the need for states to protect themselves against multiple and complex transnational challenges. The most imminent and perhaps least understood dangers come not from strong states but from weak or failed ones that are poor, divided, or disintegrating. Almost all of the violent conflicts in the post–Cold War period have been civil or internal rather than international. It was a weak state that harbored bin Laden, not a strong one. The new security dilemma arises from the fact that an increase in a country's military strength may not provide a corresponding increase in its security (see Chapters 9, 10, and 11). New security issues also arise from that fact that there are many challengers to state power and authority on the world stage. The stronger states become, the more they open themselves up to increased challenges from both globalization forces *and* international terrorism. The state is under challenge, and while the state is not obsolete and will not disappear, its security can no longer be based entirely on military capability as traditionally defined.

Diffusion of power: Globalization and nonstate actors

We have seen that the term *globalization* is widely used to describe economic and other forms of interdependence and explain various major international

[48] Robert J. Jackson and Doreen Jackson, *Politics in Canada: Culture, Instutions, Behavior and Public Policy*, 6th ed. (Scarborough, ON: Pearson, 2009), chapter 15.

[49] John Hertz, "Idealist Internationalism and the Security Dilemma," *World Politics* 2 (1950), p. 157.

events from global economic relations to world terrorism. It is also used to explain why no single state can rule the world as a hegemon. In fact, it has become so widespread and controversial as a concept that its critics refer to it as nothing more than capitalism or even "globaloney." In response, its proponents say that some people are so afraid of change they have developed "globalphobia." The proponents argue that (1) the free flow of trade, services, capital, investment, and technology around the world is increasingly making single state economies a misnomer; (2) the fragility of the modern state can be seen in every walk of life, from trade to transportation to telecommunications to entertainment; and (3) the process of economic interdependence is driving the world together into what advocates of the English School of theorists could even call an international society (see Chapter 3).

We have defined globalization broadly as a reorientation of cultural, economic, political, and technological activities and processes in such a way that they transcend state or country borders and have a global reach. There are several views of this process, but they all include expanded international trade, communications, and technical cooperation across states. A cluster of interconnected factors makes states more economically interdependent and transforms world politics, including the integration of goods, services, capital, and markets. The implications of globalization are immense. The degree of economic interdependence in the world is reflected in the fact that global trade in goods and services now exceeds US$14 trillion annually. The speed of the flow of capital around the world – calculated at about $2 trillion per day – and also the growing importance of nonstate actors undermine the ability of states to regulate their own economies.

Economic interdependence stimulates globalization with its advantages and disadvantages. All states retain their primary responsibilities in military and security fields, but increasingly they share power with broader forces in other aspects of international life. To a remarkable extent, the forces of globalization are determining which

countries and individuals win or lose in the world market. Globalization poses challenges to the world that cannot be resolved by states or their intergovernmental organizations. It has brought extraordinary economic growth to some parts of the world, notably China and India, but it has also increased disparities between the rich and poor across states and sometimes within them. Globalization has caused a resurgence of ethno-nationalism and raised international protests against capitalist organizations.

The state's overarching power in the global system is diminished by an impressive number of powerful intergovernmental and nonstate actors. This is partially because of globalization and the explosion of information technologies such as the Internet. Computers and communications enable a great many actors to compete on a world scale in economics, culture, and politics. The number of such international and transnational actors has been growing rapidly. They include a large number of global intergovernmental organizations (IGOs) that have universal membership, such as the United Nations and World Bank, and which play a greater role on the world stage than many states. The number of permanent IGOs has been tabulated at around 250, including both international and regional institutions. Each continent has its own regional institutions, such as the Organization of American States (OAS) for the states of South America, North America, and the Caribbean; the African Union (AU) and the Economic Community of West African States (ECOWAS) for Africa; the Association of Southeast Asian Nations (ASEAN) for parts of Asia; and so on. We will examine the most important of these institutions and their roles in Chapter 6, but for now, let it suffice that they mitigate the political power of individual states, (sometimes even the most powerful ones) and present new security issues.

Nongovernmental organizations (NGOs) also compete for world attention and influence. Some of them, such as Amnesty International and the Red Cross, have millions of members and considerable clout on the world stage. Last, power is also shared with multinational corporations (MNCs), which cross state borders and often have capital and political clout greater than that of most states. Energy companies such as Exxon Mobil and British Petroleum (BP) operate on more than one continent and spill oil in more than one ocean. General Motors and other automotive companies compete around the world. Wal-Mart enhances Chinese power *inside* the United States, and some renowned individuals make their voices heard in the highest chambers of most governments. The interests of these independent, nonstate actors frequently do not coincide with the interests of particular states or their leaders. We examine some of these influential institutions in Chapters 7 and 8.

Conclusion: The new global security map

The current unstable and confusing nature of the global system is due to the simultaneous existence of both traditional security challenges, such as those posed by countries like China and Iran, and new security threats emerging from subnational actors, particularly from the Muslim world, and the consequences of globalization. Those who argue that the United States is so powerful that its government is sometimes tempted to act alone in international affairs are obviously correct. Where they may err is in assuming that because America possesses this great military power, it knows how to use it wisely. Moreover, other countries and institutions are also powerful in economic and social fields. The U.S. margin of superiority is not unassailable, and in a turbulent and violent world collective action will prove more effective in the long run than individual state action. The advent of the new security challenges indicates that even the most powerful country cannot deal with world problems alone.

The new security dilemma derives from the implications of ubiquitous insecurity – violent threats coming from a number of places and sources all at the same time. With the advantages of rapid transportation and modern communications, criminals and terrorists can have a global reach. Supplied with new technology such as miniaturized weapons, they can penetrate the borders and security devices of all countries. Thus, there is a need to include the "new" set of security dilemmas along with the more "traditional" security dilemma in a framework for understanding international relations.

As we consider global politics, we also need to bear in mind that the concept of security itself has broadened. During the past decade or so, scholars and international organizations have expanded the definition to include not only physical security of persons and property but also human rights, democratic government, and possession of the basic necessities of life. Security has become associated with wider concepts of democratization – free societies, free elections, and free markets. It has also become tied to the idea of human security and basic rights and requirements of individuals and societies as well as states. There is a necessity to link the new global order with these novel concepts and theories and to revive other ideas that have fallen into abeyance.

To understand and explain the new world order, our discussion of global politics in this text is, therefore, based on a vocabulary appropriate for contemporary circumstances. While powerful states continue to dominate around the world and regional centers of power exist in some areas, they are only a part of the global system. Four interwoven trends or strands in global politics characterize the new global order. They form a kind of conceptual map, which includes the following:

1. The rise and then weakening of the United States as a hegemon and the growing opposition to this in the rest of the world, symbolized by the rise of powerful states such as China and India, the rising importance of the EU, and the revitalized Russia (i.e., traditional security issues and dilemmas)
2. The constant march of globalization, which is changing relations between rich and poor countries and between the haves and the have-nots, giving rise to violent protests (i.e., traditional security dilemmas, with global economics and capitalism as heroes or scapegoats)
3. The cultural alienation of some parts of the Muslim world, with a concomitant rise of militant Islamist groups and others with virulent anti-Western, particularly anti-U.S. prejudices and actions, as well as a resultant and concomitant growth in organizations intent on using asymmetrical warfare as a tool of international politics (i.e., new security issues and dilemmas)
4. The development of a global concern and societal action to advance human security and all the needs associated with this concept, from clean water to reduction of poverty and sustainable development, and growing acceptance of the idea that foreign intervention in the affairs of weak countries is sometimes justifiable with sovereignty considered expendable (i.e., the new "human" security issues and dilemmas)

In this chapter we have introduced the first two of these strands of global politics – the rise and then relative weakening of the United States compared to its major rivals and the march of globalization and its impact. Both are based on traditional security issues and dilemmas. In following chapters we add the third and fourth strands, which are based on globalization and new security challenges. The newly emergent hybrid global system is complex and worrying. How and even whether leaders can shape it for the betterment of all people is unclear. Nevertheless, the potential for ideas to shape complex realities is possible and should be approached with enthusiasm. In the next chapter we discuss how global governance is affecting the role of states, their power, and security.

Select bibliography

Bacevich, Andrew J., *The Limits of Power: The End of American Exceptionalism* (New York: Metropolitan Books, 2008).

Bergsten, C. Fred, Charles Freeman, Nicholas R. Lardy, and Derek Mitchell, *China's Rise: Challenges and Opportunities* (Washington, DC: Peterson Institute for International Economics, 2008).

Black, Jeremy, *Great Powers and the Quest for Hegemony: The World Order since 1500* (New York: Routledge, 2008).

Bremmer, Ian, *Every Nation for Itself: Winners and Losers in a G-Zero World* (New York: Penguin, 2012).

Brown, Archie, *The Rise and Fall of Communism* (London: Ecco, 2009).

Brown, Michael E., Owen R. Coté Jr., Sean M. Lynn-Jones, and Steven E. Miller, eds., *Primacy and Its Discontents: American Power and International Stability* (Cambridge, MA: MIT Press, 2009).

Calleo, David P., *Follies of Power: America's Unipolar Fantasy* (Cambridge: Cambridge University Press, 2009).

Friedman, Thomas L., and Michael Mandelbaum, *That Used to Be US* (New York: Farrar, Strauss, and Giroux, 2011).

Green, Michael J., and Bates Gill, *Asia's New Multilateralism* (New York: Columbia University Press, 2009).

Holslag, Jonathan, *China and India: Prospects for Peace* (New York: Columbia University Press, 2009).

Jacques, Martin, *When China Rules the World: The Rise of the Middle Kingdom and the End of the Western World* (London: Allen Lane, 2009).

Jackson, Nicole J., *Russian Foreign Policy and the CIS* (Oxford, UK: Routledge, 2007).

Johnson, Chalmers, *Blowback: The Costs and Consequences of American Empire* (New York: Metropolitan, 2000).

Kagan, Robert, *The World America Made* (New York: Knopf, 2012).

Khanna, Parag, *The Second World: Empires and Influence in the New Global Order* (New York: Random House, 2008).

Kissinger, Henry, *On China* (New York: Penguin Press, 2011).

Kurlantzick, Joshua, *Charm Offensive: How China's Soft Power Is Transforming the World* (New Haven, CT: Yale University Press, 2007).

Layne, Christopher, *The Peace of Illusions: American Grand Strategy from 1940 to the Present* (Ithaca, NY: Cornell University Press, 2006).

Layne, Christopher, with Bradley A. Thayer, *American Empire: A Debate* (New York: Routledge, 2006).

Lieber, Robert, *Power and Willpower in the American Future: Why the United States Is Not Destined to Decline* (Cambridge: Cambridge University Press, 2012).

Luce, Edward, *In Spite of the Gods: The Strange Rise of Modern India* (London: Little, Brown, 2007).

Madden, Thomas F., *Empires of Trust: How Rome Built – and America Is Building – A New World* (New York: Dutton, 2008).

Maloney, Suzanne, *Iran's Long Reach: Iran as a Pivotal State in the Muslim World* (Washington, DC: U.S. Institute of Peace, 2008).

Nilekani, Nandan, *Imagining India: The Idea of a Renewed Nation* (London: Penguin, 2009).

Overholt, William H., *Asia, America, and the Transformation of Geopolitics* (Cambridge: Cambridge University Press, 2008).

Panagariya, Arvind, *India: The Emerging Giant* (Oxford: Oxford University Press, 2010).

Sebestyen, Victor, *Revolution 1989: The Fall of the Soviet Empire* (New York: Pantheon, 2009).

Shirk, Susa, *China: Fragile Superpower* (Oxford: Oxford University Press, 2008).

Trenin, Mitri V., *Getting Russia Right* (Washington, DC: Carnegie Endowment for International Peace, 2007).

Walt, Steven M., *Taming American Power: The Global Response to U.S. Primacy* (New York: W. W. Norton, 2005).

Walton, C. Dale, *Geopolitics and the Great Powers in the Twenty-First Century* (Abingdon, UK: Routledge, 2007).

Zakaria, Fareed, *The Post-American World* (New York: W. W. Norton, 2008).

6

Global governance in transition
International law and intergovernmental institutions

While there is no international authority that can impose laws on people around the globe and force them to be obedient, there is a new kind of global governance in flux. States accept some forms of international law, sign treaties, and even join various international organizations for their mutual benefit or to approve certain norms of behavior, yet none subjects itself to a higher set of decision makers or laws than those of its own domestic authorities. This is illustrated by the fact that international institutions cannot back up their rules, demands, or threats unless member states stand behind them. They do not have courts, police, prisons, or soldiers to enforce their rulings unless states supply them. Simply put, the global community lacks the sinews of sovereignty.

International law and intergovernmental institutions are intermittently on the minds and in the emotions of informed citizens around the world, because the media carry information about them on a regular basis. Political leaders try to win the support of these international authorities in economic and security matters as they negotiate new treaties, participate in global institutions, and contribute to the evolution of new norms, rules, and practices. Yet the details about how such topics and events are handled or mishandled in international forums are neither covered well by news organizations nor followed closely by the public. Think of events such as the wars in Afghanistan and Iraq, military intervention in Libya, violent upheaval in Syria, the war-crime trials in The Hague, prisoners of war held in Guantánamo Bay, torture and humiliation in Iraq's Abu Ghraib prison, and genocide in Darfur and Rwanda. All of these topics raise issues about international laws concerning war, murder, and torture that are complex and only vaguely understood except by specialists.

The state of international law and institutions is a matter of ideological controversy. Liberals, especially liberal internationalists, argue that "the glass is half full" for many reasons. Clearly, states do attempt to find mechanisms for bringing cooperation and peace. International law helps to distinguish between illegal wars and wars of self-defense and to establish overall principles such as declarations by the United Nations that states should settle their disputes by peaceful means. International institutions have helped to nurture a relatively stable and prosperous era since World War II, even though there needs to be even more cooperation based on an institutionalized and rule-based order. "No!" shout back the realists. "The glass is half empty" – international law and global institutions exist all right, but they are weak and ineffectual. They do not replace the primacy of state sovereignty, and they have not, and cannot, replace the role of states in global politics. They have not put an end to war, even in this period of increased interdependence.

To a large extent, the institutions of international governance institutions are struggling to fulfill their mandates during this period of globalization and new security dilemmas. They sometimes appear to be out of line in a world of rising states such as China, India, and Brazil, powerful nonstate actors, and new global challenges. They constantly need to be reformed to adequately represent the changing balance of power in global politics, but the new circumstances make it difficult to do so.

In this chapter, we assess these conflicting contentions, beginning with a discussion of how international law is made, applied, and enforced in a world characterized by sovereignty and interdependence. First, we study the evolution of international law, international courts, and extraordinary courts. We then examine major international organizations, focusing on the United Nations, and regional institutions, with particular attention to the European Union. How effective is the UN in terms of peacekeeping and peace enforcement? Should it be allowed to intervene in sovereign countries for humanitarian reasons? The European Union is the most successful transnational regional organization. Is it stronger than its individual states in terms of collective action and foreign policy?

There are, of course, other important elements in global governance. In Chapter 9 we assess the role of alliances in the international security architecture, and in Chapter 12 we examine the role of international economic institutions. These chapters all help answer some important questions. How much global governance exists? Is a new system of global governance emerging? Should and can it be reformed to meet the new global challenges?

Law

Law consists of a body of rules that emanate from government institutions and are enforceable by courts. It can be seen as a body of rules for resolving disputes for the collective good of states and societies. In theory, law should apply equally to all individuals so that those who violate rules are punished, and those who have been harmed by rule breakers are compensated. In democratic states, laws are interpreted and applied by judges, who attempt to mete out justice impartially. Recognized legal authorities such as courts, the police, and sometimes the military enforce their judgments. In democracies police and security forces work for the state, but this should not give them dispensation to act outside the law.

There are two basic sources of law. Customary law, or common law, develops over time through trial and error; it is never really "made" at any specific point in time but instead develops through habit and custom. A law becomes customary after there has been long-standing practice and people begin to act in accordance with the norm because they believe that they are legally obliged to do so. Customary law may emerge from court or administrative decisions about social conflict, and it may or may not be written down or codified. But it exists and is enforced. It is law that is followed without being expressly adopted by states in the form of legislation. A good example is English common law, which developed through court decisions based on customs and usage in England, and then was disseminated through much of the world by the British Empire. In contrast, legislative or statutory, law is created according to an explicit plan to resolve actual or potential social conflict, and it can replace or supersede customary law. It is created by a high organ of government such as a congress or a parliament.

Close Up 6.1 **The first recorded code of laws**

Hammurabi, king of Babylon, who reigned from 1795–50 BCE was one of the great rulers of antiquity. He governed much of Mesopotamia (roughly today's Iraq) and created a code of laws for which he is famous. The Code of Hammurabi is found today in the Louvre in Paris. The black basalt stele almost 2.5 meters high is inscribed with 282 laws in the Akkadian language. The stele, or post, shows the king receiving the laws from the god of justice.

Students of jurisprudence (legal philosophy) are divided about the essential nature of law and what makes it differ from other customs, habits, and basic rules that affect human behavior. Does it differ because of its content or because of the procedures involved in making and enforcing it? Some theorists argue that laws are, or should be, based on natural law – a body of principles for human behavior ordained by God or nature. Religious believers and natural law theorists, therefore, argue that eternal principles of right and wrong should guide the behavior of moral people even in the event that government-made laws conflict with them. They distinguish government or secular law from the "wrong" principles for human behavior. Secular law theorists, in contrast, argue that since no one can establish absolute right and moral principles for all people over all time, law should be defined by the

procedures or rules that determine how governments and courts make and enforce rules of social behavior. In the English language the word *law* covers both natural law and man-made or positive law. However, many languages accord these things different words – in French, for example, *droit* refers to eternal principles of correct conduct, and *loi* refers to the rules enforced by government.

In democracies there is a belief that both rulers and the ruled ought to be subject to the same laws. The authority of the state should be exercised rationally and without malice, with all citizens protected from abuses of power. This notion is embodied in the concept of the rule of law, which means that the citizen, no matter what his or her transgression, should not be denied due process of law. No individual or institution ought to be above the law or exempted from it, and all are equal before it.

Historical events, culture, ideology, and religion give character to the customs and procedures of all countries and have an impact on customary law, constitutions, statutes, and regulations. The idea that the relationship between the government and the individual should be based on law (i.e., individuals possess inherent rights and can be deprived of them only by due process) was central to the rise of the modern state in Western societies. This important concept made the development of law in the West differ from that in areas where absolutist rulers were not impeded by legal restraints or other social influences such as strong aristocracies. In early Persian, Indian, Chinese, Japanese, and European societies (prior to the 17th century), the individual was simply a subject, and law was used only to enforce the power and policy of the ruler. Later, over time, Western legal concepts and the idea of citizenship had considerable influence in other parts of the world, and states adopted Western procedures and codes and blended them with their own customs. This is true in most states in Africa, Asia, the Middle East, and Latin America.

Religion provided many of the values found in early Western law. By the late Middle Ages the powers of European monarchs were circumscribed by "divine law" or "natural law," as interpreted by the Catholic Church and by enacted laws of the state itself, which conferred the right to life, liberty, and private property. Adherence to principles based on religion is found even in the modern constitutions of some so-called secular societies. The British monarch, for example, must be of the Anglican faith. In Canada, the Charter of Rights and Freedoms begins with the idea that "Canada is founded upon principles that recognize the supremacy of God and the rule of law." Other secular societies, in an attempt to avoid the divisiveness of competing religions, have been more adamant in separating church and state. In the United States, the framers of the Constitution sought to separate government explicitly from religious practice. The First Amendment stipulates that Congress is prohibited from establishing a national religion and from interfering with religious practice. Although freedom to *believe* is absolute, freedom to *practice* that belief may, in certain circumstances, be limited by government.

International law

Despite the sovereignty of individual states, international law does exist at the global level. While the relationships among states are inherently conflictual and there is no supreme government to make rules, international law incorporates many of the traits of domestic law so that states regularly use it to deal with one another and to redress grievances. The Dutch legal theorist Hugo Grotius (1583–1645) is sometimes called the father of modern international law because he declared in his famous early 17th-century work *On the Law of War and Peace* that international relations are based on international law, even if individual states are recognized as independent and sovereign.

International law can be defined as the binding rules of conduct among countries. It consists of principles and rules for regulating relations among states, institutions, and individuals on a global basis. In this sense, relations between and among states and embassies or their equivalents have existed since at least 3000 BCE, and customs have developed from these interactions that constitute primitive forms of law. Modern international law, therefore, approximates the type of law that existed in traditional societies before the development of modern states. It is expressed in treaties, the rulings of judicial bodies, the writings of scholars, and is shown particularly by the consistent and established behavior of states. The fact that there is no world government or universally accepted court system means, as we have said earlier, that there is an absence of a worldwide authority to legislate, adjudicate, and enforce international law.

International law comes from both treaty law and customary international law. Treaties are written contracts in which two or more states formally establish specific rules. Customary international laws, in contrast, are unwritten but derive from general practices. To prove that a specific rule is customary, it must be shown that it is reflected in the practice of states and that such practice is required. Private international law covers the routine activities of states and nonstate actors in fields such as international commerce, communications, and travel, whereas public international law regulates the relations among states and intergovernmental agencies.

In their ordinary, day-to-day activities states follow international rules and principles (the corpus *juris gentium* or law of nations) because they find it convenient and uncontroversial to do so. At one time no ships were safe on the high seas because of piracy, but now the principle of secure passage is accepted by all states (if not by all pirates!). States establish embassies and diplomatic missions in other countries. They join intergovernmental organizations such as the United Nations and sign trade agreements among themselves such as the General Agreement on Tariffs and Trade (GATT). Think of what the world would be like without such treaties as the Universal Postal System (1864) and the International Telegraphic Union (1865).

The evolution of international law

International law has evolved in three main ways: (1) by custom and usage concerning negotiations and practices among states, (2) by treaties made between two or more states, and (3) by the decisions and actions of multilateral organizations such as the United Nations and courts.

Custom and usage Customary international law consists of implicit rules of behavior and conduct based on usage or practice. States follow these long-established principles or norms of behavior most of the time because they have become accepted as the normal or respected way to act. Eventually, these implicit rules may be codified into treaties and, hence, written international law. When one state "recognizes" another state, it accepts its sovereign equality. This recognition may be de facto or de jure. The former is recognition based on practical or pragmatic considerations that the state is actually an independent governing entity, whereas the latter provides formal legal recognition, usually based on an acceptance of its legitimacy.

An example of recognition is found in the routine relations carried out by negotiations between diplomats and other officials who assert the claims of their states in bilateral (between two states) and multilateral (among several states) frameworks.[1] Diplomacy, the art of conducting relations between countries, is an old profession. In ancient Greece, passports called "diplomas" existed. They were made of double metal plates folded and sewn together, and carried by Greek messengers as a sign that they should be given special treatment and travel privileges. Modern diplomacy originated in Italy in the 14th century as an independent profession with countries maintaining permanent embassies in foreign countries. Today, ambassadors and diplomatic staff are given diplomatic immunity, or freedom from the laws of their host countries, and their embassies are exempt from local control because there is universal acceptance of the legal doctrine of *extraterritoriality*. While customary behavior gave rise to these concepts, they have mostly been codified in treaties such as the 1961 Vienna Convention on Diplomatic Relations.

A long-standing problem with customary international law is that large parts of the world claim that it is biased in favor of Western traditions and ideas. There is some validity to this contention. In the 16th and 17th centuries, for example, international law included the view that all Christians should be treated equally, whereas non-Christians in America, Asia, and the Muslim world could be treated according to different principles. Sometimes this distinction meant that non-Christians were treated as barbarians or savages. Even today some non-Westerners contend that such biased viewpoints dominate in discussions of international law and in actions of international organizations such as the UN and its various allied organizations.

States may normally follow internationally recognized customs and practices of behavior, but no higher political authority or international organization can settle disputes or impose solutions on individual states based on these rules. The core principle is that each state possesses sovereignty, and no authority can, or should, exist that can bind them by international law. They have to voluntarily consent to it for it to be valid. States conform to international law most of the time because they want other states to do the same. This is known as the principle of reciprocity, and it serves to make international relations stable and predictable.[2]

---

[1] For an overview of this fascinating subject, see Sir Harold Nicholson, *Diplomacy*, 4th ed. (New York: Oxford University Press, 1988). On the early history of diplomacy, see Frank Adcock, *Diplomacy in Ancient Greece* (New York: St. Martin's Press, 1975).

[2] Christopher C. Joyner, *International Law in the 21st Century* (Lanham, MD: Rowman & Littlefield, 2005).

Treaties Through centuries of interaction, states have adopted explicit forms of negotiating and bargaining that are considered part of international law. States (and individuals) carry out many global functions with a high degree of security – goods move across state borders; people move by air, sea, and land; and agreements are upheld – all under rules of international law. These principles have continued to evolve through centuries of interaction among states.

Treaties form the most important part of these international laws. A treaty – essentially a contract between two or more state signatories – binds the countries that sign it to observe the agreement if a proper legal ratification process has been carried out. Thus, treaties impose codified obligations on the signatory states to comply with the principles and details of the agreement. There is widespread attachment to the principle of *pacta sunt servanda*, which means that treaties ought to be kept. More than twenty-five thousand treaties have been signed since the middle of the 17th century, with an escalating number in the past century. Many of them have replaced rules that used to be based on customary international law, such as the rules concerning embassies and diplomats.

The crucial point is that treaties are legally binding once they have been signed and ratified. However, the fact that there are no enforcement institutions makes them binding on states only if they agree to be bound by them. The Nuclear Non-Proliferation Treaty (NPT), for example, prohibits signatory states from acquiring nuclear weapons. But when North Korea, a signatory to the NPT, wanted to produce a nuclear bomb in 2003, it simply withdrew from the treaty and proceeded to build it.

Multilateral organizations Some international institutions also create international law. The United Nations is the best example. While it does not constitute a world government, the UN does attempt to prevent disputes and preserve law and order globally. Composed of almost all states in the world, the UN may attempt to act like a government, yet it has no power of enforcement. Article 13 of the UN Charter specifies that the General Assembly may make recommendations for "encouraging the progressive development of law and its codification," but its judgments are not binding on its member states. The United Nations has no army, navy, or air force, and since no international government is in place to impose international law, adherence to UN principles is usually, but not always, contingent on the voluntary compliance of the individual states themselves.

There are several well-known recent exceptions. In 1991, the United Nations sanctioned the collective efforts of member states to attack Iraq after Saddam Hussein launched a hostile takeover of Kuwait. In 1992 it imposed a binding economic embargo on Libya because Libya refused to hand over two alleged airplane hijackers. After the 9/11 attacks in 2001, the UN sanctioned an attack on Afghanistan, but later it divided on whether to send forces to rid Iraq of Saddam Hussein. In 2012 the Security Council agreed to NATO support of the insurgents' campaign against Muammar Gaddafi in Libya but later did not support the enemies of Bashar al-Assad in Syria (see later in this chapter, as well as Chapter 10).

International courts

For international law to be effective there must be courts to determine whether laws have been violated. In exceptional circumstances, local, regional, and national courts may allow principles of international law to be argued before them. For example, in some countries, when a citizen is charged with having committed a crime in a foreign country, the case can be heard in the citizen's own national court system, despite the fact that the judges are dealing with the laws of another country.

Some courts are higher than domestic counterparts, and their judgments are considered sources of international law. The International Court of Justice (ICJ) in The Hague is the primary judicial organ of the United Nations. It was established to apply international law on an impartial basis, and its fifteen judges are appointed by the United Nations for nine-year renewable terms. The Court can issue advisory opinions on international law when requested by the UN, and it can also hear and determine cases between states based on international law. However, it can neither initiate proceedings nor act on the request of nonstate actors such as multinational corporations or individuals. Nor can it try individuals. Therefore, the parties to a dispute in the ICJ are all states, whether they are complainants or defendants.

While it hears and adjudicates disputes between states, the ICJ does not have compulsory jurisdiction. It acts only if a state requests it to do so, and a state must agree to its jurisdiction before the Court can act. In some cases, compulsory court jurisdiction is required by treaty or by an earlier formal acceptance of article 36 of the ICJ's charter, which allows states to accept its compulsory jurisdiction in what is known as the optional clause. Almost half the world's states have accepted the ICJ's jurisdiction by signing the optional cause. The United States, for example, accepts it but then qualifies its significance with the Connelly Amendment, which says that the jurisdiction will apply only "as determined by the United States." Although the voluntary compliance of states is required, rules set by such international bodies as the ICJ do have significant influence, and states usually adhere to the norms set by them. Most court cases are resolved satisfactorily, but if states believe that their interests are negatively affected by the Court's decisions, they simply disregard its strictures. This dependence on voluntary state acceptance is the Court's vital weakness.

The best example of a court with transnational importance and compulsory jurisdiction is the

Close Up 6.2 **How effective is the International Court of Justice?**

International Court of Justice judgments have been most significant in nonpolitical cases, such as boundaries and fishing disputes between states. Only rarely does the Court deal directly with major political issues. In one telling example in 1984, the leftist Sandinista government of Nicaragua brought a suit to The Hague after the American CIA attempted to overthrow the elected government by mining Nicaraguan harbors. Even though the Court concluded that the CIA had interfered in the territorial integrity of Nicaragua, the U.S. government would not agree that the Court had jurisdiction over its actions. The United States simply denied the tribunal's authority, so there was nothing the Court could do to make the United States comply. It was convicted and fined, but the fine remains unpaid.

In another similar case in 2003, the ICJ concluded that Israel was improperly infringing Palestinian rights when it began constructing a wall along and through the West Bank. However, Israel continues to build the wall, illustrating why much of the developing, poorer part of the world is skeptical of ICJ decisions, while the developed and richer states tend to applaud its international significance even though they obey its strictures only when it suits them.

European Court of Justice (ECJ), whose regional power has increased over time. It successfully imposes community law on citizens inside the twenty-seven states of the European Union, provides advisory opinions to individual state courts, and rules on treaties. Based on the 1957 Treaty of Rome, the decisions of the European Court must be obeyed even if a member state does not approve.

The Court can annul community acts and bring infringement procedures against member states that fail to comply with EU laws and obligations. It is, therefore, reasonable to claim that the ECJ has acquired aspects of a fledgling pan-European sovereignty. Another European court, the European Court of Human Rights (ECHR), has increased its importance in the area of human rights abuses, and in doing so, has become a vital part of the European system.

Disputes over the importance of international law and transnational courts highlight the world's support of both the principles of liberal internationalism and the realist principle that state power remains an important ingredient in global politics. States normally follow international law and attempt to obtain worldwide compliance with the principle of collective action because it is in their interests to do so. However, on occasion, the most powerful of them use nonlegal actions to defend their interests, or they simply do not adhere to treaties that they believe are detrimental to their national interests and sovereignty. That is, despite the existence of international law and even international courts to uphold their principles, states occasionally resort to nonlegal actions to defend their interests. A good example would be the war crimes discussed later in this chapter. Realists may claim that this is only natural, and liberals may argue that it is to be condemned, but as J. L. Brierly puts it, states normally observe international law when it is convenient to do so, and breaches generally occur "either when some great political issue has arisen between states, or in that part of the system which professes to regulate the conduct of war."[3] The inability of global institutions to prevent war and even to manage the conduct of war is a great weakness, but the fact is that states obey international law most of the time because the rules reduce uncertainty and enhance security in global affairs.

[3] J. L. Brierly, *The Law of Nations*, 6th ed. (New York: Oxford University Press, 1963), p. 72.

International law pertaining to war is discussed in Chapter 9.

Extraordinary courts

On occasion, extraordinary courts have been set up to prosecute individuals for war-crime violations. At the end of World War II, the victorious Allies set up the Nuremberg and Tokyo courts to try enemy civilian and military leaders for war crimes. A dozen Germans were sentenced to death, and seven Japanese were hanged. More recently, after a new government was elected in Iraq following the invasion by the United States and its "coalition of the willing," an Iraqi court tried and condemned President Saddam Hussein to death for crimes against his people. However, many have criticized these courts as nothing more than the revenge of the victors.

In recent years there has been a growing movement for special and even permanent international courts to be set up to prosecute war crimes and human rights violations. In 1993–94, the United Nations established ad hoc war-crimes tribunals to deal with perpetrators of atrocities in the former Yugoslavia and again later in Rwanda. Special courts were also set up to deal with Sierra Leone, Cambodia, and East Timor but with more mixed results.

The International Criminal Tribunals for Yugoslavia and Rwanda indicted more than 150 people, most of whom were arrested and convicted of war crimes. The most infamous case was the killing and maiming of thousands of Muslims by Serbs during the Bosnian conflict of 1992–95. For his part in the atrocity, the tribunal could have condemned former Yugoslavian president Slobodan Milošević for war crimes and crimes against humanity, but he died in jail in 2006 before a decision was made. In 2009 another Serbian leader, Radovan Karažić, went on trial for war crimes. He was joined in 2011 by Ratko Mladić, a former Bosnian Serb general who faced charges for war crimes, including the murder of eight thousand unarmed men and boys in

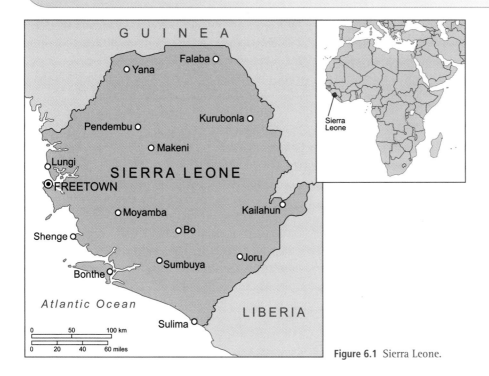

Figure 6.1 Sierra Leone.

Srebrenica in 1995. Another International Criminal Tribunal was set up in Rwanda to deal with crimes committed by the Hutu for maiming, raping, torturing, and killing thousands of Tutsis in 1994. More than eighty people have been arrested to date, and among the many people who have been sentenced by the court was the former prime minister of Rwanda, Jean Kambanda, who was convicted of genocide (see Close Up 6.4).

In 2007, after several years of warfare, much of it fueled by trade in so-called blood diamonds, the government of Sierra Leone, aided by the United Nations, set up the Special Court of Sierra Leone (SCSL) to try eight prisoners for crimes against international law (Figure 6.1). The prisoners and their followers had kidnapped, drugged, and forced children, many younger than the age of fifteen, into battle and had taught them to attack and mutilate civilians. Many thousands of children had their hands chopped off for refusing to join the rebels or for not fighting strongly enough for the cause. The

Special Court ruled that the recruitment of children younger than fifteen for hostilities was a war crime under customary international law, despite the fact that the crime of enforcement of children was not specifically included in the court's original mandate. All the convicted prisoners were sent to prison in Rwanda. It was the first time that sex slavery and use of child soldiers were recognized as international crimes, and the convictions were the first ever by an international tribunal for the recruitment and use of child soldiers.

Another notorious case took place in 2006. The trial for the leader of the Sierra Leone murders, Charles G. Taylor (former president of Liberia), was placed under the jurisdiction of the SCSL, a hybrid court which deals with both domestic and international cases. The case was moved to The Hague for security reasons but remained under the jurisdiction of the SCSL. Taylor was charged with eleven counts of war crimes and crimes against humanity during the conflict in Sierra Leone, including the use of women and girls as sex slaves and the abduction of children for fighting and labor. In April 2012 the ex-president was convicted of all eleven counts and sentenced to fifty years in jail. He was the first head of state to be convicted by such a court since the Nuremberg trials after World War II. He will serve his sentence in a British prison.

All of these ad hoc tribunals have been roundly criticized for clumsy procedures, slowness, expense, and sometimes lack of success. But given the complex nature of the cases and the international issues involved, it is fair to say that the tribunals have made significant progress in satisfying global concerns about human rights and war crimes. In these cases, not only states but also individuals and nongovernmental institutions are being called before judges, and the idea of global justice for human rights has became part of the language of international law. Worldwide support for a rapidly growing body of international law about war crimes and human rights violations has backed up these judicial proceedings and led many states to support the establishment of a permanent court.

The International Criminal Court

The permanent International Criminal Court (ICC) came into existence in 2002 after sixty countries ratified the treaty – as of 2012, 114 states had ratified it.[4] The ICC consists of eighteen judges from participating countries who meet in The Hague (Figure 6.2). The prosecutor can pursue an investigation only when he is asked to do so by a member state or by the Security Council of the United Nations. The Court can issue arrest warrants for war crimes around the world. Unlike the ICJ, it can try individuals, but not states, and it can arrest and prosecute citizens of any state that has ratified the treaty and also noncitizens who are alleged to have committed war crimes in the territory of a state that has ratified the treaty. It can even arrest

---

[4] For updates on current cases and individuals, see http://www.icc-cpi.int.

heads of governments for crimes they are alleged to have committed. However, the ICC can function only when national state courts are unable or unwilling to deal with atrocities. In other words, the ICC can try cases only when states fail to do so. This means that as long as a state investigates and prosecutes its citizens, the ICC has no jurisdiction in the case.

The ICC enforces the Rome Statute. The treaty specifies four types of criminality to come before the ICC – war crimes (crimes that international organizations and states define as illegal), genocide (systematically killing people because of their race, ethnicity, or religion), crimes against humanity (enslavement, forcible transfer of people, and torture), and undefined aggression (which was postponed pending an agreement on its definition). The Court is not a judicial institution of the United Nations, although with a supermajority of nine members the Security Council can instruct the Court to begin or terminate certain types of cases.

Many major countries – including China, India, Iran, Iraq, Israel, Japan, Russia, Turkey, the United States, and all major Arab states – decline to participate in the ICC. They reject the possibility that their leaders or military personnel should be subject to it because, as they argue, these individuals have "exceptional" obligations. While some nonsignatories attend the ICC as observers, the United States does not participate in any of its proceedings, and it has even passed a law, the American Service Members Protection Act, which prohibits American cooperation with the ICC. Washington argues that the Court lacks accountability and that it therefore will not allow U.S. leaders and military officers to be subject to what might amount to politically motivated prosecutions. If the United States were to recognize the Court, other states or individuals might attempt to punish American leaders and citizens for alleged improper and illegal behavior. Some radical critics, for example, would like to charge former president George W. Bush and his generals for acting without United Nations approval in its 2003 invasion of

Figure 6.2 The International Criminal Court was established by the United Nations in 2012, the first permanent treaty-based international criminal court to try perpetrators of the most serious war crimes – genocide, crimes against humanity, and war crimes. *Source:* Alamy.

Iraq, but they are prevented from doing so since the United States does not accept the jurisdiction of the ICC.

Some Arab leaders criticize the ICC for a different reason. They say that it is biased and has double standards – it wants to prosecute Muslims, but not Israelis, for war crimes. They claim in particular that the Court is irresponsible in not investigating Israeli war crimes in Gaza. Arab countries also condemn the Court's efforts to arrest Omar Hassan al-Bashir, president of Sudan, who has been accused of torture, rape, killing, and widespread pillaging in Darfur. In February 2009, the Court charged the president with crimes against humanity, but leaders in the Arab world have helped to prevent an arrest from taking place. The case is ongoing.

Currently, the ICC is investigating fifteen cases in seven countries with "irregular situations" (see Critical Case Study 6.1). The Central African Republic, Côte d'Ivoire, the Democratic Republic of the Congo, and Uganda have forwarded domestic cases to the Court for resolution. The Security Council has nominated two other cases – Darfur (in Sudan) and Libya – and the Court has undertaken investigations in Kenya at the request of the government there. All the cases include allegations of war crimes, genocide, crimes against humanity, and enforcing the enlistment of children in war activities (see also Chapter 14 on human rights).

Critical Case Study 6.1 **Ongoing ICC investigations and actions**

The ICC's evolution is a primary example of the growth of institutions for global governance. As of 2013, the ICC was investigating the following specific crimes (Figure 6.3):

1. **Democratic Republic of the Congo (DRC):** In January 2009, the ICC began its first trial for crimes against humanity. Three international judges, from Britain, Costa Rica, and Bolivia, sat in judgment of Thomas Lubanga Dyilo and other Congolese warlords charged with war crimes, crimes against humanity, and forced enlistment of children during Congo's civil war. They were charged with using children younger than fifteen to fight and kill in the Ituri region of the eastern DRC in 2002–03. Prosecutors claim that at the height of the conflict as many as thirty thousand boys and girls were forced to be part of the militia forces, some were abducted, and others recruited in exchange for food and drugs. The Court alleged that Lubanga and his people used the children, some as young as nine, as spies and sex slaves and sent them out to pillage, rape, and kill members of other ethnic groups. Approximately one hundred victims were expected to testify in these cases.

   Thomas Lubanga Dyilo, Germain Katanga, Mathieu Ngudjolo Chui, and Callixte Mbarushimna were arrested and put in the custody of the ICC. Another suspect, Bosco Ntaganda, remained at large. These were the first cases by the new permanent court of criminal behavior. In March 2012, after a difficult and controversial trial, Thomas Lubanga was found guilty of recruiting and enlisting boys and girls younger than age fifteen and using them in war. He was sentenced to fourteen years in prison. Meanwhile, the notorious Bosco "Terminator" Ntaganda became a general in the Congolese army. In March 2013, he surrendered to the ICC and his case is at the trial stage. The other cases are ongoing.

2. **Sudan:** Cases are being heard for five Sudanese, including Omar Hassan Ahmad al-Bashir, Ahmad Muhammad Harun, Ali Muhammad Al Abd-Al-Rahman, Abdallah Banda Abakaer Nourain, and Saleh Mohammed Jerbo Jamus. The Court charges al-Bashir, president of Sudan, and others with crimes against humanity, including torture, rape, killing, and widespread pillaging in Darfur. Leaders in

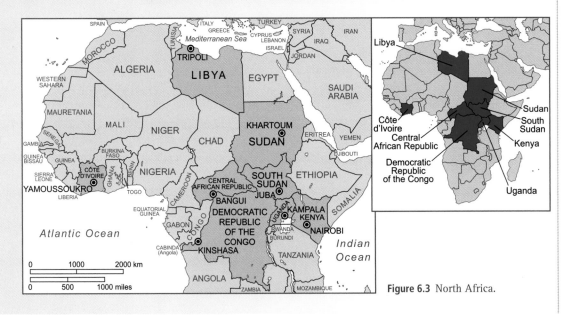

Figure 6.3 North Africa.

Arab countries condemned the Court's efforts and have actively helped prevent al-Bashir's arrest. The African Union has specifically ordered its fifty-four members not to cooperate with the ICC's arrest warrant for al-Bashir. China officially welcomed the president in Beijing! None of the suspects has been captured, and the case is ongoing. As one wag put it: The case is not so much ongoing as it is going nowhere!

3. **Central African Republic:** Jean-Pierre Bemba Gombo has been at the trial stage of proceedings since late 2010 and is currently being questioned for three charges of war crimes and two crimes against humanity.

4. **Uganda:** There are four ongoing trials concerning the top four living members of the Lord's Resistance Army (LRA): Joseph Kony, Vincent Otti, Okot Odhiambo, and Dominic Ongwen. They are cited for several crimes, including crimes against humanity and forced the enlistment of children. All four suspects are at large (see Close Up 14.2 on Kony and Invisible Children).

5. **Kenya:** In the postelection period (2007–08) there were alleged violations of crimes against humanity – murder, rape, inhumane acts, and deportations. The ICC charged several Kenyan leaders, including the country's deputy prime minister, with committing crimes against humanity in the violent aftermath of Kenya's 2007 election. The ongoing trials have caused considerable conflict in Kenya.

6. **Libya:** In 2011 The Security Council asked the ICC to investigate the situation in Libya for crimes against humanity leading up to and following the attempted revolution. After doing so, the prosecutor asked the Court to issue arrest warrants for the arrest of Colonel Muammar Gaddafi, his son Saif al-Islam Gaddafi, and the director of military intelligence, Abdullah Senussi. Libya is not a member of the ICC, and there is no compulsion for it to comply with its rulings. If Colonel Gaddafi had been charged, however, he would have been the second serving leader, after Sudan's President al-Bashir, to be indicted. Gaddafi has since been murdered and his case formally terminated, but his son is being held by one of the Libyan tribes. The Court has not yet acted. Senussi remains at large.

7. **Côte d'Ivoire:** In November 2011 the ICC issued an arrest warrant for former Côte d'Ivoire president Laurent Gbagbo. He was put on trial for four crimes against humanity committed in June 2010. He is currently being held at the detention center in The Hague with the confirmation of charges hearing set for February 2013.

Do these cases provide clear evidence that international institutions such as the International Criminal Court and human rights norms can be effective and/or enforced in global politics?

Domestic extraordinary courts also have been organized in several countries after long internal wars. South Africa, Rwanda, and Sierra Leone set up truth and reconciliation commissions to get past the standard legal approach of punishment for wrongdoing – allowing countries to heal after the trauma of war and move forward by revealing the truth of past wrong doing. The Sri Lankan government has set up the controversial Commission on Lessons Learned and Reconciliation. In Rwanda, *gacaca* – a system of outdoor community courts – was convened for genocide cases. More than twelve thousand courts adjudicated more than a million cases. These so-called courts are set up not to render criminal justice but rather to allow some emotional catharsis to be expressed by revealing the truth about the crimes.

International institutions

Since World War II, world leaders have developed significant new rules and standards for cooperation. Efforts to reduce dangerous conflicts within the international system through international law and courts have been augmented by new inter-governmental organizations (IGOs) that contribute to cooperative international activities and help resolve disputes. These IGOs allow member states to act within regional or global arenas, but they also constrain them by establishing norms and rules about their behavior. There are approximately 250 permanent IGOs. The most important of these international organizations is the United Nations, with its specialized multilateral organizations, including the World Health Organization (WHO), the International Labor Organization (ILO), the Universal Postal Union (UPU), and the International Atomic Energy Agency (IAEA). In Chapter 12 we discuss international economic institutions such as the World Trade Organization (WTO), the International Monetary Fund (IMF), and the World Bank (WB), as their activities are also a major part of the transformation that is taking place in world governance.

Two general claims can be made about IGOs and the UN in particular. First, while such organizations perform specific functions, they are also instrumental in creating new rules of global behavior and in helping set up and maintain regimes. Political scientists use the term regime to refer to agreed-on rules, norms, and procedures that emerge from high levels of cooperation. These rules may be explicit as set down in treaties or implicit as determined by general agreements about how problems should be addressed. They help to guide how political leaders act in negotiations and in particular issue areas.

International regimes are entered into because states agree that they will bring long-term benefits. The regimes consist of networks of norms, rules, and decision-making processes that act as guides for decision makers and states in solving global problems. An example of how different processes can be woven together in a regime is the way the UN adopted a set of principles in the Universal Declaration of Human Rights and set up an institution, the Office of the High Commissioner for Human Rights, to ensure that agreed-on rights and principles would be monitored. Another example is the

nuclear nonproliferation regime. The principles of nonproliferation are formally adopted by states that have signed the Nonproliferation Treaty (NPT). The International Atomic Energy Agency (IAEA) monitors the agreement and the norms and rules around the regime, reporting publicly on those countries that acquire nuclear energy for peaceful purposes and those that attempt to get around the rules.

The second general claim about the United Nations as an IGO is that it is intended to be a collective security organization, which means that unlawful aggression ought to be met by the combined military force of all the other members of the organization. If the collective security threat of retaliation is credible, member states know that they will be punished if they engage in aggression and will therefore refrain. In other words, if the theory and practice worked properly, a collective security agreement would act as a deterrent to aggression, as it would be foolish or irrational for any state to attack another.

It must be clear that a collective security organization is not the same as a military alliance. An alliance is formed by a coalition of states to combine their power against one or more adversaries. For example, NATO is a military alliance, not a collective security organization, because it does not include all the countries that could possibly be involved in a conflict. In contrast, the UN is a collective security organization. Since almost all countries are members, a call for collective security would, in principle, implicate virtually all the world's states.

Collective security has been tried before. After World War I, the League of Nations (1920–46) was set up with the overall goal of using collective security to prevent future wars. It failed. Not only did all the powerful states not join (countries defeated in World War I were not admitted as members, and U.S. members in the league was blocked by the U.S. Senate), but the organization also failed to counter several major aggressions. Without international response, Japan invaded Manchuria in 1931 and China in 1937, and Italy attacked Ethiopia in 1935. After World War II there was a general commitment that any new organization would need to avoid these fundamental mistakes of the League.

The United Nations

The United Nations (UN) was created in 1945 to provide a forum at which international grievances could be heard and peaceful cooperation enhanced. While the UN Charter calls for member states to "settle their international disputes by peaceful means," it is not supposed to be a government with the ability to use coercion to enforce compliance. The UN is intended neither to replace the state-based global system nor to become a world government. It does not tax citizens, and despite some naive expectations, it has not been able to establish its own military or police force to send abroad (UN peacekeepers are drawn from consenting member states). On the whole, however, the UN was set up without the deficiencies of the League of Nations.

During World War II, the countries that were allied against Germany and Japan signed the Declaration by United Nations, in which they pledged not to make separate peace treaties with the enemy. This preliminary step culminated eventually in the Charter of the United Nations, which fifty-one states signed in 1945. Since then, in principle, all states of the world can join the UN, but, of course, the UN itself determines their "legitimacy" to do so. The membership of the UN has continued to expand, reaching 193 countries in 2011, when South Sudan joined.

There have been some exceptions to rules about membership in the UN. The government of Taiwan was expelled in 1971 and replaced by the People's Republic of China, which maintains that only it can represent all of China. On January 1, 1965, Indonesia withdrew from the UN because of a feud over Malaysia becoming a member of the Security Council (SC). Later that year, after a coup d'état, it resumed its membership. In 1991, Russia replaced the former Soviet Union as a member of the UN. In 1998, the UN approved a special arrangement for Palestine, allowing it to take part in debates and participate in activities of the UN but not vote, and in 2012 it approved an upgraded observer state status for Palestine despite U.S. and Israeli opposition.

The political organization of the UN is based on a compromise between realist and idealist liberal principles. It is a hybrid organization, encompassing a concern for universalism in that all states are given equal status and supporting the principle that the great powers, at least as envisaged at the origin, are to be treated differently and given more power. All members of the UN, regardless of their size or significance, have seats in the General Assembly. The General Assembly is essentially a deliberating body, and its decisions have no legal, binding force on states. The significance of its decisions is based on moral suasion and the fact that they can influence international public opinion. Much of the General Assembly's work is done in committees on topics such as disarmament, security, and humanitarian and cultural affairs. Perhaps its most important institution is the fifty-four-member Economic and Social Council (ECOSOC), which supervises economic and social welfare programs and coordinates, but does not control, the activities of nineteen specialized agencies, such as the Food and Agriculture Organization (FAO), the World Health Organization (WHO), and the International Atomic Energy Agency (IAEA).

The realist position of recognizing the more powerful states is apparent in the rules for the establishment of the Security Council. This body, set up to reflect political and military realities, is given the primary responsibility for action on questions of peace and security. Since 1965, the Security Council has been composed of fifteen members: five permanent members (the P5) – France, Great Britain, the People's Republic of China, Russia, and the United States – and ten temporary members elected for two-year terms by the General Assembly. As of 2013, the elected members were Argentina, Australia, Azerbaijan, Guatemala, Luxembourg, Morocco, Pakistan, Rwanda, South Korea, and Togo. This composition attempts to square the liberal

Figure 6.4 The United Nations adopted its flag in 1947. The olive branches represent peace, and the map shows the area in which it proposes to achieve its goals of peace and security. Significant as it is in global politics, the United Nations does not constitute a world government.

notion that the UN represents the entire "international community" with the realist insistence that some states are more powerful and important than others. The Security Council may consider any action that its members decide is a threat to peace or an act of aggression and then make recommendations for the resolution of the conflict, including provisions for enforcement. It requires a vote of nine of fifteen to pass a resolution, and the more powerful P5 states are given enhanced authority with a veto over all Security Council decisions.

The UN has a permanent body of several thousand international civil servants called the Secretariat. It is situated in New York City on international territory and has its own rules, flag, and internal police force (Figure 6.4). It is led by a secretary-general whose authority has waxed and waned over the years. The secretary-general is chosen by the Security Council and approved by the General Assembly. A Korean, Ban Ki-moon, was elected in 2006 as the eighth secretary-general to a five-year renewable post and then unanimously reappointed by the General Assembly until December 2016. Attached to the UN are several specialized institutions,

including widely recognized organizations such as the International Children's Emergency Fund, the World Health Organization, the Office of the High Commissioner for Refugees, the Commissioner on Human Rights, and even a university.

The General Assembly elects new members on the basis of recommendations from the Security Council. It also approves the overall budget, passes resolutions and declarations, and sometimes signs conventions or treaties with countries. A two-thirds vote in the General Assembly is required to approve all major decisions and for membership votes. However, decisions of the assembly are not binding on the UN or on its member states; they are merely recommendations. This weakens the assembly vis-à-vis the Security Council, which can make binding decisions and follow them up with force. An example of the nonbinding nature of General Assembly resolutions was its 2008 vote (106–46) for a moratorium on the use of the death penalty in member countries. Despite the large majority against capital punishment, the resolution is only a guideline for states to consider, and many pay no attention to it – including the United States.

Collective security is enshrined in the principles of the UN and defined in two chapters of the UN Charter. Chapter VI, the "pacific settlement of disputes" clause, allows the Security Council to act when international peace is threatened. If mediation does not work, chapter VII explicitly allows the SC to enforce its decisions by imposing embargoes and sanctions or by taking collective military action against states. The Security Council can also directly sanction individuals. Senior members of al-Qaeda and the Taliban have been listed, as have family members of Libyan president Muammar Gaddafi. The named individuals have had their international assets frozen and their travel banned. Decisions of the Security Council must be taken by a majority, defined as nine members, but each of the five permanent members also has a veto, and their vetoes have often prevented any action. Since the 1950 Korean War decision, an abstention has not counted as a veto.

During the Cold War, Security Council resolutions were routinely blocked by vetoes. The explicit use of the veto has declined since then, but implicit veto challenges to resolutions have increased, and this has often prevented collective action. The Security Council's decision to support an attack on Iraq after it invaded Kuwait in 1990 is a fine example of the UN acting in concert based on the collective security principle. Its failure to approve another attack on Iraq in 2003 illustrates the necessity to get a majority of states on the Security Council to agree on collective action. The Security Council approved military action in the Yugoslavian civil war in 1992, but the abysmal failure of the UN peacekeepers to restore peace there eventually led to the employment of NATO troops. NATO's subsequent proposal to bomb Serbia in 1999 was not supported by the Security Council, but NATO proceeded anyway. In other words, in the Yugoslav case, NATO's military alliance was more effective than the UN, and the UN was marginalized. The collective security principle has had mixed results in many other war situations as well. We return to this contentious issue in the discussion of peacekeeping and peace enforcement later in this chapter.

Aside from using chapters VI and VII of the UN Charter, the most important work of the UN may be in the fields of economic and social development (Figure 6.5). In 2000, for example, the UN brought the heads of all member states together for

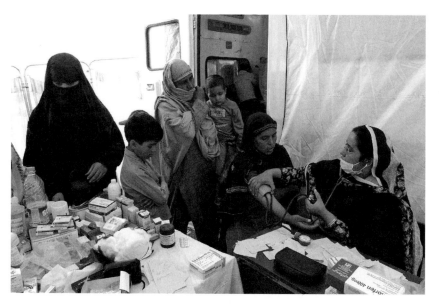

Figure 6.5 The United Nations may be accused of many faults, but even its critics acknowledge the outstanding humanitarian work it does in times of crises such as the devastating 2005 earthquake in Kashmir, Pakistan. *Source*: UN Photo/Evan Schneider.

a Millennium Summit. The leaders committed themselves to Millennium Development Goals (MDGs), measurable goals or targets that are to be achieved by 2015. As of 2013 most of the goals (e.g., reducing by half the number of people living on less than a dollar a day, achieving universal primary education, and reversing the spread of HIV/AIDS and malaria) have not been fully met. But officials continue to strive to achieve them, and in that sense, the MDGs have given focus and priority to the developmental work of UN officials (see Chapter 13).

Reform of the United Nations

The United Nations is the most advanced and inclusive international institution in existence, but even it needs to adapt to the changing world order. Critics question its effectiveness and relevancy because of two major ongoing challenges – the imbalance of power in the Security Council and failure to solve international problems that require long-term sustained financing and strategic responses.[5] However, state sovereignty remains sacrosanct and makes any change involving these major topics difficult. Moreover, the amendment procedure is very rigid, as such changes must be recommended to the General Assembly by two-thirds of the members of the Security Council, including all five permanent members.

The composition of the Security Council is hotly debated. There has been no increase or change in the permanent membership of the Council since its founding in 1945. Japan, for example, is not a member, despite the fact that it has one of the largest world economies and contributes handsomely to United Nations activities. But China does not want Japan to become a member. Given its international significance, Germany should also be a member of the Security Council, but Britain and France oppose any dilution of their European preeminence. India should be a member because of its large population

and general importance as the world's largest democracy, but the dynamics are such that it cannot obtain membership without an Islamic state such as Indonesia also being admitted. These are only a few of the complications in reforming the Security Council's membership. Many countries, perhaps even a majority, want an expanded membership. One report by the secretary-general called for an expansion to twenty-four members, with as many as eleven states wielding the veto power. But the United States is opposed to any increase in the number of vetoes. A larger membership would certainly make the body more representative, but it is hard to see how it would be more effective with more than twice as many potential vetoes. The overall issue remains in limbo and is likely to remain there.

Another issue concerns the proportion that each country pays of the approximately $20 billion UN budget. Almost all of the core budget and the peacekeeping budget are paid by the richest countries, as the rules stipulate that revenue is based on the ability of each member state to pay. The ten largest contributors pay more than four-fifths of the UN costs, while the bottom 70 percent pay only the minimum, or .01 percent of the budget. The BRICS countries (Brazil, Russia, China, India, and South Africa) pay for less than their fair share. Although they are not members of the Security Council, Germany and Japan pay more money to the UN than all the permanent members of the Security Council except the United States. The third budget (based on voluntary contributions) is approximately twice the size of the core and peacekeeping budgets. It covers UN agencies such as the United Nations Children's Fund (UNICEF) and is paid almost entirely by the richest countries. Ironically, the poorer countries – often represented by what is called the nonaligned movement – want equality in decision making without increasing their financial contributions.

Over the past few decades the UN has been severely criticized by Western democratic countries because its large membership, with equal voting rights among very unequal states, restricts what the

---

[5] Thomas G. Weiss, *What's Wrong with the United Nations and How to Fix It* (Cambridge, UK: Polity Press, 2009).

organization can accomplish. According to them, the General Assembly is too often used as a platform for denouncing the richer states rather than as a forum for rational debate and action. Clearly the UN does not have either the leadership or the resources it needs to carry out its daily responsibilities. Reform is difficult, however, because although the richer states contribute by far the most money, the poorer, less developed countries have the most votes, thus maintaining a majority on UN committees and around 120 votes in the General Assembly. Moreover, rich and poor states dispute how the money should be spent. The poorer states prefer less to be spent on political stabilization missions and peacekeeping and more on development projects. In short, the financial means for the United Nations to carry out its objectives are woefully inadequate and unlikely to be improved in the foreseeable future.

War, peacekeeping, and peace enforcement

The UN Charter is an optimistic document that calls on the Security Council to provide for the peaceful settlement of disputes among members and the collective use of military force. It allows for the use of force in two circumstances – in self-defense or as authorized by the Security Council in response to "a threat to the peace, a breach of the peace, or an act of aggression." Each sovereign country is expected to look after its own national security; this principle acknowledges the realist idea that states will do whatever is necessary to survive and will resist efforts to weaken their sovereignty. However, chapter VII of the Charter permits the Security Council to determine when enforcement measures such as sanctions or military force can be used to restore international peace. Since the UN does not have its own military, article 43 of the UN Charter calls on all members to make forces available to the Security Council under "special agreements" for the "maintenance of peace and security." A United Nations force, therefore, consists of the militaries of member countries acting under the authority and flag of the UN.

The UN's record of using Charter provisions to prevent wars has been pitiful. Only rarely has it succeeded in reducing major aggression, although two satisfactory occasions can be cited. The United Nations played a vital role in the 1950 Korean War. For years, Korea had been divided between a democratic south and a communist north. By chance, when the north attacked the south, the Soviet Union's delegate was boycotting the United Nations, so an American-inspired resolution was able to pass the Security Council without a Soviet veto. A handful of members decided to act on the resolution even though the Soviet Union later came back to the meetings and attempted to reverse the decision. Thanks in large part to that resolution, the Korean War ended in 1953 with an uneasy truce. UN advocates argue that this case proves that the UN was instrumental in preventing the forceful takeover of South Korea.

In the second case, the Security Council authorized an embargo against Iraq in 1991, and later, after Saddam Hussein invaded Kuwait, it authorized member states under chapter VII "to use all necessary means" to remove Iraqi forces from Kuwait. This decision was possible only because the Soviet Union agreed and China did not use its veto to prevent the operation. Subsequent Security Council policies enforced further embargoes on Iraq as well as weapons inspections by the International Atomic Energy Agency (IAEA). Later, in the establishment of a no-fly zone over northern Iraq and the bombing of Serbia during the war in Kosovo in 1999, the Security Council did not commission the acts but only came close to approving them.

After the terrorist attacks on New York and Washington, DC, in 2001, the UN approved retaliation by the United States "in self-defense" but did not join the ensuing war. The burdens of war and occupation in Afghanistan were taken up by the United States, NATO, and a few other like-minded countries. The UN did not, however, approve the attack on Iraq in 2003. Of the permanent members of the Security Council, only Britain supported the U.S. request for UN intervention and also participated in the invasion. China, France, and Russia opposed any action, and even NATO declined to join the American cause. The United States decided to form its own American-led "coalition of the willing" for the war. This action split the international community, led to a protracted war in Iraq, created a short-term weakening of the UN as a force for international peace, and unleashed a broad condemnation of Western policy in the Middle East (see Chapters 9 and 10).

The UN uses various techniques to quell internal state conflicts and war. In the early stages of a conflagration, it engages in reconciliation and conflict resolution, and it works with transitional governments to try to stabilize the situation. If these actions are not sufficient, it may get further involved. In 2012, the UN employed 120,988 personnel in sixteen peacekeeping, peacemaking, and peace enforcement operations. The UN Department of Peacekeeping Operations (DPKO) led these operations at a cost of almost $8 billion annually. Only the United States deploys more military personnel overseas than the UN. This grand undertaking by the UN is managed by the DPKO and the recently established UN Department of Field Support (DFS), which administers the nonmilitary parts of the program, including political and peace-building missions. As well as peace operations, the UN is increasingly engaged in reforming police, judicial and electoral processes, disarming and reintegrating former combatants, and supporting displaced persons and refugees.

During the Cold War, the United Nations found it difficult to act without one of the superpowers invoking or threatening to use its veto power to prevent action. The concept of peacekeeping arose as a way to get around this problem. Peacekeeping is a broad term used to describe the efforts of the UN and other organizations to intervene in violent conflicts such as civil wars or ethnic conflict with the goal of limiting harm to noncombatants and preventing the possible escalation to major warfare. If conflict has not yet broken out, or if there has been a temporary cease-fire among the competing parties, traditional peacekeeping may take place

in which UN peacekeepers maintain cease-fires and armistices with lightly armed UN soldiers in blue berets acting as a buffer between the militants. This occurs only after the UN has received a request from, or the voluntary agreement of, the parties to the dispute. This is called the principle of *consent of the parties.*

Enlisting UN peacekeepers is considered especially desirable when many noncombatants or innocent bystanders are being killed – and in most civil wars many more noncombatants than soldiers are injured and killed. Examples of early and traditional peacekeeping missions still operational today include the UN Peacekeeping Force in Cyprus (UNFICYP), the UN Mission in Ethiopia and Eritrea (UNMEE), and the UN Interim Force in Lebanon (UNFIL). These missions have become "frozen conflicts." Borders in Cyprus, for example, have been controlled by UN peacekeepers since 1964. Some major countries, such as Canada, pulled their troops out long ago, believing that the Greek and Turkish Cypriots can and should resolve the issues that divide them.

When there is no consent of the parties involved in a conflict, the term for UN intervention is *peace enforcement* (Figure 6.6). Chapter VII of the Charter allows the Security Council to take action by "air, sea, or land forces as may be necessary to maintain international peace and security." Such actions can take several forms. Peace enforcement (or *peacemaking*) describes actions that involve the threat or use of military force to compel the compliance of the participants to follow resolutions or sanctions designed by the UN to maintain peace and security. In these cases the UN troops engage the enemies by threatening or actually using force to stop the fighting. Disarmament, demobilization, and reintegration of the combatants (the military shorthand for this is DDR) may all be used in an attempt to end the hostilities. During the past two decades the Security Council has intervened without invitation (i.e., without consent of the parties to the dispute) in Congo, Kosovo, Timor-Leste, Somalia, Bosnia, and Haiti.

The term peace operation encompasses both peacekeeping and peace enforcement activities.

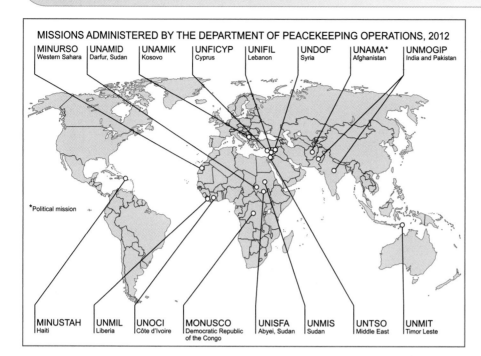

Figure 6.6 Missions administered by the Department of Peacekeeping Operations.

MISSIONS ADMINISTERED BY THE DEPARTMENT OF PEACEKEEPING OPERATIONS, 2012

MINURSO	UNAMID	UNAMIK	UNFICYP	UNIFIL	UNDOF	UNAMA*	UNMOGIP
Western Sahara	Darfur, Sudan	Kosovo	Cyprus	Lebanon	Syria	Afghanistan	India and Pakistan

*Political mission

MINUSTAH	UNMIL	UNOCI	MONUSCO	UNISFA	UNMIS	UNTSO	UNMIT
Haiti	Liberia	Côte d'Ivoire	Democratic Republic of the Congo	Abyei, Sudan	Sudan	Middle East	Timor Leste

Between 1945 and 2012 there were sixty-six UN peace operations. The 2012 budget for its fifteen operations was US$7.84 billion. While the earliest missions were fairly straightforward, consisting mainly of monitoring cease-fires, today the UN personnel are often engaged in complex nation building – training local police and military forces, guarding infrastructure, ensuring the rule of law, monitoring elections, and protecting civilian lives. The UN has engaged in this type of *complex peacekeeping* in places such as in Cambodia (UNTAC) and Namibia (UNTAG). Similarly, it has used humanitarian intervention, or the use of UN peacekeepers to protect people from violations of human rights, disintegrating order, lack of food and medicines, and mass murder or genocide.

Success and failure in UN missions

The UN peacekeeping missions to Liberia, Sierra Leone, and Timor-Leste are usually regarded as successful, while the missions to Yugoslavia and Rwanda are generally considered to have been clear-cut failures. The UN Protection Force (UNPROFOR) failed in the former Yugoslavia because it could not bring a cessation to hostilities or even prevent the genocide of Muslims by Serbs. Rwanda is cited as a failure because, although the UN Assistance Mission in Rwanda (UNAMIR) was there to monitor a 1993 cease-fire, massive violence between Hutus and Tutsis erupted throughout the country (see Close Ups 6.3 and 6.4 on Yugoslavia and Rwanda). Realists generally claim that these failures prove that the UN is weak and cannot be trusted, whereas liberal internationalists are likely to reply that such cases prove the need for the UN to be strengthened and its mandates made more robust. Both are correct, as the United Nations tends to reflect the fundamental nature of international relations as much as it influences it.

Sierra Leone is an example of a successful UN mission. A weak, corrupt government led to the outbreak of civil war in 1991. Fueled by profits from the sales of "blood diamonds," the war lasted more than a decade and caused the displacement

Figure 6.7 The former Yugoslavia today.

of more than two million people and the deaths of thousands. In 2001 the UN Mission in Sierra Leone (UNAMSIL) helped to institute a cease-fire between the government and the rebel Revolutionary United Front (RUF), allowing warriors to be disarmed, thousands of refugees to be repatriated, and elections to be held. In 2005 the country was stable enough for the UN to end the mission. This clearly was a successful outcome in that limited but laudable goals were achieved (Figure 6.1).

Close Up 6.3 Peacekeeping in Yugoslavia: A UN failure?

The United Nations did significant humanitarian work in the former Yugoslavia (1992–95), but when faced with continuing hostility, displacement of people, ethnic cleansing, civilian bombing, wanton destruction, and war, its inability to act was deplorable, a result of its weak mandate. The United Nations responded to the violence between Yugoslavia's Serbs and Muslims with relief supplies, economic embargoes, peacekeeping, and an arms embargo, but these efforts were inadequate to stem the violent conflicts that escalated into outright warfare. (Figure 6.7)

By the time UNPROFOR abandoned its responsibilities, the economy of the former communist state was in ruins; multiple cases of ethnic cleansing, mass murder, and rape had been confirmed; and almost a quarter of a million people had been killed. Sixty thousand NATO troops eventually had to be sent to forcefully maintain the peace and restore economic and social stability. In November 1995, Bosnia, Serbia, and Croatia signed the Dayton Accords to end the war in Bosnia – and divide the country into several new states.

Where did the UN go wrong in this case? Should it have sent more heavily armed troops with a more robust mandate, as was later done with NATO troops? (Figure 6.8)

Figure 6.8 SFOR, the Stabilization Force in Bosnia and Herzegovina was established in December 1996. It was a NATO-led multinational peacekeeping force tasked with upholding the Dayton Peace Agreement, which provided for the formal division of the former Yugoslavia.

Close Up 6.4 Peacekeeping in Rwanda: A UN failure?

In 1993–4 the central African country of Rwanda was party to one of the most atrocious genocides in recent history (Figure 6.9). Approximately eight hundred thousand ethnic Tutsis and moderate Hutus were murdered in only a hundred days. The weapons used were primitive – firearms, machetes, knives, hammers, screwdrivers, and clubs.

When the violence broke out, the UN Assistance Mission for Rwanda (UNAMIR) was in the country on a peacekeeping assignment, but it was not mandated to enforce peace between the Hutus and Tutsis and was unable to interfere directly in the fighting. The peacekeepers had been sent to Rwanda to monitor the 1993 Arusha Accords between the Hutu-dominated government and the Tutsi Rwanda Patriotic Front (RPF), an agreement designed to end a war that had persisted since 1990. When new violence erupted, General Romeo Dallaire, the Canadian commander of UNAMIR, asked for the "rules of engagement" for his mission to be changed and for more troops to be sent, but his requests were denied. Instead, the UN ordered all foreigners to be evacuated and ended the mission, leaving a humanitarian disaster in its wake. The movie *Hotel Rwanda* publicized the failure of the UN in Rwanda.

Who was at fault in this case? Should the UN have listened to General Dallaire, changed the mandate, and sent more troops?

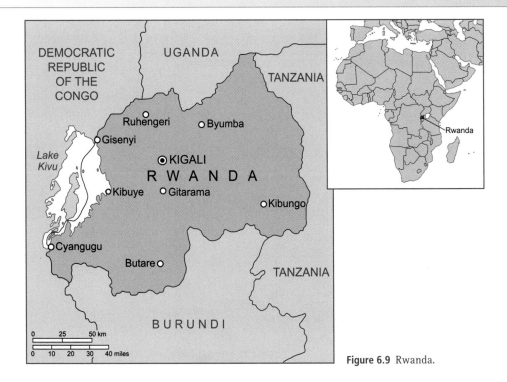

Figure 6.9 Rwanda.

Debate over United Nations humanitarian intervention

The post–Cold War period has witnessed a significant increase in the number of times that the United Nations has sanctioned the use of troops to intervene in a sovereign country *without* the state concerned having requested it. As we have seen, some of these interventions have been successful, but many have failed. In 2000, the Panel on United Nations Peace Operations issued the Brahimi Report, which concluded that "genocide in Rwanda went as far as it did in part because the international community failed to use or reinforce the operation then on the ground in that country to oppose obvious evil" and that in such cases "peacekeepers may not only be operationally justified in using force but morally compelled to do so."[6] In fact, peacekeepers themselves have sometimes been blamed for the failures. In the Congo mission, Pakistani peacekeepers accepted gold from a militia in return for letting them rearm their troops, and Indian peacekeepers reportedly traded arms for ivory. In Haiti there is evidence that poor sanitation facilities at a peacekeeping compound was responsible for the cholera outbreak that swept the island after the 2010 earthquake.

When should states intervene in the sovereignty of other states for moral or humanitarian reasons? This question has been debated for years – it is one of the serious hot-button issues that the UN has regularly confronted since the fall of the Berlin Wall in 1989. How serious do threats to human security have to be before action by the United Nations is justified? Is it *ever* acceptable to intervene in a country when there is a stable, recognized government? Should the intervention be by powerful individual states such as the United States and its allies, by regional bodies such as the African Union or the European Community, or only by the United Nations? What degree of force should they be authorized to use?

[6] http://www.un.org/peace/reports/peaceoperations/nd.

A recent doctrine called the responsibility to protect, or R2P, has been introduced to structure this debate.[7] Former UN secretary-general Kofi Annan linked the issues of state and human security together in his declaration that "not only are development, security and human rights all imperative; they also reinforce each other."[8] In 2004, the UN High-Level Panel on Threats, Challenges and Change adopted the term human security to promote the idea that the UN has a duty to protect not just states but also individuals. It expanded the list of possible reasons for intervention from military issues to economic, health, and environmental problems. In other words, the concept of security was expanded to include general threats to human survival and well-being, not just threats of death and injury. At a UN summit in 2005, more than 150 world leaders accepted the R2P principle– that states have a responsibility to protect people anywhere from genocide, ethnic cleansing, war crimes, and crimes against humanity.

The belief that not just states but also ordinary people and groups need to be protected has been increasingly accepted since the United Nations was founded. Yet this notion is contentious. It is ethically admirable to declare that massive violations of human rights are not acceptable and that something should be done in these situations, but when such violations occur *within* a state, who should intervene? The UN is based on the ironclad premise of state sovereignty, and that means that state borders are inviolable. If the UN agrees to intervene inside state borders, it can be accused of promoting the use of military force. Since the prevention of war is the main reason for the existence of the UN, a claim to the right of intervention does not seem logically consistent. The UN Charter does accept the need for self-defense, but it does not promote foreign intervention to correct wrongs inside countries.

The obligation of the UN to act in the face of human rights abuses, therefore, poses an unresolved dilemma, because intervention undermines the principle of sovereignty. Yet the UN is intervening more and more based on the doctrine that it has an obligation to protect people around the world. Some people believe the UN ought to act in all such cases, with little regard for whether this is even practically possible. Others believe that the institution should not interfere if a legitimate government exists – that is, that humanitarian interventions should never take precedence over the sovereignty of a legitimate state, even by a resolution of the Security Council.

Because of the controversy about accepting the moral principle of R2P, the 2009 General Assembly reconsidered the concept. While the UN secretary-general and staff continued to support the idea of moral duty as expressed in R2P, many critics insist that it is merely a justification for rich Western countries to intervene in the affairs of poor ones. Critics argue that the real difficulty in R2P is that since the Security Council is dominated by the veto-wielding major powers, those powers could use the concept to justify assaults on the sovereignty of smaller states, even though they would never accept international intervention in their own countries. Certainly, there is a neo-imperial aspect involved when rich and powerful countries use the United Nations to set standards for how poor and powerless countries govern their internal affairs and to back their demands with the threat of force. One such critic, the Libyan president of the General Assembly, Miguel d'Escoto Brockmann, renamed the principle as R2I, or the right to intervene. Some critics complained that it was just such a doctrine that President Bush used to justify his war on Iraq in 2003. Others claimed that Russia used the principle to justify its atrocities in the two breakaway regions of Georgia. Perhaps the real issue is not whether UN intervention should ever take place, but on what occasions and with what limitations.

---

[7] *The Responsibility to Protect: Report of the International Commission on Intervention and State Sovereignty* (Ottawa: International Development Research Centre, 2001).

[8] See Marie Joelle-Zohar, "Intervention, Prevention and the Responsibility to Protect," *International Journal* 60, no. 3 (Summer 2005), p. 725.

The two schools of thought were directly exposed in 2011, when the Security Council voted in Resolution 1973 to impose a no-fly zone over Libya and take "all necessary measures to protect civilians."[9] Although Brazil, China, Germany, India, and Russia abstained, the resolution was the clearest illustration yet of the emerging UN doctrine of R2P. If a state is failing to carry out its responsibility to protect its population – which the Libyan government was doing when it used excessive force to repress rebellion – then the Security Council can act under the UN Charter "to authorize action by member states," even though that action would normally fall under prohibitions against intervention in the affairs of a sovereign state. However, many critics interpreted this intervention as an effort to change the Libyan regime by military force. Even though the UN would not arm or actively assist the rebels, one UN diplomat told a reporter, "We're pushing the responsibility to protect civilians to extremes. When before did the UN support regime change of a member state?"[10]

Realists may see this UN policy of R2P as meddling in the affairs of sovereign countries and predict that it will, in the long term, run amok, whereas liberals and constructivists may believe that it is a groundbreaking example of the importance of a growing and vital global norm. However, its use will remain dependent on the realities of geopolitics, resources, and political determination (see "Rebellion, Civil War, and Humanitarian Intervention in North Africa and the Middle East" in Chapter 10).

Despite several instances of success in the field of war and peace, the UN has not become a world government, and it is very unlikely to do so. However, no institution has arisen to take its place, and one can be reasonably confident that none will for many decades. Despite its weaknesses, the UN remains the preeminent global institution in questions concerning peace and war. (For detailed discussions of the UN's role in wars, civil conflict, and terrorism, see Chapters 9, 10, and 11.)

The European Union

If the United Nations is the *global* institution with the widest reach, the most successful transnational *regional* organization is the European Union (EU). The EU, with its complex institutional architecture, is an extraordinary achievement. It has created a formidable economic bloc from Ireland to the Balkans, incorporating twenty-seven separate states and almost half a billion citizens in an integrated market and zone of peace. Despite multiple cultural and ethnic identities and twenty-three official languages, Europeans have a form of collective citizenship, a flag, and an anthem (which has no words, but the melody is that of Beethoven's Ninth Symphony, "Ode to Joy"). Citizens of all member states have the right to an EU passport and can vote in both local and EU elections, but they can vote only for the national legislature of their own country, not for leaders of other EU countries. In June 2009, Europeans voted for their European Parliament for the seventh time (Figure 6.10).

The European Union demonstrates how European states are attempting to adjust to the need to expand beyond their national contexts in a globalized political and economic environment without losing their sense of national identity. Liberal internationalists hail the EU's dramatic success as validating their argument that former enemy states can cooperate and develop peacefully even while guarding their local, national interests. European integration continues to develop in both economic and security fields. The EU is the world's leading exporter of industrial goods and services: some 20 percent of the world's exports emanate from the EU. Aside

---

[9] Clearly, the United States was a major backer of this proposal. On August 4, 2011, the Obama administration released the Presidential Directive on Mass Atrocities (PDA 10), which defined the prevention of atrocities as both "a core national security interest and core moral responsibility of the United States." http://www.whitehouse.gov/the-press-office 2011/08/04.

[10] Quoted in Nicolas Pelham, "Bogged Down in Libya," *New York Review of Books* (May 12–25, 2011), p. 15.

Figure 6.10 The European Union flag was adopted in 1983 by the European parliament as a symbol of European unity, solidarity, and harmony. The twelve golden stars arranged in a circle represent unity. *Source:* Photos.com.

from the obvious fact that Europe is a major player in world economics and trade, the EU member states are also extremely significant in international relations. The members contribute by far the greatest number of UN peacekeepers and international police officers. In fact, the vast majority of military personnel serving in NATO's International Security Assistance Force (ISAF) in Afghanistan today are Europeans.

The European Union and integration

The initial impetus for union came from the desire to develop Europe economically and to pool sovereignty to eliminate one of the causes of war, namely military competition among former warring European states. The early exponents of European integration, Jean Monnet and Robert Schumann, believed in a kind of "spillover" thesis in which economic cooperation would lead to cooperation in other fields such as security.[11] The initial step was taken in 1952, when the European Coal and Steel Community was constructed, bringing France, West Germany, Italy, Belgium, Luxembourg, and the Netherlands together into one economic sector in which coal resources and steel mills were harmonized.

The next step came in 1957, with the Treaty of Rome, which brought six European states together in a common market, with a level of economic integration that allowed the free movement of goods internally within the member countries. Restrictions were removed on cross-border trade, barriers to the movement of people and services were reduced, and a common transport and agricultural policy was established. Later, a customs union was added that provided a similar external tariff toward the rest of the world for all the countries in the system. Efforts of nonsignatory European countries to remain independent of the Treaty of Rome vanished when Britain joined the European Community in 1973 along with two other new members. The most expensive policy of the EU is the Common Agriculture Policy (CAP), which came into effect in 1962. It subsidizes all farmers in the European Union so that they are brought up to the level of farmers from the states with the highest subsidies. The CAP consumes

[11] There is an extensive literature on integration, or the process of shifting aspects of sovereignty from a state to regional or global institutions. See Ernest B. Haas, *Beyond the Nation-State: Functionalism and International Organization* (Stanford, CA: Stanford University Press, 1964); James A. Caporaso, *The European Union: Dilemmas of Regional Integration* (Cambridge, MA: Westview, 2000).

slightly less than half of the whole EU budget and is one of the most successful but contentious EU policies.

Two fundamental processes – known as widening and deepening – advanced the process of European integration. In 1986, twelve European states signed the Single European Act (SEA), which set a timetable for the removal of the last impediments for integrating Western Europe into a single economic market. In 1992, the Maastricht Treaty created a framework for the further deepening of integration, by creating not only the European Community but also the European Union of three pillars committed to greater political unification of Europe. The union of supranational institutions (known earlier as the European Community) formed the first pillar, and the two other pillars consisted of new forms of intergovernmental cooperation in foreign and home affairs. All nontariff barriers to the movement of goods, services, capital, and persons were removed, and foreign policy cooperation was established as a goal.

Three years later, Austria, Finland, and Sweden joined the European Union, and in May 2004, ten more new members were admitted – the Czech Republic, Slovakia, Estonia, Hungary, Latvia, Lithuania, Malta, Poland, Slovenia, and Cyprus. This made the EU the largest free-trade bloc in the world, but it also added a number of poorer countries to the association and began to compound difficulties in economic policy making. Bulgaria and Romania joined in 2007, bringing the number of member states to twenty-seven. Croatia and Macedonia are slated to join soon, and negotiations continue with Turkey. However, the admission of Turkey will be extremely difficult because of its large Muslim majority and huge underprivileged class.

The decision-making powers of the EU are based in an "institutional triangle" consisting of the European Council (which brings together the heads of each member state and sets the broad agenda for the EU) and the Council of Ministers (ministers from each member state representing particular policy fields); the members of the European Parliament (MEPs; as of 2013 there are 754, directly elected by voters in each country for a five-year term; in certain fields, MEPs share legislation determination with the Council); and the Commission, the permanent bureaucracy of some twenty-five thousand Eurocrats that initiates, administers, and oversees EU legislation and policies and is led by twenty-seven commissioners, one from each state, serving five-year terms (Figure 6.11). The EU budget exceeds $150 billion annually. The revenues come from import duties, a 1.4 percent sales tax, and a portion of the gross national product of each member state. As the member states have "pooled" their sovereignty on some questions but not others, the Council operates on some issues on a basis of unanimity and on other issues on a "qualified majority" vote, in which the largest countries have the most weight.

The Maastricht Treaty also embraced a timetable for economic and monetary union (EMU) with two institutions – a common bank and a common currency. The European Central Bank (ECB) replaced the domestic central banks in 1999 at the same time as the Community adopted a single currency, the euro. In 2002, the currencies of the participating members were "fixed" at a specific rate in relationship to the euro, which replaced the deutsche mark, franc, lira, and other national currencies of fifteen members of the Union. Britain, Denmark, and Sweden continue to opt out of the common currency, and the newest members have not yet fulfilled the conditions to join.[12] On January 1, 2011, Estonia became the seventeenth member to adopt the euro. The common currency in effect gives the European Central Bank control over monetary but not fiscal policy, as the EU cannot control the taxation and expenditure policies of its member states. All twenty-seven members of the EU, with the exceptions of Britain, Cyprus, Bulgaria, and Romania, also belong to the Schengen arrangement, which allows easy migration within the territory of the European Union, with no internal border controls.

[12] David Marsh, *The Euro: The Politics of the New Global Currency* (New Haven, CT: Yale University Press, 2009).

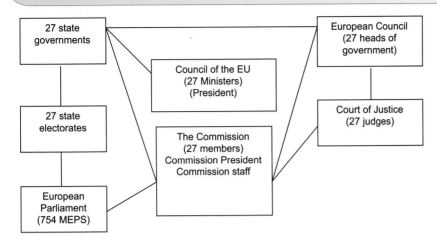

Figure 6.11 Institutions of the European Union, 2013.

European Council
The executive decision-making body decides on policy and directs the Commission. Each member state sends one minister to the Council. The president holds office for 2½ years.

The Commission
This is the executive body as its role is to execute decisions taken by the Council; however, it also prepares proposals for the decision by the Council and the Parliament. This body consists of 27 commissioners serving five-year terms. The Commission is supported by an enormous bureaucracy.

The European Parliament
There are 736 members of the European Parliament (MEPs), distributed among the member states in rough proportion to population. Different national electoral systems are used to elect them for five-year terms.

The Court of Justice
There are 27 judges on the Court of Justice, appointed for staggered six-year terms. The Court is designed to be the ultimate judge on the application of EU law.

The European Union and reform

Although the EU created a central bank and a single currency, the march to political integration has not been as quick as many "good Europeanists" would have liked. Nevertheless, it has made great strides. It has completed its internal market, abolishing nontariff barriers and providing freedom for the movement of all goods, services, capital, and people within Europe. It enforces its decisions through the European Court of Justice, the most powerful interstate court in existence (discussed earlier). In 2003, the EU adopted the Nice Treaty, which enacted various reforms in the Commission and Council and expanded the use of majority voting. Instead of relying on the earlier unanimity principle for all decisions, the Council adopted a system whereby the largest states get more votes than the smaller ones, and decisions are taken on some issues if they receive the vote of a majority of all members – 72.3 percent of all possible votes and the agreement of states representing 62 percent of the European Union's population.

Despite the fact that the EU and leaders of every member state supported it, a 2005 proposal to continue the process of European integration by adopting a constitutional treaty for the EU was defeated by referenda in France and the Netherlands, two of the founding members and original signatories of the Treaty of Rome. The defeat challenged the legitimacy of the European Union and illustrated how far removed Europe's elites seemed to be from the people. The new constitution would have gone further than just consolidating earlier treaties. It would have attempted once again to "deepen" the integration of European countries toward a "superstate," without eliminating individual state sovereignty. It would also have redistributed power within the European Union, including strengthening the EU's control over common foreign and military policies and creating two new posts: president of the Council and an EU foreign minister. During the referendum campaign complaints against the Union included disapproval of bureaucratic rules emanating from Brussels; dislike of the increased number of members in the EU; concern that further immigrants from North Africa and elsewhere might gain admittance to the European Union; and a general but persistent worry that Turkey, a relatively poor Muslim state, might be admitted if the Union continued its march toward a "deeper" Europe or perhaps even a federal union.

In 2007, the EU tried again to strengthen economic and political integration. This time it did not attempt to write a proper constitution, but it put forward the Lisbon Treaty. This proposal watered down some of the provisions of the earlier proposed constitution but still included a full-time president for the European Council with a two-and-a-half year term and a high representative (foreign minister), as well as an increase in "qualified" as opposed to "majority" votes in the European Council. To be accepted, the treaty had to be ratified by all twenty-seven member states. Ireland was the only member to put the treaty to a referendum. When the Irish citizenry voted it down in 2008, the EU leadership faced the prospect of an unreformed set of institutions. However, in 2009 the Irish voted a second time, this time approving the new treaty.

The treaty came into force in December 2009. While it includes both a new permanent president of the European Council and a high representative, their significance is circumscribed by the power of member states. As Catherine Ashton, the European Union's new foreign policy chief put it, "I am not

trying to be the equivalent of the UK foreign secretary for all Europe."[13] In the meantime, an economic turndown made the search for more integration even more difficult, as member-states had to cope with uneven levels of economic development and could not agree on how to combat the slump. The problems included protectionist pressures in some of the countries and severe economic difficulties for more profligate members. Under these pressures, discussion of further integration came to a standstill. Greece eventually had to be bailed out several times under harsh conditions, and a three-year plan had to be put in place by the European Union for other debt-laden members, most of it financed by Germany. The Greek political system faltered in mid-2012 when citizens rejected severe austerity proposals. The EU itself teetered on the verge of collapse. (This issue is covered in Chapter 12.)

The European Union and sovereignty

In the grand debates about what the "new Europe" is, the word *sovereignty* is loosely bandied about, sometimes meaning the "independence" of states in the Union and sometimes referring to a member state's "rights" to exercise or refrain from exercising certain lawmaking powers. Perhaps the most often voiced controversy concerns whether "sovereignty" is actually being "transferred" to the EU as a new state actor or is merely being "pooled." This is the essential argument of intergovernmentalists, who argue that the twenty-seven states have not ceded any final authority to the EU.[14] The supranationalists, in contrast, think that Europe should deepen its integration and head toward a type of federation similar to that of the United States or Canada.[15] To

[13] *The Economist*, February 13, 2010.

[14] See Robert O. Keohane and Stanley Hoffman, eds., *The New European Community: Decision-Making and Institutional Change* (Boulder, CO: Westview, 1991), p. 277.

[15] There is much more variety to federalism than often ascribed to it in the European and international relations literature. There are more than fifteen times more unitary states than federal states in the world. However, although there are some twenty-three federal states, they contain more than 40 percent of the world's population, and most have large territories. In a

date, however, the constitutional referenda indicate popular skepticism about such federation as the EU's ultimate goal.

There are many justifications for both the supranational and the intergovernmental arguments. Analogies with the history of federalism in other countries, however, are misleading. Sometimes federations have been created by a gradual assumption of power by the center, and sometimes they have been initiated by agreement of relatively equal units. Perhaps federalism in the European context should be conceived of not as a noun denoting a rather rigid legal construction but as a verb denoting constant renovation. If it has to be used as a noun, perhaps it should be understood as the result of political experiences in "shared learning" rather than simply a formal legal framework.

The historical evolution of the European Union provides an example of the complications entailed in integrating sovereign states. In some fields of the EU, graded sovereignty exists. In some it does not. In the integrated areas, the EU may actually legislate against the wishes of some member states. Moreover, since 1963 the European Court of Justice has moved the EU toward shared authority in even more fields. As summarized by Stephen Krasner, four points from the Court's history make this direction clear:

1. Acceptance of the doctrine of direct effect (i.e., EU legal norms may have direct effect in member states)

2. Acceptance of the doctrine of supremacy (which the Court began to uphold in 1965), which

asserts that Union law trumps domestic law and that individuals can bring domestic cases based on community law to the Court

3. Acceptance of the 1971 doctrine of implied powers, in which the Court held that the EU as a whole had the right to make and sign treaties because otherwise it could not carry out the tasks assigned in a treaty (e.g., in the field of trade, individual states cannot take unilateral action, as the EU holds exclusive power)

4. A ruling that the Court can review any measures having to do with human rights[16]

In contradiction to this apparent evolution toward increased political integration, the German Constitutional Court ruled in 1993 that the EU is not a federal state but a confederation of states (*Staatenverbund*). The German Court said that it alone could decide whether the EU had exceeded the "sovereign rights" of member states. But is this not the prerogative of the European Court? Joseph Weiler tries to get around this problem by saying that the EU accepts "constitutional tolerance": national constitutions coexist with an overarching treaty, which can impose rules and conditions.[17] But what type of state is that? Is it a federation? In June 2009, the German Constitutional Court counseled the government to pause its search for more European integration. The Court asked the Berlin Parliament to pass a new law giving it more power over the EU, declaring that the EU is not a democratic state and the EU Parliament is not a proper legislature because "no uniform people" could "express its majority will in an effective manner."[18]

For supranationalists, the effort to adopt a constitution was to have been a step toward legitimizing the EU by further connecting it with the European people. Certainly, the result would not be a homogeneous nation-state, but it could be in

---

federal system the legal powers are divided between a central government and regional governments in such a way that each level of government retains some kind of activities on which it makes final decisions. Neither level of government owes its authority to the other. Both federal and provincial legislatures may make laws that directly affect the citizens. Each level of government has more or less complete authority over some specific spheres of activity, while there may be a degree of overlapping jurisdiction on others. For a discussion of types of federal systems and comparisons see Robert J. Jackson and Doreen Jackson, *Politics in Canada*, 7th ed. (Scarborough, ON: Prentice Hall, 2009).

---

[16] Stephen Krasner, *Sovereignty: Organized Hypocracy* (Princeton: Princeton University Press, 1999) pp. 235–37.

[17] J. H. H. Weiler, *The Constitution of Europe* (Cambridge: Cambridge University Press, 1999).

[18] *The Economist*, July 25, 2009.

line with the federal constitutional design of settler states like Canada, Australia, and the United States. Detractors believe that not much has changed. Intergovermentalists do not want further integration, and they particularly do not want European states to give up their control of foreign and defense policies. The British government especially does not like the "*f*" word, and in this it is joined by a number of other states. But even the British have to admit that the speed of change in the EU during the past few years has been phenomenal. Critics do not object to the factual arguments of supranationalists that there has been an expansion of rules in the common market, justice and home affairs, qualified voting, a large expansion of members, and acceptance of the principles of subsidiarity. While there may not yet be a shared national identity, the EU is increasingly sharing policies and objectives and, on occasion, increasing its joint actions. It may not be a superstate, but clearly, the EU is considerably more than a *confederation* of equal states.[19] Is that a pooling or a gradation of sovereignty? The debt crisis of 2012 brought this issue to the forefront with discussions for a closer federation at one extreme and abandoning the EU as untenable at the other (see Chapter 12).

Foreign policy

The EU is often ridiculed as having lofty foreign policy ambitions but little consensus on action. Its ability to act in concert has been slow in coming, but there has been some movement in that direction.[20] Even the expression "common foreign policy" in the Common Foreign and Security Policy (CFSP) was added only in the 1992 Maastricht Treaty, many decades after the signing of the 1957 Treaty of Rome. Not until May 1999 did the Treaty of Amsterdam come into force, allowing the appointment of a foreign policy envoy for the CFSP and indicating a desire to move forward in unified conflict prevention and crisis management. The position supplemented that of the EU external relations commissioner. At the same time, the EU agreed to implement the so-called Petersberg tasks of strengthening crisis management for peacekeeping and security.

We have noted that the 2009 Lisbon Treaty included a new position of high representative. This is a difficult role, as state unanimity still remains the rule in EU decision making on foreign policy. However, some recent innovations in foreign policy have been startling. Examples include an agreement with NATO on combined joint task forces, which led to the goal of creating a European force of sixty thousand troops for rapid action (albeit the same troops as NATO uses), and an EU agreement on common strategies for both Russia and the Mediterranean region.[21] As well, the EU has developed coherent policies on two pressing issues, namely the ending of the embargo on military procurement for China (although national interests are protected, as the "code of conduct" is to be interpreted by national governments, not the EU) and on efforts to prevent Iran from developing nuclear weapons. The EU played a major role defending democracy in the Ukraine and held out an implicit offer of eventual membership in the European Union. There have been many recent examples of European action – police and military missions in Bosnia and Herzegovina, in the former Yugoslavian republic of Macedonia, and even in the Democratic Republic of Congo.

European foreign policy making remains complex, however. Austria, Finland, Ireland, and Sweden are not in NATO, while the other twenty-three EU members are. In contrast, some NATO members,

---

[19] See Jackson and Jackson, *Politics in Canada*, chapters 10 and 11.

[20] See Paul Cornish and Geoffrey Edwards, "Beyond the EU/NATO Dichotomy," *International Affairs* 77, no. 3 (2001), pp. 587–603; Michael E. Smith, "Institutionalization, Policy Adaptation and European Foreign Policy Cooperation," *European Journal of International Relations* 10, no. 1 (2004), pp. 95–136.

[21] In September 2004 a decision was made to set up a European Gendarmerie Force (EGF), of nine hundred personnel, whose function was to contribute police for conflict prevention, peacekeeping, and peace enforcement operations.

namely Norway, Turkey, Canada, and the United States, are not part of the European Union. Even within the EU some members are not as favorable to a European defense capability as are others. The United Kingdom, Denmark, and perhaps Poland lean more toward NATO than toward the supranationalists' position on security questions in the EU. But as former German chancellor Gerhard Schröder put it, "NATO is no longer the primary venue where transatlantic partners discuss and co-ordinate strategies,"[22] He means the EU is!

The traditional concept of sovereignty as meaning indivisibility of power and state autonomy perhaps needs revision in light of Europe's success with integration. The evolving nature of EU security and defense policies and actions do not fit easily within the neat and tidy theories of academicians or the zero-sum perspectives of realists. Are they supranationalist or intergovernmentalist? They are neither. Perhaps the Belgian surrealist artist René Magritte gave us a glimpse of the answer when he described his masterful painting of a beautiful pipe with the title *Ceci n'est pas une pipe* ("This is not a pipe.").

Regional and functional IGOs

There are many intergovernmental organizations (IGOs) other than the UN and EU. Many are regional in nature but have widespread importance and contribute to forms of global governance. Most geographical areas have important international organizations, albeit with less centralized authority than the EU. The Organization for Security and Cooperation in Europe (OSCE) has both regional and functional characteristics. It has thirty democratic members in Europe and elsewhere devoted to economic development and progress.

22 *The Economist*, February 26, 2005.

Another good example is the Organization for Petroleum Exporting Countries (OPEC), which brings together major oil-producing states to set production rules in order to protect the production and price of oil.

Regional IGOs exist on every continent. The Organization of American States (OAS) joins all states of North and South America (except Cuba) for discussions and action on various topics. The African Union (AU) and the Association of Southeast Asian Nations (ASEAN) are examples of organizations that bring states of their respective regions together in pursuit of common goals and interests. Asia has the Southeast Treaty Association (SEATO). Australia, New Zealand, and the United States are bound together in the ANZUS Pact.

Nonregional international actors are also significant. For example, the British Commonwealth, which consists of former members of the British Empire, has fifty-one members scattered throughout the world. The League of Arab States brings together Arab states in support of Arab causes and issues, and the Gulf Cooperation Council supports joint causes. The Organization of the Islamic Conference (OIC), an intergovernmental organization similar to the Commonwealth, is one of the largest intergovernmental organizations after the United Nations, with a membership of fifty-seven states on four continents. The organization serves as the collective voice of the Muslim world and attempts to safeguard and protect its interests. Its latest charter, adopted in Dakar, Senegal, in 2008, lays down the objectives and principles of the organization and establishes fundamental purposes to strengthen the solidarity and cooperation among member states. The organization has the task of galvanizing the Ummah (nation or community) into a unified body and actively represents Muslims "by espousing all causes close to the hearts" of more than 1.5 billion Muslims around the world (see Chapter 8).

Conclusion: Prospects for global governance

Is a new system of global governance emerging? This chapter clearly shows that in terms of international institutions, the global governance glass is less than half full. There is no world government, even though globalization is proceeding rapidly in many economic and social fields. States continue to be the dominant actors in world affairs, but at the same time their leaders perceive a need for the continued enhancement of international law, world institutions and regimes, and mechanisms that enhance global cooperation and problem solving. Hand in hand with the elements of global governance found in this chapter there is also a developing economic architecture (discussed in Chapters 12 and 13) and, to a much lesser degree, a security architecture (as found in Chapters 9–11).

International law continues to evolve, with customary procedures being constantly enhanced or replaced by treaties and formalized decision making. Significant work is being done by the International Court of Justice, and the seminal decisions of the International Criminal Court are dramatically affecting international criminal law, but these organizations are limited by state sovereignty – as they should be until global governance is achieved. The end of World War II brought a number of new international organizations, the most important of which is the United Nations, with its goals of preventing war and enhancing peace and development. Nearly all the states of the world belong to the UN, and it is active as a collective security organization around the globe. It has spun out many other multilateral organizations such the World Health Organization and Food and Agriculture Organization. In 2004 the UN even adopted the term *human security* to promote the idea that it has a duty to protect not just states but also individuals. This led to the principle of R2P, that states have a responsibility to protect people anywhere from genocide, ethnic cleansing, war crimes, and crimes against humanity. As laudable as this highly moral goal is, it conflicts with the premise of state sovereignty on which the UN is based. In spite of its many beneficial services, the organizational structure of the UN has many flaws that limit its activities. It is in need of drastic institutional reform, but this is extremely difficult to achieve. Despite it inclusivity and dramatic activities, the United Nations has not and will not become a global government.

There is a host of other IGOs, such as the Organization of American States and the Organization for Security and Cooperation in Europe, which provide elements of global governance but do so on a regional basis. However, states still are the primary instruments of governing, and their leaders accept or reject the decisions of such intergovernmental institutions as it suits them. The most successful transnational regional organization is the European Union, which has widened and deepened so much that it includes a common bank, a common currency, and the European Court of Justice – the most powerful interstate court in existence. Controversy continues over whether sovereignty is being transferred by the twenty-seven European states to the EU as a new state actor or is merely being pooled. So far, there is popular skepticism about the EU federating on the scale of Canada or the United States.

Realists tend to undervalue the growth of international law and global institutions such as the United Nations and European Union. Constructivists and liberals perhaps tend to weigh the significance of such institutions in global governance too highly by comparison with the power of states. Balance from scholars of all persuasions would be welcomed. In the next chapter we examine how nongovernmental actors and mass communications are also moving toward more global interaction, and in Chapter 8 we consider the role of social identity, especially religion, in this process.

Select bibliography

Ash, Timothy Garton, *Free World: America, Europe and the Surprising Future of the West* (London: Random House, 2004).

Bellamy, Alex J., et al., *Understanding Peacekeeping* (London: Polity, 2004).

Doyle, Michael W., and Nicholas Sambanis, *Making Wars and Building Peace: United Nations Peace Operations* (Princeton, NJ: Princeton University Press, 2006).

Eichler, Maya, *Militarized Men* (Palo Alto, CA: Stanford University Press, 2011).

Finlay, Trevor, *The Use of Force in UN Peace Operations* (Oxford: Oxford University Press, 2003).

Goldsmith, Jack L., and Eric A. Posner, *The Limits of International Law* (Oxford: Oxford University Press, 2005).

Ikenberry, G. John, *Liberal Leviathan: The Origins, Crisis, and Transformation of the American World Order* (Princeton, NJ: Princeton University Press, 2011).

Jolly, Richard, Louis Emmerij, and Thomas G. Weiss, *UN Ideas That Changed the World* (Bloomington: Indiana University Press, 2009).

Jolly, Richard, and Eric A. Posner, *The Limits of International Law* (Oxford: Oxford University Press, 2005).

Kennedy, Paul, *The Parliament of Man* (New York: Random House, 2006).

Kupchan, Charles A., *How Enemies Become Friends: The Sources of Stable Peace* (Princeton, NJ: Princeton University Press, 2011).

Leonard, Mark, *Why Europe Will Run the Twenty-First Century* (London: Fourth Estate, 2004).

Love, Maryann Cusimano, *Beyond Sovereignty: Issues for a Global Agenda*, 4th ed. (Florence, KY: Wadsworth, 2010).

Posner, Eric A., *The Perils of Global Legalism* (Chicago: University of Chicago Press, 2010).

Reid, T. R., *The United States of Europe: The New Superpower and the End of American Supremacy* (London: Penguin, 2004).

Rifkin, Jeremy, *The European Dream: How Europe's Vision of the Future in Quietly Eclipsing the American Dream* (London: Tarch/Penguin, 2004).

Sarotte, Mary Elise, *The Struggle to Create Post–Cold War Europe* (Princeton, NJ: Princeton University Press, 1989).

Simmons, Beth A., and Richard H. Steingberg, eds., *International Law and International Relations* (Cambridge: Cambridge University Press, 2006).

Smith, Karen E., *European Union Foreign Policy in a Changing World* (Cambridge, UK: Polity, 2008).

Weiler, H. H., *The Constitution of Europe* (Cambridge: Cambridge University Press, 1999).

Whitworth, Sandra, *Men, Militarism and UN Peacekeeping: A Gendered Analysis* (Boulder, CO: Lynne Rienner, 2004).

7

Politics beyond the state I

Nonstate actors, mass communications, and social networking

The two previous chapters focus on two major types of actors on the global stage – states and intergovernmental institutions. But these are not now, and never have been, the *only* players. There are others vying for attention – actors that are not confined by states and that often challenge states rather than support them. In this chapter, therefore, we move beyond states and their institutional creations, such as the United Nations and the European Union, to examine other significant nonstate participants in global politics.

Around the world today people are mobilizing across state borders to bring about political and social change, pressuring governments to help change social norms. They are forging new connections and organizing new institutions with novel interests. These are *transnational actors*, sometimes known as *transnational advocacy groups* (TANs), and their activities across state borders are known as *transnational relations*. TANs try to exert new pressure on states to alter their interests and change social norms. To do this, they produce new knowledge about issues, frame issues to mobilize popular support, or provide social pressure for policy change. They facilitate cooperation among states by providing information about international agreements and monitoring compliance. Their effectiveness is influenced by domestic political institutions, and they can mobilize social pressures more effectively in democracies than in autocracies. Transnational actors include both legal and illegal institutions that are involved in many types of behavior. Who are they, and what do they do?

Nonstate actors include nongovernmental organizations (NGOs). These *are nonprofit actors* – such as charities and humanitarian agencies that operate across borders. They also include multinational corporations (MNCs), which are *for-profit* international business corporations. Both these types of actors pursue their own objectives and strategies relatively free from state coercion or influence, and both are increasingly recognized as playing major roles in global politics. NGOs come in many diverse forms, ranging from advocacy groups such as Amnesty International, which supports a broad range of humanitarian causes, to criminal enterprises such as drug cartels and terrorist groups such as al-Qaeda that seek to impose a political agenda on others. (Terrorist groups, which may also be classified as international actors, are examined separately in Chapter 11.) Frequently, there are public concerns about whether MNCs and NGOs are good or bad. What are the benefits and drawbacks of their activities?

In this chapter we also consider modern mass communication technologies and social networks as nonstate actors. They create information flows across state borders and increasingly challenge the ability of states to control international politics. These technologies, including the Internet and social networking forums, have enhanced the transnational roles of individuals and the mass media in global politics. They connect people and international organizations around the world, and together they increase the interactions among citizens, creating a new form of independence from states in global affairs. For this reason some states are obsessed with filtering and controlling the Internet and prevent the dissemination of opposing views. Today tablets and smart phones are being used to record, document, and transmit internationally information and photos of atrocities that governments are trying to cover up. Table 7.1 summarizes the various types of nonstate actors.

In the next chapter we examine the contributions of nations, ethnicity, and religion to politics beyond the state. Their affiliated organizations and ideas also flow across state borders and can have a major impact on domestic and global politics.

Table 7.1 Nonstate actors and types of organization

Type of Organization	Membership	Examples
Intergovernmental organizations (IGOs)	States	United Nations, NATO
Nongovernmental organizations (NGOs) (including illegal organizations)	Individuals and groups	Amnesty International, Red Cross Drug cartels, al-Qaeda
Multinational corporations (MNCs)	Companies that operate across borders	British Petroleum, Wal-Mart
Mass media and Internet	Companies, networks, and individuals	CNN, Al Jazeera, Google, Facebook, Twitter

Nongovernmental organizations (NGOs)

Nongovernmental organizations (NGOs) carry out activities across state borders and take part in global activities such as transnational advocacy campaigns. The broad NGO category covers a gamut of international groups such as Amnesty International, the Sierra Club, Friends of the Earth, Greenpeace, Human Rights Watch, and Save the Children. These are private institutions that consist of individuals or associations linked by a common purpose – to help people, without regard for state borders. They have a strong attraction for idealistic volunteers, and their numbers are growing.

NGOs exist in practically every field of human interest. Some originate from domestic interest groups or grassroots advocacy groups at the state level. Like their national counterparts, these groups try to advance their ideas by organizing conferences; soliciting members and funding; and co-opting media, state officials, and politicians. As their name signifies, they are private actors and can operate locally, nationally, and/or globally. To achieve their goals, they collect and disseminate information, backing this up with expertise about particular issues, trained personnel, and reputation. Organizations such as the International Committee of the Red Cross, have millions of members, are admired by almost all states and do immense good; others are tiny groups of like-minded individuals who support narrower, more specific causes. Although NGOs may receive funding from governments, they are not directly tied to states or the business community. Many, however, receive tax-free status from their governments and, thus, are more indirectly tied to government largesse than they frequently admit.

The number of NGOs accredited by the United Nations continues to rise. In 2012, the *Year Book of International Organizations*, supported by the United Nations Economic and Social Council (ECOSOC), tabulated that there were 66,398 civil society organizations around the world, of which about half were not-for-profit organizations.[1] Greater transparency in international politics, a product of the global information age, has sparked immense growth and involvement in such groups by allowing them to communicate easily with their constituencies and build coalitions with other associations, IGOs, and governments.

NGOs provide an outlet for individuals around the world to take collective action in the face of shared problems. Many of the issues that NGOs address cannot be resolved by states alone but require wider cooperation. Since the capacities of governments to provide aid for humanitarian and other global crises are limited by funds and political bargaining, nongovernmental organizations play a role in offsetting some of the most devastating effects of natural disasters and other global humanitarian challenges – such as those caused by tsunamis, earthquakes, and war. NGOs publicize causes, condemn abuses, and pressure governments to act. They collect and distribute billions of dollars in aid and support, some from private sources, but much of it from governments and intergovernmental agencies such as the World Bank.

The functions of NGOs are diverse. In general terms, they are issue-oriented groups promoting causes such as human rights, humanitarian and environmental concerns, peace, justice, and women's rights. They form broad social movements or transnational advocacy groups (TANs), which include individuals or organizations that share the basic principles, normative objectives, information, and actions of the network and act across state borders.[2] They connect people, mobilize them internationally, and then attempt to alter state or IGO behavior by the way they discuss or frame issues.[3] They may also be involved in curing diseases, assisting in disaster relief, or alleviating suffering in civil wars. Their direct contributions to easing human misery enhance their reputation and, thus, the legitimacy of their political advocacy activities.

International human rights and other nongovernmental organizations use several avenues to provide effective assistance to civilians in need. Usually, governments invite NGOs to provide aid for afflicted areas. In the wake of large-scale natural disasters, for example, the governments of some stricken countries do not have the resources or capacity to provide adequate relief to their citizens. Nongovernmental organizations may well be in a position to help, since they possess professional expertise, have confirmed relationships with intergovernmental organizations, and have acquired special knowledge of local needs and customs. These organizations then raise funds from individual donors, groups, or companies to implement programs on the ground.

Since international aid groups are not affiliated with any particular government or state, their presence and efforts normally do not pose a threat to state sovereignty in the same way that foreign state intervention does. This gives some NGOs the ability to work in ways and in places where governments cannot. The 2005 Hurricane Katrina on the southern coast of the United States; the 2008 earthquake in Chengdu, China; and the 2011 earthquake and tsunami in Japan all required massive assistance

[1] *Yearbook of International Organizations* (Brussels: Union of International Associations, 2009/2010).

[2] See Margaret E. Keck and Kathryn Sikkink, *Activists beyond Borders: Advocacy Networks in International Politics* (Ithaca, NY: Cornell University Press, 1998).

[3] Miles Kahler, ed., *Networked Politics: Agency, Power, and Governance* (Ithaca, NY: Cornell University Press, 2009).

from international aid organizations such as the International Federation of the Red Cross. Such organizations are designed to respond quickly and thoroughly to disasters worldwide with resources that a devastated area may lack (see Chapters 15 and 16).

Some humanitarian challenges are so sensitive that afflicted states do not want other governments or intergovernmental bodies to help them, a fact that encourages NGOs to act independently of even their own governments. An example of the problems this can create is ongoing in Afghanistan, where NATO and its allies want aid and development NGOs to assist them with their pacification policies, but aid workers fear that doing so will bring them under suspicion of the Taliban (see Chapter 10). They do not want the military to know exactly what they are doing or to have to tell them about any enemy activities that they happen to learn about. They claim the status of political neutrality, yet they often need the help of military security forces for transportation or for delivering aid and supplies, so their neutrality is often not backed by self-reliance. This conundrum frustrates both NGOs and militaries in many civil conflict situations.

A pertinent case occurred in relation to the killing of Osama bin Laden in Abbotabad, Pakistan, in 2011. Shakil Afridi, a doctor who allegedly gave secret information to the American CIA to help identify bin Laden, also worked for international aid agencies, especially Save the Children. After bin Laden was killed, Pakistan put restrictions on Save the Children, compromising the agency's multimillion-dollar aid operations in the country. To some Americans Afridi is a hero, but to others he spied for the CIA and, therefore, is reviled. To many Pakistanis he is a traitor.

Violations of widely accepted human rights standards have raised international concern, particularly since the adoption of the Universal Declaration of Human Rights in 1948 and the establishment of the International Criminal Court in 1998. Spurred by high-profile crises such as the genocide

of the European Jewish population in the Holocaust and ethnic cleansing in the former Yugoslavia and Rwanda, nongovernmental organizations have increasingly found ways to transcend state boundaries to provide humanitarian assistance when they deem it necessary or to withhold aid from local governments when they do not. However, NGO triumphs in this field are well publicized, but their failures are not.

Some NGOs have been remarkably successful in improving the lives of people around the world. The Red Cross was established in the middle of the 19th century by a Swiss, Henry Dunant, after he saw thousands of wounded soldiers abandoned on a battlefield. The organization he formed now provides worldwide humanitarian aid in disasters caused by natural or human causes. It is often said that the Red Cross is the first organization to arrive in a crisis and the last to leave. Oxfam, too, is vital in providing aid to countries that require urgent disaster relief. It was active, for example, in Yugoslavia, the Congo, Libya, Rwanda, Sudan, and Syria when they descended into civil war. Other NGOs include Greenpeace (Figure 7.1), which fought for and won international laws to limit whaling, and the Sierra Club and Friends of the Earth, which works to keep the world's focus on the degradation of the environment and the implications of climate change. Amnesty International (Close Up 7.1) and Human Rights Watch focus public attention on alleged human rights violations around the world, including torture in Iraq and Guantánamo Bay, the plight of dissidents in China, and refugees from Libya and Syria. The International Olympics Committee organizes the world's summer and winter Olympics.

In the 1970s NGOs began to achieve wide public recognition for their work, and their prestige has increased. In 1998, the Campaign to Ban Landmines (ICBM), led by Nobel Peace Prize winner Jodi Williams and aided by 1,400 NGOs in ninety countries, helped persuade a majority of governments to outlaw antipersonnel land mines. Up to twenty thousand people are estimated to die or be wounded by land mines annually around the world. The 1999

Figure 7.1 The NGO Greenpeace has been campaigning against environmental degradation since 1971, and has a tradition of bearing witness in a nonviolent manner. Its activities are hotly contested by groups such as sealers, whose livelihoods have been seriously affected by its activities. *Source:* Corbis.

Box 7.1 **Contributions and criticisms of NGOs**

Positive Contributions of NGOs

- Collect funds and distribute aid to improve the lives of people around the world
- Provide outlets for collective action in response to shared problems
- Publicize causes and condemn abuses
- Pressure governments to act
- Act independently in sensitive areas where some governments and intergovernmental institutions are unwelcome

Criticisms of NGOS

- May contribute to weakening state sovereignty
- Policy positions may be arbitrary, based on cultural bias and ethnocentrism
- Possess no power to enforce their policy positions in global politics
- Goals may conflict with those of the very state they are trying to help, or with IGO activities
- May spend funds mostly on self-promotion

---

treaty banned the use, production, stockpiling, and sale of these deadly mines, but the agreement was weakened by the lack of support of by more than forty countries, including China, Russia, and the United States – those countries with the largest number of these weapons.[4] Another example of the growing recognition of NGOs came in 1999 when Médecins sans Frontières (Doctors without Borders) was awarded the Nobel Prize for supplying health and humanitarian work to people in need during natural disasters and political violence.

There are also negative aspects to NGO activities in developing states. Activism may contribute to a gradual weakening of state sovereignty. While most aid is carried out with the agreement or approval of the host state, it becomes extremely controversial when it is not. Sometimes NGOs provide support for humanitarian and political causes, even when such actions are *against* the wishes of official state leaders. Many critics also argue that human rights standards (usually developed by nongovernmental agencies) are arbitrary and based on Western cultural biases and ethnocentrism. For example,

---

[4] The Ottawa Convention is officially called the Convention on the Prohibition of the Use, Stockpiling, Production and Transfer Anti-Personnel Mines and on Their Destruction.

the UN Security Council is criticized for upholding a predominantly Western worldview, and many humanitarian organizations work under UN auspices and in collaboration with its agencies. This argument surfaces particularly when humanitarian aid is forced on a weak state because of the moral perceptions of the international community. In these instances, nongovernmental organizations may be subject to the limitations and even dangers of domestic and local interference. The ongoing crisis caused by migrants from the Democratic People's Republic of Korea escaping into northeastern China, for example, is hotly debated because neither the government of the DPRK nor the Chinese government will allow nongovernmental intervention to help in what activists called a refugee "crisis of unprecedented proportions." This example illustrates what many consider a major weakness of NGOs – that they do not have the power to enforce their ethical positions in global politics. However, since they are unelected and unaccountable to anyone but their own membership, perhaps that is reasonable.

In any case, the goals of NGOs often conflict with those of local or state authorities, and sometimes they even clash with those of other NGOs or even IGOs. NGOs may also have difficulty upholding their principles while trying to raise funds to keep their organizations functioning. These two endeavors may on occasion be at cross-purposes, leading some critics to contend that the real purpose of NGOs is self-promotion and the continued success of the organizations themselves. Of course, advocates respond that the organizations need to remain financially solvent if they are to pursue their principled goals.

Multinational corporations

Multinational corporations (MNCs), also called transnational corporations (TNCs), are businesses that extend across state borders, with subsidiaries (wholly or substantially owned companies) and employees in one or more other states. While they

---

Close Up 7.1 **Amnesty International (AI)**

> It is better to light a candle than curse in the darkness.
>
> – AI motto

Amnesty International is a well-known, non-profit, nongovernmental organization with a long history in the field of human rights. The NGO was founded in 1961 in Britain by Peter Benenson to fight for prisoners of conscience. In 1963 he established an international secretariat, and his organization quickly became a worldwide movement, fighting for the release of prisoners as long as they had not committed violence or exhorted others to do so (for details, see http://www.amnesty.org).

Within a decade Amnesty International had expanded to thirty-three countries, and in 1977 it was awarded the Nobel Peace Prize for its campaign against torture and ill treatment of prisoners. Amnesty began to take on human rights abuses in general and also stood up against capital punishment and, by 2000, it had broadened its scope to include a wide range of human rights issues. On its web site it contends that today "people are more likely to become victims of abuse because of who they are, rather than what they think, say or do – the biggest threat to human rights are the mass violations committed during armed conflicts." In 2010 it documented torture and ill treatment in ninety-eight countries and at least sixty-seven countries that imposed death sentences. Amnesty complained about prisoner abuse by the Bush government in U.S. prisons in Guantánamo, Cuba, and elsewhere, and in 2009 it accused both Israel and Hamas of committing war crimes.

Amnesty is a popular worldwide movement with three million members and supporters, but because it takes on states that allegedly are behaving badly, it often comes into conflict

with governments, especially those that have authoritarian tendencies. In the 1980s it was accused of espionage by the Soviet Union and of defending lawbreakers by Morocco. In recent years it has been criticized by the United States, Israel, China, Russia, Congo, and the Catholic Church, among others, for such topics as one-sided reporting, failure to take security needs into consideration in the treatment of individuals, left-wing bias, and support for abortion rights.

With its moral certitude, wide following, and modern communications facilities, AI provides a powerful, public moral compass that evaluates government policy in the field of human rights. Are NGOs like AI transforming global politics for better or for worse?

have their headquarters in one country, they operate and invest in others, buying resources, producing goods and/or services, and then selling them in other countries. Today, the largest of the MNCs consider the entire world a single marketplace. Their growing importance makes them controversial as purveyors for the wealthiest areas in the world. Issues concerning the role of MNCs in economics and trade are discussed in Chapters 12 and 13. Here we discuss them as examples of nonstate actors.

After World War II and up to the 1960s, U.S. companies dominated multinational activity in the automotive, pharmaceutical, electrical, and other industrial sectors. European and Japanese multinational corporations began to compete internationally over the following three decades and, near the end of the 20th century, changes in political regimes and ideologies brought Eastern Europe, China, and several Asian countries into the multinational arena as well. As the world became more interdependent, shareholders and managers increasingly dispersed around the world, and international involvement and corporate behavior has shifted from resource and market seeking to strategic asset seeking.

Large firms dominate multinational activity. Many are more powerful than NGOs, and a few are even more powerful and influential than many countries. In terms of foreign assets, Wal-Mart is larger than most countries, including Israel, Poland, and Greece; Mitsubishi is bigger than Indonesia; and Toyota is larger than Norway. There are approximately sixty-one thousand multinational corporations, the vast majority of which are run from bases in the United States, Japan, and the countries of the European Union. They account for about two-thirds of world trade and employ more than fifty million workers.[5] The combined sales of the world's top two hundred corporations are greater than a quarter of the entire world's economic activity. In 2012, JP Morgan, a U.S. financial holding company, was the largest public company; the largest non-financial enterprises were General Electric (United States), Exxon Mobil (United States), Vodafone (United Kingdom), Royal Dutch Shell (Netherlands and United Kingdom), Petro China (China), and Petrobras-Petróleo Brasil (Brazil).

Through what is called foreign direct investment (FDI), MNCs increasingly buy companies, buildings, land, and factories in foreign territory. While the assets of such investment companies differ, they often deal in natural resources (particularly oil and gas), manufacturing, and banking sectors. They may include large service franchises, such as McDonald's. Sometimes MNCs do not seek to control or run the companies directly, but instead they buy their stocks and bonds through foreign portfolio investments (FPIs). However, whether they are owners or investors, they may or may not share the political interests of either the host countries where they operate or their home country where they base their headquarters. Of course, some of the largest MNCs are state owned or state controlled and have to adhere closely to their government's policies, but most are free to pursue their own interests and policies wherever or however they choose. They

[5] *World Investment Report*, annual, found at http://www.unctad.org.

Figure 7.2 McDonald's is a large multinational corporation that employs about 1.5 million people in 119 countries. It is the world's largest chain of hamburger fast food restaurants, and has become a symbol of globalization and the spread of American culture and economics. *Source:* Alamy.

adopt a range of strategies to be profitable, from employing cheap labor in developing countries to seeking tax advantages from host governments. As their motive is profit, it is not surprising that multinational corporations tend to support free trade and free capital flows – in short, economic globalization.

Multinational corporations are significant actors in the international arena because they carry out economic activities that are beyond the jurisdiction of individual states. They control an immense proportion of the world's wealth, account for most of the world's exports, and dominate the world economy. Wal-Mart, the world largest retailer, with approximately fifty thousand stores, buys billions of dollars worth of goods from China every year and is a crucial world player (Close Up 7.2). Some MNCs are also important conveyors of the culture of their home country. As of 2012 there were more than thirty-two thousand McDonald's fast-food restaurants spread across more than half the world's states, the largest of which is in Beijing, China. The corporation exports U.S. values to the rest of the world along with its Big Macs and fries (Figure 7.2).

Historically, MNCs have produced products in poorer countries to take advantage of cheap labor, and today they are a major cause of outsourcing – the transfer of jobs from richer countries to the developing world to hire workers at lower wages than those paid in developed countries. It is common, for example, for North American airlines to transfer telephone calls to agents in India or the Philippines to answer queries. To cut costs, some British publishers routinely send their books to India to be edited and produced. Apple outsourced the production of its iPad and computers to China because it was profitable to do so.

Multinationals obviously possess a great deal of power in the global economy. Many civil activists and some NGOs are concerned with the negative impacts that flow from MNC activity. They fear the power of MNCs and want them to be better regulated. Their concerns are often about the environmental, human, and social damage that powerful firms can cause. In 1987 in Bhopal, India, for example, a poisonous gas leak from an insecticide plant owned by Union Carbide (now controlled by Dow Chemical) killed more than five thousand people and injured many thousands more. The company was required to pay US$470 million in settlements related to the accident. It then closed the plant but left vast amounts of untreated toxins at the site, which eventually contaminated nearby supplies of drinking water. A new legal suit demanded cleanup funds and damages for personal injury for twenty thousand more people. In 2008, after years of fighting in the courts, the U.S. Court of Appeals for the Second Circuit reinstated the claim, but as of 2013 it remained unsettled.[6]

Many academic observers criticize what they see as the increasing impotence of democratic governance and global institutions in the face of the power and mobility of rich global corporations. Whenever possible, corporations conduct their international transactions in such a way as to earn profits in high-tax countries and then declare them in states where taxes are low. At the same time, corporations regularly call for reduced taxes, deregulation, and "less government" in the name of promoting "business efficiency and confidence." Cynical observers maintain that states will soon be left only with whatever resources the global corporations and their elites are willing to contribute. Is the globalization of capitalism killing liberal democracy?

States are not totally powerless against MNCs. They may take at least two types of actions toward them. Local governments can attempt to modify corporate behavior by regulations or they can encourage corporations to invest in and improve the host country in some way.[7] In recent years, therefore, many multinationals have tried to clean up their act and establish voluntary guidelines for their conduct. For example, IKEA, Nike, Kmart, and Shell are among corporations that have adopted codes of conduct regarding social responsibility. Voluntary regulation is not legally binding, however, and with little monitoring and no enforcement mechanisms, the procedures often prove little more than window dressing.

[6] Case: Sahu v. Union Carbide, No. 06–5694, http://www.bhopal.com/chrolology.
[7] See J. H. Dunning, *The Globalization of Business* (London: Routledge, 1993).

Box 7.2 **Positive and negative impacts of MNCs**

Positive
- Stimulate research and development
- Inject capital into host economies and generate revenue for them
- Create jobs, improve living standards, and provide business for local suppliers
- Create linkages to foreign markets
- Establish high labor and environmental standards
- Raise quality and efficiency of competition

Negative
- Build branch plants in developing countries at time of high unemployment and economic downturns at home so that well-paying jobs are exported to other countries
- Use their power to block business opportunities and crowd out smaller entrepreneurs
- Exploit workers and children, with poor wages and working conditions that would not be allowed in the home country
- Damage the environment in host countries that do not have high pollution standards or other protections in place – for example, using them as a dumping ground for hazardous waste
- Use unfair accounting practices, allowing MNCs to repatriate large profits earned in the host country
- Support oppressive regimes in return for favors
- Create an economic downturn when they move out of a host area
- Are not legally accountable to host countries for damages caused
- Displace people from their land in order to set up MNC facilities

Supranational organizations have made several attempts to establish an international regulatory framework to govern MNCs. In 1976, for example, the Organization for Economic Cooperation and Development (OECD) issued guidelines on environmental protection, labor standards, tax avoidance, and human rights for all OECD-based MNCs operating abroad. But as usual, no enforcement mechanisms were included. The European Parliament made an attempt at regulation in 1999. It published general standards for all European companies with branches in developing countries, but they were never fully implemented. International regulations have been more successful when narrowly focused on specific issues. In 1981 the World Health Organization set the International Code for the Marketing of Breast Milk Substitutes. The code was the result of a long campaign by the NGO INFACT against Nestlé (the Swiss MNC), for promoting milk formula that mothers in poor countries were mixing with contaminated water, thus killing many infants.

Close Up 7.2 **A classic MNC: Wal-Mart**

Wal-Mart is a prime example of an MNC. Founded in 1962 by American Sam Walton, the company quickly developed supercenters combined with discount grocery stores. By 1990 it was the largest retail business in the United States. It expanded first to Mexico and Canada, and then in 1991 it moved into Europe, including Germany and the United Kingdom, and later in 2002 it moved into Japan. By 2003, with revenues of US$244.52 billion, Wal-Mart was the world's largest retail corporation, with nearly three times the revenue of its closest competitor. Its own publicity estimated that its imports from China in 2003 were $15 billion, representing 10 percent of total U.S. imports, but other analysts estimated that Wal-Mart's imports were much higher.

In 2012, Wal-Mart was the world's largest retail company, with more than two million employees in 10,130 stores in twenty-two countries, and US$444 billion in worldwide sales.[8] Sam Walton's recipe for making profits is simple. The company buys inventory at as low a price as possible and then passes the savings on to customers. The company makes a profit by large-volume sales and keeping costs low – that includes hiring as few people as possible, paying them minimum wages and benefits, and preventing the establishment of unions. To make employees feel that they have a stake in the company, Walton introduced a profit-sharing plan for employees, which allows them to put a percentage of their wages into the purchase of Wal-Mart stock.

Wal-Mart's high profits came with a price. It ignored local producers, which had a negative effect in small towns, where it drove out local competition. There was a growing criticism that it was cutting costs at the expense of its workers. The company was forced to fight lawsuits over its low wages and benefits, treatment of women, and allegedly for putting "Made in America" signs on goods imported from Asian sweatshops.[9]

In response to such criticisms, Wal-Mart argued, in effect, that the proof is in the pudding – shoppers want low prices and Wal-Mart provides them, and shoppers reward them by coming back for more. This love-hate relationship with the general public is fairly typical of the public relations issues around many large MNCs.

Should large MNCs like Wal-Mart be more carefully regulated by governments in both their domestic and foreign activities? What should be required of them? How would realists, liberals, Marxists, and constructivists differ in their approaches to this topic?

[8] http://www.walmart.com, accessed May 8, 2012.
[9] Anthony Bianco and Wendy Zellner, "Is Wal-Mart Too Powerful?" *Businessweek*, October 6, 2004, pp. 100–04.

Multinational firms can have other problems to contend with in their foreign work environment. When host governments change, they frequently alter their policies toward businesses arbitrarily, and sometimes they nationalize or expropriate their assets. Sometimes less developed states have provided land and tax incentives to MNCs while restricting the importation of their finished goods. Historically, governments in rich countries have often used their MNCs as instruments to extend their reach into the politics and economies of developing countries and gain access to resources and foodstuffs with deleterious effects on the corporations. Sometimes MNCs have to function in conditions of political turmoil, violence, or war.

Criminal and terrorist organizations and networks

Not all nongovernmental organizations are involved in legal or ethical practices. Despite the perhaps invidious comparison, criminals and terrorists not only organize outside the control of states and governments to a far greater extent than NGOs and MNCs but they are also involved in direct attacks on the ability of states to govern and protect their populations. International organized crime (IOC) includes activities such as trafficking in people, narcotics, small arms, and nuclear material; smuggling of illegal aliens; and money laundering. These activities threaten individual, state, and global security. Criminals who engage in them operate across international borders and thereby poison trust among states, eroding faith in democratic institutions, undermining the state by creating social instability, eroding tax bases, and diverting resources. Transnational illegal activity is growing quickly in global politics, assisted by electronic networks that allow criminal and terrorist groups to communicate easily while concealing their identity. Weak states are particularly vulnerable to these practices.

Narcotics consumption is increasing worldwide. The United Nations Office on Drugs and Crime estimates that around the world there are between eighteen million and thirty-eight million "problem drug users" between the ages of fifteen and sixty-four.[10] The market for marijuana and heroin is in rich, developed countries like the United States and Canada, but the major suppliers are principally in Colombia, Peru in South America, and Afghanistan in Asia. Drug lords in Afghanistan control about 90 percent of the world's heroin market. In Mexico drug trafficking undermines civil society through kidnappings, murders, pervasive corruption, intimidation of politicians, and the breakdown of law and order. Such drug-trafficking networks extend their violence deep into the United States.

Trafficking in humans is especially invidious. International criminal organizations such as the Mafia have networks around the world, carrying out illicit money laundering, tax evasion, and fraud in their illegal movement of people from place to place. Human trafficking has many faces; it includes forced labor in sweatshops, slavery, sale of human organs, sale of children, and sex trafficking. The sale of small arms and nuclear materials are also major issues. Since the end of the Cold War, when stockpiles of weapons became available for legal and illicit markets, their sales have been a factor in facilitating and sustaining civil wars and violence (see Chapters 9–11).[11]

These types of criminal activities pose global security threats, and international cooperation is required to counter them. This is not always easy, because when states are weak or failing and cannot help their people sufficiently, these illegal nonstate activities generate employment and may actually be major contributors to a state's overall economy. In some circumstances, therefore, governments tolerate and even support criminal activity. This is currently the case in Afghanistan with the poppy industry (see Chapter 10).

---

[10] UNODC, *World Drug Report*, 2010, http://www.unodc.org.
[11] See, for example, Nicole Jackson, "International Organizations, Security Dichotomies and the Trafficking of Persons and Narcotics in Post-Soviet Central Asia," *Security Dialogue* 37, no. 3 (September 2006), pp. 299–317.

Terrorist networks also operate across state borders. The best known among them currently (but far from the only one) is al-Qaeda, which is active in Afghanistan and Pakistan and has branches in many countries throughout the world. The UN lists all organizations related to al-Qaeda and the Taliban as terrorist organizations. Other well-known transnational terrorist organizations include Hamas in Palestine, Hezbollah in Lebanon, Euzkadi Ta Askatasuna (ETA) in Spain, and the Revolutionary Armed Forces of Colombia (FARC). The UN attempts to monitor their activities and reduce their significance, especially through restricting their financing (see Chapter 11).

Terrorist networks may be tightly structured, hierarchically organized institutions such as some criminal organizations and revolutionary communist cells, or they may be widely dispersed and decentralized, such as one might find in a franchised business like Starbucks or McDonald's. The point is that criminal and terrorist networks are nonstate actors with considerable influence and power in global politics, in large part because they adapt organizationally to local and regional circumstances.[12] They are also like NGOs and MNCs in that they are spread out around the world and are often decentralized in structure. We deal with this topic in detail in Chapter 11.

Communications and global politics

Modern communications, with their cross-border ownership, personnel, and activities, have little respect for state borders and increasingly perform as independent nonstate actors. Of course, states can and do use communications technologies for their own purposes, but today there is such a free flow of information that political leaders have difficulty imposing restrictions on such nonstate actors and countering their challenges.

In recent decades, the proliferation of new information and communications technologies (ICTs) has enhanced the impact of the mass media and the Internet in global politics.[13] An astounding quantity of information cascades around the world at lightning speed. The traditional mass media of radio, television, and print journalism provide a "top-down" fourth estate, while the Internet and social networking supplement this phenomenon and, at times, even hold the mass media itself to account with their "bottom-up" approach. The combined interactions among national governments, MNCs, NGOs, mass media, and the flow of individual commentaries from social networks around the world are assaulting historical patterns of conducting global politics. Examples are legion. In 2001, texting on cell phones was used in the Philippines to get people to attend rallies to help depose a president from power. In 2004 it was used to alert people to attend rallies challenging the Spanish government's claims about who was responsible for the 2004 bombings at train stations in Madrid. In 2012 and 2013, it was used to capture and disseminate photos of vicious government military bombing of civilian quarters in Homs and elsewhere in Syria. The widespread use of photographs and cell phones means that little government action goes undocumented.

Such empowerment of the general public appears to be growing in global politics. It can be detrimental to government authority and perhaps even undermine good policy, as occurred in the famous 1992 incident of a downed Blackhawk helicopter in Somalia. In that case, U.S. soldiers were sent to Somalia on a humanitarian mission after American journalists had reported on social distress and violence in the country. Then, after American television reported that eighteen U.S. soldiers had been killed, and one dragged through the streets in Mogadishu, U.S. public opinion shifted radically against their country's presence in Somalia, and the

---

[12] See Marc Sageman, *Understanding Terrorist Networks* (Philadelphia: University of Pennsylvania Press, 2004).

[13] See Miles Kahler, ed., *Networked Politics: Agency, Power and Governance* (Ithaca, NY: Cornell University Press, 2009).

government was forced to end the mission. Public opinion had reversed in a matter of a few weeks.

The presence of mass media and the Internet does not automatically mean that the public possesses new political power, however. People may acquire knowledge and perhaps orientation from communications, but unless that information is channeled into political action in some manner, it will not prove instrumental in effecting change in domestic or global politics. The Internet may allow individuals to communicate and network across the world by email or instant messaging, and sites like Facebook, YouTube, and Twitter may bring people together, but this in itself does not bestow power or even irresistible influence on its users. Knowledge and connections need to be harnessed and organized in order to hold leaders of governments and elite social institutions accountable for their actions. For twenty years, the dissident Aung San Suu Kyi was kept imprisoned or under house arrest by Burmese military leaders, despite constant media attention around the world. It took two decades of international and other pressure before she was freed to campaign for political office.

Mass media

Traditional mass media include communication vehicles such as radio, television, newspapers, and magazines that report news and shape public opinion and political behavior. These media are crucial sources of political information in and across most societies, suggesting not just which topics individuals should think about but even what they should think and feel about them. In 1989 the world was transfixed by the image of a lone young man standing in the road before a column of Chinese army tanks that were moving into Tiananmen Square to crush the rebellion of students and others who had gone there to demonstrate for liberal reform (Figure 7.3). This is a good example of the media's enormous access to the public and how a single photo can make a powerful and lasting impact on public opinion. Twenty years later, communism is still in place, but the Chinese government continues to take draconian steps to prevent further such demonstrations on Tiananmen Square. Similar photographs of young people committing suicide and being killed in Tunisia, Egypt, Libya, and Syria in 2011–12 fixated the international media and helped spread upheaval in the Arab world.

Figure 7.3 In 1989, a series of largely student-run demonstrations in cities throughout China ended in tragedy in Beijing when the military brutally suppressed demonstrators in Tiananmen Square. Many were killed. The crowds were protesting inflation, limited career prospects, government corruption, and authoritarianism. *Source:* Press Association.

Mass media are not nearly as neutral or objective as they like to claim, and they often act more like a pulpit than a forum. They are selective in subject and content. While they inform and persuade, coverage is rarely comprehensive. The media provide little depth, and stories appear and disappear as if on a whim. Reporting is often based on cynicism rather than neutral skepticism, so that public figures, political events, and especially foreigners tend to be discussed in stereotyped, negative terms. This magnifies the bad and ignores or underplays the good, distorting events to suggest scandal or confrontation even when there is neither. Some journalists have learned that they get more personal rewards for outrageous opinions, so they oversimplify and sensationalize in order to build their ratings and advertising dollars for their employers. Journalists in rich democracies are criticized for their tendency to see world events through "liberal" or "Western" eyes and for reporting on events as if they were games largely about winning and losing rather than about values such as equality and justice.

All political news, both domestic and international, is delivered to the public through media intermediaries – media owners – who have their own biases and agendas. The media are often owned by only a few members of the wealthy, dominant class or by multinational corporations such as Fox News in the United States, and they are relatively free and independent of government control. In authoritarian countries such as China, the state owns the media, and it censors news and information that come across its borders, making the media almost a commercial for the Communist Party leadership. In such authoritarian countries, journalists have far less legal protection when they engage in free speech. In Cuba, for example, unofficial print and broadcast outlets have been banned, and independent journalists sending stories to foreign media are treated as political dissidents and often jailed.[14] In

Russia and elsewhere today journalism is a dangerous profession in which criticism and exposure of wrongdoing can bring death. The British Broadcasting Corporation (BBC) is owned by the British government but is legally precluded from having a corporate political stance, even if commentators and individual programs appear to do so. Indeed, the BBC's reporting of Britain's role in the invasion of Iraq in 2003 was deemed by some to be subversive of the national interest.

In absolute monarchies, restrictions on the media may be severe. In Saudi Arabia, for example, before going on sale, foreign magazines are subject to censorship by the *mutawa*, an independent religious body sanctioned by the government. The *mutawa* has even been known to comb magazines such as *People* and *Better Homes and Gardens* to paint out with black markers such objectionable sights as exposed arms and legs and to draw black robes over pictures of women. Books and magazines suspected of containing explicit or subversive materials (e.g., *Time, Newsweek*) are often seized.

While the political bias of the news media in authoritarian regimes is overt and easily spotted, it can also be subversive in terms of clarity and objectivity in any country. By political bias we mean deliberate manipulation of the content and presentation of news so as to favor certain political interests over others. In Western liberal democracies this process is relatively subtle. Sometimes it is through omission – as when U.S. broadcasters omitted or only briefly mentioned the large numbers of civilian Iraqi deaths during two wars, but at the same time stressed the relatively much smaller number of American military casualties. Sometimes bias is found in an implicit, unquestioning acceptance of the system in place – for example, capitalist, democratic, or liberal principles.

Mass media may play a less significant socializing role in developing countries, especially in rural areas, where there is less television exposure and literacy is lower. But even there, leaders recognize the potential impact of the media and often use them extensively, especially radio. A government's

[14] News from the world media is found at http://www.worldpressinstitute.org.

use of the media to legitimize its actions can be very potent. In Cuba, for example, the government supplied television sets to recipients of public housing, thus providing Fidel Castro and later Raúl Castro with a vehicle to "enter" as many homes as possible. North Korean media are among the most strictly controlled in the world. The state news agency is the only source of information for all media outlets. Kim Jong Il used the media to indoctrinate his people. Radios and televisions were pretuned to government stations, and stations tuned to other broadcasters were not permitted. His son, Kim Jong Un, continues the practice. Media control is considered so important by military leaders that in planning a government takeover, one of the first things revolutionary leaders do is take over the means of communication so that all messages to the public can be censored and tightly controlled.[15]

Satellite-transmitted television has revolutionized the ability to communicate across borders and weakened government control over information. Western governments often broadcast their viewpoints in foreign countries (to counteract anti-Western news and sentiments). Voice of America (VOA) and the British Broadcasting Corporation (BBC) are available almost everywhere today, even where governments do not want them. For example, both have government-funded broadcasters that offer Persian-language reports in Iran. They both claim that they take pains to steer clear of partisanship and just report facts, but even the selection of facts can be contrary to what the local state government wants distributed, so like other foreign media, they are regularly accused of meddling or bias. Cable News Network (CNN) is available around the world and broadcasts in nine languages. In recent years, the forces of globalization have dramatically increased the scope and reach of mass media. Economically powerful countries exercise a powerful socializing influence on others, thus extending their culture around the globe. A number

of huge multimedia corporations, including such institutions as Time Warner, Disney, Viacom, News Corporation, Viendi, Sony, and Bertelsmann, have extensive control over information received by people around the world. All of these corporations are from the rich north – the first four mentioned are from the United States, Viendi is from France, Sony is from Japan, and Bertelsmann is from Germany. Their reach is immense, and they largely set the agenda for what topics people think about and how they understand the issues.[16] Viewers in the global South complain that their culture is neglected, while northern values such as consumerism and conspicuous consumption are promoted.

Through CNN (which beams its twenty-four-hour news channel around the world), newspapers such as *The New York Times* and *International Herald Tribune*, and the Hollywood film industry, the United States disseminates American culture abroad and collects international news that is of interest to Americans. When the U.S. Marine Corps landed on the beaches of Somalia in late 1992, camera crews were there waiting for them. In Canada, where most of the population is clustered within a hundred and fifty miles of the long Canadian-U.S. border, the country is deluged with American radio and television signals. Almost all international reporting is bought from American media, so that by the time it reaches the public it has been filtered through American eyes and given American perspectives. There are symbols of American cultural penetration even in much more remote locations. Isolated islands in the Pacific Ocean often have no television reception, but they do have large stocks of American videos for their DVDs.

As modern communications networks have expanded, new owners have begun to share the international communications field with those in North America and Europe. Al Jazeera, the Arab-based

---

[15] In 2011–12 Reporters without Borders listed North Korea as 178 of 179 on its Press Freedom Index. http://ed.rsf.org/press-freedom-index.

[16] Mark Crispin Miller, "What's Wrong with This Picture?" in *Global Issues 05/06*, ed. Robert Jackson (Dubuque, IA: McGraw-Hill Duskin, 2000); Eytan Gilboa, "Global Television News and Foreign Policy," *International Studies Perspectives* 6 (August 2004), pp. 325–41.

news network based in Qatar, was established in 1996 and quickly became the world's first and most popular Arabic-language television news network, providing disparate Arabs with a sense of unity. The network became famous for broadcasting hate tapes from Osama bin Laden, but perhaps much more important is that, for many people in the Middle East, it is replacing American and British sources for international news. It is particularly active in broadcasting news from troubled areas such as the Gaza in Israel, Benghazi in Libya, and Homs in Syria, for example, and it provides a view that radically differs from that of Western media on many topics. In 2006, Al Jazeera added twenty-four-hour English-language broadcasts.

New media are proliferating rapidly, and as they do, traditional journalists are having a harder time competing with new methods of reporting and interpreting the news. They are often excluded from areas or events by state governments. In Iran in 2009 foreign media were not allowed to cover the antigovernment protests without permission, were confined to their offices and hotels, and risked beatings or worse if they went into the streets. They needed visas to be there, and when their short-term visas expired, they were expelled from the country. Their role was usurped by "citizen-journalists" using the Internet and social networking to access the airwaves.

Internet technologies and social networking

Communications guru Marshall McLuhan noted decades ago that "the medium is the message," by which he meant that one must look beyond the content of media to understand its effects on lives and thinking. This observation was directed at the mass media and its importance, but McLuhan could have used the same reasoning about the modern development of the Internet and social networking. Within the past decade, some terms that are now part of everyday conversation have changed their meanings – *Twitter* and *cloud* being good examples (Figure 7.4).

The Internet was developed and promoted in the 1960s and 1970s by a U.S. government research

Figure 7.4 Globalization has penetrated all societies around the globe and the cell phone in particular is rapidly making instant communications and the ability to access information possible at all times, in all places. *Source:* Corbis.

program across several universities, including the University of California at Los Angeles and Santa Barbara, the University of Utah, and Stanford University. At the time, the government hoped that the Internet would help the United States expand its technological edge over the Soviet Union and provide a decentralized means of government communication and military command and control if traditional communications broke down during a war. The Internet was, of course, wildly successful and quickly developed largely independently of governmental bodies, allowing ideas, words, and pictures to be disseminated well beyond the locations where they were created.

Today there is a virtual cyberspace, a term or metaphor used to describe the global electronic web of people, ideas, and interactions on the Internet that, to a large extent, are uncontrolled by states and borders. Google's search engine is so widely used around the world that it makes more money from advertising than all the U.S. newspapers combined.[17] Wikipedia is a free encyclopedia on the Internet for which articles are written, edited, and regulated almost entirely by tens of thousands of unpaid volunteers around the world. The site contains some seventeen million articles, in more than 270 languages and is one of the most visited on the Internet. As most professors tell (or should tell) their students – "you may start with Wikipedia, but don't stop there. You need to double-check before using the information." Interestingly, as of 2012, no print edition of the old standby *Encyclopedia Britannica* was available; it now has to be read on line.

Ideas, information, pictures, business, and capital are increasingly moving by the Internet, computers, and mobile phones. The entire global Internet is coordinated by the Internet Corporation for Assigned Names and Numbers (ICANN), a nonprofit NGO based in California.[18] In 2012, 5.5 billion people owned cell phones, and about 2 billion used the Internet. These two-way media allow users to interact without the top-down control of institutions or governments. The Internet has created a global information highway in which diarists share their opinions globally in Internet chat rooms in blogs, (online diaries for spreading information and ideas), and in podcasts (which allow individuals to create audio and visual images and make them available as digital downloads). In 2011 there were more than 156 million public bloggers. YouTube, which was created only in 2004, has become a "virtual video village," a website where people post videos and comments. Today it airs an estimated 120 million videos and adds about 200,000 daily.

Both cell phones and the Internet are used dramatically more in the richer north than in the poorer south.[19] There is a *digital divide* both within and among countries. Large parts of the world in remote areas and rural and poor villages can neither afford computers nor access the Internet. Cell phones are much more prevalent than computers – and even in the poorest parts of the South, the rise in cell phone use is dramatic. Since new technology and communications diminish the significance of borders, people in the developing world complain that the concentration of media in the Western capitalist states means that southern values and needs are again being ignored, while northern values, including consumerism and conspicuous consumption, are being spread, thus undermining the traditional values of the South – and they blame the United States for most of this. Others, more optimistically, see the new technology as a step toward a truly global village with a more united, homogenized "world culture" that will bring the world together and rid it of the parochial hatreds that shape contemporary reality and provide the grounds for international conflict and terrorism. Certainly non-Western points of view are getting more exposure on sites such as Al Jazeera, which is now among the top two hundred most visited Internet sites worldwide.

[17] Steven Levy, *In the Plex: How Google Thinks, Works, and Shapes Our Lives* (New York: Simon & Schuster, 2011).
[18] For updates, see http://www.icann.org.

[19] See Pippa Norris, *Digital Divide: Civic Engagement, Information, Poverty and the Internet Worldwide* (Cambridge: Cambridge University Press, 2001).

Critical Case Study 7.1 Media, regional cultures, and political stability

Is the flow of information across borders destroying regional cultures and undermining governments and political stability? This is a complex question.

At a general level, the Internet helps create a sense of global community, bringing diverse people together. The Internet has the ability to inform mass audiences at relatively low cost, and it is difficult for states to regulate. It empowers nonstate actors such as advocacy groups.[20] Some optimists refer to this development of transnational associations and interests as the emergence of a new **global civil society** – a "sphere of people, events, organizations, networks – and the values and ideas they represent – that exists between the family, the state and the market, and which operates beyond the confines of national societies in a transnational arena."[21] The advent of an actual global civil society would mean that states and their policies would be subject to challenge not only from their own citizens or other states but also from transnational issue networks and organizations connected by the Internet.

Academic research on political culture has made it clear that norms and beliefs are central to explanations of stability and change, but a complete explanation has proved elusive.[22] It is difficult to provide unambiguous, empirical evidence that a specific agent such as borderless media is a direct cause of political behavior and government performance. As an explanatory variable, political culture limits the range of possibilities but does not determine specific outcomes. Political culture is not destiny – people can and do change, even if new technology is fast-forwarding this change. Today, throughout Eastern Europe, Central Asia, the Middle East, Asia, and North and Central Africa, new and fragile democratic political cultures are emerging in which citizens have entirely new expectations and beliefs concerning their government and their role in society. Their political views are "conditioned" by their country's history but not dictated by it. Increasingly global technology and global awareness are playing a part, but where this change will lead is unknown. Certainly the use of social networking proved important in the Arab Awakening in Egypt, Libya, Morocco, Syria, and Tunisia.

How important is the new media in integrating cultures? How much is it pulling them apart? To what degree can it be held responsible for social upheaval in North Africa and the Middle East?

Social networking Social networking is a distinctly 21st-century phenomenon based on new technology. The number of people online worldwide is expected to grow from 1.5 billion in 2009 to 2.2 billion in 2013. Twitter, a San Francisco–based social-networking service, has more than 300 million users.[23] Tweets can originate from text messaging on a cell phone or even blogging software, whereas Facebook operates solely as a website and can be shut down. Other broad-based social networks include Facebook and MySpace, which operate solely as websites. Governments and politicians also are making use of this phenomenon. Since 2009, U.S. Secretary of State Hillary Rodham Clinton has often

[20] Clay Shirky, "The Political Power of Social Media: Technology, the Public Sphere, and Political Change," *Foreign Affairs* 90, no. 1 (January–February 2011), pp. 29–38.

[21] The Centre for the Study of Global Governance, "Global Civil Society," http://www.lse.ac.uk.

[22] See Hans Peter Schmitz, "Domestic and Transnational Perspectives on Democratization," *International Studies Review* 6, no. 3 (2004), pp. 403–21; Julianne E. Allison, ed., *Technology, Development and Democracy: International Conflict and Cooperation in the Information Age* (New York: State University of New York Press, 2002).

[23] "Tweeting All the Way to the Bank," *The Economist*, July 25, 2009, p. 61.

talked about the power of e-diplomacy, particularly in places where mass media are repressed.[24]

Exchanges on these new social media are generally banal or inane, but on occasion they have been able to drive public opinion and challenge the traditional levers of media control. How will the ubiquity of social media affect global politics? Social networking was credited, for example, with aiding protests in the Republic of Georgia when Russia invaded in 2008, and Twitter was a crucial tool in directing the public and international journalists to video, photographs, and text related to protests in Iran in 2009. Iranians blogged, posted to Facebook, and coordinated their protests on Twitter. They used Twitter to send reports and links to photos with accounts of street fighting and casualties around the country. The tragic photos and video of Neda Agha-Soltan, a twenty-six-year-old Iranian woman shot to death in Tehran, were collected on the cell phones of her fellow demonstrators and surreptitiously transmitted over the Internet to the rest of the world, making her a martyr and an instant symbol of courageous resistance. The political regime reacted brutally and held fast, but it was shaken by the public defiance. Still, the reaction of the "international community" to the episode has not brought about decisive change within Iran.

The growth of networking among individuals is believed by some to lead automatically to empowerment. Certainly, the Internet allows information to be collected and disseminated quicker than previously, and it can inspire political activity. According to Oxford University professor of the Internet Bill Dutton, Wikipedia beat the mainstream press in reporting detailed information on the terrorist attack in Mumbai, India, in November 2008.[25] But it also should be clear that all stakeholders, government and nongovernment alike, will use the World Wide Web to reinforce their interests and claims. Blogs are only a recent online addition to the traditional

way of communicating the news. What makes the Internet differ is that it allows individuals to hold not only politicians but also the mass media itself to account. Of course, blogs themselves may be dishonest; many make unsubstantiated claims on a regular basis.

The new media can, of course, be constrained by state "filtering" systems, the most aggressive of which are erected in authoritarian systems such as Iran, Burma, China, North Korea, and Saudi Arabia, where the governments use their control over the Internet to suppress opposing views. When imprisoned Chinese dissident Liu Xiaobo was awarded the Nobel Peace Prize in 2010, the news was prevented from being disseminated on Chinese broadcasting stations, and anyone who entered the words "Liu Xiaobo" or "Nobel" into Google in China received only a blank screen as a response. States can regulate the intermediate actors that operate within their territory, including Internet service providers like cable companies and search engines like Google or Yahoo! Some Western democracies, in spite of their commitment to free speech, are also beginning to filter some "inappropriate" content. India, for example, regulates a range of content, including political satire and material that could offend religious or ethnic groups.

Authoritarian states are particularly challenged by social networking. Certainly, the Internet challenges governmental control of the flow of information. China and the former Soviet Union, like most authoritarian regions, used to own and manage all means of mass communication in their countries. Now, they don't. In North Korea, access to computers is restricted to those families most loyal to the regime.[26] While these states want to benefit from disseminating information on the Internet, they also want to control its political effects. According to Reporters without Borders, more than twenty countries use sophisticated blocking and filtering systems for Internet content.[27] While all countries

---

[24] Issues and details about the secretary and State Department embracing the new media of email, blogs, Facebook, Twitter, Flickr, and YouTube can be found at http://www.state.org.
[25] *Oxford Today* 21, no. 2 (2009), p. 15.

[26] *The Washington Post*, December 19, 2011.
[27] *The New York Times*, May 1, 2009.

may use these devices to filter some content, such as child pornography, authoritarian regimes also block political dissent and activism. The government of Iran censors more than most governments do, using elaborate technology to block millions of websites that offer news, commentary, videos, and music. In 2009, the Iranian government shut down text-messaging services to prevent them from being used as an organizing tool for the opposition. Later, it cut cell phone transmissions and access to Facebook and some other websites. Twitter was more difficult to block, because individuals do not have to visit a home site to send a message, or "tweet." Shutting down Twitter.com does not stop the offending tweeting – one would have to shut down the entire service, which only Twitter can do. Many Twitter users also share ways to evade government interference, such as programming their web browsers to contact an Internet server that relays their connection through another country.

New technologies have made state control much more difficult, and because democracies are more concerned with preserving freedom of speech, it is in some ways more difficult for them than for authoritarian states to cope with the challenges posed to government by borderless communications. They can restrict content such as child pornography but only on websites from servers in their own territory. They cannot easily limit access to images or content from servers abroad, which are out of reach of their domestic laws. All they can do is try to pinpoint the source of the offensive material that is being uploaded. It is possible to locate the server and even the computer that is involved in an upload, but the government of the state of origin would have to cooperate in order to actually stop the upload and possibly prosecute the offender. Of course, it is also possible for a state to target individuals who consume illegal material. The main point is that the Internet may empower freedom fighters, but it also allows governments to hunt them down because of their online presence.

China has long censored what citizens can read online. The government employs more than forty thousand censors and pays hundreds of thousands of students to flood the Internet with government messages and crowd out dissenters.[28] It regularly censors Internet sites of groups deemed to be state enemies, like the Falun Gong, the spiritual movement that the government claims is a dangerous cult responsible for ruining the lives of thousands of people.[29] China admits that it monitors content on the Internet but only to police illegal material such as pornography, criminal activity, and fraud – and of course treasonous propaganda. Blocking unwanted sites has become more insidious as Internet filtering technology has grown more sophisticated so that governments can block particular words or phrases without users realizing it. China successfully stopped Google from allowing unfiltered text messages by preventing sensitive words and subjects from being disseminated. One recent study showed that one-third to more than half of all postings made to three particular Chinese Internet service providers were not published or were censored.[30] There is no doubt, however, that people in China now understand a lot more about what is going on outside their borders than they did a few decades ago, and much of this is due to the communications revolution. In 2010 Google moved out of mainland China and into Hong Kong in defiance of Chinese government prohibitions on its activities.

The Chinese fight over censorship is ongoing as dissidents move beyond state borders to challenge state authority. The Global Internet Freedom Consortium is an Internet proxy service with ties to Falun Gong. It maintains a series of computers in data centers around the world to route web users' requests around sensors' firewalls. It also offers downloadable software to help evade censorship. The Internet has become a forum for state control but also for rebellion against it, and because computers have become so vital, they have spawned another industry based on infiltrating, spying, and

[28] *The New York Times*, May 1, 2009.
[29] Ibid.
[30] Ibid.

stealing documents from governments and private offices.

The impact of the Internet has come under vociferous and heated discussion in the past few years. The issues have included its role in fostering the 2010–11 anti-government rebellions in North Africa and the Middle East and the riots and fires in London in 2011. Others have concerned the digital divide, or the fact that the richest countries use the Internet as providers and consumers far more developing countries do. But perhaps the most heated discussion followed the release of more than 250,000 secret cables from U.S. embassies around the world that were posted on the Internet by the founder of Wikileaks. This international, online (self-described) for-profit organization publishes private, secret, and classified documents from anonymous sources and whistle-blowers. The founder Julian Assange is being held responsible for this dramatic Wikileaks episode, which involved the theft of classified information from a democratically elected government.

Wikileaks improperly left some names of ambassadors and their informants around the world in their leaked news reports.[31] One of the memos was by U.S. Secretary of State Hillary Clinton, who said that the Saudi government was the world's largest source of funds for Islamist groups and that its leaders were reluctant to stem the flow of money.[32] Other memos publicly identified dozens of sources of information and put their lives in jeopardy. Whereas some called the use of the Internet in anti-government rebellions in Tunisia, Egypt, Libya, Syria, and elsewhere a grand success for democracy and freedom, the leak of secret U.S. cables was termed a blow for civil liberty and freedom of speech. Many called it vandalism and said that it is destructive of the secrecy required in international diplomacy. Should the curiosity of Internet users trump the right of the American government to have its internal communications kept secure? The topic of the Internet's role in violent, civil upheaval is discussed further in Chapter 10, and cybercrime and cyberterrorism are outlined in Chapter 11.

[31] *The New York Times*, August 30, 2011.
[32] *The Times*, November 30, 2010.

Conclusion: Continuing debates about nonstate actors and communications

Many types of nonstate actors conduct flourishing regional and global operations. All international relations specialists, especially constructivists, are concerned with how ideas evolve and how they affect politics in the international system. Constructivists, liberals, and feminists are united in defending nonstate actors and applauding them for getting their issues onto the agendas of international institutions and states. Realists have more mixed views about the importance of nongovernmental actors. Radical Marxists criticize MNCs for favoring the interests of richer classes and states over poorer ones. For them, nonstate organizations may help perpetuate a core of richer and a periphery of poorer states (see Chapters 12 and 13).

As we saw in Chapter 3, constructivists study intensively how socially constructed norms of behavior and the power of ideas affect global politics. They argue that nongovernmental organizations teach people and states new norms of behavior. Realists, of course, believe that final authority resides in states, so

MNCs and NGOs should have to derive their power from them. They point to the fact that nonstate actors too operate in a semianarchic world and have to compete with states that have more wealth, military power, and generally expertise at their disposal. Liberal internationalists welcome nonstate actors because they view their networking activities as facilitating collective action and promoting peaceful relations among peoples. They do not consider them to be threats to the state; indeed, they find their humanitarian activities generally helpful to states. Feminists are cheered by their work on behalf of women around the world. All of these approaches, however, have difficulty assessing the simple fact that criminals and terrorists are also nonstate actors.

The existence of diverse nongovernmental agencies with wide and high frequency across borders raises the obvious question of how much these institutions influence or determine the direction of global politics. Are they moving the world toward a primitive but global civic culture? No doubt transnational activities are flourishing, and it is a trend that could weaken inward-looking state nationalism by encouraging wider transnational or even supranational identities. People with a cause and ready access to the media and Internet are right, perhaps, to think of themselves as *global diplomats*. On occasion, as we have shown, they have been successful in using their communication and organizing skills to influence government policy. But they are quickly disabused of their power when they confront powerful state opposition in the form of economic, political, or military action.

We turn next to nations, ethnicity, and religion – other forces in global politics that are outside direct government or state control.

Select bibliography

Barnett, Michael, and Martha Finnemore, *Rules for the World: International Organizations in Global Politics* (Ithaca, NY: Cornell University Press, 2004).

Brown, L. David, *Creating Credibility: Legitimacy and Accountability for Transnational Civil Society* (Sterling, VA: Kumarian Press, 2008).

Clifford, Bob, *The Marketing of Rebellion: Insurgents, Media, and International Activism* (Cambridge: Cambridge University Press, 2005).

D'Amico, Francine, and Peter R. Beckman, eds., *Women in World Politics: An Introduction* (Abingdon, UK: Bergin and Garvery, 1995).

Ebrahim, Alnoor, and Edward Weisband, eds., *Global Accountabilities: Participation, Pluralism, and Public Ethics* (Cambridge: Cambridge University Press, 2007).

Kahler, Miles, ed., *Networked Politics: Agency, Power, and Governance* (Ithaca, NY: New York: Cornell University Press, 2009).

Keck, Margaret E., and Kathryn Sikkink, *Activists beyond Borders: Advocacy Networks in International Politics* (Ithaca, NY: Cornell University Press, 1998).

Khagram, Sanjeev, James V. Riker, and Kathryn Sikkink, eds., *Restructuring World Politics: Transnational Social Movements, Networks, and Norms* (Minneapolis: University of Minnesota Press, 2002).

Leatherman, Janie, and Julia Webber, eds., *Beyond Global Arrogance: Charting Transnational Democracy* (New York: Palgrave Macmillan, 2005).

Meyer, Mary K., and Elisabeth Prugl, eds., *Gender Politics in Global Governance* (Lanham, MD: Rowman and Littlefield, 1999).

Moghadam, Valentine M., *Globalizing Women: Transnational Feminist Networks* (Baltimore, MD: Johns Hopkins University Press, 2005).

Nelson, Barbara J., and Najma Chowdhury, eds., *Women and Politics Worldwide* (New Haven, CT: Yale University Press, 1994).

Prakash, Aseem, and Mary Kay Gugerty, eds., *Rethinking Advocacy Organizations: A Collective Action Perspective* (Ann Arbor: University of Michigan Press, 2000).

Risse-Kappen, Thomas, ed., Bringing Transnational Relations Back. In: *Non-State Actors, Domestic Structures and International Institutions* (Cambridge: Cambridge University Press, 1995).

Risse, Thomas, Stephen C. Ropp, and Kathryn Sikkink, eds., *The Power of Human Rights: International Norms and Domestic Change* (Cambridge: Cambridge University Press, 1999).

Wolfsfeld, Gadi, *Media and the Path to Peace* (Cambridge: Cambridge University Press, 2004).

8

Politics beyond the state II
Identity – ethnicity, nationalism, and religion

Ethnicity, nationalism, and religion greatly affect global politics. They provide a sense of belonging that helps to shape political activity within states and across state borders. Families, peer groups, and educational and religious institutions all socialize new generations with ideas, values, and beliefs about social interactions, including peace and war. Together they help create a political culture that underpins the behavior of both leaders and masses in multiple and important ways. People identify with, fight for, and often even die for their blood, faith, and beliefs. Leaders of political movements and other elites target these basic identities to mobilize support or incite mass action in their attempt to achieve or thwart specific goals. Adolf Hitler infamously extolled blond Aryans as the "Master Race." Winston Churchill rallied the British people to fight the same Germans in World War II. Although their political causes were diametrically opposed, both men spoke to deeply held sentiments about national identity in an effort to steel their peoples for the horrors of war.

This chapter is concerned with transnational movements in which identity provides a sense of community and belonging. An **identity group** consists of people who share a characteristic or characteristics that define them and set them apart from others. Ethnicity, nationalism, and religion are three components of **social identity** that have gained prominence in international relations theory in recent years. Many sources of international political conflict involve one or more of them. Secular ideas and ideologies such as human rights, feminism, environmentalism, and antiglobalism movements are also significant components of identity, but we cover those topics later in Chapters 14 and 15. Here we are concerned with how transnational movements affect political choices and structure collective decisions that affect global politics.

Ethnicity and nationalism both contribute to social cohesion by providing fundamental identity and unity for societies. Ethnicity, based on extended families or kinship, was the glue that held together early civilizations like Babylon and the Greek city-states. Violence and conflict often occurred between groups that did not share the same ethnicity. Beginning with the French Revolution, **nationalism** based on the state became a primary source of identity and a unifying force for society. Ethnicity and nationalism have both positive and negative consequences – positive when combined with respect for others but negative when they teach contempt for others to justify discrimination, conflict, or war.[1]

Religion, too, is a component of social identity. In this chapter we provide a nutshell summary of the great world religions and then discuss their significance as movements in global politics. We consider

---

[1] Geert Hofstede and Gert Jan Hofstede, *Culture and Organizations: Software of the Mind* (New York: McGraw Hill, 2004); Amiram Raviv, Louis Oppenheimer, and Daniel Bar-Tal, eds., *How Children Understand Peace and War* (San Francisco: Jossey–Bass, 1999).

the impact of four religious belief systems on global politics – Christianity, Islam, Judaism, and Hinduism – as well as Confucianism, an influential cultural force in Asia. Like the nonstate actors discussed in the previous chapter, ethnicity, nationalism, and religion can be forces for stability and peace, or they can develop in ways that threaten the stability of governments and the global system. On September 11, 2001, for example, radical Islamic extremists attacked the United States and became the focus of a global "war on terror."

Belief systems influence politics only when they are expressed through organized or institutional forces. In the previous chapter we dealt with nonstate actors such as corporations, humanitarian organizations, and communications that operate within and across state borders. Now we turn our attention to different types of transnational actors, including religious, ethnic, and nationalist groups that challenge the authority of modern states. A **movement** is a collective or group that is ideologically inspired, idealistic, and action oriented. It aims at social change, sometimes through revolutionary upheaval. Some movements have no clear leadership, whereas others are actively led and directed by ideological guidelines. Sometimes these groups become political parties, as environmental movements have become Green parties in many countries, but most never become institutionalized in this manner. Some have wide social and political concerns, based on nationalism, civil rights, and environmental or human rights; others restrict their focus to particular or geographical areas or topics as specific as the prohibition of alcohol. The most radical movements aspire to fundamentally change the world and may be willing to resort to violent social conflict to achieve their ends.

Many of the world's conflict regions today – including Afghanistan, Iran, Iraq, Israel, Pakistan, Palestine, Somalia, Syria, Turkey, and Yemen – are located on fault lines that can develop when nations and states are not perfectly aligned. They are **divided societies**, where ethnic groups are not satisfied with the states in which they reside or where religious groupings harbor long-standing quarrels and hatreds about the leadership of their countries. Since the end of the Cold War, there has been considerable speculation about whether clashes between civilizations are inevitable and what can or should be done about them. Clashes between religious believers and secularists have surfaced in many countries. Within Islam, there is also growing concern about the internal divisions among moderate Muslims, fundamentalist Muslims, and violent Islamic jihadists. We examine these issues, focusing first on what has been called the "clash of civilizations" and then on the impact of radical Islamic jihadism, as well as the events and prospects of the Arab Awakening and rebellions of 2011–13. Issues directly related to conflict and war in North Africa and the Middle East are covered in Chapters 9–11.

Identity: Ethnicity and nations

Ethnicity and nation both provide a powerful sense of identity. Much of modern conflict is rooted in disputes over ideas and ideology based on ethnicity, nationalism, or religion. Often, the clashes within and across borders are instigated by movements searching for political self-determination or simply attempting to dominate rival groups. Group action can be stimulated by sudden, sensational events, such as the terrorist attacks of 9/11, which initially galvanized the American public behind the

Table 8.1 Basic patterns of identity: Cultures, religions, and regions

Culture/ Civilization	Principal Religion	Region/Countries
African	Christianity/ paganism	Africa south of Sahara
Arab	Islam	North Africa, Central Africa, Middle East
Indian	Hinduism	India
Japanese	Confucianism, Buddhism, Shintoism	Japan
Jewish	Judaism	Israel
Latin	Catholicism	Southern Europe, Latin America
Malay	Islam, Buddhism, Catholicism	Malaysia, Indonesia
Slavic	Orthodox	Eastern Europe, Russia
Sinic	Confucianism	China, Taiwan, Korea, Singapore, Vietnam
Western	Protestantism	Northwest Europe, North America, United Kingdom

Source: Adapted from Samuel P. Huntington's controversial categories in *The Clash of Civilizations and the Remaking of World Order* (New York: Simon & Schuster, 1996).

Bush administration's "war on terror" and the later wars in Afghanistan and Iraq. Identity provided by ethnicity or nation can be a driving force in international politics in less exceptional circumstances, mobilizing public opinion and stimulating citizens to be politically active. It can be a force for good or evil.

Ethnicity is primarily a subjective characteristic shared by groups of people with similar ancestral customs, language, dialect, and/or cultural heritage, and sometimes distinct racial characteristics. Ethnic groups are based on family, blood relatives, distant ancestors, or some form of kinship such as clans or tribes. They are *cultural* entities and are essentially subjective, providing common identity or a sense of "we-ness," or belonging. Ethnic groups often cross state and regional boundaries. The political manifestations of ethno-linguistic subcultures can include a range of political behaviors, from bloc voting to separatist movements and from discrimination to genocide.

Ethnic diversity, when combined with regional, religious, and linguistic differences, can become powerful enough to tear a state apart. Since the end of the Cold War, international or interstate hostilities and violence have relaxed, but there has been a corresponding rise in ethnic rivalries and demands within and across states. In recent decades, ethnic intolerance has surfaced on a scale unseen since before World War I. Yugoslavia and Czechoslovakia, for example, both disintegrated in the wake of challenges by ethnic minorities, the former in a series of secessionist wars, and the latter through peaceful negotiation and agreement.

Closely related to ethnicity are issues of race. Race is "an arbitrary social category, consisting of persons who share such inherited physical characteristics as skin color and facial features, characteristics which are charged with social meaning in some societies."[2] Racial discrimination is the imposition of handicaps, barriers, or different treatment on individuals solely because of their race; it can be embedded formally in laws or carried from one generation to the next by social prejudice. Behavioral and psychological differences are attributed to a racial grouping as a whole. History is replete with examples. There has been discrimination of gentiles against Jews, whites against blacks, Japanese against Koreans, and so on – generally based on the unwarranted assumption that a particular "race" is inherently inferior or that one's own is superior. Racial conflicts tend to become political, with

[2] James J. Teevan, *Introduction to Sociology* (Scarborough, ON: Prentice Hall, 1986), p. 196.

discriminators trying to enact regulations against the discriminated and encountering group protests, antidiscrimination movements, and affirmative-action groups taking the opposite stand. Racist ideologies have gone as far as to call for the extermination of minority groups. Nazism was a hideous example of this, as was the Hutu massacre of the Tutsis in Rwanda.

A **nation** is a cultural entity or group that shares an identity and a feeling of community. It is essentially a subjective identity, involving a sense of social belonging and primary loyalty based on a feeling of commonality. A nation is usually based on people who possess a common language, ancestry, or cultural heritage, and, therefore, share an ethnic identity. It may or may not be the same as the citizenry of a state, but it almost always involves some political consequences. Members of a nation want to govern themselves politically, yet may differ on the practical goals of political autonomy. Some states consist of basically one nation, while others consist of two or more. Canada has two nations, English and French, as well as the aboriginal First Nations, for example, while Switzerland has four language and cultural groupings or nations, French, German, Italian, and Romansch. Some countries, such as the United States, have many ethnic groups within their borders but many members of these groups believe that they share a common identity and may therefore think of themselves as one nation. Americans consider themselves as held together by their experiences and values. The motto of the United States, *E pluribus unum*, spells it out clearly. "Out of many, one" symbolizes the American view of their exceptional nationhood and gives American identity a highly evolved ideological, rather than a cultural, character.

In reality, of course, all states include more than one ethnic group within their populations; no state is entirely ethnically unified. The groups within a state may be bound by feelings of commonality but still not aspire to nation status and/or seek self-determination. However, when nations politicize their demands to redraw state borders along ethnic lines, this often results in highly emotional and sometimes even violent conflict. In other words, an ethnic group may or may not be a politically conscious collectivity of people that aspires to self-government or independent statehood. Some states are deeply divided with so little sense of national identity that they fail to function as states in practical terms. Afghanistan and Iraq, with their many ethnic divisions and divided loyalties, are prime examples today, but Afghan divisions are primarily tribal, whereas Iraq divides along sectarian lines and only secondarily over ethnic quarrels. These types of states are discussed in Chapter 10.

Nationalism and self-determination

Members of a nation, then, whether that nation coincides with the borders of a state or constitutes a smaller group within a state border, may share a sense of loyalty and psychological attachment based on a common language, history, and culture – and often on a desire for political autonomy or even independence. This identification is known as **nationalism**. Nationalism in its modern sense is defined as the collective action of a politically conscious group or nation in pursuit of increased territorial autonomy or sovereignty.

We can trace elements of nationalism throughout history, but as illustrated in Chapter 2, it emerged most strongly in the 17th century, with the growth of the modern state (see also Chapter 4). In Europe, as the unifying ability of the Catholic Church diminished, nations coalesced inside fairly distinct territories with borders. States formed and empires disappeared. People and nations became emotionally attached to the state in which they lived, and by 1800, after the American and French Revolutions, ideas of popular sovereignty blossomed, and absolute monarchies began to disappear. Gradually, people accepted the idea that nation implies equality for its members and a measure of popular participation in political life. Nations became the core unit of identity within states.

Outside the continent, however, Europeans colonized the globe and drew colonial boundaries – according to their own knowledge, interests, and administrative convenience – often subsuming people of different tribal and ethnic backgrounds within colonial borders and forming states that were doomed to internal division with perpetual conflict, violence, and fragmentation. After World Wars I and II, when these colonies became states, many of them lacked a single, cohesive nation, and their peoples' primary identification was often with a tribal, ethnic, or religious group that crossed state boundaries. Many of these states, especially in Africa, collapsed into civil war because of the difficulties of building national identities and state nationalism. Over the centuries, nationalism has appeared in many forms. It has been used positively in quests for emancipation from colonial rule and as an operative force integrating newly independent, multiracial developing countries. Negatively, it has been used to justify doctrines such as **exceptionalism** (the belief that one's state is better than other states or has a unique historical mission to fulfill), economic expansionism, protectionism, and imperialism. As an ideology it has sometimes been employed to further the supremacy of particular nations or peoples over others. Sometimes, it has led to war between and among countries.

The issue of nationalism involves the right of a nation to achieve **self-determination**, usually defined as self-government or sovereign statehood. This is not a simple issue, because many interests and claims are involved. As we saw in Chapter 6, international law is instructive but not conclusive on this point, as it recognizes the principle of self-determination but also the principle of inviolability of existing state borders. The resolutions of the United Nations support both ideas. In 1960, the UN General Assembly adopted a declaration about colonial countries stating that "the subjection of peoples to alien subjugation, domination, and exploitation constitutes a denial of fundamental human rights." Later, in 1976, the UN passed two covenants, both of which declared, "All peoples have the right of self-determination." But, in the final analysis, as we have seen in Chapter 6, it is the UN itself that determines which nations are recognized as states, and the UN organization consists entirely of states. The UN now recognizes China as a member state but not Taiwan. Israel is a member of the UN but Palestine has only observer status.

The only way to settle issues of self-determination is for individual states either to recognize a new country or to defend an existing country's right to maintain its territory intact. Even the UN policy of the right of self-determination extends only to those circumstances in which people are experiencing foreign or alien domination and exploitation or are subject to discriminatory regimes. But since the end of colonialism, the issue is no longer about old colonies or new territories wishing to become independent; rather, it is about groups within extant states attempting to secede. This conundrum haunts UN decision making concerning the admission of new states, and it is likely to grow in intensity as ethno-regional movements inside UN member states agitate for separation and recognition.

To counter separatist groups within a state, governments actively foster national identity at the state level. There are several ingredients or components of a strong **national identity**. They include emotional attachment to the geographical features of the territory; common experiences that promote pride; a common language (bilingual or multilingual nations such as Belgium, Canada, and Switzerland are rare – most have one major, official language); shared history, values, traditions, and customs; and perhaps even a common literature or sport that creates a wide sense of familiarity and belonging. States adopt flags and anthems, issue honors and medals, and sponsor parades and national days to inspire unity (Figure 8.1).

All governments foster national identity to promote cohesion and stability. However, there is a point at which such attachments can become virulent, divisive, and threatening. This development, called **hypernationalism**, occurs when nationalist sentiment fosters the belief that other nations or states are both inferior and threatening. At this point, hypernationalism, commonly called xenophobia, may threaten domestic and international peace.

Figure 8.1 Symbols that unite nations and build patriotism can include flags, anthems, buildings, constitutions, and national heroes. The architecturally unique Opera House in Sydney is a symbol of Australian nationalism along with its flag and other cultural artifacts.

Hitler's Germany is a classic example of nationalism that crossed the threshold to hypernationalism. The government preached the purity of the German race and attacked Jews, Gypsies, homosexuals, communists, and others as "enemies of the state." Nazi propaganda nourished contemptuous beliefs about the nations of surrounding states and promoted hatred toward them in order to garner support for Germany's national security policy and eventually a wave of aggression against other states.[3]

Ethno-national movements

When an ethnic group or nation does not possess its own state but is territorially based within a country, political scientists call it an *ethno-national movement*. On occasion, but not always, these groups evolve into separatist movements that seek to form their own states. Such movements are quite common inside the world's 193 states. Even in rich, developed, and democratic countries there can be pressures for autonomy from such movements. In the United Kingdom, Scottish, Welsh, and Irish nationalists form political movements, and although the country remains constitutionally united, the government has recently had to respond with administrative decentralization and separate legislatures for Wales and Scotland. As of 2012 this was also the case in Northern Ireland. The Northern Ireland Assembly (formerly Stormont) now has the full powers that it was earlier denied because of the so-called Troubles (turmoil and violence between Protestants and Catholics). Scotland, on the other hand, will have a referendum in 2014 on independence from the United Kingdom. Other well-known ethno-nationalist movements inside stable democratic countries include the Québécois in Canada, Basques and Catalans in Spain, Bretons and Corsicans in France, Sikhs in India, Kurds in Iraq and Turkey, and Flemings and Walloons in Belgium. In these and many other cases, ethnic minorities regularly make demands that cannot be accommodated.

---

[3] See Robert J. Jackson and Doreen Jackson, *An Introduction to Political Science: Comparative and World Politics*, 5th ed. (Scarborough, ON: Pearson, 2008), p. 52.

Under Joseph Stalin, the former Soviet Union forced distinctive ethnic groups underground. It physically removed people from their communities and dispersed them across the country in the guise of economic planning. Today, China imposes strong controls over Tibetan culture, ensuring that Tibetan children learn the standard Chinese version of history – namely that Tibet was "peacefully liberated" by China in 1951. However, Tibetans continue to carefully guard elements of their local culture, including their language and the Buddhist religion. In large parts of the developing world, movements exert regional and nationalist pressures on the power of the central governments. For a list of some of these groups currently in the news, see Table 8.2.

While many ethno-national movements are content to remain within their states, especially if they can obtain a degree of political decentralization or federation, some agitate constantly for self-determination and statehood. Ethno-regional movements can threaten international stability when they are based inside what is regarded as a legitimate state or when they are spread over several countries. Yugoslavia and the Soviet Union split into several independent states after their communist states fell apart. Quarrels over ethnicity separated Serbs, Croatians, and Muslims in the former Yugoslavia, and ethnic differences continue to be at the root of current problems between Russia and Chechnya. In Africa, ethnic rivalries led to the massacre of Hutus by Tutsis in Rwanda in the 1990s, and in Sudan, violence against Christians and black Muslims in the western area of Darfur was carried out by the Janjaweed militia, with the full backing of the Arab Muslim government in Khartoum (see Chapter 10).

Two particularly troublesome ethno-regional challenges today concern Kurds and Kashmiris. Their quarrels pose multiple threats. Like the case of Palestine and Israel discussed earlier, they illustrate the type of conflict that develops when ethno-national movements exist inside states they resent. Their agitation affects the politics of entire regions and global affairs generally (see Close Ups 8.1 and 8.2).

Table 8.2 Selected states and their principal ethno-national challengers

State	Ethno-national challengers
Afghanistan	Hazaras, Pashtuns, Tajiks, Turkmens, Uzbeks
Canada	Québécois
Georgia	Abkhaz, Ossetes
India and Pakistan	Kashmiris
Indonesia	Timorese, Papuans, Moluccans
Iraq, Iran, Syria, Turkey	Kurds
Israel	Palestinians
Lebanon	Maronites, Palestinians
Malaysia	People of Sabah and Sarawak
Mexico	Mayans, Zapotecs, Mixes
Moldova	Ukranians, Russians
Myanmar	Karens
Nigeria	Ibos, Yorubas
People's Republic of China	Tibetans
Russia	Chechnyans
Rwanda	Hutus, Tutsis
Serbia	Albanians
Spain	Basques
Sri Lanka	Tamils
Sudan	More than 50 ethnic groups and 600 tribes (sometimes reduced to Black, Arab, and Beja)

Identity: Religion and religious movements

Religion provides a powerful sense of identity. It is one of the most important forces shaping political culture, and it is unlimited by state boundaries. A religion consists of a complex system of faith, beliefs, ethical principles, and laws. It appeals to the head and the heart, which is a source of enormous

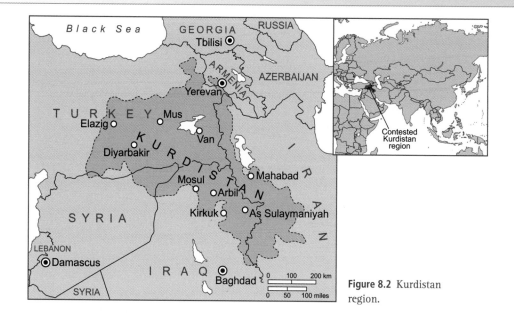

Figure 8.2 Kurdistan region.

Close Up 8.1 **Kurds**

Most of the thirty million Kurdish people are spread throughout four Middle East countries that border one another – Iran, Iraq, Syria, and Turkey (Figure 8.2). There are also small groups of Kurds in some states east of Turkey and in diasporas in much of the developed world. Kurds share an ethnic heritage and a language (Kurdish), and a majority of them share the Muslim faith. Large numbers of them are **irredentists** – that is, they want to return to their homeland and to form a new state rather than continue to be part of the state in which they reside. Some would be satisfied with an autonomous region within their present state. In northern Iraq, Kurds have achieved a federalized form of autonomy. However, the other three countries in question – Iran, Syria, and Turkey – are not prepared to cede any autonomy or territorial control to the Kurds. The Kurdish language is prohibited in some areas, and Kurdish political organizations are harassed.

Most Kurds want to separate from their Middle Eastern countries and form a new country, to be called Kurdistan. The most visible Kurdish ethno-regional movement is the Kurdistan Workers Party (PKK), which has adherents throughout Turkey and promotes pro-separatist strikes from northern Iraq into Turkey. Demonstrations and violent clashes regularly take place between the Turkish army and police and the separatist, nationalist Kurds. Kurdish militancy shows no signs of abating.

comfort and assurance to the faithful in their private lives. But religion also constitutes a belief system that involves issues of authority and justice that are factors in politics, and in certain circumstances this gives it a powerful voice in public affairs. Religion has made a major resurgence in international affairs in recent years largely given to the rise of populations in the global South (whose families tend to be both more religious and more prolific) and increased religious broadcasting

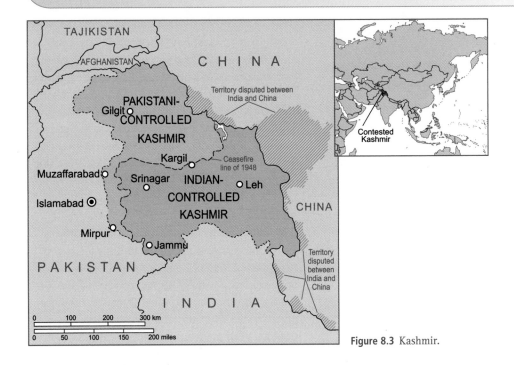

Figure 8.3 Kashmir.

Close Up 8.2 **Kashmiris**

Kashmir presents an ongoing ethno-regional challenge that confronts India, Pakistan, and, to a lesser extent, China (Figure 8.3). The case clearly illustrates the relation between major ethno-regional challenges to local state power and their impact on regional and global stability. To the dismay of the international community, both India and Pakistan have built up their militaries in preparation for war, and in 1998 both countries began to develop and deploy nuclear weapons.

This regional challenge stems from the fact that, at independence in 1947, the Kashmiri maharaja chose to join his Himalayan territory to India. Kashmiris are mainly Muslim, and most would have preferred to join Pakistan, an Islamic republic, rather than the predominantly Hindu India. Internal disputes and border wars between India and Pakistan were inconclusive

until 1972, when the territory was divided into two parts, with most of the population in the south given to India as Jammu and Kashmir, and the lesser populated northern portion given to the state of Pakistan. The so-called Line of Control (LOC) was established between the two sides, but it did not eliminate violence across the border.

In 1999 so-called freedom fighters crossed the LOC from north to south but were repelled by the Indian army and air force. On other occasions, pro-Pakistan separatist groups have been associated with terrorist activities and even suicide bombings. In 2003 India and Pakistan declared a cease-fire for the first time in more than a decade. Both governments then tried confidence-building measures, but hostilities continued. The contemporary tense situation encourages both states to keep thousands of troops on their borders; deflects possibilities for overall cooperation; and makes it difficult for Pakistan to focus its energies and troops along the border with Afghanistan, where they are needed against the Taliban. Many commentators regard the India-Pakistan standoff as the most dangerous situation in the world, especially as both states possess nuclear weapons.

via television and the Internet.[4] In global politics its most noticeable features have manifested in the uprisings in the Middle East and North Africa and in the growth of cybercrime and international terrorism.

A religion is an organized, institutionalized system of beliefs based on the superior authority of a supernatural being, or beings, the purpose of which is to instruct the faithful in morally responsible behavior. *Faith*, or complete trust, is a necessary condition to believe that basic religious tenets and teachings are infallible. Many religions have rich and long histories. Their adherents have established great civilizations and have produced significant cultural, artistic, and scientific achievements. When religion combines with ethnic and territorial issues, it can become a force for cohesion or conflict within and across states. Since organized religions express the central value system of many individuals, they can teach people to love but also to hate. Adherents may become extremists, dividing the world into believers and infidels, friends and enemies. They may oppose other religions or even secular state systems and create religious movements to proselytize or fight for their beliefs or impose them on others.

Throughout history, empires and religions often used each other to establish and strengthen a centralized grip on territory and peoples.[5] Those who adhere to strict religious practices are easily identified and may be persecuted by others. Islamic and Arab states in general are difficult for Westerners with Christian or secular beliefs to comprehend. The central concept of separation of church and state, for example, does not fit easily with universal claims of the Muslim faith. Christianity also makes universal claims, with the difference that since the 17th century the separation of state and church has been progressively consolidated in most Christian societies.

Religious leaders not only teach their faiths and beliefs but also set up institutions to support their causes. Believers may form politically active organizations, or religious movements, to promote their ideas. Christianity, Islam, Judaism, Hinduism, other smaller religions, and philosophies such as Confucianism have formed movements and even formalized nongovernmental organizations (NGOs) to promote their viewpoints. In a pertinent example of how they can come into conflict, Christianity, especially in the form of Catholicism, Pentecostalism, and other forms of evangelicalism, is currently strengthening in parts of Central Africa, moving north and confronting forces of Islam that are moving south on the continent. The certainty of religious beliefs and the desire to proselytize and convert nonbelievers to their faith through aggressive missionary activities has often promoted intolerance toward others. Religious movements can become sources of intolerance, hatred, and terror. Throughout history, wars have been fought in the name of religion, with contending forces claiming to be acting in accordance with divine authority. It was religious fanatics in the Islamic al-Qaeda global terrorist organization who initiated the events of 9/11 in the United States and led to the war against the Taliban in Afghanistan. The distribution of the world's Muslim population is indicated in Table 18.3.

---

[4] See Monica Duffy Toft, Daniel Philpott, and Timothy Samuel Shah, *God's Century: Resurgent Religion and Global Politics* (New York: Norton, 2011); and Scott M. Thomas, "A Globalized God: Religion's Growing Influence in International Politics," *Foreign Affairs* 89, no. 6 (November–December 2010), pp. 93–101.

[5] See Selina O'Grady, *And Man Created God: Kings, Cults and Conquests at the Time of Jesus* (London: Atlantic Books, 2012).

Table 8.3 Muslim population by region, 2010

	Estimated Muslim population	Estimated percentage of global Muslim population
World	1,619,314,000	100
Asia-Pacific	1,005,507,000	62.1
Middle East and North Africa	321,869,000	19.9
Sub-Saharan Africa	242,544,000	15.0
Europe	44,138,000	2.7
Americas	5,256,000	0.3

Source: "The Future of the Global Muslim Population," Pew Research Center's Forum on Religion and Public Life, ©2011, Pew Research Center. http://pewforum.org/The-Future-of-the-Global-Muslim-Population.aspx.
Note: Population estimates are rounded to thousands. Percentages are calculated from unrounded numbers. Figures may not add exactly due to rounding.

Christianity

Christianity is the largest religion today, with about 33 percent of those who claim a religious affiliation belonging to the Christian church. More than 2.2 billion of the world's approximately seven billion people are Christians, which makes the faith a global force – by virtue of both sheer numbers and the compelling message of the religion's moral code. Christianity was founded by followers of Jesus Christ, known also as Jesus of Nazareth. Christians consider Jesus, born between 6 and 4 BCE, and crucified around 28 CE, to be the Messiah predicted by the Old Testament prophets. Christianity therefore is monotheistic – that is, based on a belief in one God. Christianity is an offshoot of Judaism, which over time completely eclipsed the mother faith. Jesus was considered by Jews and Romans to be a radical rabbi.

Over time, Christianity has divided into several different branches. Many churches have prospered, and some have become formidable economic empires. Protestantism, which embodies a wide variety of beliefs, had an immense impact where it originated in northern Europe; the Roman Catholic church exercised more influence in the south; and the Eastern Orthodox Church predominated in the East, Russia, and Greece (Figure 8.4). By 1900, around two-thirds of the world's Christians lived in Europe and the United States. Today, both Protestant and Catholic churches send missionaries throughout the world. While secularism is on the rise in Europe and North America, evangelicalism and especially Pentecostalism are growing quickly in the developing South, especially in Africa. Today, two-thirds of the world's Christians live in South America, Africa, and Asia. After years of persecution, Orthodox Christianity and missionary activity have reemerged in former communist countries from Russia to Albania, providing moral teaching and strengthening national identities. Christianity has both mainstream and fundamentalist adherents. Fundamentalists of any religion believe in the literal truth of their holy text or texts, and they justify their actions as God's will. Both the horrors of the Christian Inquisition in the 15th century and the rhetoric of Muslim terrorists today are based on the belief that God's will justifies their actions.

Since the Treaty of Westphalia in 1648, the acceptance of the idea of separation of state and religion has been fairly consistent in democratic countries. Since that time, the Roman Catholic Church has had little control over geographical territory, and today it controls only a very tiny state, Vatican City. While the Christian faith and fundamentalist branches of it exist throughout the democratic world, its adherents are usually prepared to follow the adage from Jesus that one should "render therefore to Caesar the things that are Caesar's; and unto God the things that are God's."[6] The U.S. Constitution promotes the absolute principle of separation of church and state, but some countries such as the United Kingdom have an established church, an arrangement that subordinates the Church of England in some respects to the state and makes the monarch the "defender of the faith."

[6] Matthew 22:21.

Figure 8.4 The Russian Orthodox Cathedral of Christ the Saviour, first consecrated in 1883, was a memorial to the Russian people for their role in defeating Napoleon's army. Persecution of the church began in 1918 under Stalin, and the cathedral was vandalized, destroyed, and later even turned into a swimming pool. It was rebuilt 1994–2000 after the fall of the Soviet Union and the restoration of religious freedom.

Islam

Islam arose shortly after Christianity and is the fastest-growing religion in the world. It is the monotheistic religion of Muhammad (CE 570–632), whom followers consider the true Prophet of God and the last of the prophets. Adherents of Islam, called Muslims, follow the revelations and teachings of Muhammad as contained in the Koran and its interpretations, which call for the creation of a just society. Today there are estimated to be more than 1.6 billion Muslims worldwide. Islam is the second-largest religion in the world, both in terms of the number of adherents and the number of countries where it is professed by the majority of the population. Worldwide, about 21 percent of those claiming a religious affiliation are Muslim. Muslim populations are located mostly in northern and central Africa, the Middle East, central and southern Asia, and the Indonesian archipelago. Four-fifths of Muslims live outside the Arab Middle East. The three principal languages of the Islamic tradition are Arabic, Persian, and Turkish.

The **Organization of the Islamic Conference (OIC)** brings together fifty-seven states on four continents to enhance the collective voice of the Muslim world. Twenty-five of them have a population that is more than 90 percent Muslim, with the largest single state concentration in Indonesia. The organization espouses the causes of Muslims around the world. It attempts to eliminate misperceptions about Muslims and strongly condemns discrimination against them. The member states include various forms of government, including monarchies, democracies, and four Islamic republics – Afghanistan, Iran, Mauritania, and Pakistan.

Since the issue of succession arose after Muhammad's death, the religion has been split into two main branches, Sunni and Shiite, or Shia, but there are a great many other divisions apart from and within these two groupings. Essentially, **Shiites** believe that the successor or leader of the Muslim religion must be a direct descendant of Muhammad, whereas **Sunnis** do not. The vast majority of Muslims (85–90 percent) are Sunnis, who claim they

Table 8.4 Main branches of Muslim traditions and sects

Branch	Approximate number of followers	Core beliefs
Sunnis	1 billion plus	Follow the deeds and practices (Sunnah) of Muhammad)
Shias	100 million plus	Believe Muhammad's kin are his rightful successors; that the last in a line of twelve imams may reappear soon
Sufis	Unknown	Adhere to Islam's mystical tradition; may be Sunni or Shia
Salafis/Wahhabis Ismailis Alevis Ahmaddiyas	About 17 million 15 million 10 million 4 million	Strict, austere Sunnis, peaceful or violent, often followers of al-Wahhab of 18th century, mainly in Saudi Arabia
Alawites	3 million	Emphasize the Shia imams, some rites overlap with Christianity; rulers of Syria

represent the "Suna" or right path, rather than the Shiite branch of the faith. Sunnis account for most Muslims among the Turks, Arabs, Afghans, North Africans, Indonesians, Pakistanis, and East Indians. Only about 10 percent of all Muslims are members of the Shia sect, and they are concentrated mainly in Iran and Iraq. Shah Abbas (1587–1629) established Shia Islam as the state religion of Iran, and it remains so today. (Adherents of Shia Islam are called Shi'is, Shiites, or Shias). There are many other branches of Islamic thought, as Table 8.4 indicates.

Two points about Islam are vital in the study of international affairs. First, Islam is often equated with the Arab world, but it is much broader than that – fewer than 15 percent of Muslims are Arab. Twenty-two countries belong to the Arab League, which encompasses some 350 million people, of whom many are Muslims, but these countries also are home to Maronites, Copts, Berbers, Kurds, and black Christians. Arabs are not an ethnic or religious group but rather *Arab* denotes a combination of language, state, and territory into a regionally defined sense of common identity.

Second, Islam does not always coexist easily with democracy. Religious leaders, or mullahs, hold that any system that places the will of the people above the will of Allah destroys the soul and the nation. They insist on the unity of the spiritual and temporal world and therefore reject any concept of separating religion from the state. In contrast to Christians, they follow the guiding principle that Muslims are to be unified spiritually, culturally, and politically. For them, the Koran insists both on the indivisibility of God's law and the unity of any power structure based on Islam.

Because the religion developed at a time when there were very few social and governmental institutions, Islamic law assumed the role of regulating all areas of human conduct, not just religious behavior. Sharia law (Islamic law) has become a central tenet of government policy in some Muslim-majority countries. In early Islamic states, no distinction was made between the person of the ruler and the state, and the law was conceived of as simply a means to maintain official power and policy. By the 19th century, many Muslim states had modernized their legal systems to cope with new demands. For example, European legal codes were adopted in Egypt and Turkey to supplement Islamic law. In the 20th century, Turkey abolished Islamic law altogether. Egypt abolished it as well in 1956, but then in 1980 amended its constitution

Figure 8.5 Religious identity plays a powerful role in Middle Eastern political life. About 90 percent of Egyptians are Muslim and 10 percent are Christian Copts. The Mosque of Mohammed Ali dominates the Citadel fortress in Cairo and illustrates the significance of Islam in the country.

to reinstate Islamic revelations as the philosophical foundation of Egyptian law (Figure 8.5).

Islam exercises profound influence on governments in the Middle East, and also in Africa, Central Asia, and Southeast Asia. Iran has an Islamic government, and so did Afghanistan under the Taliban from 1996 to 2001. Islamic movements are active in Palestine, Lebanon, Jordan, the Gulf States, and across northern and central Africa. Several Muslim states use a blend of Islamic law and European civil law codes to meet the needs of their culturally varied populations. One of these is Indonesia, which contains almost one-fifth of the world's Muslims, but where Islam is not the state religion. Saudi Arabia, by contrast, is a monarchy, with the Koran as its constitution and Islamic Sharia law as the basis of the government and courts. Some religious fundamentalists would like to impose strict Islamic law in all Muslim countries.

Turkish, Iranian, and Arab nationalisms that developed during the late 19th and 20th centuries never entirely superseded the bonds of Islam. During that time secular nationalisms developed, but

its advocates often drew on Islam as a source of cultural strength to oppose encroachments of the West. Even today, pan-Arab nationalism and the Islamic faith are often called on in times of crisis to mobilize the faithful across national borders. After his troops invaded Kuwait in 1990, President Saddam Hussein of Iraq called in vain for a *jihad*, or holy war, against the UN forces after the Security Council authorized the use of military force against the Iraqi occupation. Both pro- and antigovernment demonstrators during the 2011–12 Arab Awakening used the Islamic faith to support their claims and demands.

Many Westerners regard radical fundamentalist Islam as a danger for the West and democracy, as well as for women's rights, and freedom of speech. They also consider it to be a source of extremist attitudes that can lead to violence, terrorism, and possibly war (see Close Up 8.3). As Figure 8.2 shows, however, in Europe and North America, majorities in the United States, Canada, Britain, France, and Russia say that they hold somewhat or very favorable views of Muslims. Many of the world's Muslims, however, believe that the West, linked to Christianity and Judaism, wants to control their lands and oil wealth. For them, Jewish control of parts of Palestine, Western dominance of Iraq and Afghanistan, and influence in other Persian Gulf states are proof of the West's ambitions to dominate the region. There is dramatic variation in these attitudes, with more extreme positions in some countries, but everywhere there is concern about Western intentions. Table 8.5 shows that predominantly Muslim countries have mixed views of Christianity and strongly negative views about Jews.

Table 8.5 Favorability ratings toward Muslims, Christians, and Jews, 2011

States	% Favorable toward		
	Muslims	Christians	Jews
United States	57	89	82
Britain	64	83	76
France	64	84	84
Germany	45	75	71
Spain	37	76	59
Russia	62	89	63
Israel	19	54	88
Turkey	72	6	4
Egypt	97	48	2
Jordan	96	57	2
Lebanon	92	96	3
Palestinian Territories	82	–	4
Indonesia	97	52	9
Pakistan	95	16	2

Source: "Muslim-Western Tensions Persist," July 21, 2011, the Pew Attitudes Project, a project of the Pew Research Center.
Note: In predominantly Muslim countries, figures are for Muslims only. Because of an administrative error, ratings of Christians in the Palestinian Territories are not shown.

Close Up 8.3 Afghanistan: Islamic law and the Taliban

By 1998, after nine years of war with the Russians, relative peace returned to Afghanistan for a few years. Until 2001, Afghanistan's law was determined entirely by the Taliban's rigid interpretation of the teachings of Islam – a more rigid code than elsewhere in the Muslim world. Those who violated the Taliban's ways were publicly beaten, maimed, or killed.

The harsh rules touched every aspect of life. In public, women had to cover themselves with burkas that provided only a screen-covered opening for their eyes. They were forbidden to work, read, or walk the streets alone. Girls could not attend schools. Men had to trim their mustaches just above their lips, trim their bangs neatly along their foreheads, and wear beards. Harsh punishments were meted out for gambling, taking alcohol or drugs, watching television, and even listening to music. Homosexuals were buried alive under walls of brick, adulterers were stoned to death, and thieves had their hands amputated. "Unclean things" included satellite dishes, kites, chess, computers, television, nail polish, photographs, any equipment that produces music, wine, and firecrackers.

After the 2001 Western invasion of Afghanistan and the inauguration of a democratic government, many of these harsh laws were rescinded. Under the government of President Hamid Karzai more girls are being educated, urban women are freer (indeed, have even been elected to Parliament), and societal regulations have been relaxed. But violence continues throughout the country and ethnic, regional, and cultural divisions are profound and destabilizing (see Chapters 10 and 11 on civil war and terrorism), and it remains to be seen whether the harsh laws will be reinstated if the West leaves the country and the Taliban regain their power and influence.

Figure 8.6 The Jewish people are divided into groupings of orthodox, conservative, and reform. There are many sects of orthodox Jews. The largest community is in Israel, where about 25 percent of Jews are orthodox. They strictly adhere to the traditional interpretation and application of the laws and ethics of the Torah and later authorities.

As we saw in Chapter 2, Muslim attitudes are deep seated in history. For much of the Middle Ages, Islam formed a thriving empire that dominated the Middle East, North Africa, much of Southwestern Asia, Spain, and Central Europe. From 1195 to 1270 European kings led major Christian crusades against Muslim rule over the Christian Holy Land in what is present-day Israel. Islamic civilizations also clashed with Christian Orthodox powers, but their decline did not begin until about 1500. The Ottoman Empire collapsed after World War I, and much of the Middle East experienced colonial domination by Christian, European powers. Even today many Muslims charge that the West, led by the United States, interferes in the Muslim world by protecting pro-Western regimes in Saudi Arabia, Kuwait, the United Arab Emirates, and elsewhere.

Judaism

Another important religion for understanding modern global politics is Judaism. Judaism is older than Christianity or Islam, but like them, it is monotheistic. Indeed, it is the oldest existing monotheistic religion today. It consists of beliefs and practices originating in the Hebrew Bible, as explained in the Talmud and other writings (Figure 8.6). Religious authority is vested not in any single person or body but in texts, law, and rabbis who interpret those texts and laws.

Judaism describes itself as the religion and philosophy of the Children of Israel or the Jewish Nation. Followers are called Jews, and they regard themselves as an ethno-religious group. The total population is estimated at more than thirteen million people, which comprises less than 1 percent of the major world religions. Jews are spread throughout the world, with slightly less than half in Israel and the next largest number in the United States. They have three main divisions: orthodox, conservative, and reform.

Judaism has had a major impact on contemporary international relations. Throughout history Jews have often been a persecuted minority. It was only after they were subjected to Hitler's genocidal policies in Germany in 1939–45 that, in 1948, they achieved their own state of Israel. Since then tensions between Jews and Muslims in the Middle East have been high. When the UN voted to create Israel from part of a partitioned Palestine, the United Nations failed to set up a Palestinian state as originally envisioned, and the neighboring Arab states refused to accept the partition or recognize the new state of Israel. The first Arab-Israeli War then made refugees of the Palestinians. The ensuing tensions have sparked a series of wars between Israel and its neighbors. Unlike Christianity and Islam, which are spread out around the world and dominate in many countries, Judaism since 1948 has been mainly linked to a particular state – although the Israeli constitution does not declare Judaism as the official state religion. However, as Prime Minister Benjamin Netanyahu put it, there will not be peace until it is recognized that Israel is a "Jewish state."[7]

The state of Israel is about the size of Massachusetts, with a population of slightly more than seven million people. Its population is more than 80 percent Jewish, with significant minorities of Muslims and other religions. Hebrew is the official language of the country, although Arabic and English are widely spoken. The dramatic political conflict between Israeli Jews and Palestinians is described in Chapter 4 and elsewhere in the text.

Hinduism

Hinduism was known as Brahmanism until the 18th century.[8] Like Judaism, it is an ancient religion. It is the world's third-largest religion after Christianity and Islam. With an estimated one billion adherents (about 14 percent of adherents of the world's major religions), the vast majority live in India, and others are spread across southern Asia. Hinduism is a *henotheistic* religion in which there is one deity that takes many forms. Hindu beliefs vary widely across many branches. Well-known characteristics include a belief in reincarnation and karma and a spiritually informed explanation for all cause and effect. Vishnu and Shiva are two of the most popular gods among Hindus. Religious living (dharma) is governed by ancient moral texts such as the *Vedas* and the *Upanishads*.

Like Judaism, Hinduism is linked to a particular state. While India contains several minority groups, such as Christians, Sikhs, Jains, Buddhists, and a large minority of Muslims, it is predominately Hindu (more than 83 percent of the population). Both Hindi and English are official languages in this land of more than a billion people. However, the ethnic and religious differences are reinforced by different languages. The constitution of India recognizes fourteen major languages, and hundreds of other languages and dialects are spoken in the rural areas. India is a classic example of a complex multiethnic society in which issues of religion, race, and ethnicity are highly politicized. Its caste system – a hereditary system delineated in terms of certain occupations, rules of marriage, and rules of interaction with other castes – dates back to the origins of Hinduism more than two thousand years ago.

The Hindu population has four main castes, which contain hundreds of subcastes based on descending levels of ritual purity.[9] *Brahmins* (approximately 12 percent) of Hindus are the highest caste, traditionally the caste of Hindu priests, now found in most professions; *Kshatriyas* (13 percent) are soldiers, governors, and landowners; *Vaishyas* are tradespeople and farmers; and *Shudras* are the service castes or artisans, including land tillers, barbers, craftspeople, and menial laborers (25 percent combined). Over time, an underclass also emerged. The *Harijan* ("untouchables"), who are outcasts, and tribes who belong to none of the castes, make up the remaining 50 percent of Hindus. Within the broad caste groups are *jati* (literally "born") – thousands of occupation-based groups. The *jati* form the basis of strict rules about social contact and intermarriage.

Although caste-based discrimination has been illegal since India became independent in 1947, its impact continues and incidents of social discrimination are common. Caste discrimination begins early

[7] http://www.jpost.com.
[8] A. C. Grayling, *Ideas That Matter: A Personal Guide for the 21st Century* (London: Weidenfeld & Nicolson, 2009).
[9] See, for example, Yogendra K. Malik, Craig Baxter, et al., *Government and Politics in South Asia*, 6th ed. (New York: Westview Press, 2008). India stopped collecting statistics on caste in the 1931 census, so all figures about caste are extrapolations from that time.

in life and extends to all parts of life. Untouchables are sometimes barred from wells and temples and live in the semislavery of debt-bonded labor. Attempts to eliminate even some of the worst injustices of the Indian caste system regularly meet with resistance, which has political repercussions, but affirmative action is beginning to raise opportunities for untouchables. Similar caste systems also govern the lives of 240 million people in Bangladesh, Japan, Nepal, Pakistan, Sri Lanka, and other parts of southeast Asia and Africa.

The Indian Sikh population, followers of a religion founded by Guru Nanak, is strongly concentrated in the north of the country in the Punjab region and is relatively prosperous economically. Their struggle for independence has often led to violence between Sikh extremists and antiseparatists. In 1984, for example, Sikh extremists occupied the Golden Temple in Amritsar. Its recapture by the Indian army left many dead. That same year, Prime Minister Indira Gandhi was assassinated by her Sikh bodyguards. The anti-Sikh riots that followed her death caused more than a thousand additional deaths. In 1985, the struggle also reached the level of international terrorism, with the bombing of an Air India plane and the attempted bombing of a second, both taking off from Canadian airports. Today, the prime minister is a Sikh.

Hinduism was traditionally a very tolerant religion, but in recent decades some branches have become more political, intolerant, and terroristic. Some Hindu political parties advocate violent political struggle against other religious groups, particularly Muslims in Pakistan. They have, for example, provoked Muslims by calling for Hindu law to be imposed throughout India. In Kashmir tensions between Muslims and Hindus continue to create instability (see Close Up 8.2).

Confucianism

Confucianism is not a religion based on faith but a cultural force that has had a powerful effect on politics in many states in Asia, especially in China, Japan, North and South Korea, Singapore, Taiwan,

and Vietnam. It is a Chinese political and moral philosophy based on the teachings of the scholar Confucius (551–479 BCE), who advised rulers that they could obtain stable government by instilling correct moral behavior in both rulers and the ruled. It is, however, compatible with formal religions, and this has helped it spread throughout Asia. Confucianism was the official creed of China in the 2nd century BCE – a guide both for statecraft and moral instruction. It became the official state belief system for the Han Dynasty in 136 BCE, dominated Chinese political and ethical thought until the early 20th century, and is a central component of East Asian political culture today.

Confucianism does not have a formalized structure or organized worship. As an abstract guide to a way of life, it stresses management of society through a carefully defined system of social and familial relationships. It teaches that each person has a role to understand and perform obediently. Sons are subservient to fathers, wives to husbands, and subjects to rulers. As the highest authority, rulers must set a moral example by demonstrating a pure spirit and manners above reproach. If the ruler has good thoughts and is utterly sincere, good government will follow. When things go wrong, it is an indication that rulers have not been sincere. The emphasis on right thinking remains important in China today, even though Confucianism has been replaced by Marxist thought as the formal state orthodoxy.

Confucianism as a cultural tradition is extremely varied. Each Asian country developed its own distinctive version, and these diverged even more as the countries modernized and modified the doctrinal teachings of Confucianism without eliminating its essence. In this way the evolution of Confucianism contributed to distinct political cultures, while strands of Confucian culture visible throughout Asia are said to be conducive to economic achievement (see Close Up 8.4). Some cultural characteristics and socialization patterns of Confucianism have significant political consequences. In politics, perhaps the most important aspect of Confucianism is respect

Close Up 8.4 **Confucianism in Singapore and Japan**

The tiny city-state of Singapore illustrates the relationship of Confucianism, culture, and politics. When Lee Kuan Yew was elected prime minister in 1959, Singapore's future was uncertain. Its two-year federation with Malaysia had collapsed, and many doubted Singapore's ability to exist as an independent country. Today, however, three million Singaporeans enjoy one of the highest living standards in Asia.

The Western goal of democracy played little role in Singapore's remarkable transition. Lee's thirty-one-year leadership was based on strict, authoritarian methods. He did not believe that democracy had a place in his country, or anywhere in the developing world, because, he said, checks and balances interfere with governing in a developing country, "where executive action must be swift to forestall disorder."[10] In the three decades in which he transformed Singapore, the tightly controlled structure that he crafted rested heavily on his own incorruptibility and "the innate entrepreneurship and pragmatism of the ethnic-Chinese majority and its Confucian father-knows-best ethic."[11] In late 1990, Lee Kuan Yew installed his protégé, Goh Chok Tong, as prime minister, and he was followed in 2004 by Lee Hsien Loong (son of Lee Kuan Yew), who remains in office. All three prime ministers of Singapore have been from the People's Action Party, and authoritarian capitalism continues to direct the Singapore economy.

Japan is a country in which the Shinto religion and Confucianism exercise an important influence on politics. Both buttressed the authority of the emperor throughout much of Japan's history and had a role in training suicide kamikaze bombers during World War II. A democratic form of government was introduced there after the country's defeat and occupation at the end of World War II. However, religious influence is still to be found in political and social relations. Characteristics such as obedience, achievement, and respect for authority are important in Japanese society, and these are reinforced by intense competition in national examinations for students at all levels of education and by loyalty to corporations in the workplace.

The Japanese culture also includes Buddhist and Shinto religion and philosophies, both of which inspire habits of cleanliness and extraordinary discipline and are often credited with playing a significant role in the Japanese economic "miracle." It is common, for example, for priests and engineers to gather in a ceremony outside a temple to burn pictures of worn-out computer chips to thank the chips and other electronic devices for their uncomplaining service. The Japanese culture is often perceived as consensual – an attitude considered vital in the conduct of political parties, cabinet formation, and decision making in foreign policy.

for loyalty and authority, as hierarchy is considered critical to both personal discipline and social harmony. All social relations are structured by the status of subordinate and superior, and due respect and obedience are honored, providing a tendency to value the collective over the individual.

The clash of civilizations: Supporters and critics

According to one influential and controversial group of scholars, the global order has entered a new phase in which the decisive forces that dominate

---

[10] Quoted by Lewis M. Simons in "Brave New Singapore," *Atlantic*, 268, no. 1 (July 1991), p. 26.
[11] Ibid.

international conflict are culture and religion rather than democracy versus communism or capitalism versus Marxism. When the Cold War ended, many Americans began to speak triumphantly about the universal triumph of Western liberal capitalism.[12] Others saw the world as a more varied and, to some extent, more frightening place. For this latter group, a clash of civilizations seemed to be developing between the forces of secularism and religion, between Western liberal democracy and Islamic fundamentalism.[13] According to this argument, cultural and religious differences among the major civilizations create violent conflict. Samuel P. Huntington's controversial and classic book *The Clash of Civilizations* provides the most thorough and persuasive presentation of this argument:[14]

Spurred by modernization, global politics is being reconfigured along cultural lines. Peoples and countries with similar cultures are coming together. Peoples and countries with different cultures are coming apart. Alignments defined by ideology and superpower relations are giving way to alignments defined by culture and civilization. Political boundaries increasingly are redrawn to coincide with cultural ones. … Cultural communities are replacing Cold War blocs and the fault lines between civilizations are becoming the central lines of conflict in global politics.[15]

According to Huntington, the main civilizations or cultural blocs are Nordic or Western (including North America and Europe), Arab, "Sinic" (including Confucian cultures and China, Korea [North and South], and Vietnam), Indian, Slavic-Orthodox (with

Russia as the core state), Japanese, Latin, and African. Some states, of course, do not fit any of these categories exactly; however, Huntington estimates that at least 85 percent of the world's population live in national societies that fit reasonably well into one of his categories (see Table 8.1). Each of the groupings has its own pattern of political and economic development and goal achievement. Huntington argues that conflicts are most likely to occur *between* or *among* states and groups that represent these different civilizations. They are the battlegrounds of the future. What ultimately counts for people is not abstract political ideology or even economic interest. "Faith and family, blood and belief, are what people identify with and what they will fight and die for."[16] He therefore predicts a clash among Islam, the West, and a revitalized Confucian China as the most likely scenario of global politics after the fall of communism. This prediction taps into a view of each as necessarily hostile to the "other" – a view that dates back to the Crusades. Huntington goes on to point out that the ideal image in developed Western society is to be wealthy, equitable, democratic, stable, and autonomous, but that for countries that have different cultures the image of a good society may differ quite markedly – for example, it may be one that is simple, austere, hierarchic, authoritarian, disciplined, or even martial.

Contrary to many liberal ideas, Huntington contends that modernization does not necessarily mean democratization. Western values and goals therefore may not actually provide a meaningful model in modern Islamic, Confucian, or Hindu societies. Neither China nor the authoritarian states of the Middle East may choose to become democratic. He suggests that the time may have come to stop trying to change these societies and instead to develop models of a modern society that would be more relevant to them. In that sense, his ideas are a harsh criticism of both liberals and the neoconservatives who argue that democratic values could be spread to the Middle East by a Western victory in Iraq and elsewhere.

[12] Francis Fukayama, *The End of History and the Last Man* (London: Hamish Hamilton, 1992).

[13] *Civilization* was first used as a term and published by French scholars in the mid-18th century. It is a controversial term because it is often used to imply a contrast with odorous characteristics such as barbarism. Using different definitions of the term, multiple writers have used many different forms of it. See Niall Ferguson, *Civilization: The West and the Rest* (London: Allen Lane, 2011).

[14] Samuel Huntington, *The Clash of Civilizations and the Remaking of World Order* (New York: Simon & Schuster, 1996). Huntington's reputation rests on other books as well, especially *Political Order in Changing Societies* (New Haven, CT: Yale University Press, 2006) and *The Soldier and the State* (Boston: Harvard University Press, 1981).

[15] Huntington, *The Clash of Civilizations*, p. 194.

[16] Ibid., p. 194.

Huntington's suggestion is that new cultural divisions create barriers that drive people apart. But intolerance is not new, and many would argue to the contrary that globalization is pushing societies closer together, such that some form of global or world culture is developing that will subsume these differences. The latter contend that knowledge of other cultures and languages actually brings people together and reduces interpersonal conflict. All critics maintain that Huntington's argument divides peoples too rigidly into crude differences and that his approach stereotypes cultures and religions and portrays the world in terms of Christian and Muslims, good and evil – as one critic put it, into the "West versus the Rest."[17] Another concern is that such stereotypes might easily become self-fulfilling, leading to further hatred and conflict.

Amartya Sen, a Nobel Prize–winning economist, has argued that focusing on religious and cultural differences robs us of our plural identities. It "not only reduces us; it impoverishes the world."[18] Sen disputes Huntington's thesis, saying that his emphasis on religious civilizations is misleading, that many other factors such as class, language, and economic status overlap, thus blurring religious lines and creating new ones in society. He points out that India, for all its religious diversity, has many common and shared practices. Although the Hindu religion dominates in India with more than 80 percent of the population, there are still 145 million Muslims in India, the world's third largest grouping, and the world's largest Muslim-minority population.

We believe that the characteristics of a civilization do not necessarily predict how all people in it will act and that most violent clashes of modern history have been *within* civilizations or religions rather than *between* civilizations. Europeans fought

the 20th century's bloodiest wars among themselves from 1914 to 1918 and from 1939 to 1945. Most of the wars since then have been internal or civil wars, and only a handful have conformed to Huntington's argument. We examine modern warfare and internal wars in Chapters 9 and 10. Huntington's political analysis, however, is much more nuanced than his critics claim. He does not hold that his paradigm explains *all* events in global politics – nor is he a simpleminded warmonger. His policy position is that the United States should work to forge strong alliances with those cultures with which it shares common ground and a common inheritance in order to spread its values as widely as possible. For him, all civilizations will have to learn to live together and tolerate one another.

As for those civilizations with which the United States shares no common ground, Huntington argues that U.S. policy should be cooperative when possible, but strong willed and confrontational when necessary. He rejects the concept of a universal value system and the related global ambitions that have dominated U.S. foreign policy for many decades. The belief in the universality of any particular culture, he says, is false, immoral, and dangerous. Empirically, Western culture is not universal, and morally, the idea of universality is unjustified because imperialism is the logical and necessary consequence of universalism. It is extremely dangerous for the United States to seek to impose its values and traditions on other countries, overriding local interests, culture, and leadership. Doing so could even provoke a major intercivilizational war.

Huntington argues that instead of seeking the universality of Western culture, we should accommodate the differences between civilizations and create a system of order and power that acknowledges their differences and dividing lines. For him, these claims were demonstrated in the Soviet-Afghan war of 1979–89 and the first Gulf War of 1990–91. Both began as straightforward invasions but quickly transformed into wars of civilizations. They began an era of ethnic conflict and fault-line wars between groups from different civilizations.

---

[17] Among the sophisticated criticisms of work such as Huntington's is that by Edward Said. In his book *Orientalism* (London: Penguin, 1995), Said argues that the West depicts the Muslim world as exotic and unidimensional in a way that creates negative stereotypes of all Muslims.

[18] Amartya Sen, "A World Not Neatly Divided," *New York Times*, November 23, 2001.

Following the premise that a third world war is highly unlikely but not impossible, Huntington outlines three rules to manage foreign affairs and avoid intercivilization wars in a multicivilization world. The first rule is that core states should refrain from intervening in conflicts in other civilizations. Spheres of influence among civilizations should be recognized and respected, much as they were during the Cold War domination of the United States and the Soviet Union. The second rule is that where religious regions overlap and are prone to create instability, such as in the former Yugoslavia, the Middle East, and Central Asia, core states must engage directly with one another in joint conciliation to contain or to halt fault-line wars between states or groups that are part of these civilizations. Despite his grave rejection of universality, Huntington's third rule is that peoples in all civilizations should search for and strive to expand the values, institutions, and practices they have in common with peoples of other civilizations. Huntington holds this responsibility as imperative if we are to avoid the doomsday conflicts that could destroy the new world order. In his view, since clashes of civilizations are the greatest threat to world peace, an international order based on civilizations is the best safeguard against world war.

Inevitable encounters between civilizations might be manageable, Huntington argues, if we can find some way to replace traditional forms of community and autonomy. Within most modern religions there exist communities that are emphatically against violence. If their voice is strong enough, and the costs of hostility toward outsiders are fully recognized as unacceptable, these communities may defuse the most serious threats. Meanwhile, since no civilizations are prepared to withdraw from the exchanges that characterize globalized international relations, the West should continue to spread its values wherever possible. In fact, Huntington goes so far as to claim that the West must create a stronghold with which to defend its civilizational heritage. To this end, he believes, controversially, that the United States should reaffirm its Western

identity by rejecting multiculturalism at home and cooperating closely with its European partners to protect and advance the interests and values of their shared civilization.

Herein lies an apparent and serious contradictory flaw in Huntington's thinking, for this idea would seem to promote violence. Rather than building barriers around civilizations, establishing or reaffirming the connections between them would do more to provide the foundations for an ideal global village that presumably would offer the best hope for humanity. Huntington's prescription gives credence to the inevitability of conflict between and among civilizations or states as we know them. The world is a hostile place, he is saying, and the United States must be ready to take it on unless it wishes to lose its own values. In practical terms, Huntington's ideas provide leadership to those who believe that the world can be described in terms of cultural differences and support the argument that the United States must act to protect its own values in a sea of conflicting viewpoints.

To summarize, Samuel Huntington argues that cultural rather than economic differences are the most important issues dividing states and peoples in the post–Cold War world. He claims that the communist-democratic divide has been replaced by cultural identities – by civilizations based on different worldviews and religious tenets. Despite Huntington's obvious humanity and concern for global peace, his book predicts growing clashes between Western countries and those of Muslim and Chinese cultures in particular. The events of 9/11 and the ensuing wars in Afghanistan and Iraq buttressed his claim that conflict will emerge along cultural lines.

Benjamin Barber puts forward an interesting opposing argument about the cause and character of broad clashes in global politics.[19] He argues that the sharp Cold War division between communism and democracy was replaced by an ideological schism based on two forces, both of which threaten the democratic way of life. They can be visualized as

[19] Benjamin R. Barber, *Jihad vs. McWorld: Terrorism's Challenge to Democracy* (Toronto: Random House, 1995).

Jihad and McWorld. In Barber's terminology, the word *jihad* refers to the forces of self-righteous, fanatical devotees of religious, ethnic, national, or political groups. *McWorld* refers to the forces of greed and global capitalism. Barber thinks both of them threaten democracy and civil liberties. For him, corporate power and American consumerism have given rise to institutions like McDonald's fast-food restaurants, which symbolize unfettered and uncontrolled global capitalism. They have inspired hatred and resentment and even calls for jihad from groups that feel threatened by globalization and the spread of Western culture and values. Barber concludes that the world is being pulled apart much more by these two forces than by any clash of civilizations. Since Barber wrote in 1995, he did not consider the greatest threat from global capitalism: the interconnectedness of markets, speculative investment, and outright fraud that brought on the global financial crisis of 2008 (see Chapter 12).

Both Huntington and Barber are controversial authors. Which do you think has the better argument for what divides states and peoples in the post–Cold War world? Critical Case Study 8.1 considers ongoing religious and cultural divisions in Europe. Would Huntington's or Barber's arguments tell us what kinds of decisions Europeans should make to unite their societies?

Critical Case Study 8.1 **Europe's fears: Eurabia and Londonistan?**

The terrorist events carried out in the United States on 9/11, combined with shifting patterns of global power and even migration, stimulated fears that a Christian-Muslim "clash of civilizations" might be developing that would jeopardize world peace. As of 2013 there were an estimated forty-four million Muslims in Europe, and sixteen million in the European Union. Muslims constitute only about 6 percent of the total population of Europe, but that percentage is growing because of a higher birthrate than other Europeans and continued immigration. A Pew Forum study in 2011 forecast an increase of Muslims in Europe from 6 percent in 2010 to 8 percent in 2030, but other projections have been much higher. Concern about the implications of this demographic change is ongoing.

Europe's Muslim population is concentrated particularly in France, Germany, and the Netherlands and also in large cities like London, Paris, and Amsterdam. Whereas the Muslim population in the United States is estimated to be less than 1 percent of the population, and in Canada just over 2 percent, it is much higher in some European countries: France, 7.5 percent; Germany, 5 percent; the United Kingdom, 4.6 percent; and the Netherlands, 5.5 percent. These Muslim communities are far from monolithic; their populations come from quite different homelands. In Germany many Muslims are from Turkey; in the United Kingdom most are from Pakistan; in France the majority originate from North Africa, and so on.[20]

Muslim immigrants first came to Europe as guest workers recruited after World War II. They eventually benefited from asylum and family reunification laws put in place on the expectation that they would be absorbed into European society. However, some fear that the Muslim communities are not integrating but are becoming increasingly culturally and economically isolated. They tend to congregate in impoverished areas that suffer from severe unemployment, high crime rates, and poor education, all of which make their

[20] See Melanie Phillips, *Londonistan: How Britain Is Creating a Terror State Within* (New York: Encounter Books, 2006); Bruce Bawer, *While Europe Slept: How Radical Islam Is Destroying the West from Within* (New York, Doubleday, 2006).

youth particularly vulnerable to the lure of radical Islamic fundamentalists. Studies of Dutch Muslims, for example, suggest that feelings of "indignation and humiliation" among Muslims are growing and are especially strong among second-generation Muslims who feel isolated and rejected in Dutch society.

Opinion polls show that Islam is increasingly important as a symbol of identity for European Muslims, and their feelings for their former homelands compete with their loyalty to the European Union.[21] Governments are increasingly aware that they need to make policy changes that will assist immigrants to integrate into their new communities. For example, the UK has five Islamic Sharia courts, the first of which opened in 2008. However, political assimilation is a slow process, accompanied by heated debates on freedom of speech, women's rights issues, and foreign practices such as honor killings. It is not yet clear how long it might take or how much it will change the face of Europe.[22]

Meanwhile, there has been a growing public backlash across Europe against the growing Muslim population that has led to restrictive policies. In Switzerland, where 5.7 percent of the population is Muslim, a referendum was held in 2009 in which more than 57 percent of voters chose to ban Muslims from building new minarets in the country. The French banned the hijab (headscarf) in the public education system. The British in 2009 elected two representatives of the fascistic, anti-Islamic British National Party to the European Parliament, and Italy introduced a bill to ban mosque construction and restrict the call to prayer.[23]

The likely scenario is for a long period of tension and sporadic violence while degrees of integration continue. Governments and the media need to explain to the public better what the underlying issues are and to foster the idea that while freedom of speech is an important right, it has to be exercised prudently and responsibly. How might that be done? Is it an issue for leaders in your country?

Islamic fundamentalism and radical Islamic jihadism

Religion often forms the core of a nation's value system, and when it does, violent conflicts can find expression as religious issues, especially when they are based on economic grievances and territorial disputes. Issues pertaining to Muslim thought and militancy have become acute in global politics in recent decades. In the end, many hostile stereotypes have been adopted about Muslims, and especially their political goals and intentions. In other regions

of the world, anti-Western and particularly anti-American attitudes have flourished.

Islamic fundamentalists are not to be confused with radical Islamic jihadists. Both base their beliefs on the Koran and Islamic law, but jihadists politicize their beliefs and use the Koran to justify jihad or holy war and violence to obtain their objectives. Religious fanatics have formed, joined, or assisted networks of terrorists in carrying out acts of violence to spread their belief that governments and societies should be based on the strict teachings of the Koran and Islamic (Sharia) law. Therefore, the term radical Islamic jihadists, not *Muslims*, should be used to describe Islamists who are prepared to use violence. They are militant radical fundamentalists who politicize religiosity. They use the Koran to justify jihad, or holy war, to

[21] Pew Polls, July 14, 2005.
[22] Jackson and Towle, *Temptations of Power*, chapter 4.
[23] Europe's Islamic dilemma is analyzed by Christopher Caldwell, *Reflections on the Revolution in Europe* (New York: Doubleday, 2009).

obtain their objectives, and they believe they are authorized to kill and perhaps die as martyrs for their cause.

The Pakistani ideologue Abu Ala Maududi (1903–79) was the first major Muslim thinker to equate jihad with "holy war." The traditional meaning of *jihad* was "struggle" or "striving" for self-betterment, which is a sacred Islamic duty.[24] Maududi and the Egyptian Sayyid Qutb (1906–66) were influential in spreading this controversial concept throughout the Muslim world, believing that it was justified by "Western imperialism and the secularizing policies of rulers such as Egyptian President Gamal Abdel Nasser."[25] Qutb developed and spread this extreme ideology in the concentration camps where he was interned by Nasser along with thousands of Muslim Brothers. The Muslim Brotherhood today encompasses several factions, including Qutbists and other puritanical strands of Islam, particularly Salafism and Wahhabism, which is common in Saudi Arabia, as well as more moderate elements. Within the Salafis in particular, some extremists advocate waging violent jihad, and there is "ample" evidence of the ideology's increasing popularity in many circles, including Europe and the Middle East.[26] Their ideas provide legitimacy for martyrdom operations.[27] Throughout history when groups have been attacked militarily or verbally, they almost invariably have become more extreme.[28] In the 1970s, Sayyid Imam al-Sharif and Ayman al-Zawahiri became the new thinkers behind the concept of radical jihad. Al-Sharif's story illustrates the division within the militant Islamists (see Close Up 8.5).

Close Up 8.5 Divisions among Muslim militants: Sayyid Imam al-Sharif

In 2009, Sayyid Imam al-Sharif, an Egyptian founder of al-Qaeda, was named by *Foreign Policy* magazine as one of the top one hundred "Global Thinkers." To a large extent, it was his ideas that provided Muslim militants with justification for terrorist jihad.

In the 1970s Sharif, along with Ayman al-Zawahiri, authored two books that "laid the ideological foundation for a global religious war."[29] Both men were studying to be medical doctors in Cairo when Sharif joined Zawahiri's militant group al-Jihad. They eventually ended up in Afghanistan when the Soviets were there, and Sharif took over the al-Jihad group. It was at this time that Sharif and Zawahiri completed the two books, *The Essential Guide for Preparation* and *The Compendium of the Pursuit of Divine Knowledge*. The first focused exclusively on martyrdom and was taken up as "a new legal compass for the global movement." Both books were later used to teach in al-Qaeda's Afghan training camps.

In 1994 after a quarrel over the content of the second book, Sharif quit the group.[30] He was arrested in Yemen in 2001 and sent to prison in Egypt, where he changed his mind about Islam and jihad. In 2007, he published a revision of his previous ideas called *Rationalizing Jihad in Egypt and the World*, a tract that undermines the legitimacy of al-Qaeda and similar groups. Having constructed the ideological justification for jihad, he is now trying to demolish it. He argues:

---

[24] Karen Armstrong, "God," *Foreign Policy* (November 2009), p. 56.

[25] Ibid., p. 56.

[26] Assaf Moghadam, "Motives for Martyrdom: Al-Qaeda, Salafi Jihad and the Spread of Suicide Attacks," *International Security* 33, no. 3 (Winter 2008–9), pp. 46–78.

[27] See Gilles Kepel, *Jihad: The Trail of Political Islam* (Cambridge, MA: Harvard University Press, 2002); Oliver Roy, *Globalized Islam: The Search for a New Ummah* (New York: Columbia University Press, 2004).

[28] Armstrong, "God."

[29] Jarrett Brachman, "Al Qaeda's Dissident," *Foreign Policy* (December 2009), p. 40.

[30] Quoted in ibid.

> *Ramming America has become the short-est road to fame and leadership among the Arabs and Muslims. But what good is it if you destroy one of your enemy's buildings, and he destroys one of your countries? What good is it if you kill one of his people and he kills 1,000 of yours?*[31]

Confusion about Islam arises from the fact that all believing Muslims, not just radical Islamic jihadists, consider the Koran as the unmediated word of God. Since not all believing Muslims are militant, however, a clear distinction needs to be drawn between fundamentalists who are violently militant and those who are not. Most believers, who are nonmilitants, focus on belief rather than action. They do not interpret the Koran as commanding them to undertake holy war but rather highlight statements in it that support peaceful behavior – prohibition of the direct killing of innocents, for example. Extremist views, they argue, do not represent principles inherent in the faith.

As we have noted, the tendency for religious extremists to claim divine or scriptural justification for their actions is not limited to Islam. It was used by Christians against Muslims in the Crusades and by both Catholics and Protestants when they clashed throughout the Middle Ages. More recently, it was used to justify the terrorism of Catholics against Protestants in Northern Ireland, and literal interpretations from the Torah are used today by some Jews in Israel to justify actions against what they perceive as threats to their homeland.

A great many Muslims, not just radical jihadists, dislike and suspect the worst from the United States and Israel. A vast majority believe that Palestinians are treated unfairly in Israel and that the United States dominates politics in the Middle East because it wishes to control oil reserves in the region. Many believe that some states, such as Saudi Arabia,

---

[31] Quoted in ibid.

Egypt, and the United Emirates, should be forced to change their pro-Western stances, and some believe that this will occur only if the present-day rulers in those countries are replaced. Many condemn the invasions of Iraq and Afghanistan by the United States and its allies. Many also object to the fact that the West opposes Iran obtaining nuclear weapons, while India and Israel are allowed to do so. This set of beliefs does not make these Muslims violent militants, but it does provide support for radical Islamic extremists.[32]

Besides understanding that not all Muslims (even if they are fundamentalists) are terrorists, observers of the current conflation of Muslims with terrorism should bear in mind that over time considerable terrorism also has been committed in the name of nationalism and ideology. Blaming religion for terrorist activity is a much too simple explanation, as it may actually be less of a motivation than other factors, such as poverty. We examine the causes of contemporary terrorism, and in particular radical Islamic jihadism, in Chapter 11.

The clash of values inside the Muslim world

The Muslim and non-Muslim worlds both contain people who seek to turn their counterparts into enemies. To a large extent, the West and Islam have developed simplistic "mirror images" of each other. But as in the West, there are many divisions in the Islamic community. Muslims do not take a uniform stand on issues of theology or government organization. Moreover, leaving aside the radical jihadists, a heated debate is currently underway between fundamentalist Islamists and reformers about the need to modernize Islamic teaching and politics. Some wish to adopt more inclusive and secular forms of governing, while others maintain that Islam requires some form of theocratic government.

---

[32] For details on the role of religion in global politics, see "What to Read on Religion and Foreign Policy" at http://www.foreignaffairs.com/readings/religion.

The desire to throw off dictators has also been prevalent in recent years. The cases of Iran and Turkey testify to the continuing divisions over secularism. We explore these cases first and then turn to the clash of values in the so-called Arab Spring or Arab Awakening of 2011–12.

Iran and Turkey

Iran Iran provides a good example of the internal conflicts that some states are going through as they try to reconcile Islam with modern life. As in many Islamic countries, in Iran there is conflict between fundamentalists who insist on a strict interpretation of the Koran in every facet of life and secularists who prefer a more liberal interpretation and want to keep religion separate from politics. Some fundamentalists are militants and are prepared to use violence to get their way; others are not.

Throughout the 1980s, after the Shah of Iran was ousted in 1979 and replaced by a vehemently anti-Western Islamic regime, Iran became a showcase of Islamic fundamentalist rule – one in which virtually all of life's decisions were based on literal interpretations of the Koran. Ayatollah Ruhollah Khomeini, the spiritual leader, became the head of state, and Shiite clerics filled political offices. Khomeini, a fundamentalist ideologue, set up a revolutionary Islamic government in Iran. He held the office of *faqih*, a divinely inspired imam who is recognized by the constitution as the best person to lead the country. Khomeini maintained that "there is not a single topic in human life for which Islam has not provided instruction and established norms."[33] With the help of the Islamic Republican Party (IRP), he instigated a cultural revolution and oversaw the "Islamization" of educational institutions, city planning, media and entertainment, and also such details as clothing, food habits, manners, and family relations. Terror was an accepted tool of government under the IRP, and the Revolutionary Guards were established as a highly trained domestic police force to attack anyone who threatened Islamic unanimity.

The terror extended beyond the borders of Iran. In 1989 Khomeini broadcast a *fatwa* (religious decree) concerning Salman Rushdie, a British citizen, declaring all involved in the publication of his book *The Satanic Verses* "sentenced to death," and a $2.5 million bounty was placed on Rushdie's head by a radical religious foundation in Iran. Rushdie was forced to live in hiding for nearly a decade, and some consider that he is still at risk today because under Iranian law the government has no authority to revoke a fatwa. Hard-liners claim that Muslims are still duty bound to execute the sentence. When government is based on "God's word," it cannot be challenged.

When Khomeini died in 1989 and was replaced by Ali Khamenei, Iran became a somewhat less ideological and more traditionally authoritarian regime. Elections are now allowed, but the Revolutionary Guards enforce Islamic law using intimidation and repression. Today, President Mahmoud Ahmadinejad is in power, but he can be overruled on major issues by Ayatollah Khamenei, the supreme religious guide. Islamic fundamentalists in Iran speak of wanting a classless society and promoting collective choice over the rights of the individual. However, while the fundamentalist rulers tolerate a "middle class" and allow private property that is "nonexploitative," religious structures still dominate.

Incumbent President Ahmadinejad easily won the 2009 presidential election in Iran. However, contrary to his claims that the election had been free and fair, large portions of the Iranian public and international media believed that the election had been rigged and votes manipulated. Citizens held protests in major cities throughout the country in support of popular opposition candidates Mir-Hossein Mousavi and Mehdi Karroubi. Rallies in support of the president also took place. Supreme Leader Ayatollah Ali Khamenei called for unity and promised that there would be an investigation by the Guardian Council.

[33] Quoted in Cheryl Benard and Zalmay Khalilzad, *The Government of God* (New York: Macmillan, 2006).

The contest between the president and his opponents was widely characterized as reflecting divisions in Iranian society over free speech and democracy. The protesters were largely young and made extensive use of Twitter and Internet sites to communicate and plan demonstrations. Their demonstrations were harshly suppressed by police and paramilitary groups, and many died. Universities were closed, websites blocked, and text messages and phone transmissions stopped. The clash was termed "the Persian Awakening" or the "Green Revolution" by some, but the government held fast and made few changes. Smaller demonstrations have continued to take place.

Turkey   In Turkey, the conflict between religious values and secularism is at the core of current political life. The country is 99 percent Muslim, and yet it is a secular state. Fundamentalist parties are strong, and today they control the government. The country wants to join the European Union but is encountering significant resistance largely because of Europeans' perceptions of a threat of instability that might be caused by militant radical Islamists or even simply by fundamentalist Islamists. Yet at the same time, Turkey is a member of NATO and a significant ally of the United States.

The background to this situation is that after World War I Turkey was defeated and partitioned, but Mustafa Kemal rallied the Turkish military, drove out the occupying forces, and took political control. The next year, 1923, he founded the Republic of Turkey from the ruins of the six-hundred-year-old Ottoman Empire. Kemal abolished Islamic-based laws and separated church and state. In doing so, he paved the way for peaceful coexistence of the Muslim factions and liberated women to participate openly and freely in society. The national assembly honored Mustafa Kemal by giving him the name Ataturk (father of the Turks) (Figure 8.7).

Although weakened in recent years, the Turkish military still sees itself as the guardian of the secular state, and it has a say in the National Security Council, a senior policy-making body. In 1997 it engineered the overthrow of Turkey's first Islamic-

Figure 8.7 Ataturk was an Ottoman, a Turkish military officer, and first president of Turkey 1881–1938. He is famous for making Turkey a secular state even though it has a predominantly Muslim population.
Source: Photos.com.

oriented government and banned the pro-Islamic Welfare Party. However, in 2002 an Islamic party, the Justice and Development Party (AKP), led by Recep Tayyip Erdogan, won the election to the Turkish parliament. The party was formed from banned Islamist parties, but its leadership insisted that it no longer based its policies on Islamic ideology. Prime Minister Erdogan and his administration struck a decidedly moderate stance, but their claims did not satisfy fearful critics who urged the Turkish military to intervene to maintain a secular government. It did not. The AKP won control of the government again in 2007, sending another wave of concern across Europe and giving opponents ammunition with which to sabotage Turkey's bid to join the EU. It won a third decisive term in 2011, winning more votes than all the other parties together, but not enough votes to write a new constitution without the cooperation of other parties.

The current constitution, written by generals three decades ago, needs to be replaced, and Erdogan wants to change the current parliamentary system into a strong presidential regime and then run for president himself. If he can reach consensus on a constitution that guarantees free speech, women's rights, judicial independence, and cultural freedom for ethnic and religious groups, he will make Turkey a successful model for Muslim democracy. The country now has the world's seventeenth-largest economy.

Erdogan's first electoral victory in 2000 raised fears in Europe about the election of a governing Islamist party. The anxiety was fueled particularly by the example of theocratic Iran and also Afghanistan under the extremist Taliban from 1996 to 2001. Taliban edicts were so pervasive and all-encompassing that they swept aside social traditions and political forms. They enforced their laws with brutality and allowed al-Qaeda to establish bases within their borders. It took a UN-sanctioned and U.S.-led attack after the events of 9/11, 2001, to dislodge the Taliban from office. European fears are therefore understandable. But Turkey is already a vibrant democracy. If Erdogan achieves his goals, he may be able to demonstrate that a stable democratic Muslim state can be a significant power and a leader in the Middle East.

Arab Awakening or Arab Spring?

In early 2011, protests began and escalated in Tunisia, Egypt, Morocco, Jordan, Libya, Bahrain, Syria, and Yemen. The context for each uprising differed, and the protesters' demands differed from country to country, with one exception. Whether they were ruled by monarchs or authoritarian dictators, all wanted a voice in their government. Since there were no established political parties and few civil society institutions in these countries, the revolts consisted of a few committed people who wanted change and much larger groups with

broad resentments against the regimes and individual leaders. There was considerable debate about whether the events they initiated should be called an *Arab Spring*, which seemed too temporary and even patronizing to some participants; the *Arab revolutions*, which seemed too substantive and premature to some scholars; or *Arab civil wars*, which implied very high levels of violence and open armed struggle, which was not true in some cases. To avoid this argument, we have used the phrase Arab Awakening, which is relatively neutral. Regardless of the nomenclature, the consequences of the uprisings will not be absolutely clear for some time. The transitions are far from over, and the region as a whole is extremely fragile.

In Chapter 10 we examine these uprisings in detail as part of the discussion of the context of civil wars. What is important here is to understand that civil wars tend to last for a long time, and these upheavals are only at their beginning stages. The bases of a stable state include security, literacy, food, and health care for the population, and these cannot be achieved amid civil strife. The essential questions to be resolved by the leaders of these uprising are how to frame relations between Islam and the state and how to incorporate different ethnic and religious minorities. Mainstream Islamists claim to be a new generation who are moderate and will respect ethnic and religious minorities and not impose Sharia law universally. However, many secular Arabs are skeptical, as are Christians in Egypt and Syria. Critics argue that devout Muslims seek a global caliphate in which one seat of religion or political authority will rule the whole Islamic world. Perhaps this is not realizable, so they aim for the development of religious states such as Iran or Saudi Arabia. Even this limited vision is impossible to reconcile with liberal democracy, where authority flows from the people regardless of religion. Islamists are divided, and all groups claim that they will seek coalitions with secular and other parties in the transition to democracy.

Perhaps the most significant aspect of the Arab revolts is the historical, unresolved conflict between Sunnis and Shiites that is reemerging. The split that became so volatile in Iraq after Saddam Hussein is surfacing in other Arab states where it had long been kept in check by brutal authoritarian governments. Shiites want greater rights in Lebanon, Bahrain, and Saudi Arabia. The Sunnis seek more recognition in Iraq and Syria. Saudi Arabia considers itself the guardian of Sunni Islam, Iran the guard- ian of Shia Islam. In many of these countries the largest and best-organized political organizations are religious associations such as the Muslim Brotherhood in Egypt and the Nahda Party in Tunisia. The possibility for instability and escalating violence on a sectarian basis is a serious and ongoing challenge (see Chapter 10).

Conclusion: Interpreting conflicts over identity

What do the levels of analysis and the main theoretical approaches that we discussed in Chapter 3 tell us about what causes identity conflicts over ethnicity, religion, and nationalism and what can be done to resolve them? Neal Jesse and Kristen Williams conducted five different case studies to show how levels of analysis can help uncover the factors that contribute to ethnic conflict. Their original contribution illustrates how to apply the levels of analysis to selected issues. After examining conflicts in Northern Ireland, Bosnia, Sudan and Sri Lanka, they concluded that international, domestic, and individual factors all can play a role in conflict resolution. At the individual level they examined the decisions of elites and political leadership and leadership styles. At the domestic level they considered factors such as regime type, political parties, armed forces, social movements, and small organizations and groups. At the international level they focused on "the nature of the international system, the structure of power within the system, international organizations, international regimes, and diffusion/escalation of conflict."[34]

The levels-of-analysis approach was useful in helping to understand the causes of ethnic conflict and the means with which to manage it. In particular, Jesse and Williams discovered the following:

1. Ethnic ties across borders (where a diaspora exists because an ethnic group has migrated and where ethnic groups have been divided by a recognized border) are important in conflict mediation.
2. States and other political actors may intervene positively in an ethnic conflict if they perceive it to be in their national interest to do so.
3. Third-party mediation (by states or international institutions) can ameliorate conflict.
4. International intervention (coercive or noncoercive) can also ameliorate conflict.

Realists generally consider that identity conflict is relatively hardwired, based on ancient hatreds and cultural differences that are deep and cannot easily be changed. Their response to such conflict might be to try to create a secure balance of power

---

[34] Neal G. Jesse and Kristen P. Williams, *Ethnic Conflict: A Systematic Approach to Cases of Conflict* (Washington, DC: CQ Press, 2011).

to prevent conflict and/or to try to partition hostile groups if they seem incapable of reconciliation. The downside of partition is that it can lead to ethnic, religious, or nationalist cleansing by encouraging dominant groups to drive others out from the territory. This happened in Bosnia following the dissolution of Yugoslavia in 1991, when Serbs, hoping to annex Bosnian territory to Serbia, slaughtered several thousand Muslim men and boys in Srebrenica. In contrast, fifteen Soviet republics successfully separated and became independent states when the Soviet Union fell apart in 1991.

Neo-realists focus less on human nature and identity and more on the anarchic structure of the global system and the balance of power. They consider that the end of the Cold War changed the balance of power and made it possible for national, ethnic, and religious conflicts that had been minimized during East-West conflict to erupt in full force. Barry Posen, for example, applied realist theory about ethnic conflict in situations where the state had broken down (in the Soviet Union and Yugoslavia). He concluded that the *security dilemma* that exists in the international system also plays out for ethnic groups. When the state breaks down, ethnic groups gather weapons and mobilize troops for defensive purposes, and this action makes other groups fearful and motivates them to increase their military capabilities as well, so that the issue escalates. The security dilemma, therefore, offers a useful explanation for ethnic conflict.[35] However, critics warn that focusing narrowly on this realist interpretation risks missing other socioeconomic processes that might also be at work and therefore neglects policy tools that might help ameliorate security fears.[36]

Liberals reject the notion that identity conflict is hardwired and consider that it may be the result of elite manipulation, distortion, and/or institutional failure. They point out that political elites often play on fears based on ethnic and religious differences, inciting violence that becomes self-perpetuating. Like realists, liberals see the state as a major actor in the international system, but they stress that institutions can help states cooperate. Their preferred solution to conflict is to look to state institutions such as federalism or consociationalism to decentralize power and accommodate divisions in societies and to emphasize the processes within existing institutions. They seek ways to accommodate differences short of secession.

Internationally, liberals support intervention by international institutions such as the United Nations to relieve identity and conflict tensions through peacekeeping and peace enforcement missions. Such missions were successful in Cyprus, Timor-Leste, Sierra Leone, and Liberia, for example. But international interventions are limited in what they can achieve, and ultimately such identities must be reconstructed and reconciled to achieve long-term peace (see Chapter 10). Liberals also believe that democratic institutions encourage cooperation and compromise,

[35] Barry R. Posen, "The Security Dilemma and Ethnic Conflict," *Survival* 35, no. 1 (Spring 1993), pp. 27–47.

[36] Jack Snyder, "The New Nationalism: Realist Interpretations and Beyond," in *The Domestic Bases of Grand Strategy*, ed. Richard Rosecrance and Arther A. Stein (Ithaca, NY: Cornell University Press, 1993), pp. 179–200.

and this enables societies to be relatively peaceful in spite of social differences. However, although established democracies are relatively peaceful, states going through a transition to democracy are rife with ethnic and religious tensions that often lead to war. Bosnia, Azerbaijan, and Chechnya are relevant recent examples. Liberals believe that when states are members of international institutions such as the European Union, those institutions provide mechanisms for dealing with issues of ethnicity and nationalism.

We have seen that constructivists consider that a central issue of the post–Cold War period is how different groups conceive their identities and interests.[37] They, therefore, focus on what social processes generate changes in normative beliefs and how beliefs and norms influence international behavior. They consider that ethnic, nationalist, and religious conflict is ideationally constructed and can change over time, so in their view the solution to conflict is to find new ideas that in the long term will supersede and replace those at the root of the problem. To inspire loyalty across diverse ethnic and religious groups, new concepts such as democracy or pluralism or tolerance must be strong enough to embrace everyone within a state.

Identity can be multilayered, and in strong states citizens are able to separate their loyalties and support the larger nation or state in their public lives while they identify with more immediate religious or ethnic groups in their private lives. To do so, they must have faith that state institutions will protect them. When a public conflict occurs, they need to be able to turn to their local or national government for help, not to their ethnic or religious group. This is not easy to achieve, and it requires a long time to develop. This contention is also shared by feminists who argue for the need for government roles in protecting against gender discrimination.

Building a national identity is crucial for creating stable states out of failed ones. Contemporary Afghanistan is an illustration (see Chapters 9 and 10). Government institutions are weak; politicians are considered corrupt; and loyalties are severely divided among regions, ethnic groups, clans, and religious and other interests. Peaceful resolution requires the people of Afghanistan to figure out whether they want a religious or a secular regime and whether they want a democratic or authoritarian government. From an identity perspective, growth in attachment to democracy is a long-term goal, but it may also be the only answer for resolving ethnic conflicts.

In the final analysis, these theoretical perspectives contribute competing ways to understand and perhaps resolve difficult issues involving ethnic nationalist and religious conflict. They all contribute to our ability to construct a more complete picture of an identity conflict. There is no one answer, just as there is no agreement among states of different political persuasions about which form of government is the best one to unite a multiethnic society.

[37] Stephen M. Walt, "International Relations: One World, Many Theories," *Foreign Policy* 110 (Spring 1998), pp. 29–46.

Select bibliography

Barber, Benjamin R., *Jihad vs. McWorld* (Toronto: Random House, 1995).

Booth, Ken, and Tim Dunne, eds., *World in Collision: Terror and the Future of Global Order* (Basingstoke, UK: Palgrave, 2002).

Brumberg, Daniel, and Dina Shehata, eds., *Conflict, Identity, and Reform in the Muslim World* (Herndon, VA: U.S. Institute of Peace Press, 2009).

Felman, Noah, *The Fall and Rise of the Islamic State* (Princeton, NJ: Princeton University Press, 2009).

Fetzer, Joel S., and J. Christopher Soper, *Muslims and the State in Britain, France and Germany* (Cambridge: Cambridge University Press, 2005).

Haleem, Harfiyah Abdel, et al., eds., *The Crescent and the Cross: Muslim and Christian Approaches to War and Peace* (New York: Palgrave, 1998).

Huntington, Samuel P., *The Clash of Civilizations and the Remaking of World Order* (New York: Simon & Schuster, 1996).

House, Karen Elliott, *On Saudi Arabia: Its People, Past, Religion, Fault Lines – and Future* (New York: Alfred A. Knopf, 2012).

Jesse, Neal G., and Kristen P. Williams, *Ethnic Conflict: A Systematic Approach to Cases of Conflict* (Washington, DC: CQ Press, 2011).

Kadri, Sadaket, *Heaven on Earth: A Journey through Shari'a Law from the Deserts of Ancient Arabia to the Streets of the Modern Muslim World* (New York: Farrar, Straus, and Giroux, 2012).

Kidd, Thomas S., *American Christians and Islam: Evangelical Culture and Muslims from the Colonial Period to Terrorism* (Princeton, NJ: Princeton University Press, 2008).

Lewis, Bernard, *The Crisis of Islam: Holy War and Holy Terror* (New York: Random House, 2004).

Maloney, Suzanne, *Iran's Long Reach: Iran as a Pivotal State in the Muslim World* (Washington, DC: Institute of Peace Press, 2008).

Midlarsky, Manus I., *Origins of Political Extremism: Mass Violence in the Twentieth Century and Beyond* (Cambridge: Cambridge University Press, 2011).

Norris, Pippa, and Ronald Inglehart, *Sacred and Secular: Religion and Politics Worldwide* (Cambridge: Cambridge University Press, 2004).

Ozkirimli, U., ed., *Nationalism and Its Futures* (London: Palgrave, 2003).

Popovski, Vesselin, et al., *World Religions and Norms of War* (Tokyo: United Nations University Press, 2009).

Roy, Olivier, *Globalized Islam: The Search for a New Ummah* (New York: Columbia University Press, 2004).

Ruthven, Malise, *Islam: A Very Short Introduction* (Oxford: Oxford University Press, 2000).

Shin, Doh Chull, *Confucianism and Democratization in East Asia* (Cambridge: Cambridge University Press, 2011).

Smith, A., *Chosen Peoples: Sacred Sources of National Identity* (Oxford: Oxford University Press, 2004).

_____, *National Identity* (London: Penguin, 1991).

_____, *Nations and Nationalism in a Global Era* (Cambridge, UK: Polity, 1995).

Part III Global conflict and war

Woe to the statesman whose reasons for entering a war do not appear so plausible at its end as at its beginning.

– OTTO VON BISMARCK, GERMAN CHANCELLOR

Part III examines the causes and consequences of the breakdown of international law and order. The character of war has changed dramatically in recent years not only in terms of technology and strategy but also with regard to the security dilemmas political leaders face when they try to protect their states and their citizens. What has not changed is the need to comprehend the sacrifices that are required as states strive to maintain their security. U.S. General Dwight Eisenhower once said, "I hate war as only a soldier who has lived it can, as one who has seen its brutality, its futility, its stupidity."[1]

Chapter 9 focuses on international war, its causes, conduct, and consequences. The advent of the nuclear era changed the basic concepts of national security, brought new arms-control issues, and forged new security organizations. With the end of the Cold War, internal wars became more frequent and international terrorism erupted with new intensity. International conflicts since 9/11 have brought new security dilemmas that make security perhaps even more elusive. Issues such as weapons of mass destruction, alliance formation, and the ethics of war are all part of this discussion. Archibald MacLeish, the poet, honored the human cost of war in a poem called *The Young Dead Soldiers Do Not Speak* where he expressed the wishes of the dying: "We leave you our deaths. Give them their meaning."

Chapter 10 examines civil wars and insurgencies, in particular the ongoing violent conflicts in Afghanistan, Iraq, Libya, Syria, and elsewhere in North Africa. It deals with failing states such as Somalia, Sudan, and South Sudan, as well as the role of private armies and new technologies such as drones. Chapter 11 focuses on terrorism and counterterrorism, including nuclear terrorism, and novel issues relating to al-Qaeda, enemy combatants, Yemen as a terrorist haven, modern-day pirates, and suicide bombers.

[1] *The New York Times*, December 1, 2009.

9

War
Causes, conduct, and consequences

Since no ultimate international authority is in place to enforce the will of the majority of the world's seven billion people, international politics is largely about the capacities and relative powers of the individual states that constitute the global system. Conflict between and among states emerges when interests are challenged and states respond by exercising power in bargaining situations or, occasionally, by threatening or engaging in military confrontation. The search for security is never ending. A writer of the Roman Empire, Vegetius, once recommended, *si vis pacem para bellum*, "if you desire peace, prepare for war." In fact, it might be said that states prepare for conflict more than they do for peace and harmony. It is unfortunate that governments often misuse the concept of war for rhetorical purposes – as when they speak of a war on drugs, poverty, or terrorists – a practice that does little to illuminate the nature of war.

This chapter builds on the concepts of old and new security dilemmas to discuss what happens when security fails. Violent state conflicts are frequent, and come in many types, but here we focus primarily on those between and among states. There are many questions to answer, perhaps the most basic of which are the following: What causes war? Can it be prevented or is it inevitable? We use the three levels of analysis discussed in Chapter 3 to determine whether they can advance our understanding of what causes war.

Weapons of war have changed dramatically over the centuries, from bows and arrows to weapons of mass destruction, thus changing the very nature of war. In this chapter, we discuss 21st-century technologies, their proliferation, and their implications for security. The global landscape is littered with nuclear weapons. What disarmament and arms-control agreements are in place to prevent their use, accidental or otherwise? How effective are they? The United States launched an antiballistic missile defense system under George W. Bush. President Obama revised it in 2011. What is it intended to do? Can it keep the United States safe? There are several security organizations, but the only major one today is the North Atlantic Treaty Organization (NATO). We examine its successes and failures, looking particularly at its role in Libya in 2011.

One of the most important questions about war is whether there is such a thing as a *just* war. Are there things so vile that war is morally justified? John Stuart Mill wrote that war is an ugly thing, but not the ugliest of things. Consider the war to abolish slavery during the U.S. Civil War. We examine arguments for and against war and apply them to the 2003 Iraq War. There are international laws about war, but they do not limit the prospect of war or even regulate war in general, they only attempt to protect certain people in specific ways during times of war. Chapter 10 expands the topic of state war to internal or civil wars and insurgencies and Chapter 11 deals with international terrorism.

War

Violent conflict and war are endemic in world history and modern global politics. War, the use of organized military force in clashes between two or more states, is as old as the human species. The Greek philosopher Plato famously warned that only the dead have seen the end of it. Yet discussion of war is often prudish and moralistic to an extent that impedes an appreciation of its never-changing nature. There are regular meaningless bromides about the "futility" or "senselessness" of war, but even our understanding of history is structured largely around the major and minor conflicts that have shaped, and occasionally reconstituted, international relations. Some contemporary authors believe that war is almost extinct (John Mueller), others that "industrial war" is a thing of the past (Rupert Smith), and still others that the 21st century will witness considerable conflict and violence (Colin Gray).[2]

Wars are not aberrations, and they can have beneficial as well as horrific results. Wars of independence, or liberation, as they are now often called, helped draw the contemporary map of states. Americans became independent by fighting the British; the Irish fought the English; the Algerians fought the French; the Western Allies and the Soviet Union destroyed Nazi Germany to free Europe from its horrors. Yet why do states keep resorting to something that is so profoundly ugly and perhaps even mad? As Chinese leader Mao Zedong is alleged to have observed, "War is not crochet." To accept the idea that war can be justifiable is to agree that weapons of supreme deadliness should be produced, that people should be systematically trained to kill thousands of other humans for a cause, and that it is acceptable in certain circumstances for organized slaughter be carried out on a massive scale.

Carl von Clausewitz, a Prussian general and theorist of war, is often cited to explain that war is not independent of regular public policy. In his book *On War* he claims, "War is the continuation of policy by other means."[3] In other words, war or its threat is not an aberration but rather an integral part of political affairs. States use military force because they believe that their objectives are worth the costs, and sometimes this has meant fighting to prevent other countries from going to war. Threats of force may induce countries to settle disputes peacefully and may be just as efficacious as the actual exercise of war.[4] The threat of coercion moves states beyond the level of peaceful negotiation to the possibility of war. Wars are always connected to politics and choice, a continuation of a political strategy. But they are destructive and may cause massive human suffering. The political calculations that lead to war may be rendered irrelevant by the sheer destructiveness of the strikes themselves.

States regard security as a primary function, and every state in the world supports a military, or in a small number of cases, a powerful police force, to make it less vulnerable to attack from outside or inside its territory. Leaders consider that it is their primary duty to defend their people from physical violence or the threat of it. In recent decades, the scope of the term *security* has broadened to include individuals and groups as well as states, and we consider this change in Chapters 10 and 11, but here we limit ourselves mainly to an exploration of war between or among states.

War is the most violent form of international competition. Estimates of the total number of past wars vary, with estimates of up to 559 international and civil wars in the past two hundred years. While the frequency of wars has remained fairly constant over time, their severity in terms of the number of victims has increased, culminating in World War I, with an estimated 51 million deaths. Weapons have become so powerful that one nuclear bomb dropped

---

[2] Colin Gray, *Another Bloody Century: Future Warfare* (London: Weidenfeld & Nicolson, 2005); Rupert Smith, *The Utility of Force: The Art of War in the Modern World* (New York: Vintage, 2008); John Mueller, *Retreat from Doomsday: The Obsolescence of Major War* (New York: Basic Books, 1989).

[3] Carl von Clausewitz, *On War* (Princeton, NJ: Princeton University Press, 1984), p. 87.

[4] Sun Tzu, *Art of War* (New York: Basic Books, 1994).

by the United States on Hiroshima is estimated to have caused about 200,000 deaths within five years, and another 140,000 Japanese died in Nagasaki died from a second bomb within the same time frame.[5] Most scholars contend that the 20th century was the bloodiest in history. Ploughshares Monitor estimates that there were 250 wars and more than 109 million war-related deaths in the 20th century. Nearly three times as many people were killed in conflict in that century as in the previous four centuries combined. According to a recent Human Security Report, however, there has been a rapid reduction in the number of wars and war related deaths in recent decades.[6]

There have been few international wars in the 21st century, and none of a world or hegemonic nature. The major contests in Iraq and Afghanistan were vital to world peace and stability, but even they were mixtures of international and regional wars and insurgencies. With the exception of these two wars and perhaps the protracted conflict in Israel, recent fighting in Africa (Central African Republic, Democratic Republic of the Congo, Ethiopia, Mali, Somalia, and Sudan), Libya and Syria in North Africa, Yemen in the Middle East, and Colombia in South America is more akin to civil wars or insurgencies. Despite the atrocities they perpetuate, these internal wars are unlikely to affect international peace. These limited wars are discussed in Chapter 10. The number and length of such internal wars and insurgencies has shown a huge increase as the number of international wars has declined. Other forms of violence, such as global terrorism and international criminal violence, have also greatly increased during the same period. Close Up 9.1 illustrates how domestic civil wars can flow across borders and become regional or international.

In a search for security, almost all states prepare for war even at the risk of provoking an arms race, a competitive buildup of weapons and military

[5] Graham Allison, *Nuclear Terrorism: The Ultimate Preventable Catastrophe* (New York: Henry Holt, 2004), p. 51.
[6] *Human Security Report, 2005* (New York: Oxford University Press, 2005), p. 153.

Close Up 9.1 International or civil war? Kosovo, Serbia, and NATO

Domestic and international wars are often interrelated. Examine the following set of facts:

1974 Kosovo becomes an autonomous province within the federal country of Yugoslavia.

1987 Slobodan Milosevic assumes leadership of Serbia.

1989 Milosevic revokes Kosovo's autonomy. Ethnic Albanians riot.

1990 Serbia closes Kosovo's Parliament. Kosovo's Albanians start parallel government.

1991 Slovenia, Croatia, and Macedonia secede from the Yugoslav federation. Kosovo Albanians approve independence.

1992–93 Bosnia-Herzegovina declares independence from Yugoslavia.

1995 NATO begins air-bombing campaign against Bosnian Serbs. After forty-three months, Bosnian war ends with the Dayton Accords.

1996 Pro-independence Kosovo Liberation Army (KLA) emerges.

1998 KLA seizes control of much of Kosovo before being routed by the Serbian military. Massacres and fighting start in Kosovo.

1999 Peace talks fail. NATO begins Operation Allied Force against Yugoslavia, bombing throughout the territory for seventy-eight days.

1999 Serbia signs a UN-approved peace agreement on Kosovo. Kosovo continues to be governed by UN mission (UNMIK), and as of 2013, Serbia continued to oppose its transition to autonomy despite free elections, a pro-independence referendum, and UN support.

This timeline illustrates how domestic and global factors can be intertwined in contemporary wars. At what point did this internal war become a regional and then international war?

Table 9.1 **The ten countries with the highest military expenditure in 2011**

Rank 2011	Country	Spending (US$ billions)
1	United States	711
2	China	[143]
3	Russia	[71.9]
4	United Kingdom	62.7
5	France	62.5
6	Japan	59.3
7	India	48.9
8	Saudi Arabia	48.5
9	Germany	[46.7]
10	Brazil	35.4
	World	1,738

Note: Brackets indicate estimated figures. The figures for Saudi Arabia include expenditure on internal security. *Source*: 2011 SIPRI data, http://www.sipri.org.

forces between and among states in a search for security. The 2011 estimated world military expenditure was US$1,738 billion. The U.S. military budget soared during the presidency of George W. Bush to the highest level since the World War II, and it has continued to climb. In 2011 U.S. military expenditure was $711 billion, greater than the combined spending of the next nine countries. It accounted for 41 percent of the total world military outlay. China followed at $143 billion, with Russia, the United Kingdom, and France next in order (Table 9.1).

Old and new security dilemmas

As discussed earlier, a central principle of international relations is that when states try to protect themselves they create a security dilemma. While they negotiate with other states in attempts to find agreement in regional and international organizations, they may also continue to augment their militaries, security apparatus, and police to ensure the greatest possible security for their sovereign territory, people, and government. As each state protects its security and survival, it frightens others, encouraging them to strengthen their own militaries and security apparatuses. As realist John Herz summarized it, in the anarchy of world states, "striving to attain security from [such] attack, they are driven to acquire more and more power in order to escape the power of others. This, in turn, renders the others more insecure and compels them to prepare for the worst."[7] In short, each state's security is defined and rests on other states' insecurity. Despite some nuanced criticisms of this realist principle, most scholars of international relations adopt security as a starting point for understanding activities in the field of international relations.

After World War II the security dilemma was interpreted as being essentially about the East-West conflict, and Western policy was based on protecting interests without aggravating relations with Russia or its allies. The bipolar configuration of the Cold War period reflected the security dilemma as both sides attempted to increase their security by enhancing their power and alliance strengths, and in so doing, they made their counterpart feel less secure. The NATO alliance and the Warsaw Pact developed mirror images of each other's intentions and enmity.

Recall from Chapter 1 that a new security dilemma has arisen from the realization that an increase in a country's military strength may not provide a corresponding increase in security. The stronger a state becomes, the more it opens itself up to challenges from globalization forces and international terrorism. The state is under challenge, and while the state is not obsolete and will not disappear, its security can no longer be founded entirely on weapons and soldiers. The current difficult and unstable security situation is due to the simultaneous existence of *both* traditional state challenges (e.g., the rise of new powerful states

---

[7] John Herz, "Idealist Internationalism and the Security Dilemma," *World Politics* 2 (1950), p. 157.

such as China and the quest for nuclear weapons by Iran) and new security threats emerging from subnational actors (e.g., from parts of the Muslim world in terms of international terrorism and from internal wars in weak or failed states). This changing nature of security brings novel challenges to political leaders – ubiquitous insecurity and violence that may come from a number of places and sources at the same time. This change underlies our discussion of civil wars and terrorism in the following two chapters.

Types of war

A classification of warfare is necessary but controversial. Is a particular war international or internal? Few wars can be classified in such a straightforward manner, however, the terms general war or world war are used to depict wars that involve a number of great powers, massive destruction of combatant and civilian lives and property, and extensive objectives such as destroying enemies or installing favorable governments. Limited wars involve fewer great powers, entail somewhat less destruction, and are generally fought for restricted goals such as preventing an enemy from taking over new territory. Civil wars, the third type, discussed in detail in Chapter 10, are internal wars fought between rivals for control of individual states or regions within states. World Wars I and II, which involved all of Europe and North America and much of the rest of the world, were classic examples of general wars, while the Korean War, which was about stopping Chinese communist aggression in southern Korea, was a pertinent case of a limited war. Although outside powers aided some parts of the country in the American Civil War, and also in the Chinese Revolution, these, too, may be classified as civil wars.

The distinction between whether a particular war is defensive (protecting a state's territory) or offensive (trying to get control of another country's territory) is another distinction that is not always simple. It may appear reasonable to declare that the United States' war on Japan after being attacked at Pearl Harbor in 1941 was defensive and that Iraq's 1990 invasion of Kuwait was offensive. But most wars have complicated histories and mixed motives that are difficult to disentangle. Usually, both sides claim to be victims acting justly out of a necessity to protect themselves. In the 1930s, for example, the Nazis invented foreign threats against Germany in order to justify and wage aggressive wars in both Western and Eastern Europe.

Although the motives for fighting are often confused or unclear, another distinction that needs to be made is between preventive and preemptive wars. A preemptive war is a war begun to forestall an *imminent* enemy attack. Preemption is the legal right to repel a potential, imminent aggression by another state or nonstate actor. A preventive war is undertaken to stop a long-term increase in the power of a potential enemy and, thus, to prevent a *future* attack. The first is legal under international law; the second is not. It is a confusing and controversial issue. Nuclear weaponry and terrorist attacks have to some extent blurred the lines between preemptive and preventive war. The economic and military balance among states changes all the time, and, thus, to condone preventive war would provide an excuse for constant fighting. However, a state cannot be expected to remain inactive when it knows that enemy forces are preparing to launch an attack against it in the coming few hours or days. In their attacks on Poland in September 1939 and the Soviet Union in June 1941, German forces used the advantage of surprise to realize their plan of colonizing Eastern Europe. In this case it was not necessary for Germany to take the initiative to preempt enemy aggression; whatever their claims, these strikes were intended to advance massive territorial expansion, not to forestall imminent attacks by their opponents. They were offensive and therefore preventive wars.

As the world's only superpower, the United States is constantly being tempted to make preventive attacks on states that may be developing the capability to threaten it sometime in the future.[8] The terrorist events of 9/11 dramatically increased that temptation. After that attack, President Bush announced his so-called Bush doctrine, which states that the United States would, if necessary, act preemptively to forestall or prevent further hostile acts. In his 2002 State of the Union address, he declared, "The United States will not permit the world's most dangerous regimes to threaten us with the world's most destructive weapons," and mentioned three countries as forming an "axis of evil" – Iraq, Iran, and North Korea.[9] In his State of the Union speech on January 29, 2003, he said:

Some have said we must not act until the threat is imminent. Since when have terrorists and tyrants announced their intentions, politely putting us on notice before they strike? If this threat is permitted to fully and suddenly emerge, all actions, all words and all recriminations would come too late.[10]

Should the United States or any other great power act to prevent possible future aggression? Where is the line to be drawn – when a sworn enemy possesses nuclear weapons? Russia has nuclear weapons and so does China. Are preventive attacks to be used only against less powerful countries? Countries do sometimes strike first to forestall an attack, but it is a dangerous strategy, and it has been recognized as such for many decades. The modern international legal system and many international institutions were developed to discourage such wars. A broad policy of preventive war could induce an enemy state to increase its military preparedness, escalate its hostile actions, and even perhaps goad it into escalating its production of weapons of mass destruction. This could be argued in the current cases of both North Korea and Iran. From those countries' point of view, they must develop nuclear bombs precisely to deter a preventive attack on their country.

Causes of war

Why have wars occurred so often throughout history, and why do they remain with us today? Realists tend to argue that states act in the pursuit of security and power, not according to ethical and legal principles. Liberals, in contrast, tend to believe that wars are caused by ideologies, nationalism, and poor leadership. But was World War I caused by the assassination of Austrian Archduke Franz Ferdinand or by social and political trends such as great power politics and imperialism? Wars are highly complex, and the paths leading to them are interwoven with multiple factors and events.

Many controversies about the causes of war are simply debates about the background factors that make war possible and the details of the events that precipitate them. Historians and political scientists have found many reasons for the outbreak of particular wars, but there is no universally agreed cause for all of them.[11] Wars may start through the calculated policy decisions of leaders and/or result from ridiculous accidents. Perhaps even both. Some writers say the Battle of Jahra in the 1920s was launched because the Saudis did not like the fact that Kuwaitis were smoking cigarettes. Obviously, individual wars erupt for a variety of specific reasons, and there is rarely unanimous agreement about their causes. Why can war be neither avoided nor prevented entirely? Why are there periods of peace?

The causes of war and conditions of peace are highly controversial but extremely important, as they hold the key to the prevention of war. There are several distinct issues in analyzing what causes war. First, the question is perhaps too general. There are at least three ways to approach it. First, there are *permissive conditions* about why war is possible,

---

[8] See Robert J. Jackson and Philip Towle, *Temptations of Power: The United States in Global Politics since 9/11* (Basingstoke, UK: Palgrave, 2006).

[9] Ibid., p. 37.

[10] Micah Sifry and Christopher Cerf, *The Iraq War Reader* (New York: Touchstone Books) p. 385.

[11] Stephen Van Evera, *Causes of War: Power and the Roots of Conflict* (Ithaca, NY: Cornell University Press, 1999; Kalevi J. Holsti, *Peace and War: Armed Conflicts and International Order* (Cambridge: Cambridge University Press, 1991); Hew Strachan and Sibylle Scheipers, eds., *The Changing Character of War* (Oxford: Oxford University Press, 2011).

such as might be found in the nature of the international environment or global politics. Second, there are the *core or root causes* of war, such as power, economics, land, ethnicity, nationalism, and religion. And third, there are the actual triggers or *decisions* to go to war. The latter may be the responsibility of groups or individuals depending on the nature of the political system and may be based on accurate information, misconceptions, or perhaps plain ignorance.

The level-of-analysis approach discussed in Chapters 3 and 4 can be helpful in analyzing the causes of war. Are individuals, states, or the global system responsible for causing war? Or is it more likely that wars arise from a combination of factors at all three levels, with individuals, states, and the international system all playing a part?

Level 1: Individuals

Some take the view that aggressive behavior is innate, as it has been "hardwired" into the human personality through evolution and genetics. Despite the fact that behavior is mostly learned, humans demonstrate the same tendency to violence as other animals do. They fight over food, territory, and even mates. But humans are unique in killing their own kind in large numbers and in highly organized ways. They conscript, enslave, torture, and kill their opponents, even in gas chambers. Is there some common flaw in humans that makes them aggressive?

To prove that war is natural or inevitable in the human species, one would have to show that collective violence is the sum of individual aggressiveness. This is very difficult to prove or justify scientifically. Efforts to discover peaceful, conflict-free societies have found only a very few primitive groupings in small, isolated geographical regions of the world. The history of almost all areas, and absolutely all those with sizable populations, demonstrates that man is essentially aggressive in nature. But if aggression is natural and learning cannot keep it in check, then violence should be the norm over time and location. Clearly there are periods

of cooperation and peace across time and place, so presumably aggression is not innate but somehow learned behavior. It is also the case that all modern state institutions, such as laws, courts, and prisons, are based on assumptions about the flawed character of humankind. Could human aggression be deterred by more knowledge and better education?

Perhaps it is not ordinary people who cause wars but rather aggressive, ignorant, or demented leaders. States do not go to war accidentally. Someone or some group makes that choice. Of course, such a decision is always couched in terms of war being the best possible alternative – other choices would be worse or all efforts at peace have been exhausted.[12] But while sometimes the choice to declare war proves beneficial or at least advantageous, at other times it harms a country more than it does good. Why do leaders make the decisions they do?

We examined the general issue of decision making in Chapter 4, but it is common to explain war in terms of the foolish or selfish behavior of leaders. Perhaps some leaders do deliberately choose to lead their country into war. Napoleon is often portrayed as a warmongering megalomaniac. Adolf Hitler similarly is blamed for starting World War II. But in each of these cases other explanations for initiating wars were also possible – such as satisfying or fulfilling a country's national interests in terms of economics or territorial expansion. In the decision to go to war, individual leaders may simply be nervous or suspicious of the motivations of leaders of other countries, or perhaps they are attempting to satisfy the desires of some particular interests or ethno-nationalist group within their own country.

War may also provide the glue for national integration. While the underlying motive may be a leader's own aggrandizement, identifying an enemy facilitates the leader's ability to mobilize resources and people. Or a war may be a mere diversionary tactic. Leaders may also cause war by mistake.

---

[12] Philip Towle, *Going to War* (London: Palgrave 2010).

Misperceptions of the intentions of foreign leaders or even misunderstandings of their own country's national interests are among mistakes that have led to wars. Such examples have been documented in both World Wars I and II. But while a demagogue may goad individuals into going to war to satisfy personal interests of wealth and power, even the most dictatorial regimes seek some measure of popular approval for risking lives and national treasure in war. As for the popular argument that it is the military that favors wars, this has been proved false. It is more common for civilian government employees to favor war.[13]

In recent years, radical feminists have focused on the role of gender in causing war. They have challenged the underlying principles of the realist interpretations of international order, and they have drawn attention to some basic facts about the role individuals play in causing war.[14] Throughout history and across all cultures, males have played the predominant role in making war. Because of this, some feminists have wrongly attributed human aggressive behavior, and thus war, to the male sex hormone testosterone. However, there is no biological argument that proves that males are more aggressive than females. Testosterone does not cause aggression; its level is raised and lowered by human social interactions, not vice versa. Another argument put forth by some radical feminists is that because women are more socialized into nurturing roles by pregnancy and caregiving, they develop superior qualities of reconciliation and negotiation than men do. But women's roles have differed across states, societies, and history. In some societies women have engaged directly in warfare, and in others they have acted in more supporting roles. Rarely, however, have they been wholly passive in conflict situations. In contemporary Israel, women are conscripted into the military and fight on the front lines in a manner similar to men. In World Wars I and II women provided much of the personnel for armament factories, and many shamed men who would not fight for their country and Western values. Posters showed women declaring "Your Country Needs You!"

Level 2: Middle range – states and societies

Perhaps the causes of war are to be found not in individuals or the personalities of leaders but rather in societies and states. According to middle-range theories, these collectivities harbor within them ongoing contests over identity based on differences such as ethnicity, tribe, ideology, religion, and nationalism. We examined the importance of these and other social forces of global politics in Chapter 8. Here we stress the role that contesting groups may play in causing wars. If the nation is the primary unit of allegiance or subjective loyalty (feelings of togetherness or "we-ness"), then there will invariably be internal and international conflict, as there are dramatically more nations than states. History proves this to be the case. Nationalism has been involved in many modern wars because groups or nations desired to break away from the country to which they belonged and form their own state. Nationalists don't want to remain subservient to majorities of other nations or considered second-class citizens within their own state.

The recent Yugoslavian wars are a pertinent example. Individuals made the choices that led to war, but ethnicity, religion, and nationalism all played a part in generating hostilities. Throughout the Cold War, Yugoslavia had been held together

[13] See Peter D. Feaver and Christopher Gelpi, *Choosing Your Battles: American Civil-Military Relations and the Use of Force* (Princeton, NJ: Princeton University Press, 2005). Also see Philip Towle, *Going to War: British Debates from Wilberforce to Blair* (Basingstoke, UK: Palgrave, 2009).

[14] There is a growing literature in this field. A few useful volumes include Joshua S. Goldstein, *War and Gender: How Gender Shapes the War System and Vice Versa* (Cambridge: Cambridge University Press, 2001); Adrienne Harris and Ynestra King, eds., *Rocking the Ship of State: Toward a Feminist Peace Politics* (Boulder, CO: Westview, 1983); Judith Stiehm, ed., *Women's and Men's Wars* (Oxford, UK: Pergamon, 1983); Wenona Giles and Jennifer Hyndman, eds., *Sites of Violence: Gender and Conflict Zones* (Berkeley: University of California Press, 2004); Cynthia Enloe, *Maneuvers: The International Politics of Militarizing Women's Lives* (Berkeley: University of California Press, 2000); Jean Bethke Elshtain, *Women and War*, 2nd ed. (Chicago: University of Chicago Press, 1995).

Figure 9.1 NATO deployments played a key role in implementing the Dayton peace agreement, which ended the Yugoslavian war. NATO camps in Bosnia had to be set up quickly in very harsh conditions. The soldiers in this photo camped in tents inside a dismantled flour factory.

by a communist ideology and a tight-knit oligarchy of communist leaders led by Tito. In 1991 after the Soviet collapse, Yugoslavia's ethnic and religious divisions erupted into claims for independent state-hood, or "self-determination." Slovenia and Croatia declared independence first, followed by Bosnia-Herzegovina and Macedonia a year later. Fighting broke out among the former Yugoslavian repub-lics and ethnic and religious groups, leading to a three-year war that was ended by the Dayton Peace Accord in 1995. Until that point the United Nations and NATO had both failed to restore peace to the area, some two hundred thousand individuals had been killed, and more than four million displaced (Figure 9.1).

Even today the ethno-religious contest continues in Kosovo. As we saw in Close Up 9.1, NATO forces bombed Serbian targets in 1999 until it withdrew its troops from Kosovo and the United Nations Interim Administration for Kosovo (UNMIK) could take control of the small landlocked area (Figure 9.1). Since then, Kosovo elections have made clear that its predominantly Albanian Muslim people wish to

be independent of Serbia, which is predominantly Orthodox Christian. Serbia, however, continues to claim that Kosovo has always belonged to it and still contains large numbers of Orthodox Serbs who wish to remain part of their Serbian homeland. The situation remains frozen, as Russia supports Serbia's claim but most members of the Security Council support Kosovo's right to be independent. Nation-alism has not always been the strongest force in world history, but some form of group identity such as ethnicity or kinship or religion has always been present to strengthen the claims of some groups over others. Leaders may make the final decision to go to war, but when an ethnic group or nation believes that it must rule itself or achieve its own statehood, then conflict is inevitable. In Yugoslavia all of these social forces were involved in the wars of secession.

Civil wars and insurgencies are often permeated by social forces. While the U.S. Civil War of 1861–65, for example, was not fought over nationalism and ethnicity, it certainly involved arguments about identity, race, ideology, and slavery. The current conflict in Afghanistan is essentially about contesting ideologies concerning who should govern and how the country should be ruled. In contrast, among other things, Iraq's recent internal warfare has been about quarrels over religious identity – Sunnis, Shiites, and Kurds fighting one another for spoils and property. Many central African civil wars have been caused by mixtures of materialistic motives combined with primary allegiances based on religion, ethnicity, and tribe. Colonialism, too, has played a role in Africa, as to a large extent the state boundaries of these countries were set by Europeans without concern for basic identities and loyalties. Despite UN efforts to bring peace to some particular regions and states, hostilities and deaths continue and even proliferate. Some conflicts have led to genocide, the systematic killing of an ethnic group. The best-known recent case of genocide is the 1994 Rwanda crisis, when Hutu radicals set about systematically murdering hundreds of thousands of Tutsis. Such internal wars and insurgencies are discussed in detail in the following chapter.

Another middle-range argument about the cause of war is based on the idea that the form of government itself may be a cause of, or hindrance to, war. Leaders cannot make war if their citizens will not follow them. Following this argument, some American theorists in particular believe that wars do not develop between or among states that are democratic. The classic position on this topic is called the democratic peace theory.[15] Its advocates argue that the mere existence of democracy promotes peace and reduces the possibility of war. Indeed, of the 416 wars between sovereign countries between 1816 and 1980, only 12 were arguably between democracies. But the theory used to explain this set of facts is only partly valid. The data clearly show that democracies rarely go to war with other democracies, but they do go to

war with states that have other forms of government (e.g., authoritarian). Moreover, the data also confirm that authoritarian states do not usually go to war with other authoritarian states.

The term zone of peace is often used in political circles to describe geographical areas in which countries do not go to war with each other because they share democratic values. If only democracy could be spread to other countries, particularly in the Middle East, advocates say, peace would be enhanced. This was one of the major arguments made by American neoconservatives and the Bush administration for the Iraq War. A democratic outcome in Iraq would make the war worthwhile, they argued, because it would help spread democracy in the Middle East, thus making the whole region more peaceful. In other words, going to war would be worthwhile because it would reduce the likelihood of war in the future. Obviously, this is a controversial form of analysis.

Level 3: The global system

The global system itself may itself be the cause of war. If, as realists say, the international system is made up of sovereign states in an anarchical world with only weak international law and institutions, then each state will automatically seek to build up its own security forces and structures. It will be in each country's self-interest to protect itself – to look after its own security needs – but in doing so, a country may frighten others into doing the same. Liberals may counter that, despite the fact that there is no overall arbiter such as a world government, there are still multiple, global organizations and regimes for mediation, arbitration, and peace operations. The body of customary international law continues to grow, and the UN, for example, is increasingly involved in settling violent disputes around the world. Global norms about proper behavior are embedded in the International Criminal Court and in international commitments such as the responsibility to protect (R2P) principle adopted by the United Nations (see Chapter 6). Of course, states retain the ultimate power, but they are subject to

---

[15] There is a considerable literature on this topic. For data and contending arguments, see Bruce Russett, *Grasping the Democratic Peace* (Princeton, NJ: Princeton University Press, 1993); Edward D. Mansfield and Jack Snyder, *Electing to Fight: Why Emerging Democracies Go to War* (Cambridge, MA: MIT Press, 2005).

persuasion and codes of proper behavior that are developing slowly but surely.

If all states were satisfied with their situation in the international order, they would obviously not choose to go to war. States go to war only when they are very dissatisfied with some conditions. The United States and Canada are separate states in this anarchic world, but they no longer prepare to go to war with each other. The same is true of states in the European Union. In both cases the states involved used to be enemies but today are not. However, the fact remains that these situations are not the norm, and the international system is basically anarchical. Within it, states continually build up their military and security apparatuses and compete with other states for importance and influence in the international area.

Many sophisticated arguments have been made about global system change and its effect on war. Does rapid economic change or a weakening hegemon increase the likelihood of war? Historians have contributed to our understanding of particular wars by studying the changing nature of the world system, including arguments about the rise and fall of states. They have been less successful in explaining or predicting all wars. Social scientists have also posited a number of theories of war, including cyclical theories, power transition, and bargaining models. We encountered the cyclical theories in Chapter 2. There are many versions of these theories. Recent long-cycle theory holds that cycles of major wars have occurred at irregular intervals approximately once every century. A state rises to a hegemonic position roughly every hundred years, monopolizing military power, trade, technology, and the rules of the global system. Challengers then arise, competing with the hegemon, and a war ensues. Later, another hegemon arises and the cycle begins anew. Even if this theory were accepted as valid (and many scholars contest it), it explains only very general patterns about the causes of war.[16]

Perhaps some countries are more aggressive than others simply because their leaders believe that the structure of the global system, or the balance of power, is not to their country's benefit. Perhaps their state's significance has increased dramatically because of economic or technological change. Might they go to war to establish what they regard as the proper distribution of power in the world? Shifts in the global distribution of power may help explain their choice of war. In fact, historically, when major changes have occurred in the major state's capability, war has often broken out.

Such a power transition theory has been used by neorealists to explain why some countries have caused wars, but this theory also has its critics.[17] They argue that one could just as easily posit a power transition thesis by which states go to war when they think their power position is being weakened. In other words, either strengthening *or* weakening could lead to war. Since all states are characterized by one of those two characteristics at all times, the argument is a truism. Scholars of the public choice tradition view war as a product of rational choice, because state leaders weigh the costs and benefits of their interests and actions (see Chapter 3). A bargaining model therefore posits that the decision to go to war is part of a process between adversaries to settle disputes and disagreements over items of value such as territory or resources.[18]

Radicals, Marxists, and some economic historians attribute the cause of wars to contests among capitalist states over resources and markets. Arguing that economic interests cause war, these theorists claim that, by their very nature, capitalist states must expand, employ cheap labor, and gain access to sources of raw materials to survive and prosper. The political left uses the words

---

[16] George Modelski, ed., *Exploring Long Cycles* (Boulder, CO: Lynne Rienner, 1987).

[17] Charles F. Doran, "Economics, Philosophy of History, and the 'Single Dynamic' of Power Cycle Theory: Expectations, Competition, and Statecraft," *International Political Science Review* 24, no. 1 (2003), pp. 13–49.

[18] Darren Filson and Suzanne Werner, "A Bargaining Model of War and Peace," *American Journal of Political Science* 46, no. 4 (2002), pp. 819–38.

imperialism and *colonialism* to describe how richer states have obtained control over the resources of poorer ones; for example, states in Central Africa that have copper, diamonds, gold, and iron ore have been and continue to be exploited by richer states today. Economic liberals claim exactly the opposite. They argue that expanding free trade and markets knit people together and reduce the need for war because conflict is costly and impedes commerce. In other words, open markets and free trade reduce the need and prospects for war. Fascinating as these approaches are, both right and left versions have proved unsuccessful in generating empirical and particularly statistical conclusions to back up their predictive claims. The issues of economic development, capitalism, and colonialism are covered in Chapters 12 and 13.

Each war has unique properties. The participants, cultures, leadership, objectives, economies, and technologies differ from case to case, which makes comparison difficult and analysis complex. Wars begin, develop, and end in diverse ways. It is beyond the ability of the leadership of either side to control or direct a war's trajectory, as modern technology and events sometimes seem to take on a life of their own. Perhaps war is not even a generic type of human phenomena. Certainly, it is caused by disagreements over something – territory, population, prestige, power, form of government, leadership, and so on – but so far at least, the variation in types of war makes generalization about *all* wars tenuous. Different factors are involved at different levels. Because of this analytical problem, analysts continually shift their level of explanation, depending on their theoretical perspectives, from the individual level to the state and society level to the overall global system. There can, therefore, be several valid but different explanations of even the same war, but in general, scholars have been gaining understanding of what does and does not lead states and people to go to war. Table 9.2 summarizes the competing explanations and essential arguments in history and social science about what causes war.

Table 9.2 **Interpretations of the causes of war – levels of analysis**

Individual	Human characteristics – innate behavior or flawed character; males Leaders – aggressive personalities, misperceptions, mirror images
States and/or societies	Ethnicity Nationalism Religion Economics, class system, aggressive states
Global system	Anarchy – lack of world government Economic factors; capitalism Colonialism Lack of democratic peace Cycle theories, global power transition and bargaining models

Fighting wars: Conventional weapons and weapons of mass destruction

Over time the methods of fighting wars have followed the technological advances of weapons as they evolved from simple sticks and stones to gunpowder, tanks, ships, and air forces. Today they include high-tech conventional weapons, drones, and nuclear warheads. The word *conventional* is often used to describe traditional weapons such as pistols and rifles, but even these continue to evolve and improve as killing machines. Today's conventional high-powered jet aircraft were certainly not in use during World War II. Weapons of mass destruction (WMD), whether nuclear, chemical, biological, or radiological, have become part of the arsenal of warfare, yet they have a fundamentally different nature from that of conventional weapons, as their primary effect is to produce massive carnage without discriminating between military and civilian targets. Modern technology also has enabled both conventional weapons and WMD to be miniaturized, thus allowing them to be easily exported and used in insurgencies and terrorist activities.

In recent decades there has been a revolution in military technology (RMT), with new weapons that are able to hit targets with a very high degree of accuracy and reliability. Such precision-guided bombs and missiles are controlled by lasers, satellites, and other guidance mechanisms. Precision-guided bombs were used by NATO to attack Serbian targets in the war over Kosovo, and they caused relatively few civilian casualties. They have been used in Afghanistan, Libya, Pakistan, Yemen and elsewhere, directed by operators in the United States who controlled small, unpiloted "drone" aircraft. The U.S. military claims such weapons save American lives, but their use is condemned by most host countries. Despite the alleged accuracy of the technology, one high-tech bomb destroyed the Chinese embassy during raids on Serbia over Kosovo, and countless noncombatants have been killed by drones in Afghanistan, Iraq, Pakistan, and Yemen during raids on Taliban and al-Qaeda forces (see Chapter 10).

Focusing on modern weapons may disguise or detract from the reality that low-tech conventional weapons remain vital in warfare, especially in the least developed countries (LDCs; see Chapters 10 and 13). Some countries are far superior to others in terms of military hardware, including high-tech delivery systems and WMDs. Other states seek status through having these weapons, but almost all wars fought since the end of the Cold War have also had to make use of low-tech weapons and improvised explosive devices (IEDs). With few exceptions, high-tech weapons have had less significance than might have been expected in internal wars in Africa, North Africa, the Middle East, and South Asia.

After the Cold War there was a rapid growth in the global arms business as arms manufacturers directed their sales to places where high-tech weapons could not be afforded or used effectively. The trade in rifles, grenade launchers, and mortars was astounding.[19] They strengthened rebellious ethnic and nationalist groups, criminals, and terrorists. In Afghanistan, Iraq, and Pakistan, roadside bombings and suicide bombs increased significantly partly because of the availability of these weapons, but

also because of the use of IEDs made from widely available, inexpensive materials.

Weapons of mass destruction

Along with the proliferation of smaller arms and more accurate means of delivering weapons payloads, recent years have also seen an increase in the numbers of weapons of mass destruction (WMDs). These modern weapons include chemical, biological, radiological, and nuclear weapons (CBRNs). They are highly lethal, can be made small and transportable, and are not prohibitively expensive. More than a half century ago, in 1945, President Truman ordered nuclear bombs to be dropped on Hiroshima and Nagasaki to end the war with Japan – the only times the bomb has been employed in hostilities. The consequences of those two atomic bombs were devastating: seventy thousand people in Hiroshima (Figure 9.2) and thirty-five thousand in Nagasaki died immediately. Many more died because of radiation. Yet these casualties resulted from only two bombs, and deaths from lingering radiation continue even today. Some scholars now put the total number of Japanese deaths at a quarter million. This first use of nuclear bombs provoked considerable apprehension around the world and made it clear that new approaches to military strategy would be required (see Close Up 9.2).

Many traditional ideas about military strategy, both defensive and offensive, were made redundant by the existence of nuclear weapons. Policy makers realized that nuclear weapons could not and should not ever be used again because they would cause too much death and destruction. Foreign policies and strategies began to focus on the idea that while there could not be a prudent or rational exchange of bombs, nuclear arsenals could still play a role in deterrence. Since their introduction in 1945, nuclear weapons have become more accurate and lethal, yet they have actually killed only a fraction of the number of deaths accounted for by conventional weapons. Conventional weapons still account for about 80 percent of world military expenditure, and they are becoming deadlier, more accurate, and more abundant.

---

[19] See reports on arms sales put out by the Federation of American Scientists at http://www.fas.org.

Figure 9.2 In August, 1945, the United States dropped nuclear bombs on Hiroshima and Nagasaki in Japan, immediately killing more than a hundred thousand civilians. Six days after the attack on Nagasaki, Japan announced its surrender to the allies, ending World War II. These are the only two times in history that nuclear weapons have been used in warfare. *Source:* Alamy.

Close Up 9.2 **How to build a nuclear bomb**

Nuclear "fission" was discovered by a German physicist, Otto Hahn, in 1938. This scientific breakthrough eventually led to the first nuclear explosion, carried out in the desert of New Mexico in 1945 as part of the secret World War II–era Manhattan Project.[20] Three countries – Canada, the United Kingdom, and the United States – assembled the resources necessary to develop the bomb. The technology to make the weapons is, therefore, more than sixty years old – it cannot be wished away by well-meaning citizens or politicians.

A nuclear weapon works by creating a powerful explosion in which a large amount of energy is released in a very short time. The physics are well understood and are used in the production of electricity in civilian nuclear reactors. In both cases, atoms of uranium or plutonium are split (i.e., undergo fission) to create a chain reaction. The difference in the two processes is that fission is *controlled* in a nuclear reactor but not in a nuclear weapon.

Uranium-235 and plutonium-239 are the key materials used in nuclear weapons programs. When a neutron enters the nucleus of an atom of either uranium or plutonium, it creates a self-sustaining fission chain of splitting atoms. The size of the explosive yield is determined largely by the amount of material "fissioned." Given appropriate construction, the critical mass of material required to achieve an explosion can be remarkably small – "about the size of a small orange."[21] A fission nuclear weapon made from approximately ten pounds of plutonium-239 would explode with the equivalent of twenty thousand tons of TNT, the power of the nuclear bomb dropped on Nagasaki.

Obtaining the required amounts of uranium-235 to build a nuclear weapon is difficult. Extracting enough fissionable uranium-235

---

[20] David Albright, *Peddling Peril: How the Secret Nuclear Trade Arms America's Enemies* (New York: Free Press, 2010).

[21] Frank Barnaby, *How to Build a Nuclear Bomb* (London: Granta Books, 2003).

from natural uranium (i.e., enriching it) to weapons grade is complex, slow, and expensive. Plutonium-239, however, is readily available and easily obtained. It comes from low-grade uranium used in nuclear power reactors. However it also must be "separated" from uranium in special plants, and bombs based on plutonium are more difficult to build than uranium-enriched bombs.

Nuclear "fusion" is the opposite of nuclear fission. It occurs when the nuclei of atoms of hydrogen fuse together to form nuclei of helium. This takes place when the nuclei are affected by extremely high temperatures, such as those that take place on the sun, or by exploding plutonium. Fusion is used to "boost" the explosive power of the fission process by up to five to ten times. Atomic bombs are "fission" weapons, whereas thermonuclear or hydrogen bombs are boosted "fusion" weapons sometimes referred to as "thermonuclear" bombs.

All types of nuclear bombs kill people first by their explosions and then by the heat and radiation that follow the blast. A **radiological weapon** is not, strictly speaking, a nuclear bomb, as it creates neither an explosion nor heat. A radiological, or "dirty," bomb is set off by a conventional explosion – caused by some material such as dynamite or TNT – along with a quantity of radioactive material. The conventional explosion causes the radioactive material to be taken into the atmosphere and blown about by the wind. There are thousands of sources for obtaining such radioactive materials, as they are used in medical, industrial, and agriculture facilities.

Nuclear weapons

The development of nuclear weapons profoundly changed the notion of security for all countries. Offensive and defensive strategies were turned on their heads. Even the concept of *balance of power*

no longer had the same meaning or importance it once had. When the superpower rivalry between the United States and the former Soviet Union ended, the two countries continued to possess the most powerful military machines on Earth. Together they have 95 percent of the world's nuclear weapons. In 2011 the United States was estimated to have 8,500 total deployed and undeployed warheads, whereas Russia had an estimated total of 11,000 warheads. Britain, France, and other countries also have many nuclear weapons (Table 9.3).

The destructive capability of nuclear bombs is well known. The atomic bomb used to destroy Hiroshima had the power of fifteen thousand tons of TNT, and the Soviet Union once actually built a device with the explosive power of fifty-seven million tons of TNT. To put this in perspective, one

Table 9.3 Estimated world nuclear forces by number of deployed warheads, 2011

Country	Deployed Warheads[a]	Other Warheads[b]	Total Warheads
United States	2,150	6,350	8,500
Russia	2,427	8,530	11,000
United Kingdom	160	65	225
France	290	10	300
China	–	200	240
India	–	80–110	80–100
Pakistan	–	90–100	90–110
Israel	–	80	80
N. Korea	–	–	–[c]
Total	5,027	15,500	20,530

[a] Deployed warheads are those placed on missiles or located on bases with operational forces.
[b] Includes warheads in reserve, waiting preparation or dismantlement.
[c] There is no public information to verify that North Korea has operational nuclear weapons.
Source: Adapted from Shannon N. Kile, Vitaly Fedchenko, and Hans M. Kristensen, "World Nuclear Forces," *SIPRI Yearbook 2011* (Oxford: Oxford University Press, 2011), pp. 319–59.

ten-megaton nuclear bomb would yield the destructive power of ten million tons of TNT, destroy buildings within a range of twelve miles from the target, and produce some hundred thousand square miles of radioactive fallout. More than one thousand times as much explosive power is stockpiled today than was used in all the wars since the invention of gun powder. Just one nuclear submarine of the American Poseidon or Trident class carries enough nuclear warheads to destroy every major city in the former Soviet Union.

A bitter debate continues about the strategic implications of nuclear weapons.[22] Does their mere existence mean that war is more likely? It is clear, for example, that the world came close to a nuclear disaster at the height of the Cuban Missile Crisis.[23] Or does the existence of nuclear arsenals mean that all states fear the consequences of nuclear warfare so much that they will strive to prevent their use? The Cold War between the nuclear superpowers ended peacefully after an arms race of more than forty years, and no nuclear exchange took place. The question remains therefore, are nuclear weapons a stabilizing or destabilizing force in global politics? Would a growth in the number of nuclear states change the situation? Certainly, the international community accepts the premise that a spread of nuclear weapons would be harmful. But would they? Before trying to answer this question, we survey other WMDs for sale on the market.

Biological, chemical, and radiological weapons

Chemical and biological weapons have been around for a long time, but radiological weapons are more novel. All three are weapons of mass destruction and pose dangerous threats because they are relatively easy to obtain and less expensive than nuclear weapons to produce.

If they are effectively disseminated in sufficient quantities, chemical weapons can cause mass casualties. During World War I several chemical agents were employed, including mustard gas and nerve gas. After that war, the international community attempted to eliminate some of the most odious of these weapons. The 1925 Geneva Protocol, which was signed and ratified by more than 132 states, bans warring parties from using chemical weapons such as poisonous gases or liquids such as mustard gas and chlorine. Since production and stockpiling of such weapons are not prohibited, however, many states continue to amass them. Mustard gas was used in the 1980–88 Iran-Iraq War, for example. More recently, in 1995 the nerve agent sarin gas was dispersed in a Tokyo subway, killing twelve people and injuring thousands. The most urgent threat today is the possible use of complex synthetic materials such as those used for toxic industrial products as chemical weapons of mass destruction. The commercial use of these materials means that their costs are low and that they can easily be obtained by rogue states or terrorists.

Biological terrorism refers to the deliberate dispersal of pathogens through food, air, water, or living organisms to cause disease and death. The materials required to produce such biological weapons are readily available in laboratories worldwide. Anthrax attacks in the U.S. mail system after 9/11 indicate how relatively easily an attack can be mounted and with what profound significance. The assaults killed only five people and infected seventeen, but their economic impact was enormous in terms of costs and social disruption. Efforts to limit biological weapons have been successful. The 1972 Biological and Toxin Weapons Convention (BTWC), ratified by 155 states, committed the signatories to prohibit the development, production, stockpiling, and acquisition of biological agents or toxins. The lack of verification methods in the BTWC was rectified in the 1993 Chemical Weapons Convention

---

[22] Scott D. Sagan and Kenneth N. Waltz, *The Spread of Nuclear Weapons: A Debate Renewed* (New York: W. W. Norton 2003); Michael Krepon, "The Mushroom Cloud That Wasn't," *Foreign Affairs* 88, no. 3 (May–June 2009), pp. 2–6; Amitai Etzioni, "Tomorrow's Institution Today," *Foreign Affairs* 88, no. 3 (May–June 2009), pp. 7–14.

[23] Michael Dobbs, *One Minute to Midnight: Kennedy, Khrushchev, and Castro on the Brink of Nuclear War* (New York: Vintage 2009).

(CWC), which has been ratified by almost every state in the world. The convention mandates the destruction of all chemical weapons and sets up unprecedented on-site verification provisions. The United States accepts the treaty despite its concern that the treaty's compliance mechanisms may be too weak given the sophistication of modern biological weapons.

Some weapons fall between conventional weapons and WMDs. A "dirty bomb," for example, uses conventional explosives to disseminate radioactive material (see Close Up 9.2). Such bombs are easy to assemble and much easier to acquire than actual nuclear devices. They have dangers beyond their potential to kill and maim individuals. The dispersal of radiation by a conventional bomb in an urban area would trigger widespread panic and economic disruption. Materials for making them are considerably easier to obtain than the fissile materials that are required for nuclear bombs, or most chemical and biological agents, because they are widely available for use in power plants, cancer therapy treatments, food and blood irradiation, and radiography.

Security concepts in the nuclear era

The chief purpose of security policy is to avert violence and war and to avoid vulnerability to coercion by a stronger or more aggressive state. States prepare defensive strategies such as shielding their borders with fortifications, security guards, and militaries. All states equip and train soldiers to defend their territories, which makes it as costly as possible for other states to attack them. We have noted, for example, the historical role of border protection by fortifications from Hadrian's Wall to the Great Wall of China and the Berlin Wall in Germany. States also actively prepare to go to war by preparing offensive strategies and tactics in case they are needed. In Chapters 2 and 5, we introduced the concept of **balance of power**, a term that refers to a relatively equal distribution of power among

states sufficient to maintain security and peace among rivals. It also refers to the tendency of states to form coalitions or take actions to prevent any single state or coalition from dominating others. If one state or coalition tries to assume sufficient power to dominate the system by obtaining more territory or resources or military strength, others will try to constrain it through negotiation, new alliances, or war.

The development of nuclear bombs complicated this balance of power equation. After the United States dropped two nuclear bombs on Japan in 1945, the use of nuclear weapons became questionable from a policy point of view. While war has never had many admirers, nuclear war was viewed as so abhorrent that even military strategists thought it should never be considered as a policy option again. This realization brought a new concept to the idea of balancing one state against another – there was a shift from the idea of fighting wars to the idea of deterrence. **Deterrence** means that war is to be avoided by each side posing a threat great enough that it never needs to actually carry through with it. Deterrence strategies, therefore, are adopted to dissuade an adversary from doing what it otherwise might do or to create such an enormous cost for military aggression that it would not be deemed rational. In other words, adoption of deterrence as a policy accompanied a new nuclear doctrine and a special vocabulary.

Nuclear strategic doctrine

Modern military weapons have changed many of the strategies and even the tactics of warfare and public policy. The strategic doctrine underpinning the theoretical use of nuclear weapons during the Cold War was known as **nuclear deterrence** – the ability of each superpower to persuade the other not to attack it by threatening retaliation with nuclear weapons. The paradox was that for each side to feel secure, it had to make the other feel insecure. In other words, deterrence rested on each side being able to deter the other because it, too, possessed nuclear capabilities. There had to be a balance of nuclear power. Neither side could be allowed to produce a perfect defense system because that would give it an advantage that could lead to war.

Over time, the United States and the Soviet Union established a rough nuclear parity, and deterrence worked because each side was capable of obliterating the other even if it sustained a first nuclear strike. This situation was considered *stable* because neither side would wish to launch a first strike that could not be successful. In military language, deterrence works when each side has a second-strike capability – that is, when each side is able to withstand a strike and still be able to retaliate at a level unacceptable to the aggressor. Since under these conditions neither side could win a nuclear war, so goes the argument, mutual deterrence is achieved. Hence, nuclear war was not to be waged; only its threat was reasonable or rational. Indeed, a nuclear weapon has not been used since the U.S. attacks on Hiroshima and Nagasaki in 1945, and there are few realistic ways that one could actually be employed on the battlefield.

The peace movement calls nuclear deterrence theory nothing but a "game of chicken," because any miscalculation or irrational act could result in human annihilation. Some policy makers call this strategic doctrine mutual assured destruction (MAD), as there is no advantage to the country that attacks first. Only the threat of using nuclear weapons retains utility. Any attack on countries with even a small number of nuclear weapons, such as Britain, France, China, Israel, Pakistan, and India, would be irrational, since the level of retaliation would be too devastating to make a nuclear attack worthwhile. Of course, this is the major reason both India and Pakistan retain nuclear weapons.

To have any utility or threat value, both nuclear and conventional bombs must be able to be delivered to their target. Weapons in modern military arsenals are able to travel long or short distances. A strategic weapon is one that travels over large distances to strike an enemy; intercontinental bal-

listic missiles (ICBMs), submarine-launched ballistic missiles (SLBMSs), and long-range bombers that can travel from the United States to Russia, or vice versa, are examples (Figure 9.3). An intermediate-range weapon such as a cruise missile travels between 500 and 5,500 kilometers. A short-range weapon is sometimes called a tactical weapon because it travels only short distances, usually less than 500 kilometers. Examples of short-range weapons are artillery shells, mines, and short-range nuclear missiles that can be used as battlefield weapons.

Even when treaties prohibit an increase in the number of missiles, new technologies often provide ways around the restrictions. To evade agreed-on rules, for example, both the United States and Russia equip their ballistic missiles with multiple independently targetable reentry vehicles (MIRVs) that allow the missile to carry multiple warheads aimed at different targets. For example, a U.S. MIRV missile (Peacekeeper) can carry ten nuclear weapons. In the past three decades nuclear-armed tactical air-to-surface missiles (TASMs) and air-launched cruise missiles (ACMs) have also become standard military equipment.

The sheer variety of modern conventional weapons is astounding. Smart bombs, which can penetrate bunkers and caves and detonate explosives at a precise moment underground, were used to destroy Taliban weapons caches in Afghanistan. Laser and antisatellite weapons can be used in outer space, and American pilotless aircraft or predators were and are being used in the Middle East and South Asia (see Chapter 10). The United States is developing a conventional weapon, called Prompt Global Strike, a combination of a Minuteman missile with a glider guided by satellite, which would allow the United States to release a thousand-pound conventional bomb on a target after traveling halfway around the world in less than an hour.[24]

In 1983 the United States announced its Strategic Defense Initiative (SDI), known as "Star Wars," which was to compliment its deterrence theory.

[24] *The New York Times*, April 23, 2010.

Figure 9.3 A cruise missile is an intermediate range delivery vehicle. It can carry a conventional or nuclear warhead and can reach a land-based or sea-based target with a high degree of accuracy. *Source:* Photos.com.

Under this policy the United States was to build a high-technology shield to defend American territory against incoming nuclear missiles. So far the policy has been an expensive albatross that will not, in the conceivable future, be capable of preventing all missiles from landing on American territory. The project is ongoing, however, in the form of an antiballistic missile defense system that the United States continues to build to prevent an attack from overseas, possibly from North Korea or Iran. Other defense issues were involved in the U.S. decision to put a ballistic missile defense system in Poland and the Czech Republic. This project was canceled by the Obama administration in 2009, when it switched from a land- to a sea-based system, but the administration did not cancel missile defense for Eastern Europe entirely (see Critical Case Study 9.1).

The spread of WMDs and conventional weapons

There has been a rapid increase in numbers of conventional high-tech weapons and WMDs since World War II. Much media attention has focused on the proliferation of WMDs, but the rising numbers and killing power of conventional weapons have been just as significant and perhaps more so. Lethal conflict around the world has also been facilitated by the proliferation of low-tech weapons such as machetes and rifles, which, for example, killed almost a million Rwandans during that country's 1994 civil war, and by improvised explosive devices (IEDs) made of readily available materials and used in Iraq, Afghanistan, Pakistan, and several areas of central Africa and the Middle East. Killing by WMDs remains basically theoretical, whereas daily loss of life from conventional and low-tech weapons is actual and widespread.

The international market for weapons is brisk, with trade in conventional weapons continuing to grow, especially in LDCs, with a sizable percentage flowing not to governments but to civilian combatants and terrorists around the world. Tanks, self-propelled guns, armored cars, aircraft, helicopters, and surface-to-air missiles are examples of conventional weapons. The worldwide value of such sales in 2010 was $40.4 billion, of which $30.7 billion were sold to developing countries. The United States and Russia are the largest exporters of such arms. The next three major exporters are the United Kingdom, France, and China (Table 9.4). The top five

Critical Case Study 9.1 **U.S. antiballistic missile defense**

In 2001, President George W. Bush announced that his administration would develop and deploy an extensive and expensive antiballistic missile defense system. It would include land, sea, and air components, and it would, in theory, be able to knock out incoming hostile missiles. The government argued that such a defense system was necessary because there had been an increase in the proliferation of the technology used for building weapons of mass destruction and for delivering nuclear, chemical, and biological bombs. For the United States to develop and deploy such a defense system, it needed to annul the 1972 bilateral Anti-Ballistic Missile Treaty with Russia, which allowed each country only one site from which to protect its capital. In 2001 it withdrew from the treaty. Critics argue that this decision resulted in the remilitarization of international relations and could lead to a new arms race and perhaps even the weaponization of space.

What would a new U.S. missile defense do? In theory it would destroy incoming ballistic missiles that might potentially emanate from Iran or North Korea. Radar stations were placed in Alaska and California in the United States, at Flyingdales in the United Kingdom, and in Greenland. Antimissile missiles, or interceptors, were placed in Alaska and California and on ships. The most controversial proposal was to locate a radar system in the Czech Republic and put interceptors in Poland. On coming into office in 2009, U.S. president Barack Obama canceled part of the European project, declaring that it was not necessary because ship-based systems could be used to counter any threats. Russia, which had vehemently protested the radar system next to its border, reported this as a diplomatic victory.

As part of the new NATO strategic doctrine, in 2011 President Obama declared a "reset" with Russia and proposed that it join an antiballistic defense shield with NATO. At the core of the revised system is the SM-3 missile, which is borne on ships, and by 2015 interceptor missiles will be placed on land sites in Romania and by 2018 in Poland. Russia continues to regard NATO expansion to parts of the former Soviet Union as offensive, and NATO has been affronted by Russia's recognition of the independence of Abkhazia and South Ossetia after the 2008 Russian-Georgian war.

Change in the European part of the project did not mean that the overall antimissile system was eliminated. The U.S. government has already spent more than $100 billion on the project, and it continues to claim that the Alaskan and California interceptor missiles will be able to destroy their incoming targets. Since the closing speed of an incoming missile will be approximately fifteen thousand miles per hour, there are many critics of the feasibility of the plan, who say that it will be like trying to hit a bullet with another bullet. Such critics say that it will never work, claiming that it could never stop all missiles and that it will trigger a new arms race. Suffice it to say that missile defense is still in its infancy, and nobody has a complete measure of its potential or whether it will merit its cost.

What are the merits and demerits of the antimissile system from your point of view? Should it be eliminated or continued? Could it provoke an arms race between the United States and Russia?

Table 9.4   Conventional arms shipments to developing nations in 2010: leading suppliers (in millions of constant U.S. dollars)

Rank	Suppliers	Value of Agreements
1	United States	21,255
2	Russia	7,800
3	United Kingdom	1,400
4	France	1,300
5	China	900

Source: U.S. government. Congressional Research Service, http://www.fas.org.

buyers in 2010 were India, Taiwan, Saudi Arabia, Egypt, and Israel.[25]

Nuclear proliferation can result from a state making, buying, or stealing a weapon. Currently, at least nine states are capable of detonating a nuclear bomb: China, France, India, Israel, Pakistan, Russia, the United Kingdom, the United States, and (as of the fall of 2006) North Korea. Several other countries, including Brazil and South Africa, have nuclear capability but have given up the pursuit of nuclear weapons. Another half dozen states could develop this capacity, including Canada, Germany, Iran, Iraq, Libya, and Taiwan. In May 1998, India and then Pakistan set off several nuclear devices, to the consternation and criticism of the world community. Later, Ali Khan, a Pakistani nuclear scientist, sold equipment and expertise to build a nuclear bomb to Libya and Iran. After leaving the Nonproliferation of Nuclear Weapons Treaty (NPT), North Korea tested its first nuclear device in 2006, and it has since tested more powerful weapons. By 2010 it had produced about ten nuclear bombs, ordered UN weapons inspectors out of the country, announced that it planned to restart its plutonium production facility, and launched new rockets.

The number of deadly WMDs makes even the most sanguine pragmatist nervous about the possibility of nuclear, chemical, or biological warfare. While realists and liberals argue profoundly over whether more weapons in the world increase or decrease the potential for war, political leaders and international statesmen have no such doubts. Essentially, political leaders believe that the fewer WMDs there are in the hands of states and people, the less chance there is that they will be used. Many commentators fear that an accident or bad judgment, stupidity, or miscalculation by political actors could lead to their use with catastrophic effects. However, a prohibition (even a taboo) also seems to have developed on the *first use* of nuclear weapons, which may prevent them from ever being employed.

The fact that North Korea possesses several nuclear weapons and that India and Pakistan are armed against each other is particularly fearful to Western leaders and the UN. The possible spread of nuclear weapons to middle-rank powers such as Iran is also feared, but from Tehran's point of view, such weapons would give the country both prestige and deterrence against an outside attack (see Chapter 4). From the political position of Iran, North Korea, and some other countries such as Syria, the developed Western countries deny them the right to have nuclear energy and bombs in order to keep them subservient. However, the rise of international terrorism has dramatically increased concerns about proliferation (see Close Up 9.3). Fortunately, most countries accept the argument that the proliferation of nuclear weapons is dangerous because a "rogue" state or perhaps terrorists could get hold of one and use it. It is difficult to contest the argument that terrorist groups without territory and people to defend are more likely to use nuclear weapons, as they have no location against which a retaliatory strike could be directed. As President Obama put it in April 2009, "In a strange turn of history, the threat

[25] Bates Gill, "Diffuse Threats, Frail Institutions: Managing Security in the New Era." *Current History* (November 2010), pp. 329–35.

Close Up 9.3 Belfer Center's myths of nuclear theft and terrorism

1. **Myth:** Terrorists do not want to carry out a nuclear attack.
   Reality: Some terrorists are actively seeking nuclear weapons and materials for use in such an attack.
2. **Myth:** Terrorists could not realistically get a nuclear bomb or nuclear material to make one.
   Reality: Around the world, enough nuclear material for thousands of nuclear weapons is inadequately protected against terrorist and criminal threats.
3. **Myth:** Terrorists could not make a nuclear bomb if they had the material or set off a bomb if they had one.
   Reality: Numerous authoritative studies have concluded that if they obtained the needed nuclear material, a well-organized terrorist group could plausibly make and use a crude nuclear bomb.
4. **Myth:** Only state-sponsored terrorists could plausibly carry out a nuclear attack.
   Reality: A state sponsor would not be needed either to steal nuclear material or to make it into a bomb.
5. **Myth:** Border defenses can reliably prevent nuclear bombs or materials from being smuggled into the United States.
   Reality: There are many routes into the United States, and nuclear materials and bombs are so easy to hide that border security can never be more than a very porous last-ditch line of defense.
6. **Myth:** Nuclear terrorism can reliably be prevented with offensive military action.
   Reality: The activities involved in making a bomb are small and easy to hide so the world can never be confident that a group building a bomb would be found and stopped before it was too late.

7. **Myth:** States will not seek to obtain stolen nuclear material
   Reality: States have in fact attempted to buy nuclear weapons or materials when making their own seemed too difficult, dangerous, or time consuming.

Source: Adapted from Mathew Bunn and Anthony Weir, "Securing the Bomb: An Agenda for Action" (Belfer Center, John F. Kennedy School of Government, May 2004), p. viii, http://www.nti.org/cnwn.

of global nuclear war has gone down, but the risk of a nuclear attack has gone up."[26]

Disarmament and arms control

The question of how to maintain security in the post–Cold War world is daunting. The arms race, in which the two superpowers and their allies sought security by competing to produce more and more nuclear weapons, has been abandoned, but the deadly weapons continue to be stockpiled around the world. Many states remain armed to the teeth with nuclear and conventional weapons, as well as biological and chemical weapons. Controlling nuclear material and expertise is very difficult and controversial – an analysis by the Belfer Center at Harvard found that only two of eighteen indicators for controlling nuclear materials had reached the 50 percent threshold for safety.[27]

The two broad options for reducing the proliferation of weapons of mass destruction are general disarmament and arms control. Pacificism, a liberal idealist school of ethical thought, defends the view that all violence and war is morally wrong

---

[26] *The New York Times*, April 6, 2009.
[27] Mathew Bunn and Anthony Wier, *Securing the Bomb: An Agenda for Action* (Belfer Center, John F. Kennedy School of Government, May 2004).

and upholds the first of these options, calling for worldwide unilateral disarmament to prevent world destruction. Pacifists tend to take the view that armaments themselves are a fundamental cause of hostility in international politics. They promote the idea that the West should take the first step in the peace process by destroying all its weapons. However, most government policy makers counter with the argument that such weapons will continue to exist as long as there is hostility between major states. For them, nuclear weapons are not the cause of hostilities but the result of it. Moreover, they argue that even if all nuclear weapons were totally destroyed, they could be remade, and, thus, states would produce them again quickly if they needed to ensure their security. In other words, nuclear weapons cannot be "disinvented" because the technology is widely understood. Despite this fundamental disagreement, however, there is widespread consensus that fewer and less powerful weapons would enhance security by making war much less likely and less destructive. International agreements reduce the uncertainty that one state could be tempted to strike first against another out of fear of being attacked itself. The acceptance of this principle by both the Soviet Union and the United States during the Cold War meant that, despite their ideological hostilities, the countries found it in their interests to engage in arms-control measures.

Since no major state is willing to accept the vulnerability associated with total disarmament, the pragmatic option has been for governments to adopt policies of limited disarmament (reducing WMDs) or arms control (preventing proliferation and reducing the growth in number of arms). These policies offer the prospect of reducing threats and increasing stability in international affairs without the danger posed by outright disarmament. Arms-control agreements have been around for centuries. As early as 1139, Pope Innocent II called an international conference to control a new, awesome weapon – the crossbow!

In the past four decades, several bilateral and multilateral arms-control treaties have been com-

pleted that require states to eliminate or reduce the number and type of nuclear weapons. Many of them are weak in terms of monitoring and verification. The 1968 Nonproliferation of Nuclear Weapons Treaty (NPT) prohibits the sale, acquisition, and production of nuclear weapons to countries that are not already in the nuclear club. By this treaty the nuclear powers pledge not to disseminate nuclear devices or expertise to nonnuclear countries. States without nuclear weapons agreed not to develop or acquire them and to accept international inspections so that other states could be assured that they were fulfilling their obligations under the treaty. Signatories, however, remained free to develop nuclear energy for peaceful purposes. The International Atomic Energy Agency (IAEA), part of the UN system, is responsible for monitoring nuclear facilities to prevent noncompliance with the treaty. It has a legal duty to report violations of the NPT, but on occasion its monitors have found it exceedingly difficult to distinguish peaceful nuclear energy programs from their nuclear weapons counterparts.[28] Better ways to detect and prevent cheating by some states, and new fueling methods for peaceful nuclear power plants that will lower the risk of material being diverted for arms production, have yet to be developed.

As of 2013, almost all states, including those with the largest nuclear weapon arsenals, have signed the NPT agreement, even nuclear states in the former Soviet Union. However, Israel, Pakistan, and India have not acceded to the agreement and continue to develop new ballistic and cruise missiles capable of delivering nuclear weapons. North Korea withdrew its agreement in 2002, when the United States ended its shipments of fuel oil to the country. It then started up a nuclear reactor that could process weapons-grade nuclear material, and dictator Kim Jong Il announced that

[28] The major difference between nuclear material used as fuel in producing nuclear energy and in producing nuclear weapons is the level to which it is enriched. The IAEA monitors the amounts of uranium and plutonium available for use in enrichment programs.

he would build nuclear weapons and test short and long-range missiles. The country experimented with its first nuclear explosion in 2006 and then in 2009 tested a more powerful device estimated at between ten and twenty kilotons, approximately the size of the bomb dropped on Hiroshima. Today, North Korea possesses some ten nuclear warheads and a thousand missiles of various ranges to transport them. Taepodong 2, a long-range missile, was tested in 2009. It flew over Japan and had an estimated range of 2,500–4,000 kilometers.

A U.S.–North Korean ballet of nonnegotiations over nuclear issues continues. Experts believe that North Korea does not yet have a nuclear device small enough to fit onto its missiles, but the United States is taking no chances, and after the testing of Taepodong 2, it immediately placed a floating radar system off the coast of Hawaii. The U.S. Navy also began monitoring North Korean ships in case they were carrying arms or nuclear technology. North Korea declared that if the United States forced inspections of its ships it would be considered an act of war. So far no confrontations have taken place. In 2012, after an embarrassing missile failure, North Korea's leader Kim Jong Un (son of the former dictator) announced that he would suspend nuclear weapons testing and uranium enrichment and allow IAEA inspectors to do their work in exchange for an American pledge to ship tons of food to his country. While significant, such agreements have been stillborn in the past.[29]

Every five years the countries that have signed the NPT get together to discuss their progress in nuclear disarmament. Aside from issues regarding rule breakers such as Iran and North Korea, there has been considerable concern over the spread of purely civilian nuclear technology. Issues such as the arms race in India and Pakistan are not on the agenda, as these countries are not signatories to the NPT. There are no mandatory international standards for nuclear facilities or for institutions

such as hospitals whose radioactive waste could be used for making a dirty bomb. Thirty-eight countries possess weapons-usable nuclear materials, and experts estimate that roughly 2,100 tons of weapons-grade material exist around the world that together could make 120,000 nuclear weapons.[30] The IAEA reported that more than 250 cases of unauthorized possession, theft, and loss of nuclear and other radiological materials took place in 2009. Many argue that even the United States may have offended the spirit of the NPT by allowing India access to civilian nuclear energy and high-level technology despite its refusal to sign the NPT. The United States pushed the deal through the Nuclear Suppliers Group (NSG), the forty-six-state organization that sets rules for world nuclear trade. Pakistan considers this arrangement inappropriate and is preparing to greatly expand its production of weapons-grade fuel. The arms race therefore continues in South Asia.

Much more needs to be done to keep all nuclear materials under strict control.[31] In an ideal world the NPT would have legally binding amendments, but that would require a new consensus and take many years to achieve. Most countries have signed on to additional protocols concerning nuclear materials, but new international agreements are needed to ban the production of weapons-usable material and provide at least minimum security for all nuclear reactors, fuel plants, and storage facilities, as well as hospitals and laboratories that work with radiological materials.

In 2009 President Obama announced ambitious targets and later the UN General Assembly passed a resolution to support them. The plan calls for all existing nuclear warheads to be secured and for the United States and Russia to cut back their weapons programs. In four years, if it were implemented, all weapons-usable nuclear material could be secured, and there would be an internationally monitored

[29] *International Herald Tribune*, March 1, 2012.

[30] *The New York Times*, April 12, 2010.
[31] An excellent source of all issues and continuous updating on nuclear security is found at the Belfer Center's website (http://www.belfercenter.org).

bank of nuclear fuel for countries to draw from rather than continuing to produce weapons-grade materials themselves. The role of the IAEA needs to be enlarged to enable it to secure access to all suspected nuclear sites and data. Opponents of such new security treaties complain about compliance and inspection rules; about the peaceful use of nuclear energy; and about expanding the treaty to include India, Pakistan, Israel, and North Korea. It will prove difficult to overcome these broad objections, but despite formidable challenges, the goal of protecting all stocks of nuclear weapons, highly enriched uranium (HEU), and plutonium so that they never fall into the hands of terrorists could be achieved.[32]

In 1996, a large majority of countries signed the Comprehensive Test Ban Treaty (CTBT), which bans the testing of all nuclear weapons and provides a world monitoring system. As of 2013, 157 countries had ratified the treaty, but many powerful countries such as China, India, Iran, Israel, North Korea, Pakistan, and the United States are not among them. Because of these and other naysayers, the CTBT has never come into force. President Obama has vowed to pursue ratification as soon as possible, but obtaining the two-thirds vote of the Senate has proved difficult. As we have seen, in 2006 North Korea tested a nuclear device. Western leaders complained, but few commentators referred to the U.S. opposition to the CTBT – which perhaps was a missed opportunity in arms-control progress. Various international agreements already prohibit military activities in the Antarctic, and nuclear tests are not allowed underwater, in the atmosphere, or in outer space. Nuclear weapons are also prohibited in Latin America, the South Pacific, Southeast Asia, and Africa. But the world has yet to write a treaty that would end the production of nuclear fissile material for bombs, and there is little likelihood of one being accepted in the near future.

[32] See reports of the Institute for Science and International Security at http://www.isis-online.org.

Bilateral agreements between the United States and Russia (formerly the Soviet Union)

The United States and Soviet Union made considerable progress in reducing their stockpiles of strategic missiles. In 1972 they signed two bilateral agreements based on the Strategic Arms Limitation Talks (SALT). The agreements did not reduce the number of weapons, but they did slow the rate of increase by freezing them at the then existing levels. The SALT-1 treaty put a freeze on the total number of fixed land-based ICBMs (intercontinental ballistic missiles), SLSMs (submarine-launched ballistic missiles), and bombers. This reduced the possibility that one side could attack and win a nuclear war. However, although the treaty froze the number of missiles, it did not regulate the number of warheads that could be put on each missile. The Anti-Ballistic Missile (ABM) Treaty limited the deployment of antiballistic missile systems to two sites in each country (later reduced to one) so that neither side could knock the other out with a first strike. The United States withdrew from the ABM Treaty in 2001, but the Russians still operate an antimissile defense system outside Moscow.

The 1991 Strategic Arms Reduction Treaty I (START I) was the first agreement by each side to make major cuts in long-range nuclear weapons. It reduced the number of strategic nuclear warheads held by the United States and the Soviet Union by a third, to six thousand deployed warheads each. The rules were complicated, but essentially they established limits on strategic nuclear delivery systems. Each side was to possess no more than 1,600 strategic nuclear delivery vehicles (e.g., booster rockets, jets) and 6,000 "accountable" strategic warheads (actual nuclear bombs). The purpose of START was to lower the risk of war by making a preemptive nuclear attack less likely than had been achieved with the earlier SALT treaty. The treaty contained basic rules of verification that allowed both the Soviet Union and the United States to be confident that the other side was not cheating. Then the Soviet Union fell apart and further negotiations were required between the two superpowers. START II followed. It called for bans on multiple-warhead, land-based missiles. The treaty was ratified by the United States in 1996 and by Russia in 2000, but it never entered into force because of disagreements over the U.S. withdrawal from the ABM Treaty.

In May 2002, the United States and Russia again discussed reducing their nuclear arsenals. This time each agreed to a two-thirds reduction, to about 2,200 warheads each by 2012. This Strategic Offensive Reduction Treaty (SORT), negotiated by Presidents Bush and Putin, was ratified in 2003. When completed, the treaty would have further reduced the number of nuclear weapons to between 1,700 and 2,200 for each country, but this success was superseded by the fact that the earlier START I agreement came up for renewal during the presidencies of Obama and Medvedev, so in April 2010 the United States and Russia signed the New Strategic Arms Reduction Treaty (New START) agreement. This ten-year agreement commits the two countries to slashing their nuclear warheads to the lowest level in a half century and adds a new inspection or monitoring regime; the parties agreed further that within the coming seven years they would reduce their strategic warheads to 1,550 from the 2,200 presently allowed and their launchers or delivery vehicles to 700 from 1,600. Despite some objections that the treaty might prevent the development of a national missile defense program, the U.S. Senate ratified the treaty in 2010. In the meantime, in April 2010, the Obama government announced a new "nuclear posture" that narrows the conditions in which the United States will use nuclear weapons.[33] This declaratory policy vows that the United States will not use, or threaten to use, nuclear weapons against nonnuclear states that are in compliance with the NPT, even if they attack the United States with biological or chemical weapons or mount a cyberattack.

---

[33] For a critique of this declaratory policy, see Peter D. Feaver, "Obama's Nuclear Modesty," *The New York Times*, April 9, 2010.

The intermediate-range nuclear forces (INF) agreement is the most comprehensive of the treaties, covering missiles that travel 500–5,500 kilometers. In December 1987 NATO and the former states of the Warsaw Pact agreed to eliminate all land-based INFs in their arsenals. The treaty included an asymmetrical compromise by the former Soviet Union and a verification regime that included on-site inspection of the destruction process. By May 1991 the destruction of all these missiles in Europe was complete. In practical terms, having destroyed the 859 U.S. Pershing II and ground-launched cruise missiles, as well as 1,752 Soviet SS-20s, SS-5s, and SS-4s means that there are no nuclear-tipped missiles with a range of between 500 and 5,500 kilometers left in Europe.

Short-range nuclear forces include all weapons with a range of less than five hundred kilometers. In 1989, President George H. W. Bush announced that on completion of the Treaty on Conventional Armed Forces in Europe, talks would begin on the reduction of short-range nuclear weapons in Europe. NATO agreed with the proposal in 1990. Finally, the United States, acting on its own, decided to remove these weapons. The basic argument was that such short-range devices were not needed in Europe, as they could strike only Germany or the newly founded democracies of Eastern Europe. With Soviet troops removed from these regions there was no purpose for them. The United States got rid of all ground-launched nuclear weapons, including artillery shells, and reduced the number of its air-launched missiles in Europe. NATO agreed to limit its air-launched nuclear missiles to 1,100.

At the conventional level, too, there has been considerable progress in the past three decades. In 1990 the Treaty on Conventional Armed Forces in Europe (CFE) signed between NATO and the Warsaw Pact countries sharply reduced levels of conventional forces in Europe. The treaty limited each alliance to equal inventories in five areas – 20,000 tanks, 29,000 artillery pieces, 30,000 armored vehicles, 7,200 combat aircraft, and 2,000 attack helicopters. According to the treaty, the twenty-two participating states from the Atlantic to the Urals had to adhere to the ceilings and destroy any surplus forces. Destruction and verification was conducted under the auspices of the Organization for Security and Cooperation in Europe (OSCE). For all practical purposes, this agreement made either a NATO or former Warsaw Pact land offensive in Europe impossible. Along with the INF agreement, the CFE realized the greatest single demilitarization of security in Europe since the Napoleonic Wars. In 2007 Russia unilaterally suspended its participation in the program.

The continued lessening of tensions between the East and West and the end of Soviet aggressive intentions and capabilities further affected the arms balance in Europe. When the Warsaw Pact ended in April 1991 five hundred thousand Eastern European troops were released from its command, and as part of an agreement with Germany, Russia removed all its troops from Eastern Germany by 1994. NATO, in response, overhauled its military structure, reduced its troop levels in Europe, set up a rapid reaction corps to handle future confrontations in Europe, and began to invite Russia and other former communist countries to participate in its activities.

As well as these bilateral agreements, there have also been major breakthroughs concerning international treaties on conventional weapons. The 1991 UN Register of Conventional Arms requires states to list all major weapons exported or imported. The 1995 Wassenaar Export-Control Treaty monitors transfers of some weapons technology. And as of 1999, under the Inter-American Convention on Transparency in Conventional Weapons Acquisitions, member states of the Organization of American States are required to report on the export and import of all weapons. The international campaign to ban land mines also led many governments to outlaw antipersonnel mines. The treaty, Antipersonnel Landmines Treaty (APLT), which bans the use, production, stockpiling, and sale of antipersonnel land mines, came into effect in 1999 without the support of major countries such as China, Russia,

and the United States. The United States refuses to sign the treaty because it deploys plentiful and cheap antipersonnel mines, and this allows it to reduce the number of military personnel required to defend South Korea against a possible attack from North Korea. In 2008 a majority of the countries of the world signed the Convention on Cluster Munitions (CCM), which prohibits the use, production, stockpiling, and transfer of cluster munitions (Table 9.5). However, as of 2012, only seventy

Table 9.5 **Major bilateral and multilateral arms control agreements (mentioned in text)**

Treaty	Year
Nonproliferation of Nuclear Weapons Treaty (NPT)	1969
Biological and Toxic Weapons Convention	1972
Strategic Arms Limitation Treaties	
SALT 1 and Anti Ballistic Missile (ABM)	1972
Strategic Arms Reduction Treaty 1 (START 1)	1991
Strategic Arms Reduction Treaty 11 (START 11)	1996
Strategic Offensive Reduction Treaty (SORT)	2002
New Strategic Reduction Treaty (New START)	2010
Intermediate Nuclear Forces Europe (INF)	1987
Conventional Forces in Europe (CFE)	1990
United Nations Register of Conventional Arms	1991
Chemical Weapons Convention (CWC)	1993
Wassenaar Export-Control Treaty	1995
Comprehensive Test Ban Treaty (CTBT)	1996
Antipersonnel Landmines Treaty (APLT)	1997
Inter-American Convention on Transparency in Conventional Weapons Acquisitions	1999
Convention on Cluster Munitions	2008

states had ratified the agreement. Fourteen powerful countries that possess cluster munitions, including China, Russia, and the United States, oppose the treaty on technical and policy grounds.

Without going as far as total disarmament, arms-control measures have proved useful in providing pragmatic solutions to reduce both nuclear and conventional weapons. Unless and until states learn to live with the values and philosophies that separate them, a sound defense policy accompanied by arms-control agreements is the best that can be expected on all sides. This does not mean that there cannot be more or better safeguards. The world would still profit from further reductions in overall nuclear warheads, a major reduction in short-range nuclear weapons, an enhanced monitoring system, a strengthened nuclear nonproliferation treaty, an American ratification of the Comprehensive Test Ban Treaty, prevention of an arms race in outer space, and a comprehensive treaty for the Arctic region. There is still much to do to make the world a safer place!

Alliances and security organizations

It takes more than arms-control measures to achieve international peace and security. States join in alliances and other organizations to achieve mutual advantages in a search for international stability. A balance of power among states may be maintained by an alliance or by a power distribution that exists outside formal alliance structures. We have seen that for more than half a century, global security has been maintained by the nuclear deterrent. As only slightly more than half a dozen countries have nuclear weapons and the ability to deliver them, nuclear states exercise power and balancing influences throughout the world. The rough parity in nuclear weapons between the United States and Russia balances the relations among the great powers in Europe and elsewhere. Some realists would argue controversially that the fact that both India and Pakistan have nuclear bombs actually balances power

in South Asia, too. In such arguments balances of power are expected to decrease, not increase, the likelihood of war, as neither side can begin a war and expect to escape unharmed.

The international system encompasses many organizations, some of which have regional security as one of their objectives. They provide a balance of power in their specific geographic area and sometimes outside it. In Europe the European Union (EU) was formed primarily to promote trade and economic and political integration, but in recent years it has taken on a security and military component. For example, it has been the key organization carrying out peacekeeping in Kosovo. Apart from the EU, the Organization for Security and Cooperation in Europe joins thirty democratic states of Europe and elsewhere to work on peace-building endeavors. Most other geographical areas also have important regional organizations, albeit with much less centralized authority than the EU but sometimes with greater roles in security issues. For example, Africa has the Organization of African Unity (OAU), which carries out peace enforcement and peacekeeping in Africa, and Asia has the Southeast Asia Treaty Organization (SEATO). Australia, New Zealand, and the United States are bound together in an Australia–New Zealand–U.S. Pact (ANZUS). All the states of North and South America, except Cuba, are members of the Organization of American States (OAS). The United States and Japan have a treaty that guarantees the two countries' cooperation on defense issues.

There has been an increase in new multilateral institutions among states outside the European and U.S. system. The 2002 Shanghai Cooperation Agreement (SCO) combines China, Russia, Kazakhstan, Kyrgyzstan, Tajikistan, and Uzbekistan in a Central Asian security organization. It declares its focus to be terrorism, separatism, and extremism. India, Iran, and Pakistan are official observers. Iran has asked to upgrade its status in the SCO so that it can receive assistance from other members if it is ever attacked. Such a policy position would change this cooperation agreement into a mutual defense alliance, but that is some way off, and Iran's wishes are unlikely to be fulfilled. Nonregional international actors are also significant but tend to be political institutions, not security structures. For example, the British Commonwealth, which consists of former members of the British Empire, has fifty-one members throughout the world. The League of Arab States joins Arab nations in support of Arab causes and issues and the Gulf Cooperation Council supports joint causes in the Middle East. The BRICS Summit includes Brazil, China, India, Russia, and South Africa.

North Atlantic Treaty Organization (NATO)

Since the breakdown of the Soviet Union and the collapse of the Warsaw Pact, the only major security organization remaining is the North Atlantic Treaty Organization (NATO). This alliance of Western states was set up in 1949 against the threat of communist aggression. As stated in article 5 of the treaty establishing NATO, "an armed attack against one or more of the parties to the treaty in Europe or North America shall be considered an attack against them all." Until the breakup of the Soviet Union in 1991, the competition between East and West, or, as it was often phrased, between democracy and communism, was best understood in the context of the historical development of the international system discussed earlier. The division of Europe by the Iron Curtain gave rise to two powerful military alliances – NATO and the Warsaw Pact. However, in purely military terms, since the disintegration of the Soviet Union the basic global pattern can be characterized as one of sharply decreased East-West hostility in the developed world and continuing competition and conflict in many developing countries or the LDCs. In view of these changes, NATO has had to reevaluate its role and change its membership and mission. Defying those analysts who thought NATO would dissolve after the Cold War, NATO has simply reinvented itself several times.

At its 1991 meeting in Rome, NATO agreed on a new strategic concept to replace its Cold War strategy. The alliance members concluded that a full-scale, surprise attack from the East had effectively been removed and that the new threats would be more multifaceted and multidirectional. Risks, they calculated, were more likely to emerge from economic, social, and political issues, including ethnic rivalries and territorial disputes, than from communism. This thinking led to a reduction in the overall size of alliance forces, a reduced forward presence in central Europe, and less reliance on nuclear weapons. The Euro-Atlantic Partnership Council (EAPC) also emerged, with a membership of forty-six countries of diverse backgrounds and security traditions, as a forum for cooperation on security issues in Europe.

NATO's membership also shifted eastward and nearly doubled. In April 1999, Hungary, Poland, and the Czech Republic joined the alliance, bringing it to nineteen members, and in November 2002 seven more new members were admitted – Bulgaria, Estonia, Latvia, Lithuania, Romania, Slovakia, and Slovenia. The new body of twenty-six members expanded NATO's responsibility for Eastern European territory and made the organization more cumbersome to administer.[34] In 2009 Albania and Croatia joined, increasing the membership to twenty-eight. NATO also developed the Partnership for Peace with Russia and former members of the Warsaw Pact and the Mediterranean Dialogue to enhance its geographical reach.

NATO is now more than sixty years old. Although it continues to be based on a treaty that commits each member to come to the defense of the others in the event of an attack from without, this is no longer its primary objective. The organization's purpose began to change when it agreed to its first-ever violent use of air and naval forces to back up UN peacekeepers in Bosnia-Herzegovina,

---

[34] Zoltan Barany, "NATO's Post-Cold War Metamorphosis: From Sixteen to Twenty-Six and Counting," *International Studies Review* 8, no. 1 (March 2006), pp. 165–78; Piotr Dutkiewicz and Robert Jackson, eds., *NATO Looks East* (Westport, CT: Greenwood, 1998).

Figure 9.4 This Bosnian guard post shows the human face of war. A young NATO guard at the entrance of an SFOR camp peers from his machine gun nest while the camp mascot enjoys a break.

then its first-ever ground-force operations in the Dayton Implementation Force (IFOR) – later called the Stabilization Force (SFOR) – and eventually its first-ever joint operation within *Partnership for Peace* (Figure 9.4).

In 1999, without UN authorization, NATO carried out seventy-eight days of massive air strikes against Yugoslavia, which had attacked Albanian civilians in Kosovo. This was the largest operation NATO had ever carried out. All member states supported a pullback of Serbian troops from Kosovo, autonomy for the Albanian region of Kosovo, and an armed force to monitor the agreement. The war resulted in the overthrow of Slobodan Milosevic, who later died in The Hague after being accused of war crimes by a war crimes tribunal. Kosovo remains under UN, NATO, and EU guarantees but has not been made a member of the UN. In the meantime, NATO became more multifunctional, undertaking "out of area" assignments, ranging from enforcing peace in Bosnia and Kosovo to patrolling the seas for pirates and weapons smugglers.

In response to the events of 9/11, and for the first and only time, NATO invoked article 5 (the mutual defense principle) in response to the events of 9/11, calling on member states to support the United States in its fight against terrorism. Despite not being involved in the Iraq War, the alliance began training Iraqi security personnel in 2004, and in 2006 it took command of the International Stabilization Force in Afghanistan (ISAF), providing muscle for Hamid Karzai's government and becoming the first NATO mission outside the Euro-Atlantic region. Such out-of-area peacekeeping, peacemaking, and peace enforcement activities are not explicitly mentioned in NATO's legal charter. The exercise in Afghanistan is extraordinary, and to a large extent, its eventual success or failure will mark a turning point for NATO. The continuing work of NATO in Afghanistan is discussed in Chapter 10, but it must be understood here that a U.S. general is both the commander of NATO's operations and head of Operation Enduring Freedom, the exclusive U.S. command in Afghanistan and elsewhere, which does not come under NATO command.

In 2008, NATO leaders announced that Ukraine and Georgia would eventually become members. Russia did not accept that prospect and later that year invaded South Ossetia, a breakaway province of Georgia, and also interrupted gas supplies to the Ukraine. Since NATO was not prepared to defend either of these countries, the altercation left Russia more powerful in the area – and NATO weaker. One sign of NATO strength was shown in 2009, however, when France reentered the integrated military command of NATO, which Charles de Gaulle had deserted forty-three years earlier as a token of France's independence. In 2010 NATO unveiled its "New Strategic Concept," which bound the alliance, where possible or necessary, to prevent crises, stabilize postconflict situations, and support

Close Up 9.4 **NATO in Libya**

In early 2011 internal war broke out in Libya, and many members of the UN called for action to halt government atrocities against those rebelling against the Gaddafi regime. The UN Security Council passed Resolution 1973, which called for all necessary military action, short of invasion, against Libyan forces. The resolution allowed the imposition of a no-fly zone, strikes against Gaddafi forces, and external military action in support of the rebels. The vote in the Security Council was 10–0, as five members of the council abstained. Brazil, China, Germany, India, and Russia argued that intervening in the affairs of a sovereign state presented considerable risks.

NATO took on the responsibility of enforcing UN Resolution 1973. However, splits within NATO soon surfaced over what tactics would be used to help the anti-Gaddafi rebels. The United States declared that it was ready to let France and the United Kingdom take the

lead in the mission, but it was not long before other issues appeared. After two months, the Italians, backed by the Arab League, claimed it was time for a cease-fire so that humanitarian aid could be provided for the civilian casualties in Tripoli. France had to admit that, against NATO decisions, it had been supplying weapons to the forces on the ground. The U.K. government faced challenges at home that it was spending too much money on the mission, and the Obama administration in Washington had difficulty showing that it had acted properly with regard to the War Powers Act, which requires the president to obtain approval from Congress within sixty days of the outset of any war. Debates in U.S. Congress indicated a sharp division in the United States over the mission. The secretary-general of NATO warned, however, that the country "must be ready" to step in when Gaddafi falls.[35]

Other voices began to chime in that the mission was getting out of hand. Russia, a permanent member of the Security Council, said the NATO attack raised "serious doubts about coalition members' statements that the strikes in Libya do not have the goal of physically annihilating Mr. Gaddafi and members of his family."[36] The mission continued, however, until the rebels succeeded in defeating the progovernment forces, killing Gaddafi and ending his regime. The Libyan upheaval is discussed further in Chapter 10.

Was NATO's action in Libya justified? Did NATO overreach the UN mandate?

reconstructions. It put these principles into force in Libya in 2011 (see Close Up 9.4).

From these cases it is clear that NATO is quickly becoming a multifunctional, three-tiered, and perhaps confused organization. The United States

[35] *The Guardian*, June 16, 2011.
[36] *The New York Times*, May 2, 2011.

is forced to do the heavy lifting both inside and outside the alliance. With the exception of the Libyan case, Europeans seem to have lost their taste for war, and especially for paying for it. The United States is carrying most of the burden in Afghanistan, for example. Secretary-General Anders Fogh Rasmussen from Denmark has warned against unequal burden sharing and has said that continued disparity between American and European defense spending might lead to a "two-tiered alliance" in which troops from the two regions would not be able to fight effectively together. He pointed out that the United States pays for 75 percent of all defense expenditures in the alliance.[37] NATO is in need of strategic review. Some Atlantic alliance partners such as Canada, Denmark, Netherlands, and the United Kingdom helped significantly in Afghanistan, but then the Dutch and Canadians pulled their combat troops out of the country in 2011. A third group of NATO members did less than its share, preferring to do police training, economic assistance, and development assistance in Afghanistan. Some in the latter group want NATO to revert to operating strictly in the Euro-Atlantic area and to focus in particular on what some regard as the growing Russian challenge on the European continent.

[37] *The Guardian*, June 16, 2011.

In summary, NATO remains the most coherent, well-integrated, and powerful military-security alliance in the world. It now has twenty-eight members, and France has returned to full participation in NATO's integrated military structure. Despite cynical claims that it will soon disappear, the alliance has already lasted sixty years. It helped unite the West, secure Europe against invasion by the Soviet Union and end the Cold War, and it has taken on new challenges outside of the Euro-Atlantic region. It currently faces several challenges, including ending the war in Afghanistan, managing relations with Russia, and coming to grips with new security issues such as terrorism and cyberattacks. NATO has never been far from the verge of falling apart, but so far it has always managed to solve its difficulties and continue as the preeminent military-security organization in the world.[38]

Should NATO restrict its activities to Europe and remain led by the United States?

[38] Zbigniew Brzezinski, *Second Chance: Three Presidents and the Crisis of Superpower* (New York: Basic Book, 2008). For earlier periods of crises in NATO, see Robert J. Jackson, ed., *Continuity of Discord: Crises and Responses in the Atlantic Community* (New York: Praeger, 1985) and *Europe in Transition: The Management of Security after the Cold War* (New York: Praeger, 1998).

Conclusion: Ethics and war

Critics of a particular war ask, "Is it ethical or just?" This may seem like a contradiction (like "jumbo shrimp"), but some wars do seem justifiable, such as World War II, because of the aggression and genocide against Jews and others in Germany. Can there be an unambiguous set of principles about when war is justified? Could such principles be placed into law – that is, can states or international organizations limit the inhumanity and destructiveness of war by legal agreement? These questions and themes have a long history, dating back to the ancient Greeks, and the Muslim Koran as well as medieval Christian thought (especially in the work of St. Thomas Aquinas). The arguments were summarized brilliantly by Michael Walzer, who said that the theory of just war is based on five premises:[39]

[39] Michael Walzer, *Arguing about War* (New Haven, CT: Yale University Press, 2006).

1. Fought only for a good or just cause
2. Chosen by a legitimate authority
3. Entered into only as a last resort
4. Undertaken only if it is likely to succeed
5. Proportionality should be adhered to – that is, human suffering should be avoided as much as possible and a clear distinction ought to be made between combatants and noncombatants

A just cause might, for example, be based on self-defense or to prevent a massive violation of human rights. A legitimate authority might be a state, combination of states, or a global organization such as the United Nations. The consequences of going to war need to be considered as well, as there is no justice in choosing to go to war if there is no reasonable chance of success or if too many noncombatants will be killed.[40] Just war theorists examine armed conflicts under three headings: the cause – *jus ad bellum*; the conduct – *jus in bello*; and the consequences – *jus post bellum*. These three Cs determine whether a war is to be considered just or unjust.

Let us briefly examine the 2003 Iraq War employing the just war theory. (See Chapter 10 for a comparison of justifications for wars.) The United States and its allies needed to find a cause or justification for going to war and especially for justifying the use of preventive war when no threat was imminent – so they argued that the Iraqi government was cooperating with terrorists and had WMDs. The credibility of these justifications for the war was challenged almost immediately.[41] There were no terrorists in the country and the claim that Iraq possessed WMDs also proved faulty. Before the war, early IAEA inspections revealed that many weapons had been destroyed and the nuclear program ended. When inspectors were allowed to return for another inspection, their reports were ambiguous about whether Iraq possessed WMDs. The United States attacked the actions of the new director of the UN inspection commission, Hans Blix. Blix fought back, insisting that the inspectors needed more time to evaluate Iraqi claims that no weapons existed. In the end, all the information on weapons programs that took the United States into the war proved false, including reports about aluminum tubes, "yellowcake" uranium, and mobile labs.[42]

When the link between the 9/11 terrorists and the Iraqi regime did not hold up to scrutiny, the U.S. administration and its allies changed the justification to one based on the nature of the Iraqi regime itself. Saddam Hussein's regime was undemocratic and had engaged in human rights violations, even killing his own citizens.

---

[40] One serious weakness in this argument is that it seems to favor stronger states. If a weak state resisted invasion by a strong one the war would not be "just," because it would be unlikely to succeed.

[41] Bob Elgar, general secretary of the National Council of Churches, representing fifty million American Christians, used the just-war doctrine to denounce the attack on Iraq when he declared, "Before we justify going to war, we need to see that Iraq poses a clear and present danger, and I just don't see it." Congressional Quarterly, *Global Issues* (Washington DC: CQ Press, 2005), p. 275.

[42] Hans Blix, *Disarming Iraq* (New York: Pantheon Books, 2004), pp. 232–34.

This gave a humanitarian justification for the war. It clearly was an evil regime, but many other governments throughout the world were just as inhumane as Saddam Hussein's, and there was no intent to attack them. Moreover, the major human rights violations had occurred many years earlier. A war based on this argument could be seen only as delayed revenge or punishment of Iraq for its earlier actions.

In short, there was no clear-cut justifiable cause for the war.[43] This was not a war of *necessity*, then, but a war of *choice* that should be considered unjust.

Finally, the just war theory also requires that the conduct of a war be handled appropriately – that the amount of violence employed should be proportionate to the ends to be achieved only to the degree necessary to attain the war's goals. This is the proportionality principle. Noncombatants should be harmed as little as possible. During the initial, conventional operations in Iraq, the United States made great efforts to ensure that this was the case, but the ensuing urban insurgency was extremely violent, with many noncombatants killed (see Chapter 10).

To complete our just-war appraisal we need to know the final result, or consequence, of the war in Iraq, but that remains uncertain. If it becomes a stable democratic regime, will the invasion have been worthwhile? Some will say yes and others no. The just war theory helps with the analysis of a particular war, but it does not provide easy or absolute answers. Indeed, the consequences and full political meaning of most wars are often not known or appreciated until decades later.

The United Nations recently adapted just war principles to determine whether any particular war is justifiable.[44] The new UN guidelines set out the following five criteria for deciding when to use military force:

1. Seriousness of the threat – Is the threat serious enough to justify the prima facie use of force?
2. Proper purpose – Is the primary purpose of the use of force to halt or avert the threat in question?
3. Last resort – Has every nonmilitary option been explored and exhausted?
4. Proportional means – Is the proposed force the minimum necessary to meet the threat?
5. Balance of consequences – Is it clear that the consequences of action will not be worse than the consequences of inaction?

The attack on Iraq did not meet these criteria. Under the first principle, if there had been a link between the 9/11 terrorists and Iraq, then there might have been an argument for war based on the internationally recognized right of self-defense.

---

[43] Well after the attack, the 9/11 Commission concluded there were no WMDs in Iraq. *The 9/11 Commission Report: Final Report of the National Commission on Terrorist Attacks on the US* (New York: W. W. Norton, 2004). See also Anonymous [Michael Scheurer], *Imperial Hubris: Why the West Is Losing the War on Terror* (London: Brassey's, 2004); Richard A. Clarke *Against All Enemies: Inside America's War on Terror* (New York: Free Press, 2004).

[44] See the UN report on providing a secure world at http://www.un.org/secureworld.

However, there was no way to link the invasion of Iraq with the defeat of terrorism, and so the second criterion, proper purpose, was undermined.[45] Third, the war was not a last resort because the UN inspectors had not completed their work, and they were hopeful that increased Iraqi cooperation would facilitate their operations. Fourth, following the new UN principles, the violence expended should have been only to the degree necessary to attain the war's goals. During the initial, conventional operations, the United States made great efforts to ensure that this was indeed the case, but the ensuing urban insurgency and counterinsurgency tactics were extremely destructive, and many commentators would argue that minimum force was not always employed. Fifth, inaction would have left Saddam Hussein in power along with his horrific, authoritarian regime, but this has to be weighed against the thousands of civilian casualties caused by the invasion, an unstable new regime in Iraq, massive expenditures in terms of resources and people, and increased Muslim anger against the West.

In other words, if one follows either the just war principles or the new UN code, a strong case can be made against the commencement, conduct, and conclusion of the Iraq War. The UN did not agree to the 2003 Iraq War. Many believe that the UN principles need to be applied to major powers as well as the weaker ones, but this is unlikely to happen, and that is one of the reasons some people regard just war principles as impractical and inoperative – and perhaps even regard other UN declarations as a failure.[46]

Can one make a clear and compelling case in favor of any war? Should the just war approach be used? Do you have other suggestions about whether or when a war should be called justifiable? Do the laws of armed conflict need to be amended for present circumstances? There is room for debate on all these questions. Unfortunately, war still happens. In Chapter 10 we turn to contemporary civil wars and insurgencies in which the use of war as an instrument of public policy, new instruments of war, and the laws of war are hotly debated.

---

[45] Clarke, *Against All Enemies*, p. 56.

[46] For details of these problems, see the International Committee of the Red Cross summaries at http://www.icrc.org.

Select bibliography

Blainey, Geoffrey, *The Causes of War* (New York: Free Press, 1973).

Bobbitt, Philip, *Terror and Consent: The War for the Twenty-First Century* (London: Allen Lane, 2008).

Cohen, Eliot, *Conquered into Liberty: Two Centuries of Battles along the Great Warpath That Made the American Way of War* (New York: Simon & Schuster, 2011).

Comaroff, John L., and Paul C. Stern, eds., *Perspectives on Nationalism and* War (Amsterdam: Gordon and Breach, 1995).

Cushman, Greg, and Leonard C. Washington, *An Introduction to the Causes of War: Patterns of Interstate Conflict from World War I to Iraq* (Lanham, MD: Rowman & Littlefield, 2007).

Friedman, Lawrence, ed., *War* (Oxford: Oxford University Press, 1994).

Gat, Azar, *War in Human Civilization* (Oxford: Oxford University Press, 2006).

Gill, Bates, Hans Born, and Heiner Hanggi, eds., *Governing the Bomb: Civilian Control of Nuclear Weapons* (Oxford: Oxford University Press, 2010).

Gilpin, Robert, *War and Change in Global Politics* (Cambridge: Cambridge University Press, 1983).

Gray, Colin, *Another Bloody Century: Future Warfare* (London: Weidenfeld & Nicolson, 2005).

Gross, Michael L., *Moral Dilemmas of Modern War: Torture, Assassination, and Blackmail in an Age of Asymmetrical Warfare* (Cambridge: Cambridge University Press, 2009).

Howard, Michael, *The Causes of War*, 2nd ed. (Boston: Harvard University Press, 1983).

Junger, Sebastian, *War* (New York: Twelve, 2010).

McMahan, Jeff, *Killing in War* (Oxford: Oxford University Press, 2009).

Mueller, John, *Atomic Obsession* (New York: Oxford University Press, 2010).

_____, *Retreat from Doomsday: The Obsolescence of Major War* (New York: Basic Books, 1989)

Pinker, Steven, *The Better Angels of Our Nature: The Decline of Violence in History and Its Causes* (London: Allen Lane, 2011).

Reiter, Dan, and Allan C. Stram, *Democracies at War* (Princeton, NJ: Princeton University Press, 2002).

Rodin, David, and Henry Shue, eds., *Just and Unjust Warriors: The Moral and Legal Status of Soldiers* (Oxford: Oxford University Press, 2008).

Rose, Gideon, *How Wars End: Why We Always Fight the Last Battle* (New York: Simon & Schuster, 2010).

Sagan, Scott, and Kenneth Waltz, *The Spread of Nuclear Weapons* (New York: W. W. Norton, 1999).

Slim, Hugo, *Killing Civilians: Method, Madness and Morality in War* (London: Hurst, 2008).

Smith, Rupert, *The Utility of Force: The Art of War in the Modern World* (New York: Vintage, 2008).

Stachan, Hew, and Sibylle Scheipers, eds., *The Changing Character of War* (Oxford: Oxford University Press, 2011).

Walzer, Michael, *Arguing about War* (New Haven, CT: Yale University Press, 2006).

_____, *Just and Unjust Wars: A Moral Argument with Historical Illustrations*, 4th ed. (New Haven, CT: Yale University Press, 2006).

10

Civil wars, insurgencies, and counterinsurgencies

Political leaders and their security advisers are constantly obliged to make choices about how to maintain order in light of their citizens' expectations and actions. In responsible and viable political systems the resulting transactions are relatively clear and harmonious, but when public demands cannot be met, political order may break down. Bombings, riots, rebellions, and even civil wars may ensue, and the political system may fail or collapse. A few countries engage in perpetual strife and violence that trigger insurgencies or wars. Such local warfare cannot always be kept within state boundaries today, as it is to some extent internationalized by the forces of globalization and the new security issues.

Armed conflict and wars within and among states are endemic in world history. In much of the academic literature on warfare there is an assumption of a degree of symmetry among protagonists. This is because most scholarship is about **general war**, the relations and conflict between and among states, or **limited wars**, those that involve states but have restricted objectives, such as the Korean War (1950–53), which was fought to prevent a China-backed Korean army from taking over the entire peninsula. Countries that are relatively weak are thought to be unlikely to go to war with more powerful states; they are more apt to capitulate or negotiate their way out of disagreement and conflict. But wars come in various types, and many are among distinctly uneven military forces.

Chapter 9 dealt with interstate wars. This chapter focuses on wars that occur basically *inside* states – civil wars, insurgencies, and counterinsurgencies that remain within the territory of one country or sometimes spread to neighboring states, thus inviting international involvement.[1] After outlining the context, causes, and conditions of civil wars around the world, we examine failing and failed states in which governments are losing or have lost their monopoly of coercive power. These states are hotbeds of violence and frequently the location of present or future civil wars. Critical Case Studies of Somalia and Sudan illustrate how failing and failed states often coincide with internal war. Insurgencies are closely related to civil wars, and it is difficult to distinguish between the two. To understand what can be learned about victory and defeat in insurgencies, we compare the successful British counterinsurgency measures in Malaya with the failed measures adopted by the United States in Vietnam and elsewhere.

Most important, perhaps, this chapter examines the context and arguments for and against the wars in Afghanistan and Iraq. Both began as limited interstate wars, but after the initial foreign invasion they began to take on the characteristics of civil wars or insurgencies. Postconflict countries such as these

---

[1] There are many contending definitions of types of wars. For a brief survey, see World Bank and Human Security Report Project, *Mini Atlas of Human Security* (Washington, DC: Myriad Editions, 2008)

are dangerous and often revert to internal violence as contesting domestic groups struggle for power. It is happening in Iraq, and Afghanistan also threatens to erupt when international troops withdraw. In 2011–12, several other internal wars overthrew authoritarian regimes in North Africa and the Middle East. We analyze the volatility of rising expectations in the region, the impact of the United Nations and NATO in the contests, and include Critical Case Studies about the events of the Arab Awakening in Libya and Syria. A discussion of responsibility to protect (R2P), counterinsurgency, drones, and targeted killing strategies concludes the chapter.

Modern weapons systems and tactics have produced many new issues about who can and does engage in civil warfare. For example, nonmilitary personnel may be hired to fight, and new technology such as drones and robotics are increasingly being employed. Are these new approaches and technologies changing the nature of warfare? This topic concludes the chapter. In Chapter 11 we examine terrorist situations.

Civil wars and insurgencies

As of 2013, only the war in Afghanistan could be called *international*, and perhaps even it should be considered domestic, as the fighting is localized. All the rest are civil wars or insurgencies, despite that fact that other states and international actors such as the United Nations and NATO are to various degrees involved in them. Civil or internal wars are those that occur between parties inside extant states and are likely to involve two or more groups within a country fighting each other or the government, with unequal armies.[2] They often occur when states and nations are not aligned or when ethnicity, sectarian, and religious claims cannot be accommodated within a particular state (see Chapter 4 on states and Chapter 8 on ethnicity, nationalism, and religion). To complicate the matter, civil wars become entangled with international politics when violence and refugees cross national borders and regions. Today, international organizations such as the UN often get involved in trying to solve civil conflicts, as they did recently in Libya, Mali, Somalia, Syria, Sudan, and Yemen. Individual states or groups of states often use conflicting arguments about sovereignty and human rights when they support one side or the other.

Whenever groups wish to form a separate state from an already existing one, or when regional alienation and desire for increased autonomy are present, political activism often spills over into political violence. Examples can be found throughout history and in many countries, including in stable democracies. In Canada during the 1970s, the now-defunct Front de Libération du Québec used bombings, kidnappings, and murder in its quest for an independent Québec. The Irish Republican Army in Northern Ireland and the Palestinian Liberation Organization are more recent examples of groups that have used violence for political purposes. Coups d'état, or military strikes at governments, are also widespread. One scholar has tabulated 357 successful coups since 1945, 82 of them in Africa.[3] Since that tally at least one more has occurred in Mali in 2012.

[2] To some extent, the term *civil war* has changed its meaning over time. In the 19th century and the first half of the 20th century civil wars were basically thought of as conventional wars, and then in the post–Cold War period they became associated with the idea of irregular warfare. See Stathis N. Kalyvas, *The Logic of Violence in Civil War* (New York: Cambridge University Press, 2006). Perhaps internal war is a safer neutral concept, but it implies that no outside forces are involved at all, and that is usually not the case and was not true even in the U.S. Civil War.

[3] Paul Collier, *War, Guns and Votes* (New York: Harper Collins, 2009), p. 8.

Well-known examples of civil wars include the Russian Revolution of 1917–19 and the twenty-two year struggle between Chinese communists and nationalists, from 1927 to 1949. Sometimes, as in the American Civil War (1861–65), the two sides in the combat have similar or roughly equal capabilities, but most internal wars involve a substantial degree of inequality. The term asymmetrical warfare refers to such conflicts between two or more relatively unequal contestants, whether they are states or other groups. The strategies and tactics in asymmetrical wars differ from those in regular wars. They are contests between government forces and irregular rebels; the government is usually the much more powerful entity, with the rebels trying to bring it down or claim some territory from it. Contemporary examples of very weak forces confronting strong governments are the Karens in Myanmar, the Naxalites in India, and the now-defunct Tamil Tigers in Sri Lanka. Most such forces fail simply as a result of their relative weakness.

Civil wars and revolutions may begin as insurgencies, in which relatively small and weak rebel forces engage in low-level asymmetrical warfare against state authorities and their more powerful militaries.[4] Amateur dissidents know they cannot win open battles with professional soldiers, so they try to weaken the government, make the civilian populations feel insecure, and entice foreigners to leave the country. The insurgents use myriad harassment techniques against government troops. To raise the costs of government security, they may not directly confront government forces in "pitched" battles, but rather they live and hide among the population with supportive groups. The irregular

troops live off the people, attacking the government forces with hit-and-run strategies that make them appear weak and unable to provide security. Mao Zedong, the communist leader who used such tactics to defeat the Nationalist's forces in the 1949 Chinese war, called on his guerilla followers to live among the people "as fish live in the water." The government or occupying power opposes these irregular attacks with counterinsurgency measures such as trapping guerillas in accessible places and putting spies among them.

During the Cold War there was little concern about failing states. Attention to collapsing states began in the 1990s and came from experts on poorer, developing countries in specific areas of the world, especially sub-Saharan Africa and South Asia. The West's lack of attention to the plight of Afghanistan after the Russians left in 1989, for example, was breathtaking but can be explained partly by the West's preoccupation with the transition of post-Soviet Europe to democracy. However, the events of 9/11 and the rise of radical Muslim jihadism focused attention on weak states like never before. Pressing issues concerning international terrorism and human security drove scholars and diplomats to conclude that development and security issues go hand in hand and must be tackled together. Development workers began to accept that security is essential for economic prosperity, and military leaders promoted economic development to increase security – although, to be frank, the two professional groups often did not, and still do not, trust each other in all situations.

Insurgencies and civil wars often take place in states afflicted with internal turmoil so great that their governments cannot function and eventually disintegrate. According to analysts in *The Economist* magazine, military strategists today concern themselves with the "ungoverned, under governed, misgoverned, and contested areas" of the world.[5] The European Union concurs: "Neighbors who are engaged in violent conflict, weak states where

---

[4] In political science the word *revolution* is normally used to refer to massive or fundamental changes in society based on the use of violence. Examples include the French Revolution (1789), the Russian Revolution (1917), and China (1949). Of course, the term is also employed to depict any form of social change, from haircuts to musical tastes, and in politics for major nonviolent change such as the toppling of the Soviet regime in 1991. See Robert J. Jackson and Doreen Jackson, *Comparative and World Politics*, 5th ed. (Toronto: Pearson/Prentice Hall, 2008), chapter 20.

[5] *The Economist*, January 31, 2009.

organized crime flourishes, dysfunctional societies or exploding population growth on its borders all pose problems for Europe."[6] We turn to an analysis of such failing states before examining contemporary insurgencies and civil wars.

Weak and failing states

Failing and failed states are defined in many, often controversial, ways.[7] The World Bank, the U.S. Department of State, Britain's Department of International Development, the CIA, and the Brookings Institution, for example, all use different definitions and to a large extent come to different conclusions about such countries. In this chapter we use the term failing states to mean countries close to disintegration because their governments have lost (or never had) adequate authority over their peoples and territories. These countries lack law and order, and their people face varying levels of violence escalating to anarchy. However, although such instability may breed significant degrees of violence, it does not always lead to an absolute collapse of authority or outbreak of major armed conflict or civil war. Failed states differ in that they have disintegrated to the point that their government has collapsed and the country has fallen into civil war. In practice, this distinction is not always clear, and it varies according to which social and political indicators are used in the analysis.

Using twelve indicators of state cohesion and performance, in 2012 the Fund for Peace ranked 177 states in order of their risk of failure and

breakdown.[8] It found that the most endangered or failed states among them were Somalia (which was number one five years in a row), Democratic Republic of the Congo, Sudan, Chad, Zimbabwe, Afghanistan, Haiti, Yemen, Iraq, and Central African Republic. These ten most failed states are mostly grouped in sub-Saharan Africa, but two are in South Asia, and Haiti alone is in the Americas. Africa contains seven of the most unstable states, sixteen of the top twenty, and more than half of the sixty worst scoring countries (see Table 10.1). A majority of the top twenty failed states have Muslim majorities. The differences among them are significant, however; Somalia's dysfunction is a result of state failure, whereas the conflict in Sudan is tied to state policies and political differences between the north and south.

What characteristics lead weak or failing states to collapse or fall into armed conflict?[9] On this issue, too, there is considerable controversy. As Robert I. Rothberg points out, failed states, as opposed to failing ones, have two defining criteria: they provide very low quantities and qualities of political goods to their citizens and they have lost their monopoly on violence.[10] Many of the top twenty countries on the Fund for Peace's list are weak but have not lost their monopoly of coercive force and are not engaged in armed conflict or civil war. They may be failing, but they have not yet collapsed. However, their potential for collapse is great because internal revolts bring displacement, mass migration, and death; they also force refugees into neighboring countries and cause regional instability. As their institutions of law and order weaken, these states may become havens for corruption and illegal activities. Some, therefore, become centers of criminal activities in such fields as human trafficking and sales of narcotics and weapons. Others

---

[6] Ibid.

[7] There are several indexes to choose from in studying the pattern of failing states. U.S. law requires the secretary of state to provide an annual analysis of terrorist havens. This report called *Country Reports on Terrorism* replaces the earlier *Patterns of Global Terrorism*. It lists major countries with an assessment of their likelihood for breakdown and terrorism. It is found at http://www.state.gov; Brookings also has an Index of State weakness in the developing world, at http://www.brookings.edu. Freedom House organizes world data on levels of freedom around the world, at http://www.freedomhouse.org; and Transparency International keeps abreast of corruption at http://www.transparency.org.

[8] See "The Failed States Index," *Foreign Policy* (July–August 2012), pp. 85–99.

[9] Ashraf Ghani and Clare Lockhart, *Fixing Failed States: A Framework for Rebuilding a Fractured World* (Oxford: Oxford University Press, 2008).

[10] Quoted in "Disorder in the Ranks, *Foreign Policy* (July–August 2009), p. 91.

Table 10.1	**Top twenty failed states 2012**
1.	Somalia
2.	Democratic Republic of the Congo
3.	Sudan
4.	Chad
5.	Zimbabwe
6.	Afghanistan
7.	Haiti
8.	Yemen
9.	Iraq
10.	Central African Republic
11.	Côte d'Ivoire
12.	Guinea
13.	Pakistan
14.	Nigeria
15.	Guinea-Bissau
16.	Kenya
17.	Ethiopia
18.	Burundi
19.	Niger
20.	Uganda

Note: The indicators include demographic pressures, refugees and internally displaced people, group grievances, human flight, uneven development, economic decline, delegitimization of the state, public services, human rights, security apparatus, factionalized elites, and external intervention. The researchers used data from 130,000 sources.
Source: "Failed State Index," Fund for Peace, http://www.fundforpeace.org.

Practical and ethical questions about humanitarian intervention in these weak states are at the top of the United Nations' agenda. Is it important for the UN to prevent leaders in weak states from killing, raping, and plundering their own citizens? Or does foreign intervention in the sovereignty of failing states merely increase long-term violence?[11] We know that many states have reverted to anarchy and division years after foreign interventions, and that failing states are tragedies for their own people but not necessarily others. Using information from West Point's Combating Terrorism Center, *Foreign Policy* magazine concluded that Somalia is so weak in terms of infrastructure, excessive violence, criminality, and basic services that even al-Qaeda finds it too difficult to operate there.[12] Their argument is that al-Qaeda leaders prefer to operate in weak, broken states not completely failed ones.

Armed conflict and civil war

In Chapter 9 we examined the nature and causes of wars between and among states. World War II (1939–45) was the last extensive international war, but as we shall see the wars in Afghanistan and Iraq shared some of its characteristics, especially length of duration. During the Cold War (1945–91) there was a continual increase in the number of civil wars, especially in Africa. By its end there were seventeen of them, as well as thirty-five smaller conflicts.[13] Since then, however, the total number of civil conflicts has been dropping. The end of the clash between democracy and communism terminated some of the ethnic contests and brought the beginnings of peace to countries such as Burundi

harbor terrorists or collapse totally. In short, failing governments are havens for gangsters, pirates, warlords, terrorists, and insurgents. They may or may not collapse into civil war, but they pose major problems for their immediate neighbors and the international community at large.

[11] The question of which factors ensure stability after civil war is complex and contentious. See Monica Duffy Toft, "Ending Civil Wars: A Case for Rebel Victory," *International Security* 34, no. 4 (Spring 2010), pp. 7–36.
[12] "The Failed State Index," *Foreign Policy* (July–August 2009), p. 82.
[13] Collier, *Wars, Guns and Votes*, pp. 4–5. Other research substantiates these figures. James D. Fearon and David Laitin count 127 civil wars between 1945 and 2003, in "Ethnicity, Insurgency and Civil War," *APSR* 97 (February 2003), pp. 75–90.

and Sierra Leone; others simply petered out from exhaustion or negotiation.

Sophisticated data about countries in armed conflict or civil war are found in the annual studies by the Stockholm International Peace Research Institute (SIPRI) and Ploughshares. Their data are similar, but there are marked differences in their conclusions because of contrasting definitions and collection methodology. In 2010 Ploughshares counted twenty-four civil wars in twenty countries (defined as a combat between at least one state military and other groups in which at least one thousand people were killed; Table 10.2).[14] This was the smallest number of major armed conflicts that Ploughshares had identified since 1987. SIPRI also found that the number of wars has diminished over the past decade, and even with a more restrictive definition it supported Ploughshares' conclusion that there were fewer major armed conflicts in 2010 than earlier.[15] The only armed rebellion in the Americas remained in Colombia.

Civil wars come in various guises and with a variety of causes and justifications. They tend to be extremely violent, kill mostly noncombatants, and last a long time – averaging around a decade in recent years. Civil wars last longer than interstate ones because they are often resistant to negotiated settlements, and short of one side achieving a decisive victory, there is often continued violence even after a peace settlement.[16] Recent examples include clashes between ethnic groups or clans over control of weak or failing countries, such as in Ethiopia and Rwanda; fighting between political factions for control of a state, such as in Somalia; hatred-fueled violence and genocide of one group over another, as in the Darfur region of Sudan; ethno-national challenges to established states, such as by the

[14] Ploughshares is a project of the Canadian Council of Churches. Data found at http://www.ploughshares.ca.

[15] http://www.sipri.org/yearbook/2009/02/02A. For yet another approach, see the Human Security Report, at http://www.hsrgroup.org.

[16] See ibid.; James D. Fearon, "Why Do Some Civil Wars Last So Much Longer Than Others," *Journal of Peace Research* 41, no. 3 (2004), pp. 275–301.

Table 10.2 Major armed conflicts, 2010

SIPRI	Ploughshares
Afghanistan	Afghanistan
Algeria	
Chad	
Colombia	Colombia
Dem. Rep. of Congo	
Ethiopia	
India (Kashmir)	India (Kashmir, Naxalite, Nepal)
Iraq	Iraq
Israel (Palestinian territories)	Israel (Palestinians)
Kenya	
Myanmar (Karens)	Myanmar
Nigeria	
Pakistan	Peru
Philippines (Mindanao)	Philippines (Mindanao)
Rwanda Russia (Chechnya)	
Somalia	Somalia
Sudan	Sudan (Darfur)
Thailand	
Turkey (Kurdistan)	Turkey
Uganda	
Yemen	
United States (overseas wars)	

Source: SIPRI information adapted from "Patterns of Major Armed Conflicts," http://www.sipri.org/yearbook/2010. Ploughshares data from "Armed Conflicts Report 2010," http://www.ploughshares.ca.

Kurds in Turkey and Chechens in Russia; secession movements such as the Eritrean rebels in Ethiopia and the defeated Tamil Tigers in Sri Lanka; and economic justifications, such as control of trade in diamonds, oil, and other resources as in Central and West Africa. The contemporary wars in Afghanistan and Iraq pit international forces against insurgents inside states, while in Libya NATO supported the insurgents against the government.

Critical Case Studies 10.1 and 10.2 highlight the interrelationships between domestic and international factors in current civil wars in Sudan and Somalia. International public opinion about internal wars can be fickle. When humanitarian issues of hunger, homelessness, death, and rape are first reported, there is almost always immediate moral revulsion and concern that "something must be done." But when rapid solutions fail to achieve results and the factors behind the conflicts become complex, commentators and concerned citizens become disillusioned and lose interest, often claiming that the problems are insoluble and not the responsibility of the world community. Such has been the experience in Somalia, Sudan, and North Africa, where, to a large extent, international fatigue has taken hold and civil conflict still rages unabated.

Critical Case Study 10.1 **Somalia**

In 2012, the Fund for Peace ranked Somalia as the most failed state in the world for the fifth straight year. Located in Africa between Djibouti, Ethiopia, and Kenya, Somalia holds a strategic naval location along the southern route to the Red Sea and the Suez Canal (Figure 10.1). It is home to about

Figure 10.1 Somalia.

nine million people, most of whom are of Somali ethnicity. A small minority are Arabs.[17] All share the Somali language and Sunni Muslim religion. Despite this degree of homogeneity, the people are divided into traditional rival social units or clans, which are subdivided into subclans and even sub-subclans.[18] Although there are significant numbers of workers in business, trade, and fishing, Somalis are largely pastoral people, and many are nomadic. The major clans are armed, and several of them are ruled by warlords. Political struggles among these groups are essentially contests over power and resources, often accompanied by the occupation of land, banditry, and targeted atrocities.

In 1991 a civil war broke out, leading to the collapse of the repressive government of President Mohamed Siad Barre. President George H. W. Bush sent twenty-five thousand troops to Somalia to lead a peacekeeping mission there, but the mission came unhinged on October 3, 1993, when two American Blackhawk helicopters were shot down in the capital of Mogadishu. Eighteen Americans were killed, and several of their bodies were dragged through the streets of the capital in triumph. Under public pressure, the new president, Bill Clinton, withdrew all U.S. forces from Somalia. This fiasco led to serious complaints about U.S. foreign policy and UN peacekeeping generally. The lack of direction and concerted action by the world community affected the response by the UN and the United States in the next humanitarian crisis in Rwanda when neither was prepared to authorize military force sufficient to stop the massive genocide of Tutsis by Hutus.

For more than a decade Somalia had no permanent government and no national armed forces. Anarchy, turmoil, famine, and fighting were the norm. The northwest portion of the country, Somaliland, declared its independence, but despite the fact that it has remained relatively calm, the UN has not recognized its sovereignty. Meanwhile, Puntland, in the northeast, has begun acting as a semiautonomous region. Persistent violent conflict among the various clans and ideologies in the rest of the country in 2006 led to an Islamist group, known as the Islamic Court Union, gaining control of much of the capital and country. It promised to unite the clans under Islam. Order was restored in many parts of the country, including the capital Mogadishu, and Sharia law was briefly instituted. However, the Islamic Courts held control for only six months, before Ethiopian forces backed by U.S. covert groups invaded and ended their rule.

Many Western leaders believed that the Islamic Court contained extreme Islamic leaders and al-Qaeda operatives bent on bringing violent jihad to East Africa. The Christian Ethiopians were accused of conducting a religious crusade in a Muslim country, and their military left the country after only two years. Lack of a functioning government and continual internal war led the United Nations to sanction international action in Somalia in 2009. This time the work was carried out by about nine thousand African Union (AU) soldiers, who remained in the country guarding parts of the city, port, and airport, as well as the shaky, unelected Transitional Federal Government (TFG) with Sharif Sheikh Ahmed as leader. In mid-2012, with the help of the AU soldiers and a moderate religious movement (Ahla Sunna Waljama), Ahmed's government managed to get control over some territory. Despite improvements in the capital, Mogadishu, the situation remained extremely tenuous. Later in 2012, Hassan Sheik Mohamud, a political activist and academic, was elected president. The AU gained control of the capital and gradually forced the Islamic militants out of the major towns along the coast.

---

[17] There has been no census there since 1975.
[18] See *World Bank Report*, "Conflict in Somalia: Drivers and Dynamics," http://www.world bank.org.

During this decade of turmoil thousands of Somalis have been killed and more than a million displaced. The military force from the African Union (mostly Ugandans and Burundians) receive funds and support from Western governments. War continues with **al-Shabaab**, a radical Muslim militia that combines nationalist sentiments and religious ideology and is supported by al-Qaeda, controlling much of the south and centre of the country. The border between the Shabaab-controlled south and Kenya is porous and worrying for Western leaders, and the waters off Somalia are a major zone of piracy that has disrupted shipping to and from the Suez Canal (see Chapter 11).

After more than a decade of civil war, with at least a third of the country in need of humanitarian aid, and with terrorism and piracy on the rise, a massive famine hit the area in the summer of 2011 caused by "the worst drought in a half-century."[19] Thousands of children died and 16 percent of the population was displaced. Most of the famine-stricken people are in the south, much of which is controlled by al-Shabaab rebels who have sometimes blocked aid to them. The world's largest camp for displaced people – the Dadaab refugee camp in nearby Kenya, built to accommodate ninety thousand people – has swollen to a half million, mostly from Somalia.

Should Somalia be classified as a failed state, or is it simply a country engaged in a civil war? Is it time for the United Nations to act more vigorously by sending in blue-bereted peacekeepers to force an end to warfare and warlordism? Or is the situation, including the massive famine, none of the world's business? Does anyone have both the resources and the stomach for intervention? Would theorists such as liberals and realists differ or coalesce in their answers to such questions?

Critical Case Study 10.2 **Sudan, South Sudan, and Darfur**

Sudan is one of the most failed states in the world.[20] It is located in northeastern Africa and until 1956 was a British colony (Figure 10.2). In early 2011 it was the largest country geographically on the African continent, with nine states on its borders. The huge territory housed forty-one million ethnically diverse groups, including black (51 percent), Arab (39 percent), Beja (6 percent), and many others. Arab Sunni Muslims dominated in the north, at about 70 percent of the population. Various indigenous religions such as animists reside throughout the south, and Christians, constituting between 5 percent and 10 percent of the population, are located mostly in the south and in the northern capital of Khartoum. Sudanese Arabs include Nubians in the north, Bejans in the northeast, and Fur in the west. The non-Muslim blacks including the Dinka, Nuer, and numerous smaller ethnic groups live mostly in the south. Arabic is the primary and official language, English is second, but Bedawiye is spoken by the Beja, and there are many minor languages and dialects.

Sudan has been explosive since its independence from Britain. Its pronounced ethnic and tribal identities divide the country. Historically, the northern Arabs were nomadic and the southern blacks were more often settlers or farmers. After severe climate conditions affected their livelihoods, intense competition began over the best grazing land for cattle, thus exacerbating the tribal and religious divisions.

[19] *The Globe and Mail,* July 22, 2011.
[20] The 2012 Fund for Peace ranked Sudan as the third most failed state in the world.

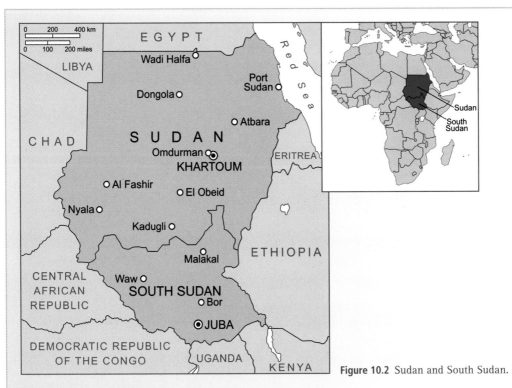

Figure 10.2 Sudan and South Sudan.

Hostilities escalated, with armed soldiers and warlords supporting the major tribes. The country has had two major civil wars since independence, both concerning the political and economic domination of the north over the south. The wars were fought over resources, power, the role of religion, and self-determination. The second war broke out in 1983 and resulted in the deaths of an estimated two million people and the displacement of double that number.

A Comprehensive Peace Plan (CPA) was signed in 2005 between the government of Sudan and the Sudan People's Liberation Movement (SPLM) in the south, which confirmed a temporary split between north and south. The agreement established a six-year transition period leading to two separate states. A new temporary constitution allowed southern autonomy and power sharing, with some rebels holding government positions until a referendum on independence could be held. Northern leaders remained authoritarian in their approach to political issues, and the new government of Southern Sudan in Juba was reportedly corrupt. The latter spent much of its share of oil revenues on soldiers and weapons, preparing, it said, in case the north would not accept the results of a future pro-independence referendum. Violence and intertribal fighting did not cease.

A referendum was held in January 2011 in which some 98 percent of the voters of South Sudan voted for independence. On July 9, 2011, President Salva Kiir declared South Sudan free of northern control. Within a short period the United Nations accepted the Republic of South Sudan as its 193rd member and authorized a peacekeeping mission for the area. The new country is one of the poorest in Africa; a majority of its people live on less than a dollar a day; it has one of the world's highest maternal and infant mortality rates; and illiteracy is extremely high, as more than three-quarters of adults cannot read.

Major issues remain unresolved, particularly over resource sharing. Before the referendum, Sudan as a whole had major petroleum reserves and small amounts of other important minerals. This presents a difficult problem, as most oil reserves are in the south, whereas the refineries and pipelines are primarily in the north. In the interim period revenues from oil were split fifty-fifty between the two governments. Disputes also remain over borders, and especially over Abyei, a border town that has significant oil fields. The two sides are deadlocked over who owns the oil-rich territories between the two countries and how much South Sudan should pay to use the north's oil pipelines. Fighting has resumed along the border on several occasions, and there have been reports of villages being slaughtered by northern forces. In May 2011 the Security Council passed a resolution demanding that the two sides cease hostilities, and as of July 2012 both parties had accepted to participate in negotiations. The UN and African Union have threatened Sudan and South Sudan with sanctions if they cannot reach an agreement. The outlook is dismal as both sides are locked into irrevocable viewpoints on the future of the two countries.

The Sudanese government in Khartoum is controlled by Arab Muslims and led by Omar al-Bashir, a military ruler who has been running the country since 1989. He has abolished political parties, banned associations, and implemented Sharia law in the north. Al-Bashir was elected president in 2010 with some 68 percent of the votes in a campaign that had many irregularities. The recent election results allow him to maintain that the Sudanese people support him.[21]

While north-south issues have dominated the news recently, a separate and very bloody conflict took place earlier in Darfur in the north-west of the country. In 2003 the Sudan Liberation Movement (SLM) and the Justice and Equality Movement (JEM) attacked government offices. The government retaliated by ordering the national army and various militias, including the Janjaweed, to crush the rebels. Much of Darfur was destroyed, and civilians were abducted, raped, and murdered. An estimated two hundred thousand to half a million people died, and more than two million were displaced, many of whom are still in camps scattered around Darfur.

The Sudanese government blocked UN efforts to prevent killing in Darfur, claiming that it had a sovereign right to determine what happened on its territory. While the administration of George W. Bush in the United States accepted the term *genocide* to describe the actions of the Sudanese government in Darfur (in contrast to President Clinton's negative decision on this topic for Rwanda), the UN was very slow to act. The UN Security Council was divided, and none of the major powers was prepared to act decisively, perhaps for selfish interests – China coveted Sudanese oil; Russia wanted to sell arms; and the United States wanted members of the Security Council to support it in other conflicts including Afghanistan, Iraq, and Iran. However, in 2004 a UN Commission of Inquiry concluded that while the Sudanese government had not pursued a policy of genocide, its forces and allied Janjaweed militias had carried out "indiscriminate attacks, including killing of civilians, torture, enforced disappearances, destruction of villages, rape and other forms of sexual violence, pillaging and forced displacement."[22]

A small African Union (AU) contingent entered the country in 2004 a year before the CPA was signed between north and south, and efforts by it and others finally led to a humanitarian cease-fire agreement over Darfur. In 2007 the Security Council approved the United Nations Mission in Darfur (UNAMID), a

---

[21] See "Situations and Cases" at http://www.icc-cpi.int/Menus/ICC/Situations+and+Cases/.
[22] Cited in "UNMIS: United Nations Mission in the Sudan – Background," http://www.un.org/en/peacekeeping/missions/umis/background.html.

larger peacekeeping force of some twenty-six thousand troops. Since they have been present the number of attacks and deaths in Darfur has reduced dramatically, but security remains erratic. The outgoing commander of the joint UN–African Union peacekeeping force, General Martin Luther Agwai, declared the conflict essentially over in late 2009, but approximately three million displaced people remain in dire circumstances – perhaps the world's worst humanitarian crisis.[23] Recently, the International Criminal Court in The Hague indicted Sudan's president, Al-Bashir, for war crimes in Darfur (see Chapters 6 and 14), but he has not gone to The Hague to face the charges, and most Arab African leaders continue to defend him.

What factors contributed to this highly complex and unstable situation? Is there any way the International Criminal Court can apprehend President Al-Bashir? Should the UN use force to capture him? If the north does not accept the independence of the south, and civil war breaks out again, should the UN intervene? Should the countless victims of the violence in Darfur be helped? Would international relations theorists differ in their approaches to these topics?

Insurgencies and counterinsurgencies

Insurgency and counterinsurgency situations involve two or more armed forces in a contest for the "hearts and minds" of people within a state. With the support of the population, insurgents can move without notice inside the territory and carry out hit-and-run-type missions. Sometimes they terrorize the population in an effort to shatter traditional structures of authority, but this can backfire. If the counterinsurgents can get the public on side, individuals may feel safe enough to inform on insurgents' movements, plans, and tactics and prevent them from hiding among the population, moving freely, and getting supplies. The historical success of counterinsurgency measures is exceedingly varied. Government leaders, and especially foreign occupiers who support the status quo, often fail because they cannot separate their enemies from their friends. In the 1950s, France failed to put down rebellions in both Algeria and Vietnam, and Britain failed in Palestine, Cyprus, and Aden. Later, the United States lost in Vietnam, Lebanon, and Somalia, and Russia was humbled in Afghanistan. In these cases and many others, the occupiers decided that the price of staying was not worthwhile and

finally just took their troops and military equipment home.

Governments often do manage to crush rebellions, however. Russia has been able to check dissent in both Chechnya and the Caucuses. Agitation and government repression continue, but insurgencies there have essentially ended. In India, the government has not been able to suppress the Naxalites, a Maoist group (named after the village of Naxalbari in West Bengal, where this Maoist group was formed), or stop them from fomenting trouble on behalf of what they call deprived people. However, there is no possibility that the Naxalites can destroy or take over the government of India. In Sri Lanka, for twenty-six years the Liberation Tigers of Tamil Eelam (LTTE) attempted to establish a homeland (Eelam) in the north and east of the island.[24] They engaged in terrorist tactics from suicide bombings to assassinations, extortion, and press-ganging children until 2009, when the Sri Lanka government finally defeated the group despite their massive overseas support. After ceding defeat, the Tamil representatives demanded a federation in which they would be allowed to control everything except foreign policy, trade, and the military, but the government declared

---

[23] For more details, see Mahmood Mamdani, *Savior and Survivors: Darfur, Politics, and the War on Terror* (New York: Pantheon, 2009).

[24] For decades the Tamil minority suffered discrimination and violence from the Sinhalese government. Although the Sinhalese constitute about 70 percent of the island's population, they felt threatened by the three million Tamils because there are some fifty million Tamils in continental India.

this a nonstarter, asserting that the country would be run as a unitary government out of Colombo. In Vietnam, however, the northern rebels were victorious despite government support from the United States, a superpower. So, the question remains – why do some insurgencies succeed while others fail?

Ending insurgencies: Classic historical examples

Britain has been one of the most successful democracies at ending insurgencies. Between the two World Wars, Sir Charles Gwynn emphasized that the key to victory in such cases is winning over the potential supporters of the insurgents. His book *Imperial Policing* was the basic military text on the subject in the United Kingdom for many years. Its principal argument was that in guerrilla warfare

excessive severity may antagonise this element, add to the number of rebels, and leave a lasting feeling of resentment and bitterness. On the other hand, the power and resolution of the Government forces must be displayed. ... Mistakes of judgement may have far-reaching results. Military failure can be retrieved, but where a population is antagonised or the authority of the Government seriously upset, a long period may elapse before confidence is restored.[25]

Gwynn's successor as guru of antiguerrilla operations in the United Kingdom was Sir Robert Thompson, who was involved in British operations in Malaya in the 1950s. His 1974 book *Defeating Communist Insurgency* was studied closely by generations of British army officers. Unfortunately, its prescriptions were not remembered or adopted; indeed, almost every one of the errors that he identified was repeated later by the United States in Vietnam and then again in the early stages of both wars in Iraq and Afghanistan.

Thompson set out four principles. First, the government should have a clear political aim. Without that, short-term and ad hoc measures would be adopted that would undermine long-term objectives.[26] Second, the government should operate with-

in the law despite temptations to behave otherwise: "the excuses being that the processes of law are too cumbersome, that the normal safeguards in the law for the individual are not designed for an insurgency and that a terrorist deserves to be treated as an outlaw anyway."[27] Third, the government should have a plan coordinating all aspects of its effort against the insurgents, "otherwise a situation will arise in which military operations produce no lasting results because they are unsupported by civil follow-up action." Fourth, the defeat of political subversion is more important than attacking the insurgents themselves.

Thompson's four principles underline the central dilemma. If a government uses "excessive" force against rebels, this may encourage those who are neutral to join the insurgency. However, "the power and resolution of the government must be displayed. Anything that can be interpreted as weakness encourages those who are sitting on the fence to keep on good terms with the rebels."[28] This means that once a government has become involved in a conflict, it should pursue it to victory if at all possible.

Applied to contemporary issues, Thompson's ideas suggest that winning the sympathy of the Muslim world is more important than capturing radical jihadist terrorists, because more terrorists can always be recruited. As we shall see in Chapter 11, however, the West's difficulties have been compounded by the fact that even minor defeats or signs of weakness encourage terrorists, who repeatedly cite American failures in Vietnam, Lebanon, and Somalia to rally supporters and show that the United States can be cowed and defeated. In Vietnam, in the 1960s, a small and relatively undeveloped Asian country forced Washington to abandon its South Vietnamese allies, withdraw its forces, and sign a humiliating peace treaty. In Lebanon in the 1980s, the destruction of the U.S. marine barracks persuaded Washington to withdraw its peacekeeping force; and in Somalia in the 1990s the death of a handful of U.S. soldiers had a similar effect. Bruce Hoffman has outlined the lessons the

[25] Major General Sir Charles Gwynn, *Imperial Policing* (London: Macmillan, 1934), p. 7.
[26] Robert Thompson, *Defeating Communist Insurgency: Experiences from Malaya and Vietnam* (London: Chatto and Windus, 1974), p. 51.

[27] Thompson, *Defeating Communist Insurgency*, p. 52.
[28] Gwynn, *Imperial Policing*, p. 5.

United States should have learned about counterinsurgency from these defeats:

First, always remember that the struggle is not primarily military, but political, social, economic and ideological. Second, learn to recognize the signs of a budding insurgency, and never let it develop momentum. Third, study and understand the enemy in advance. And fourth, put a strong emphasis on gathering up-to-the-minute local intelligence.[29]

Afghanistan and Iraq wars

This section focuses on the causes, conduct, and consequences of recent wars in Afghanistan and Iraq. We examine the two situations from a distance and up close, paralleling them and comparing them to earlier counterinsurgency efforts. This gives both historical perspective and immediacy to questions about the efficacy and justice of these wars. Bearing in mind the apology of former U.S. defense secretary Robert McNamara for the errors in conducting the war in Vietnam, and particularly the American failure to win the "hearts and minds of people,"[30] we ask how the wars were fought and how they will end. Will the countries achieve democracy and stability, or will they join the ranks of other failed states with the potential to do great harm in the long run to American and Western interests? We conclude with a comparative examination of the lessons to be learned from the wars in Afghanistan, Iraq, and Vietnam before turning to contemporary events in the Middle East and North Africa.

Justification for the wars in Afghanistan and Iraq

On September 11, 2001, nineteen men armed only with box cutters hijacked four U.S. airplanes. They flew three Boeing 757 and 767 aircraft into several large buildings in New York and the Pentagon in Washington, DC, killing at least 2,996 people. The fourth plane was brought down by passengers before it could reach its target. Since the perpetrators were from the terrorist group al-Qaeda, an organization and not a state, the U.S. government set out to wreak vengeance on any countries that had trained or harbored them. In the first instance this meant Afghanistan, the staging point for the attack on 9/11, but it left open the possibility of an attack on any country that the U.S. administration considered might be aiding anti-American terrorists. For some officials in President George W. Bush's administration, this meant that the United States should also consider attacking Iraq or other countries in the so-called "axis of evil," namely Iran and North Korea. Government policy and action began with the premise that 9/11 had "changed everything" and ushered in a "new age of terrorism."

A month after the attack, the United States, with the concurrence of the United Nations Security Council, launched Operation Enduring Freedom (OEF), an attack on the territory and government of Afghanistan (Figure 10.3). Then, one and a half years later, on March 19, 2003, without UN agreement, the United States invaded Iraq in Operation Iraqi Freedom (OIF). Operation Enduring Freedom (OEF) is the official name of the U.S. war in Afghanistan and all other military actions emanating from the global war on terrorism. The operation was never merged with the International Security Assistance Force (ISAF), which is the combined members of NATO and allies in Afghanistan. Both wars lasted longer than World War II, though not as long as the Vietnam War. The costs of the two wars have been estimated as of 2012 at about $3 trillion, with more than six thousand Americans dead and forty-six thousand wounded.

The Iraq War is now over, while the one in Afghanistan continues, but in both cases the same question arises – why did the insurgents prove so difficult to defeat? Some of the answers are found in the context of the wars, and others in the foreign policies of Western countries in the Middle East

---

[29] Bruce Hoffman, "The War on Terrorism," *Atlantic Monthly* (July–August 2004), p. 42.

[30] In Robert McNamara, *Retrospect: The Tragedy and Lessons of Vietnam* (New York: Times Books, 1995).

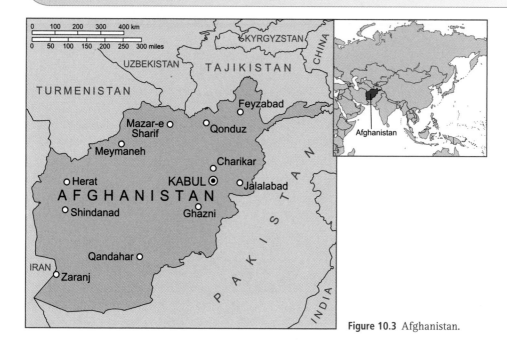

Figure 10.3 Afghanistan.

and South Asia. We look next at the context of both wars.

Context of the war in Afghanistan

Afghanistan occupies the heartland of Eurasia. Its high mountains and desertlike plains are surrounded by Pakistan on the East, Iran on the west, and China and former Soviet republics in the north. Over the centuries the territory of Afghanistan has been the battleground of armies invading from different directions. For a time in the 19th century, the country was a buffer state between the British and tsarist Russian empires.[31] It was the centerpiece of what was termed The Great Game, meaning the competition between Britain and Russia over power and influence in Central Asia, and especially over the routes to India, long considered the jewel in the British crown. When British power in South Asia

---

[31] James Lunt, *Bokhara Burns* (New York: Barnes and Noble, 1969); Dorothy Woodman, *Himalayan Frontiers* (London: Cresset Press, 1969); Charles Miller, *Khyber: The Story of the North West Frontier* (London: Macdonald and Jane's, 1977).

ended in 1947, Soviet influence in Afghanistan gradually increased until 1978, when radical army officers took over the government, forming a coalition with the Marxist People's Democratic Party. In 1979 the Soviet Union intervened massively in the country, with an estimated eighty thousand troops, allegedly to help the radical Afghanistan government. This episode and the subsequent defeat of the Soviet Union proved defining moments of the Cold War.

Afghanistan is riven with divisions based on ethnicity and clan allegiances. The efforts of the pro-Soviet government to centralize and modernize the country gave rise to an Islamic insurgency with tribal and sectarian violence. The precise numbers of each ethnic group are disputed, but figures provided by the Asia Foundation for the largest groups are as follows. Pashtuns constitute approximately 41 percent of the population. They live in the south and east separated from their ethnic brothers in Pakistan by the Durand Line, the unverified border between the two countries. The Tajiks, with 37 percent of the population, and the Uzbeks, with 9 percent, are settled in the north, while the Hazara,

Figure 10.4 Small arms have always been an important part of the culture in Afghanistan and Pakistan. During the Soviet occupation of Afghanistan and afterward, small arms and particularly Kalashnikov rifles (the AK 47) poured into both countries. They were readily available for purchase here in Peshawar and elsewhere.

at 9 percent, live in the west. These four large ethnic groups are divided into many tribes or clans and large extended families. In total they speak some thirty-two different languages and dialects, and although Pashto is the language of the largest group of Pashtuns, the second official language, Dari, is actually spoken by more Afghans. Various forms of the Turkic language also exist, and Farsi, an Iranian language, is important in parts of the country.

The ethnic groups are territorially divided and spread into neighboring countries. While there are some ten million Pashtuns in Afghanistan, there are even more in Pakistan, with some estimates of more than eighteen million. There are several rungs in the traditional Afghan tribal system. For example, the two largest Pashtun tribes are the Durrani and Ghilzai. These confederations are subdivided into primary identity groups or tribes, such as the Populzai (home of Hamid Karzai), Alikozai, Barakzai, Hotak, Zadran, Kharoti, Mohammadzai, Nurzai, Shinwari, and Tokhi, among others. These are further divided into subtribes that consist of hundreds or thousands of people and extended families. An unwritten code of social conduct, called the Pashtunwali, governs the relations among them.

By the mid-1980s several of these Afghan factions – most to varying degrees Islamic fundamentalist – united in overt opposition to the Soviet occupation. The most powerful were the Afghan partisans, or mujahideen, who resisted Soviet occupation with the help of generous American technical and financial support. The Pashtuns formed the majority of early opponents, while the three other major ethnic groups were more prevalent later. Muslim radicals also were recruited from other countries to fight the Russians. Journalist Ahmad Rashid has claimed that before the Soviets left Afghanistan, more than one hundred thousand foreign Muslims had joined the cause.[32] Resistance bases against the Soviets formed in and around Peshawar, Pakistan (Figure 10.4).

With congressional approval the United States administration supplied advisers and

---

[32] Ahmed Rashid, "The Taliban: Exporting Extremism," *Foreign Affairs* 78, no. 6 (December 1999), pp. 22–36.

American-made Stinger antiaircraft missiles to shoot down Soviet planes.[33] Enormous sums of American and Saudi money were funneled through Pakistan: the CIA aided various Afghan factions and helped recruit the person who would later become America's number-one enemy – Osama bin Laden. When bin Laden arrived, the wealthy and well-connected Saudi aided the Islamist Taliban with weapons and money. He helped to set up al-Qaeda (which means "military base") to welcome Afghans and other Arabs. After the victory over the Soviets, bin Laden was allowed to set up terrorist training camps inside Afghanistan so that, in effect, a terrorist obtained control of much of a state.

In April 1988, the United Nations brokered a cease-fire agreement that required Russia to withdraw from Afghanistan, and the last forces left in April 1989. The Soviet Union and United States were coguarantors of the accord, and both agreed not to interfere in the internal affairs of the country. However, stability did not ensue. A civil war broke out among rival Tajik, Hazara, Pashtun, and Uzbek warlords, leaving most of the capital, Kabul, in rubble. The various factions of the mujahideen divided regionally (north and south), linguistically (Dari, Pashto, and Farsi), and doctrinally (Shia and Sunni). Rather than come together to forge a new unified regime, the clans, subclans, and mujahideen fought one another in a vicious civil war. Of a population of 20 million people, as many as 1 million died, 1.5 million were injured, and approximately 5 million became refugees.

Amid regional disputes and continual violence, a new Afghan government run by the Taliban was set up. Pakistan supported the Taliban economically, militarily, and diplomatically. With Russia out of the war, American interest in Afghanistan evaporated. Even when the Islamists took over the country, the West at first showed little concern about the rise of radical jihadist groups in the area. The Taliban core was an Afghan Islamic and Pashtun

tribal movement that had originated in Pakistan during the Soviet occupation. (The word *Talib* means student and referred to the student movement cultivated in the madrassas, Islamic schools, and nourished by the Cold War; Figure 10.5). By the time of the 9/11 attacks the Taliban controlled about 90 percent of Afghanistan. They had rejuvenated Islamic religion and ideology in all aspects of society – politics, law, economy, and foreign policy – and had implemented a radical interpretation of Sharia law. Among other things, the Taliban opposed television, films, and singing. They enforced strict dress codes, banned women from public life and girls from schools, and outlawed games with balls and most music.[34] It was in this 1998 setting that Osama bin Laden declared "jihad" or holy war "against Jews and Crusaders."

The 9/11 terrorist attacks revived dormant U.S. strategic interest in Afghanistan. Al-Qaeda was identified as responsible for the atrocities almost immediately, and its host, the Taliban regime, was marked as the first target for reprisals. A month after 9/11 the war in Afghanistan began. Since the Taliban were organized in small, dispersed groups of two hundred fighters, the United States welcomed the local support of the mujahideen and other anti-Taliban figures, especially the Northern Alliance forces. The Taliban regime was quickly vanquished, and the al-Qaeda network dispersed throughout Afghanistan and Pakistan and around the world.[35]

Hamid Karzai, a Pashtun royalist from the south, was chosen to head an interim government, and in December 2001, the United Nations invited a variety of Afghan factions to Bonn to develop a power-sharing arrangement and plan the future of the country. The Bonn Agreement, or Afghanistan

---

[33] Philip Towle, *Pilots and Rebels: The Use of Aircraft in Unconventional Warfare* (London: Brassey's, 1989), pp. 190ff.

[34] For details, see Ahmed Rashid, *Militant Islam, Oil and Fundamentalism in Central Asia* (New Haven, CT: Yale University Press, 2001). Also see John K. Cooley, *Unholy Wars: Afghanistan, America and International Terrorism* (London: Pluto Press, 2002).

[35] For an overview of the country after the defeat of the Taliban, see Pankaj Mishra, "The Real Afghanistan," *New York Review of Books* (March 10, 2005), pp. 44–48.

Figure 10.5 *Madrassa* is an Arabic word for any type of educational institution. In English, the word generally refers to the colleges of Islamic learning that arose in the 11th century. They are seminaries that teach mostly Islamic subjects. Some madrassas fomented anti-Russian, and later anti-American, ideas and activities. *Source:* Press Association.

Compact, established the legitimacy of the interim government and paved the way for Hamid Karzai to take office as president. Karzai was officially elected in October 2005, and elections for the 249-seat Wolesi Jirga (lower house of parliament) and thirty-four provincial councils took place in relative peace. In August 2009, after a very heated electoral contest troubled by allegations of electoral fraud and corruption, the people reelected Karzai as president for a second term.

Context of the war in Iraq

During World War I (1914–18) the Ottoman Empire fought alongside Austria and Germany against Britain, Russia, and France. After their victory the British and French divided the former Turkish colonies in the Middle East between themselves. Britain received a League of Nations mandate to control Mesopotamia, today's Iraq (Figure 10.6). Over the following two decades Iraq was granted independence, a constitutional monarchy was set up, and the country benefited economically from its

oil.[36] Already, however, the Iraqi army was giving evidence of its brutality, conducting a mass murder of Assyrian Christians who had worked for the British.[37] The 1937 Treaty of Saadabad temporarily reconciled the Sunnis of Iraq with the Shiites of Iran, and Britain tried constantly to reconcile the various interests in the region to obtain secure access to Middle East oil.

The Iraqi monarchy did not last long. In 1958 Emir Faisal II and his advisers were murdered by a mob in Baghdad.[38] Internal instability and factional fighting followed, leading to a military coup in 1968 that in turn allowed the Baathist Party and Saddam Hussein to take control of government. Saddam Hussein became president in 1979 after destroying all opposition to his rule. The next three

[36] Peter Slugett, *Britain in Iraq 1914–1932* (London: Ithaca Press, 1976).
[37] Paul P. J. Hemphil, "The Formation of the Iraqi Army," in *The Integration of Modern Iraq*, by Abbas Kelidar (London: Croom Helm, 1979), pp. 88–110.
[38] Elie Kedourie, "Arab Political Memoirs," *Encounter* (November 1972); Archie Roosevelt, *For Lust of Knowing: Memoirs of an Intelligence Officer* (London: Weidenfeld & Nicolson, 1988), p. 138.

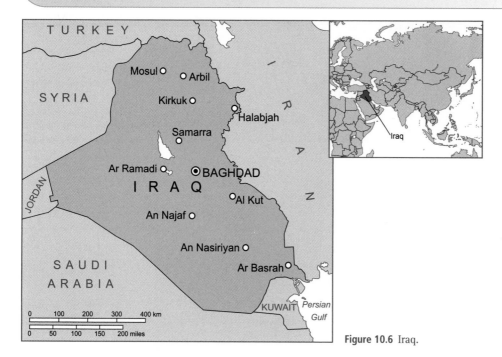

Figure 10.6 Iraq.

decades of Iraq's history were bloody both inside and outside the country. In 1980 Iraq attacked neighboring Iran to gain control of its oil fields and the Shatt al-Arab waterway. Iran was just recovering from the overthrow of the Shah by Ayatollah Khomeini and other religious leaders and Hussein obviously believed that the instability would allow him a quick and easy victory. But it was not to be: Shiite patriotism and fervor prevailed as the Iranians pulled together. The war dragged on for eight years with no clear winner and more than a million dead. It was followed by an unsteady peace.

A decade later, in August 1990, Iraq invaded Kuwait in an attempt to gain control of its oil fields and obtain funds to pay off the debt that it had built up during the war with Iran (Figure 10.7). With UN Security Council approval, many Arab states on side, and almost no opposition, the United States mobilized an impressively large coalition to free Kuwait. In four days the allies smashed the Iraqi army with little difficulty, but they did not occupy Iraq or even advance into its heartland.[39]

Hussein lost Kuwait but his authoritarian regime was intact.

International efforts to control Iraq's weapons development began shortly after the Gulf War. Hussein promised the United Nations that he would disclose and destroy all weapons of mass destruction. However, Richard Butler, the head of the UN inspection teams, reported at the end of 1998 that, in the "absence of full co-operation by Iraq, the mission is not able to conduct the disarmament mandated by the Security Council."[40] Finally, in 2002 the UN Security Council unanimously passed Resolution 1441 criticizing Iraq's noncompliance with the treaty that had ended the fighting more than a decade earlier and demanded that the inspectors be allowed to return to Iraq. In the meantime, the 9/11 attacks on the United States had occurred.

In early 2003 the United States, Britain, and Spain proposed a Security Council resolution authorizing military force against Iraq for noncompliance with resolutions about WMDs but then withdrew it when France threatened to veto

[39] Colin L. Powell, *My American Journey* (New York: Ballantine Books, 1995), p. 508.

[40] Richard Butler, *Saddam Defiant* (London: Weidenfeld & Nicolson, 2000), p. 222.

Figure 10.7 A small museum in Kuwait, set up to memorialize the Iraqi invasion and the seven-month occupation of 1990, includes the dramatic exhibition of an unexploded Iraqi bomb embedded in a book on a student desk.

it – Germany, Russia, and China also strongly opposed the idea.[41] The American administration maintained that the situation in Iraq could not be tolerated, and it began to link Iraq to the events of 9/11. Despite the fact that the Security Council could not be persuaded to support the American position, Britain, Australia, and a handful of other countries joined the United States in going to war with Iraq on March 20, 2003, in a so-called coalition of the willing.[42]

War in Afghanistan

The 2001 invasion of Afghanistan, unlike the later attack on Iraq, was sanctioned by the Security Council of the United Nations. The forces of Prime Minister Mullah Omar were swiftly defeated. NATO assumed control of the **International Security Forces (ISAF)** in Afghanistan and shared a large part of the fighting with the U.S. troops under the **Enduring Freedom** mandate. In 2003 thousands of American troops were pulled out to prepare for an imminent war in Iraq. In 2006, the **Afghanistan Compact** established the international legitimacy of the Hamid Karzai government and committed the international community and the Islamic Republic of Afghanistan to collective goals regarding security, governance, and economic and social development. It would have been possible for NATO, the United States, and its allies to have left the job to warlords and simply gotten out of the country at that time, but instead they decided to set up an Afghan political system that was viable enough to endure without international support. Despite their initial military successes in the country, an agreement on a constitution, two Karzai governments, and functioning parliaments, there have been many failures, reflecting a lack of purpose and realism in the overall approach to Afghanistan.

[41] Hans Blix, *Disarming Iraq* (London: Bloomsbury, 2005), p. 248.
[42] A strong case for the war is found in Kenneth M. Pollack, *The Threatening Storm: The Case for Invading Iraq* (New York, Random House, 2002). A further defense of what the United States chose to do after the war is found in Noah Feldman, *What We Owe Iraq: War and the Ethics of Nation Building* (Princeton, NJ: Princeton University Press, 2004).

The most direct consequences of the 9/11 attack were two long wars, multiple insurgencies, and the destabilization of weak and fragile states. The United States government originally listed its four major goals in Afghanistan as capturing Osama bin Laden, capturing Mullah Omar, closing down al-Qaeda in Afghanistan and elsewhere, and releasing U.S. prisoners in Afghanistan. A decade later, only two of these objectives had been accomplished. Bin Laden was dead and the U.S. prisoners released, but Omar remained at large, Islamists continued the war on "Jews and Crusaders," and international terrorism had spread to several countries (discussed in Chapter 11). *The Economist* magazine later described the Afghan war as "the hapless accumulation of failures."[43] To a large extent, bin Laden has had some success in putting radical Islam and the West on a collision path.

The threat of insurgency is ongoing, and much of Afghanistan remains insecure. Al-Qaeda operatives and copycats have dispersed to Yemen and elsewhere. Warlords control much of the country, while insurgents linked to the former Taliban have regrouped and gained strength, especially along and across the Pakistan border, their presence destabilizing an already weak and fragile Pakistan.[44] Casualties among the U.S. military and its allies as well as the local Afghan population have been substantial.[45] Suicide bombings and improvised explosive devices are common, and on occasion, the rebels have reached into the capital Kabul, destroying government buildings and killing government officials without significant resistance. U.S. army officers complain that the enemy is "like a hydra – you cut off one snake's head and it grows back again."[46]

As of 2013, the West has largely failed to prevent the Taliban resurgence and block its threat to provide a future haven for terrorists. American and NATO military have killed thousands of insurgents but also many hundreds of civilian bystanders. The Taliban still include two broad groupings – the "Afghan Taliban," which hosted bin Laden and al-Qaeda and now wants to oust President Karzai and foreign troops so an Islamist state can be reestablished, and the "Pakistani Taliban" (called Tehrik-i-Taliban), whose goal is to overthrow the Pakistani government. Both groups include hard-core members with links to al-Qaeda, including "rent a Taliban," or Afghan mercenaries hired from funds from opium production who fight for wages higher than those paid by the government, and Afghan religious jihadists willing to die for their beliefs and their country, which they perceive to be dominated by foreign occupiers. Two million Afghan refugees inside Pakistan constitute a large pool from which recruits can be drawn.

The contemporary economic and social state of Afghanistan is appalling: illiteracy, poverty, land mines, and illness are everywhere. Eighty percent of the population is illiterate, and the average schoolteacher has the equivalent of only a sixth-grade education. The country has severe terrain and a dilapidated infrastructure. Roads, schools, power supplies, and sewage systems are in drastic need of repair. Only 36 percent of the country's residents have electricity. Poppy cultivation has increased so much that Afghan militants control around 90 percent of the world's heroin supply. The opium trade is likely to grow after foreign troops depart in 2014. The upper-level Afghan bureaucracy has been decimated by decades of Soviet and Taliban control. There is a lack of administrative capacity because of a narrow human resource base of skill and expertise. Only about a quarter to a third of government ministries are effective. The country lacks the funds to run an effective civil service and cannot pay for its own military or police. Despite the country's desperate needs, the Afghan government and supporters are conducting a war or counterinsurgency and are not able to focus entirely on reconstruction and

[43] *The Economist*, September 13, 2003.
[44] Admed Rashid, "The Mess in Afghanistan," *New York Review of Books* (February 12, 2004), pp. 24–27.
[45] The number of U.S. casualties in the Afghan and Iraqi wars can be found at http://www.icasualties.org.
[46] Catherine Philip, "They Expected an Easy Rise," *The Times*, July 30, 2005.

Figure 10.8 Rural Afghans are rebuilding their lives, making a living from dried fruits and nuts. This peaceful area near the Hindu Kush Mountains is still littered with armaments and tanks left behind after the Soviet exodus in February 1989.

aid. The people are developing a survival culture – protecting themselves by hedging their bets with all three sides, Karzai, NATO, and the Taliban (Figure 10.8).

In December 2011, representatives of eighty-five countries met in Bonn, Germany, and declared their intention to help Afghanistan after Western troops leave in 2014.[47] The representatives committed to a framework agreement for future aid. President Karzai said his country will need at least US$10 billion annually to pay for security forces and basic services, and this would have to last a decade. After that, further political support and financial aid would be needed until 2030. The United States, Saudi Arabia, and Qatar are expected to pick up more than half the tab. The World Bank estimates that 97 percent of Afghanistan's $29 billion gross domestic product comes from military and development aid and in-country spending of foreign troops.

[47] *The New York Times*, December 6, 2011.

To convince foreign donors to continue providing such vast sums of money, three controversial issues need to be addressed. First, there are the complaints that the Afghan government is corrupt and incapable of handling large sums of money from international donors. Second, there should be some reconciliation with the Taliban – so that some of its more moderate members join the government. President Karzai said he will negotiate with Mullah Omar, the leader of the Taliban, but only if he and the Taliban renounce the use of violence and terrorism. The Taliban, however, say they will negotiate only when all foreign troops have left the country. (They eventually did agree to negotiations, setting up an office in Qatar, but broke them off after an incident in which a U.S. soldier murdered several Afghan civilians). Third, Pakistan has to be part of any long-term solution. There are ungoverned territories along both sides of the Durand Line as well as terrorist bases inside Pakistan. When Western troops depart, this will further destabilize nuclear-equipped Pakistan and allow radical jihadists to claim victory in the propaganda war.

Military strategies: From counterinsurgency (coin) to counterterrorism (ct) and targeted killing

Military strategy in Afghanistan has changed dramatically since the beginning of the war. Lessons have been learned, basically through trial and error. The intervention forces and their civilian partners lacked an understanding of the social structure of Afghanistan – including appropriate language skills and knowledge of the culture, tribes, and local warlords. However, the primary error was mixing up the logic and requirements of counterinsurgency and/or counterterrorist measures with those of peacekeeping missions. They were slow to comprehend that Afghanistan was a war zone with an insurgency and not ready for peacekeeping or reconstruction.

Because of these strategic mistakes, several errors were made early in the war. Western leaders

- acted incrementally by responding to specific Taliban challenges
- misunderstood the endurance of the Taliban
- lacked knowledge of enemy sanctuaries in neighboring Pakistan
- underestimated how difficult it would be and how long it would take to build up the central government, the Afghanistan National Army (ANA), and police
- underestimated the financial expenses and costs in terms of the lives of NATO soldiers
- killed thousands of insurgents but also relied so heavily on air power, killing many civilian bystanders
- did not have enough troops in the early stages. The thirty-seven thousand soldiers in Afghanistan as part of ISAF, and the eleven thousand American-led Operation Enduring Freedom troops, were inadequate for the task. In successful counterinsurgency strategies such as Malaysia and Timor-Leste, the number of foreign troops was much higher vis-à-vis the local population and insurgents.
- accepted a divided military approach. Some NATO countries – the United States, Canada, Britain, Australia, Denmark, the Netherlands, and even Romania – were effective, but Germans, French, Italians, and Turks were not allowed to go in "harm's way" because of "caveats" placed on their military participation by their governments.

The military strategy in Afghanistan was devised by General David H. Petraeus (later head of the CIA) and other U.S. military leaders in 2006 after studying seventy-three earlier insurgencies. Their report concluded that in counterinsurgency the people, not the enemy insurgents, are the prize! Petraeus's ideas were applied first in Iraq when he commanded U.S. troops there,[48] and then in Afghanistan. The counterinsurgency policy was based on the principle that the United States should abandon the doctrine of using overwhelming force to smash enemies in short, winnable wars and concentrate instead on how to win victories in longer, irregular warfare. The new doctrine, bolstered by a surge in troops, was credited with turning the war around in Iraq. These ideas were also guided by the counterinsurgency strategy that had earlier proved successful for the United Kingdom in Malaysia. The main underlying idea is not to spend too much energy trying to kill terrorists but rather to engage in a Comprehensive Counterinsurgency Strategy (COIN). The principles of counterinsurgency are relatively simple – capture an area; create a zone of security within which good governance, rule of law, and economic activity can flourish; and then spread out from this area to the next one, like an "ink spot."[49] It is an expensive, troop-heavy, and time-intensive policy. For success there needs to be approximately one trained counterinsurgent for every fifty members of the population.

General Stanley McChrystal, who replaced Petraeus as commander of NATO and U.S. forces

---

[48] Summarized in Steven Simon, "Can the Right War Be Won?" *Foreign Affairs* 88, no. 4 (July–August 2009), pp. 130–7.

[49] Hew Strachan, "Campaign Plans, War Plans and British Defense Policy," *RUSI* 153, no. 66 (December 2008), pp. 28–31.

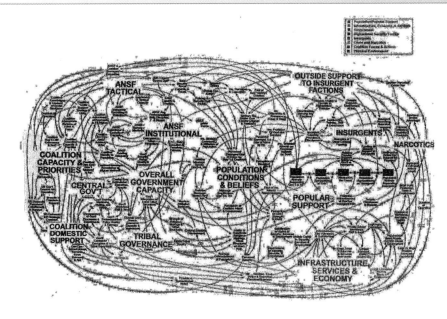

Figure 10.9 Dynamic planning for COIN in Afghanistan 2009. *Source:* Office of the Joint Chiefs of Staff, United States, 2009. This figure is a slide that is meant to portray the complexity of military strategy in Afghanistan. When General Stanley McChrystal was shown the slide, he is alleged to have said "When we understand that slide we will have won the war."

in Afghanistan (until he was dismissed for talking publicly to the press), believed that these counterinsurgency tactics worked to stabilize the country. His COIN had three components – a "hearts and minds" campaign, a commitment to increasing indigenous Afghan forces, and a drive to eliminate corruption in government. It meant that Western troops had to learn to live among the population, adapt to local and tribal customs, and do excellent intelligence work. The complexity of this task is illustrated by the diagram shown in Figure 10.9, used by Mc-Chrystal and the U.S. military in Kabul.

After his 2008 election, President Barack Obama authorized a comprehensive review of U.S. policy. He downplayed previous American goals (even those he had championed himself such as security, opportunity, and justice), stating that the United States was not going to "rebuild Afghanistan into a Jeffersonian democracy," and announced that the "core goal of the U.S. must be to disrupt, dismantle, and defeat al-Qaeda and its safe havens in Pakistan, and to prevent their return to Pakistan or Afghanistan."[50] The United States would do this, he declared, by disrupting terrorist networks capable of

launching international attacks; promoting a more capable, accountable, and effective government in Afghanistan; building up Afghan security forces; nudging Pakistan toward greater civilian control; and getting the international community to help achieve these objectives under UN auspices.

In 2009 President Obama listed Afghanistan as his number-one foreign policy priority. He increased the U.S. troop commitment by an extra thirty thousand for a "surge," bringing the total number of U.S. troops there to around one hundred thousand.[51] The surge had a dramatic effect, reducing insurgency activities by 30 percent the next year and increasing the number of Afghans who signed up for the police and army. But Obama then declared he intended to begin troop withdrawal by the middle of 2011 and have all combat troops out of the country by 2014. Canada and the Netherlands, therefore, withdrew in 2011 and 2010, respectively. France departed in 2012; Italy, Germany, the United Kingdom, the United States, and other NATO countries will leave in 2014.

By 2010, Obama had narrowed the Afghan mission to its barest elements. State-building was

[50] Summarized in Simon, "Can the Right War Be Won?"

[51] *The New York Times*, December 2, 2009.

dead. The global war on terrorism was narrowly focused as a campaign against the remnants of the al-Qaeda network. The United States began to cut back its combat roles and slowly hand over power to the Afghans. By late 2012, ten thousand troops were already gone, and more than twenty-three thousand were to depart by the summer of 2013. The remainder of some seventy thousand will leave in 2014. A residual force of perhaps fifteen thousand to thirty thousand U.S. troops will be kept in the country until 2024 to help put down militants and provide air cover, intelligence, logistical support, and training. [52] The 2012 "strategic partnership" agreement between the United States and Afghanistan establishes the outlines for a long-term relationship and framework, but it leaves many details to be sorted out in the future.[53] The plan estimates that about 352,000 Afghan Security Forces (including national army and police) will be in place by that time. The United States and NATO made a commitment to continue funding the Afghans for another five years, providing US$4.1 billion annually.

There remain doubts about aspects of Afghan security. The army is plagued with low enlistment and desertions. There are many parts of the country where government forces cannot operate effectively. Afghan women have made some progress – they can hold office, study in university, and walk the streets of major cities without wearing a burka, but many experts worry that such rights will be lost when the U.S. troops are removed and the Kabul government is forced to seek a settlement with the Taliban. The country has also had major problems with corruption. In 2012, a Tokyo conference provided a promise of US$16 billion in aid over the next four years – or two years after most U.S. and NATO troops will have left the country in exchange for a promise to fight corruption.

Planned or not, as of mid-2013, the United States was headed toward the traditional strategy of counterterrorism (trying to disrupt or kill terrorists with the use of covert special forces – now including drones). COIN, the counterinsurgency strategy of Petraeus and McChrystal was abandoned – even if no politician would say it was dead.

Targeted killing Over the past few years the United States has steadily eroded al-Qaeda's leadership, not by capturing and imprisoning leaders but by killing them.[54] As well as the special forces killing of Osama bin Laden (covered in Chapter 11), the United States has stepped up drone missile attacks in an effort to kill large numbers of senior al-Qaeda leaders. According to information leaked to *The New York Times*, every week about a hundred top intelligence officers under the leadership of the Pentagon allegedly rank order the worst terrorists and how they should be targeted for killing by special forces or drones. This memo goes to the White House, where President Obama meets with his security advisers and personally micromanages the policy, determining who will be "nominated" for kill or capture and personally approving every name on the "kill list."[55]

Attorney General Eric Holder defends such killings, arguing that the government has the clear authority and responsibility to defend the United States through the use of lethal force. "We are a nation at war. And, in this war we face a nimble and determined enemy that cannot be underestimated."[56] Holder and others in the Obama administration approve the targeted attacks as lawful

---

[52] *Daily Telegraph*, August 19, 2011.
[53] Stephen Hadley and John Podesta, "The Right Way Out of Afghanistan: Leaving Behind a State That Can Govern" *Foreign Affairs* 91, no. 4 (July/August 2012), pp. 41–53.
[54] See the detailed research of Bryan C. Price, "Targeting Top Terrorists: How Leadership Decapitation Contributes to Counterterrorism," and Patrick B. Johnston "Does Decapitation Work? Assessing the Effectiveness of Leadership Targeting in Counterinsurgency Campaigns," *International Security* 36, no. 4 (Spring 2012), pp. 9–79.
[55] *The New York Times*, May 29, 2012.
[56] Eric Holder, speech to Northwestern University School of Law, March 5, 2010. Holder's complete speech can be found at http://www.justice.gov.

acts of war and self-defense under established principles of the right to self-defense in the fight against the Taliban and al-Qaeda. These actions are legal because of the "Authorization for the Use of Military Force" laws passed by Congress in a Joint Resolution on September 14, 2001, and signed into law by President Bush on September 18, 2001. The resolution gave the president carte blanche to use all "necessary and appropriate force" against individuals and groups he deemed to have "planned, authorized, committed or aided" the 9/11 attacks or who provided a haven for such groups.[57]

Holder also claims that the authority granted to the president is not limited to battlefields in Afghanistan, as the United States faces existential threats from "stateless enemies" prone to shifting operations from country to country. His Justice department asserts that the U.S. government may lawfully kill a U.S. citizen abroad if three points are covered: (1) a high-level U.S. official decides the target is a top-ranking al-Qaeda figure or affiliate, (2) the named figure poses an "imminent" threat of a violent attack on the United States, and (3) capturing him/her is not feasible.[58]

Is this too much power for a president to possess? How can the world know whether the individuals chosen are truly terrorists or simply people who have the wrong political affiliations or who happened to be in the wrong place at the wrong time? Should the United States be in a perpetual war against terrorism with no limitations of time or geographical space? Critics claim that President Obama has sacrificed American core values in the name of security. Should outside courts be required to review the evidence before a targeted assassination takes place against foreigners or U.S. citizens?

Arguments for foreign involvement in Afghanistan The situation in Afghanistan is complicated, including even defining success itself. A minimally successful end to Western involvement presumably would mean leaving Afghanistan in such a condition that it would not implode when the West leaves. The Afghan government must be able to deliver basic services and maintain adequate security after all the foreign troops are gone.

There may be different perceptions of what is happening on the ground, contested estimates of government and enemy strength, and varying opinions over what should or should not be done, but an essential question remains: what is the strategic goal of Western military troops in Afghanistan? The initial objective was to remove the Taliban government and end the al-Qaeda training camps. This was successful. But will it be a lasting success? Some Western political leaders and almost all Afghan politicians fear that a premature Western exit from the country will result in another Afghan war and that the Taliban will return to power and allow al-Qaeda to train terrorists once again. The Afghan defense minister General Abdul Rahim Wardak told *The Wall Street Journal*, "Nobody at this moment based on any type of analysis can predict what will be the security situation in 2014. That's unpredictable."[59] While negotiators are trying to develop guidelines about the details of leaving, they are blurring the principles about what the future of Afghanistan will be like. How one answers the primary question about strategic goals will determine the answer to the question about whether the West should stay in Afghanistan for the long haul or depart as soon as possible.

There has also been some evolution in the minor goals for Afghanistan. What are they? Do they include ensuring political rights for minorities and women? Is it acceptable, for example, that "men are fundamental and women are secondary" as the Afghan government's own appointed council of 150 leading Muslim clerics recently concluded?

[57] U.S. Congress, *Special Joint Resolution of September 2001 Authorization for Use of Military Force* (P.L. 107–40,115 Atat.224 (2001). Also see Thomas Billitteri, "Drone Warfare," *Global Issues 2010* (Washington, DC: CQ Press, 2010).

[58] Department of Justice, "White Paper on the Lawfulness of a Lethal Attack against a U.S. Citizen," leaked to Michael Isikoff of NBC News Feb. 4, 2013.

[59] *The Wall Street Journal*, February 18, 2012.

Arguments against foreign involvement in Afghanistan
Opponents of the Afghan war claim that the West has not learned from history. All former invading empires, from Great Britain to the Soviet Union, found it much easier to enter Afghanistan than to remain there. Such critics believe that the international community should depart as soon as possible and let Afghanistan look after itself. They argue that Afghans do not want to be under the tutelage of foreigners; they have never accepted them in the past and will not do so in the future. Britain fought three wars in Afghanistan between 1839 and 1919, defending its interests in India, and each time it was defeated.[60] Possibly the greatest humiliation ever suffered by the British army was when it was defeated at Gandamak, Afghanistan, in January 1842. In each case the foreign invaders met local resistance that sealed the fate of young soldiers, as depicted in Rudyard Kipling's 1892 poem "The Young British Soldier," and produced "the grave-yard of empires":[61]

When you're wounded and left
On Afghanistan's plains
And the women come out
To cut up what remains
Jest roll to your rifle and blow
Out your brains
An' go to your Gawd like a soldier.

Opponents of foreign involvement in Afghanistan make several other specific allegations. They claim that the situation there is more difficult to solve than in Iraq. The country never was stable, they argue, and it cannot be changed. It is much larger and poorer; it has longer, more porous borders than Iraq; and terrorists can cross the border with ease

from neighboring Pakistan and elsewhere. Unlike Iraq, Afghanistan has no revenue from oil or any other major resources. The country is fragmented by multiple ethnic groups and clans, and it has never constituted a "state" in the same sense as Iraq. For thousands of years it has been stable only when ruled by ruthless, authoritarian leaders. Professor Andrew Bacevich calls Afghanistan a "sinkhole," consuming resources neither the U.S. military nor the U.S. government can afford to waste.[62] Today, the government is corrupt and cannot control vast parts of the country. There is only a very thin national identity and little loyalty to the capital of Kabul or to political leader President Hamid Karzai.

According to these assessments, there are three faces to Western policy in Afghanistan. The first is the one accepted by naive optimists who believe the present-day policy will provide a self-reliant, stable Afghanistan. The second, shared by hard-boiled realists, is that the West may attempt to construct a vibrant Afghanistan, but the project will fail eventually. This view is often expressed in the phrase, "We cannot set up a Jeffersonian democracy there." The third, shared by pessimistic realists, and perhaps the most cynical of all, argues that the West may pretend to build a vital Afghanistan, but what it actually wants to do is keep the country fragile for geopolitical reasons. According to this argument, a weak, fragile Afghanistan is a boon for the West in the new "Great Game" of power politics in South Asia.

Perhaps the most sophisticated opposition to the current strategy in Afghanistan comes from those who contend that the present policy of top-down state building will never ensure long-term stability in the country. These critics argue that Western policy is based on a fundamental misunderstanding of Afghan culture and social structure. As Seth G. Jones put it, the current strategy "must take place alongside bottom-up approaches, such as reaching out to legitimate local leaders to enlist them in

---

[60] Opponents of this argument claim that the British won the second Afghan War in the Battle of Kandahar in 1880 and that the third Anglo-Afghan War (1919) was not a defeat in the sense of 1842, as both sides got what they wanted from the settlement (for the British, acceptance of the Durand Line was a key point).

[61] Seth G. Jones, *In the Graveyard of Empires: America's War in Afghanistan* (New York: W. W. Norton, 2009).

[62] *Newsweek*, November 29, 2008.

providing security and services at the village level. Otherwise, the Afghan government will lose the war."[63] In *Empires of Mud*, Antonio Giustozzi also concludes that only a combination of top-down and bottom-up co-optation of local approaches will bring stability and security to the country.[64]

Realists believe that ordinary Afghans are now "hedging their bets" by pretending to be with the West while not completely abandoning the Taliban – they have to protect themselves because of uncertainty about what will happen next in their country. It seems reasonable. How can ordinary Afghans believe that the West will not one day merely pack its bags and leave? Given the history of Afghanistan, is this not a rational approach for Afghans to take toward foreigners? What they fear is that the U.S. will leave behind an undefeated Taliban insurgency, a dysfunctional government, and a country dependent on foreign help and aid. The reality is, there is no coherent U.S. or NATO policy about how to deal with the consequences of a 2014 withdrawal.

War in Iraq

Members of NATO and most other states agreed that the events of September 11, 2011 in the United States justified a military response – as two unanimously adopted United Nations Security Council resolutions substantiated. As long as the U.S. government targeted only proven terrorists in Afghanistan, UN and NATO cohesion was assured. However, when Iraq was called a co-conspirator of the 9/11 attack, this unity quickly disintegrated. When the Security Council and NATO could not be persuaded to extend their support to an attack on Iraq, Britain, Australia, and a handful of other countries joined with the United States in a "coalition of the willing" to declare war on Iraq.

Close Up 10.1 **Summary questions about Afghanistan: Discuss, debate, decide**

The role of NATO and the United States is drawing to a close in Afghanistan. Only a handful of foreign troops will remain after 2014. The consensus to continue the mission has gradually diminished with growing disillusion about the future of the country and economic downturns in most of the NATO countries, including the United States. The war in Afghanistan began as a "war on terrorism" and an effort to punish the Taliban for harboring al-Qaeda, but as the realities of nation-building became clearer, people began to believe the task was not reachable within a reasonable time frame. Polls throughout NATO countries, including the United States, continually show very large majorities favor pulling all troops out of Afghanistan.

Clearly, a departure scramble from Afghanistan is underway. Has an intermediate end state, somewhere between ideal and intolerable, been achieved?[65] Should NATO have fought in Afghanistan for minimal goals, nation-building, or long-term occupation? Should the goals have included protecting U.S. and Western interests; extinguishing al-Qaeda; or setting up a viable, democratic state in the country? Even if al-Qaeda is weakened or defeated, what will the Western response be if the Taliban take over again in parts or all of Afghanistan or if there is massive instability in Pakistan? Will Western troops be sent back to the region? Is a democratic government in Kabul something Afghans will fight and die for?

[63] Seth G. Jones, "It Takes the Villages: Bringing Change from Below in Afghanistan," *World Affairs* 9, no. 3 (May–June 2010), pp. 120–7.
[64] Antonio Giustozzi, *Empires of Mud* (New York: Columbia University Press, 2010).

The actual war lasted only a few weeks, and by May 2003, Iraq was fully occupied. Within a year it had an interim government, and in February 2005 the country successfully elected a transitional assembly that appointed Iraqis to draft a constitution to be ratified by referendum in October 2005. The Iraqi people voted in the affirmative for the new constitution, elections for the National Assembly were held, and a permanent government led by Nouri al-Maliki took office in December of the same year. Only one year later Saddam Hussein was executed after being found guilty of crimes against humanity. The next election in March 2010 proved divisive. Prime Minister Maliki, a sectarian Shiite, would not accept his defeat by Iyad Allawi's Iraqiya coalition. Allawi (a secular Shiite), with the support of Sunnis, received ninety-one seats in the Council of Representatives, two more than Maliki, but Maliki clung to power with the support of the Iraqi National Alliance, a group of pro-Iran religious Shiites that includes the followers of Muqtada al-Sadr, the leader of Iraqi Shiites who had earlier fought coalition forces in Iraq.

During the 2008 election campaign in the United States, Barack Obama said that the United States had completed its responsibility in Iraq.[66] He committed to withdraw all U.S. combat troops from there by September 2010 and all other military by the end of 2011. Conservatives, who opposed the withdrawal of U.S. troops, claimed that Obama's policies might increase long-term Sunni violence against the fragile Shiite-dominated government. In the meantime, Iraqi security forces had increased to 670,000.[67] When a compromise agreement on future U.S. deployment issues could not be resolved, all U.S. forces were withdrawn from the country in 2012 and the mission ended. Domestic violence resumed while the first U.S. combat troops were preparing to leave.[68] Some have called the Iraq war

a success, others a self-inflicted tragedy. As of 2013, only a few U.S. troops remain in the country at the U.S. embassy.

Arguments for foreign involvement in Iraq Americans who favored the Iraq war believed that inaction after 9/11 would have been an evasion of responsibility. Led by neoconservatives, think tanks, journalists, and President George W. Bush, they contended that the United States had to respond to terrorism on American territory. Throughout the prewar period and the war President Bush stressed three justifications for the invasion. First, Iraq had WMDs (unconfirmed by UN weapons' inspectors and later disproved by investigations). Second, Iraq had links to the al-Qaeda terrorist organization and perhaps the 9/11 attacks (later proved false by official investigations in Britain and the United States). Third, the brutal dictatorship of Saddam Hussein had to be destroyed before he attacked another country. As President Bush proffered, "You can't distinguish between al-Qaeda and Saddam when you talk about the war on terrorism. They're both equally bad, and equally as evil, and equally as destructive."[69]

From the neoconservative point of view, the United States won the war and reduced the terrorist threat. They regret that many lives were lost on both sides but maintain that defeating Saddam Hussein's authoritarian government was worth it. Although the insurgency continued for some time, they argue, violence has diminished considerably. They point out that there has been measurable progress in Iraq since it almost collapsed in sectarian war – security incidents have fallen from a weekly average of 1,600 in 2007–08 to fewer than one hundred today.[70] Further, the country has experienced a new constitution, free elections, and a consensus government. The March 2010 election

---

[65] This is the essence of the question asked by Stephen Biddle, Fotini Christia, and J. Alexander in "Defining Success in Afghanistan: What Can the United States Accept?" *Foreign Affairs* 87, no. 6 (July–August 2010), pp. 48–60.

[66] *The New York Times*, September 1, 2010.

[67] *The New York Times*, July 29, 2011.

[68] For a pessimistic analysis of Iraq's future, see Bruce E. Moon, "Long Time Coming: Prospects for Democracy in Iraq," *International Security* 33, no. 4 (Spring 2009), pp. 115–48. According to a USA Today poll, 60 percent of Americans respond "no" to the question "Do you think the situation in Iraq was worth going to war for?" *USA Today*, August 27, 2010.

[69] *Washington Post*, September 26, 2002. See also Stephen Watts, "Military Interventions and the 'Lessons of Iraq'," *PS: Political Science and Politics* 40, no. 2 (April 2007), p. 419.

[70] Antony Blinken, "Morning in Mesopotamia," *Foreign Affairs*, 91, no. 4 (July/August 2012), p. 152.

provided Nouri al-Maliki with a minority government supported by other major party leaders, and since then Maliki has concentrated power in his office by his direct control over the security forces. Oil production is up 50 percent. From this point of view, Iraq has become a beacon for democracy and freedom in the Middle East. Some even argue that the later Arab Awakening in North Africa vindicates this form of analysis.

Arguments against foreign involvement in Iraq Many liberals and some conservatives do not believe there was adequate justification for the war in Iraq. They point out that sectarian violence continues and do not believe that long-term political stability in the country is assured. Arguments for why the invasion was ill advised include the following:

- The country is riven by division and suspicion over religion, ethnicity, and geography.[71] Sunnis, Shiites, and Kurds fight for power; believers and secularists contest Islamic law; and all have their own contending militias.
- The Shiite Maliki government has shown disregard for civil liberties since the 2010 election. There is no transparency in government and, nongovernmental agencies have been raided and journalists arrested.
- The ongoing sectarian violence and reprisals show that there may not be enough political compromise and trust to produce a viable democracy. In September 2012, the Sunni vice president of Iraq was convicted and sentenced to death. Tariq al-Hashimi was convicted in absentia after he had escaped to Turkey, a Sunni country. Al-Hashimi called the trials a "witch hunt," and sectarian violence has escalated.
- The country is not self-reliant. It cannot protect its borders, airspace, or territorial waters without foreign assistance.

- The Bush administration argued that democracy in Iraq would solve other problems in the Middle East, but the so-called road map for Israeli-Palestinian relations has not progressed since the invasion of Iraq. The region remains as highly unstable as before the war was launched – perhaps more so.
- It is questionable whether the new constitution can win the sustained loyalty of Iraqis and provide a shared vision for the future. Solutions or mechanisms to overcome the country's fault lines are not apparent, and the once-powerful Sunni minority is now angrily dispossessed of power.

The country remains divided over specific questions:

1. Centralization versus regional autonomy, essentially disagreements about how much autonomy should be given to the regions and religious groups inside Iraq.
2. Which institutions should have power over oil resources – the constitution put the central government in charge of administering current oil and gas fields but provided no agreed-on formula for dividing oil profits among the new political entities. Disputes continue about some areas, especially the oil-rich region of Kirkuk.
3. The role of Islam, and particularly the question of civil rights for women, are vague in the constitution, which says that "Islam is the basic source of law" and that no law should contradict its "principles of jurisprudence." But under article 30, Iraqis are given the choice of defining their own "personal statuses" according to their own beliefs.
4. The role of former Baathists in the country – the constitution banned ex-members of Saddam's Baath Party from government positions but left open the possibility that they might be allowed to disown their affiliation and restore their opportunities. However, the arrest of six hundred suspected former Baathists in 2011 and the conviction of the Sunni vice-president in 2012 were not good signs for future sectarian relations.

[71] Larry Diamond, *Squandered Victory: The American Occupation and the Bungled Effort to Bring Democracy to Iraq* (New York: Times Book, 2005); David L. Phillips, *Losing Iraq: Inside the Postwar Reconstruction Fiasco* (New York: Westview Press, 2005).

5. Violence in postwar Iraq continues. Apart from northern Kurdistan, there are few secure areas in the country. The militant Sunni community is both anti-Shiite and anti-American. It is buttressed by three million former members of the Baath Party and seven hundred thousand former army and security forces – a large pool from which insurgents can be drawn.

Close Up 10.2 Summary questions about Iraq: Discuss, debate, decide

Pessimists claim that only a miracle will prevent Iraq from breaking up or falling into a prolonged civil war now that the U.S. has left the country. Of course, prediction is foolish because nothing is absolutely certain, but the following four possibilities constitute the parameters of future outcomes:

1. A stable liberal democracy with federal institutions
2. A shaky liberal democracy with confederal institutions
3. Fragmentation and inertia
4. Civil war

The first two scenarios are based on the optimistic idea that security can be established permanently along with satisfactory postwar reconstruction, thus allowing the process of democratization to continue smoothly and satisfactorily. The third relies on the argument that the three sectarian groupings will decide that there is not enough national identity or consensus to maintain one country. The last and most pessimistic scenario is that religious and political differences will eventually lead to a civil war between and among the groups.[72]

What is a realistic prognosis for the future of Iraq? Should the United States have delayed its departure from Iraq to postpone a civil conflict? Will a bloodbath come eventually as Shiites continue to marginalize Sunnis?

Critical Case Study 10.3 Lessons of insurgency and counterinsurgency in Afghanistan, Iraq, and Vietnam

Afghanistan and Iraq are textbook cases of countries divided by ethnicity, religion, conflict, and historical injustices. Whether they can be rebuilt into durable states is far from certain. The issue for the Afghan and Iraqi governments and their allies is how to protect peaceful citizens and eliminate insurgents. Keeping the population on side is vital for counterinsurgency and the most important step is determining the motivation behind the violence and responding to it in a way that is proportionate and likely to provide a solution. To stop insurgencies the rebels must be isolated and discredited. But insurgents, too, learn from their experiences, discovering how not to repeat their mistakes. In the early stages in Iraq and Afghanistan the insurgents adapted continually, moving from one type of attack to another and taking advantage of the weaknesses of the government.

When insurgents kill and pillage they alienate people, and when counterinsurgents harm the people, they too can lose public trust. Indeed, the United States' policy in both Iraq and Afghanistan went

---

[72] For further discussions of each option, see James Dobbin, "Winning the Unwinnable War," *Foreign Affairs* 84, no. 1 (January–February 2005), pp. 16–25; Edward N. Luttwak, "Iraq: The Logic of Disengagement," *Foreign Affairs* 84, no. 1 (January–February 2005), pp. 26–36; Ahmed S. Hashim, "Iraq: From Insurgency to Civil War?," *Current History* (January 2005), pp. 10–18.

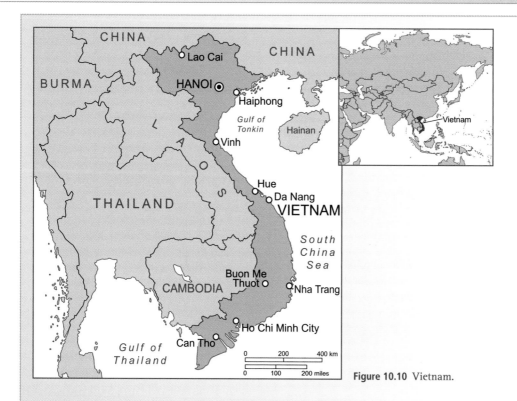

Figure 10.10 Vietnam.

through two phases. The first followed the doctrine used in Vietnam, in which the local people were essentially seen as the enemy (Figure 10.10). In the second phase, called COIN, the U.S. military adopted a policy of trying to win the hearts and minds of the people as outlined in their new counterinsurgency manual *FM 3-24*.[73] In Iraq, U.S. forces faced up to the necessity of obtaining local support when they had to convince members of the Sunni population to report on rebel actions by paying them large sums of money. Winning counterinsurgencies requires ensuring the well-being of the civilian population even if it means taking more casualties, and in encouraging his soldiers to adopt this policy, General Petraeus said, "I count on each of you to embrace the warrior-builder-diplomat spirit."[74] In Afghanistan, the killing of bystanders, especially by unarmed drones, has eroded support for the United States and NATO among the population.

The wars in Afghanistan, Iraq, and Vietnam are reasonably parallel. There are striking similarities. In all cases the United States had

- difficulty building a strong, viable state
- difficulty obtaining information about what was going on in the country – policy makers were bewildered by intelligence failures in Vietnam, and they are today in South Asia
- difficulty understanding why the number of insurgents continued to grow, despite significant battle victories

---

[73] See the latest U.S. Army and Marine Corps counterinsurgency manual *FM 3-24* at http://www.fas.org/irp/doddir/army/fm3-24.pdf.
[74] *National*, February 21, 2008.

- difficulty in accepting that the battle for the hearts and minds of people is or was failing and that, among the populace, ethnicity, religion, and nationalism continue to count more than loyalty to the state
- difficulty understanding why reconstruction plans did not reduce the number of insurgents as they had in some other war-torn countries

The main difference among the three wars is that the United States used conscription only in the Vietnam War. Today's U.S. military does not include unwilling and hostile conscripts; it is a paid, professional army. The soldiers have chosen to join the army (although the reserves, for example, had no idea that they would see active service overseas so often). Moreover, the number of U.S. service members killed in Vietnam was far higher than in Afghanistan or Iraq and that turned a vast majority of Americans against the war. In the end, Vietnam lost about a million lives while the United States lost fifty-eight thousand. The American public found this cost intolerable and the United States withdrew from the contest.

In Vietnam, the United States was not prepared to use adequate numbers of troops or to engage in an effective counterinsurgency strategy. In fact, it may have lost because it spent too much energy hunting down Vietcong guerillas. Counterinsurgency is not like fighting frontline battles in which the enemy is readily identifiable. Winning battles and attacking ordinary people are not the major goals in counterinsurgency.

Perhaps the greatest error in all three wars was the inability of the United States and its allies to plan for a viable end game. In all three cases the United States did not recognize how long a commitment it would take nor to what extent human and financial resources would be required to succeed.

How long should the United States have remained in Afghanistan and Iraq? What will the results be now that the Iraq war has been concluded and the Afghanistan military campaign is to end in 2014? Will keeping a few U.S. noncombat troops in Afghanistan make a difference?

Rebellion, civil war, and humanitarian intervention in North Africa and the Middle East

In Chapter 8 we discussed the protests and rebellions that shook Arab states in 2011–12 and examined their social and religious characteristics. Here, we first note how some of the uprisings were successful without massive upheaval and then discuss in more detail those in Libya and Syria, which required high degrees of violence to overthrow, or attempt to overthrow, their governments.

All of the countries affected by the uprisings were/are authoritarian and predominantly Muslim (Figure 10.11). Like most North African and Middle East Arab countries they were run by regimes that exercised power in a fairly similar way. At the top

was a single authoritarian ruler (monarch, president, ruling party, or royal family) bolstered by a large intelligence service (mukhabarat) with a coterie of informers. At the second level was a large government bureaucracy that dispensed money, employment, and patronage. At the third or mass level, the countries usually possessed the trappings of democracy with political organizations and sham elections to channel and control dissent.

While the media to a large extent characterized these rebellions as similar, there was no coherent "Arab Spring." In retrospect, the rebellions may look as though they were inevitable, but few experts predicted them.[75] Factors such as a very young

---

[75] See F. Gregory Gause III, "Why Middle East Studies Missed the Arab Spring," *Foreign Affairs* 90, no. 4, pp. 81–90.

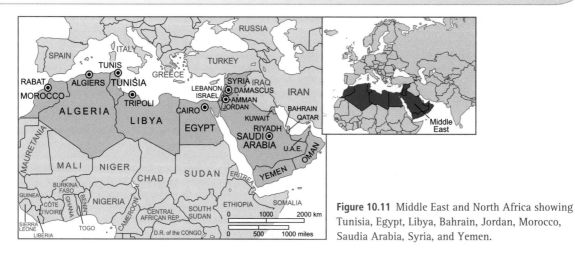

Figure 10.11 Middle East and North Africa showing Tunisia, Egypt, Libya, Bahrain, Jordan, Morocco, Saudia Arabia, Syria, and Yemen.

population, high unemployment, poverty, corruption, and the use of the Internet and social networking by protesters were present in all cases, but the dynamics differed in each case because of history, local conditions, social organization, government institutions, religion, and military structures.[76] The uprisings electrified the world, but their outcomes remain uncertain. The Middle East is in the midst of historic change, but permanent political reform will emerge only when a new and stable balance of power exists inside and among these countries.

The problem in North Africa and the Middle East is not simply how to overthrow authoritarian leaders but also how to shape the political order that follows without replicating its flaws. The Arab states involved in the recent uprisings may end up following quite different paths. If they follow the trajectory of many of the great revolutions of the past, these diffuse and essentially leaderless revolts may prove to be forerunners of more profound transitions. However, civil wars tend to last a long time, and these conflicts are only in their initial stages. The specter of prolonged bloody conflict could yet dampen the optimism that has been raised. The authoritarian governments that have been overthrown

or are still under challenge were guilty of suppressing individual rights and concentrating power in the hands of minorities. Protesters above all revealed the frailty of government authority. The new leaders of even the most peaceful of the uprisings need to solve basic issues about the relations between religion and state; how to incorporate ethnic and religious minorities; how to share proceeds from sales of petroleum; and how to provide security, literacy, jobs, food, and health care for their populations.

One of the most significant aspects of the Arab revolts is the historical unresolved conflict between Sunnis and Shiites. The split that became so volatile in Iraq after Saddam Hussein is resurfacing in other Arab states, where it had long been kept in check by authoritarian governments. Shiites want greater rights in Lebanon, Bahrain, and Saudi Arabia. Sunnis seek more power in Iraq and Syria. Saudi Arabia considers itself the guardian of Sunni Islam, and Iran the guardian of Shia Islam. In many of these countries the largest and best-organized political organizations are religious associations such as the Muslim Brotherhood in Egypt and the Nahda Party in Tunisia. The possibility for instability and escalating violence on a sectarian basis is a serious and ongoing challenge.

Western policies such as supporting an Arab-Israeli truce and the maintenance of order at the expense of freedom in allied Arab countries once served mutual interests, but that is changing. Israel,

[76] Lisa Anderson, "Demystifying the Arab Spring: Parsing the Differences between Tunisia, Egypt and Libya"; Jack A. Goldstone, "Understanding the Revolutions of 2011: Weakness and Resilience in Middle East Autocracies," *Foreign Affairs* 90, no. 3 (May–June 2011), pp. 2–16.

in particular, is fearful of what the change might bring. Regional stability is at stake and conclusions to the civil wars in Libya and Syria will be crucial. There are some good precedents. The Turkish government, with roots in Islam, shares a democratic commitment to free enterprise and good relations with the West. It is also a model admired by many of the Arab protesters. The government of Turkey emphasizes the moral rules of Islam, but it downplays its political prescriptions and law. Neighboring Jordan and Morocco have taken preemptive initiatives to democratize, while Kuwait and Algeria are locked in continuing crises, albeit without money worries. Saudi Arabia is a firm ally against violent Islamic extremism, but it, too, has a serious democratic deficit. King Abdullah is nearly 90 years of age, and his crown prince, Salman, is in poor health.

The revolutions are a challenge for the West, especially the United States. For half a century the United States and Europe have been able to deal with only two kinds of leaders in the Middle East and North Africa – the opponents (Syria, Libya, Iraq, and Iran) and the friends (Egypt, Tunisia, Morocco, Saudi Arabia, Jordan, and the United Arab Emirates). The friendly, stable, authoritarian-led countries provided predictable access to oil and relative security for Israel. The political landscape has changed significantly, however. It is uncertain whether the countries undergoing revolutions will become stable or democratic, and dealing with them will be more complicated than in the past. Islamist parties are showing strength throughout the region. The cocktail of democracy and religion may be more difficult to deal with than the West has anticipated.

Tunisia

The first revolt was in Tunisia, sparked by the self-immolation of Mohamed Bouazizi, a poor and desperate street vendor on December 17, 2010. His plight struck a chord with young people, many of whom, like him, had no hope of decent employment to pay for a family or a modestly comfortable life. After his death, a relatively spontaneous Tunisian uprising took place in which rural areas joined with the urban labor movement to overthrow dictator President Zine el-Abidine Ben Ali. Many of the protesters demanded more employment opportunities, especially for the young. The military's role in the revolt was minimal. The majority Sunni population supported the revolt because they said the government was "prostituting the country for foreign exchange," but many of their leaders were old, or out of the country, and their direct role was limited in the early stages of the rebellion.[77]

After President Ben Ali resigned and left the country, a state of emergency was declared, and Mohamed Ghannouchi became prime minister, to be quickly replaced by Beji Caid el Sebsi. Public protests and tribal divisions continued, but an election for a constituent assembly took place in October 2011. This assembly was given eighteen months to write a new constitution. It appointed Moncef Marzouki, a former civil rights worker, as president and Hamada Jebali, secretary-general of the Islamist movement, as prime minister and head of government. A coalition government was then set up, combining members of both the moderate religious organization Ennahda and the left-of center Ettakatol. Despite this progress, political order remains in disarray and the country has been afflicted by civil violence and large numbers of Libyan refugees. Conflict between fundamentalist and moderate Islamists continues with Salafist and other fundamentalist groups putting pressure on the government to move the country closer to Sharia law with restrictions on alcohol and the role of women. Elections for a permanent assembly and government are set to take place in 2013.

Egypt

The revolts spread eastward. In Egypt, disgruntled young people in the major urban centers, especially

---

[77] Anderson, "Demystifying the Arab Spring," p. 3.

Cairo, gathered for weeks in Tahrir Square in early 2011, demanding an end to the Hosni Mubarak regime and the authoritarian rule they held responsible for their extreme poverty and unemployment. Their protests escalated and they were joined by other groups, including the Muslim Brotherhood. The military did not take sides in the early stages but took charge after the rebellion was established. Mubarak was soon ousted from power, and the Supreme Council of the Armed Forces (SCAF), headed by Field Marshall Mohamed Tantawi, stepped in to run the country.[78]

Parliamentary elections to the People's Assembly of Egypt were held between November 2011 and January 2012. The results showed the strength of Muslim parties. In the run-off, the Freedom and Justice Party, led by Mohamed Morsi, captured 37.5 percent of the vote, and Al-Nour, led by Abdel Moneim El Shat, received 27.8 percent. The main function of the new assembly was to choose members for a Constitutional Assembly to write a new constitution. When it could not reach an agreement, Field Marshal Mohamed Hussein Tantawi, leader of the Supreme Council of the Armed Forces, told the squabbling political leaders that if they did not come up with a hundred-person Constitutional Assembly the ruling military would either declare its own constitutional annex or revert the country back to its 1971 constitution. The contest ended with the assembly approving a power-sharing deal that gave Islamists and secular politicians equal representation in the Constitutional Assembly.

The election for the Egyptian presidency was forced to a run-off second ballot on June 16–17, 2012, with a former air force general, Ahmed Shafiq, facing off against the Muslim Brotherhood candidate, Mohamed Morsi. Morsi won the election with 52 percent of the vote. Soon after his election, Morsi set out to purge the military. On August 12, 2012, he retired Field Marshal Tantawi, chairman of the supreme council of the armed forces, and the heads of the air force, army, navy, and air defense. This allowed Morsi to promote officers more likely to follow his lead and showed the country that he was in charge.

Chaos continues in the country. Civil war is unlikely, but the economy is on the brink of collapse. Debt is mounting, unemployment rates are soaring, and tourism has plummeted. Defence Minister Abdel Fattah El Sissi has warned that the Egyptian state could collapse.[79] The balance of power among elected politicians, the Muslim Brotherhood, and the Egyptian military will take many more years to sort out. Anti-Americanism continues even though the United States continues to give Egypt US$ 1.3 billion in annual funding for military assistance. In a private discussion with *The New York Times*, Morsi said that the United States needed to change its approach to the Arab world and show greater respect for its values. He declared that he would not accept the categorical approach to free speech that President Obama had urged at the United Nations.[80]

Bahrain, Jordan, Morocco, and Saudi Arabia

The monarchies of Bahrain, Jordan, Morocco, and Saudi Arabia also experienced protests, but they have remained fairly stable after offering various deals to placate dissidents. So far, there has been no split in military ranks, and the major social institutions have sided with the governments. Bahrain has had the most difficulty. It is ruled by a Sunni-minority monarchy, and the protests come from the majority Shiites, who claim they are treated as second-class citizens and want democracy and equality. However, the overwhelmingly Sunni military sides with the government, and Saudi Arabia, which supports Sunni monarchs throughout the region, helped the Bahrain government put down the protesters quickly and violently. The United

---

[78] In 2012 the Supreme Court condemned Mubarak to a life sentence of fifty years in prison, but that sentence was appealed and he is to get a new trial. To the chagrin of many Egyptians, his son and many top security officials were not found guilty.

[79] *The New York Times*, January 30, 2013.
[80] *The New York Times*, September 22, 2012.

States, which bases the navy's Fifth Fleet there, was particularly silent on the Bahrain issues. In Jordan, protests were minimal and organized mostly by Palestinians until the Syrian crisis produced thousands of refugees there. Saudi Arabia has stayed calm throughout the unrest.

Libya, Syria, and Yemen

Libya, Syria, and Yemen are clan-based societies run by ruthless military regimes supported by complex security institutions. They all erupted in various states of violent upheaval and civil war during this period. In Libya, there were no national civic organizations to lead the rebellion because they had been silenced or destroyed by President Muammar Gaddafi. When the protest began, the country's tribal groups and military effectively split on a regional basis. Gaddafi responded by brutally attacking the protesters. NATO, backed by a 2011 UN Security Council resolution, defended the rebels from the air, bombing Gaddafi's troops, military installations, and even his headquarters in Tripoli (see Critical Case Study 10.4).

Yemen also faced daunting challenges from rebels. In 2011 the president, Ali Abdullah Saleh, was wounded by insurgents and driven out of the country. Like Libya, Yemen is split along tribal lines, and those ties are stronger than loyalty to the country as a whole or abstract concepts such as democracy and civil institutions. The country's Muslim population is further split between Sunni and Shiite traditions. Yemen is the poorest of the Arab countries, with no significant resources, an inadequate supply of freshwater, limited agriculture, and a huge population for its tiny land base. The economy is a shambles, and most people are desperately poor. Al-Qaeda has cells in parts of the country that benefit from the turmoil. The scope for ongoing chaos is immense. See Critical Case Studies 10.4 on Libya and 11.1 in the next chapter, where Yemen is discussed in the context of its growing importance in international terrorism.

Critical Case Study 10.4 **Libya and R2P**

In Libya, mass protests among its 6.5 million people escalated into wholesale rebellion in 2011. Demonstrators set up a quasicapital in Benghazi and demanded that Colonel Muammar Gaddafi step down and end his more than forty-year dictatorial rule. He responded by brutally attacking them, calling them "cockroaches" and "rats." Civil war ensued. When Gaddafi mobilized his troops outside the city of Benghazi, it provided a justification for international humanitarian action. International condemnation of his attacks was swift. Britain and France, supported by the Organization of the Islamic Conference, the Gulf Cooperation Council, and the Arab League, led a public campaign calling for the UN to authorize NATO to impose a no-fly zone over Libya. On March 17, 2011, the UN Security Council passed Resolution 1973, authorizing action against Gaddafi and allowing a no-fly zone over Libya. The resolution instructed members "to take all necessary measures to protect civilians" while excluding a foreign occupation force of any form on any part of Libyan territory. Ten council members voted in favor, but Russia, China, India, Brazil, and Germany abstained.

NATO actions led by the French, American, and British began immediately, with air strikes and cruise missile attacks against military targets to prevent Gaddafi from flying planes or shooting down NATO aircraft. The alliance also defended the rebels from the air, bombing Gaddafi's troops and even his headquarters. The Mediterranean became a war zone, with ships and air forces from the United States, France, United Kingdom, Italy, Canada, Belgium, Denmark, Spain, Qatar, and the United Arab Emirates participating. NATO maintained that its strikes were strictly designed to protect civilians as authorized by the Security Council, but they also prevented Gaddafi from making sustained ground attacks on rebel forces. The alliance attacked government "command centers" and appeared to side with the rebels. What began as a UN effort to prevent a tragedy soon developed into a "regime change" operation, even if Western leaders would not admit it. By April, NATO planes were bombing targets in Tripoli while still denying they were trying to kill Gaddafi.

In the course of the war NATO and President Obama shifted the goals in Libya from protecting civilians to regime change. On May 24, 2011, Obama asserted "The goal is to make sure that the Libyan people can make a determination about how they want to proceed, and that they'll finally be free of 40 years of tyranny and can start creating the institutions required for self-determination."[81] The president argued that all the conditions for action were in place – an international mandate to act, a broad coalition, the support of Arab countries, and a plea for help from the Libyan people themselves. By now it was also clear that Gaddafi had no support from other Arab leaders. Security Council Resolution 1973 called for "all necessary measures" to be used to protect civilians and enforced a no-fly zone and an arms embargo, but the resolution was stretched to include a naval blockade, arming the rebels (France claimed it did), training (special forces were on the ground), and close air support for rebel attacks (by knocking out Gaddafi's missiles, tanks, armed cars, and troops).

This was the UN's first major explicit test of the new principle of **responsibility to protect** (R2P), which holds that when a sovereign state fails to prevent atrocities to its own people, foreign governments led by the UN have the right to intervene and stop them (discussed in Chapter 6). The United Nations Security Council urged the Libyan government to meet its responsibility to protect its citizens and then expressed its "determination to ensure the protection of citizens." Advocates of R2P applauded the statement, claiming it was vital for humanitarian action, while its opponents argued that the principle could too easily be abused and on other occasions might even be used as an excuse for Western imperialism. Undoubtedly, future application of R2P will remain selective and highly dependent on the political context. The leaders of many developing countries believe that R2P is just a new label for the traditional practice of great power intervention in the affairs of weaker countries. Whether the action in Libya will strengthen or weaken the R2P principle may be determined by the war's long-term consequences. Brazil has since advocated a supplementary principle called *responsibility while protecting* (RWP), which calls for a new set of procedures to ensure that R2P is properly used on future occasions.

During the conflict, the International Criminal Court indicted Gaddafi, his son Saif al-Islam Gaddafi, and the director of military intelligence Abdullah Senussi for crimes against humanity (see Critical Case Study 6.1: Ongoing ICC Investigations). The chief judge said that there were reasonable grounds to charge the three Lybians for the murders of hundreds of civilians. This indictment reduced Gaddafi's options and made a deal with the rebels or international authorities impossible for him. He had no safe haven, and his troops were quickly defeated. On August 22, 2011, jubilant rebel forces poured into central Tripoli and declared victory. On October 20, 2011, Gaddafi was captured and killed without trial. His son Saif al-Islam Gaddafi is still being held by a Libyan tribe.

The overthrow of this dictator was a remarkable, if fragile, achievement. There are no verifiable accounts of how many Libyans died in the uprising, but estimates vary at around thirty thousand people. The Libyan people could yet suffer years of violent conflict, largely because the capital of Tripoli and much of Libya are divided among groups of rebel fighters with clan links to the various geographical

---

[81] *International Herald Tribune*, May 27, 2011.

regions of the country. Local identities and loyalties that were suppressed under decades of Gaddafi rule have resurfaced and clashed. Elections for a general national congress were held in July 2012, the country's first free elections in six decades. The role of the new congress was to appoint an interim government and a constituent authority to draft a constitution. The congress elected Mohammed Magarief of the liberal National Front as chairman, making him the first interim head of state, but other leaders came and went rapidly with government instability characterizing the regime.

The new Lybian transitional government does not control an effective army, while some sixty armed militias or brigades that were never demobilized continue to run parts of the country, essentially out of control. The militias are both the guardians of order in Libya and the main menace to it. Some Islamic gangs have tortured and executed black Africans for supporting the deposed regime. As Talal Atrissi, a political analyst in Lebanon, put it, "The next era will witness battles and conflicts between actors inside countries bent on crushing each other. ... It will be full of challenges large and severe."[82] The shattering of the Gaddafi regime has slipped the country into an unstable situation with an uncertain future. Getting rid of Gaddafi may prove to have been the easy part.[83]

On September 11, 2012, the American consulate in Benghazi was attacked and the U.S. ambassador and three other Americans were killed by radical jihadists. The date of the 9/11 attack implicated al-Qaeda armed militias in Libya and invoked U.S. memories of the horrific 1979 Iranian hostage crisis in which fifty-two Americans were held hostage for four hundred and forty-four days in the embassy in Tehran by a group of Islamist students and militants.

Has this United Nations operation in Libya raised serious questions about international support and the use of R2P for similar interventions? Has toppling an unpopular dictator solved anything in Libya, or has it merely exposed a toxic mix of tribalism, Shiite-Sunni sectarianism, fundamentalism, and oil problems? Will old rivalries and divisions be revived? What role will and should NATO and the UN play in future transitions of this type?

The situation differs substantially from that in Syria. Most of the military has stood with the ruling leader and (so far at least) prevented an overthrow of the government by protesters. The ongoing government crackdown by authoritarian President Bashar al-Assad is bloody and brutal. He is a member of the minority Alawite sect, a branch of Shia Islam, and his response has targeted the majority Sunni population. Iran and Iraq are providing support for Assad. Protests have engulfed the country and Syrian refugees are flooding into Turkey and Lebanon. As in the other neighboring rebellions, the major issue is whether the military forces will stay loyal to the government or join the rebels (see Critical Case Study 10.5).

Critical Case Study 10.5 **Syria**

Syria's situation is vastly more complicated than that of Libya. It is encircled by Middle Eastern hot spots and has a much larger population of about twenty-one million. Its social divisions are even more complex, with a complicated web of religions and sects. Syria's Muslim population is divided into

---

[82] *The New York Times*, August 25, 2011.
[83] For NATO's viewpoint, see Anders Fogh Rasmussen, "NATO after Libya," *Foreign Affairs* 90, no. 4 (July–August 2011), pp. 2–7.

Figure 10.12 In 2012, protests and violent upheaval began in Syria to overthrow the government of President Bashar al-Assad. The UN Security Council was divided over how to deal with the issue, and internal war is ongoing. *Source:* Press Association.

roughly 74 percent Sunni (including Sufis), 13 percent Shiite (including Alawites, Ishmailis, and Twelvers), 3 percent Druze, and about 10 percent Christian. President Bashar al-Assad is a member of the minority Alawite sect, a subgroup of Shia Islam. While a large majority of the population is Sunni, both the government and military are domin ated by Alawites. Their minority position binds them together against the majority Sunnis, so that unlike in Egypt, the military and intelligence agencies stand firmly behind the ruling leaders to prevent an overthrow of the government. The dominant Alawites recall earlier persecution of their sect by Sunnis and are frightened that some version of ethnic cleansing would result if they were defeated. Many non-Sunni Muslims and Christians also support the Alawite leadership for security reasons. Government leaders are backed by Iraq and Iran in the Middle East and Russia and China in the United Nations.

The ongoing crackdown in Syria by al-Assad is brutal (Figure 10.12). According to the UN, as of March 2013, more than seventy thousand Syrians had died in the uprising.[84] Up to half a million Syrians had left their homes, and some two hundred and fifty thousand were refugees in Jordan, Lebanon, and Turkey. The economy was shattered, with inflation soaring and exports collapsing.

Syria shares borders with the most volatile regimes in the Middle East – Iraq, Israel, Jordan, Lebanon, and Turkey. It was crucial in helping jihadists enter Iraq during the recent war there, and the issue of the Israeli annexation of the Golan Heights is still unresolved between Syria and Israel. Damascus, the capital, is the headquarters of various Palestinian groups, and Hamas had its headquarters there until recently, despite the fact that it governs the Gaza Strip. The Shiite militant group Hezbollah in Lebanon has offered its full support to the regime. Its leader, Hassan Nasrallah, lashed out against Assad's

[84] *The New York Times*, August 27, 2011.

enemies in December 2011, saying that he was leading a "resistance regime" against outside enemies.[85] Lebanon's prime minister backs Assad, because he needs the support of Hezbollah, which dominates his government and is a close friend of Syria and Iran. In other words, Syria's stability has implications for Israel, Iraq, Lebanon, and other countries in the Middle East.

While there has been grumbling by Western states and even significant economic sanctions, the United Nations has not proposed R2P, and overt military action is extremely unlikely. While the United Nations has found ways to condemn the Assad regime for atrocities, Russia and China vetoed three moderate Security Council resolutions that would have allowed unspecified measures. As relations with Syria have been close over several years, the Russian foreign minister said he would not even read the draft of Security Council resolutions. Russia uses the Syrian port of Tartus as a supply and maintenance base for its warships and over the years Syria has purchased Russian aircraft, artillery, and antiaircraft missiles. An aerial attack on Syria, therefore, is out of the question because of the country's integrated air defense system supplied by Russia. There is also considerable evidence that Iran is providing massive support for Assad; the two countries signed a mutual defense pact back in 2006, and the European Union has accused Iran's Quds Force of aiding Syria's intelligence and security branches.[86] Iran has publicly declared that Syria is part of its "Axis of Resistance" and that it will not tolerate any division of the country.

In August 2011, the United States and several allies called on President Bashar al-Assad to stand down, and the United Nations Commissioner for Human Rights said that Syrian authorities had committed crimes against humanity. A group of states calling themselves the Friends of Syria (including the United States, Saudi Arabia, and Qatar) has contributed aid such as communications equipment to the insurgents. The United States has banned importation of Syrian oil, sanctioned top government officials, barred Americans from business there, and allowed the CIA to help opposition fighters acquire weapons and logistics. The wisdom of such actions is questionable as there is little cohesion in the opposition forces, and they even include the Al Nusra Front, a terrorist off-shoot of al-Qaeda that is condemned by the United States.

Various avenues for negotiations have been suggested by the Arab League and representatives of the UN, but all have proved futile. The United Nations has sent cease-fire monitors, major countries have withdrawn their ambassadors from Damascus, and former UN secretary-general Kofi Annan drew up a six-point cease-fire and peace plan. When nothing was achieved, Annan resigned and was replaced as the UN negotiator by Lakhdar Brahimi. In short, unless the unlikely happens and the Syrian military divides, al-Assad may stay in power, as neither regional nor international military forces are likely to be used directly against him. If the Syrian government is going to change hands, it will have to implode from within.

The Syrian president defends his actions by declaring that he is being attacked by a "war from abroad," and says he has no intention of "relinquishing power." The ruler is equally as brutal as Gaddafi was, and many thousands of innocent civilians have been killed, so why has R2P not been applied in Syria as it was in Libya? Did lightly arming some of the rebels by the United States in June 2013 make a difference? For the better or worse?

[85] *The New York Times*, December 7, 2011.
[86] *Los Angeles Times*, August 25, 2011.

Conclusion: The changing character of war?

While to some extent globalization and new security issues have changed the character of warfare, other novel and disquieting issues have also arisen concerning the methods for fighting wars. The use of private armies and drones are two dramatic changes. The "unmanning" of warfare is giving rise to new questions about strategy, tactics, and ethics. However, perhaps the greatest challenges come in assessing the legal right of Americans to use targeted killing in the ongoing war against terrorism, and the new techniques for fightning wars.

Mercenaries Mercenaries, or private fighters, have long been part of warfare. They are civilians who fight for personal, usually financial, gain.[87] Historically, private companies were often used for transportation, housing, catering, training, and guarding high-profile officials and foreign leaders; however, in recent years governments have begun "outsourcing" strictly military operations to them as well. For these companies, war is a money-making business. Their number and especially the importance of private security companies (PSCs) have increased substantially since the end of the Cold War. Western governments have turned more and more to private companies such as Executive Outcomes and Xe (formerly Blackwater and Dyn Corp) to carry out basic military tasks. The private company Executive Outcomes, for example, helped defeat insurgencies in both Sierra Leone and Angola during the 1990s. In 2004 the CIA hired the firm Blackwater to locate and assassinate al-Qaeda operatives. None was captured or killed, but one CIA officer told *The New York Times*, "There was a feeling that Blackwater eventually became an extension of the agency."[88] The same firm is alleged to have carried out full-service military activities in Iraq between 2007 and 2009.[89]

The use of private companies has mushroomed to the extent that they may sometimes actually displace the role of the military, even though mercenaries may not be directly responsible to military command and control. Some commentators question whether extensive use of civilians to do military work is justifiable. Certainly, further oversight of their activities is warranted. Among the reasons given for using them is that national militaries are held to such a high standard of accountability that it may be politically prudent to outsource some of the more gruesome tasks of counterinsurgency to outsiders. Should states and/or UN overseas expeditions use paid mercenaries in place of their own militaries or those of donor countries? What ethical issues are involved in this growing practice?

---

[87] Sara Percy, *Mercenaries: The History of the Norm in International Relations* (Oxford: Oxford University Press, 2007).

[88] *The New York Times*, August 23, 2009.

[89] Suzanne Simons, *Master of War: Blackwater USA's Erik Prince and the Business of War* (New York: HarperCollins, 2009).

Drones and robots   The traditional adversarial shape of battlefields may be a relic of history. Miniaturized weapons, drones, and robots are the latest technological developments in weapons of war. Today, army units use handheld devices to peer over hills and buildings. Robots move forward and backward, climb stairs, and even swim to carry out routine surveillance and rescue missions. As P. W. Singer points out, the number of such robots in Afghanistan was forecast to reach twelve thousand by 2008,[90] and the numbers have gone up steadily since then. Robots may be programmed to kill autonomously, and computer viruses may be launched that could not be stopped by anyone.

Remotely piloted planes are not new, but their significance has grown enormously. They date back to near the end of World War I, when inventor Charles Kettering tested a pilotless biplane that he called the Kettering Bug. The term drone encompasses an array of technical terms for machines such as unmanned aerial vehicles (UAVs), remotely piloted vehicles (RPVs), and remotely operated aircraft (ROA). Larger drones the size of Cessnas (such as Predators and Reapers) are employed for both military missions and intelligence work. These drones carry two Hellfire missiles and precision-guided bombs to attack militant groups or even individuals. As we have seen earlier in this chapter, the U.S. president micromanages the use of drones by personally choosing their targets. American government planners are preparing for remotely piloted larger planes that could replace bombers and cargo planes, and even smaller ones – the size of butterflies – for spying inside closed spaces. U.S. infantry soldiers use five-pound backpack drones for tactical surveillance purposes, and even small surveillance drones, Cicadas, are used for collecting data on the ground.

The use of drones is proliferating. Not only have they been approved for domestic purposes inside the United States, but at least forty other countries, including Britain, China, India, Iran, Israel, Italy, Spain, and Turkey, are developing drones comparable to those used by the United States. The Pentagon says that it has about 7,500 drones that it has used to collect information and kill anonymously in Afghanistan, Iraq, Pakistan, and Yemen. The military and CIA have carried out more than three hundred strikes – both overt and covert – and killed an estimated three to four thousand people in a half dozen states (Figure 10.13). Both the military and CIA use these drones along with the more traditional U-2 spy planes to obtain detailed information about the enemy.[91] In theory, the Pentagon was supposed to act only in the war zones of Iraq and Afghanistan, while the CIA was allowed to act in other countries thought to be harboring terrorists, such as Somalia, Yemen, and Pakistan.

War has always been about enemies confronting each other with new technologies that create moral dilemmas. Clearly, the new pieces of equipment will not replace soldiers fighting on the ground, but they do present new issues. Battles can

[90] P. W. Singer, "Robots at War: The New Battlefield" in Strachan and Scheppers, *The Changing Character of War*, p. 334.

[91] P. W. Singer, *Wired for War: The Robotics Revolution and Conflict in the 21st Century* (New York: Penguin, 2009).

Figure 10.13 A recent exhibition of new security technology in Manama, Bahrain, included drones and other unmanned vehicles, anti-riot equipment, and weapons detection systems for airports. Some of these items were used in Manama for putting down demonstrations in 2010–12.

now be fought without any contact between the combatants, and unmanned vehicles, ships, and warplanes are troubling for many reasons. In the early 20th century the bombing of civilians by aircraft became acceptable to the mass public – if, of course, it was done for a supposedly right or just cause. Hiroshima and Nagasaki followed. In the war in Afghanistan, U.S. missiles from unmanned drones have killed more than seven hundred civilians in Pakistan.[92] Killing enemies in warfare is not a crime, but killing people who are not proven to be members of al-Qaeda or affiliate operatives in countries that are not part of the battlefield is questionable. The use of drones in sovereign countries that are not at war with the United States raises contentious legal issues, and many experts believe that explicit rules need to be developed for targeting individuals, whether foreigners or U.S. citizens.

The new forms of weaponry concern not just how countries fight but even whom they fight. They keep their own soldiers out of danger while making it easier to kill enemies – a sop to the casualty-averse Western publics. But, this gives rise to new complex dilemmas. The *unmanning* of war affects both sides – the attackers and the attacked. There is already an impression in some countries that Americans are cold blooded or coldhearted, and the use of unmanned drones has increased this perception. The use of drones has been a radicalizing force in some Muslim countries.

[92] For a critique of this policy, see Peter Bergen and Katherine Tiedemann, "Washington's Phantom War: The Effects of the U.S. Drone Programme in Pakistan," *Foreign Affairs* 90, no. 4 (July–August 2011), pp. 12–18.

There are many unanswered questions. How is international law affected by the use of this technology? What is the human role in war if autonomous robots or planes kill combatants? How would a court or judge apportion blame for noncombatants killed by drones? How does one establish accountability when pilotless planes in Afghanistan, Pakistan, and Yemen are manned from buildings inside the United States? If a missile hits the wrong target, who is responsible? The operator? Senior military commanders? Political leaders? The inventor?

Questions concerning these new weapons and the purposes to which they are put seem almost endless.[93] What exactly is the extent of the battleground in an expansive war on terrorism? Has the use of such weapons changed warfare permanently? Is riskless warfare a change as significant as the invention of nuclear weapons? Is it evolutionary or revolutionary? Does it tell us anything about the nature of security policy and perhaps even humanity today or is it just one more minor change in the character of war?

[93] For a fascinating account of the roles of these drones, see Jane Mayer, "The Predator of War," *The New Yorker* (October 26, 2009), pp. 36–45.

Select bibliography

Ashraf, Ghani, and Clare Lockhart, *Fixing Failed States* (Oxford: Oxford University Press, 2008).

Barfield, Thomas, *Afghanistan: A Cultural and Political History* (Princeton, NJ: Princeton University Press, 2010).

Billitteri, Thomas J., "Drone Warfare," in *Global Issues* (Washington DC: CQ Press, 2011).

Boot, Max, *Invisible Armies: An Epic History of Guerilla Warfare from Ancient Times to the Present* (New York: Liveright, 2013).

Bruton, Bronwyn E., *Somalia: A New Approach* (Washington, DC: Brookings Institution, 2010).

Collier, Paul, and Nicholas Sambanis, eds., *Understanding Civil War: Evidence and Analysis*, 2 vols. (Washington, DC: World Bank, 2005).

David, Steven R., *Catastrophic Consequences: Civil Wars and American Interests* (Washington, DC: Johns Hopkins University Press, 2008).

Evans, Gareth, *The Responsibility to Protect: Ending Mass Atrocity Crimes Once and for All* (Washington, DC: Brookings Institution Press, 2009).

Friedman, George, and Meredith Friedman, *The Future of War: Power, Technology, and American Dominance in the 21st Century* (New York: St. Martin's, 1998).

Freedman, Lawrence, *A Choice of Enemies: America Confronts the Middle East* (New York: Public Affairs, 2008).

Gordon, Michael, and Bernard Trainor, *Cobra II: The Inside Story of the Invasion and Occupation of Iraq* (Washington, DC: Vintage, 2006).

Hagan, John, and Wenona Rymond-Richmond, *Darfur and the Crime of Genocide* (Cambridge: Cambridge University Press, 2009).

Hass, Richard N., *War of Necessity, War of Choice: A Memoir of Two Iraq Wars* (New York: Simon & Schuster, 2009).

Hersch, Seymour, *Chain of Command: The Road from 9/11 to Abu Ghraib* (London: HarperCollins, 2005).

Holmqvist-Jonsater, Caroline, and Christopher Coker, eds., *The Character of War in the 21st Century: Paradoxes, Contradictions and Continuities* (London: Routledge, 2009).

Ignatieff, Michael, *Empire Lite: Nation-Building in Bosnia, Kosovo, and Afghanistan* (London: Vintage, 2003).

Jackson, Robert, and Philip Towle, *Temptations of Power: The United States in Global Politics after 9/11* (New York: Palgrave, 2006).

Jones, Seth G., *In the Graveyard of Empires: America's War in Afghanistan* (New York: W. W. Norton, 2009).

Kaldor, Mary, *New and Old Wars: Organized Violence in the Global Era* (Cambridge, UK: Polity Press, 2009).

Kilcullen, David, *The Accidental Guerrilla: Fighting Small Wars in the Midst of a Big One* (Oxford: Oxford University Press, 2009).

Lieven, Anatol, *Pakistan: A Hard Country* (London: Allen Lane, 2011).

Murphy, Martin N., *Somalia: The Barbary? Piracy and Islam in the Horn of Africa* (London: Eland, 2011).

Nagel, John A., *Counterinsurgency Lessons from Malaya and Vietnam: Eating Soup with a Knife* (Westport, CT: Praeger, 2002).

Ramadan, Tariq, *Islam and the Arab Awakening* (Oxford: Oxford University Press, 2012).

Rashid, Ahmed, *Descent into Chaos: The United States and the Failure of Nation Building in Pakistan, Afghanistan and Central Asia* (New York: Viking, 2009).

———, *Fiasco: The American Military Adventure in Iraq* (New York: Penguin, 2006).

Ricks, Thomas E., *The Gamble: General David Petraeus and the American Military Adventure in Iraq, 2006–2008* (New York: Penguin, 2009).

Sanger, David, *Confront and Conceal: Obama's Secret Wars and Surprising Use of American Power* (New York: Crown, 2012).

Sarkees, Mersith Reid, and Frank Whelon Wayman, *Resort to War* (Washington, DC: CQ Press, 2009).

Semple, Michael, *Reconciliation in Afghanistan* (Herndon, VA: U.S. Institute of Peace Press, 2009).

Singer, P. W., *Wired for War: The Robotic Revolution and Conflict in the Twenty-First Century* (New York: Penguin, 2011).

Slim, Hugo, *Killing Civilians: Method, Madness, and Morality in War* (London: Hurst, 2008).

Stiglitz, Joseph E., and Linda Bilmes, *The Three Billion Dollar War: The True Cost of the Iraq Conflict* (New York: Norton, 2008).

Walter, Barbara F., and Jack Snyder, eds., *Civil Wars, Insecurity, and Intervention* (New York: Columbia University Press, 1999).

Walter, Barbara, *Committing to Peace: The Successful Settlement of Civil Wars* (Princeton, NJ: Princeton University Press, 2002).

Woodward, Bob, *Bush at War* (New York: Simon and Schuster, 2002).

Wright, Lawrence, *Looming Tower* (New York: Vintage, 2006).

11

Terrorism and counterterrorism

On September 11, 2001, the world watched in horror as terrorists hijacked commercial aircraft and flew them into the twin towers of the World Trade Center in New York's financial district and the Pentagon in Washington, DC, and caused another plane to crash in Pennsylvania. Foreign terrorists took at least 2,996 American lives that day, and their audacity thrust terrorism firmly into public consciousness. Until then, studies of global security had been based primarily on analysis of state power as measured by factors such as economic, diplomatic, and military capabilities. Since then, there has been a shift to try to understand new forms of warfare, and international violence has become an important focus of global studies. Today, terrorism and counterterrorism are central features of international security.

Terrorism is not a goal or end in itself. It is a means or tactic to achieve a desired consequence or end state. Terrorists, by definition and necessity, employ asymmetrical warfare: while great powers have vast sums of money and advanced weaponry at their disposal, all terrorists possess is their commitment; their lives (which they may sacrifice in suicidal attacks); and relatively small, unsophisticated weapons. There are, however, grave concerns that terrorists may obtain weapons of mass destruction (WMD). Unlike insurgencies and civil wars (discussed in Chapter 10), terrorism is not aimed at obtaining control of a territory or state. Its proponents attempt to frighten governments into believing that unless they change their approach to politics there will be further violence. Terrorist methods commonly include kidnapping, bombings, arson, and hijacking airliners to create public fear and to force governments to respond to their demands; today they include cyberattacks on computer and data systems. Since terrorists do not represent states, and by definition are less powerful than the states they attack, standard patterns of responding to them may be inappropriate and ineffective. Against whom or what does a state retaliate? Dealing with terrorists has also created new issues in the fields of prisoners, torture, civil liberties, and international law.

Basically, there are two contrasting public policy approaches to terrorism: a military response and a more moderate approach based on a combination of diplomacy, aid, intelligence, and law enforcement. The response of the United States to 9/11 included both – President George W. Bush declared a "war on terror," but he also set up a new government department of Homeland Security to be responsible for domestic security, and initiated other less aggressive approaches. Over time, he modified his vocabulary so that the initial declaration of a "war on terror" became a "global struggle against violent extremism."[1] Later,

---

[1] Debates about how to conquer terrorism are extensive. See, for example, Philip B. Heyman, "Dealing with Terrorism: An Overview," *International Security* 26, no. 3 (Winter 2001–2), pp. 24–38; Barry R. Posen, "The Struggle against Terrorism: Grand Strategy, Strategy and Tactics," *International Security* 26, no. 3 (Winter 2001–2), pp. 39–55; Stephen M. Walt, "Beyond bin Laden: Reshaping U.S. Foreign Policy," *International Security* 26, no. 3 (Winter 2001–2), pp. 56–78.

President Barack Obama modified this further to "overseas contingency operations," before eventually reverting to the earlier terminology of the United States "at war."

In this chapter we survey the definition and history of terrorism, explain who today's terrorists are, and explore the causes of terrorism before turning to a discussion of counterterrorism. We include data and analysis of worldwide terrorist organizations, in particular radical Islamist movements such as al-Qaeda, and analyze the policy approaches to terrorism taken by the United Nations and the United States. The possible use of WMDs by terrorists, especially strategies to confront nuclear terrorism, are also explored, as well as specific controversial issues related to these topics – including the pros and cons of homeland security measures, unlawful enemy combatants, and prison abuses. Cyberterrorism and piracy are considered, and we take a Close Up look at relevant issues in Yemen. Throughout the chapter, arguments about whether terrorism can be defeated are foremost, but, however desirable, terrorism can never be eliminated entirely, as witnessed by the 2013 bombings at the Boston marathon.

Terrorism as a concept and history

Terrorism is a controversial and ambiguous concept. It tends to embody such an odious perception of a designated enemy that it justifies a broad array of violent responses. A standard academic definition (there are many from which to choose) is that terrorism is the systematic use of violence or threat of violence against civilians and/or states to obtain political concessions.[2] The concept does not include spontaneous, purposeless violence such as riots or other random or criminal activities. It can be carried out by individuals, nongovernmental organizations, and groups, or even covert government agents, but the term does not include acts by military personnel in wartime. The Japanese kamikazes, or suicide pilots, in World War II who killed more than fifteen thousand people were not terrorists because they were military personnel attacking enemy military personnel, not civilians. Nor is it called terrorism when military actions accidentally result in civilian

deaths, because there is no intent to kill innocent bystanders. Such acts are classified as war crimes, coming under principles about the proper conduct of war (discussed in Chapter 9).

Terror was not always considered the activity of subnational groups against states or individuals. When the term *La Terreur* was first coined for Robespierre's Committee of Safety during the 18th-century French Revolution (Figure 11.1), it referred to the indiscriminate murder of civilians and bystanders by the government of the day.[3] In other words, the authorities used mass executions by guillotine or drowning to terrorize their own people. It was state-inspired and state-condoned terrorism. Authoritarian regimes in Nazi Germany and the communist Soviet Union perfected this form of terrorism against their own citizens. Over the years, however, the term *terrorism* evolved to its present meaning of nonstate actors, not states, being its main perpetrators. Today, political scientists use the term state terrorism to describe violence carried out by governments or clandestine operatives working for governments against other states or their

[2] Bruce Hoffman, "Defining Terrorism," in *Terrorism and Counterterrorism: Understanding the New Security Environment*, ed. Russell D. Howard and Bruce Howard (Boston: McGraw-Hill, 2012), p. 5; Robert J. Jackson and Doreen Jackson, *Introduction to Political Science: Comparative and World Politics* (Scarborough, ON: Prentice Hall, 2008), p. 439.

[3] A scholar has traced the history of terrorism back to the Sicarii sect of Zealots in the years 66–73 CE. See Grant Wardlaw, *Political Terrorism* (Cambridge: Cambridge University Press, 1989), p. 18.

Figure 11.1 Execution by decapitation, the major method of execution during the French Revolution, was used in France until 1981. The first conception of terrorism, therefore, was based on the idea that states execute their own citizens. *Source:* Alamy.

citizens. The U.S. Department of State lists countries it deems guilty of state terrorism, as do other countries. Over the years, the U.S. list has included Cuba, Iran, Libya, North Korea, Syria, and Sudan. Iran is constantly included, as it sponsors the Islamic Revolutionary Guard's Qods Force, which cultivates and supports violent jihadist Islamic groups in the Middle East.

Terrorism is based on motivations such as ideology, religion, and nationalism, and its targets include politicians, statesmen, and innocent bystanders. The term has come to imply that all acts of terrorism are heinous, but it must be borne in mind that in some cases (e.g., the French Resistance during World War II), the purpose behind the action may be noble, even when the methods

are horrific. In fact, a proposed UN convention on terrorism has been stalled since 1997 precisely because some member states will not allow terrorism to be defined by the *nature* of the act but only by its *purpose*. These states believe that struggles against occupation or a racist regime or for national liberation do not constitute terrorism. A suicide bomber should not be considered a terrorist, according to these observers, if the act is carried out for a righteous reason such as liberation or to resist foreign occupation. Opponents of a UN definition argue that governments anathematize all asymmetrical warfare, and therefore any definition of what terrorism is, or who terrorists are, is automatically politically motivated and biased. As the cliché goes, "one person's terrorist is another person's freedom fighter." However, in 2001 the UN set up a counterterrorism committee and has developed international rules to try to contain such violent behavior. It has passed conventions to protect airports, diplomats, and transportation of people and goods (especially nuclear material), and it has found ways to block the funding of terrorist organizations, even though it has not been able to agree on a definition of terrorism.[4]

The events of 9/11 showed that the world was more dangerous and less predictable than imagined. The United States began to focus intensively on al-Qaeda and the elimination of terrorism. Shortly after 9/11, U.S. president George W. Bush declared, "Our responsibility to history is already clear: to answer these attacks and rid the world of evil."[5] This extremely broad goal led to the Global War on Terror. The wide American net included "evil" enemies of the civilized world; the al-Qaeda network; other terrorist organizations of a global, regional, or local scope; rogue states (including Iraq, Iran, and North Korea, and other unnamed countries); as well as, in a general way, terrorism as a phenomenon and WMDs. All of these groups and states were

[4] See http://www.un.org on terrorism, and http://www.un.org/secureworld on high-level threats.
[5] United States, *National Security Strategy* (Washington D.C., 2011), p. 5.

mentioned at one time or another as undifferenti-ated threats to the United States – evils that had to be totally eliminated. The approach involved more than mere rhetoric and political propaganda; it had a direct effect on U.S. foreign and defense policy. Officially, the U.S. government defined terrorism as "premeditated, politically motivated violence perpe-trated against noncombatant targets by sub-nation-al groups or clandestine agents, usually intended to influence an audience."[6] This definition excluded states or countries as perpetrators.

This comprehensive approach to terrorism was accompanied by a U.S. switch from the established foreign policy strategy of containment and deter-rence to a preventive strike strategy. This new, preventive counterterrorism policy found its first expression in the 2003 invasion of Iraq. As we saw in Chapter 10, Iraq did not provoke the aggres-sion, but rather the United States used the new antiterrorism policy and a belief that Iraq possessed WMDs to justify a preventive war on Iraq. When no WMDs were found in Iraq, the U.S. administration shifted its justification for the attack to the need to eliminate the regime of Saddam Hussein and destroy its supposed nexus with terrorism. The claim that Iraq posed a direct or imminent threat to the United States was quietly dropped.[7] U.S. Secretary of State Colin Powell made a powerful speech at the United Nations in defense of the idea that there were WMDs in Iraq, but later he called the speech a painful blot on his record.[8]

From old to new terrorism

Today, we are more familiar with hostage taking and suicide bombing as terrorist tactics than with

[6] The U.S. government published three documents that structured the U.S. response to terrorism after 9/11: (1) *The National Security Strategy of the United States of America*, (2) *The U.S. National Strategy for Combating Terrorism*, and (3) *National Strategy to Combat Weapons of Mass Destruction*. See U.S. National Counterterrorism Center site at http://www.nctc.gov.

[7] For a retrospective view of the period, see Melvyn P. Lafler, "9/11 in Retrospect: George W. Bush's Grand Strategy, Recon-sidered," *Foreign Affairs* 90, no. 1 (September–October 2011), pp. 33–44.

[8] *The Globe and Mail*, September 10, 2005.

the French guillotine or the Russian gulag, but their objectives are similar. Terror is used by individuals or groups, and sometimes states, in an attempt to force governments, domestic or foreign, to alter their policies according to the terrorist demands or sometimes for revenge. Their methods are varied. Well-known examples from the past quarter-century include the following:

- 1973: Arab terrorists killed thirty-two people while trying to attack a U.S. aircraft at a Rome airport.

- 1976: Terrorists hijacked a French plane, flew it to Uganda, and said they would kill the hostages unless prisoners in Israel were released.

- 1984: Extremists of the Irish Republican Army blew up the Grand Hotel in Brighton, England, where the Conservative Party was meeting with Prime Minister Margaret Thatcher.

- 1985: An Air India plane was bombed off the coast of Ireland and 329 people died.

- 1988: Pan Am Flight 103 was blown up over Lockerbie, Scotland, by a concealed bomb placed aboard by a Libyan.

- 1995: Bombing of a federal building in Oklahoma City, Oklahoma.

- 1995: Sarin gas was used to attack passengers in a Tokyo subway – thousands were infected and twelve died.

- 1998: American embassies were bombed in Tan-zania and Kenya.

- 2001: Chechens took over a school in Beslan, Russia, and more than three hundred people (in-cluding many schoolchildren) were killed during the rescue attempt.

- 2008: Terrorists attacked hotels and other estab-lishments in Mumbai, India, killing more than 160 people.

- 2009: A single-person assault at Fort Hood mili-tary base resulted in thirteen deaths before the terrorist was killed.

- 2009: The Nigerian "underwear bomber" tried to set off a bomb on a Northwest Airlines aircraft en route to Detroit on Christmas Day.

Figure 11.2 The recent rise in terrorist bombings can be explained by several factors, including the appeal of radical jihadist ideology and al-Qaeda. The 7/7 attacks in London, UK, created immediate widespread fear but, like 9/11, they were not accompanied by any specific political demands. *Source:* Corbis.

These examples illustrate that terrorism has become a frequent occurrence and that its definition and form vary dramatically (Figure 11.2).[9] Violence sometimes has been used to demand specific or general concessions, but at other times it has been employed as a form of reprisal against the citizens of a state because of its foreign policies or even its very existence. The 1976 hijacking of a French airplane was accompanied by specific demands, while the Tokyo subway terrorists and Air India bombings were not. On September 11, 2001, terrorists escalated the magnitude and carnage of the attacks when they flew hijacked commercial aircraft into the twin towers of New York's World Trade Center and the Pentagon in Washington, DC, without making any demands. Innocent bystanders were the targets of hatred because they symbolized the perceived wickedness of the United States.

Terrorism is disproportionally feared because it seems random, sudden, indiscriminate, and lethal. "Kill one; frighten ten thousand," as a Chinese proverb described it. Terrorists use fear as a weapon. In fact, fear became so great in the years immediately following 9/11 that the terrorists did not need to do anything. Mere media reports about possible terrorist attacks were frequent and hysterical enough to cause stock markets to fall, aircraft flights to be canceled, and even hospitals and schools to be closed. State and police actions followed up on such reports to meet public demands that "something had to be done," and governments feared that they would be accused of complacency if they did not act decisively. Clearly, terrorism today needs to be understood in terms of both the actual violence used and that which is implied or feared.[10] But perhaps people and governments today are more worried about terrorism than they should be; both are continually prodded by a media fascination with terrorism often bordering on the macabre. They tend to be particularly nervous of irregular, dramatic events such as terrorism but less so of everyday events such as driving down the highway

[9] Russell D. Howard and Margaret J. Nenckek, "The New Terrorism," in *Weapons of Mass Destruction and Terrorism*, 2nd ed., ed. J. F. Forest and Russell D. Howard (New York: McGraw-Hill, 2013).

[10] Andrew H. Kydd and Barbara F. Walter, "The Strategies of Terrorism," *International Security* 31, no. 1 (Summer 2006), pp. 49–80.

Close Up 11.1 **The new face of terrorism**

"Once upon a time even terrorism was subject to certain rules. True, they were not always observed, but few people boasted of openly defying them. Terrorism was mainly directed against individuals representing tyrannical regimes (or those believed to be tyrannical). If innocent bystanders were killed or wounded, this was not done intentionally."[11]

The author of this quotation, Walter Laqueur, argues that the rules for terrorism have changed dramatically with the growth of religious fanaticism and the development of weapons of mass destruction. "New terrorism" is better financed than earlier terrorism, and weapons are more sophisticated and lethal. Innocent bystanders have become targets.

Consider the destruction of the World Trade Center in New York on September 11, 2001; the attacks on transportation systems in Britain and Spain in 2005; on hotels in Mumbai, India, in 2009; or the Boston marathon bombings of 2013. Do these incidents indicate that the nature of terrorism has changed? How? If so, what can and should be done about it?

Table 11.1 **Terrorists methods**

1. Hostage taking
2. Hijacking aircraft or other means of transportation
3. Explosive Attacks: improvised bombs, "dirty" or radiological bombs, nuclear detonation
4. Biological attack: anthrax, flu pandemic, pneumonic plague
5. Chemical attack: blister agents, toxic industrial chemicals, nerve agent, food contamination, foot-and-mouth disease, chlorine tank explosion
6. Cyberattack
7. Violent, sophisticated simultaneous strikes, including "swarming" – small units hitting a target from several directions or attacking several targets at the same time
8. Suicide missions

or going to a ball game. Yet people are more likely to die from murder, suicide, a car accident, or even a lightning strike at a sports match than they are by terrorism in the United States. The "new" terrorism described by Walter Laqueur (discussed in Close Up 11.1) and the variety of "methods" listed in Table 11.1 have increased this public fear.

Modern terrorist incidents

Successful terrorist attacks reap massive publicity for their perpetrators' ideologies and causes. Terrorism is a low-cost activity with a high potential for winning useful tactical and perhaps even strategic objectives. Successful ventures have the potential to attract

followers, impress donors, and sometimes extort large sums of money to finance the purchase of weapons and expand their campaigns. Despite the evident difficulties of achieving worldwide agreement on definitions, and therefore an objective standard for describing the phenomenon of terrorism, the overwhelming conclusion is that there has been considerable terrorism during the past decade. The **Global Terrorism Database (GTD)**, the most comprehensive database, recorded 11,604 attacks worldwide in 2010. Its definition of terrorism was "premeditated, politically motivated violence perpetrated against noncombatants by subnational groups or clandestine agents." These attacks resulted in at least 49,901 people killed, injured, or kidnapped (see Table 11.2) . The same year the number of terrorist attacks in Afghanistan and Iraq held steady, with 2,688 attacks in Iraq that killed or injured 15,109 people. In Afghanistan there were 3,307 attacks and 9,016 people killed or injured. Sunni Muslim extremists accounted for 60 percent of worldwide violence, and suicide bombing was the most lethal method used.

---

[11] Walter Laqueur, "The New Face of Terrorism," *Washington Quarterly* (Autumn 1998), p. 169.

Table 11.2 Incidents of terrorism worldwide, 2008–10			
Incident	2008	2009	2010
Total attacks worldwide	11,662	10,969	11,604
Attacks resulting in death, injury, or kidnapping of at least one person	8,358	7,874	8,249
People killed, injured, or kidnapped as a result of terrorism	54,263	58,711	49,901

Source: Adapted from data published by the U.S. Department of State's Country Reports on Terrorism 2010 (National Counterterrorism Center: Annex of Statistical Information), http://www.state.gov.

Thousands of volumes have been written on terrorism, and research in the field is diverse and sometimes contradictory. The major topics that experts examine are organization, leadership, demography, ideology, operations, communications, weapons, funding, and external support.[12] As Table 11.3 shows, terrorism occurs throughout the world and comes in many guises. While the primary goals of terrorists vary immensely, all attacks are intended to signal that they have the strength and will to carry out their purposes.[13] Historically, terrorism has been associated with a variety of economic goals, such as destroying the capitalist system, and with messianic goals, such as holy war. In the 21st century, terrorism has been used less to obtain political concessions and more as a manifestation of rage and revenge against the citizens and leaders of despised states. This has brought a rise in suicide bombings, which currently account for about half of all deaths caused by terrorism (see Tables 11.3 and 11.4).

[12] Bonnie Cordes, Brian M. Jenkins, and Konrad Kellen, *A Conceptual Framework for Analyzing Terrorist Groups* (Santa Monica, CA: RAND, 1985).

[13] Andrew H. Kydd and Barbara F. Walter, "The Strategies of Terrorism," *International Security* 31, no. 1 (Summer 2006), pp. 49–80.

Causes of terrorism

Many ideas have been put forward to explain why people become terrorists and what motivates their actions. Because the paths to radicalization are many and complex, the approaches have been at the individual, group, state, and global levels and are often a mix of all four explanations.

At the individual level, one prominent view argues that terrorism is psychopathological, proffering that crazy people and fanatics engage in such seemingly purposeless slaughter of strangers. Some, therefore, attribute terrorist activities to personality imbalances or specific motivations, such as revenge or deep and perhaps psychotic attachment to extremist causes. At the group or organizational level, it has been posited that some groups simply believe that terrorism is the best or even most rational strategy to fulfill their goals or objectives. After all, even a partly botched terrorist operation gets publicity from sensational news coverage.[14] However, neither theory has proved why some individuals or organizations choose violent means to obtain their goals while others do not. The reasons people join terrorist organizations, and especially why they are prepared to die for their causes, are complex. Both personal motivations and the ideology of the organization are obviously involved, but while these are useful arguments, others have found conclusively that neither personal nor rational group arguments are *sufficient* explanations for terrorism.[15] It is well known that

[14] See Max Abrahams, "What Terrorists Really Want: Terrorist Motives and Counterterrorism Strategy," *International Security* 32, no. 4 (Spring 2008), pp. 78–105; and subsequent debates on the topic in "What Makes Terrorists Tick," *International Security* 33, no. 4 (Spring 2009), pp. 180–202.

[15] See Martha Crenshaw, "Theories of Terrorism: Instrumental and Organizational Approaches," in *Inside Terrorist Organizations*, ed. David C. Rapoport (London: Frank Cass, 1988); Farwaz A. Gerges, *The Far Enemy: Why Jihad Went Global*: (Cambridge: Cambridge University Press, 2005), *Suicide Bombers in Iraq* (Washington, DC: United States Institute of Peace, 2007); Mohammad M. Hafez Assaf Moghadam, *The Globalization of Martyrdom* (Baltimore: Johns Hopkins University Press, 2008); Amy Pedahzur, ed., *Root Causes of Suicide Terrorism: The Globalization of Martyrdom* (New York: Routledge, 2006). Marc Sageman, *Leaderless Jihad: Terror Networks in the Twenty-First Century* (Philadelphia: University of Pennsylvania Press, 2008).

Table 11.3 Types of ideological and nationalist terrorist groups

Non-Islamic Organizations	Primary State/Region	Targets/Actions
Emarat Kavkaz (radical Islamist Chechen)	Chechnya, Russia	Separatist
Communist Party of Philippines/ New People's Army (CPP/NPA)	Rural areas in northern Philippines, cells in cities	Ideological – opposes U.S. military presence and targets U.S. personnel
Euzkadi Ta Askatasuna (ETA)	Spain, mostly in Basque north-east	Nationalist
Irish Republican Army (IRA) (defunct)	Northern Ireland and United Kingdom	Nationalist and separatist – bombings
Kurdish Workers' Party (PKK)	Turkey, Iraq, and Syria	Nationalist – violence and bombings, advocates a Kurdish homeland
Revolutionary Armed Forces of Colombia (FARC)	Colombia; some activities in Brazil, Venezuela, and Panama	Marxist – kidnapping, extortion, bombings, murder, drug trafficking
Tamil Tigers (LTTE) (defunct)	Sri Lanka	Defeated nationalists – suicide bombings
Weather Underground and Symbionese Liberation Army (defunct)	United States	Ideological – anarchical and leftist

terrorism is sponsored by some countries such as Iran and Syria. This fact alone is sufficient to support the contention that the state level of analysis needs to be examined to explain terrorism. Many scholars also believe that globalization and increasing integration are making terrorism more likely.

Following radical or Marxist approaches, some believe that economic deprivation and poverty are powerful incentives to violence, and they point to the fact that terrorism is often associated with the least developed parts of the world. However, such group or class action has often been shown to correlate more closely with middle-class ideologies and professions than with poverty. Fidel Castro was a teacher. Ernesto "Che" Guevara was a doctor. Most of the nineteen 9/11 terrorists were financially relatively well-off; Osama bin Laden himself was from a family of millionaires, and Ayman al-Zawahiri, who eventually became the leader of al-Qaeda, was a surgeon. Moreover, not every economically deprived or discontented group becomes violent. Nor does every grievance lead to terrorist action.

Most of the time, people are reconciled to their grievances or join in low-level political participation and do not participate in violence. Since many discontented groups do not become violent, even though they possess some or all of the expected characteristics, how can one determine which of them are inclined to be strife prone or violent? The literature is fairly conclusive that they are likely to be groups that seek an ideologically defined transformation of society. The objective conditions of economic and social deprivation alone do not predispose them to violence. As Peter C. Sederberg expresses it, discontent is less an objective condition than a state of mind.[16] Or as Ted Gurr put it, "What we expect more than what we experience affects our feelings of discontent."[17]

Discontent, strife, and eventually violence occur, therefore, when group identity and cohesion are

[16] Peter C. Sederberg, *Terrorist Myths* (Englewood Cliffs, NJ: Prentice Hall, 1989), p. 85.
[17] Ted Robert Gurr, *Why Men Rebel* (Princeton, NJ: Princeton University Press, 1970), pp. 217–49.

Table 11.4 **Types of radical Islamic terrorist organizations**

Radical Islamic Organizations	Primary State/Region	Targets/Actions
Abu Sayyaf	Southern Philippines	Terrorists – nationalist and Islamic, bombings.
Al-Qaeda: in Iraq, Saudi Arabia, the Arabian Peninsula, North Africa, the Magreb, and Yemen	Dispersed; Afghanistan, Indonesia, Iran, Iraq, North Africa, Pakistan, Syria, and Yemen	Formed by bin Laden; 9/11 attacks and bombings in North Africa, United States, Spain, United Kingdom, India, Yemen; Sunni foreign fighters active against U.S. forces
Asar Dine	Mali	Committed to destroy the Mali government
Hamas (Islamic Resistance Movement)	Israel and Palestine (Gaza)	Committed to create a Palestinian state; kills Israeli civilians, controls Gaza Strip; wins Palestinian elections (Sunni)
Hezbollah (Party of God; Islamic Jihad)	Lebanon	Links to Iran; dominates Lebanese politics
Islamic Courts	Somalia	Controlled most of Somalia in 2006; ousted within months (Sunni)
Al-Shabaab	Somalia	Radical jihadist militia – nationalist and religious ideology
Islamic Republic of Iran	Iran	Islamic revolution; since 1979 controls the state of Iran
Mahdi Army	Iraq	Active against government forces (Sunni)
Lashkar-e-Jhangi	Pakistan and tribal areas bordering Afghanistan	Active against Pakistan, United States
Lashkar-e-Taiba (LeT)	Pakistan and India	Ideology is to create a Muslim caliphate over the entire subcontinent of South Asia; Mumbai attack in 2008
Taliban: in Pakistan, Tehrik-e-Taliban	Afghanistan and Pakistan	Controlled Afghanistan; housed al-Qaeda until after 9/11; regrouped in Pakistan (Sunni)

motivated by an ideology. Ideology is defined as an organized set of ideas and values that purport to explain and evaluate social conditions and to propose guidelines for action. Violent extremist ideologies include beliefs that actions by an enemy may justify violence in the name of high moral principles. Identification refers to the way individuals empathize with the political conditions that affect others.[18] Studies of group alienation indicate that historical experiences

and normative convictions may interact with a group's relative economic deprivation to promote dissent and cause terrorism. A deprived group feels systematically blocked from obtaining what it considers its due. Such discontent – based on ideology and identification – may be found in many ethno-cultural, nationalist, and religious groups and individuals.

From this literature, one can conclude that the greater the ideological opposition to persistent deprivation, the greater belief there may be in the illegitimacy of the state and its institutions. The

[18] Sederberg, *Terrorist Myths*, p. 85.

more this ideology is buttressed by facilitating structures such as coherent organization, committed leadership, adequate resources such as weapons and funding, geographical proximity, and external support, the greater is the possibility that a strife-prone group can develop. Belief in a transformational ideology reduces terrorists' moral reservations and inhibitions about using violence. Osama bin Laden's message, "Hostility towards America is a religious duty, and we hope to be rewarded by God," is precisely the type of maxim that builds on ideology and identification.[19] Suicide bombers perhaps represent these broad characteristics at their most extreme. True, they cannot have the same satisfaction as a serial bomber, who is able to witness the mayhem he or she produces, but they generate great fear in their opponents because their desire to kill is greater than their will to live. As we see later in this chapter, large numbers of individuals are prepared to engage in suicide terrorism and have made this the choice method of modern terrorism.

Alienated individuals or groups that use violence should not necessarily be viewed as mentally deranged or psychotic. Their behavior is seldom, if ever, radically senseless or absurd.[20] Their choice of terrorism as a tactic is based on a calculation of its possible impact and that makes them rational acts.[21] Instead of dismissing terrorism as the product of deviant personalities or criminal behavior, we need to understand violent groups in terms of their social psychology.[22] Indeed, there have been very few lone terrorists; almost all have been linked to a group to which they had prior connections through other networks such as sports clubs, social organizations, schools, and religious affiliations.[23] Cycles of violence in the Middle East, North Africa, and South Asia are not isolated incidents provoked by the mentally deranged and fanatics; such high levels of violence are the result of widespread anger, hatred, and frustrations – emotions that are fomented over time through group suffering and often, but not always, are accompanied by experiences, sometimes vicarious, of extreme economic or social deprivation and persecution. Becoming a terrorist is obviously an individual choice and can be explained in terms of frustrations, grievances, religious piety, belief in political and economic change, nationalism, and even revolution. It can be learned in groups or on the Internet.

In this regard, one needs to be aware that perceptions of realities may be constructed. The distinction between myth and reality is not simple. Violence-prone individuals have unique understandings of what constitutes reality and unique interpretations of what is of value. In their "rational" understanding, all things come together in a worldview of good versus evil. Their mind-set provides elaborate explanations of why they hate someone or something, but it is the group's impact or influence on the individual that is most significant. Throughout history there have been hostile groups whose violent acts were based on feelings of injustice or hatred. Almost all religions, philosophies, and ideologies have attracted adherents prepared to shed the blood of others or die themselves for their cause. This at least partially explains why radical Islamist terrorists who hate what America stands for believe that jihad is reasonable – even necessary.

The increasing number and ferocity of religious terrorist groups may be difficult to comprehend in the West because the norms, rules, and organization of Western societies are to a large extent based on a well-established doctrine of separation of church and state which is reinforced by widespread secular

---

[19] Philip Jenkins, *Images of Terror: What We Can and Can't Know about Terrorism* (New York: Aldine de Gruyter, 2003); Walter Laqueur, *No End to War: Terrorism in the Twenty-First Century* (New York: Continuum, 2003).

[20] Michael Stohl, ed., *The Politics of Terrorism*, 3rd ed. (New York: Marcel Dekker, 1988), pp. 8–11. See also Charles Townshend, *Terrorism: A Very Short Introduction* (Oxford: Oxford University Press), p. 98.

[21] Mark Abrahms, "What Terrorists Really Want: Terrorist Motives and Counterterrorism Strategy," *International Security* 32, no. 4 (2008), pp. 78–105.

[22] See, for example, Richard E. Rubenstein, *Alchemists of Revolution* (New York: Basic Books, 1989).

[23] See Marc Sageman, *Leaderless Jihad: Terror Networks in the 21st Century* (Philadelphia: University of Pennsylvania Press, 2008), p. 86.

values. Religious terrorists derive inspiration, commitment, and resistance to compromise from their strong beliefs; if death for their cause is sacred, there is little to trouble them when it comes to destroying themselves and others in a suicide bombing.

Born of insecurity, terrorist organizations must, first, ensure their survival. Thus, they are usually loosely linked by a decentralized power structure that prioritizes secrecy and allows the subunits considerable autonomy of action. Individuals receive the benefits of group membership – camaraderie, a cloak of anonymity, the likelihood of diffusing blame within a large organization, collective meaning for their endeavors, support and justifications for their actions, the sharing of risky decisions, and perhaps the promise of salvation in a glorious afterlife.[24] At the very least, media coverage ensures a certain notoriety. Terrorist organizations have an amazing ability to regenerate themselves when attacked by the forces of power and authority. Because of their deep sense of threat and generational experiences of direct violence, they are always preparing for the worst. It is not just rational calculations that make a terrorist; individuals require loyalty and devotion to a cause greater than themselves. Fanaticism, the excess of loyalty to a cause and the will to risk anything for it, provides the glue for terrorist organizations – a desperate longing for a meaningful life.

A violent group must have both an ideology that can guide the actions of its members and the ability to attract financial resources. It has to believe that there are no other means of achieving its goals or policies. It needs committed leadership, adequate resources such as weapons, and geographical proximity to external support. Terrorists try to delegitimize the state and its institutions and often believe that only shocking and violent actions can gain them the respect and attention they think they deserve. If the government tries to repress them with brutality, a retribution-revenge cycle may begin in which the actions of each side are fueled by escalating

---

Box 11.1 Ingredients of terrorism

Ideology
Financial resources
Coherent organization
Leadership
Economic deprivation

---

demands for vengeance. In such a situation, the original reasons for the terrorists' actions may become less significant than the desire for revenge, and their persecution may widen their support among those who share their religion, ethnicity, nationality, or political beliefs.[25]

As we have seen, terrorism has come to refer to both the threat and the use of violence. Terrorists use the media or Internet to gain attention for their acts in the hope that they can intimidate a particular population or put enough pressure on the government to achieve their political desires. The growth of international media, especially television and the Internet, has made it much easier for terrorists to communicate to large audiences. The 1972 Palestinian attack on the Olympic Games in Munich was watched throughout the world because international television covered it from beginning to end – along with the Olympics. The event was filmed as *One Day in September*, one of the best documentaries of a terrorist attack and its aftermath. Similarly, the horrific image of the collapsing World Trade Center in New York on September 11, 2001, riveted attention around the world on that terrorist attack and remains an impartial symbol of success for future terrorists.

---

[24] Jonathan L. Freedman, J. Merrill Carlsmith, and David O. Sears, *Social Psychology* (Englewood Cliffs, NJ: Prentice Hall, 1970).

[25] Robert Pape's study of 315 suicide bombers worldwide has shown that suicide bombing has increased dramatically in the past two decades and that while these actions account for only 3 percent of all incidents, they produce 48 percent of all deaths caused by terrorism. He also shows that in recent years, suicide terrorism is more a product of foreign occupation than of Islamic fundamentalism. But it is almost certainly affected by both these variables. Robert A. Pape, *Dying to Win: The Strategic Logic of Suicide Terrorism* (New York: Random House, 2005).

Close Up 11.2 **Are pirates terrorists?**

Pirate attacks off the Horn of Africa have drawn the attention of security experts and military planners (Figure 11.3). Some have even called the region the new "Wild West." Of course, piracy is not new.[26] We are all familiar with books and entertainment about pirates of the 17th and 18th centuries, such as *Treasure Island* and *Captain Blood*, and are well acquainted with stereotypes of pirates with peg legs and eye patches. But there has been a modern revival of the practice.

Max Boot shows that 265 ships were attacked by pirates between 2007 and 2009. High-profile cases from his survey include a Saudi oil supertanker, a Ukrainian freighter loaded with tanks and other weapons, and the first attack against a U.S.-flagged ship in more than two hundred years (or since the Barbary pirates).[27] In the latter case, the twenty-member crew of the MV *Maersk Alabama* prevented pirates from taking over the boat but not before they had escaped with their captain. The USS *Bainbridge*, a guided missile destroyer, followed the pirates until naval snipers were able to shoot the pirates and rescue the captain.

Piracy has negative impacts on coastal and regional states and on the states whose flag vessels ply the waters. Why are cargo ships so vulnerable? First, the ships' personnel cannot prevent attacks – automation has reduced the size of crews, and civilian ships do not carry appropriate weapons. In fact, due to their inherent weaknesses, crews are instructed not to resist attacks. Second, local naval forces do not have the resources to protect shipping through their waters. Third, as Max Boot has

pointed out, international naval forces are supposed to protect shipping lanes, but they cannot cover the large stretches of sea between Somalia and India. Just off East Africa alone there are a million square miles of water that are "transited by over 33,000 cargo vessels every year."[28] Somalia's coast is some three thousand kilometers long, stretching from the Indian Ocean to the Gulf of Aden. It funnels a huge volume of shipping to and from the Strait of Bab el Mandeb leading to the Red Sea and the Suez Canal (through which 7.5 percent of the world's trade passes).

These pirates are called criminals, not terrorists, because their sole motivation is extortion, not forcing changes in government policies or personnel. However, they have links with terrorism. Somalia and Yemen (discussed in Chapter 10) are failing states with known jihadist training camps. Many of the pirates have ties to Al-Shabaab, an Islamic extremist group that controls much of southern Somalia and is alleged to have links with al-Qaeda.

The international response to piracy includes warships and other assets of thirty states or organizations, including the United States, NATO, and the European Union, as well as Russia, India, and Japan. They are coordinated through the **Shared Awareness and Deconfliction (SHADE)** program, which is located in Bahrain. The United Nations has passed several chapter 7 resolutions that authorize military forces to pursue pirates into Somalia's territorial waters and ashore, but so far they have had little effect.[29] The UN **Convention on the Law of the Sea (UNCLOS)** provides a comprehensive legal and political framework for the use and

---

[26] See Max Boot's excellent summary, "Pirates, Then and Now: How Piracy Was Defeated in the Past and Can Be Again," *Foreign Affairs* 88, no.4 (July–August 2009), pp. 94–107.
[27] *The New York Times*, April 13, 2009.
[28] Boot, "Pirates Then and Now," p. 95.
[29] UN Security Council Resolution 1851 provides authority for warships to enter the territorial waters of Somalia to deal with pirates with permission of the transitional government of Somalia.

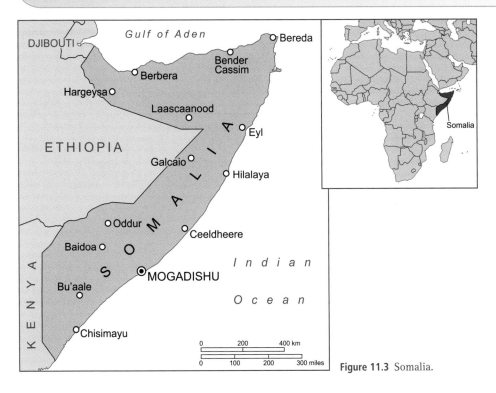

Figure 11.3 Somalia.

governance of all the oceans.[30] It confers rights and places obligations directly on coastal states and flagships but is inadequate for coastlines such as those of Somali and Yemen, where there is no effective government. The key general rule is that sailors from warships can board vessels of other states on the high seas only with the consent of the flag state. The waters off Somalia and Yemen may have become the most notorious, but piracy is also rife in many other parts of the world. Indeed, it is damaging commerce in practically every other water choke point in the world, especially in the area of the Strait of Malacca.

Is the growth of piracy just a minor nuisance, or should and can international organizations do something about it?

Who are the contemporary terrorists?

Terrorists have changed very little over time in terms of age, socioeconomic background, and education. This is not surprising. During the Cold War period, terrorists were overwhelmingly young, male, educated, and often from at least middle-class backgrounds.[31] Terrorism has always been dominated by young people. Indeed, that may be the only thing that has characterized all terrorists over time. Radical youth willing to devote their lives to the pursuit of universal goals in groups such as the German Baader-Meinhof Gang or the Italian Red Brigades have been prevalent over the years, and they are a fact of modern times. The average age of the nineteen terrorists who carried out the 9/11 attacks was 24.2.[32]

[31] Congressional Research Service, "Characteristics of Terrorists in the Cold War Period," http://www.fas.org/irp/threat/frd.html.
[32] Bruce Hoffman, "Who Fights? – A Comparative Demographic Depiction of Terrorists and Insurgents in the Twentieth and Twenty-First Centuries," in *The Changing Character of War*, ed. Hew Strachan and Sibylle Scheipers (Oxford: Oxford University Press, 2011), pp. 282–301.

[30] More than one thousand Somali pirates are serving prison sentences in eighteen different states. UNCLOS has been ratified by 160 members of the United Nations.

Box 11.2 **Basic characteristics of terrorist leaders**

Young
Homegrown or travelers
From financially well-off families
Well educated

Indeed, terrorists are nearly always in their twenties, and their leaders in their late twenties or early thirties. Bin Laden was twenty-seven when he first arrived in Pakistan.[33]

Terrorists can be home grown or travelers. The variety is astounding. In the July 2005 terrorist attack in London, three of the perpetrators were ethnic Pakistanis born in Britain, and the fourth was a British citizen born in Jamaica and converted to Islam. In the failed attack that followed two weeks later in the same city, the attackers included a British resident born in Somalia, an Ethiopian who posed as a Somali refugee to obtain residency, and a British citizen born in Eritrea and radicalized in prison. In the 2004 terrorist bombing of a train in Spain, most of the perpetrators were Moroccans, but there were also Spanish natives with no connection to international jihadism. Not all the leaders have been found, but among those arrested one was from Tunisia, and the others included both radical Muslims and petty criminals.

Porous borders, fake documents, and worldwide sympathizers provide global mobility for organized groupings of jihadist militants. They mix with diasporas in Western countries, nourishing and being nourished by them. Mobile immigrants and frustrated members of diasporas combine, providing recruits and sanctuaries for terrorist causes. Many offer no easy or obvious target for governments to attack, as they have no headquarters or perhaps even training sites in foreign countries.[34] So while

terrorists can come from many places, they are essentially of the same age and from a similar type of background. The popular stereotype that terrorists tend to be from poor backgrounds and be poorly educated is not true. As we have seen, their leaders tend to come from financially well-off families; to be employed; and to be well educated, if not highly educated.[35] Two-thirds of the terrorists involved in planning and hijacking the four aircraft on September 11, 2001, had attended university, two were enrolled in a PhD and two had obtained their doctorate.[36] As Bruce Hoffman puts it, "Persons with higher incomes and more education are more, not less, likely to join terrorist and insurgent groups."[37] And again, "The top leadership and mid-level command strata are populated by the educated (or relatively well educated) and financially well-off, while the majority of foot soldiers are less well educated and often from more modest socio-economic and educational backgrounds."[38]

Suicide bombers

Suicide bombings have increased significantly in the past decade and are one of the most shocking tactics in the terrorist arsenal. In modern times, this phenomenon can be said to have originated in Lebanon in the 1980s and spread around the world, but especially throughout the Middle East, North Africa, and Asia. It has been linked to radical religion-based groups such as Hezbollah, Hamas, al-Qaeda, and the overall radical Islamic jihad movement. During the past ten years, suicide attacks have occurred in at least thirty-five countries, with much greater loss of lives than in earlier suicide operations. As Assaf Moghadam has demonstrated, this increase is related to the rise of martyrdom on an international scale and is explained by two factors: the evolution of al-Qaeda as a global terrorist movement and a growth

---

[33] Ibid., p. 285.

[34] Martha Crenshaw, "Theories of Terrorism: Instrumental and Organizational Approaches," in *Inside Terrorist Organizations*, ed. David C. Rapoport (London: Frank Cass, 1988).

[35] Walter Laqueur, *Guerilla* (Boston: Little, Brown, 1976); Walter Laqueur, *The Age of Terrorism* (Boston: Little, Brown, 1987); Hoffman, "Who Fights?" pp. 286–7.

[36] Hoffman, "Who Fights?" p. 287.

[37] Ibid., p. 289.

[38] Ibid., p. 290.

Figure 11.4 Suicide bombing has become a tactic of choice in civil wars, particularly in Iraq and Afghanistan. This scene is from a suicide bomb attack in Kabul in May 2012. *Source:* Alamy.

in the appeal of *Salafi jihad*, the basic ideology of al-Qaeda and its affiliates.[39] The attack of 9/11 and later events in Afghanistan, India, Iraq, Pakistan, and Yemen indicate the degree to which suicide attacks have become entwined with modern global politics (Figure 11.4).

Al-Qaeda, perhaps more than any other terrorist group in history, has instilled a spirit of martyrdom among its followers. They are willing to give up their lives to carry out their missions. For them, suicide bombers are noble. They do not kill themselves for personal reasons, because that is forbidden by Islam; instead, they die for a cause, which makes suicide morally acceptable. They attain "martyrdom in the cause of God." As bin Laden put it, "Those youths know that their rewards in fighting you, the USA, is double their reward in fighting someone else. ... They have no intention except to enter paradise by killing you."[40]

In the November 2008 attack in Mumbai, India, one of the ten suicide bombers of the Pakistan-based Lashkar-e-Taiba (LeT) was captured

alive.[41] In his testimony to the court, he said, "Sir, I plead guilty." Azam Amir Kasab, a twenty-one-year-old Pakistani, then described how he joined the terrorist group for money and martyrdom. He learned how to use weapons in camps in Pakistan and then was selected to be one of the ten terrorists who sailed from Karachi, Pakistan (using inflatable dinghies) to launch the raid on India's financial capital, Mumbai. Under instructions from LeT leaders, he and his colleagues killed more than 160 people in attacks at the railway station, expensive hotels, a popular café, and a Jewish center with used AK-47 rifles and hand grenades. "Everything is being recorded by the media," one of the handlers told the gunmen. Inflict maximum damage. Keep fighting. Don't be taken alive. ... For your mission to be a success you must be killed."[42]

Recently, suicide bombings have been carried out mostly by followers of the philosophy of Salafi jihad, whose adherents adopt a strict interpretation of

[39] Assaf Moghadam, "Motives for Martyrdom," *International Security* 33, no. 3 (Winter 2008–9), pp. 46–78.
[40] Ibid., p. 61.

[41] For further discussion of the Mumbai massacre, see Bruce Riedel, "The Mumbai Massacre and Its Implications for America and South Asia," *Journal of International Affairs* 63, no. 1 (Fall–Winter, 2009), pp. 111–26.
[42] *The New York Times*, January 6, 2009.

Islamic law (see Chapter 8). They believe that there should be no division between state and religion, and they advocate violence rather than peaceful means of obtaining their objectives. They support suicide operations against both infidels and apostates. Assaf Moghadam's research on 1,857 suicide attacks between the years 1981 and 2008 found that 788 (37.7 percent) of incidents were justified in terms of the Salafi ideology. These jihadists were followed in numbers of suicide attacks by nationalist and/or separatist groups (18.5 percent) and hybrids (17.8 percent). Of the remaining 1,069 suicide incidences, 74.4 percent occurred in Iraq and were undoubtedly influenced to some extent by Salafi jihadism. In short, this one religious ideology has supplied the rationale for most suicide terrorism in recent years, and there has been a concomitant decline in other ideological justifications for suicide bombing (e.g., from nationalist and/or separatist and leftist and/or Marxist groups).

Al-Qaeda, affiliates, regional jihadists, and copycats

Al-Qaeda is the best-known terrorist group today.[43] Of the many types of terrorists groups, including nationalist, secessionist, and revolutionary, it is clearly of the religious variety.[44] While its followers come from many ethnicities and nationalities, they are true believers, fully committed to the cause and immune to compromise. Radical Muslim militants in general and al-Qaeda in particular profess disgust with the moral degeneracy of the West. Their actions are buttressed by the conviction that they are doing God's work and their acceptance of messianism – the imminent transformation of the world. Dying for a cause and killing enemies is believed to be not only rational but also sacred, hence their propensity for martyrdom and suicide bombing.

The al-Qaeda movement, more than a quarter-century old, is based on a radical internationalist ideology that combines theological justifications with political demands, focused especially on anti-Americanism. It was inspired by the teachings of the deceased Palestinian cleric Abdullah Azzam (bin Laden's mentor) to create an Islamic fighting force whose task was to defeat infidels and apostates wherever they were. Its religious thought is based on a radical fringe of Islam, a Salafist ideology of extreme antimodern fundamentalism. The movement quickly spread from the Middle East to Afghanistan and elsewhere in the 1980s. With at least partial support from the U.S. government, these young, radical Muslims converged on Afghanistan to carry out a jihad (holy struggle) against the Soviet occupiers. Many of them were led by Osama bin Laden (Figure 11.5), who redirected and subsequently prepared them to wage violence against the United States.

Al-Qaeda was initially funded from bin Laden's personal wealth, with additional financial support gradually coming from other contributors around the world. In the 1980s, neither the Saudi Arabian nor the Pakistani government tried to thwart al-Qaeda's efforts to recruit and train terrorists, raise money, and establish clandestine cells. Pakistani officials even provided military and intelligence assistance to both the Taliban and al-Qaeda in their fight against the Soviets in Afghanistan. After the war with Russia ended, many of the so-called Afghan Arabs returned to countries such as Egypt, Saudi Arabia, and Yemen and began to form clandestine pockets of radicals in their own countries. However, the top al-Qaeda leaders came to a strategic decision not to attack local Arab regimes but rather to concentrate on attacking Western infidels, especially Americans. To do so, they created widespread links with insurgents in South Asia and the Middle East. They set up terrorist training camps in Afghanistan and established a sophisticated global network of bank

---

[43] For an overview and conclusions about what policies to adopt toward this terrorist movement, see Audrey Kurth Cronin, "How al-Qaeda Ends: The Decline and Demise of Terrorist Groups," *International Security* 31, no. 1 (Summer 2006), pp. 7–48.

[44] Jonathan Randal, *Osama: The Making of a Terrorist* (New York: Knopf, 2004); Jason Burke, *Al-Qaeda: Casting a Shadow of Terror* (London: I. B. Tauris, 2004); Townshend, *Terrorism*, p. 98.

Figure 11.5 Osama bin Laden, the mastermind of 9/11, was killed by a U.S. Special Forces team on May 1, 2011. The debate today focuses on whether his ideas died with him or whether they live on in the minds of others. *Source:* Alamy.

accounts to allow money to move easily across borders.

The 9/11 terrorist attacks on the United States were the culmination of this escalating Islamic jihadist offensive. The year before, there had been an estimated 423 terrorist events around the world, almost half of which involved interests or citizens of the United States.[45] Many direct threats and three major terrorist offensives were made by radical Islamist groups against U.S. interests over the decade previous to 9/11. In February 1993, a group led by Ramzi Yousef tried to bring down the World Trade Centre; using a truck bomb, his group killed six and

injured more than one thousand. In August 1998, al-Qaeda terrorists drove truck bombs into U.S. embassies in Kenya and Tanzania, and in October 2000, al-Qaeda followers used explosives to blow a hole in the destroyer USS *Cole* in the Persian Gulf, killing seventeen military personnel.

In 1995, President Clinton signed Presidential Decision Directive 36, authorizing the unilateral use of force against terrorists. He later used it to justify missile attacks in response to the attacks in Kenya and Tanzania. However, bin Laden escaped, and plans for Special Force Operations to capture the terrorist leader were shelved without explanation. Between February 1993 and April 1998 the new Taliban government of Mullah Omar in Afghanistan declined to hand bin Laden over to the United States, despite several requests to do so. Then, on August 6, 2001, President Bush received a daily brief warning – "Bin Laden Determined to Strike in U.S." However, the warning was not taken seriously enough to prepare new emergency plans or to strengthen domestic security.[46]

The appalling events of 9/11 surpassed those at Pearl Harbor in 1941: at least 2,996 people died at the World Trade Center, the Pentagon, and on the aircraft downed in Pennsylvania. Whereas the Pearl Harbor attack was directed at military targets, the 9/11 attacks targeted civilians. As bad as it was, the high number of deaths was not unprecedented: the 1993–98 Rwanda massacres, for example, resulted in as many deaths of Tutsis and Hutus as took place in New York and Washington – but every day for one hundred days. What was unprecedented on September 11 was that the most powerful state in the world proved vulnerable to attack from outside its borders. It was the worst-ever terrorist attack on the United States, and it provided inspiration for other dissident groups around the world.[47]

[45] Each year the State Department reports to Congress on terrorism. See the annual *Patterns of Global Terrorism*. Of course, it may make mistakes in their assessment. See Alan B. Krueger and David D. Laitin, "Misunderstanding Terrorism," *Foreign Affairs* (September–October 2004), pp. 8–13.

[46] Robert J. Jackson and Philip Towle, *Temptations of Power: The United States in Global Politics since 9/11* (Basingstoke, UK: Palgrave, 2006), chapter 7.

[47] The second-largest terrorist attack on the United States killed 168 people in the Oklahoma City Federal Building in 1995, but it was planned and carried out from within the United States by an American citizen, Timothy McVeigh.

Much has been learned about al-Qaeda since 9/11. The organization has proved flexible, adaptive, and durable. After the U.S. invasion, some al-Qaeda members and their allies moved across the border to the remote regions of the Pakistani frontier, where they still continue their activities (see Chapter 10). According to the annual *Strategic Survey*, at least eighteen thousand individuals who trained in al-Qaeda camps remained at large in sixty countries after the invasion of Afghanistan.[48] Despite Western claims to have reduced the group's finances, bin Laden had stashed away billions of dollars before 9/11, of which only several million were confiscated. Since the United States destroyed the group's training bases in Afghanistan, al-Qaeda has attempted, mounted, or been blamed for terrorist attacks in Indonesia, Kuwait, Libya, Mali, Morocco, Saudi Arabia, Spain, Tunisia, Turkey, the United Kingdom,[49] Yemen, and the United States, as well as Afghanistan, Iraq, and Pakistan.

Al-Qaeda is not a hierarchical organization with a classic pyramid-style structure. It is not able to exercise absolute command and control over its branches and franchises. However, there is a degree of devolved authority over the network and the continued power of al-Qaeda's ideology.[50] Audrey Kurth Cronin summarizes the uniqueness of al-Qaeda as comprising three new components: the hybrid structure of a central core, the nebula, and indigenous volunteers. She stresses the importance of its radicalization and recruitment methods and its means of communication.[51] Al-Qaeda groups worldwide include al-Qaeda in the Arabian Peninsula, al-Qaeda in Iraq, al-Qaeda in the Islamic Maghreb, and al-Qaeda in Mesopotamia. It is known to have worked with the following extremist and insurgent groups: Afghan Taliban, Pakistani Taliban, Haqqani Network, Lashkar-e-Taiba, Harakat-ul-Jihad Islami, Islamic Movement of Uzbekistan, and Islamic Jihad Union.

Mali The actions of al-Qaeda in Islamic Maghreb (AQIM) may illustrate that al-Qaeda is making a comeback in parts of Africa (Figure 11.6). Mali is a critical country, as it is bordered by seven other fragile states that could also be threatened by al-Qaeda supporters. It has often combined tendencies to armed rebellion, poverty, and radical Islam. After the collapse of Gaddafi's Libya, nomadic Tureg and other fighters left that country with heavy weapons and moved back to their homes in the broad north African region known as the Sahel, and especially to Mali, which has often been considered one of the most stable democracies in Africa. In the spring of 2012, the AQIM joined forces with the other Islamist groups, especially the Ansar Dine, or Defenders of the Faith. The Tureg formed the National Movement for the Liberation of Azawad (NMLA) and took over control of much of northern Mali, including the historic cities of Timbuktu, Kindal, and Gao. The weak government forces of Mali could do little about the situation, because they were in disarray after a coup d'état in the capital Bamako. The AQIM quickly outmaneuvered the NMLA and began to impose strict Sharia law throughout the central and northern Saharan regions of Mali.

By spring 2012, the country was divided with three Islamist militias, dominated by al-Qaeda in the Mahgreb, holding the north while weak government

---

[48] Cited in Bruce Hoffman, "Al Qaeda and the War on Terrorism: An Update," *Current History* (December 2004), pp. 423–6.

[49] Prime Minister Tony Blair found parallels between the July incidents in London and the actions of the Irish Republican Army invidious. In the thirty-six years of the IRA's war, more than 3,600 people were killed in the name of national self-determination. The last bombs were set off in 1995, and the IRA said it would end its war in July 2005. In 1998 Sinn Féin, the political wing of the movement, signed the Good Friday Agreement and began to contest elections. Blair maintained that the IRA philosophy and methods differed entirely from those of the jihadist terrorists, as the freedom fighters had illegitimate demands and provided a different level of threat, especially in the use of suicide bombers. His distinction between freedom fighter and terrorist is one that many scholars contest.

[50] Leah Farrall, "How al Qaeda Works: What the Organization's Subsidiaries Say about Its Strength," *Foreign Affairs* 90, no. 2 (March–April 2011), pp. 128–37.

[51] Audrey Kurth Cronin, "What Is Really Changing? Change and Continuity in Global Terrorism," in *Changing Character of War*, Hew Strachan and Sibylle Scheipers (eds) (Oxford: Oxford University Press, 2011), p. 135.

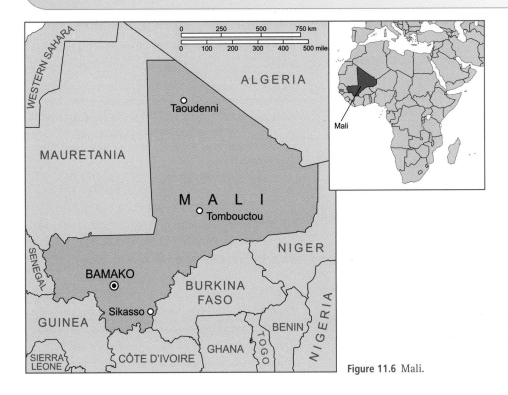

Figure 11.6 Mali.

forces controlled the south. The United Nations called for the consolidation of the country, and support for interim president of Mali, Dioncounda Traoré. It also helped with mediation efforts by African institutions, but the country was quickly developing the characteristics of a failed state. The UN Security Council unanimously approved a resolution supporting a French- and African-led military force to retake the country. By January 2013, they had taken over most of central Mali. However, holding the territory will be difficult with rapidly shifting developments in the vast desert and savanna of northern Mali, an area roughly the size of France.

What does al-Qaeda want? Does a worldwide al-Qaeda network exist and has it "franchised"? There certainly is a vast global audience for its exploits and those of its affiliates, with the Internet acting as a multiplier. What is startlingly new today is that there are now large Muslim diasporas born in or living throughout the developed world, and especially in Europe. Unknown numbers of them

– hundreds or perhaps thousands – have turned to radical jihadist Islam. Looking for universal truth, uprooted from their culture, frustrated by Western society, dejected, and not integrated in their homelands, these malcontents are a receptive audience for al-Qaeda and its messages. Radical Islamists include members and converts to al-Qaeda or regional organizations, disaffected youth with various levels of loyalty and commitment to jihadist causes, and simply angry and disoriented youth. There is no one type.

Because of their inchoate and ever-changing nature, the cells of such groups are difficult to penetrate or even monitor, as they often have no connection to a broader terrorist network and only minimal or no outside assistance with their attacks. They are often merely embryonic in nature, frequently existing without any defined organization. They are linked by their perceptions of injustice toward Muslims and their suffering, especially in Iraq, Afghanistan, Pakistan, and Palestine. One British Muslim reflected this when he pointed to his head and said of the underground bombers in London that "al-Qaeda is inside."[52]

Such alienated individuals can never be eliminated entirely in a free and democratic society. Their sanctuaries are ethnic or religious ghettos in which displaced immigrants and their children are cut off from the culture of their homeland – "internal colonies" as the *Economist* calls them.[53] In Britain, for example, Muslims constitute about 4.6 percent of the population (recall Close Up 8.1). To understand terrorists from such areas, there is a need to identify and address the fundamental causes of their violence and rebellion, why some are recruited to the jihadist cause, and how they are funded.

While individuals may be disaffected through poverty and isolation, we have seen that they also require an ideology to justify violence before they will act. Globalization, modernization, and Western imperialism provide these justifications, and there is no doubt that the war in Iraq and Afghanistan has helped radicalize a section of Muslim youth. Deep hatreds arise from fundamental grievances caused by perceived humiliation, poverty, and exclusion.[54] Former British prime minister Tony Blair referred to this idea when, after the London bombings of July 7, 2005, he admitted, "I'm not saying these things don't affect their warped reasoning and warped logic as to what they do, or that they don't use these things to try and recruit people."[55] They obviously do!

Modern terrorism as exemplified in al-Qaeda is an unwanted and unforeseen consequence of globalization, Western interventions in the developing world, and the steady march of modernity. The combined effects of these three circumstances on disaffected people, and especially religious groups, cannot be vanquished by war or occupation. Intervention in Muslim countries by those of other religious persuasions only compounds the problems and does not diminish them.

But what exactly does al-Qaeda want? In 1998, bin Laden explained his specific political grievances:

For over seven years the United States has been occupying the lands of Islam in the holiest of places, the Arabian Peninsula, plundering its riches, dictating to its rulers, humiliating its people, terrorizing its neighbours, and turning its bases in the Peninsula into a spearhead through which to fight the neighboring Muslim peoples.[56]

He went on to cite U.S. pro-Israel policies and its oppression and lack of recognition of the Palestinian people. His supporters defend Islamic states and Islamic causes in Asia and the Middle East, advance Palestinian causes, and advocate punishing the United States and its allies for supporting Muslim countries such as Saudi Arabia and the United Arab Emirates, which they consider corrupt. Yet the very terrorism employed against the American presence in the Muslim Middle East, climaxing in the 9/11 attacks, had the result of massively increasing that presence.

The death of Osama bin Laden

After a decade of trying to find and kill Osama bin Laden, the mastermind of 9/11 and the man who said "We – with God's help – call on every Muslim who believes in God and wishes to be rewarded to comply with God's order to kill the Americans and plunder their money wherever and whenever they find it,"[57] bin Laden was finally located and killed by a U.S. Special Forces team on May 1, 2011.[58] His body was flown to the USS *Vinson* and buried at sea. However, the death of bin Laden did not end terrorism or do away with al-Qaeda or its copycats. It may lead to its eventual decline, but threats of revenge quickly reverberated around the world. Anger and shame were especially pronounced in Pakistan, especially among its military and intelligence

[52] *The New York Times*, July 31, 2005.
[53] *The Economist*, July 16, 2005.
[54] Robert S. Leiken, "Europe's Angry Muslims," *Foreign Affairs* 84, no. 4 (July–August 2005), pp. 120–35.
[55] *The Globe and Mail*, July 27, 2005.

[56] Fatwa urging jihad against Americans. Cited in Jackson and Towle, *Temptations of Power*, pp. 131–2.
[57] *Los Angeles Times*, May 2, 2001.
[58] Mark Owen, *No Easy Day: The Firsthand Account of the Mission That Killed Osama bin Laden* (New York: Dutton, 2012).

Critical Case Study 11.1 **Yemen: Emerging safe haven for terrorists?**

Failing states are ideal havens for terrorist movements and suicide bombers. In Chapter 10 we discussed the cases of Somalia and Sudan. Yemen is another excellent example (Figure 11.7). Its own leader said that ruling the country was like "dancing on snake heads."[59] Osama bin Laden is popular there even today, and his advocate, American-born radical cleric Anwar al-Awlaki, brandished the slogan that American is "a nation of evil."[60] Until al-Awlaki was killed by a missile in 2011, he was widely feared by the West because of his perceived ability to shape the emotions of alienated Muslims and convert them into enemies of the United States.

The leader of the terrorist group **Al-Qaeda in the Arabian Peninsula** (AQAP), Nasir Abd al-Karim al-Wahayshi, is a Yemeni. The group's headquarters is in Yemen, and it is quickly enhancing the country's reputation as an emerging safe haven for terrorists. To complicate the situation, Yemen is the location of choice for militants leaving Afghanistan, Iraq, and even Egypt, and, despite the lack of a common border, thousands of Somalis are seeking refuge there. The country has been implicated in several recent attacks on the United States, including the Fort Hood massacre by Nidal Hasan and the failed "under-wear bomber" mission of Umar Farouk Abdulmutallab.

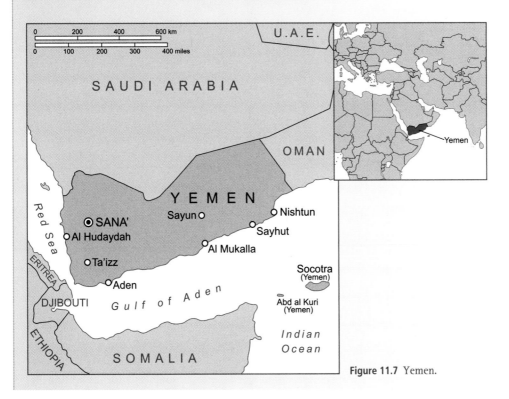

Figure 11.7 Yemen.

[59] Iris Glosemeyer, "Dancing on Snake Heads," paper prepared for the Canadian Defense and Foreign Affairs Institute, May 2009.
[60] *The New York Times*, May 9, 2010.

The ethnic and religious makeup of Yemen is extremely diverse, and the socioeconomic challenges daunting. The population of more than twenty-two million is predominantly Arab, and the official language is Arabic. The country is divided by religion with Shiites located mainly in the north and west and Sunni in the south and southeast. Tribal and clientelistic systems permeate all aspects of government, including the state bureaucracy in the capital Sanaa. Al-Qaeda has thrived in the south of the country, which is known to hate the government, and in areas where tribal authority has eroded.

The country has few resources, and the economy is in dire straits. Yemen is the poorest country in the Middle East, and oil production has been depleted. A small amount is being replaced by natural gas. A humanitarian crisis exists. More than half the population lives below the poverty line of US$2 per day. The GDP is decreasing annually and a half million people have been displaced from their homes. A high fertility rate means that more than half the country is younger than fifteen years of age and almost a million children younger than five years of age experience acute malnutrition.

Yemen has been plagued with violence, secession movements, and civil wars throughout its long history. The central government has never been able to maintain a monopoly on violence throughout the country. President Ali Abdullah Saleh (who came to office in 1978) and his successor, Abed Rabbo Mansour Hadi, have three distinct security challenges.[61] In the north there are several armed tribes and an insurrection from the Houthis, who want to restore a religious leader as head of the country. In the south there is a long-established separatist movement. Al-Qaeda has been operating in several locations since the early 1990s. Tribal leaders are wary of foreign intrusion, and Islamic radicals have declared foreigners, Western interests, and oil facilities to be legitimate targets of violence. In October 2000 Yemeni suicide bombers attacked the USS *Cole*, which was refueling in Aden, killing seventeen Americans.

The Yemeni government officially supports the U.S. war on terrorism but tries to remain only minimally confrontational with radical Islamists and mujahideen returning from wars in foreign lands. It has had to tread a fine line between ignoring terrorists and attacking radical Yemeni strongholds. President Obama signed an executive order in 2010 creating the Joint Unconventional Warfare Task Force, which authorizes the U.S. military to use covert methods to "penetrate, disrupt, defeat or destroy" al-Qaeda in the Arabian Peninsula.[62] Obama has also agreed to CIA and Pentagon drone strikes against al-Qaeda subject to top administration consent.

Yemen has the potential to be the next Afghanistan for terrorist training camps. What should the United Nations or the United States do about it? Allow terrorists to move freely in the country? Aid the government with special operation forces and equipment to attack the militants, including missile-launching drones?

services, because U.S. authorities had not alerted Islamabad about the operation to go after the al-Qaeda leader, had clearly engaged in duplicity, and violated Pakistan's sovereignty. While the caches of information found at the site gave the CIA and other intelligence agencies access to information about the organization's membership and finances, within two months Ayman al-Zawahiri, an Egyptian-born theorist, was proclaimed the new leader of al-Qaeda and spiritual leader of the worldwide

[61] In 1912 Saleh and his family were given immunity from prosecution and have the right to live and work in Yemen with the honor of a former president. The new president was elected in a referendum in which he was the only candidate – he received 99 percent of the vote.

[62] Ginny Hill, "Avoiding Freefall," *World Today*, July 2010, http://theworldtoday.org.

network and the various extremist groups that co-operate with it. The United States continued to use its elite special forces and drones to kill al-Qaeda operators, or, as the military calls them, high-value targets. However, on the anniversary of 9/11 in 2012, terrorists got away with attacking the U.S. consulate in Benghazi, killing the American ambassador and three others.

Terrorism and weapons of mass destruction

Terrorists usually rely on small conventional weapons such as guns, bombs, and relatively more sophisticated arms such as shoulder-propelled rockets. The importance of low-tech weapons has been demonstrated by the successful use of improvised explosive devices (IEDs) in countries like Iraq and Afghanistan. However, the diffusion of high technology is making more sophisticated and powerful weapons available around the world. In Chapter 9 we discussed the four general categories of weapons of mass destruction (WMDs): nuclear, radiological, chemical, and biological. Perhaps the greatest fear of Western policy makers is that terrorists might use WMDs to attack infrastructures or places where large numbers of people congregate. A successful major terrorist attack on such a site would result in massive casualties and create serious economic and political consequences as well as global fear. Al-Qaeda has openly expressed a desire to acquire nuclear weapons.

If a small nuclear weapon were to be detonated in an attack on New York City, all major structures would be destroyed. Within one second, at least seventy-five thousand people would die, and within four seconds, roughly three hundred thousand people, everyone within direct line of sight of the blast, would be dead. Those outside the direct line of sight would receive lung and eardrum injuries. By the end of the explosion, there would be roughly eight hundred thousand casualties, nine hundred thousand injuries, and twenty square miles

of property destruction. The impact of the detonation of a nuclear weapon or a terrorist attack at a nuclear power plant would be even worse.[63]

Graham Allison brilliantly demonstrated in *Nuclear Terrorism* that the potential terrorist use of nuclear weapons is a dangerous threat to security.[64] While developing a nuclear weapons program is expensive and time-consuming (as it involves the acquisition of fissile material and information about how to manufacture a working bomb), such materials and knowledge have become widespread. The public dissemination of nuclear technology has made the production of nuclear weapons relatively easy if the appropriate ingredients are available (see "How to Make an Atom Bomb" in Chapter 9). To test how difficult it would be to make a bomb, the U.S. military asked two physics graduates to attempt to produce a nuclear weapon without the aid of any secret information. While the graduates had no experience in atomic energy, they were able to demonstrate that the project could, in theory, be completed within thirty months if the fissile material were available.[65] If potential proliferators had access to classified weapons schematics and one or two experienced scientists, the production of nuclear weapons could be completed even faster.[66]

In addition to the threat posed by loose nuclear weapons, there are also risks related to fissile materials in nuclear energy plants. These facilities use enriched uranium, a necessary ingredient in nuclear weapons. There are more than 430 fission reactors

---

[63] Atomicarchive.com, "New York City Example," available at http://www.atomicarchive.com/Example/Example1.shtml.

[64] Graham Allison, *Nuclear Terrorism: The Ultimate Preventable Catastrophe* (New York: Henry Holt, 2005). Michael Krepon warns that dire warning of impeding nuclear dangers could actually worsen U.S. defenses. See Michael Krepon, "The Mushroom Cloud That Wasn't: Why Inflating Threats Won't Reduce Them," *Foreign Affairs* 88, no. 3 (May–June 2009), p. 4.

[65] *Guardian Unlimited*, June 24, 2003: "How Two Students Built an A-Bomb," http://www.guardian.co.uk/nuclear/article/0,2763,983714,00.html.

[66] Various guides on nuclear issues, including *An Encyclopedia for the Preparation of Nuclear Weapons*, have appeared on Islamist websites. They are made available and translated from Arabic at http://www.emritv.org.

Figure 11.8 Unlike nuclear weapons, the subject of nuclear waste is often overlooked in public discourse, yet its significance cannot be doubted. One of the major issues to be faced on a multilateral basis is how to dispose of dangerous radioactive nuclear waste. *Source:* Photos.com.

in the world, producing an estimated 345 gigawatts of electrical power. Enough highly enriched uranium and plutonium already exists (produced by civilian nuclear power plants) to create a significant number of nuclear weapons. With every new nuclear power plant constructed, the amount of fissile material grows.[67]

Inadequate storage security at nuclear power plants poses additional threats. Nuclear waste, in the form of spent fuel cells, is cooled by being immersed in water for roughly ten years and then moved to dry lockers (Figure 11.8). These fuel rods can produce weapons-grade plutonium that can be used in high-yield nuclear devices. Russian nuclear power plants, for example, produce more than one ton of plutonium every year as a by-product of heating and powering communities. An estimated fifty-two thousand tons of waste are not securely stored, providing potential nuclear terrorists with a virtual shopping mall for theft.[68]

Even today, Russia and the former Soviet states lack adequate security measures for dealing with existing nuclear fuel. North America, too, is relatively insecure in this regard. To test the security of American nuclear facilities, the United States military sent a Special Forces team to breach the Los Alamos National Laboratory. The unit incapacitated the guards and stole enough highly enriched uranium to produce several nuclear weapons. The main problem encountered was that the fissile material was too heavy for the team to carry, so they stole a cart from a local Home Depot store and used it to move the dangerous material.[69]

States that possess a WMD program and sponsor terrorism present another serious problem. In 2003, the United States and others interdicted a shipment of WMD-related material destined for Libya's then-active nuclear weapons program. It was part of a nuclear proliferation network (developed by Pakistani nuclear scientist A. Q. Khan) that reached from Southeast Asia to Europe. Khan made sensitive technology and WMD-related materials available to states that were willing to pay for them.

[67] David Albright and Kimberly Kramer, "Fissile Material: Stockpiles Still Growing," *Bulletin of the Atomic Scientists* (November–December 2004).

[68] Michael Long, "Half Life: The Lethal Legacy of America's Nuclear Waste," *National Geographic* (July 2002), p. 14.

[69] Allison, *Nuclear Terrorism*, p. 64.

The reach of his network illustrated how globalization can nourish terrorism. The trends that drive globalization – improved communications and transportation links – enable the development of networks for acquisition of WMD by terrorists or rogue states. In 2004, the United Nations Security Council unanimously adopted Resolution 1540 under chapter 7 of the UN Charter, obliging states "to refrain from supporting by any means, non-state actors for developing, acquiring, manufacturing, transferring, over-using nuclear, chemical, or biological weapons and their delivery system."[70]

In 2006, U.S. President Bush and Russian President Putin announced the Global Initiative to Combat Nuclear Terrorism (GICNT) to strengthen defenses against and respond comprehensively to the nuclear terrorist threat. By 2010, seventy-six countries representing all regions of the world had joined the initiative and were working to improve such areas as accounting, control, and physical protection systems for nuclear and other radioactive materials and substances. This is just one of many international initiatives designed to mitigate against nuclear terrorism by identifying, securing, and removing or disposing of vulnerable nuclear and radioactive materials around the world. Much

is also being done to provide radiation detection systems and training to deter, detect, and interdict illicit trafficking of nuclear and other radiological materials across international borders. Global threat reduction programs are active in Pakistan, Afghanistan, and other regions vulnerable to proliferators, working to prevent terrorists from acquiring WMDs expertise, materials, and technology.

As Graham Allison has shown, many more policies could be developed to reduce the threat of nuclear terrorism. They include the following:

1. Taking a firm stand against the further spread of nuclear weapons and unguarded nuclear materials
2. Securing existing nuclear sources by working with international institutions, such as the International Atomic Energy Agency (IAEA), to safeguard existing nuclear weapons, production facilities, and civilian power plants
3. Increasing funding to secure loose Russian nuclear weapons
4. Focusing more on preventing proliferation than on developing new weapons technologies
5. Making it a priority to remove highly enriched uranium (HEU) and plutonium from nuclear

Critical Case Study 11.2 Cyberterrorism and cyberwarfare: New global threats?

The Internet facilitates extensive and rapid human interaction, and cyberspace provides immense opportunities. It means people can connect instantly with others wherever they are, through text and photos, or can access information of all types, including maps and satellite photos. Businesses, commerce, and international trade – including banks, hospitals, transportation and electrical systems – can no longer operate without it. Governments, international organizations, and even military defense systems are linked electronically via the Internet. All this connectivity has great advantages, but it also makes people and their institutions vulnerable to attacks from outside sources, including alienated and unemployed youths, extremist or terrorist groups, organized criminals, and rogue states. Rather than physically assaulting harbors, railroads, transportation hubs, and airports as in the past, massive harm can now be done by using the Internet to facilitate the planning, coordination, and execution of low-tech attacks. The attacks of 9/11 demonstrated this more vividly than any other terror event.

[70] http://www.un.org/sc/1540/.

The prefix *cyber* is used to distinguish between that which is conducted by computer and that which is "real." The distinction is moot. In 2011, Sony announced that the user files of seventy million customers had been stolen from its computers by hackers; in 2012, Saudi Armaco was attacked by a virus that erased three quarters of the company's files and replaced them with an image of a burning American flag. In 2010, it was discovered that the highly sophisticated "Stuxnet" and "Flame" computer viruses had been used by the United States and Israel to target and disrupt nuclear facilities in Iran. A global figure of US$1 trillion annually has been attributed to cybercrime.[71] Computers, indispensable to an advanced peacetime economy, are becoming even more vital during political conflicts and warfare. Effective defense against cybercrime, cybertheft, cyberespionage, and cyberwarfare are being discussed by policy makers everywhere. It is difficult to know how to anticipate or intercept an attack of this nature. Much of the time it will be impossible to know in advance that a cyberattack is coming, or even where it is coming from, as it can be routed through other countries' websites. There is no front line or border to use as a bulwark against an attack. There are many problems to consider, such as how long will it be before the United States and China start playing cyber-Chicken, or India and Pakistan engage in cyberwarfare over the subcontinent?

Clearly, the dissemination on the Internet of more than 250,000 secret cables from U.S. embassies around the world by the founder of WikiLeaks Julian Assange was a case of theft. The website disclosed secret information, but it did not physically attack state institutions or infrastructures. **Cyberterrorism**, in contrast, involves attacks on a state's telecommunications and computer networks to destroy the technological systems considered vital to economic and defense institutions. Cyberattacks on energy, nuclear, transportation, banking, and commerce sites could prove disastrous, conceivably even escalating to **cyberwarfare**.

A new international race, that some compare to the development of the atomic bomb, is therefore underway to develop cyberweapons and systems to protect them.[72] China has announced the creation of a cyberunit in the People's Liberation Army (PLA), and Canadian researchers at the University of Toronto claim that a vast electronic spying operation located in China has stolen documents from computers in 103 countries, including many belonging to government offices including embassies.[73] In the United States the **National Cybersecurity Center** (NCSC) in the Department of Homeland Security and the **National Security Agency** (NSA) in the Department of Defense co-ordinate US efforts in the field of cyberspace security. Former U.S. Secretary of Defense Leon Panetta frightened many Americans when he claimed, "We could face a cyberattack that could be the equivalent of Pearl Harbor."[74]

There is no international legal framework for the Internet that enables pursuing investigations across country's borders. The WikiLeaks case showed that there was no clear way to safeguard private communications, classified information, or even military defense secrets. The leak provided classified files about Iraq that gave a fascinating but distorted view of the war. It also put lives in danger. Who is to be blamed for a cyberattack? Who is responsible for monitoring and responding to attacks? If origins can be determined, to what extent is a state-sponsored cyberattack the equivalent of a declaration of war? If the source of a cyberattack were known, could a response with noncyberweapons be triggered?

---

[71] Claire Yorke, "Cybersecurity and Society," *World Today* (December 2010), http://theworldtoday.org.
[72] *The Times*, April 28, 2009.
[73] *The Times*, March 29, 2009.
[74] Thomas Rid, "Think Again: Cyberwar," *Foreign Policy*, no. 192 (March–April 2012), p. 81.

The question of whether cyberterrorism is a global threat is a major issue in government circles. One side argues that it is overblown and that designating cyberattacks as terrorism should be avoided. Another side makes the alarmist argument that while the world has not yet witnessed a devastating cyberattack on a country or its infrastructure, it is just a matter of time before it will occur.

Where do you stand on this issue?

reactors (the United States could expedite the conversion of nuclear reactors to low-enriched uranium; there is enough American HEU in forty-three countries for the development of one thousand nuclear weapons)

6. Aiding in the disposal of radioactive nuclear waste (a multilateral team could establish and maintain secure holding facilities in nuclear countries; to keep highly radioactive materials out of unsafe storage facilities, Allison suggests fuel cycling, a process by which some states would receive processed fuel rods as long as the material would be returned and the enrichment facilities dismantled)

7. Establishing internationally controlled enriched-uranium or spent-fuel banks that would allow countries to produce electricity with nuclear materials

Particularly since the breakup of the Soviet Union more than two decades ago, concerns have grown that a rogue state or terrorists might acquire material to make a radiological weapon, or a *dirty bomb*, which uses conventional explosives to disperse radioactive material over a large area. Radioactive materials are readily available because they are used in medical facilities and industries in nearly all countries, and the IAEA has confirmed several cases of theft and trafficking in stolen radiological material. Fortunately, most radioactive material is too weak to pose a significant health risk when spread widely. The most dangerous materials would require great expertise in handling them, or the terrorists themselves could be incapacitated by doses of radiation.

Bioterrorism refers to the deliberate dispersal of pathogens to cause disease. It is another serious threat because it is difficult to control the proliferation of biotechnologies and information about biological agents. Small quantities of chemical and biological agents are easily transportable and highly toxic and have the ability to cause mass casualties. Chemical ingredients are relatively inexpensive and easy to obtain and deliver. They were used in World War I and during the Iran-Iraq War.

Antiterrorist strategies

Terrorism can never be completely eradicated, and there can be no absolute security from it, but it can be reduced, and countries can be more resilient to its consequences. The security and intelligence apparatus can do much better. To respond effectively to terrorist attacks, governments need to understand the impact of historical grievances and attempt to undermine the myths that perpetuate violence. Diplomacy is an integral part of security. Since security policy often involves the use of armed force and may deal with the symptoms rather than the causes of terrorism, it is important to consider whether military intervention in foreign countries itself may be a cause of terrorism rather than an answer to it. Indeed, many counterterrorism successes have been fostered by good intelligence and overt and covert police action, with the military acting only in a supporting role.

Analyzing the response to 9/11

In theory, there was an entire spectrum of possible responses to the terrorist events of 9/11, but the U.S. government chose to respond militarily with a global "War on Terror." Immediately after the attack the U.S. government announced that the initial goals of that war would be the following:

1. Capture Osama bin Laden
2. Capture Mullah Omar (the Taliban leader)
3. Close down al-Qaeda in Afghanistan and elsewhere
4. Release U.S. prisoners in Afghanistan

Of these goals, only the fourth was accomplished quickly. It took nearly a decade for bin Laden to be killed by U.S. Special Forces, in 2011, and Mullah Omar currently is still at large (see Chapter 10). Moreover, the war on terror would be considered successful only if it met certain strategic objectives that were perceived as realistic. It would need to do the following:

1. Diminish terrorist organizations rather than increase their attraction to potential recruits
2. Avoid damage to the United States, its citizens, its image in the world, and its alliances
3. Remain cost-effective and avoid undermining the U.S. economy and the ability of the U.S. armed forces to perform other important functions
4. Ensure that it was seen as just by not causing excessive "collateral" damage by killing or injuring too many civilians
5. Reduce the prospects for conflict between the Muslim world and the West

As of 2013, these five strategic objectives have not been met. Al-Qaeda has not been able to execute another major terrorist attack inside the United States since 9/11, but terrorist activity has not appreciably decreased around the world. Significant damage has been done to the U.S. economy, its image, and its alliances. The intervention in Iraq increased the attraction of copycat asymmetrical warfare for many radical Muslims. The failure to discover weapons of mass destruction in Iraq or any evidence that Baghdad was involved in the events of 9/11, combined with large numbers of civilian deaths during the insurgency, undermined

---

Close Up 11.3 **Counterterrorist measures**

Apart from sanctions, the following counterterrorist measures are common:

1. Strengthening regional and transnational partnerships and cooperating in the fields of intelligence and law enforcement coordination as well as financial sanctions, norms, and standards of financial regulation
2. Cooperating with states to deny **safe havens**, defined as ungoverned, undergoverned, or ill-governed areas where terrorists are able to organize, plan, and raise funds in relative security, allowing them to plan acts of terrorism around the world. Fourteen terrorist safe havens are monitored in Africa, the Middle East, East Asia and the Pacific, South Asia, and the Western Hemisphere, as well as terrorist use of the Internet for propaganda, recruiting, fund-raising and training as "virtual" safe havens.
3. Promoting international cooperation to block the funding of terrorists and their supporters
4. Offering rewards for information that prevents or resolves incidents of international terrorism
5. Pushing counterradicalization as a priority, where there is considered to be potential for violent extremism that could threaten the United States or its allies
6. Setting up long-term goals and programs under the U.S. **Antiterrorism Assistance Program (ATA)** to provide partner countries with training, equipment and technology to find and arrest terrorists

the claim that this was a "just" war and greatly exacerbated tensions between Muslims and the West, leading to attacks in London, Madrid, and elsewhere.

Trying to stop terrorism by attacking and "democratizing" other lands is self-defeating.[75] Military attacks on terrorists are usually clumsy, killing too many innocent bystanders and doing little to resolve the basic social, economic, political, and religious issues that nourish terrorists. Since the early military success in ending Taliban rule in Afghanistan, intelligence and police work arguably have done the most to damage the al-Qaeda network. Eventually, al-Qaeda will end,[76] but other groups can be expected to take its place.

In view of this argument, the U.S. State Department claims that terrorism is being fought on four fronts apart from the military: "diplomatic, intelligence, law enforcement, and financial."[77] The U.S. government imposes four sets of sanctions on countries that support international terrorism. It bans arms-related exports and sales to them, it prohibits economic assistance, it places controls on exports of dual-use items, and it requires congressional notification for questionable goods or services. Close Up 11.3 lists six counterterrrorist measures that continue to be pursued.

Since 9/11 the international community has undertaken a great many significant initiatives to identify and monitor possible hostile organizations. International cooperative initiatives have been carried out in the areas of intelligence, law enforcement, and targeted financial sanctions. Besides the activities of individual states, organizations working in the field of counterterrorism include, among others, the United Nations, the Group of Eight (G8), the European Union (EU), the Organization for Security and Cooperation in Europe (OSCE), NATO, the African Union, Asia-Pacific Economic Cooperation (APEC), and the Organization of American States

Inter-American Committee against Terrorism, to name only a few of the most prominent.

After 9/11 the United Nations established the Counterterrorism Committee to help member states combat terrorism. Specialized UN agencies, such as the International Civil Aviation Organization, which controls passport security standards, were engaged. The Security Council was particularly concerned with nuclear terrorism, and after 9/11 passed important resolutions. Resolution 1373, for example, requires all member states to refrain from providing support, active or passive, to terrorists, and to attempt to limit terrorists' movements and safe havens. Resolution 1540 requires all UN member states to refrain from providing support to nonstate actors that attempt to develop or acquire WMDs or their means of delivery.

Homeland security

In the aftermath of 9/11 most states reviewed their domestic laws to determine whether they were adequate for the surveillance of potential terrorist activity. Canada, for example, entered into new agreements with the United States to strengthen its activities to prevent terrorism. There was a renewed emphasis on security and enhanced programs at borders, transportation systems, and preparedness globally.[78] Since dissent and terrorism can never be fully abolished in open societies, Western leaders tried to find ways to make their countries more secure from attacks but also more resilient if they should occur. Many parts of government were reorganized. The United States was the most affected by terrorism, and it made the most expansive changes in organization. For example, it created the Department of Homeland Security and added the U.S. Northern Command to the military structure to coordinate homeland defense. The intelligence community was also thoroughly revamped, with the appointment of a national intelligence director

---

[75] For a cogent argument that adopting democracy will not reduce terrorism, see F. Gregory Gause III, "Can Democracy Stop Terrorism," *Foreign Affairs* 84, no. 5 (September–October 2005), pp. 62–76.

[76] Audrey Kurth Cronin, "How al-Qaida Ends: The Decline and Demise of Terrorist Groups," *International Security* 31, no. 1 (Summer 2006), pp. 7–48.

[77] U.S. Department of State, *Patterns of Global Terrorism*, 2002, p. iii.

[78] Ashton B. Carter, "The Architecture of Government in the Face of Terrorism," *International Security* 26, no. 3 (Winter 2001–2), pp. 5–23.

as principal adviser to the president. The National Counterterrorism Center (NCTC) was set up in the State Department to collect, analyze, and share relevant information and consolidate terrorist watch lists from the various agencies.[79] Around the world similar steps were taken, and all developed countries took measures to protect critical infrastructures and provide medicines and vaccines in the event of a biological, nuclear, chemical, or radiological attack.[80]

Worldwide, new institutions proliferated to protect states against future terrorists and other harmful repercussions from the new security dilemma. Perhaps the most important administrative change in the United States was the new large and complex Department of Homeland Security (DHS), with its responsibility for securing American borders and protecting ports from illegal immigration, security risks, drug smuggling, and human trafficking. It is staffed by about 180,000 employees and combines twenty-two agencies, including immigration, coast guard, customs, emergency preparedness, and the Secret Service. The new department has tightened airline security with measures such as reinforced airplane cockpits, U.S. marshals on flights, and new systems including sophisticated passenger prescreening that includes cross-checks of information. The department directs the agency U.S. Customs and Border Protection, which consolidates all border activities, as well as the coast guard. Although their surveillance procedures have increased, ports remain vulnerable to terrorist attacks. Cargo containers are not adequately searched when they enter U.S. ports or cross Canadian and Mexican land borders, and other forms of transportation for passengers and goods have not undergone adequate security upgrades. The rail transportation system, in particular, continues to bring unsecured goods, such as dangerous toxic chemicals, into large cities. There are also more than one hundred unsafe chemical plants around the country where an attack could take the lives of a million or more people.

The impact of terrorism on civil liberties

A particularly divisive issue is the extent to which governments should intrude on people's privacy to improve security from terrorism. Former U.S. president Jimmy Carter's administration established the Foreign Intelligence Surveillance Act (FISA) to allow the federal government to use electronic methods in the surveillance of citizens and resident aliens alleged to be acting on behalf of foreign governments. In the atmosphere of frenzy after 9/11 a new act, the Patriot Act was rushed through Congress. It provided extensive tools to track down and prosecute terrorists by increasing the government's capacities for law enforcement and intelligence collection. For example, under the new act the government only has to claim that persons are being investigated as part of a foreign intelligence operation to be able to legally infringe on their civil liberties. It also made surveillance much easier. Section 206 permits roving wiretaps, and section 215 allows governments to search business and computer activities of citizens suspected to be involved in terrorist cases. It permits the government to subpoena library, medical insurance, and even university student records. Section 216 expands this right of access to the Internet. While surveillance of Internet content is prohibited, extracting information about citizen transactions is not. The law permits the government to obtain search warrants even when there is no evidence that a crime may have been committed, and noncitizens suspected of terrorism can be detained before deportation proceedings commence.

Civil libertarians claim that this law permits spying on American citizens and provides tools for suppressing political dissent. They argue that

---

[79] Available at http://www.state.gov/s/ct/rls/crt/2008/122452.htm. The NCTC draws together information from more than eighty databases across the U.S. government. Its early successes were marred by its failure to prevent the Christmas Day "underwear bomber" from almost carrying out his suicide mission.

[80] Information is available at http://www.state.gov/s/ct/rls/crt/2008/122452.htm.

the law was passed too quickly and should be reviewed and sections repealed. According to the Homeland Security website, however, the act has been important in finding and dismantling terror cells.[81] In 2008, Congress overhauled the Foreign Intelligence Surveillance Act to bring federal statutes in line with what the Bush administration had been doing secretly. Governments often find it convenient to retain authority established by their predecessor, and in 2010 President Obama signed legislation to temporarily extend provisions of the Patriot Act that had been set to expire, among them warrantless wiretapping. However, a federal judge ruled that surveillance without warrants was illegal and rejected the Obama administration's request that the program be kept in place.[82] In spite of this, wiretapping U.S. citizens was extended for an additional five years on December 28, 2012.

Absolute security from terrorism can never be achieved in an open and democratic country, and, therefore, success should be defined in terms of reducing threats, not absolutely eliminating them. Frank P. Harvey makes this point in a telling fashion. For him, a security paradox arises because the more security you have, the more you will need. In other words, enhancing security raises public expectations and amplifies public outrage about subsequent failures, and therefore the public demands more security.[83] Since terrorism can never be totally eliminated, perhaps what is needed is a new kind of containment policy. What also may be required is a campaign to create a more positive image of Western interests in a democratic and just world. Soft power, including diplomacy, education, foreign and development aid, may be needed to make headway against the causes of terrorism rather than more homeland security institutions.

---

[81] http://www.whitehouse.gov/homeland/.

[82] *The New York Times*, April 1, 2010.

[83] Frank Harvey, *The Homeland Security Dilemma: Fear, Failure and the Future of American Insecurity* (Abingdon, UK: Taylor and Francis, 2010).

Close Up 11.4 Summary of Geneva Conventions

The First Geneva Convention covers the wounded and sick personnel of armed conflict on land.
The Second Geneva Convention deals with the wounded, sick, and shipwrecked.
The Third Geneva Convention handles prisoners of war.
The Fourth Geneva Convention concerns the protection of civilians in time of war.
Additional Protocol 1 of 1977 relates to the protection of victims of armed conflict.
Additional Protocol II of 1977 covers victims of noninternational armed conflicts.

International humanitarian law and terrorism

The current core of international humanitarian law is based on the Geneva conventions drawn up in 1949 after World War II. The four conventions and their two important additional protocols shown in Close Up 11.4 form the basic laws of armed conflict. While these conventions have been ratified by 194 states, they do not regulate war in general; they only attempt to protect various classes of people in a limited way during and after war. The conventions do not prevent or limit war or deal specifically with terrorists, and they relate almost exclusively to interstate warfare and the amelioration of conditions.[84] The conventions require, for example, humane treatment for prisoners of war (POWs) and persons with no active part in hostilities. The right not to be arbitrarily deprived of life and the prohibitions against murdering or maiming civilians are included in human rights treaties and humanitarian law, and

---

[84] Henry Shue, "Laws of War," in *The Philosophy of International Law*, ed. Samantha Besson and John Tasioulos (Oxford: Oxford University Press, 2010), pp. 511–28.

given power by the common article 3 of the Geneva Conventions, which declares, "Persons taking no active part in the hostilities ... shall in all circumstances be treated humanely, without any adverse distinction based on race, color, religion or faith, sex, birth or wealth, or any other similar criteria."

While the conventions have been adapted by courts in international legal judgments over the years, there remains considerable doubt about their relevance to modern warfare. For example, the two 1977 protocols have been interpreted to include wars *within* states, but the United States, Israel, Pakistan, Iran, and Iraq, for example, have not ratified them. The U.S. government did not apply the Third Geneva Convention to prisoners at Guantánamo, and there has been considerable difficulty in determining how to apply the Geneva rules to prisoners who have been involved in terrorism. It is debatable whether these prisoners come under the clauses based on war between states and indeed whether they meet the conditions to be considered prisoners of war. There are other major unresolved issues in the Geneva Conventions concerning security detention, the activities of multilateral peace enforcement forces, and even the privatization of war.[85]

One of the most baffling of these issues has been how to deal with captured individuals whom the U.S. administration terms unlawful enemy combatants. These are not military personnel fighting on behalf of a state but rogue terrorists (who consider themselves freedom fighters). A 2001 classified presidential document declared the U.S. president had the power to incarcerate any noncitizens the government had reason to believe had engaged in planning, executing, or harboring individuals associated with terrorism or simply if it was in the interest of the United States to incarcerate them.[86] Captives in the ensuing Afghanistan and Iraq wars, therefore, did not come under the 1949 Geneva Conventions on the protection of noncombatants in war, nor did they have the rights of prisoners of war (discussed in Chapters 10 and 14). If these prisoners had been brought to the United States, they might have had access to American courts. To prevent this, they were often held in selected prisons and military bases around the world. The best-known prisons, and the only ones for which significant information is available, are in Guantánamo Bay in Cuba, Bagram Airfield in Afghanistan, Belmarsh in the United Kingdom, and Abu Ghraib in Iraq – but other secret prisons may exist. The effort of the U.S. government to deal with these unlawful enemy combatants is outlined in Critical Case Study 11.3.

Critical Case Study 11.3 **Dealing with captives during the war on terror**

The George W. Bush administration established military commissions inside its offshore military prisons to judge prisoners – those the government called enemy combatants. Attorney General Alberto R. Gonzales, claimed that the president would refer only noncitizens to these courts and only those who were members or active supporters of al-Qaeda or other international terrorist organizations. They would be charged with offenses against the international laws of war, such as targeting civilians, hiding among civilians, and refusing to bear arms openly.

---

[85] For details of these problems, see the International Committee of the Red Cross summaries at http://www.icrc.org.

[86] "Detention, Treatment and Trial of Certain Noncitizens in the War against Terrorism," in *The Superpower Myth, The Use and Misuse of American Might*, ed. Nancy Soderberg (Hoboken, NJ: Wiley, 2005), p. 320.

Holding unlawful enemy combatants without charge poses serious questions of legitimacy. [87] In June 2004, the U.S. Supreme Court ruled that its jurisdiction extended to Guantánamo and that detainees there had a right to contest their detention in the courts, thus raising the prospect that prisoners might have their status resolved in the regular U.S. court system.[88] The **military review tribunals** that had been set up to determine the status of each prisoner were then suspended. However, on July 15, 2005, a federal appeals court (the U.S. Court of Appeals for the District of Columbia) ruled unanimously that the military could resume trials of Guantánamo suspects. It said it was well established in the United States that the Geneva Conventions "do not create judicially enforceable rights" – that is, accusations based on them cannot be brought forward in lawsuits in the United States. By the spring of 2006, the claim that 9/11 justified such harsh measures was under severe attack. Prominent figures such as former president Bill Clinton, many Democrats, and some Republicans were saying publicly that Guantánamo should be closed. The United Nations joined the chorus with a human rights report that concluded that the prison should be closed because it allowed torture and placed prisoners in a legal no-man's-land without recourse to legal standard proceedings. The British House of Lords called it a "legal black hole."

The Guantánamo prisoners were in legal limbo until June 2006, when in the *Hamdan v. Rumsfeld* case, the U.S. Supreme Court ruled that the prisoners were prisoners of war and did come under the Geneva Conventions and should be treated as such.[89] In 2008 the U.S. Supreme Court reaffirmed that prisoners in Guantánamo had a right of access to the legal system. If they had been in a battlefield or war zone, then the U.S. constitutional procedures and habeas corpus would not have applied to them. Barack Obama, in his bid for the presidency in 2008, said he would close Guantánamo on his first day of office, although it would take many months to resolve some difficult cases. After his election in 2009, he signed three orders – suspending the military commissions, declaring that Guantánamo would be closed within a year, and determining that each prisoner would be prosecuted or released.[90]

In January 2010 Attorney General Eric Holder announced that five suspected 9/11 terrorists, including the alleged leader of the attack, Khalid Sheikh Mohammed, would be tried in a New York Court rather than by a military commission. This raised howls of dissent from Republicans, New York officials, and many family members of 9/11 victims who wanted him tried by the military, especially as he had already confessed to the crime. In March 2011 President Obama reversed his order and signed the Congress-inspired National Defense Authorization Act (DAA), which placed restrictions on transferring prisoners to the mainland or other foreign countries and ensured that the prisoners would be tried by military courts.

Then, in April 1012, the Pentagon authorized a military commission trial at Guantánamo prison for Khalid Sheikh Mohammed and four other prisoners accused of orchestrating the 9/11 attacks. The charges include murder in violation of the laws of war and terrorism. If convicted, the five could receive the death sentence. The other prisoners wait in "indefinite detention." There is a kind of legal catch-22. The remaining prisoners cannot be sent home because the war on terror has not ended. Yet there may

---

[87] For an overview of this topic, see Kenneth Jost, "Prosecuting Terrorists," in *Global Issues, 2010 Edition* (Washington, DC: CQ Press, 2010), pp. 49–72.

[88] *The New York Times*, June 29, 2004.

[89] Adam Roberts, "Changing War, Changing Law," *World Today* 65, no. 8–9 (August–September 2009), pp. 6–8.

[90] William Lietzau, U.S. deputy assistant secretary of defense for rule of law and defense, "Detention in the 21st Century Armed Conflict." Lecture at "Changing Character of War," University of Oxford, May 8, 2012.

not be enough evidence to ever convict them of a war crime. They cannot get a trial and yet they cannot be sent home because they are not POWs. The war on terror has not ended, and the government believes that if released these prisoners might join the terrorist cause again.

The two major wars in Iraq and Afghanistan are ending, so the government can claim that it has delivered on President Obama's campaign promises. But his government's expansive definition of war leaves in place executive power to detain individuals without charge and to exercise war powers around the world. Military commissions, rendition, and indefinite detention continue. Indeed, President Obama left in place almost all of his predecessor's counterterrorism policies.

As of mid-2013, the Guantánamo prison was still operative, although efforts to close it continue. The controversy is ongoing, but the idea of holding the trials on the mainland United States appears to have been shelved. Most of the original 779 prisoners at Guantánamo have been transferred, only 169 remain in captivity. They are under strict rules regarding their right to legal counsel and other, perhaps unconstitutional, limitations. About 45 prisoners have no prospect for release. Military assessments and files leaked through WikiLeaks indicate that confusing and contradictory tainted evidence, as well as harsh interrogation methods may make it impossible to convict these prisoners in either civilian or military trials.[91] *The New York Times* calls Guantánamo "a festering sore on this country's global reputation."[92]

How to handle prisoners from the war on terror has been a new and serious problem that flows from the new security dilemmas. Should legal justice systems or military courts be used? How long can individuals captured in war be kept in indefinite detention? How would you grade the United States on how it has handled the issue?

Even before 9/11, the CIA was authorized to carry out renditions – sending noncitizen combatants to other countries for interrogation even though they might be tortured there. After 9/11 this right was expanded by presidential directive to include secret programs allowing the CIA to transfer suspected terrorists to foreign locations, including Egypt, Jordan, Libya, Pakistan, Saudi Arabia, and Syria, for imprisonment and interrogation. This measure has not been rescinded. In the meantime, in May 2010 a U.S. appeals court ruled that the U.S. Constitution and right of habeas corpus did not apply to foreign prisoners held by the U.S. military in Afghanistan because it is a war zone.[93] In other words, the U.S. government could hold terrorism suspects at Bagram Airfield in Afghanistan indefinitely and without legal oversight. At least 645 prisoners have been held in Bagram, some of whom have been transferred to and from other jurisdictions and countries. The court decision allowed the U.S. government to evade judicial review by simply transferring detainees into an active war zone. Civil liberties advocates denounced the ruling. Detailed information about the prisoners, including their citizenship, locations, circumstances of their capture, and how long they have been held, is still unknown, as it is the government's intention to try them eventually by military or civilian courts.

Another humanitarian law concerns the treatment of prisoners. Abuses in Abu Ghraib, Guantánamo, and other prisons have been well documented.[94] Clearly, the prisoners were often not accorded their

---

[91] *The New York Times*, August 7, 2011.
[92] *The New York Times*, April 26, 2011.
[93] *The New York Times*, May 21, 2010.

[94] See Seymour M. Hersh, *Chain of Command: The Road from 9/11 to Abu Ghraib* (New York: HarperCollins, 2003); Mark Danner, *Torture and Truth: America, Abu Ghraib and the War on Terror* (New York: New York Review of Books, 2004); Sanford Levison, ed., *Torture* (Oxford: Oxford University Press, 2004); Meron Benvenisti et al., *Abu Ghraib: The Politics of Torture* (Berkeley, CA: North Atlantic, 2004).

rights under international law or U.S. constitutional principles. Many were subjected to abuse and some even torture. According to the Red Cross, "Methods of physical and psychological coercion were used by the military intelligence in a systematic way to gain confessions and extract information or other forms of cooperation" from persons who had been arrested in connection with the suspected security offenses or deemed to have "an intelligence value."[95] The Bush administration justified the treatment by maintaining that the "intelligence obtained by those rendered, detained and interrogated has disrupted terrorist operations. ... It has saved lives in the United States and abroad, and it has resulted in the capture of other terrorists."[96]

After shocking photos documenting prisoner mistreatment at Abu Ghraib were released, military inquiries were held. In 2009, President Obama

released official files detailing tactics that the CIA had followed regarding captives. The tactics included the sexual humiliation of naked prisoners, use of "stress positions" during interrogations, threats from dogs, yelling, loud music, light control, isolation, misuse of the Koran, cramped and solitary confinement, and water boarding.[97] Most senior military officials escaped punishment, but a few minor officers were reprimanded, fined, or court-martialed. Amnesty International called Guantánamo "the gulag of our times."[98] To many observers, these events portrayed the United States as occupiers and tormenters, not liberators. The abuse and the lack of civil rights accorded to prisoners tarnished America's reputation for justice throughout the world and may have provided a motive for further terrorist attacks.

[95] Mark Danner, "What Are You Going to Do with That?" *New York Review of Books*, June 23, 2005, p. 53.
[96] *The New York Times*, March 6, 2005.

[97] *The New York Times*, August 27, 2004; *New York Times*, April 17, 2009. To the chagrin of some in the security field, President Obama outlawed the use of water boarding later the same year.
[98] *International Herald Tribune*, June 6, 2005.

Conclusion: Can international law regulate antiterrorist policy?

We have written in this chapter about the causes and perpetrators of terrorism. We have seen how terrorist methods and tactics have evolved to the use of IEDs and suicide bombers. We have also found that dealing with terrorists after 9/11 revealed many flaws within security systems and sometimes led to the infringement of human rights. One of the perplexing issues in counterterrorism is how to deal with enemy prisoners.

International law was not and is not prepared to deal with terrorism and unlawful enemy combatants. Prisoners of war (POWs) come under the Geneva Conventions and are sent home at the end of the war. But unlawful enemy combatants provide an entirely different case. Prisoners from the war on terror are not POWs. They might be accused of international crimes against humanity, but charges are problematic because most of the prisoners were arrested either in Afghanistan or in Iraq for defending territory that they claim had been attacked by the United States. In their view, and in the eyes of many Muslims, they are freedom fighters.

These issues are debated by two competing schools of thought. Proponents of continued imprisonment give priority to obtaining intelligence and ensuring security over human rights. The most important thing, they argue, is to prevent illegal combatants from returning to the battlefield and carrying out future terrorist actions. In 2012 officials from the Pentagon estimated that 27 percent of released prisoners have become recidivists. Critics such as human rights activists, following the standard criminal justice model, argue that prisoners should be tried and either released or punished, and they reject inhumane treatment of prisoners on any ground. They condemn long imprisonments without trial from both legal and ethical viewpoints. Where do you stand on this fundamental question?

Select bibliography

Allison, Graham, *Nuclear Terrorism: The Ultimate Preventable Catastrophe* (New York: Henry Holt, 2004).

Barnaby, Frank, *How to Build a Nuclear Bomb* (London: Granta, 2003).

Berger, Peter L., *The Longest War: The Enduring Conflict between America and Al-Qaeda* (New York: Free Press, 2011).

_____, *The Osama Bin Laden I Know: An Oral History of Al Qaeda's Leader* (New York: Free Press, 2006).

Bloom, Mia, *Dying to Kill: The Allure of Suicide Terror* (New York: Columbia University Press, 2005).

Burke, Jason, *Al-Qaeda: Casting a Shadow of Terror* (London: I. B. Tauris, 2004).

Burnett, John S., *Dangerous Waters: Modern Piracy and Terror on the High Seas* (London: Plume, 2003).

Clark, Victoria, *Dancing on the Heads of Snakes* (New Haven, CT: Yale University Press, 2010).

Clarke, Richard A., *Against All Enemies* (New York: Free Press, 2004).

Danner, Mark, *Torture and Truth: America, Abu Ghraib, and the War on Terror* (New York: New York Review of Books, 2004).

Forest, James J. F., and Russell D. Howard, eds., *Weapons of Mass Destruction and Terrorism*, 2nd ed. (New York: McGraw Hill, 2013).

Gerges, Fawaz, *The Far Enemy* (Cambridge: Cambridge University Press, 2005).

Heymann, Philip B., *Terrorism, Freedom and Security: Winning without War* (Cambridge, MA: MIT Press, 2003).

Howard, Russell D., et al, eds., *Terrorism and Counterterrorism: Understanding the New Security Environment* (New York: McGraw-Hill, 2009).

Jenkins, Philip, *Images of Terror: What We Can and Can't Know about Terrorism* (New York: Aldine de Gruyter, 2003).

Kilcullen, David, *The Accidental Guerilla: Fighting Small Wars in the Midst of a Big One* (Oxford: Oxford University Press, 2011).

Klaidman, Daniel, *Kill or Capture: The War on Terror and the Soul of the Obama Presidency* (New York: Houghton, Mifflin Harcourt, 2012).

Kurth Cronin, Audrey, *How Terrorism Ends: Understanding the Decline and Demise of Terrorist Campaigns* (Princeton, NJ: Princeton University Press, 2009).

Laqueur, Walter, *The New Terrorism: Fanaticism and the Arms of Mass Destruction* (New York: Oxford University Press, 1999).

Litwak, Robert S., *Regime Change: U.S. Strategy through the Prism of 9/11* (Baltimore: Johns Hopkins University Press, 2007).

Nacos, Brigitte L., *Terrorism and Counterterrorism*, 2nd ed. (London: Penguin, 2008).

National Commission on Terrorist Attacks upon the United States et al., *9/11 Report* (New York: St. Martin's Press, 2004).

Pape, Robert, *Dying to Win: The Strategic Logic of Suicide Terrorism* (New York: Random House, 2005).

Pape, Robert, and James K. Feldman, *Cutting the Fuse: the Explosion of Global Suicide and How to Stop It* (Chicago: University of Chicago Press, 2010).

Sageman, Marc, *Understanding Terrorist Networks* (Philadelphia: University of Pennsylvania Press, 2004).

Stern, Jessica, *Terror in the Name of God* (New York: HarperCollins, 2003).

Townshend, Charles, *Terrorism: A Very Short Introduction* (Oxford: Oxford University Press, 2002).

Wardlaw, Grant, *Political Terrorism* (Cambridge: Cambridge University Press, 1989).

Part IV The politics of global economics

Injustice anywhere is a threat to justice everywhere.

– DR. MARTIN LUTHER KING JR.

Part IV introduces the international aspects of economics, explaining its importance in the global sphere and relating it to questions of development, prosperity, poverty, and hunger.

Chapter 12 outlines traditional and scholarly concepts and theories in the field and assesses the contemporary importance of liberal internationalism, economic nationalism, neo-Marxism, and the rise of state capitalism. The prospects for global economic governance are controversial, and they are evaluated in terms of the benefits and criticisms of organizations such as the World Bank, the International Monetary Fund, and the World Trade Organization. The current global economic downturn and issues of government debt and financial reform provide a sense of urgency to these global economic issues.

Chapter 13 deals with global inequalities. It assesses winners and losers among states and peoples in the global economy and discusses issues of poverty and hunger, how they are being addressed by the UN Millennium Development Goals, and what progress is being made. On the basis of income earned per day, more than one of every four people on Earth lives in extreme poverty. The overall gap between rich and poor continues to grow, with 1.4 billion people now living below the global poverty line of US $1.25 per day. Forty-two million people are currently displaced by conflict or persecution.

Global poverty is a harbinger of disease and environmental degradation – roughly one billion humans are malnourished, more than 10 million children a year die before the age of five, 1.5 billion people do not have access to basic sanitation, and 8.8 million child deaths are due to HIV/AIDS. Poverty is associated with political instability on a massive scale. What international organizations can and will do about this deplorable state of affairs is of key importance.

12

Global economics and governance

Chapter 1 introduced the idea that the world has become more interdependent and discussed the term *globalization*, a broad term that refers to a reorientation of cultural, economic, political, and technological activities in such a way that it transcends state or country borders. The term has become so popular that it is used to explain various major international trends from social relations to world terrorism.[1] In fact, the term *globalization* has become so pervasive and controversial that critics have termed it nothing more than capitalism or even "globaloney." In response, its proponents claim that fear of change has led to "globalphobia."

Much of the recent change in global politics comes from developments in economics. This chapter, therefore, focuses on **international political economy** (IPE), a field that studies the complex interrelationships of politics and economics. It highlights the significance of globalization and shows how the study of international political economy has become central to international relations. The current global market for widely used products and financial services developed rapidly as a result of reduced barriers to cross-border trade and investment, increasing similarity in state economic regulations and laws, and technological advances in transportation, telecommunications, microprocessors, and the Internet.

Economic globalization refers to the integration of goods, services, capital, and markets. The speed of capital flow around the world (calculated at about US$2 trillion per day) and the growing importance of nonstate actors also contribute to economic globalization, undermining the ability of states to regulate their own economies. Multinational corporations have made **outsourcing** (contracting services from one corporation to another and thereby moving jobs out of a company) and **offshoring** (setting up production in another country to employ cheaper labor or escape regulatory rules) commonplace.

This chapter begins with a discussion of the fundamental concepts of traditional economics. It then outlines four approaches to international economics – liberal internationalism, economic nationalism or mercantilism, neo-Marxism, and state capitalism – and analyzes their theories in relation to economics, politics, and international political economy. It then examines global economic governance and key

---

[1] The term was popularized in Thomas L. Friedman's *The Lexus and the Olive Tree: Understanding Globalization* (New York: Farrar, Strauss, and Giroux, 1999), and *The World Is Flat: A Brief History of the Twenty-First Century* (New York: Farrar, Strauss, and Giroux, 2006).

organizations such as the International Monetary Fund, the World Bank, and the World Trade Organization. Economic integration is discussed in terms of regional agreements such as the European Union and the North American Free Trade Agreement. The next sections of the chapter highlight the benefits and drawbacks of these institutions. The chapter concludes with a discussion of the impact of the 2008–09 global economic turndown, as well as ongoing issues of government debt and economic reform. Since the impact of economic globalization is uneven, Chapter 13 examines how the continuing march toward one global system affects states and people differently, sometimes contributing to increased prosperity and sometimes to global inequalities.[2]

Traditional economic concepts

IPE specialists agree with much of the language of traditional economics, even though, as we shall see, there are divisions among them over explanations and judgments about the global economy. Certain concepts, principles, and beliefs underpin most discussions of global economics and are basic. They include money, markets, and trade. Of course, each school of thought thinks that its approach to these topics is superior.

Money and markets

Almost all states print money, which becomes the sole legal currency in their country. Currency is a measurable means of exchange that can take various forms. During World War II, soldiers used cigarettes, silk stockings, and chocolate bars as forms of payment for specific services because mere pieces of paper were less acceptable as a means

of payment. For much of European world history, precious metals such as gold and silver were used as legal tender. Then states developed their own currencies such as francs, pounds, marks, and, eventually, dollars. Since there was no international currency, countries continued exchanging gold and silver among themselves as forms of payment for the exchange of goods and services. For some time, this gold standard was the equivalent of an international currency.

After World War II, international currency exchange rates were based on the U.S. dollar, which was set at a fixed value equal to one-thirty-fifth of an ounce of gold. This "adjusted gold standard" lasted until 1971. Since then, state currencies have been valued against one another with no reference to the price of gold. Today, the exchange rate is not fixed but changes daily according to how much traders value a particular currency relative to others. Fixed exchange rates are rare, and on the whole, currencies float in relation to the value of one another. Currency changes are tied to comparative trends in economies and speculation about their future value.

There are advantages and disadvantages to the relative strengths of a currency. A strong currency, for example, means lower prices for domestic consumers when they buy imported goods or services. But it also has the disadvantage of making export products more expensive and, therefore,

[2] Unless otherwise mentioned or cited, four basic reports are used for the background data and analysis in these two chapters of Part IV and in Chapters 14–16 of Part V. These reports comprise the most rigorous and up-to-date data available on global statistics and analyses. United Nations, *The Millennium Development Goals Report 2010* (New York: United Nations, 2010); United Nations Development Program, *The Real Wealth of Nations: Pathways to Human Development* (New York: Palgrave, 2010); World Bank, *2011 World Development Indicators* (Washington, DC: World Bank, 2010–12); and World Bank, *World Bank Report 2012: Gender, Equality, and Development* (Washington, DC: World Bank, 2011).

less attractive in world markets. When you visit a foreign country, you need to be aware of the value of your currency compared to others because you will exchange it at the prevailing exchange rate. If you are visiting Britain, you will need to determine how many pounds your dollar will be worth or, if you are visiting France or Germany, you will need to assess how many euros you can get for your dollar. Exporters and importers also need to know the value of currencies so they can operate in a relatively stable environment. The value of currencies must be able to fluctuate freely according to changing economic conditions but in a stable manner so that traders know how much to pay to buy and sell products or services in the global marketplace.

For students a strong currency at home means that it is less expensive to study and travel abroad. A weak currency makes it more expensive. A weak currency also means that it will cost more to buy foreign goods and services, but it likely will attract more foreign students and visitors to your country and enhance the attractiveness of your country's exports. Today, only a very few states do not have freely convertible currencies. If a currency is not allowed to fluctuate according to international standards, bearers may be able to exchange it only illegally on the black market. Money that can readily be converted to the value of the major currencies is hard currency. If conversion is difficult or subject to a poor exchange rate it is soft. A soft currency can result if a country suffers a major devaluation caused, for example, by a high inflation rate.

Globalization requires, and is aided by, the integration of finances around the world, a trend that since the 1980s has been accelerated by the Internet and Internet-driven trading practices. Problems can arise when severe difficulties in one part of the market affect the value of currencies elsewhere. This happened in 2008–09, when the economic meltdown caused by the U.S. housing and mortgage crisis triggered economic calamity around the world. When a country does not play by the internationally accepted rules, there can also be problems. China's currency, the yuan, is not fixed, but it does not exactly float freely either. China has allowed some rise in the value of the yuan in recent years, but it continues to manipulate its exchange rate, keeping it artificially low relative to other currencies to support its exports and to discourage foreign imports.

The basics are clear. China keeps the value of its currency artificially low by selling its own currency and buying foreign currency, a practice common to state capitalism (discussed later in this chapter). This creates a conundrum for countries like the United States. It cannot force China to act differently because China could withdraw its support for U.S. instruments such as Treasury bills, thereby causing their value to drop and making it difficult for Washington to finance its deficits and debt. Such state management or manipulation is more common than is acknowledged. The United States, too, has played this game: in 1985 and 1987 President Ronald Reagan intervened with others to devalue the dollar against the deutschmark and yen and then to end the devaluation. In September 2010, Japan chose to spend a record $23 billion on foreign exchanges in a single day rather than leave the value of the yen entirely to market forces. The yen dropped markedly against the U.S. dollar.

World economy, trade, and markets

How big is the world's economy? People interested in economics have used various techniques to try to measure its size for five hundred years. The total world economy in 2012 was estimated at around $70 trillion using gross domestic product (GDP) with purchasing-power parity (PPP) figures (the sum value of all goods and services produced in the world, valued at prices in the United States). A large proportion of these products is sold across state borders. Although global trade plummeted because of the world financial crisis in 2008–09, world merchandise imports and exports still continued to account for an estimated $25 trillion, calculated on an exchange-rate basis.[3] This vast sum of money involved in world trade is greater than the amount spent on the world's combined annual military budgets.

Economists study the exchange of commodities for other goods or for money. Individuals and companies make decisions about which products to make and how much to pay or charge for what they buy and sell. The concept of market refers to terms on which such exchanges are carried out. If governments avoid managing the economy, and if all the conditions of a free market are assumed, prices for buying and selling should reach a stable level, or equilibrium, at which sellers know that they cannot sell their products if they increase the prices, and buyers know that if they try to drive the price too low, the seller will look elsewhere for buyers. In traditional economic terms, this point is the meeting point or equilibrium between supply and demand.

Foreign trade refers to the export and import of goods and services or the exchange of commodities among states. Merchandise trade consists of the import and export of tangible items such as primary goods, raw materials, and manufactured goods. Services, which are also part of trade, and include such items as education, medical services, and transportation, are not tangible but are still sold and purchased in the marketplace. As states trade with one another, there are winners and losers. The balance of trade is the value of a country's exports relative to its imports. China, for example, has a surplus or positive balance of trade because it sells more than it imports. The United States has a negative balance in large part because of large oil imports from around the world and merchandise imports from China. In turn, China uses its surplus dollars to purchase U.S. Treasury bills and shares in American companies.

Perhaps the most fundamental concept employed by professional trade economists is that of comparative advantage. The idea, first put forward by British economist David Ricardo in his book *On the Principles of Political Economy and Taxation* (1817), was that since businesses differ in their ability to produce goods, it is better for each business to produce the goods that it can make most efficiently. This is the case even if businesses have an absolute advantage and can produce every good more efficiently than every other company or country. According to this argument, there is a supply and demand for each commodity, and individuals and businesses competing in a free market determine the point at which the two will meet – or the price at which a product will be bought and sold. The theory of comparative advantage is that, if each country concentrates on producing those goods for which it has a comparative advantage, an international division of labor will develop in which all goods traded will tend toward better quality at lower prices.

To maximize its total wealth, a country should produce and sell its most efficiently produced products in a free market so that everyone can benefit. Following the theory of comparative advantage, efficient automobile producers should not make bicycles even if they can make them better than other companies. Instead of countries trying to remain economically self-sufficient by producing all their own goods, each state should specialize in what it can do most efficiently and then export those goods in order to buy goods from countries that specialize in other products. If Britain can make automobiles more efficiently, and the Netherlands can grow tulips more efficiently, it would not be wise for the United Kingdom to grow tulips or for the

---

[3] Despite differences over the various theories and approaches of international political economy, some economic ideas are consistent in them all. The idea that a country's wealth can be measured, for example, is accepted by economists, albeit it with different degrees of confidence. Here are some examples: Gross domestic product (GDP) is the economic term used for the total monetary value of all economic activity (production of goods and services) in a state over a year, including domestic and foreign companies. Gross national product (GNP) is the value of all domestic and international activities (production of goods and services) by one state's businesses and citizens. These two measures are often adjusted for purchasing-power parity (PPP). This figure adjusts the statistics to bear in mind how much a given amount of money can buy. It does this by adjusting the GNP or gross national income (GNI) figure to a relative value that takes into account the cost of local purchases of products such as food and housing.

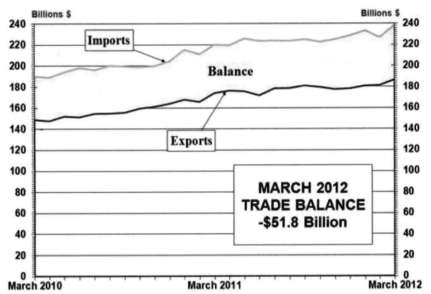

Figure 12.1 U.S. International trade in goods and services. *Source:* http//www.census .gov/indicator/www/img/ ustrade.jpg.

Netherlands to make automobiles. Economists call this a "positive sum" situation, in which all potential competitors could theoretically be winners.

According to these fundamental ideas, trade among states ought to be determined by the forces of the international market, without protection from governments. Professional economists since Ricardo have agreed that following this principle would minimize the costs of production, as only the most efficiently produced goods would be sold. Gains from trade would be maximized, and the free exchange would raise living standards throughout the world. Everyone would benefit from international trade with minimum barriers because protectionist measures would not be used to shield uncompetitive industries from overseas competition. Currencies such as dollars, euros, and yen should also be sold freely like all other goods, and money should be bought and sold in a system of *floating exchange rates*. In reality, such traditional principles cannot be maintained as governments are required to regulate the relations among buyers and sellers, to at least some extent, in order to provide security for their citizens and necessary infrastructures such

as roads and education. There is no such thing as a totally free self-regulating market. Markets cannot exist in a political or institutional vacuum, nor can they guarantee the provision of public goods, such as security, stability, health, and education.[4]

As countries trade with one another, they create a balance of payments. This concept is defined by the flow of money into and out of a country through trade and investment. When more money flows into a country than out of it, the country experiences a surplus. When more money goes out than in, it has a deficit in its balance of payments. (Figure 12.1) International investments may come in two forms: foreign direct investment (FDI), which includes buying ownership or partial ownership of foreign companies or real estate, and foreign portfolio investment (FPI), or shares in stocks and bonds in foreign countries. We examine the impact of these types of foreign investments in Chapter 13.

[4] As the authors of the *Human Development Report 2011* argue, "Firms that produce cheap labour-intensive goods or that exploit natural resources may care little about their workers' health if there is an abundant supply of labour." United Nations, *Human Development Report 2011* (New York: United Nations, 2011), p. 5.

According to mainstream economists, capitalism is the economic system that has most transformed modern societies. It is defined as an economic system that encourages the private control of business and minimal governmental regulation of private industry. It refers to both an economic system and an ideology. Although capitalism is not a complete ideology, it is a powerful force in parties, governments, international organizations, and education. The German sociologist Max Weber believed that the rise of capitalism in the West was in part the impact of Protestantism. The Protestant religion encouraged thrift and the saving or reinvestment of profits, and Weber said that these values embedded in society facilitated the growth of capitalism in the West – that is, ideas affected economics, not the reverse.[5]

These contentions about capitalism are contested. They are defended most vociferously by liberals as part of the global debate about trade and finance policy. As seen earlier, even such problems as how to measure the size of a country's economy are debated. Historically, governments often have protected their home industries for political reasons. To do so, they restrict free trade by imposing tariffs or quotas on incoming products, manipulate exchange rates by pegging currencies at fixed exchange rates, and change interest rates to affect the supply and demand of their currencies. Although outright tariff barriers to trade are now comparatively rare, currency manipulation and regulatory barriers are still common.

As globalization continues, the advantages of following the theory of comparative advantage and free trade among countries become more evident, but so may its disadvantages from a political standpoint. One sector, class, or region of a country can benefit from free trade while others suffer. The North American Free Trade Agreement (NAFTA) may benefit U.S. manufactures that move their plants to Mexico to obtain cheap labor, but U.S. workers might lose jobs in the deal. Even if the overall effect of free trade in North America benefits the economies of all three countries, workers, left-wing political parties, and even some industries may continually agitate to end it. Surveys conducted in Canada, Mexico, and the United States have revealed that a majority of those interviewed in each country believe that the other two countries benefit more from NAFTA than their own.

Approaches to international economics

Initially, international political economy was coterminous with the discipline of economics. But as formal university economics increasingly concentrated on statistics and abstract models of the economy, more economists began to study the controversial intersections between politics and economics. Their core questions include issues such as "what drives and explains events in the global economy?" and "what is more important, governments or markets?" Three approaches dominate the debate – economic liberalism or economic internationalism, economic nationalism or mercantilism, and neo-Marxism.[6] Of course, the approaches are not ironclad divisions, and all contain unique analytical styles, methodological approaches, and often political judgments.

In the actual world of government policy, economic nationalism (often called mercantilism), a state-centered philosophy of economic and government relations dominated economic thought from the development of the Westphalian state system until about the pre–World War II period. During the Cold War, and especially the period after it, liberal internationalism and capitalism dominated the world stage. This approach evolved from classical nationalistic economic theories (discussed later in this chapter) and it held sway as the most important pattern of economic thought in the 20th century. Throughout this period, radical or neo-Marxist

---

[5] Max Weber, *The Protestant Ethic and the Spirit of Capitalism* (London: Allen & Unwin, 1930).

[6] As well as these three traditional approaches and state capitalism, the IPE discipline was also influenced by rational choice analysis, institutional, and social constructivist theories (see Chapter 3).

theories continued to be influential in intellectual circles and in many of the least developed countries. In short, two approaches dominated global economics, but three main theoretical approaches were used by academic political economists to describe, explain, justify, and critique arguments about them. However, a massive change occurred in the late 1990s. The shift of economic power that was taking place in the early 21st century gave rise to a fourth competing approach, called state capitalism (discussed later in this chapter).

Economic nationalism or mercantilism

Economic nationalism is essentially about the struggle for supremacy among states. The idea that the state should act to support its own people and their interests goes back to at least the 17th century. From the rise of the modern state at Westphalia in 1647, state leaders concentrated their efforts on pursuing wealth for themselves and their countrymen. Their governments tried to protect homeland industries by encouraging exports over imports and protecting domestic production against foreign competition by state regulation. Economic nationalism or mercantilism, therefore, has some common features with the theory of realism, as competition and conflict are considered a natural part of politics in the domestic and international environment.

From the founding of the state, trade was seen as a way to increase the financial capacity of one's own country, and since trade was essentially considered a zero-sum game (one state could win only if another lost), imports were to be discouraged whenever possible. Mercantilism was an early government strategy to accumulate state wealth by encouraging exports and discouraging imports. Mercantilists believed that the total volume of trade was fixed – it could not grow larger – and success meant obtaining the largest share of what already existed. European states tried to accumulate the maximum amount of gold and silver possible – by taxing their citizens, robbing their neighbors, or accumulating wealth by means of a trade surplus. Trade was largely channeled via monopolies that could be monitored by state bureaucrats and promoted by regulations, subsidies, and tax rebates.

Colonies and their resources were used to augment the power of states, and home industries were protected with tariffs, quotas, and taxes on imported goods. Colonies guaranteed that the home country would have unfettered access to their resources and provide uncompetitive markets for their goods. The 17th-century British and Dutch East India companies were prime examples of mercantilist enterprises; monopoly partnerships promoted by the British and Dutch monarchs. They received royal privileges, carrying their state flags around the world and returning with precious metals and goods to enrich their home countries. They were privately owned but royally commissioned. States supported the principle of using military power and policies to protect these manufacturing firms, and their profits were used to build powerful militaries, in particular blue ocean navies.

The dominance of the mercantilist view began to fade with the industrial revolution and the rise of democracy, but it never really died. Most modern states continued to advocate policies to protect the growth of their manufacturers. In Europe and even in the United States, which later became the beacon for free trade and minimum protectionism, leaders advocated policies that would protect their own manufacturers. States believed that regulating economic life was important and that economics should be subordinate to state interests. While economic liberals supported the idea of shared interests in free trade, economic nationalists defended a conflicting view of the interests involved in it. They continue to believe that the distribution of wealth among countries is the most important goal – not the overall size of the global economic pie. Although contested by those who favor free trade, protectionist policies of the mercantilist style continue and have powerful advocates today.

In the classic nationalistic or mercantilist approach, states use protectionist measures to prohibit or restrict foreign imports. The strategy can be put into effect by many diverse types of government policies for manipulating foreign trade. A foreign good may simply be prohibited from entering a country – thus preventing any supply issues or questions from arising. A sanction may be placed on the goods of another country. Iran, for example, is prohibited from selling many goods in Europe and North America, and the United States imposes economic sanctions on Cuban goods. A foreign good or product may have a quota placed on it so that only a certain amount of it can be imported. Such limitations on a product increase its value or cost and make local equivalents less costly and more competitive. A government may put a tariff (or tax) on a foreign good or service, thus raising its cost and making domestic equivalents more acceptable to consumers. Other methods for discouraging imports may include nontariff barriers, such as imposing special rules for heath and security on incoming goods. This may either prevent the import of goods or make them less competitive because of their cost and availability.

Another approach is for a government to promote its own country's products and services by supporting or subsidizing them. Subsidies may include providing money to companies to lower their costs of production. Loans or tax relief may also make their own products less costly than imports. Such protectionist strategies have a decidedly "populist" appeal, especially during downturns in the economy, as in periods of unemployment, recessions or depressions, and elections. Economic nationalists are also likely to oppose free trade and international organizations such as the World Trade Organization (WTO) and NAFTA, as they make it difficult for their government to find ways to aid uncompetitive or failing industries and workers. They reduce the ability of states to act independently and, thus, diminish their sovereignty.

Economic liberalism or economic internationalism

Economic liberalism and its extension in global affairs to economic internationalism can be contrasted with various forms of mercantilism and economic nationalism. Essentially, classical liberals believe in

minimizing government intervention in the marketplace. Domestically, they push for capitalism and minimum regulations and taxes. Externally, they argue that governments should foster a free exchange of goods and services and refrain from protectionist measures, insisting on the same philosophy from other countries. Economic liberals believe that all regulations such as tariffs and subsidies distort the advantages gained by freedom in the marketplace and the possibility of prosperity for all. What matters is that all states gain from free trade and not whether one state wins over another. Liberals thus stress a shared interest in global free trade and the development of institutions to protect this principle.[7]

The case for liberal economics is posed in the same language as traditional or mainstream studies of economics. We have seen that, following David Ricardo's ideas about comparative advantage, traditional economists believe that states should make and export those goods that they can produce most efficiently and then import those that can be produced more efficiently elsewhere. Each state should take advantage of its own resources and gain from specialization. Unregulated enterprise and the free flow of trade among countries will achieve increases in overall economic prosperity for everyone. Goods and products that do not have a comparative advantage should not be allowed to hide behind protectionist walls.

The 18th-century age of Enlightenment provided many scholars and ideas of classical liberal economic theory. Particularly notable was Adam Smith, the father of laissez-faire economics (Figure 12.2). A British economist, Smith believed, like many in his time, that human beings act in rational ways to maximize their self-interest and that the resulting

---

[7] While popular in traditional economics and IPE discourse, the term *liberalism* is challenging because it is used differently from country to county – in the United States it is used popularly to mean a greater role for the state and even "socialism," in academia and government policy circles it refers to individualism and free markets, and outside the United States it is used in both senses. The Canadian Liberal Party is a centrist party much like the U.S. Democratic Party, but so-called liberal parties in Europe are often right-wing conservative parties.

Figure 12.2 Adam Smith (1723–1790) was a Scottish philosopher whose most influential work, *The Wealth of Nations*, inquired into the nature and causes of national prosperity. He invented the concept of the invisible hand, which underlies the classical liberal idea that unrestricted individual initiative serves the common good and that state direction is unnecessary. *Source:* Photos.com.

competition produces an *invisible hand* that creates the most efficient economies in terms of production, exchange, and consumption. His volume *The Wealth of Nations* (1776) made the case against state mercantilism and economic nationalism and had major influence on the development of the economies of Western states and capitalism in general.[8] He argued that wealth did not grow from the accumulation of precious metals but from the capital and goods they could buy. He expounded the policy of laissez-faire, essentially that there should be minimum intervention by government in economic affairs so that competition and markets would be free to act efficiently in the distribution of goods. According to this

theory, if individuals do what is best for themselves, this "rational" behavior will result in what would be best for the country as a whole and, by extension, the world. In other words, the free working of the market would provide the most prosperous life for the greatest number of people.

Smith's ideas included an economic reflection of the classical liberal idea that unrestricted individual initiative serves the common good and that state direction is unnecessary. Thus, free markets are a key element of his classical liberalism, as competition allows individuals to compete in the buying and selling of goods, and that will ensure the lowest possible cost. Individuals will act rationally in their own self-interest and in doing so will maximize economic efficiency. In other words, his argument is not only an economic theory but also forms part of a larger comprehensive philosophy integral to the liberal political tradition.

Society, Adam Smith said, is governed by natural laws, just like the physical universe. One of them is the law that prices in a free market are determined by supply and demand. If a government interferes with this law – for example, by trying to regulate markets, restrict competition, or assist the inefficient or unsuccessful – the natural balance of the economic system will be upset. Ideally, the government should leave the economy to adjust itself entirely through the free market. Governments, he said, had only three duties: (1) to defend against foreign attack, (2) to establish the administration of justice, and (3) to provide goods and services that are not profitable in a free society but have collective benefits (e.g., a beautiful, clean city). These three deviations from the general rule of noninterference were justifiable on humanitarian, security, and administratively pragmatic grounds, not from the standpoint of economic efficiency.

Smith's ideas about free trade and open competition were adopted and extended by John Stuart Mill in his *Principles of Political Economy*,[9] a book

---

[8] Adam Smith, *The Wealth of Nations*, rev. ed. (Lawrence, KS: Digireads, 2009).

[9] John Stuart Mill, *Principles of Political Economy* (Amherst, NY: Prometheus Books, 2004).

Figure 12.3 Friedrich Hayek (1899–1992) was an Austro-Hungarian economist and defender of classical liberalism. His famous book is *The Road to Serfdom*. He believed that central planning is dangerous because there is a tendency for it to lead to serfdom and forms of dictatorship. *Source:* Corbis.

Figure 12.4 Milton Friedman (1912–2006) was an American economist who taught at the University of Chicago and was an advisor to President Ronald Reagan. His book, *Capitalism and Freedom,* and other works made him perhaps the second most important economist of modern times after John Maynard Keynes. He rejected the Keynesian school of thought and promoted monetarism as a foundation for conservative economic policy making. *Source:* Alamy.

that helped justify the virtues of the market system in Europe and North America. In more recent times, modern economists such as Alfred Marshall, Friedrich Hayek (Figure 12.3), and Milton Friedman (Figure 12.4) have developed further such arguments for economic freedom.[10] As they argued – markets work; governments don't! Modern liberals maintain that governments cannot be as efficient as individuals in directing societies or in responding quickly to change and that the market should therefore be as free of government regulation as possible. For them, government intervention in the economy results in regulatory sclerosis, overspending, and rising inflation.

Classical liberalism, then, holds that spontaneous individual choice is more effective than government direction in coping with the demands of complex societies. This means that the marketplace should not be controlled by any individual or the government but should be allowed to adjust itself naturally to bring supply and demand into

equilibrium. Only minimal government interference is required to enforce basic rules of conduct for the general welfare, such as respect for individuals and contracts. To protect the market, the state should promote competition, prevent monopolies, provide consumers with information, and provide a few basic public amenities such as roads. But governments should not interfere with or provide benefits for society. Government-provided collective goods are a problem because governments have to finance them by taxing the people, which takes away money that could profitably be invested in the private market.

Classical liberals believed that the economic advantages generated by entrepreneurs would filter down in one form or another to the poorer elements of society. They thought that governments had no mandate to transfer wealth by subsidizing the weak or ill. They found government redistribution economically inefficient and incompatible with equality

[10] Friedrich A. Hayek, *The Road to Serfdom* (Chicago: University of Chicago Press, 2007).

of rights in that they would have to treat people differently before the law. Economic inequality was unavoidable, classical liberals said, but eventually the free-market system would create wealth and raise living standards for everyone. Individuals may not understand what is in their own best interest, but they will at least know better than the state, and they can learn from, and build on, their own failures.

John Maynard Keynes In 1936, John Maynard Keynes (Figure 12.5) published his general theory about how governments should act to prevent depressions.[11] Keynes radiated optimism about economics and life generally.[12] Contrary to traditional economic reasoning, he argued that governments should increase spending in bad times and reduce it in good times. Keynes's classic argument was that supply did not always create its own demand and that some inflation might be acceptable to keep unemployment rates down. In other words, Keynes believed that governments sometimes needed to step in to prevent persistent unemployment. It took the Great Depression and World War II for Keynesian ideas to become part of government policy. After World War II, most governments in the West accepted various combinations of private and public enterprises and fostered a broad oscillation in government policy between pro- and anti-Keynesian ideas about how governments should or should not interfere in the economy.

Historical shifts have shown that capitalism is based on a tidy theory, yet it produces a messy reality. Indeed, even during the Great Depression the argument for government restraint and letting the market prevail was overturned only when war broke out and the large defense spending provided the needed fiscal stimulus for economic growth.

Figure 12.5 The ideas of John Maynard Keynes (1883–1946) form the basis of an important school of economics. In his 1936 book, *General Theory of Employment, Interest and Money*, he provided theoretical justifications for government intervention in the economy. The global crisis of 2008 brought a resurgence of Keynesian thought. *Source:* Alamy.

The audience for Keynes's ideas gradually waned, however. The dominant approach to economic theory among economists and businesspeople from the 1970s on has been that free and open markets without intrusive government regulation produce the greatest market efficiency and hence the greatest good, or at least will cause less harm than government intervention. Among intellectuals, the so-called Chicago school, for example, has been more concerned with economic principles and how markets produce strong economies than with questions of fairness or justice. A near-unanimous move to economic liberalism and liberal internationalist thinking was achieved with the fall of the Soviet Union, only to be challenged again by a minor shift back to Keynesianism after the great recession of 2008–09 (see later in the chapter).

[11] John Maynard Keynes, *The General Theory of Employment, Interest and Money* (White Fish, MT: Kessinger Publishing, 2010).

[12] See Robert Skidelsky, *John Maynard Keynes, 1883–1946: Economist, Philosopher, Statesman* (London: Penguin, 2005).

To a large extent, the post–World War II period saw governments withdraw in favor of markets and globalization. Global trade in goods, services, and capital expanded rapidly, and an interdependent world seemed to have arrived along with a belief in the global idea. However, pure capitalism never existed in reality. Even in the United States, governments continued to act as the guardian of the financial system, providing public goods such as a legal system; national defense; public education; air-traffic control; and many aspects of social welfare, from unemployment benefits to Medicare and Medicaid. This combination of free-market competition and limited but necessary government services is called a mixed capitalist economy. Even Adam Smith believed that there was a role for the state in the economy. In *The Wealth of Nations* he wrote of how pride, envy, respect, and other emotions influence people's decisions.[13] Recognizing that human judgment is not purely rational, he argued that markets never work perfectly in reality and that collective goods such as security cannot be provided by the market. In short, Smith believed that the solution to many problems was some level of government intervention in a mostly privately run economy.

The traditional principles of economic liberalism and liberal internationalism are alive and well today, but they are increasingly moderated by the belief that abuses of capitalism require government regulation to prevent monopolies and unfair competition. All states provide minimum levels of services in security, transportation systems, education, and health. At the global level, liberals may espouse unfettered free trade, but they also favor the use of international institutions such as the WTO and the International Monetary Fund (IMF) to promote and regulate this trade. Thus, while liberal internationalists argue for the basic principles of freedom, capitalism, and free trade, they also accept the need for regulation to ensure cooperative behavior on the domestic and international stage.

[13] Adam Smith, *An Inquiry into the Nature and Causes of the Wealth of Nations* (Lawrence, KS: Digireads, 2009).

Radical, Marxist, and neo-Marxism approaches

The third broad approach to IPE is based on a structuralist argument that economics govern the way the world is organized politically. As well as accepting the idea that globalization continues (although they may condemn it), radical Marxists and neo-Marxists tend to stress the differences that persist among states and peoples in the world economy and build their philosophy around that idea.

The origins of radical economic interpretation are found in modern European political thought. In the early 19th century, the poor living and working conditions of the new industrial class gave rise to a new philosophy. Industrial workers wanted help from the state, but liberal principles held that they should be helped as little as possible, so that the effect of the "invisible hand" on the efficiency of the market would be attained for the benefit of all. Workers had to struggle for even the most basic government protection against abuses such as child labor, unsafe, dirty factories, and long working hours. The working class was fertile ground for the advancement of a new ideology.

Basically, two radical economic approaches arose: a "utopian" version found in Britain and France and a "scientific" version originated by Karl Marx. To improve the lot of the working class in society, the utopian socialists wanted industrial technology to advance by government action. In Britain, Robert Owen (1771–1858) and others organized model factories to demonstrate that under improved conditions labor could be more efficient and more productive. In France, Louis Blanque (1805–88) and others advocated that government should set up workshops to employ the jobless. By the end of the century, however, the so-called scientific socialists, led by the highly influential German intellectual Karl Marx (1818–83), dominated leftist thought. Within these two groups, a doctrinal split emerged over the appropriate means for achieving agreed-on ends. Those who wanted to work within the framework of parliamentary democracy became known as democratic socialists. Those who clung to Marx's

Pure communism ↑	The means of production are restored to the workers. When perfected, there would be no need for a state apparatus; it would wither away	**Figure 12.6** Marx's stages of economic evolution toward a communist utopia.
Capitalism ↑	Introduced when the means of production shifted to factories.	
Feudalism ↑	Large landowners need many laborers – serfs have somewhat more freedom than slaves.	
Slavery ↑	Some individuals acquire control of the means of production. Others exist in a state of slavery and absolute drudgery.	
Primitive communalism	Means of production and power are shared.	

revolutionary prescription were labeled communist. Both groups sought public control of the means of production and the abolition of the exploitation of labor under capitalism. But communism went beyond this to promise the equalization of material conditions for everyone.

Karl Marx Marx's thesis was based on a scientific claim that social and historical developments are determined by basic economic laws that inevitably lead to a revolutionary transition to socialism. He predicted that the exploitation of workers would eventually lead them to rise up and overthrow the capitalist systems. For Marx, class was the fundamental unit of analysis. As defined by him, a class was a group of people sharing the same relationship to the means of production – an idea that implies the existence of hierarchical economic stratification. Marx attributed the misery of the working class to oppression and exploitation by the rich capitalist class, maintaining that in capitalist systems, workers were psychologically alienated – cut off from their creative potential, from the products of their labor and from their fellow citizens as a result of the material conditions of their working life. To end this exploitation, he said, the working class should and would take control of the government, and government

in turn should take control of all industry. In this way the workers would control the industries themselves and share benefits equally. His thought was easily simplified and adapted into a political program that promised power to the working class.

Marx based this prescription on a dialectical theory of materialism that offered great hope for the working class. According to this theory, conflict generates change and accounts for historical development. There are two types of conflict: man against nature and man against man in a class struggle. History progresses according to a pattern; the domination by one group eventually leads to revolution against that group, followed by domination by the successful new group, which in turn leads to another revolution, until a perfect state is reached. Because of these inevitable historical conflicts, Marx said, societies pass through a series of predictable stages, eventually culminating in a communist utopia (Figure 12.6).

As proof of his hypothesis, Marx noted that the earliest societies lived a primitive, communal existence until a few individuals acquired control of the means to produce things people needed. They then created an underclass of slaves to perform the labor they required. Marx noted that in Europe a feudal society based on a nobility-serf relationship dominated Europe throughout the Middle Ages. This system, he said, created and then eventually was overthrown by a capitalist class in the Industrial Revolution. The capitalists, in turn, created a working class to supply cheap labor for their factories. Eventually, as the workers were exploited more and more, they would stage a revolution, seizing the means of production, ending the alienation of their class, and establishing majority rule.[14] In the final stage, according to Marx, the proletariat would do away with private property, which is the basis of class. Without classes there would no longer be any need for the state, since it is the instrument of the dominant class. At that point the state would "wither away."

Marx saw communism as a higher, more radical stage of socialism. Only communism would provide the equalization of material abundance that would allow true freedom for all human beings. His goal was to establish a revolutionary, international working-class movement. With Friedrich Engels he published *The Communist Manifesto* (1847), a short tract that held that the evils of capitalist society could not be ameliorated by reform and that only by destroying the entire capitalist economy could a new, classless society be created. This tract had enormous influence in the development of communist ideology (Figure 12.7). Twenty years later, Marx published *Das Kapital*, his major work. When Marx died, Engels took over his mission. At that point, they still had not agreed on whether the working class should take over the state peacefully by elections or violently through revolution.

In 1917, Vladimir Lenin (1870–1924) and the Bolsheviks took control of the Russian Empire and turned it into a socialist state – the Union of Soviet Socialist Republics (USSR) (Figure 12.8). This was a turning point in socialist development. Lenin was greatly influenced by Marxist thought, and the revolution gave him the opportunity to implement

Figure 12.7 Friedrich Engels (1820–1895) was one of the founders of communism. He was co-author with Marx of the *Communist Manifesto*, claiming that class struggle is the basis of history. *Source:* Shutterstock.

it. Socialists who supported progress through revolution established communist parties, and the Communist Party in the Soviet Union became the inspiration and leader of revolutionary communist groups throughout Europe and elsewhere. Lenin revised Marx's theory, believing that Marx's conception of socialism as a mass democratic struggle was insufficient to achieve the desired political ends; there also had to be revolutionary leadership from an efficient, tightly controlled professional elite within a Communist Party.

In the short run, Lenin said, an emerging socialist society would need a strong state to defend itself against a capitalist counterrevolution. Eventually, however, classes would disappear, the means of

---

[14] For a technical discussion of the failure of revolution to occur in the manner predicted by Marx, see Mancur Olson, *The Logic of Collective Action: Public Goods and the Theory of Groups,* rev. ed. (Boston: Harvard University Press, 1971).

Figure 12.8 Vladimir Lenin (1870–1924) was a revolutionary Bolshevik who became leader of the Communist Party, took control of the Russian Empire, and turned it into a communist state. He was succeeded by Stalin in 1924. *Source:* Photos.com.

production would be held by all, and there would be no further need for the state. If the expected European revolutions did not take place, richer countries would try to extend their power over other states. Lenin claimed that advanced capitalist economies would manage to postpone social and economic chaos only because they would expand into new markets in other parts of the world such as Asia, Africa, and Latin America. He saw colonialism and imperialism as consequences of monopoly capitalism; they were methods to delay the social disintegration and economic collapse that eventually would take place in capitalist nations. He outlined these ideas in *Imperialism: The Highest Stage of Capitalism* (1916).[15]

Modern neo-Marxists developed such reasoning much further. This is a rich and important field of enquiry, but we have space here only to deal with a portion of their theory and research. Global capitalism, they said, would lead to the developed capitalist states exploiting the lesser developed ones. The poorer states would become *dependent* on the richer

countries for capital, and the richer states would *exploit* the resources and cheap labor of the lesser developed countries. A kind of dependency would be worked out between a *core* of rich states and a *periphery* of poor states in a dependency relationship. The richer states would sell their expensive manufactured goods to the poor states and in return receive the benefits of cheap labor and resources in the poorer countries. The new proletariat would in fact be the poorer states themselves, where resources could be harvested and cheap products produced by workers. Even today, neo-Marxists argue that the poorer states are kept in a neocolonial situation akin to earlier imperialism. They conclude that the exploitation of states and classes should be ended by a fundamental restructuring of global economic power. Some neo-Marxists object as well to the attention paid to globalization – arguing either that it is nothing new or that it is used as an ideological weapon in the struggle for advantage.[16] These ideas and the theory of dependency are discussed in

---

[15] V. I. Lenin, *Imperialism* (London: Pluto Press, 1996).

[16] For a comprehensive set of views, see Richard Wyn Jones, ed., *Critical Theories and World Politics* (Boulder, CO: Lynne Rienner, 2000).

Chapter 13, where we examine inequalities in global economics.

State capitalism: The rise of a new system?

In the past decade there has been a shift in global economic power. As we saw in Chapter 5, emerging economies, especially China, are playing a more important role in trade and finance, and many other countries have begun to emulate their approach. The term state capitalism has come in vogue to describe the approach of some of the most important states in the global economy. But the concept means different things to different people. It is not a complete theory of the global economy but rather a belief in the power of the market combined with authoritarian rule. It is a redesigned capitalism sharing traits of both liberal internationalism and economic nationalism.

Ian Bremmer defines state capitalism as "a system in which the state plays the role of leading economic actor and uses markets primarily for political gain."[17] He describes such states as threats to the liberal global economy. Some authoritarian leaders, he argues, know that communist or state-directed economies will fail eventually, but they do not trust free-market capitalism either because to do so would mean empowering other political institutions. In short, such leaders cannot accept ideas that are linked with free-market capitalism, but neither can they accept other values such as the rule of law, independent courts, transparency, and a free media, which tend to be associated with democracies. Consequently, they have compromised, accepting some parts of the free-market system while maintaining political control overall. Their leaders accept the need for free world trade and recognize its importance for prosperity, as they know that globalization is bringing an increasingly free flow of goods, services, capital, and labor across borders, and they want to capture its

benefits for their own empowerment. They are not mercantilist, however, as they do not favor a return to overt protectionist measures.

The governments of such state capitalist countries control the commanding heights of their economies and possess large sums of capital. They run most of the leading energy companies in the world. They own the thirteen largest oil companies in the world; control three-quarters of the world's crude oil reserves; and compete strongly in the global marketplace in aviation, shipping, power generation, arms production, metals, minerals, telecommunications, and petrochemicals. They use the wealth from state-owned national oil and gas companies, other state enterprises, and privately owned but politically loyal "national champion" companies to increase their political control over the system.[18] In China, Russia, and India the state also owns most of the banking system.

The profits from these government ventures are kept in sovereign wealth funds (SWFs), which are state-owned pools of money that can be invested strategically for political purposes. Such funds date back at least to 1953 in Kuwait and today there are about fifty of them. The International Monetary Fund estimates that before the economic downfall there were more than US$7 trillion in these reserves in 2007.[19] By 2008 China held about a quarter of the funds in SWFs while the United Arab Emirates, Saudi Arabia, Kuwait, Russia, and Norway controlled about half of the rest.[20] Sovereign wealth funds are held in many forms – foreign currency, stocks, bonds, precious metals, real estate, and other assets. The funds come from foreign currency earned from selling natural resources such as oil and gas, profits

---

[17] Ian Bremmer, *The End of the Free Market: Who Wins the War between States and Corporations?* (New York: Penguin, 2010), p. 33.

[18] See Bremmer, *End of the Free Market*; for a more complete application of a similar argument to China, see Stefan Halper, *The Beijing Consensus: How China's Authoritarian Model Will Dominate the Twenty-First Century* (New York: Basic Books, 2010).

[19] Cited in Bremmer, *End of the Free Market*, p. 71. Alberta Canada and Alaska in the United States also possess SWFs, which come from their sales of oil and gas.

[20] For a complete listing, see http://www.swinstitute.org/fund-rankings/.

from state-owned enterprises, and, in China's case, from the profits of selling manufactured goods to the United States and elsewhere – that is, from a positive balance of trade.

A distinction should be drawn between these state-capitalist countries and others such as European social welfare countries, which mix free markets with government control of many aspects of their economies. Norway, for example, channeled money from its oil and gas revenues into a pension fund to keep the country stable when resources ran out and now has one of the largest sovereign wealth funds in the world. As we have seen, every country regulates its economy to some degree, and government intervention in the economy increased markedly even in countries such as the United States after the 2008–09 financial crisis. But there is a distinction to be made between the degree and intentions of government interventions around the world. Most state-capitalist countries are authoritarian and exhibit little or no tolerance for liberal-democratic constitutional limits on their governmental authority and in many cases punish even the mildest dissent or press criticism. While liberal internationalists and free-market proponents accept the need to interfere in the market to save it, state capitalists see the market primarily as a venue in which to compete for their country's national interest. In short, they combine characteristics of both the liberal and the nationalistic schools of economic thought.

China, Russia, Saudi Arabia, and the United Arab Emirates provide the most important examples of state capitalism, and Venezuela and Iran come close to mimicking the model. South Africa is adapting aspects of the model. According to Ian Bremmer, Chinese communist leaders believe that to maintain their political power, they must control a large share of the wealth that the markets can achieve. "This is a form of capitalism but one in which the state acts as the dominant economic player and uses markets primarily for political gain."[21] It has worked. China's share of global trade has increased tenfold since its

1970s adoption of free-market reforms. At the same time, like earlier mercantilists, China has been using its economic power to obtain control of raw materials such as oil, gas, metals, and strategic minerals in the developing world.

By 2011, three of the world's four largest banks by market capitalization were Chinese firms – the Industrial and Commercial Bank of China (ICBC), the China Construction Bank, and the Agricultural Bank of China. The country also owned two of the five largest companies by market value – the Industrial and Commercial Bank of China (ICBC) and Petro China. Beijing competes successfully by subsidizing exports heavily. It gives businesses favorable loans and provides favorable exchange rates to those who buy Chinese products. It also imposes controls on the investments of Chinese citizens so it can funnel capital into Chinese businesses. Trade profits and cash inflows have resulted. Chinese Premier Wen Jiabo described his economic policy as giving full play to the basic role of market forces in allocating resources under the macroeconomic guidance and regulation of the government.[22]

China's financial foreign policy is based on two strategies: to accumulate foreign currency reserves and to provide direct investment abroad in the form of aid, assistance, and loans, in order to secure raw materials, new technologies, managerial know-how, and distribution networks that will bolster domestic growth and the Communist Party's legitimacy.[23] To a large extent this strategy has worked, evidenced by its phenomenal 8 percent annual growth rate. After three decades of spectacular growth, in 2010 China passed Japan to become the world's second-largest economy, and some forecast that it will pass the United States as early as 2030. It is now the biggest trading partner in Asia, and in 2010 it passed Germany to become the world's biggest exporter. The belief that state capitalism is a threat to the global economy is underlined by Stefan Halper,

[21] Bremmer, *End of the Free Market*, p. 5.

[22] Halper, *The Beijing Consensus*.

[23] Ken Miller, "Coping with China's Financial Power: Beijing's Financial Foreign Policy," *Foreign Affairs* (July–August 2010), pp. 96–110.

who believes that China has successfully created imitators in the developing world. He believes that several authoritarian leaders have accepted the Chinese model based on the idea that the best way to achieve sustainable economic development is for the state to control public wealth, investment, and enterprise.

China, therefore, has accepted capitalism along with international markets and free trade, but it is also an authoritarian country that forbids freedom of speech, belief, and assembly, and even the idea of a loyal opposition. For Stefan Halper this is a direct challenge to the idea that free markets and democracies are mutually reinforcing. Growing numbers of countries in Africa, Asia, and Latin America are embracing relations with China. They admire China or are adopting its model of government. As Halper puts it, "While its leaders follow a path of progressive engagement with the liberal international order, Beijing's leaders are also leading a formidable assault on this order."[24] A battle is emerging between free-market capitalists and state capitalists, and the latter are winning.

The Chinese sell consumer goods to the United States and then use the funds to buy American dollar assets, such as Treasury bonds and mortgage-backed securities (Table 12.1). The United States profits from this, as Chinese investments enable the American government to fund large deficits, keep interest rates low, and make credit easier to obtain. It also makes it easier for Americans to buy more Chinese imports. The Chinese government keeps the value of the yuan low to encourage the sale of their products and enhance the value of its U.S. assets.[25] This means that Chinese goods are kept artificially cheap outside the country and that foreign goods are costly inside it. Chinese leaders sometime talk about selling their American dollars and setting up a new super sovereign reserve fund, but this is

Table 12.1 **China's trade in goods with United States, 2012 in millions of US$**

China	Imports	Exports	Balance
Total	110,590.1	425,643.6	315,053.5

Source: Adapted from U.S. Census at www.census.gov.

unlikely to happen. China is in a *dollar trap*. If it sells its U.S. dollars, it will decrease their value and thus weaken its own portfolio, which is about 70 percent dollar denominated.

Exchange rates are a serious point of tension between China and other countries. Both Americans and Europeans claim that Beijing's management of its currency is responsible for their growing trade deficits. Currency trading with China is controlled by the People's Bank of China. The bank sets the daily rate for the yuan against the dollar, and the currency is permitted to trade no more than 0.5 percent above or below that rate. China let the yuan rise 21 percent against the dollar between 2005 and 2008, but the U.S. Congress still argues that the currencies should be completely delinked. Economists disagree that delinking the yuan would fix America's trade deficit.

In the early 1970s Japan was pressured to let its currency fluctuate against the dollar to rectify the U.S. trade deficit with that country. Japan did so, but the deficit continued to grow. By 2006, the Japanese yen was more than three time as expensive as in 1971, and the deficit was at an all-time high of $90 billion. It could prove the same with China today. Alternatives suggested are for the United States to increase its exports and encourage China and other countries to increase their direct investment in the United States. In 2010, China allowed its currency to rise to the strongest level since 2005. This gave only a small improvement but was considered significant by analysts of global monetary issues.

In a manner similar to mercantilist practices, China also attempts to gain control of resources in the developing world, putting billions of dollars

[24] Halper, *The Beijing Consensus*, p. 2.
[25] In 2010, China allowed its currency to rise to the strongest level since 2005. This proved a small improvement but was considered significant by analysts of global monetary issues. *The New York Times*, June 25, 2010.

into regimes in Africa and Latin America, where it asserts greater and greater influence. In return for resource contracts, it supports dictators in some of the most repressive regimes in Central Africa and sells them manufactured products. It approaches these countries with a long-term strategy, providing incentives that cannot be matched by other institutions. As President Abdoulaye Wade of democratic Senegal put it, "China's approach to our needs is simply better adapted than the slow and sometimes patronizing post-colonial approach of European investors, donor organizations and non-governmental organizations."[26]

China's financial policy is set up to stimulate economic growth and job creation at home. It has pursued growth single-mindedly, on the basis of the premise that rapid growth is the best way to reduce poverty. As long as this is successful, results will give it legitimacy and help its people forgive corruption, inequality, restricted freedoms, and a host of other negative issues.[27] China, however, has huge challenges to meet. Economists say that its economy relies too heavily on exports and that it needs to stimulate greater domestic consumption.

China's global rise means that the state capitalism approach needs to be understood and examined alongside the three traditional approaches to global economics discussed earlier in the chapter. China has even set up an "overseas propaganda campaign" to sell "the China model" as a contrasting brand to that of liberal internationalism. It is already serving as a model for other Asian countries. Whether one calls it state capitalism or market authoritarianism, the idea is gaining ground both in the real world of economics and in academic commentary. Some call the approach the Beijing Consensus and claim that it is beginning to replace liberal ideas about the world economy – the Washington Consensus (discussed later in this chapter) – as the favored approach to the world economy. There now are two types of capitalism – one based on liberal ideas about government and freedom and another based on an antiliberal

philosophy. The newly rising model is authoritarian state-led capitalism inspired by Asian values rather than a product of Western capitalism based on Western values and leadership. Which model will prove the most effective at generating economic growth and will be emulated by the rest of the world?

There are times when governments are required to deliberately shape market incentives to reflect social objectives, and in this task authoritarian-led capitalism is becoming a model of choice for many countries in Asia and elsewhere.

Global economic governance

The international economic environment is not without rules, regulations, and institutional forms of governance. As the global economy grows, so, too, does the importance of international economic institutions. The first contemporary organizations were set up at the end of World War II to foster cooperation in the global economy. These intergovernmental organizations (IGOs) were designed to enhance international trade and avoid the problems that gave rise to the Great Depression of the 1930s that preceded World War II.

Near the end of the war, in July 1944, forty-four allies met at Bretton Woods in the United States to reorganize the war-torn economies and facilitate worldwide economic coordination of the trading world. The Depression had left an indelible impression that the world should not be allowed to return to the kind of nationalist and protectionist measures that had plagued it in the years leading up to the rise of Nazism. The purpose of the meeting was to establish rules to govern the postwar economic order and to provide open trade and free financial markets. A decision was taken to set up a triumvirate of institutions – the World Bank, the International Monetary Fund (IMF), and the General Agreement on Tariffs and Trade (GATT) – to make rules, settle disputes, and punish wrongdoers in the global economy. It was at this time that it was also decided to fix (peg) the exchange rate

[26] Cited in Halper, *The Beijing Consensus*, p. 103.
[27] Miller, "Coping with China's Financial Power," p. 96.

of the American dollar to the gold standard, and other currencies to the dollar. The currencies could be "unpegged" only within stipulated regulations. Eventually, however, these rules unraveled as a result of pressures on the American dollar, and in 1972 the entire exchange system became unregulated when the United States announced that it would no longer convert dollars to gold or vice versa. Since then, as we have seen, currencies have floated freely, and states have had less authority to regulate the world economy, as supply and demand is the chief determinant of the exchange rate of currencies.

This overall liberal approach to the world economy was called the Washington Consensus (a term invented in 1989 by John Williamson), which refers to a philosophy or set of ideas emphasizing that free markets enhance global development. According to this philosophy, all states and the three new global governance institutions should push for the privatization of public enterprises, reduction of government expenditure, liberalized trade by the elimination of trade barriers, minimal restrictions on foreign direct investment, the reduction of government regulation over the economy, open competition, and tax reform. There have been many attempts to summarize the meaning of this Washington Consensus. Niall Fergusson, in *The Ascent of Money: A Financial History of the World*, states that the various elements were to impose fiscal discipline, reform taxation, liberalize interest rates, raise spending on health and education, secure property rights, privatize state-run subsidies, deregulate markets, adopt a competitive exchange rate, remove barriers to trade, and remove barriers to foreign direct investment.[28] In accordance with these principles, Western countries began reducing the role of the public sector and regulation. Efforts were made to privatize rail, postal services, airlines, banking, and utility networks. Internationally, the ideas of the Washington

Consensus included a reduced role for the state and an outward orientation that demanded stabilization measures and structural adjustment programs in the poorest states of the world.

The impact of the Washington Consensus on development policies is evident in most international organizations, but it has increasingly been questioned as a model. The 2008–09 financial crisis caused thirty-four million people around the world to lose their jobs, moving sixty-four million more people below the poverty threshold level of $1.25 a day. It is being challenged as a set of beliefs by the new philosophy of state capitalism. As a top British economist, Anatole Kaletsky, put it:

> If market forces cannot do something as simple as financing home mortgages, can markets be trusted to restore and maintain full employment, reduced global imbalances or prevent the destruction of the environment and prepare for a future without fossil fuels?[29]

General Agreement on Tariffs and Trade and the World Trade Organization

The General Agreement on Tariffs and Trade (GATT) was established in 1947 as both a treaty and an institution. As a treaty, it set out a code of rules for the conduct of trade. Its aim was to promote free trade by working to remove barriers to trade such as tariffs, quotas, and legal restrictions. As an institution in Geneva, it provided a forum for discussing trade problems and negotiating solutions. In 1995 the GATT became the World Trade Organization (WTO), and today its membership comprises almost all countries of the world and covers most global trade. As of 2013 there were 153 members in the WTO, including China, which had been prevented from joining for many years, and Russia, which finally joined after seventeen years of negotiations. Each country has one vote in the organization, but action requires a two-thirds majority. A country can withdraw from the WTO by giving six months' notice of its intentions.

---

[28] Niall Fergusson, *The Ascent of Money: A Financial History of the World* (London: Allen Lane, 2008), pp. 308–09.

[29] Anatole Kalensky, "Blaming China Won't Help America," *International Herald Tribune*, September 28, 2010, p. 6.

The GATT attempted to establish a world trading order based on reciprocity, nondiscrimination, and multilateralism, and the WTO continues that work. The primary governing assumption is that liberalization, or the removal of barriers to trade, will provide increasing prosperity for all countries. States can file complaints against other member states for alleged violations of the treaty, and sanctions can be imposed if a two-thirds vote of the whole membership is obtained. This idea is fleshed out by the most-favored-nation concept, which requires states to treat all members of GATT the same as their most favored trading partners. If the United States, for example, imposes a tariff on automobiles coming into the country, it must impose the same tariff level on automobiles from all other GATT members. World trade grew steadily after the GATT was founded and then slowed in the 1970s, with the Organization of Petroleum Exporting Countries (OPEC) showing the most rapid growth during the following decade. In 1981, for the first time since World War II, there was no real growth in world trade. However, the world economy soon grew with increased international competitiveness, and the volume of global trade increased handsomely for about three decades. It slowed significantly only with the 2008–09 recession.

To reduce protectionism, GATT officials and state governments have held eight successful multilateral rounds of negotiations, amending the trading rules and reducing tariffs. The last completed round of these discussions states among 109 states began in 1986 in Uruguay. Named the Uruguay Round, it lasted nearly a decade, completing its work only in 1994. The treaty made major breakthroughs, solving difficulties in the service sector, including banking, insurance, telecommunications, broadcasting, and so forth, and on intellectual copyright for patents and licenses. Tariffs on manufactured goods were reduced by 37 percent over ten years. However, nontariff barriers based on health and safety rules continued, to some extent, to protect home industries, and agriculture was hardly reformed at all.

The Uruguay participants also agreed to transform the GATT secretariat into a somewhat more powerful World Trade Organization (WTO) with authority to administer the multilateral trade agreements. The organization set up a Trade Policy Review Mechanism (TPRM) to scrutinize trade practices and Dispute Settlement Panels (DSPs) composed of experts and to hear trade disputes among the members and exercise enough power to demand the end of the practices and authorize retaliatory sanctions on violators. The disputants often negotiate directly with each other to try to settle their cases out of court.[30] If a country has problems meeting the standards because of balance-of-payment issues or domestic political pressures, it may be allowed to claim exemptions or safeguards.

The current ninth round, or the Doha Round, on trade and development has had its ups and downs. Negotiations began in Doha, Qatar, in 2001 with the overall goal of helping developing countries. By strengthening the rules on agricultural subsidies, the developing countries hoped that the WTO would reduce the barriers that richer countries place on their agricultural imports. They claim that they are prevented from selling their agriculture products at reasonable prices, pointing to U.S. and Japanese subsidies to farmers and to the European Union's protectionist Common Agricultural Agreement as evidence for their argument. Such policies, they contended, allow farm products to be sold at artificially low prices, thus undermining the sales of products from poorer regions. Farmers in developed countries have had considerable success blocking trade reforms in agriculture before, and the WTO has been less successful lowering barriers in this field than in others. The developed countries wanted the Doha Round to deal with issues such as lowering tariffs, enforcing intellectual property rights, and reducing investment

---

[30] On average, more than thirty cases are filed annually. See Kara Leitner and Simon Lester, "WTO Dispute Settlement from 1995–2005: A Statistical Analysis," *Journal of International Economic Law* 9, no. 1 (2006), pp. 219–31.

restrictions.[31] The process stalled over these and other issues that separate the North and South members, and negotiations are still at an impasse. As Pascal Lamy, director general of the WTO, put it:

Although 80 percent of the job is done, negotiations are considering the remaining 20 percent, staring at each other waiting for the other side to move first. Obviously, nobody wants to move first by fear that its moves could be pocketed by others without obtaining anything in return.[32]

Progress is unlikely.

Criticisms of the WTO The WTO is not without critics. The principles of GATT should, in theory, disallow free-trade agreements that are limited to only some members of the organization, but the treaty is logically incoherent and inconsistent. It exempts regional organizations such as the EU and NAFTA from its rules on the basis that they are helping to liberalize overall trade and are leading the world toward more overall free trade. Moreover, the WTO as an organization is not as egalitarian as is suggested by its formal institutional structures. The great powers dominate the decision making – the Quad, consisting of the United States, Japan, the European Union, and Canada, often meets privately, comes to an agreement, and then works out a consensus with the other states based on their prior agreement. Some states also believe that the WTO endangers their sovereignty because of its ability to make trade regulations, settle disputes, and assign penalties.

Outside government circles, many groups such as trade unions, leftist organizations, and some NGOs find that the WTO supports corporations over people, businesspeople over workers, rich over poor (often phrased in terms of North over South), economic growth over environmental concerns, and so on. These clashes over fundamental values have come to a head during recent meetings of the WTO.

Protesters almost shut down the Seattle meetings in 1999, and ever since, demonstrators have been out in force at every meeting of the WTO and at other major international economic meetings that could be construed to be in favor of liberalization, free trade, or globalization.

The International Monetary Fund

The purposes of the International Monetary Fund (IMF) are to foster stability in money markets, to encourage cooperation among states on monetary matters, to aid in the establishment of a payment system, and to promote international trade. Currently, 187 states are members. The IMF funds its operations with money received from member countries and interest from its loans. The funds' unit of account is called Special Drawing Rights (SDRs), a virtual currency whose value is based on an average value or market basket of several currencies, including the U.S. dollar, the EU euro, the British pound, and the Japanese yen. In 2012 one SDR was worth US$1.54. The reason for using SDRs is that its value is insulated from significant fluctuations is any single currency. In 2011 the overall estimated budget from which loans could be made was 238 billion SDRs. The importance of each individual state in the IMF is measured by its voting strength, which is based on the financial contributions it makes to the fund. Each country has a "quota" based on the size of its economy. The United States holds the largest single share of the votes, as it contributes the largest amount of money. Its contribution is more than 17 percent of the total, or $42 billion SDRs in 2012.[33]

The IMF lends money to member states that are seriously affected by balance-of-payment difficulties due to trade deficits or other profound difficulties in loan repayments. It also provides technical assistance concerning their economies. Large and persistent deficits cannot be maintained, as sooner or later indebted countries will be unable to borrow

[31] Aaditya Mattoo and Arvind Subramanian, "From Doha to the Next Bretton Woods: A New Multilateral Trade Agenda," *Foreign Affairs* 88, no. 1 (January–February 2009), pp. 15–27.
[32] http://www.wto.org.
[33] See the IMF for the most recent figures, which are constantly changing; http://www.imf.org.

the capital required to pay for their inflow of goods and services. As their currency weakens in the global exchange, imports will become more expensive and put inflationary pressures on their domestic economies. In such cases, the IMF invokes liberal economic principles and calls on state recipients of funds to diversify and restructure their economies, achieve fiscal equilibrium, improve balance of payments, and reduce public-sector expenditures. In recent years, the IMF has also been very active in helping relieve the debts of the least developed countries and in assisting the transition of former socialist directed economies to market economics. Concentrating most on the lesser developed countries over time, the IMF devotes a large part of its budget to the very poorest of the poor countries. Its program Poverty Reduction and Growth Facility (PRGF) provides loans at extremely low rates to low-income countries, and another special program lends money at concessional rates to the most indebted countries or heavily indebted poor countries (HIPCs). Critical issues related to these topics and economic development are discussed in the next chapter.

Criticisms of the IMF The IMF has long been criticized as an instrument of Western domination, especially since voting strength in the organization is determined by financial contributions. The United States contributes 17 percent of the budget, so it gets 17 percent of decision-making votes. Together the eight largest contributors and richest countries in the world contribute more than half the funds, so they control all final decisions. Critics contend that this deprives poorer countries of a satisfactory voice in decisions.

The IMF also has been savagely attacked for its insistence on the principles of capitalism. Indeed, the central criticism concerns the very basis of the IMF philosophy – the liberal principles of eliminating obstacles to an efficient market and free trade, founded on the traditional views expounded by Adam Smith and later scholars such as Milton Friedman. For a state to receive money from

the IMF, it is often required to adopt structural adjustment policies, which typically require it to enact severe economic reforms to eradicate the causes of its financial difficulties. These may include devaluing their currency, eliminating subsidies, introducing limits on credits, making tax and financial sector reforms, reducing the size of government, and – most important – liberalizing their trade policies by removing high tariffs.

The conditionality of IMF loans requires aid recipients to fix the conditions and practices that led to the need for the loan in the first place and to adopt policies that will lead to improvement in economic growth. As such requirements are likely to demand reductions in government programs that redistribute wealth and/or increase taxes, it is not surprising that they are often not well received. The IMF's policies are also criticized as being "cookie cutter," as they tend to enforce general rules that may not bear in mind local economic and political conditions. For this reason, some economists claim that IMF policies sometimes do more harm than good. Stringent conditions have caused governments to reduce social services, an act that has often lead to internal unrest and on occasion has even destroyed governments. Indeed, the IMF's policies are attacked as violating the sovereignty of the recipient countries because they interfere in their social institutions and political processes. Christine Lagarde became the new IMF managing director in July 2011, and her most pressing job was to deal with whether, and how, to give Greece and other debt-ridden EU countries emergency funding to keep them from declaring bankruptcy (see later in the chapter).

Trade unions and leftist intellectuals often lead the fight against IMF-imposed and IMF-enforced austerity measures. Since its rules are based on and promote theories of liberal capitalism, the loans are subject to the criticism that borrowing money from the IMF means that a country has to accept the "pure" capitalist philosophy of classical economics. At an even more general level, some theorists complain that IMF rules increase the dependency of

The travels of a T-shirt in the global economy

Debates on globalization and its effects have often lacked complexity and nuance. In her thought-provoking book, business professor Pietra Rivoli follows the voyage of a single T-shirt around the world. Her conclusions debunk many of the myths of both pro- and antiglobalization camps by showing the interrelated roles of history, markets, and politics in world trade.[34]

Rivoli sharply contrasts the views of antiglobalization activists such as student, labor, religious, environmentalist, and human rights groups about the evils of business corporations with those of the IMF, World Bank, and economists who enthusiastically tout the economic advantages of free markets and the theory of competitive advantage. The first group adopts a high degree of moral certitude about how free international trade leaves human lives and societies ruined in its wake, whereas the second group concerns itself basically with gross economic and statistical considerations. Of course, both ideas are simplified and exaggerated. Even the role of markets is contestable.

As the author demonstrates, the life of her T-shirt proved less about competitive markets than about "politics, history, and creative maneuvers to avoid markets." While the life of the T-shirt is evidence of the wealth-enhancing possibilities of globalization, the markets themselves are found to be embedded in "historical and political webs of intrigue" and are not the neutral mechanisms well-loved by classical economists.[35]

Rivoli makes a strong case for both the virtues and defects of globalization in improving the human condition. Where do you stand on this vital topic?

[34] Pietra Rivoli, *The Travels of a T-Shirt in the Global Economy: An Economist Examines the Markets, Power, and Politics of World Trade* (Hoboken, NJ: John Wiley & Sons, 2009).
[35] Rivoli, *Travels of a T-Shirt*, p. xii.

the developing countries on the rich world. Loans from the IMF tend to require recipients to open their economies to world trade and investment and to accept capitalist solutions to their difficulties. Is this a form of neocolonialism? The important key concepts and relevancy of dependency and neocolonialism in the global economy are discussed in Chapter 13. See Close Up 12.1 on the lessons to be learned from this.

The World Bank

The initial purpose of the World Bank was to aid the reconstruction of Europe after World War II, but over time, the bank shifted its focus to development goals. It lends money to states that commercial banks or other lenders might not support, and it generally tries to reduce poverty in middle-income and creditworthy poorer countries. The bank consists of three institutions – the International Finance Corporation (IFC), the International Development Agency (IDA), and the Multilateral Investment Guarantee Agency (MIGA). A total of 187 countries belong to the World Bank. It makes its decisions in a manner similar to that of the IMF, with voting strength relative to financial contributions. The five countries that contribute the most to the World Bank's capital are the United States, Germany, Japan, France, and the United Kingdom. The World Bank tends to support problem projects and has large holdings with developing countries.

Like any bank, it makes loans that require interest payments, but it concentrates on large, long-term infrastructure projects such as highways and bridges, energy supplies, telecommunications, and agricultural business. The IDA also makes interest-free loans – for up to fifty years – to the very poorest countries so that they have an opportunity to reach economic stability and sustainable growth. In recent years an additional stress has been placed on sustainable development – focusing on developmental economics that demand a concern for renewable resources and the environment while protecting Earth's biosphere (see Chapter 15). The IDA also encourages private capital to flow to the developing countries.

Criticisms of the World Bank The World Bank is criticized in the same terms as the IMF. It, too, allows richer contributing countries more authority in decision making. Since the United States contributes almost 17 percent of the total budget, it obtains an almost equal percentage of the votes in policy decisions. The World Bank's president has always been an American. Even in 2007, when Paul Wolfowitz was forced to resign in a cloud of criticism, President Bush simply nominated Robert Zoellick, another American, to replace him, and he was quickly confirmed. This overt American power is condemned throughout the developing world as illustrating the problems with global financial institutions. The practice was continued in 2012, when Jim Yong Kim, a Korean American, was appointed president of the bank. Kim is well known as president of Dartmouth College and a leading medical specialist.

Moderates criticize the World Bank's inability to improve its finances. Despite pious statements about raising developmental goals in the 1990s, there has been no significant change in how much it spends and lends. Some moderates claim that too large a share of the bank's loans go to too few countries – especially to countries such as Brazil, China, and India, which have already achieved high takeoff positions in comparison to the vast number of poor countries around the world. Radicals argue that the World Bank has one basic purpose – to support the dominance of rich northern countries over poorer southern ones. Critics maintain that the World Bank, like the IMF, acts in a manner similar to earlier colonial powers by insisting that development funds follow the North's prescriptions. Indeed, they argue that not been much serious development has been achieved by the World Bank's work – but that is plainly exaggerated. The World Bank, like the IMF, has brought considerable support to the leaders of states who have asked for its assistance. Unfortunately, some funds have ended up in the hands of kleptocracies – states ruled by criminals and thieves.

Institutions for economic cooperation

Besides the GATT, the IMF, and the World Bank, the countries of the world have also organized themselves into many other intergovernmental financial institutions. These include the Organization for Economic Cooperation and Development (OECD), as well as clubs of states starting with the Group of Seven (G7), Group of Eight (G8), and, more recently, the Group of Twenty (G20). Their members and other countries form many bilateral and regional organizations, such as the North American Free Trade Agreement and the European Union. Indeed, at the time of writing there were 167 bilateral and regional free-trade agreements in the world.

Organization for Economic Cooperation and Development

The Organization for Economic Cooperation and Development (OECD) was created in 1961 by the United States, Canada, and Western European countries to discuss economic issues, collect data, carry out studies, and provide members with economic and technical advice. Today the organization has thirty-four members. According to the OECD, its mission is to bring together governments of countries from around the world that are committed to democracy and the market economy. Together they work to support sustainable economic growth, boost employment, raise living standards, maintain financial stability, assist other countries' economic development, and contribute to growth in world trade.[36]

The G7, G8, and G20

Some of the largest economic powers have been meeting annually at economic summits since 1975. These meetings provide an occasion for leaders to discuss major, often complex, international issues and to develop the personal relations that might help them respond collectively to disasters and other crises. The summits also give direction to the

---

[36] http://www.oecd.org.

international community by setting priorities, defining new issues, and providing guidance to international organizations. Increasingly, the summits have taken on urgent economic development issues.

The six countries at the first summit in 1975 met at Rambouillet, France. They included the leaders of Britain, France, Germany, Italy, Japan, and the United States. They were joined by Canada at the Puerto Rico summit in 1976, and by the European Community at the London summit of 1977. Since then, membership in the Group of Seven, or G7, has been fixed. Russia first participated with the G7 in 1991. Full Russian participation followed, and since the 1994 Naples summit, the G7 has met with Russia at every summit, giving rise to the name Group of Eight, or G8. Although the G7 or G8 has no permanent secretariat, the summit has legitimized itself with large media events at which the most important economic and even political events of the day are discussed. Throughout the year, the leaders' personal representatives (known as *sherpas*) meet regularly to discuss the agenda, monitor progress, and prepare the background for the summits.

As well as macroeconomic management and international trade, questions of East-West economic relations, energy, and terrorism have also been a focus of continual concern. From these initial topics, the agenda has broadened to include microeconomic issues such as crime, drugs, and a host of political-security issues ranging from human rights to regional security, arms control, and even the Internet. In addition, the G7 and/or G8 has developed a network of supporting meetings, which allow individual departmental ministers to meet regularly throughout the year to continue the work set out at each summit; these include meetings of the finance ministers, foreign ministers, and environment ministers, among others. G7 and G8 ministers and government officials also meet on an ad hoc basis to deal with pressing issues such as terrorism, energy, and development; from time to time, the leaders also create task forces or working groups to focus intensively on specific issues of concern, such as drug-related money laundering, nuclear safety,

and transnational organized crime. Although to a large extent the G8 summits have become publicity shows, members generally comply with the decisions they have generated and codified. Compliance is particularly high in regard to agreements on international trade and energy. Summit decisions also help create and build international regimes to deal with international challenges and reform existing international institutions.[37]

The G7 or G8 has been criticized for not reflecting the current economic balance of power in the world. Therefore, since 2000, leaders of countries such as Brazil, China, India, Mexico, and South Africa have attended the meetings, and the G8 summits have expanded to twenty members (see Table 12.2). The G20 was created as a response to the global financial crises of the late 1990s and to ensure that key emerging-market countries were adequately included in the core global economic discussions and governance. The G20 is composed of the finance ministers and central bank governors of nineteen countries plus the European Union. It declares its mission as promoting discussions between industrial and emerging-market countries on key issues related to global economic stability.

Criticisms of the G7, G8, and G20 Both positive and negative comments have been generated by these summits. They have been applauded (usually by themselves) for integrating the world economy and showing leadership on difficult issues. However, they are also criticized as elitist and for trying to act like a world government without representation from the poorest countries. Clearly, the leaders and their spokespersons exaggerate their accomplishments, as there is no significant monitoring of promises made at the summits, and targets are set in a very general, elastic manner.

The most critical view is that they are nothing but "photo ops"– opportunities for world leaders to get together and get their pictures taken while making

[37] For an analysis of compliance with decisions, see http://www.g7.utoronto.ca, a website devoted to studying this topic.

Table 12.2 2013 Membership in the G20

Argentina
Australia
Brazil
Canada
China
France
Germany
European Union
India
Indonesia
Italy
Japan
Mexico
Russia
Saudi Arabia
South Africa
Republic of Korea
Turkey
United Kingdom
United States of America

loud noises about the world economy. The G8 system did not represent all the most economically powerful countries in the world, and the G20 may have too many countries to obtain compromises and accomplish much. The fact that its members include advocates for both liberal internationalism and state capitalism complicates the situation. Dominique Strauss-Kahn, former director of the IMF, criticized the summits for having "no follow-up" to their decisions, "borrowing" their communiqués, and then simply calling another meeting. "Making declarations is just not enough if you want to change the system," he concluded.[38] Some critics ask, "why not just act at the United Nations?" But that, perhaps, is obvious, too, since self-interest is involved.

Regional economic integration

Economic integration comes in many forms. There has been a proliferation of bilateral (between two countries) and regional (among more than two countries) trade agreements in recent years. Most countries of the world now belong to one or more such trading arrangements. The degree and nature of this form of economic integration can be briefly depicted in five ascending stages as follows:

1. The lowest level of integration is free trade, an agreement in which two or more countries substantially eliminate trade barriers. This can be accomplished sector by sector, as in a preferential trade agreement, or more broadly in a free-trade zone. The 1965 Canada-U.S. Auto Pact increased the flow of Canadian automobiles and parts across the U.S. border. Comprehensive approaches such as the 1989 Free Trade Agreement (FTA) between Canada and the United States, followed by the 1994 North American Free Trade Agreement among Canada, the United States, and Mexico, allowed goods and services from the hemisphere to flow freely across borders with basically no tariffs or other trade barriers. Note that such agreements do not allow the free movement of labor.

2. More integration is attained in a customs union, in which countries adopt a free-trade zone between participating countries and a common external tariff for imports from the outside world. Such a system promotes further economic integration because it prevents a good from being imported into the country with the lowest tariff and then reexported to other countries inside the free-trade zone without ever facing a new or

---

[38] *The New York Times*, October 5, 2009.

higher tariff. A customs union consequently has a protectionist dimension, as it promotes trade within the union while shielding the membership with a common tariff against nonmembers. Several Latin American countries participate in the Southern Common Market (MERCOSUR), which, since 1991, has established a regional free-trade area with a customs union.

3. A single market or common market comprises a free-trade arrangement and a customs union, as well as common policies on capital, labor, and the movement of goods and services. Economic barriers are removed to the maximum possible to allow for the free movement of all factors of production – land, labor, and capital. The Caribbean Community Single Market and the European Union are single markets.

4. An economic and monetary union is a treaty system with free trade, a customs union, a single market, and a common currency. The European Union provides an economic and monetary union for all the countries that join this part of the treaty and most countries share the euro as their currency.

5. A *state* has complete economic and political integration. A federal state with units such as provinces in Canada or states as in Australia and the United States integrates all aspects of economics inside one federal state so that the country functions as a unitary state (a state with a single unit) would. Such an arrangement ideally gives the domestic system free trade within its borders; a customs union; a single market; similar monetary, banking, and fiscal policies; and political integration. The integration of the European Union has not "deepened" to this extent.

Regional economic institutions

Despite globalization and declared commitments to worldwide free trade, political leaders continue to protect their own state's interests by joining in regional arrangements.[39] In other words, they form organizations in their own geographical areas with different levels of economic integration. Most states attempt to gain economic leverage in the global economy by forming such regional trading blocs. They are committed to organizations like the European Union (EU), the North American Free Trade Agreement (NAFTA), and the Southern Common Market (MERCOSUR), which we examine in detail here. There are many other important examples, such as the proposed Trans-Pacific Partnership (TPP) and the Trans Atlantic Trade and Investment Partnership (TATIP), which are currently attempting to forge greater economic cooperation between the two sides of the Pacific and Atlantic Oceans, drawing Canada and the United States closer to Asia and Europe. As of mid-2013 there are no formal negotiations on these ideas, but there are agreements to proceed.

NAFTA includes only Canada, Mexico, and the United States, but in 2001 the thirty-four democracies of the Americas agreed to try to extend the principle of regional free trade to include the entire Western Hemisphere. A Free Trade Area of the Americas (FTAA) would have created the world's largest free-trade area. However, despite several summits, discussions began to flounder in 2005, when Venezuela's former president, Hugo Chávez, rallied opposition to the treaty by claiming that the FTAA would lead to an increase of American dominance of the region. He argued that the United States is a hegemon that unjustly shapes global economics and politics. Other countries expressed fear that giving up their protections might allow U.S. companies to buy local properties and industries, thus flooding the South with American imports and services. American trade unions shared similar worries, namely that U.S jobs would end up moving south to Latin America if the FTAA were implemented. Specifically, the South demanded the removal of agricultural subsidies in the United States in return for an agreement, but on this topic it received no significant American response.

[39] David A. Lynch, *Trade and Globalization* (Lanham, MD: Rowman & Littlefield, 2010).

Although leaders of the countries of North America, the Caribbean, Central America, and South America continue to meet regularly in summits, there has been no significant progress since the original target date of 2005 passed without agreement. After several years without a meeting, the leaders met again in 2012. Leftist leaders from Ecuador and Nicaragua boycotted the meeting, and those who did attend were so divided on political issues such as Cuba that they could not even issue a joint declaration.

Other important trading blocs include the Andean Community grouping of Colombia, Ecuador, Peru, and Venezuela; the Association of Southeast Asian Nations (ASEAN), of Brunei, Cambodia, Indonesia, Laos, Malaysia, Myanmar, the Philippines, and Vietnam; and the Asia-Pacific Economic Cooperation (APEC), with twenty-one members, including the most powerful Pacific countries of China, Japan, Russia, and the United States. These organizations are based mostly on cooperative agreements and function somewhat like the G8 or G20.

The North American Free Trade Agreement

The North American Free Trade Agreement (NAFTA), signed in 1994, joined Canada, Mexico, and the United States together in an agreement to completely eliminate tariffs and other trade barriers by 2009. The treaty created the largest free-trade area in the world at that time, producing $17 trillion worth of goods and services annually.[40] Tariffs were to be eliminated in more than nine thousand categories of goods and services. NAFTA was not intended to become a customs union with an external common tariff or a single market like the EU; it was intended to foster trade, eliminate restrictions on foreign investment, and lead to growing prosperity in all three countries. The treaty has been an economic success, but it is not without critics. Trilateral trade has increased greatly since NAFTA's origin with merchandise trade passing the $1 trillion mark in 2008. More than 360 million people were

[40] Robert J. Jackson and Doreen Jackson, *Politics in Canada: Culture, Institutions, Behavior and Public Policy*, 7th ed. (Scarborough, ON: Pearson, 2009).

Close Up 12.2 **NAFTA principles**

Tariffs: Tariffs were to be eliminated over a fifteen-year period. Levies on half of the more than nine thousand products were phased out immediately, and 65 percent of levies were gone within five years.

Agriculture: Some tariffs on all farm products were phased out, but producers were given fifteen years to adjust to duty-free status on sensitive products.

Automobiles: To qualify for duty-free treatment, the North American content of cars (then 50 percent) had to reach 62.5 percent within eight years.

Financial services: Mexico allowed American and Canadian banks, brokerage firms, and insurance companies free access after a six-year transition period, during which bans on foreign ownership were phased out.

Textiles: Mexico avoided high duties on clothing shipments to the United States and Canada, as long as the material was made from yarns and fabrics from North America.

Trucking: Mexico allowed foreigners to invest in its trucking firms, and American, Mexican, and Canadian trucking companies were allowed to do business on cross-border routes that previously were prohibited.

affected in the three countries, and their combined annual economic output was almost $9 trillion. In 2011 this rose to an estimated $18 trillion (purchasing power parity [PPP]). The basic principles of the agreement are in Close Up 12.2.

In 2005, Canada, Mexico, and the United States signed the ambitious Security and Prosperity Partnership (SPP), an initiative aimed at deepening the integration of the three countries. The initiative called for governments to increase competitiveness in three hundred fields, from removing specific trade irritants to establishing common standards in products and tighter border controls. Some critics called the SPP a "grand conspiracy" to fashion a North American union such as the European Union by stealth, without any significant popular consultation. Others said such arguments were nothing but fear mongering, that the SPP constituted neither a treaty nor an agreement, and that much more needs to be done in erecting a security perimeter, building a customs union to eliminate rules-of-origin difficulties, and reducing the unnecessary discrepancies in regulations. Recent summits continued efforts to increase security and prosperity across the region, but as of 2009, the SPP has been dormant.

United States and Canada: Special relationship? To understand the vital significance of North American security and examine related issues, it is helpful to understand the special relationship between Canada and the United States. The two countries have the most extensive economic relationship in the world, and their geographical alignment makes them susceptible to both the benefits and the dangers of globalization and increased transnational terrorism.

Since 9/11, the United States, Canada, and, to a lesser extent, Mexico have been forging an enhanced North American or continental security network. The issue is how to keep North America's borders as free and efficient as possible while providing a security framework for all three countries. New structures and procedures sprout almost daily. A thirty-point plan between Canada and the United States calls for integration of Canadians into the U.S. foreign terrorist tracking task force, new visitor visa policies, joint units to assess information on travelers, more immigration control officers overseas, new biometric identifiers for documents, safe third-country agreement, expansion of border enforcement teams, and enhancement of the project North Star (i.e., to improve communication and cooperation between Canadian and American law enforcement personnel).

Canada and the United States are connected in many ways that create mutual vulnerability in security.[41] Since NAFTA was implemented in 1994, trade between the two countries has increased 265 percent, thereby greatly increasing economic interdependence.[42] The economic relationship relies on the efficient movement of goods, services, and people across the border. We have seen that it generates close to half a trillion dollars in trade per year, more than $1.5 billion a day, or slightly more than $1 million a minute.[43] Together the two countries form the largest two-way trade relationship in the world, even larger than that between the United States and the European Union – which has a much greater population than Canada. Canada is the largest foreign market for the United States, absorbing one-fifth of all its exports – more than the EU and China combined. Virginia sells chemicals to Canada, making it the U.S. state's most beneficial economic sector. Canada sells engines for cars in Kentucky and provides outdoor filming locations for Hollywood films.[44] The unique aspect of the Canada–United States relationship is that the countries both have tremendous stakes in each other's success; 43 percent of Canadian foreign investment is in the United States, and 61 percent of foreign investment in Canada comes from the United States.

The relationship between the two countries goes beyond general trade. The exchange of capital between them also has important political implications. Bilateral economic exchange has integrated the two countries in such a way that a violent attack on either of them would be devastating to the other. Canada is a major source of energy for the United States, providing oil, natural gas, and

---

[41] Jackson and Jackson, *Politics in Canada*, chapter 5; Robert J. Jackson and Doreen Jackson, *Canadian Government in Transition*, 5th ed. (Toronto: Pearson, 2010); Charles F. Doran, *Forgotten Partnership: U.S.-Canada Relations Today* (Washington, DC: Johns Hopkins University Press, 1971).

[42] "Canada-US Trade Relationship." U.S. Department of Commerce, http://www.buyusa.gov/canada/en/traderelationsusa-canada.html.

[43] James Morrison, "Embassy Row: Parking Lot," *Washington Times*, November 22, 2007.

[44] Government of Canada, Trade and Security Partnership Map.

electricity.[45] Canadian exports account for 9 percent of all U.S. energy demands, and the annual two-way trade in energy is worth approximately $100 billion.

Canada has the second-largest oil reserves in the world, behind Saudi Arabia, and exports about two million barrels of oil to the United States every day. Any problem with Canada's oil production and sales would force the United States to rely on less secure sources, thus subjecting it to the political machinations and ambitions of countries that have the ability to raise the price of oil. Neither has the United States been able to meet its own demand for natural gas, although significant discoveries in the past few years have created optimism that it will soon do so (see Chapter 15). Canada has supplied 82 percent of American natural gas imports. The production and sale of natural gas has required implementation of an expensive and dangerous infrastructure that includes extensive pipelines that transport oil and gas from as far as offshore Nova Scotia to the rest of Canada and the U.S. northeast.[46] Last, Canada and the United States share an integrated electricity grid that provides energy for New York, New England, the Midwest, and the Pacific Coast.[47] An attack on the grid in Canada could cause a complete blackout of Manhattan. Both countries have to work together in securing these institutions: a terrorist attack on oil, natural gas, or electricity supplies would make American and Canadian lives very difficult – even "nasty, brutish and short," as Thomas Hobbes would have put it.

Criticisms of NAFTA Critics of NAFTA exist in all three countries.[48] In Canada the major complaints come from trade unions concerned about job losses, from agricultural interests that fear the loss of their marketing boards, and from members of the general public who believe that Canada lost considerable sovereignty in the NAFTA and will eventually be forced to reduce core elements of its welfare society. Many Mexicans also complain about the NAFTA treaty on similar grounds. Mexico has been forced to diversify its economy to include more manufacturing, especially by strengthening the role of business in the northern *maquiladora* border region, and this development, too, has many critics.

In the United States, NAFTA is criticized on similar grounds. Even before the treaty was signed, labor unions complained about American businesses putting manufacturing plants in Mexican *maquiladoras*. Ross Perot, for example, who ran as a third-party candidate for presidential office in 1992, contested the deal as one that would produce a "giant sucking sound" of jobs heading to Mexico. He won 19 percent of the U.S. vote. The political left, led by labor unions and their supporters, joined the right and some business people in making savage attacks on NAFTA based on the contention that U.S. industries would jettison jobs since workers could not compete with Mexicans paid lower wages. Many observers in the United States are also concerned that NAFTA is lowering environmental and safety regulations. They point to lower standards of regulations in Mexican companies, arguing that their Mexican trucks coming into the United States, for example, are not up to the safety standards of American trucking companies, even though their trucks must be allowed to cross the borders virtually unimpeded.

MERCOSUR

The Southern Common Market (MERCOSUR), established in 1995, is the largest trading bloc in South America (Figure 12.9). It is the world's fourth-largest trading area after the European Union (EU), the North American Free Trade Agreement (NAFTA), and the Association of Southeast Asian

---

[45] U.S. State Department, "Canada," http://www.state.gov/r/pa/ei/bgn/2089.htm.

[46] Ibid.

[47] Ibid.

[48] For detailed positive proposals for reform, see Robert A. Pastor, "The Future of North America: Replacing a Bad Neighbor Policy," *Foreign Affairs* 87, no. 4 (July–August 2008), pp. 84–98.

Figure 12.9 MERCOSUR is the southern common market of the Americas, an economic and political agreement among Argentina, Brazil, Paraguay, and Uruguay to promote free trade. Controversies continue in the organization over admitting Cuba and Venezuela and about forming a free-trade area with the Americas, including NAFTA. *Source:* Corbis.

Nations (ASEAN). Its primary interest has been eliminating obstacles to regional trade and intra-MERCOSUR trade has continued to rise.

The purpose of MERCOSUR, as stated in the Treaty of Asunción, is to allow free trade among member states, with an ultimate goal of full South American economic integration. MERCOSUR's original membership included Argentina, Brazil, Paraguay, and Uruguay. Venezuela's entry as the fifth full member was accepted in 2012 while Paraguay was suspended because of the impeachment of the country's leftist president, Fernando Luago. MERCOSUR's five associate members – Chile, Bolivia, Colombia, Ecuador, and Peru – do not enjoy full voting rights or complete access to the markets of MERCOSUR's full members. Associates receive tariff reductions, but they are not required to impose the common external tariff that applies to full MERCOSUR members. The objectives of the agreement are very lofty. It proposes a customs union with a common external tariff and movement toward an arrangement similar to that of the European Union with a common market and an elected parliament.

MERCOSUR's annual summits provide an arena for critical debate about the future role of neoliberalism and free trade in South America. The possibility of Venezuela's entrance as a full member increased tensions within the trade area over relations with the United States and will play a major role in blocking the development of the FTAA. Venezuela's former president Hugo Chávez began advocating an anti-American stance as the focus of the bloc in 2006, and Brazil and Argentina are also concerned about possible free-trade deals with the United States.

The European Union

We discussed the European Union in terms of its institutional, political, and global roles in Chapters 5 and especially 6, but here we consider it strictly as a major economic institution. The origin and history of the European Union follow, to a large extent, the stages of economic integration discussed earlier. The European states gradually abolished all internal tariffs, established a common external tariff, began to negotiate with other countries on many subjects as if they were one country, and raised revenue for the European Union by imposing a value-added tax (VAT) on all EU countries. The evolution and transition has changed the EU's mission and membership.

Highlights of European economic integration can be summarized as follows:

- 1952: Belgium, France, Italy, Luxembourg, the Netherlands, and West Germany formed the European Coal and Steel Community (ECSC), which created a common market or sectoral free trade in coal, iron, and steel.
- 1957: The Treaty of Rome, signed by the same six states, established the European Economic Community (EEC) with internal free trade and a customs union and added a new institution, Euratom, in the field of nuclear energy.
- 1962: The Common Agriculture Policy (CAP) came into effect. It was and is the single most important policy for the Union. It subsidizes all European farmers to the extent that they must be brought up to the level of farmers from the states with the highest individual subsidies.
- 1992: The Maastricht Treaty was signed, creating a framework for the further "deepening" of integration by creating not only the European Community but also a European Union of three pillars committed to greater political unification of Europe. The union of supranational institutions formed the first pillar, and the two other pillars consisted of new forms of intergovernmental cooperation in foreign and home affairs. All nontariff barriers to the movement of goods, services, capital, and persons were removed, and foreign policy cooperation was established as a goal. European citizenship was put in place, and citizens of any EU state could vote in elections to the European Parliament in the state in which they lived.
- 1997: The Treaty of Amsterdam made substantial changes to the Treaty of Maastricht. It amended the Treaty of the European Union, the Treaties establishing the European Community and certain related acts. It was signed in 1997 and entered into force in May 1999.
- 1999: The European Central Bank (ECB) supplemented domestic central banks, and the European Union adopted a single currency, the euro. The aim was to have a single currency for business in order to facilitate cross-border investment and to promote economic and political integration. Individual countries in the eurozone could no longer have an independent monetary policy.
- 2002: Most EU members adopted the euro as their currency, eliminating francs, marks, liras, and so on, leaving only the United Kingdom, Denmark, and Sweden as members of the EU with their own legal currencies (and the three states continue to opt out of the common currency). The currencies of the participating members were immediately "fixed" at a specific rate in relationship to the euro.
- 2003: The EU adopted the Nice Treaty after its initial rejection by Irish voters was overturned. This treaty instituted various reforms in the commission and council, expanding the use of majority voting. The largest states obtained more votes than the smaller ones, but decisions could be made on some issues if they received a majority vote regardless of the views of the larger states.
- 2005: A proposal to continue further European integration by putting in place a constitutional treaty was defeated by referenda in France and the Netherlands, although the EU and leaders of every member state supported it.
- 2007: The EU tried again to strengthen economic and political integration. It did not attempt to write another constitution but put forward the Lisbon Treaty, which watered down the provisions of the earlier proposed constitution but still included a full-time president for the European Council (with a two-and-a-half year term), a high representative (foreign minister), and an increase in "qualified" votes in the European Council. To be accepted, the treaty had to be ratified by all twenty-seven states. Only the Irish put the treaty to a referendum. It was defeated in 2008, and the EU leadership once more faced the prospect of an unreformed set of institutions. However, in 2009 the Irish voted again, this time approving the new treaty, which came into force in December 2009.

Figure 12.10 Turkey's membership in the European Union has met several impediments. Many conservative Europeans are concerned that the EU is not ready to absorb the large, relatively poor Muslim population of Turkey. Others are not convinced that Turkey will remain stable, given the contest between religious and secular forces in the country. *Source:* Getty.

- 2008–09: The worldwide economic turndown made the search for further integration impossible, as member states had to cope with uneven levels of economic development throughout the EU and could not agree on how to combat the slump. The financial ramifications of the economic turndown are discussed in Critical Case Study 12.1. Countries in the eurozone could not employ individual strategies such as vigorous monetary stimulus or devaluation of their currency. The problems included protectionist pressures in some of the countries and severe economic difficulties for several of the weaker members.

EU membership The membership of the EU has expanded greatly since its inception. The six original members increased to nine in 1973, when Britain joined, along with Ireland and Denmark. In 1981 Greece joined, followed quickly by Portugal and Spain in 1986. These twelve states signed the **Single European Act (SEA)**, which effectively removed the last impediments for integrating Western Europe into a single economic market. Norway applied to join and was accepted, but its citizens turned down

the idea in a referendum. In 1995 Austria, Finland, and Sweden joined.

In May 2004, the EU admitted ten new members (the Czech Republic, Slovakia, Estonia, Hungary, Latvia, Lithuania, Malta, Poland, Slovenia, and Cyprus). These additions made the EU the largest free-trade bloc in the world, but having a number of poorer countries in the association also compounded the difficulties of economic policy making. Bulgaria and Romania joined in 2007, bringing the number of member states to twenty-seven. Croatia and Macedonia are slated to join. Negotiations continue with Turkey; however, its admission will be extremely difficult because of its large Muslim majority and huge underprivileged class (Figure 12.10). All twenty-seven members of the EU, with the exceptions of Britain, Cyprus, Bulgaria, and Romania, also belong to the Schengen Agreement, which allows migration within the territory of the European Union with no internal border controls.

The EU continues to expand and develop. While the internal fight between intergovernmentalists and supranationalists over the political future of the European Union continues, the economic role of the EU in international politics grows. The EU is the world's leading exporter of industrial goods and services: some 20 percent of the world's exports emanate from there and its overall gross domestic product (purchasing-power parity) makes it the largest economy in the world (see Chapters 5 and 6).

The financial crisis and its impact on the global economy

Every major business cycle ends in a downturn. Booms and busts occur because as economies grow they produce more money than can be consumed. This surplus of money causes a rise in the price of goods, stocks, bonds, and homes that is accompanied by a fall in interest rates. Eventually prices collapse, money becomes scarce, and the business cycle begins again. The cascades of economic woes lead to public fears of another Great Depression as bills and mortgages cannot be paid and massive runs on banks ensue. Because the global economic and financial systems are highly interconnected, problems in one part of the world can quickly reverberate elsewhere – causing reductions in trade and economic activities generally and risking the collapse of banks, financial contagion, and contracting credit.

In 2008 a global financial downturn that many considered the worst since the Great Depression of the 1930s originated in the United States and soon engulfed the global economy. Recession spread. Economies around the world slowed, credit tightened, and international trade declined. Large financial institutions collapsed, banks had to be bailed out by national governments, and stock markets collapsed precipitously. Businesses failed, and many citizens lost saving and homes. For most economists, the U.S. recession ended in mid-2009, but the recovery has been uneven, and the global financial system is still shaky and experiencing the weakest recovery since World War II. The possibility of a "double dip," or a second recession, lingers in the United States and has already occurred in Europe, with massive implications for the EU and especially poorer members such as Greece.

The trigger for the financial downturn was the U.S. real estate market, which peaked in 2007 and then collapsed as home values declined and people defaulted on their loans. Speculative markets and instruments built around real estate plummeted as well. The downturn spread to foreign banks because they also owned high-risk, complex financial products associated with risky U.S. mortgages. People stopped spending. Economies that depended on U.S. consumers to buy their goods lost sales. Banks and investors literally ran out of money. The liquidity shortfall in the U.S. banking system spread like a virus around the world. Negative effects spilled into most countries and raised worries about political stability.

The normal response in a recession is for the central government – such as the Federal Reserve Bank, the Bank of England, or the European Central Bank – to cut short-term interest rates so that market-determined long-term interest rates fall, and the private sector responds by borrowing and spending more. The 2008 recession was so severe that the standard response was not enough. As banks failed, governments borrowed to bail them out of their difficulties, creating huge budget deficits and debts. To mitigate the recession, the U.S. Federal Reserve Bank (the Fed), which is charged with controlling inflation and maintaining employment and growth while supporting the government's broader objectives, typically slashed interest rates almost to zero and held them there. This was intended to stimulate consumption and spur economic growth. Since interest rates could not fall any lower, the Fed adopted the unprecedented policy of quantitative easing (QE) to force interest rates extremely low.[49] Essentially, QE means that a central bank buys large amounts of government and corporate debt and pays for it with money it creates, and that money is released into the wider economy. The Bank of England also used QE. Critics fear that this measure will spark inflation before it stimulates

---

[49] This is something Federal Reserve Chair Ben Bernanke, when he was an academic, had concluded should have happened during the Great Depression. "Top 100 Global Thinkers," *Foreign Policy* (December 2010), p. 52.

growth – and inflation is like a tax because it affects everyone as it erodes living standards.

As of 2012, global growth was "at its weakest since the recovery began" almost two years earlier, and unemployment remained high.[50] Yet governments were reluctant to implement further stimulus. Many emerging economies, including China and Brazil, had already tightened their monetary policy to ward off high inflation. Criticism of the free-market-oriented Washington Consensus increased. Marxists took advantage of the occasion to underline once again their views of the inherent instability of capitalism and the need for strong state intervention.

Economist John Kenneth Galbraith is alleged to have said that the only function of economic forecasting is to make astrology look respectable. This was close to the truth in the global financial collapse of 2008–09, as both economists and bankers were blamed for mistaken analyses and policies. But the recession was caused by many factors other than dismal forecasting. Uncertainties in the financial markets, bank failures, tight credit, falling home prices, collapsing asset values, low consumer confidence, and a worldwide drop in trade greater than during the first year of the Great Depression all played a part. The World Bank forecast a decrease of 2.9 percent in global economic activity and a 10 percent drop in trade volume. In fact, between 2007 and 2009 world GDP fell by 4.1 percent. The interaction was deep and complex. People in rich countries lost jobs and homes, and people in poorer countries continued to starve and die.[51] However, fears that the world would experience another 1930s-style Depression proved incorrect. The Great Depression witnessed the stock market crash of 1929, saw world trade contract by 60 percent, and industrial production drop by more than 35 percent in Europe and the United States. At that time most governments raised taxes and cut spending in an effort to balance budgets, making the situation even

> ### Close Up 12.3 **Glossary of basic financial terms**
>
> **Bailout:** A decision by financial institutions to pay a country's debt or interest owed.
>
> **Contagion:** When default by a country hurts banks that hold its debt and prompt credit markets to freeze, so that banks virtually stop lending to each other. The problem in one country ricochets onto others.
>
> **Credit default swap:** A form of insurance that protects the buyer in case of a loan default.
>
> **Debt:** A government's total accumulated deficits over time.
>
> **Default:** A failure to repay principal or interest owed.
>
> **Deficit:** A government's revenues minus its expenditure on an annual basis.
>
> **Fiscal policy:** Government tools and decisions for managing the economy, essentially government control of taxation and expenditure.
>
> **Monetary policy:** Policy tools and decisions made by central bankers to manage the economy; changing the country's money supply (the amount of money in circulation) and/or interest rates to control inflation.

worse. Unemployment topped 35 percent in Germany, a circumstance that helped elect Adolf Hitler.

The 2008–09 recession was not as bad as it might have been. An elaborate system of international trade rules and the WTO were in place to prevent worldwide protectionist barriers. Some lessons had been learned from the Great Depression. In 2008–09, interest rates were not raised to stop stock market speculation, and, on the whole, states did not erect corrosive trade barriers as they had in the 1930s. The multilateral organizations worked well enough to keep the trading system open, and globalization continued. The impact of the financial downturn differed around the globe. Emerging countries such

---

[50] *The Economist*, June 18, 2011, p. 15.
[51] Roger C. Altman, "The Great Crash, 2008: A Geopolitical Setback for the West," *Foreign Affairs* 88, no. 1 (January–February 2009), pp. 2–14.

as Brazil, India, and China fared best of the larger economies, perhaps because they were somewhat insulated from the global financial order.

A great many economic and political factors have been blamed for the crash, especially the very complex investment instruments, undisclosed conflicts of interest, and failures in credit rating agencies. Regulatory instruments were not sufficient or were not enforced. Because the crisis originated in the United States, the leadership of the United States and the dollar as the leading currency in the global financial system were questioned. China hinted that the dollar could be replaced as the major currency in the global marketplace.

This is not the place to point fingers and discuss crooks and "banksters," but after 2008–09, many developed states, including the United Kingdom and the United States, imposed new regulations on banks and investment firms. Debates took place throughout the world about the need to develop new institutions that could act as "shock absorbers" for dramatic shifts in domestic and global economies. There were vociferous disagreements about which monetary and fiscal measures would be effective – indeed they involved fundamental clashes of philosophies about the role of government and the private sector. Economists in Britain and the United States could not agree on such fundamentals as whether reduction in government deficits would accelerate or slow growth.[52] The U.S. government thought governments should borrow billions of dollars to stimulate growth, whereas European governments argued that a little short-term stimulus followed by measures to balance budgets and restore confidence was a better approach. The Obama administration said that such a policy would risk a long depression.

[52] *The Times*, September 29, 2010.

Critical Case Study 12.1 The Eurozone in crisis: Greece and the euro

In the aftermath of the global economic crisis, unsustainable debt levels were experienced in Greece, Ireland, Italy, Portugal, and Spain. The EU tried various measures to help solve the problems, but the severity of the situation raised fundamental questions about the future of their currency in all seventeen euro countries and even speculation about a possible breakup or a split of the EU into a two-tiered system.

In 1981, when Greece was accepted as a member of the European Union, it won a new lease on prosperity, a chance to return, some thought, to its former glory days. But under shelter of the euro it did not put its economic house in order, and the global financial crisis of 2008–09 pushed Greece's fragile economy deep into debt. In 2010 the EU and the IMF arranged a 110-billion-euro bailout, in return for which the Greek government was to cut spending deeply and privatize large sectors of the economy. Critics argued that this would only throw Greece into a cycle of spiraling debt and recession. They were right. After a year of political stalemate, Greece's economy was even worse. The debt had reached more than 350 billion euros, more than the country's entire annual economic output. Unemployment was at more than 16 percent, and the economy was predicted to contract. Greece was not only Europe's worst performing economy; it was one of the worst in the world.

As the world watched nervously, two possibilities were considered. One, financial austerity (slashing public-sector jobs and salaries and raising taxes) was rejected by parliament and the Greek people, who faced the prospect of further economic hardship and fraying social fabric with strikes, violent riots, and increasing support for radical political parties (Figure 12.11). The other possibility was for Greece to

Figure 12.11 Since 2010, the economy of Western Europe has been a shambles. When Greece was forced to adopt either harsh economic restraints or drop out of the euro zone and return to the use of the drachma, protests were widespread. *Source:* Press Association.

default on its loans. EU leaders wanted desperately to avoid this because they thought it might disrupt financial markets in ways that would be unpredictable and impossible to control. They feared that "contagion" would cause other financially precarious EU countries – namely Portugal and Ireland, and even Spain and Italy, to possibly follow suit.

World markets reacted to the insecurity. Yields on two-year Greek bonds (the interest rate the Greek government would have to pay lenders) soared to nearly 28 percent. EU countries, concerned about the euro, dithered. The German government, backed by the Dutch, Austrians, and Finns, wanted private holders of Greek bonds to be forced to bear some of the costs of a new bailout so that German taxpayers would not have to bear the burden of a rescue (i.e., take a "haircut" or a forced loss on their bonds). The **European Central Bank** (ECB) suggested that such a move against private lenders (banks) would be construed as default and create panic in financial markets.

Greek bonds are widely held by banks across Europe. The ECB is a pan-European institution able to act quickly and independently, but it is limited because primary decision making over wide areas of economic and finance policy is left to member states. Its leverage comes from its ability to give low-cost loans to institutions in financial difficulty. In 2010 the ECB bought huge quantities of Greek, Irish, and Portuguese government bonds to try to stabilize markets for them. Like other banks, it stands to lose considerably by any default. If that were to happen, the ECB would have to be bailed out by Europeans, especially German taxpayers. The ECB therefore moved in concert with the national governments, who created a 500-billion-euro bailout fund for the distressed countries, but by then Greece needed even more help.

The eurozone was in crisis. There were suggestions that all twenty-seven countries should lend Greece money. Britain's Prime Minister David Cameron declared he was "absolutely determined" to avoid getting dragged into eurozone efforts to prop up Athens and proposed a 2017 referendum on the future of the UK membership in the EU.[53] The eurozone finance ministers could not agree on how to rescue Greece. The very survival of the euro, which was considered key in uniting Europe and provided peace and security, was at stake. Former French prime minister Nicolas Sarkozy underlined the gravity of the situation somewhat hysterically by asserting, "Without the euro there is no Europe, and without Europe there is no possible peace and stability."[54]

Much of the problem was caused because, as a member of the eurozone, Greece did not have the ability to change the value of its currency to keep the government debt in check. Low interest rates worked well for Germany's large economy because it led to a surge in German exports, but low interest rates allowed the Greeks to borrow more than they should have. Huge trade deficits were built up with Germany by the weaker EU members, including Greece. Germany profited. However, Germans do not feel responsible for bailing out the defaulting economies, and the Greek people feel they are being asked to pay a huge price for a disaster not solely of their making. Critics of the Greek case believe that this is a classic example of **moral hazard**. In economic theory the term *moral hazard* is used to depict the tendency to take undue risks because the costs are not borne by the party taking the risk. The Greek government and people put in place public spending measures that did not take into account the consequences and impact of their actions.

Some argue that a small economy like Greece should never have been allowed into the eurozone. There was no precedent for a monetary union among such radically divergent economies without the support of a fiscal or political union. During "boom" years, peripheral economies like Greece's did not gain competitiveness but instead amassed huge, unsustainable debts. In bad years the facts became unavoidable. By 2011 the immediate worries were over. The Greek parliament, with rioters outside its doors, voted for a severe austerity plan, thus paving the way for another rescue package. Critics predict the austerity plan would make life too difficult for ordinary Greeks and "almost certainly condemn Greece to recession, strife and an eventual debt default."[55] Greek debt was set to surpass 160 percent of GDP. The pressure was on to come up with another bailout plan that would do more than simply delay the reckoning for a few years. The first 2012 election results prevented the formation of a stable government, and new elections had to be held. The public was divided over whether Greece should pay its loans or simply drop out of the eurozone altogether.

Finally, Greece and the EU got their act together. The second 2012 Greek election ushered in a coalition government ready to support a bailout for the country's failed economy and in exchange for a 'fiscal compact," an EU treaty was agreed on to toughen budget discipline by agreeing that a state's deficits should not exceed 3 percent of GDP. A temporary reserve plan, the European Financial Stability Facility (EFSF), was to be followed by a permanent **European Stability Mechanism** (ESM). In partial exchange for this decision, twenty-six countries agreed to sign, or agreed to consider, a "fiscal compact" that would commit them to keeping their budget deficits to less than 3 percent of GDP. The United Kingdom opted out of the agreement.

[53] *The Times* June 21, 2011, and *The Economist*, February 2, 2013.
[54] *The Times*, June 17, 2011.
[55] *The Economist*, July 2–8, 2011, pp. 9–10.

In September 2012, the European Central Bank announced that it would buy unlimited amounts of government bonds to relieve pressure in troubled EU countries and effectively spread responsibility for repaying national debts to the euro zone countries as a whole. This daring approach was criticized by the German Bundesbank, but the German government backed the new bond program. As of early 2013, Greece is in recession for the sixth consecutive year and misery continues to mount in all southern European countries.

This complex situation comes down essentially to four questions and unpalatable choices. First, are Greece and other countries guilty of moral hazard when they allow their governments to spend more than they are willing to pay in tax? Second, is the economic problem caused because the EU is only partially integrated economically? After all, member states have given up control of economic policy-making instruments such as devaluation and monetary policy, but the institutions of the European Union do not yet have the instruments for coping with economic shocks like the recession. Third, does this scramble for an adequate policy prove that European federalists, who argue for deeper integration, are correct and without it Europe will "fail"? Fourth, should Greece drop out of the eurozone and return to the use of drachmas, or would that only worsen the situation? Policy experts are divided, some calling for a controlled breakup of the euro, while others argue that the situation can be resolved without a fundamental restructuring of the EU. However, international businesses are already developing contingency plans in case of a "Grexit" – a rapid departure of Greece from the EU.

Conclusion: International economics as a discipline

Because of its failure to anticipate the crash in 2008–09 and its run-on into 2013, the academic discipline of economics came under challenge, as did the study of international political economy. Two central parts of the discipline, macroeconomics and financial economics, were challenged by the crisis. The most important ideas of traditional economics as a discipline– the rational, utility-maximizing autonomous individual whose actions supposedly cause functioning of the the *invisible hand* (rational actors buying and selling in a free market) and the *efficient market hypothesis* – have been questioned. Not only the profession's usefulness but also its central principles are being challenged by analysts who concentrate on the "irrationality" of the choices and decisions that are part of economic decision making.

The school of critical thought behind these radical challenges is sometimes called behavioral economics. Its advocates argue that humans tend to be too confident of their own abilities and to make choices and decisions based on irrational impulses rather than rational ones. They challenge the central thesis of Adam Smith and traditional economists and join with others who demonstrate that humans are not the perfect processors of information about which classical economics theorize. Psychologists, sociologists, and even neuroscientists have joined the fray with the essential charge that economics deals with perceptions, expectations, motivations, and uncertainties that are not amenable to rational actors or actions. Ben Bernanke, chair of the U.S. Federal Reserve, claims that this challenge is wrongheaded:

Although economists have much to learn from this crisis, calls for a radical reworking of the field go too far. The financial crisis was more a failure of economic engineering and economic management than of economic science. I don't think the crisis by any means requires us to rethink economics and finance from the ground up. [56]

However, something did go wrong in the world economy that was unanticipated, and international economists are reevaluating their field, rendering the entire study of IPE an exciting challenge. First there was the dot-com bubble, then the mortgage finance bubble, and then a fiscal bubble. States around the world have a debt-to-GDP ratio approaching 90 percent. Is this sustainable? If the economic and financial crisis has a lasting effect, it may be to reduce confidence in economics as a discipline to predict global economic crises and conclude what to do about them. At the present time, social science is not able to anticipate rare events such as the Great Depression, the Recession of 2008, or, for that matter, other important political events such as the collapse of the Soviet Union. In the field of prediction, an old adage may be helpful: if you want to be a successful prognosticator, never mention a number and a time in the same sentence!

[56] Cited in *The Times*, September 29, 2010.

Select bibliography

Bhagwati, Jagdish, *In Defense of Globalization: With a New Afterword* (Oxford: Oxford University Press, 2007).

Blinder, Alan S., *After the Music Stopped* (New York: Penguin, 2013).

Bremmer, Ian, *The End of the Free Market: Who Wins the War between States and Corporations?* (New York: Penguin, 2010).

Cassidy, John, *How Markets Fail: The Logic of Economic Calamities* (New York: Farrar, Straus and Giroux, 2010).

Clark, Ian, *Globalization and International Relations* (Oxford: Oxford University Press, 1999).

Clarke, Peter, *Keynes: The Twentieth Century's Most Influential Economist* (London: Bloomsbury, 2009).

Cohen, Stephen S., and J. Bradford DeLong, *The End of Influence: What Happens When Other Countries Have the Money* (New York: Basic Books, 2010).

Eichengreen, Barry, *Globalizing Capital: A History of the International Monetary System* (Princeton, NJ: Princeton University Press, 2008).

Ferguson, Niall, *The Ascent of Money: A Financial History of the World* (New York: Penguin, 2008).

Frieden, J., and D. A. Lake, eds., *International Political Economy: Perspectives on Global Power and Wealth* (New York: St. Martin's Press, 2000).

Friedman, Jeffrey, *Global Capitalism: Its Rise and Fall in the Twentieth Century* (New York: Norton, 2007).

Friedman, Thomas L., *The Lexus and the Olive Tree: Understanding Globalization* (New York: Farrar, Straus and Giroux, 1999).

_____, *The World, Is Flat: A Brief History of the Twenty-First Century* (New York: Farrar, Straus, and Giroux, 2006).

Germain, Randall, *Global Politics and Financial Governance* (New York: Palgrave Macmillan, 2010).

Gilpin, Robert, *Global Political Economy: Understanding the International Economic Order* (Princeton, NJ: Princeton University Press, 2002).

Gray, John, *False Dawn: The Delusions of Global Capitalism* (London: Granta, 1998).

Grieco, Joseph, and John Ikenberry, *State Power and World Markets: The International Political Economy* (New York: Norton, 2003).

Halper, Stefan, *The Beijing Consensus: How China's Authoritarian Model Will Dominate the Twenty-First Century* (New York: Basic Books, 2010).

Held, D., A. McGrew, D. Goldblatt, and J. Perrator, *Global Transformations: Politics, Economics and Culture* (Cambridge, UK: Polity Press, 1999).

Irwin, Douglas, *Free Trade under Fire*, 3rd ed. (Princeton, NJ: Princeton University Press, 2009).

Krugman, Paul, *Pop Internationalism* (Cambridge, MA: MIT Press, 1998).

Mahbubani, Kishore, *The New Asian Hemisphere: The Irresistible Shift of Global Power to the East* (New York: Basic Civitas Books, 2009).

Ohmae, Kenischi, *The Borderless World* (New York: Harper, 1999).

Posner, Richard A., *The Failure of Capitalism: The Crisis of '08 and the Descent into Depression* (Boston: Harvard University Press, 2010).

Rajan, Raghuram G., *Fault Lines: How Hidden Fractures Still Threaten the World Economy* (Princeton, NJ: Princeton University Press, 2010).

Skidelsky, Robert, *Keynes: The Return of the Master* (New York: Public Affairs, 2009).

Stiglitz, Joseph, *Freefall: America, Free Markets, and the Sinking of the World Economy* (New York: Norton, 2010).

Stiglitz, Joseph, and Andrew Charlton, *Fair Trade for All: How Trade Can Promote Development* (New York: Oxford University Press, 2006).

Woods, N., *The Globalizers: The IMF, the World Bank, and Their Borrowers* (Ithaca, NY: Cornell University Press, 2006).

Global inequality
Winners and losers

The field of developmental economics is characterized to a large extent by the same controversies and differences in perspectives that confront governments in global politics generally. Is the economic pie growing or contracting? How is it shared? Is its distribution just, or are there major global intra- and interstate inequalities? These issues are central to the study of international political economy; however, to a great extent, specialists who examine inequality tend to be little interested in macroeconomic issues such as global trade and the supply of credit.

Despite impressive improvements in the global economy since World War II, inequalities remain within and across states. Overall, the gap between rich and poor around the world has increased, and poverty, hunger, and disease are more prevalent in some specific, marginalized parts of the world than others, creating complex patterns of winners and losers. Significant economic inequalities inside many states have also grown. Contrasting perspectives on these facts are widespread. As we saw in Chapter 12, despite other differences, liberals, nationalists, and even state capitalists focus on the overall economic gains of states, especially the huge improvement in per capita incomes in both developed and developing countries over the past half century. Radical, Marxist, or critical theorists, in contrast, emphasize the unequal patterns in the distribution of gains within global society and within states rather than overall growth patterns. They point to facts from the UN's *Millennium Development Goals Report* that confirm the extent to which disadvantaged people are trapped in poverty: 1.4 billion people live below the global poverty line of $1.25 a day, and the numbers are likely to increase by 2015; every few seconds a child dies from malnutrition somewhere around the world.[1]

To a large extent, the conflicting arguments come from measuring different things – with some scholars analyzing the overall economic growth of the global economy and individual states, while others are more concerned with cross-state differences and cross-class inequalities within states. In the last chapter we examined features of the global economy studied by the first group. Here we examine the economic themes covered by the latter group. We begin by outlining basic concepts such as development, modernization, poverty, and dependency before moving on to answer some fascinating questions. How do we categorize countries in the study of developmental economics, and why? Why do some countries have so much wealth and others so little? Is colonial history a factor? What international strategies are employed to level the playing field, and how well are they working?

[1] United Nations, *The Millennium Development Goals Report 2010* (New York: United Nations, 2010), p. 4.

Two main approaches are used to explain development, modernization and dependency theory, and we assess their major contributions. At the practical level, there is a deep disparity in levels of economic development of states around the world, and there has been mixed success in fulfilling the objectives of the UN Millennium Development Goals project. The chapter concludes with an assessment of the impact of globalization on global inequalities. To what degree is globalization responsible for the improvements or lack of progress in reaching these goals? The chapter raises important questions about the important topic of economic fairness and introduces the tools for more comprehensive analyses of the complex issues involved.

The development dimension

One of the most important, and most contentious, issues in global politics concerns how and why some individuals and states do well and others do not. As we look around the globe, it is evident that a minority of states and their people are vastly wealthier than the rest. Poor countries are characterized by low incomes, low literacy, high infant mortality rates, and low life expectancy. Many of their people endure poverty, unemployment, inadequate housing, poor health, limited education, and impure water. In some poorer countries, citizens live mainly in rural, agricultural communities, while in others great masses of them scratch out a living in huge cities. Many of these countries have highly vulnerable economies that are dramatically affected by changes in the international economy, especially if they export only one or two major commodities.

The gap between richer states and their poorer counterparts is so significant that the two groups are often described as belonging to different worlds. Various classifications have been used to study them. The prevalent one for many years prior to 1991 was based on the concept of first, second, and third worlds. These rubrics essentially described the capitalist democratic countries, the communist countries, and some that belonged to neither grouping yet lagged behind both in economic development.

After the end of the Cold War, which had divided states into communist or capitalist camps, that

Close Up 13.1   **Who gets what?**

The enormity of the wealth of some people is overwhelming. Not long ago, a *Human Development Report* found that the three richest individuals in the world had assets that exceeded the combined gross domestic product (GDP) of the forty-eight least developed countries. The fifteen richest individuals had assets that exceeded the total GDP of sub-Saharan Africa. The richest thirty-two people had wealth that exceeded the total GDP of South Asia. The richest eighty-four had assets that exceeded the GDP of China. In summary, the richest 225 individuals in the world had a combined wealth of more than US$1 trillion – equal to the total annual income of almost half of the world's poorest people, or almost 2.5 billion individuals.[2]

Is this distribution of wealth reasonable? Desirable? Reformable?

controversial schema became woefully inadequate. Many of the new states that arose from the old Soviet Union abandoned communism and became fledgling democracies with market economies, and as a result, the distinction between first and second worlds blurred and, to a large extent, became

[2] United Nations, *Human Development Report* (Oxford: Oxford University Press, 1988), p. 30.

meaningless. As we shall see, only the third world category continued to have any relevance, and today most scholars find the term pejorative and unhelpful, as it seems to refer to these countries as a backward and lamentable part of the natural order of the globe. To a large extent, the term was also misleading, as it avoided serious analysis of the relationships between wealth and deprivation and therefore did not provide a deep historical understanding of how some states and their people became poor. Indeed, with the recent improvements in economic life in Brazil, China, India, and elsewhere, it may also be more instructive to concentrate on the changing characteristics within the third world rather than those of the entire group.

States of the first world category were considered to be both politically and economically developed. They were liberal democracies with open, competitive elections. As they also had free-market economies they profited from the forces of supply and demand and operated to a high degree without government regulation, while the profit motive provided incentives for diligence and entrepreneurial activity. Of course, in reality, no pure market economy existed anywhere. To some extent all countries had (and have) mixed economies, with governments controlling the money supply and regulating their economies through taxation and expenditure, but, in a nutshell, first-world countries were the politically stable democracies with rich economies based on the profit motive. Moreover, almost all the states in this category had maintained stable, democratic institutions over many decades. The United States was usually considered the prototype for political systems in this category, as it had been politically stable and increasingly wealthy since its Civil War of 1861–65.

Broadly speaking, states of the second world included those that were communist and had neither a competitive party system nor a free market. On the whole, they were based on one-party dominance and embraced controlled or centrally planned economies. Both the first- and second-world states had industrialized economies, but the second world adhered to a philosophy of socialism – or some form of Marxist-Leninist ideology – backed up by the command structures required by authoritarian leadership. The collapse of Soviet and Eastern European communism in 1989 depleted the number of states in the second world category. The political distinction between the first and second worlds faded, so that today many of the postcommunist states differ from the first world mainly on economic performance rather than economic philosophy. The states that constituted the second world are now commonly described as "economies in transition." There are only five significant communist states remaining – China, Cuba, Laos, North Korea, and Vietnam. North Korea retains a Soviet-modeled dictatorship, but political leaders in both Beijing and Hanoi have introduced capitalist practices into their state-run economies; in fact, in China much of the economy is actually less regulated than that of many European states. Cuba remains the only communist government in South America, and it, too, has been toying with economic and political reforms.

The now-defunct third world classification included all the countries that remained outside the first two categories. The term *le tiers monde* – the third world – was coined by French demographer Alfred Sauvey in 1952. It was almost shorthand for powerlessness and poverty. The concept of the third world was a typical product of the Cold War era, which reflected an obsession with the superpowers and their allies but a lack of interest in the less powerful, more populous states. More than 3.5 billion people living in the buffer zone between the two great global rivals were deemed part of the third world, yet there was considerable disparity within this category. For example, it included the oil-rich Gulf states of Saudi Arabia and the United Arab Emirates; industrializing countries such as South Korea, Taiwan, and Singapore; and dozens of very poor states scattered throughout Africa, Asia, and Latin America.

The political and economic heterogeneity of this catchall category made generalization difficult, but, on the whole, these states were not industrialized and were termed traditional rather than modern societies. They were found in or close to the Southern Hemisphere and were often (but not always) characterized by the military having an important role in political affairs. In most of the third world, government structures and institutions were weak, whether they were based on capitalist or socialist models of development. For most of their citizens, economic problems, including sheer survival, were more significant than the structures and processes associated with democracy or communism.

Most, but not all, third-world states had been part of a colonial empire. In the 19th century, the Latin American states obtained their independence from Europe, and in the 20th century much of Africa and Asia threw off the yoke of Western domination. The new states were often patterned on the institutions of their colonial history – institutions that generally were inappropriate for local conditions. Often the states were based on borders drawn for the convenience of a colonial power that ignored hostile tribal divisions, which made governing difficult.

Democratic stability proved elusive in many third-world states. Government legitimacy, and even geographic borders, remained shaky. Even after independence from colonial rule, the primary loyalties of their populations were more to tribes, regions, or even families than to the states themselves. The countries in this category had marginal relevance internationally, and after the Cold War they lost what little leverage they had as ideological allies or enemies of the superpowers. As well, the industrialized states began to focus more attention and aid dollars on the economic transformation of Eastern Europe, thus further marginalizing the third-world countries. The classification was dying but not yet dead. As David Landes put it succinctly in *The Wealth and Poverty of Nations*:

We live in a world of inequality and diversity. This world is divided roughly into three kinds of nations: those that spend lots of money to keep their weight down; those whose people eat to live; and those that don't know where the next meal is coming from.[3]

[3] David S. Landes, *The Wealth and Poverty of Nations* (New York: Norton, 1999).

Levels of economic development

Today, social scientists tend to categorize the world's states as "developed" and "developing" (or "less developed" or "underdeveloped"), in other words, according to their level of economic development rather than the three worlds classification that implied political and cultural backwardness for members of the third category. The term *development* is used because it implies optimistically that if a country can produce economic wealth, it can transform its society from a subsistence economy to one in which manufactured goods and services create more wealth – that is, economic development. This process combines several factors, including the adoption of capitalist principles, growth in per capita incomes, adoption of new technologies, and new values and work habits (see Chapter 12). The logic dictates that when economic wealth is generated by the manufacturing and service sectors, a country can develop a literate, urban, well-fed population. Using development as the key concept, then, the world's states are categorized as "developed" and "less developed." Such words are important not only in academia; they are crucial to the way the states, intergovernmental institutions, and nongovernmental agencies distribute their resources and money to poorer states. Without such practical distinctions, these organizations would not know which countries to help.

The terms *developed* and *developing* are used for convenience and to distinguish between countries that have or have not achieved the highest human development levels.[4] The Human Development Report (HDR) categorizes countries into four roughly equal groups: very high human development; high human development, medium human development, and low human development (often called the least

[4] For definitions and data, see United Nations, *The Millennium Development Goals Report 2010*; UN Development Program, *The Real Wealth of Nations: Pathways to Human Development* (New York: Palgrave, 2010); UN Development Program, *Human Development Report, 2011: Sustainability and Equity* (New York: Palgrave, 2011; World Bank, *2010, 2011, and 2012 World Development Indicators* (Washington, DC: World Bank, 2010 and 2011).

Figure 13.1 Contrasts of tradition and modernity exist side by side in Dubai, which boasts ultramodern shopping malls and the tallest building in the world, yet has vestiges of earlier, more primitive, culture evident almost within their shadows. *Source:* Shutterstock.

developed countries, or LDCs). In 2011, the highest levels of development were present in forty-seven countries with a total population of about 1.1 billion people; the remaining less developed countries had a combined population of about 5.9 billion.[5] The very high development countries had a gross national income (GDI) per capita of $33,252 annually based on purchasing-power parity (PPP). This high-income category includes principally the member states of the Organization for Economic Cooperation and Development (OECD), countries characterized by peace, wealth, and democracy, and some non-OECD countries that have wealth but may lack the political, technological, or demographic characteristics of the OECD members. These include oil-exporting countries (Brunei, and members of the United Arab Emirates), newly industrialized economies (Hong Kong, South Korea, and Singapore), and Andorra, Barbados, and Cyprus (Figure 13.1). In 2011 those countries with the lowest levels of human development (i.e., LDCs) had a per capita GNI of US$1,585. This category produces a list of countries that is essentially the same as the one defined formerly as the third world. The United Nations identified forty-five countries in the LDC category. The vast majority of these states were in Africa; the only such country in the Americas was Haiti.

The comparative terminology has changed from the pejorative "third world" to less developed countries (LDCs) or lowest least developed countries (LLDCs), but the countries concerned, and many of their main characteristics, remain the same. The extreme poverty that characterizes the LLDCs has many implications. Their population growth, at an average of 2.2 percent from 1990 to 2008, was far in excess of the world average of 1.3 percent. At this rate, the population of the LLDCs will double in about twenty-five years, while it will take two and a half centuries for the developed countries to grow that much. Because of the persistent disparity in population and economic growth between

---

[5] There is considerable difficulty over definition and data collection to define these groups. In this text we follow the latest decision of the World Bank to use the term *gross national income* (GNI) in place of gross domestic product (GDP). Gross national income measures the production of goods and services within a given time period. It measures production by a state's citizens or companies regardless of where the production occurs. The per capita figure is reached by dividing a country's total production of goods and services by its population.

the LLDCs and the developed countries, the richest states get wealthier and the poorest of the poor do little to improve their wretched conditions.

As of 2011, life expectancy at birth is 58.7 years in the LDCs, compared with 80.0 years in the highest developed countries. Illiteracy rates in the lowest category are the worst in the world, with an average of 4.2 years of schooling, about half the world average. Moreover, one of the main characteristics of the LDCs, besides their comparatively low economic performance, is their tendency to be "zones of turmoil," in which poverty, war, organized crime, tyranny, and anarchy dominate. Violent conflict is often present both within and between the countries in this category. None of the thirty-seven states the World Bank described as fragile in 2010 is in the developed world; most are among the LLDCs, with about two-thirds of them in Africa.[6]

Apart from these economic and demographic characteristics, there are also major differences among states in terms of their governments and politics. Democracy and economic progress have not advanced in tandem in the world, as many optimists had hoped. Developed countries tend to have fairly stable institutions, as well as governments based on the rule of law, popular legitimacy, and the ability to govern. The very least developed states are generally chronically unstable, with contested governments and institutions. In many of the poorest of them, one ethnic group holds power over others. Their governments tend to be repressive and to abuse human rights. Political violence, torture, assassinations, and war are prevalent, and, except in Latin America, free speech and a free press are often absent in the LLDCs of the global South.

Overall, the beginning of the 21st century brought massive economic and political change to developing countries. Many parts of the underdeveloped world have democratized, while others have stagnated in authoritarian rule. In Latin America, all countries except Cuba have had democratic

elections in recent years. Although the trappings of democracy are found almost everywhere in Latin America, the level of human rights abuses remains high in countries such as Colombia, El Salvador, and Guatemala. Less democratic progress has been made in Africa and Asia, but considerable movement toward democracy is visible there as well. Much of sub-Saharan Africa has nonetheless remained under military or one-party rule. The end of apartheid in South Africa was a major shining exception to the rule. In Asia, despite their impressive economic progress, China, Laos, Vietnam, and North Korea retain communist governments and repress political and personal freedoms. Famine, hunger, and war continue to devastate peoples throughout much of Africa and Asia.

Perhaps the main question that specialists in development studies seek to answer is why some countries and areas of the world have so much wealth while others have so little. What are the origins of this inequality, and what, if anything, can be done about it? These are complicated but fascinating questions, which we address later in this chapter. Questions about inequality in the modern world were reformulated by Jared Diamond in *Guns, Germs and Steel* as follows:

Why did wealth and power become distributed as they are, rather than in some other way? For instance, why weren't Native Americans, Africans, and Aboriginal Australians the ones who decimated, subjugated or exterminated Europeans and Asians?[7]

Global deprivation and poverty

While most of the richest people live in the Northern Hemisphere, poor people are found in all parts of the world. There are pockets of unemployment, homelessness, and even hunger in the developed world, but large-scale poverty is most prevalent in the LDCs and LLDCs, usually in the global South. As Figure 13.2 shows, the vast majority of the extremely poor live in sub-Saharan Africa and South

[6] World Bank, *World Development Indicators 2010*, pp. 320–1.

[7] Jared Diamond, *Guns, Germs and Steel* (New York: Vintage, 2005).

Asia. Poverty is one of the most significant issues in development studies. As the 2010 Human Development Report put it:

A person born in Niger can expect to live 26 fewer years, to have 9 fewer years of education and to consume 53 times fewer goods than a person born in Denmark. While the Danes have elected their parliament in free and open elections since 1849, Niger's president dissolved parliament and Supreme Court in 2009 – and was then ousted in a military coup. More than 7 out of 10 people surveyed in Niger say there were times in the past year when they did not have enough money to buy food for their families. Very few Danes would be in such straits.[8]

On the basis of income earned per day, more than one of every four people on Earth lives in extreme poverty. But income is not the only relevant indicator of wealth. Poverty is often defined as a combination of level of income, food, health, education, housing, and quality of life below the minimum standards for life and decency. Global poverty has serious consequences, as it brings disease, environmental degradation, and political instability on a massive scale (see Table 13.1). In the current decade roughly one billion humans are malnourished. More than 10 million children a year die before the age of five. Meanwhile, 1.5 billion people do not have access to basic sanitation; 8.8 million child deaths are due to HIV/AIDS; 42 million people are displaced by conflict or persecution; 69 million children (of whom 53 percent are female) are not in school – even with all the progress that is being made, 1.1 billion people are predicted to live on less than $2 per day in 2015 (Figure 13.2). With little or no purchasing power, many of these people are destitute.[9]

The global poor have little hope of escaping their condition. The rate of progress in fighting poverty is measured by two factors: economic growth and the share of wealth that goes to the poor. According to the *2010 World Bank Report*, income poverty has been falling over the past two decades, but global

Table 13.1 Global deprivations in many aspects of life

Health
1 billion people malnourished (2009)
1 billion people without access to improved water sources (2002)
1.5 billion people without access to basic sanitation (2010)
10 million children die before their fifth birthday (2006)
8.8 million child deaths due to people living with HIV/AIDS (2008)
42 million people displaced by conflict or persecution (2009)

Education
781 million illiterate adults, 64% of them women (2006)
69 million children not in school – 53% of them female (2008)

Income and poverty
1.4 billion people living on less than $1.25 a day (2005)
1.1 billion people predicted to live on less than $2 per day (in 2015)

Source: Adapted from United Nations, *The Millennium Development Goals Report 2010* (New York: United Nations, 2010); UN Development Program, *The Real Wealth of Nations: Pathways to Human Development* (New York: Palgrave, 2010); UN Development Program, *Human Development Report, 2011: Sustainability and Equity* (New York: Palgrave, 2011); World Bank, *2011 and 2012, World Development Indicators* (Washington, DC: World Bank, 2010 and 2012).

inequality remains extremely high. Much of the overall change has come from poverty reductions in China and India, because of their high economic growth. Despite India's economic takeoff and a reduction in the incidence of poverty in the country, there has not been a reduction in the absolute number of poor people.

---

[8] United Nations, *Human Development Report 2010*, p. 42.
[9] *World Bank Indicators 2010*, p. 4.

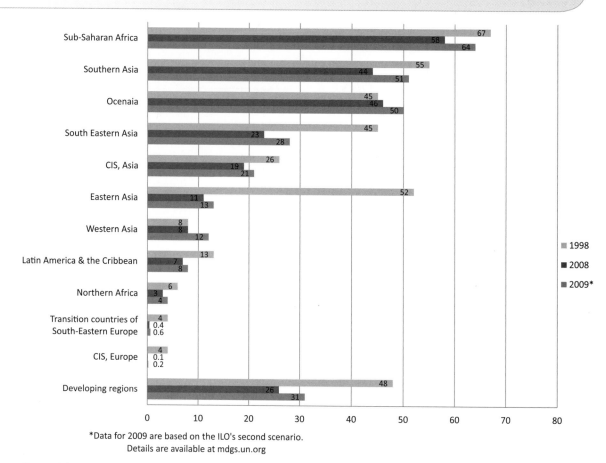

*Data for 2009 are based on the ILO's second scenario.
Details are available at mdgs.un.org

Figure 13.2 Proportion of employed people living below $1.25 a day, 1998, 2008 and 2009 (percentage).

Human development

The extent of human poverty does not necessarily equate with the average level of income because aggregate income data do not correlate perfectly with a deprived lifestyle. The United Nations therefore constructs the annual Human Development Index (HDI) to overcome this weakness. In 2011 the HDI measured three basic capabilities: to live a longer and healthier life, to be educated, and to enjoy a decent standard of living. GNI is used to measure standard of living, education is measured by mean years of schooling and expected years of schooling, and life expectancy at birth is used to measure health standards. The 2011 HDI rankings are shown in Table 13.2. Notwithstanding some technical difficulties, this index of countries

shows clearly that wealth is very unevenly distributed around the world. With the exception of Afghanistan, which is at war, all of the twenty lowest-ranked countries are in Africa.

Recent studies have confirmed that equity and human development are related – that is, countries that do well on the Human Development Index (HDI) also tend to be more equitable, but that is not always the case. Indeed, despite constant improvements in average human development, inequality has increased in many states around the world. For this reason, the authors of the *2010 Human Development Report* added two new indexes that not only examine the average state of a country's human development but also show how it compares with the distribution of inequalities within a state.

Close Up 13.2 **The bottom billion**

In his classic book *The Bottom Billion*, Oxford economist Paul Collier analyzes several countries that together house a billion people who live in persistent poverty, searching for answers to why they are failing, and what can be done about it. These countries, he says, are "not just falling behind, they are falling apart."[10] If nothing is done to change their direction, they will remain ghettos of discontent and misery for the 21st century and beyond.

As we have seen elsewhere, the developing world is normally depicted as containing more than five billion of the seven billion people on Earth. Collier narrows in on the bottom one-fifth of this group – a billion people caught in the most extreme poverty. The countries they live in are mostly in Africa. Their average life expectancy is about fifty years, and the proportion of children who die before their first birthday is about 14 percent.

The key to Collier's argument is that he does not believe that the standard tools of economic development such as economic aid will be able to solve the problems of most of these countries. Applying what he calls four major "traps," Collier shows how these factors explain the worst-off countries and peoples of the world. The four main traps include conflict, natural resources, being landlocked with bad neighbors, and a bad government in a small country. Because there are entrenched interests and powerful people opposed to change involved in each of the traps, he argues that global institutions and rich countries will have to consider using tougher measures than usual, such as military intervention, international standard setting, and trade policies to strengthen the hand of reformers. Collier also contends

that this is unlikely to happen, because Western development agencies and their officials do not want to narrow their focus toward the bottom billion. They have entrenched interests in avoiding change and do not want to take personal risks. In short, Collier wants to narrow the target of countries to be helped and broaden the types of instruments used.

This may take considerable pressure, and it may even be impossible. Collier is discussing the standard difficult problem one must address in supplying global public goods. Should his classification and policy recommendations be considered? Should aid agencies concentrate more on the bottom billion even if it means less help for other developing countries? Is international intervention reasonable in a sovereign country? Is it practical?

[10] Paul Collier, *The Bottom Billion* (Oxford: Oxford University Press, 2007), p. x.

The Inequality-Adjusted Human Development Index (IHDI) is a measure of the average level of human development that takes inequality into account. It measures how income, education, and health are "distributed." Under perfect equality, HDI and IHDI would match, but they never do. The IHDI measure is applied to countries to illustrate that, even when development takes place, a degree of inequality still exists in states. The Multi-Dimensional Poverty Index (MDPI) is designed to complement money-based income studies. An average income statistic can be useful but in some contexts is insufficient. The MDPI therefore examines the number of deprived people and the intensity of their deprivation in terms of health, education, and standard of living. In 2010, the authors found that in their sample of 104 countries, 1.75 billion people endured acute deprivation, a greater number than the 1.4 billion who lived on less than $1.25 a day. The highest percentage of people with acute deprivation was found in sub-Saharan Africa – ranging from 3 percent in South Africa to 93 percent in Niger. Yet half the world's people who endured multi-dimensional poverty (844 million) live in South Asia. While China's per capita income rose

Table 13.2 Human development index 2011

Very high human development	High human development	Medium human development	Low human development
1. Norway	48. Uruguay	95. Jordan	142. Solomon Islands
2. Australia	49. Palau	96. Algeria	143. Kenya
3. Netherlands	50. Romania	97. Sri Lanka	144. São Tomé and
4. United States	51. Cuba	98. Dominican	Príncipe
5. New Zealand	52. Seychelles	Republic	145. Pakistan
6. Canada	53. Bahamas	99. Samoa	146. Bangladesh
7. Ireland	54. Montenegro	100. Fiji	147. Timor-Leste
8. Lichtenstein	55. Bulgaria	101. China	148. Angola
9. Germany	56. Saudi Arabia	102. Turkmenistan	149. Myanmar
10. Sweden	57. Mexico	103. Thailand	150. Cameroon
11. Switzerland	58. Panama	104. Suriname	151. Madagascar
12. Japan	59. Serbia	105. El Salvador	152. Tanzania, United
13. Hong Kong;	60. Antigua and	106. Gabon	Republic of
China (SAR)	Barbuda	107. Paraguay	153. Papua New
14. Iceland	61. Malaysia	108. Bolivia,	Guinea
15. Korea	62. Trinidad and	Plurinational	154. Yemen
16. Denmark	Tobago	State of	155. Senegal
17. Israel	63. Kuwait	109. Maldives	156. Nigeria
18. Belgium	64. Libya	110. Mongolia	157. Nepal
19. Austria	65. Belarus	111. Moldova, Republic	158. Haiti
20. France	66. Russian	of	159. Mauritania
21. Slovenia	Federation	112. Philippines	160. Lesotho
22. Finland	67. Grenada	113. Egypt	161. Uganda
23. Spain	68. Kazakhstan	114. Occupied	162. Togo
24. Italy	69. Costa Rica	Palestinian Territory	163. Comoros
25. Luxembourg	70. Albania	115. Uzbekistan	164. Zambia
26. Singapore	71. Lebanon	116. Micronesia,	165. Djibouti
27. Czech Republic	72. Saint Kitts and	Federated States of	166. Rwanda
28. United Kingdom	Nevis	117. Guyana	167. Benin
29. Greece	73. Venezuela,	118. Botswana	168. Gambia
30. United Arab	Bolivarian	119. Syrian Arab	169. Sudan
Emirates	Republic of	Republic	170. Côte d'Ivoire
31. Cyprus	74. Bosnia and	120. Namibia	171. Malawi
32. Andorra	Herzegovina	121. Honduras	172. Afghanistan
33. Brunei	75. Georgia	122. Kiribati	173. Zimbabwe
Darussalam	76. Ukraine	123. South Africa	174. Ethiopia
34. Estonia	77. Mauritius	124. Indonesia	175. Mali
35. Slovakia	78. Former Yugoslav	125. Vanuatu	176. Guinea-Bissau
36. Malta	Republic of	126. Kyrgyzstan	177. Eritrea
37. Qatar	Macedonia	127. Tajikistan	178. Guinea
38. Hungary	79. Jamaica	128. Viet Nam	179. Central African
39. Poland	80. Peru	129. Nicaragua	Republic
40. Lithuania	81. Dominica	130. Morocco	180. Sierra Leone
41. Portugal	82. Saint Lucia	131. Guatemala	181. Burkina Faso
42. Bahrain	83. Ecuador	132. Iraq	182. Liberia
43. Latvia	84. Brazil	133. Cape Verde	183. Chad

Table 13.2 (cont.)

Very high human development	High human development	Medium human development	Low human development
44. Chile	85. St. Vincent and the Grenadines	134. India	184. Mozambique
45. Argentina	86. Armenia	135. Ghana	185. Burundi
46. Croatia	87. Columbia	136. Equatorial Guinea	186. Niger
47. Barbados	88. Iran, Islamic Republic of	137. Congo	187. Congo, Democratic Republic of the
	89. Oman	138. Lao People's Democratic Republic	
	90. Tonga	139. Cambodia	
	91. Azerbaijan	140. Swaziland	
	92. Turkey	141. Bhutan	
	93. Belize		
	94. Tunisia		

Source: The HDI rankings here were published in the *Human Development Report 2011*, statistical annex, along with the components of the index, pp. 127, 128, 129, 130, http/hdr.undp.org/en/reports/global/hdr2011/download/.

twenty-one-fold between 1970 and 2010, the number of people there living in multi-dimensional poverty was still an astounding 12.5 percent.

A large majority of the states of the United Nations originated only after 1945, after having been colonies of European empires. Along with a few older but equally poor states, they make up the developing world. Since many of them are located in the Southern Hemisphere, their shared problems are often referred to as southern issues to distinguish them from those of the northern democratic capitalist and former communist states. Much of the economic hierarchy of states is highlighted by the differences between the North and South.[11] The North provides high incomes, high life expectancy, and good levels of education while the South endures poverty, short lives, poor health, and low education levels. One *World Development Report* on the North-South divide says that the global South has 85 percent of the world's population but controls only 20 percent of the wealth.[12] Mired in abject poverty, most of these countries have little hope of significant progress for the coming half century.

The global South is not all poor, however. Some of the states regarded as in the south, such as those rich in oil, like Saudi Arabia, are quite unlike their poorer cousins even in the same region. Others such as South Korea, Singapore, Taiwan, and Hong Kong, which are known colloquially as the Asian tigers, or more correctly as the newly industrializing countries (NICs), have become more prosperous by their ability to produce and export manufactured goods to the developed world. In short, they have created modern industrialized infrastructures and can compete with the richer countries of the world. One of the keys to their development was the ability to attract foreign investments and then translate them into a powerful export sector that created strong economic growth in the 1980s and 1990s. In recent years, China and India have replicated these successes. China adopted market-oriented reforms and opened its economy to world trade. India generated export revenues by its strength in services. Its software companies, call centers, and professional services have contributed heavily to the country's rapidly growing economy (see Table 13.3). What are the political and policy

[11] The South is sometimes described as those countries south of the equator. It might be more appropriate to say south of the Tropic of Cancer or even further north, as many poor and populated countries are north of the equator. However, the term is very elastic and used for many purposes.

[12] *World Bank Report*, 2006, p. 292.

Table 13.3 **China and India compared**

	China	India
Population (2012)	1.35 billion	1.24 billion
Population growth (2010–15)	0.4%	1.3%
Human Development Index Rank (2012)	101	134
Infant mortality (2012)	19/1,000	66/1,000
Life expectancy (2012)	73.5	65.4
Mean years of schooling (2012)	7.5	4.4
Total GDI (in billions) (2008)	US$3.8	US$1.2
GNI per capita (2008)	US$2,940	US$1,040
GDP growth, (2007–8)	9.0%	6.1%
Internet users (per 100 people, 2008)	22.5	4.5
Energy use (million tons of oil equivalent 2007)	1,814	594.9
Seats in national parliament (2012) (% women)	21.3	10.7

Source: Adapted from data in *Human Development Report*, up to 2012; the World Bank data source for India and China in World Development Indicators, 2010.

implications of having a huge development gap between North and South?

Trade and investment

Developing countries have little capital to invest in their own economies and need help to grow and become sustainable. International strategies to resolve this problem come essentially in four forms – improved trade arrangements, new investment, foreign aid, and debt relief.[13]

Most observers agree that economic growth in developing countries requires much more trade with the richest parts of the world. But from the developing countries' perspective, their economic future is limited by Western protectionism, which denies them market access for their products. Moreover, as leaders of the developing world often argue, while

they are denied access to Western markets, developed countries often employ aid as a lever to gain access to the markets of the developing countries. We discussed the importance of the World Trade Organization and international rules for commerce in Chapter 12, but it is important to highlight here that, although there has been a major increase in free trade around the world and numerous new free trade agreements have been signed, the latest discussions in the Doha Round have stalled to near collapse, especially over opening northern markets to southern agricultural products.

Another possible source of development assistance comes in the form of foreign direct investment (FDI) – which was discussed in the previous chapter. There has been considerable growth in such foreign investment capital in recent decades, and it has helped to lift many countries out of their worst difficulties. However, the 2008–09 financial crisis and its fallout halted much of this investment and revealed how much the economies of the world have

---

[13] For an excellent treatment of the various options for aid enhanced development, see Anup Shah, "Foreign Aid for Development Assistance," *Global Issues* (April 25, 2010), http://www.globalissues.org/article/35/foreign-aid-development-assistance.

Figure 13.3 NGOs and the UN deliver food and supplies to stricken areas after natural and human-made disasters. Governments are often divided over how much aid they should supply to foreign countries, but many NGOs have no doubt. The International Red Cross, for example, is often first to arrive in times of need and the last to depart. *Source:* Alamy.

become intertwined. These types of investments come with many perplexing questions, among them, "who will benefit most from the arrangements?" While local governments may obtain a share of the profits or even tax foreign corporations, investors repatriate the profits, taking the income earned back to their home corporations or lenders. Since most FDI comes from the private sector, critics worry that multinational corporations will get more out of their transactions than the people of the developing country. Governments, too, often worry that they may come under the control of foreign companies or be forced into arrangements that are against the national interests of their people.

Aid and debt relief

Foreign aid consists of grants of money, loans or technical help from a donor state to a recipient country for a variety of reasons or purposes (Figure 13.3). There is considerable controversy about this form of assistance, but there is much evidence that it does help with economic development when given properly and with safeguards for its use. While most foreign aid or official development assistance (ODA)

is bilateral (i.e., goes directly from the contributor to the recipient), a growing amount goes to developing countries as multilateral aid from international organizations, especially the World Bank and the International Monetary Fund (IMF). The targets of such aid include economic development projects, poverty reduction, and others as specified by the donor. These goals are not always pursued without selfish motivations. Development aid may be "untied" or "tied." Recipients prefer untied aid, but most donor countries insist that large proportions of their economic assistance be accompanied by the purchase of goods and services from their own countries, that is, that the assistance be tied. This means that recipients often have to accept inappropriate or overpriced goods and services with their "tied" aid. Moreover, the United States often includes military assistance as foreign aid, and while it may be accepted, it is often criticized as interference in the country's politics. A recent example was the huge increase in American foreign aid for those countries prepared to help in the "global war on terror" after 9/11. In other words, wealthy donor states often use foreign aid to enhance

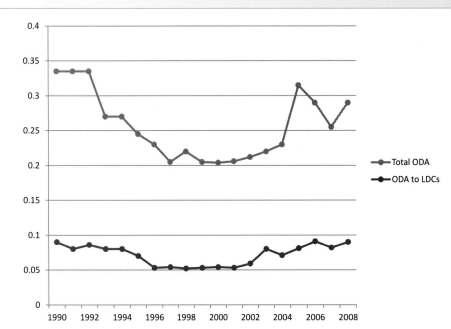

Figure 13.4 Net official development assistance from OECD countries.

their political or military influence over a recipient or increase their strategic leverage in a whole region.

Much of the general criticism of how the richer countries handle aid issues is justifiable. In 1970, the world's richest countries (i.e., the OECD countries) agreed to provide 0.7 percent of their annual gross national income (GNI) as official international development aid. Since then, despite the many billions given each year, few developed states have met their promised targets (Figure 13.4). While the United States is by far the largest donor in dollar terms, it ranks among the lowest in terms of meeting the agreed 0.7 percent target. As of 2010, only Sweden, Norway, Luxembourg, Denmark and the Netherlands had reached the GNI target. The United Kingdom provided 0.52 percent and the United States 0.2 percent. President Barack Obama has promised to double his country's aid contribution by 2015, and Britain has agreed to reach the goal of 0.7 percent by 2013. The largest donors by dollar volume rather than per capita were the United States, France, Germany, the United Kingdom, and Japan. The slowdown in economic growth since 2008 reduced the expected levels and dollar values of the aid.

The LDCs have been especially prone to the problem of debt. In the 1970s many of them borrowed heavily; then in the 1980s some found they had overestimated their ability to repay the loans, and others had simply mismanaged them. More loans were given to offset these debts, and a spiral of unpayable debt quickly developed. The situation reached a crisis when Brazil, the world's largest debtor state, threatened that it would not pay back its loans at all. In 1982 Mexico, the second-largest debtor state announced that it could not repay its loans or even the interest on them. This turned many commercial bankers into much more conservative lenders, and LDCs found themselves more dependent than ever on intergovernmental organizations.

Many leaders of developing countries complain about the insistence on the principles of capitalism that accompany loans from intergovernmental organizations, saying that it is nothing more than neocolonialism. To receive money from them, they are often required to adopt structural adjustment policies, which require them to engage in what they consider unreasonable economic reforms to eradicate the causes of their difficulties. The reforms, for example, might include devaluing their currency, eliminating subsidies, introducing limits on credits, making tax and financial-sector reforms, reducing the size of government, and, most important, liberalizing trade policies by removing high tariffs. As we saw in the previous chapter, however, the IMF and World Bank are controlled by member countries according to the amount of their respective financial commitments. They are conservative institutions that require poorer countries that obtain loans to "reinvigorate" their economies, basically by swallowing the bitter pill of economic austerity and accepting the same principles of market economics that donors consider to be the source of their own success. To meet these demands of *conditionality*, many LDCs have had to cut public services even in such vital fields as health care and education.

By 2006 the developing world owed many billions of dollars, calculated at about 80 percent of the value of its combined exports of goods and services. This debt load impeded development plans, and it became evident that the loans might never be repaid. The twenty-eight most heavily indebted poor countries (HIPCs) had arrears of $782 billion. The IMF organized a program, Poverty Reduction and Growth Facility (PRGF), which provided extremely reduced rate loans to low-income countries, and another special program loaned money at concessional rates to the most indebted poor countries. By 2010, all forty HIPCs had qualified for a new program, the Multi-Lateral Debt Relief Initiative. The MDRI is intended to assist the 2015 Millennium Development Goals endeavor by ensuring that no poor country is burdened with a debt it cannot manage by allowing 100 percent debt relief on eligible debts.[14]

Population and food

The developing world contains more than three-quarters of the world's population, and China and India each have more than a billion people. Population growth is much more rapid in these developing areas than in the industrialized North and is forecast to continue for the next few decades. Between 2003 and 2015 the population of high-income OECD countries

[14] http://www.imf.org.

is forecast to grow by only 0.5 percent, while the developing countries will grow by 1.3 percent. Globally, the past century has seen fantastic progress in longevity and quality of human life. In the economically developed parts of the world, the fall in the death rate and increased life expectancy have been accompanied by overall low fertility rates. However, these trends have not yet developed in most LDCs, where the population is expected to double in the coming century. Rapid population growth threatens to undermine the governments of many of these countries, as finding employment and food for so many people is proving nearly impossible (Figure 13.5). In the large cities

Figure 13.5 Slum development on the fringes of large cities is a significant problem in many countries as unskilled rural workers flood to cities in search of jobs creating desperate social conditions. The favellas of Rio de Janeiro in Brazil are growing even though the Brazilian economy is now booming. *Source:* Alamy.

overpopulation will lead to even greater problems in housing, transportation, sewage disposal, and garbage collection.

Most developing states are not yet prepared to take on the issues that cause overpopulation. For various reasons, they continue to encourage fertility and large families. Only in a very few places does the state intervene to limit family size. Historically, the Chinese government used policies such as birth control programs as well as penalties and even enforced sterilization and abortion in an attempt to force compliance to its policy of one child per family, but that policy has been modified in recent years. Other states have used less intrusive programs. Cuba, for example, has restricted movement from rural to urban areas in an attempt to control rapid population growth in certain regions of the country.

Population growth translates into hunger and even starvation in many developing countries. Data for the world as a whole show that there is a satisfactory amount of food for everyone, everywhere, but that its *uneven distribution* leaves millions of people hungry and condemns others to starvation. In theory, if better transportation and distribution systems existed, there would be no starvation. However, without significant advances in agriculture food production, supply will not keep up with population growth. To ensure long-term self-sufficiency and stability, less developed countries will have to develop their own independent sources of food and water close to large population centers.

Population and food are only two of the vital issues facing LDCs. Pollution of the environment is another obvious problem. Domestic and international politics are interwoven in these issues, which cannot be solved by single states. Only comprehensive changes at the international level would allow satisfactory and permanent solutions. Chapters 14 and 15 focus on some of the major environmental and social issues confronting the globe.

The politics of North-South relations

Much of the debate about development or lack thereof has been led by the global South. These states are distinguished not only by their geographical location and their low level of performance but also by their continual economic dependence on the countries of the industrialized North and their overall approach to world politics. In many of these states, the desire for economic improvement is accompanied by a search for identity at home and recognition abroad that is reflected in their foreign policies. Many of these states have historically pursued a policy of nonalignment. During the Cold War they refused to join either superpower bloc and were united only in asserting their independence. As a stated policy, nonalignment with the superpowers was first articulated by these countries at a 1955 conference in Bandung, Indonesia. Twenty-nine countries refused to participate in Cold War maneuvering, and as nonaligned states, they agreed not to join any alliances with the great powers and to remain neutral on issues that separated democratic and communist countries.

The so-called Nonaligned Movement (NAM) was founded in 1961 and eventually grew to more than one hundred states, ranging from African and Asian countries to the former Yugoslavia, which wished to escape from the clutches of the Soviet Union, and others such as Cuba, which relied on the Soviet Union for security. Regardless of their claims to neutrality, however, many nonaligned states actually did rely, and continue to rely, on one of the great powers for economic and military support, and they often buy their military equipment and arms from their patron state. In 2012, the NAM met in Tehran, Iran. President Mohamoud Ahmadinejad then became the movement's representative at international organizations such as the UN.

During the 1970s the Group of 77 (G-77), a coalition of developing countries, brought its demands to the UN and received considerable support for what it termed a New International Economic Order (NIEO), calling for dialogue and reform to bring greater equality in trade rules and international economic policy. The group's complaints about the world economy echoed the views of radical and critical theorists that major changes had to be made before progress would be possible. Essentially, they called for changes in the terms of international trade, regulation of multinational corporations, restructuring of debt burdens for the poorest countries, increased foreign aid, democratization of international economic institutions such as the World Bank and IMF, and the establishment of a common fund to aid countries adversely affected by price declines.

The developing countries won on a few of these issues. The 1975 Lome Convention gave developing countries preferential access to European markets, and plans were put in place to help the most heavily indebted countries. But most of the South's demands went unmet. Meanwhile, the end of the Cold War in 1989 did not end the desire of the South to form a non-Western coalition of like-minded countries. Economic issues of poverty and inequality continued to unite them even when ideological differences did not. By the turn of the century, the language of southern dissent had become part of the international dialogue on the future direction of the global economy. While liberalism and its focus on economic growth continued to be the dominant philosophy of much of the world, new conceptions about economic development were introduced. The role of nongovernmental organizations in development were recognized, as was the role of innovative institutions such as the Grameen Bank in Bangladesh (see Close Up 13.3). Issues of gender equity, democratic participation, empowerment, and environmental sustainability, for example, gradually became part of the language of deliberations at the United Nations.

But while the language of reform has changed somewhat in the 21st century, many developing counties have adopted the pro-growth philosophy of economic liberalism, while rich donor countries and intergovernmental agencies have made only moderate adjustments in their development policies. The principle pragmatic arguments about economic development remain constant despite these philosophical innovations. The essential issue remains – would economic development be better enhanced by economic growth, official aid, a global tax on financial transactions, or a radical restructuring of the world economy? The 2008–09 economic crises have

Close Up 13.3 **Poverty and credit**

Microcredit (small loans to very poor people) has become very popular in recent years. The practice is based on the idea that capital dispersed at the lowest levels of society will increase economic self-sufficiency and spur overall economic growth. It may also help counteract the operation of criminal leaders in poorer countries. In 2006, the Bangladeshi banker Muhammad Yunus was awarded the Nobel Peace Prize for his activities on behalf of people in extreme poverty. He believes that access to financial credit should be a human right, and he argues that much of world poverty could be eradicated if people only had more credit. Yunus contends that self-employment through borrowing money is the way out of poverty.

Operating on the definition of poverty as the inability to take care of one's basic needs, such as housing, food, and nutrition, the Grameen Bank has loaned billions of dollars to millions of poor borrowers – mostly women. The bank has had some outstanding successes, but it has also encountered some problems with religious militants, especially radical Islamist groups, concerning repayment of credit. Recently, charges of illegality and corruption have arisen in the microcredit field.

What do you think about the idea that poverty can be eliminated by providing more microcredit to impoverished people?

temporarily removed this rancorous debate from the North-South dialogue, but it is slowly returning.

The millennium development goals, 2015

In light of sustained evidence that poverty and inequalities are not being eliminated quickly enough, world leaders at the United Nations in 2000

Table 13.4. Summary of UN millennium development goals

Goal	Method
Goal 1 Eradicate extreme poverty and hunger:	- Reduce extreme poverty by half
	- Productive and decent employment
	- Reduce hunger by half
Goal 2 Achieve universal primary education:	
	- Universal primary schooling
Goal 3 Promote gender equality and empower women:	
	- Equal girls' enrollment in primary school
	- Women's share of paid employment
	- Equal representation in national parliaments
Goal 4 Reduce child mortality:	
	- Reduce mortality of children under five by two-thirds
Goal 5 Improve maternal health:	
	- Reduce maternal mortality by three quarters
	- Access to reproductive health
Goal 6 Combat HIV/AIDS, malaria and other diseases:	
	- Halt and reverse spread of HIV/AIDS
	- Halt and reverse spread of tuberculosis
Goal 7 Ensure environmental sustainability:	
	- Reverse loss of forests
	- Halve proportion without improved drinking water
	- Halve proportion without sanitation
	- Improve the lives of slum dwellers
Goal 8 Develop a global partnership for development	

Note: For a detailed Millennium Development Goals: 2010 Progress Chart, see http://unstats.un.org/unsd/mdg/Resources/Static/Products/Progress2010/MDG_Report_2010_Progress_Chart_En.pdf; for the regional groupings and country data, see http://mdgs.un.org.
Source: United Nations, Millennium Development Goals.

committed themselves to achieve eight global goals by 2015. These eight **Millennium Developments Goals (MDGs)** were then subdivided into twenty-one measurable targets with sixty indicators to track development progress.[15] The goals and their major targets are shown in Table 13.4.

MDG progress report

In 2010, two-thirds of the way through the mandate, the UN assessed its progress in meeting these eight goals. The general conclusion was that progress had been made in some fields but that much more would need to be done if all the targets were to be met. The report concluded that renewed global commitment would be required to slash poverty, hunger, disease, and a host of other ills by 2015.[16] UN Secretary-General Ban Ki-moon declared, "It is clear that improvements in the lives of the poor have been unacceptably slow, and some hard-won gains are being eroded by the climate, food and economic crises."[17] He summarized the situation as follows: "the clock is ticking, with much more to do."[18]

These are laudable goals, but the world is not on track to meet all or even most of its targets by 2015. In 2008–09 the global economy contracted for the first time since World War II, and economic growth in some formerly fast-growing developing countries plummeted. As a result, the trend in some categories is getting worse. Progress has been uneven among regions, as well as between and within countries. The poorest groups, those without education or who live in remote areas, have been most neglected and have not had adequate opportunities to improve their lives.

Of the eight UN goals, the first six have shown slight improvement and there is hope that at least some of them can be achieved. Overall progress is greatest in China and India, but the addition of their data to the overall statistics distorts the fact that other countries are far from reaching their goals. Indeed, inside these two countries their large population figures mask large pockets of poverty. Together the two states accounted for 62 percent of the world's poor in 1990, so clearly their progress markedly affects the gross numbers.[19] Despite this caveat, the goal of reducing world poverty to less than a billion people by 2015 is quite conceivable, even though the long-term effects of the 2008–09 economic crisis and its knock-on effects are still unknown. Some countries are progressing much faster than others, while the worst are struggling. Sub-Saharan Africa, for example, is not likely to reach the MDGs on poverty in the foreseeable future, so poverty, unemployment, and hunger in that area will remain severe at least until near the 22nd century.

Around the world, improvement is uneven and easily reversible. World hunger and malnutrition rose from 2008 through 2009, partially eliminating earlier gains. In 2008 more than a quarter of the children in the developing world were underweight, mainly because of either lack of food or poor nutritive quality; a sixth of the world's population lacked access to safe drinking water; and just under half used unsanitary toilets or none at all. Improved sanitation is barely noticeable in the poorest households. There were significant developments in increased primary school enrolments and some sluggish shifts toward gender equality. Enrolment in primary education reached 89 percent in 2008, up from 80 percent in 1991. There has also been considerable improvement in reducing communicable diseases, malaria, HIV/AIDS, tuberculosis, and measles immunization. Between 2003 and 2008, the number of people receiving antiretroviral therapy increased tenfold, to four million people.

Improvements in maternal and child health have not been satisfactory, despite the fact that achieving this goal could help to accomplish all the others. Between 1990 and 2008 the mortality rate of children younger than five years of age in developing countries declined from 10 percent to

---

[15] For ongoing discussions and details on the evolution of the progress towards these goals, see http://www.undp.org.

[16] United Nations, *The Millennium Development Goals Report* (New York: United Nations, 2010).

[17] Ibid., p. 3.

[18] *The Guardian*, September 21, 2010.

[19] *Economist*, September 25, 2010, p. 31.

Figure 13.6 The 1999 world trade ministerial meeting in Seattle provoked the first large-scale demonstration against globalization. While world trade organizers stress the economic benefits of globalization, opponents highlight defects such as maldistribution of world income and trade benefits, increasing environmental degradation, and human rights concerns. *Source:* Corbis.

only 7.2 percent, and maternal mortality reduced from 480 deaths per 100,000 live births in 1990 to 450 deaths in 2005. While in the developed world almost all births are attended by skilled health personnel, fewer than half the mothers receive this care in developing countries. Contraceptive use is four times higher among women with a secondary education than among those with no education, and negative progress has been observed on this issue.

The seventh and eighth goals met with the least success. Environmental sustainability measures to contain carbon emissions, deforestation, and the mining of water aquifers have been slow to gain ground. Yet climate change is increasingly affecting vulnerable populations – those who have contributed least to the problem (see Chapter 15). Changes in global governance structures such as the World Bank and the IMF have been rare. The growth in the membership of the G8 to the G20 was for political, not developmental, reasons, and only the richest of the poor countries were allowed to join.

We have seen that the process of globalization has both blessings and harmful effects. But could it eventually lead to a narrowing of the gap between the developed and developing worlds? Would more globalization increase or decrease inequalities among and within states? This debate is not limited to economic repercussions but involves other social and political consequences. Are there, for example, proven established and empirical links between poverty and violence or poverty and terrorism? The contest between antiglobalizers and global advocates came to a head in the 1990s with protests at international meetings of the IMF and World Bank (Figure 13.6). The demonstrations in Seattle in 1995 were a kind of watershed, as the protestors acted as a lightning rod for antiglobalist opinion worldwide, and there have been protests at every individual meeting ever since. The dissent has certainly made people more aware of the questions and about what could or should be done about the global divide between rich and poor.

We have seen that success in fulfilling the goals of the MDGs process has been mixed. Preliminary report cards indicate that only a few objectives will be met. They also show that some regions and countries are on track to meet the specific targets, while others are not. While Brazil, India, and China weathered the recent financial storm better than most countries, other states lost momentum in their quest to improve the lives of their citizens. The year

2015 will be pivotal, as it is likely to show highly differentiated development around the world, with some regions achieving very positive development and others very little. Several goals will not be met by the specified dates, and as indicated, some regions are unlikely to meet their targets for perhaps a half century or more.

Explanations for development

What accounts for the tenacious existence of a rich and poor world? In an epoch characterized by a global economy, global communications, global ecology, and global weapons systems, why does gross economic imbalance persist? Why, when knowledge, technology, and capital are easily transferable, has there not been a major shift in world wealth? Political and economic development is the broad rubric under which many controversial answers relating to these questions are placed. It is an umbrella concept that covers both close-linked phenomena concerning political change everywhere and more specific analysis of the growth, or lack of growth, and development in LDCs. It is no wonder, then, that there is no accepted definition of *development* and that the very term itself is criticized as inappropriate by some scholars.[20] There is considerable agreement that leaders of more developed states should be able to accomplish their goals more successfully, but there is considerable disagreement about what objectives should be sought.

Whether the term used is *development, developing,* or *underdeveloped,* the concept is said by critical and radical academics to have ideological overtones. There is some validity to their argument. In a nutshell, the question is often put as follows: Does the economic and political modernization of poorer states necessitate Westernization, or do countries that wish to improve their economies and politics necessarily have to follow the same models

of development as Western liberal democracies? Did communist states such as China – which at times in its history has been more technologically advanced than European countries – have to switch to full-blown capitalism to develop further? For many experts, the answer is yes.

Many individuals simply assume that states that wish to achieve a high level of economic and political development should adopt the same model that rich states did in the past. But many countries have value systems, cultures, histories, and economies that differ vastly from those of democratic and capitalist states. To avoid social disruption, these states need to find a model for development that is compatible with their own societies. One of the persistent questions, then, is whether political leaders in LDCs can create institutions that are capable of sustaining both economic growth and political stability. While some states have escaped from the conditions associated with low economic development and poverty, the sources of both are many and differ greatly from one national circumstance to another.[21] They may be based in low productivity, inadequate national resources, famines, corruption, wars, or even economic inequality within the country. The debate is intense.

In the view of some observers, the focus of such studies should simply be on the South rather than on development. The problem with using this approach is that it focuses not on the primary issues of world politics but rather on several specific geographical regions. The South approach takes us to many of the right places – Africa, Asia, Latin America, the Middle East, and most of the islands of the Pacific Ocean – but this does not tell us which questions to ask when we arrive. Why do similar circumstances prevail in much of the South? Is it possible for poorer states there and elsewhere to move to higher levels of economic and political development? What is the best policy route to escape from these conditions and circumstances?

[20] See Fred W. Riggs, "The Rise and Fall of 'Political Development,'" in *The Handbook of Political Behavior,* ed. Samuel Long (New York: Plenum Press, 1981), pp. 289–348.

[21] Christopher Clapham, *Third World Politics* (London: Croom Helm, 1985), p. 2.

Modernization and dependency theories

Development is a complex and contentious concept. We define it as the economic and political steps required to increase a state's capacity to meet its people's basic human requirements and raise its standard of living conditions. Applying these concepts to the diversities of states and societies characterized as either developed or developing is controversial. It is not surprising, therefore, that two basic schools of thought clash in explaining why some states remain in a less developed condition than others. The two groups can be broadly characterized as following either the traditional theory of *political modernization* or the more "radical" perspective of *dependency theory.*

On the whole, the political modernization school of global politics depicts a state's development in terms of its *internal* changes over time; its advocates ask by what processes and institutional changes a developing state evolves into a richer or more modern country.[22] The central academic question is whether one can describe and account systematically for the patterns of its various stages.[23] Many descriptions of the conditions of developed states have been suggested. They tend to include such social conditions as greater urbanization and higher literacy, as well as economic conditions such as greater industrialization and productive capacity. More developed political systems tend also to be associated with organizational sophistication (e.g., specialization, differentiation of roles and functions in organizations and government), technological improvement (e.g., an increase in means of producing goods and services), and attitudinal differences (e.g., modern attitudes are characterized by increased knowledge, rationality, secular values, and individualism). These distinctions are used in the specialist literature to define both the state of development and the process through which states must evolve to become developed.

Modernization theory is based on the premise that wealth is created through the same principles as capitalism – namely efficient production, free enterprise, and free trade. Its intellectual roots go back to classical economic liberalism based on Adam Smith's arguments about the importance of supply and demand in the market, the comparative advantage doctrine of professional economics, and laissez-faire principles in commerce and trade. The modernization school of thought is thus based essentially on the idea that LDCs will have to follow the path of Western states if they wish to modernize. They will need to accept modern ideas about political processes, education, technology, and the economy. These changes will only come about, such theorists argue, if values and structures in these developing societies can become more similar to those in the developed countries.

In purely economic terms, so the theory goes, once a poor society can create enough capital for investment purposes, the benefits of capitalism will "trickle down" to large parts of society. Western or classical economists back up this notion by arguing that the way for LDCs to develop is by competing with developed states in worldwide free trade. If domestic producers in these countries are exposed to international competition, they will become more efficient and effective; that is, they will be forced to modernize. According to this reasoning, the problem with many LDCs is that their leaders have misled them into socialism, state-directed economies, cronyism, and corruption. These arguments are backed up by international organizations such as the World Bank and the International Monetary Fund, which lend money only to countries that conform to certain norms about capitalism, government, and markets. Many of their arguments present a linear model of development that is essentially based on Western experiences. However, the idea that states follow a single, inevitable sequence of stages toward modern development is challenged. In contemporary

[22] The best-known earlier exponents of this view are G. A. Almond and G. B. Powell, *Comparative Politics: A Developmental Approach* (Boston: Little, Brown, 1966); and S. P. Huntington, *Political Order in Changing Societies* (New Haven, CT: Yale University Press, 1968).

[23] The original book on this topic was Gabriel A. Almond and James Coleman, *The Politics of the Developing Areas* (Princeton, NJ: Princeton University Press, 1960).

studies, more attention is paid to the key problems in the developmental process and to the choices that leaders make to resolve these challenges.

Whereas modernization theory largely attributes the causes of underdevelopment to domestic factors, the dependency school blames the plight of LDCs on their having been incorporated into the global, capitalist economy during periods of colonization and subsequent neocolonialism. They are dependent because they need to borrow capital to produce goods, and then they have to make debt payments, a combination that prevents them from breaking away from the richer world. Moreover, the dominant core states export their finished goods to the poorer countries in exchange for raw materials. Advocates of the dependency school therefore reject the idea that LDCs must follow the Western route to development. For them, underdevelopment is a product of unequal relationships between the richer capitalist states and the poorer undeveloped ones as a by-product of the Western model. The capitalist states maintain their economic dominance by manipulating factors such as wages, resources, capital, markets, prices, and technologies. The developing states are kept as suppliers of raw materials and providers of cheap labor for the benefit of the capitalist states. In some of the more radical of these approaches, the world economy is seen as actually *creating* underdevelopment and poverty in developing countries.[24] Thus, opening up markets in the LDCs only exacerbates the differences between rich and poor countries. According to this argument, it is existence on the *periphery* that plagues these states.

Several issues dominate discussion of these problems, but the essential one is this – why did these countries not develop economically when colonialism ended? The dependency school answers as follows. First, the economic links between colonies and colonizers were not broken by the process of independence. The new countries continued to trade with their foreign colonizers and the economic and

administrative class continued its close relations with former bosses. In this neocolonial situation the colonizers did not govern the newly independent states, but they indirectly controlled them because their institutions and leaders had been determined earlier by their colonial status. Indeed, in many former colonies a kind of *comprador* class developed. This term is used to depict indigenous people who are "bought" by former colonizers and become part of the exploitation carried out in the neocolonial period. This class tends to support the interests of those in the richer countries because they personally depend on them for their power and wealth. Second, the territorial borders of the newly independent states were drawn by colonizers, which left interethnic rivalry in place, which in turn prevented the development of coherent strategies for economic development. Many of these states only produce one or two products for export – such as coffee, oil, copper ore, or diamonds. Only a few developing states have been able to successfully break away from producing the same products for export as they did under colonialism.

Table 13.5 illustrates development issues. In the past decades many companies had their products, such as running shoes, produced in poorer countries where labor costs were very low compared to in the United States or Western Europe. Social pressures have brought "fair trade" policies in some areas, but the practice continues in others.

Colonialism and imperialism

The worldwide economic conditions that affect rich and poor countries are part of a long historical pattern that stemmed initially from the development of the modern state system and was extended by the history of colonialism and imperialism (see Chapter 2). To an extent, contemporary inequality can be traced to the European conquest of indigenous peoples and their lands beginning in the late fifteenth century. Even today's perspectives on global politics in the developing parts of the world are largely based on how colonialism affected development patterns in the world. Colonialism was a result

[24] This group would include the classic by Immanuel Wallerstein, *The Modern World-System*, 3 vols. (Maryland Heights, MO: Academic/Elsevier, 1989).

Table 13.5 Basketball shoes and workers in developing countries in the 1990s (US$)

U.S. rubber shoe industry average wage	$6.94 per hour
Indonesian rubber shoe industry average wage	$0.14 per hour
Cost of manufacturing one pair of Nike basketball shoes in Indonesia	$0.12
Sale price of one pair of Nike basketball shoes in the United States	$80.00
Michael Jordan's multiyear endorsement fee for Nike shoes	$2 million

Source: Data assembled from information in Jeffrey Balinger, "The New Free Trade Hell," *Harper's Magazine* (August 1992), pp. 46–57. Nike has since moved toward fair-trade practices.

of the economic nationalist/mercantilist strategies adopted by European states in order to build up their own countries in competition with each other and at the expense of poorer ones. Today the word neocolonialism is used by radicals and many others to describe the postcolonial indirect control exercised by richer states and their industries as they exploit people in weaker countries. As noted, almost all of today's poorest states were colonies of Northern states at one time.

European colonialism began in the late fifteenth century and continued in one form or another for over 500 years. Dutch, English, French, Portuguese, and Spanish sea explorers and adventurers roamed the Southern Hemisphere in search of booty. They were sponsored by governments and commercial interests that took advantage of their successes. A profitable transatlantic slave trade also developed. Wealth and resources from the colonies were sent to Europe for the benefit of monarchs and elites, supporting the development of state armies and navies. Companies such as the British East India Company

were chartered and financed, and navies protected their interests; for a time the British East India Company even had its own army and flag. By the late nineteenth century the United States, and to some extent Japan, had joined the Europeans in colonizing territories throughout the world.

The pattern of global politics in the 20th century was fashioned in the preceding century from the clash of competing imperial powers and their effects, beneficial or harmful, on the societies they dominated. The European wars over territory and authority, along with their overseas exploits, led to a period of massive globalization. Expansion in the Americas, Africa, and to some extent Asia was accompanied by growing commercial integration. There were no political institutions such as the League of Nations or the United Nations to provide a wider perspective. States were all-powerful, but commercial activity in the form of trade and banks forced interdependence even as they contested territories and peoples. In 1800, European power covered about one-third of the world's land surface. By the beginning of World War I, Europeans had imposed some form of political or economic ascendancy over 80 percent of the globe.[25]

By World War I, Britain alone had power over about a fifth of the world's land area and perhaps as much as one-fourth of the world's population.[26] Africa was almost completely controlled by European powers, and in the Far East only Japan and Thailand were never conquered. China was divided into zones of European dominance. The United States extended its power to Hawaii, obtained Puerto Rico and the Philippines from Spain, controlled much of the Caribbean, and obtained authority to perpetually lease the Panama Canal. Meanwhile, Japan occupied Korea and Taiwan. Both countries had fought wars against old imperial powers in the process, the United States against Spain, and Japan against Russia.

[25] Carl Cavanagh Hodge, ed., *Encyclopedia of the Age of Imperialism, 1800–1914* (Westport, CT: Greenwood, 2007).
[26] D. K. Fieldhouse, *Economics and Empire, 1830–1914* (Ithaca, NY: Cornell University Press, 1973).

The impact of this global colonization was profound. Indigenous peoples and cultures were ravaged. Slaves who had been taken to perform menial work in the richer countries were left far from their homes. Raw materials such as oil, silver, and sugar were extracted to the benefit of the colonizers. State borders, especially in Africa, often left people of diverse identities inside single states, which sometimes collapsed into mismanaged governments and periods of civil war. Colonialism and Western imperialism left deep scars of resentment, and most important, almost every colony remained poor in comparison with the developed world. Whether causation should be attributed to colonization alone remains debatable, but the reality is that the world was divided essentially into the developed Northern Hemisphere and the unequal Southern Hemisphere.

Economics, religion, and politics all were factors in colonization, but beyond that, theorists weigh and assess overseas expansion differently. Realists attribute colonial activities to the constant search of states for more security and power. Liberal theorists ascribe the development of world trade to the requirements of capitalism and the need for raw materials and new markets to absorb their products. Radicals, Marxists, and especially those who have been called theorists of the world-system approach judge colonialism as a means by which the bourgeois of the North escaped from being overthrown by a people's revolution in their own countries. The richer countries simply developed a worldwide division of labor with an inner "core" of industrialized states exploiting the poorer or nonindustrial states on the "periphery."[27]

Some colonies, such as the United States, managed to obtain independence during the 18th century. Colonization effectively ended in the rest of the Americas by the beginning of the 19th century, but the European process of imperialism continued in Africa, Asia, and elsewhere. After World War I, growing competiveness over colonies in Africa and Asia led to the beginnings of decolonization, or the freeing of colonial peoples from their dependent status as colonies. The 1919 Treaty of Versailles, which ended World War I, unleashed this process, which was embedded in a philosophy of liberalism. Mercantilism (or economic nationalism) was blamed for causing the war, and the United States and other Western powers declared that free trade and political freedoms were inextricably linked. U.S. President Woodrow Wilson called for self-determination, the ethical right for all peoples to be able to decide on their own form of government. The concepts of authority (ability to govern) and legitimacy (the moral right to govern) were linked together at the League of Nations. This institution gave credence to the idea that people in the colonies had inalienable rights and should not be treated as the property of richer states, so those territories should be held as mandates by members of the League until self-rule could be achieved.

The next major wave of decolonization coincided with the end of World War II at a time when the UN was making declarations of rights and the West was occupied with containing communism. Anticolonial movements flourished, and the appeal of liberation and nationalism grew. Mahatma Gandhi led a nonviolent movement in South Asia, and in 1947 India and Pakistan gained independence from Britain. Within a short period, nearly all of Africa overthrew European white rule. South Africa was the largest African state still ruled by whites – despite its independence in 1961. Afrikaner rule and apartheid over indigenous peoples was not terminated there until 1994, when Nelson Mandela wrestled power away from the whites. Eventually, the number of independent states in the world approached two hundred. The principle of self-determination had been translated into a right to sovereign statehood.

Assessing the theories: Modernization and dependency

The conflict between these two basic schools of development begins with their basic concepts and assumptions. Traditional theories focus on modernization, whereas more radical ideas address the dependence of LDCs on wealthier states. Both include slippery concepts. What is development? What is dependency?

---

[27] Immanuel Wallerstein, *The Modern World-System*.

Central to this dispute are fundamentally contrasting views about international political economics. As we have seen, modernization theories are based on the capitalist notion that capital and investment are required for economic growth and that this necessitates free economies and markets. Before internal inequality issues can be resolved, a country needs to accumulate enough capital to invest to provide economic growth. According to this logic, questions of equality should be set aside in the early stages of development. In contrast, radicals and others who support dependency theories believe that economic development should be accompanied by an equitable distribution of wealth. In other words, the two schools differ as to whether adopting the goal of equality will produce economic growth or slow it down. The modernization, or capitalist, idea is based on the idea that unequal economic distributions inside states and in the global economy will provide quicker and higher economic growth, whereas radicals maintain that higher growth will create more equal income distributions.

At the international level, therefore, one school of thought believes that if Southern economies are integrated with the North, the poorer countries will have to learn to compete in a free market and be forced to modernize. This will result in economic growth that will trickle down to their people. This school, therefore, argues in favor of a liberal international economy, free-trade agreements, and intergovernmental organizations such as the IMF and World Bank. Radicals believe that such reasoning keeps developing countries poor – it is precisely because they are in a global economy dominated by the richer North that their subjection and poverty continues.

There is not enough empirical evidence to support either of these positions conclusively. Some states with fairly equitable income distributions have very high growth rates (e.g., the NICs, some Scandinavian countries) but others with very unequal distribution also have vibrant economies (the United States and, more recently, China and India). Some developing countries have tied themselves to the capitalist principles of world free trade and have been successful (China and India), but others have been unable to escape from their dependence on richer countries even though they accept liberal economics. Many are linked to the developed world in terms of single-crop economies or are caught in a resource trap.

The analytical problems with the dependency school are just as significant as those with the modernization school. While modernization theorists assume the validity of capitalism and stress the developmental stages of state evolution, dependency theory advocates tend to leave the internal dynamics of each state out of their analysis. Ideologically, they seem to be saying that the poorer states ought to break with the global capitalist system in order to achieve a higher degree of economic independence. However, they mistakenly assume that the state of dependency remains unaltered for all countries throughout history. Perhaps this is because scholars of this tradition tend to concentrate on Africa and Latin America to the near exclusion of Asia. They homogenize the experience of all LDCs into one preconceived pattern arising from colonization. Some even limit their research to the colonial past to explain how that period actually created today's world without discussing today's world in any detail.[28] Last, dependency theorists do not explain why less developed states differ so greatly in their public policy choices, nor do they explain why some states have succeeded in achieving their developmental goals while others have failed.

The simple fact is that neither development theory has proved uniquely capable of explaining economic and political development around the world. Ideological differences seem to characterize both sides. Internal factors such as class, ethnicity, religion, and especially culture are often omitted in both types of analysis. Modernization theory rose and then declined as an accepted theory among political scientists. As its significance fell, dependency became a primary focus

---

[28] For a discussion of the various theories, see Vicky Randall and Robin Theobald, *Political Change and Underdevelopment: A Critical Introduction to Third World Politics* (London: Macmillan, 1985). For a discussion of debates within the dependency school, see J. Edkins, *Poststructuralism and International Relations* (Boulder, CO: Lynne Rienner, 2000).

of argument in global studies. No sooner did this take place than several developing countries began to enrich themselves by accepting and applying the principles of capitalism and modernization theory.

Several Asian countries obtained considerable economic growth by participating in the global market as both producers and consumers. The Asian tigers, or newly industrializing countries (NICs) – Singapore, Taiwan, Korea, and Hong Kong – maintained greater growth in the 1980s than did the developed world. The NICs soon became important exporters of manufactured goods and important markets for the developed world's products. This development was followed by the 21st-century rise of China, India, and Brazil as emerging countries that adopted capitalist strategies for global economic competition. The success of these and other countries has been so great that there has been a massive outsourcing of jobs from the developed to developing countries, where workers can be hired for low wages, and this has stimulated further the growth in these countries.

Clearly, a new theory that combines the arguments of both these theories is required. Development surely is tied to both internal and international factors. The rapid modernization of East Asia and parts of South Asia involved major changes not anticipated by scholars of either tradition. Neither was the emergence of democracy in the former Soviet Union and Eastern Europe or earlier in Latin America predicted by scholars of either tradition. Several countries modernized "economically" without adopting Western culture and values. Notwithstanding their economic difficulties at the end of the 1990s, the NICs demonstrated that dependency can be overcome. Brazil, China, and India have made tremendous strides in development and already rival Western states in terms of the size of their economies. Certainly, no one argues that these states are dependent on the West, that they have followed the same path of modernization as the West, or that they have abandoned their cultures in pursuit of prosperity.

To a minor degree, the two literatures on development have been synthesized in recent years. Both the impact of the Western World on poorer countries and the internal dynamics of these countries have been recognized as significant. At the same time, the quest for a universal theory of development that could be applied to every country is in disrepute as scholars search for more middle-range theories regarding specific states in particular historical periods. It has become clear that states confront development and industrialization processes at different times, and with different effects, than earlier universalistic theories had presupposed.

There seems now to be a rough consensus that attention should be paid to both international *and* domestic factors in explaining political development. Both schools have also accepted the argument that development is affected by international trade patterns, finance, and investment, but they differ on whether this is good or bad for the developing world. The belief that worldwide economic explanations alone can prove conclusive for analyzing developmental processes has been seriously questioned. Context has proved to matter.[29] The dependency school has shifted some of its focus away from economic growth controversies toward economic distribution within LDCs and the need to study domestic politics.

As well, as Samuel P. Huntington maintained some time ago, there is a proven need to explore systematically the relations between culture and development, as well as between the economy and development.[30] In other words, a richer form of explanation is required, one that not only respects the findings of area specialists about history, culture, and economics but also continues the search for meaningful generalizations about political development and the world economy. Few scholars deny that the unequal distribution of wealth and poverty in the world is affected by the attitudes of people and their local elites as well as by the domestic and international economy, but exactly how this process works continues to be controversial.

[29] See United Nations, "Diverse Paths to Development," in *Human Development Report 2010* (New York: United Nations).
[30] Samuel P. Huntington, "The Goals of Development," in Myron Weiner and Samuel P. Huntington, eds., *Understanding Political Development* (Boston: Little, Brown, 1987).

Conclusion: Globalization and global inequality

Could globalization be both the cause of the progress in the Millennium Development Goals and the lack thereof? It is time to revisit the arguments on both sides.

Advocates of globalization argue that it provides higher standards of living for people around the world by increasing economic efficiency and productivity. Free trade has been associated with higher growth and reduced poverty.[31] As trade and investment increased, the principle of comparative advantage produced what classical economists have always maintained – a trickling down of gains that affected almost everyone. Certainly, the period from the 1990s to the onset of the financial crisis of 2008 saw a marked increase in both globalization and overall growth of per capita income in the developing countries, as well as a decrease in the number of people living in extreme poverty. China and India made enormous strides in their economies. And while both China and India remain developing countries based on their overall per capita levels of income, the two countries have achieved growth within twenty years not unlike that experienced by the United States in the 19th century. At the same time, the developing world as a whole is still far from sharing the advantages of richer countries, although there have been significant improvements. The reduction of the total number of people living in poverty has been staggering.

In short, globalization proponents find that while there are differing degrees of material success around the world, capitalism and economic liberalism have proved beneficial in raising the living standards of people worldwide. Radical alternatives have failed. Even authoritarian state capitalists have embraced the free-market idea. The interdependence and mutual relationships created by globalization have also reduced conflict and war in the developing world.

In opposition, however, a diverse group of scholars, labor unions, environmentalists, farmers, and human rights and women's groups contend that globalization has not taken the world on the right course. Indeed, they believe that it has driven the world economy in the wrong direction. To highlight their opposition they have organized protests at every international meeting on the global economy in recent years. They criticize globalization not only for protecting inequality but also for privileging economic issues over other values and interfering in state sovereignty.

Even if they accept that economic growth and standards of living have increased, critics still contend that globalization leads to inequalities among states and peoples. While the overall number of people in the world living in extreme poverty is expected to decline by 2015 (and poverty rates are expected to fall to around 5 percent in China and 24 percent in India), sub-Saharan Africa, Western Asia, and parts

---

[31] Jagdish Bhagwati, *In Defense of Globalization* (Oxford: Oxford University Press, 2007).

of Eastern Europe and Central Asia will not achieve the MDG target of $1.25 per day for their people by that date.[32] Moreover, inside both China and India there are enormous disparities in income and quality of life. In interior and western China and in northern India extreme poverty and hunger persist despite their countries' overall economic improvements.

Antiglobalizers contend that the main beneficiaries of globalization are multinational corporations and their shareholders in the developed world. Adjusting to the demands of foreign investors is not easy, and it often tears communities and even states apart. Some individuals may not benefit at all, as they are forced to move to new locations to find work (inside or outside their own countries) and sometimes have to work in poor conditions and even sweatshops. The recent economic crises illustrated what is wrong with globalization. States and people in the developing world found it impossible to adapt to the deleterious effects of the serious financial issues emanating from other countries. In short, the housing bubble in the United States and the paralysis in the global financial system became a labor market problem for both developed and developing countries. The cascading crises crippled economies and forced millions of people out of work, swelling the numbers of working poor and undoing many effects of a decade of economic growth in the developing countries.

Globalization has not solved the problems of malnutrition in the developing world. The number of undernourished people rose to about a billion in 2010, and thousands continue to die every day from hunger-related causes. The latest figures about undernourished and underweight children show extreme differences across regions. Although globalization has seen an outstanding increase in world's food supply, hunger has not been eliminated, and it may even have increased. Last, economic globalization values profit over other human needs such as equity, human rights, cultural and religious traditions, environmental protection and sustainability, and political empowerment. Indeed, profit is seen as the primary human need to be satisfied above all the others.

As for security issues, antiglobalizers believe that economic interdependence and globalization can actually increase tensions among groups within societies and states and thus cause violence and war. In other words, societal and global integration can be conducive of conflict, not peace. The growth of globalization did not prevent the rise of global jihadist movements, upheaval in North Africa and the Middle East, ethnic conflict in sub-Saharan Africa, or the terrorist attack of 9/11. The global economic crisis exacerbated problems in developing countries, increasing hostilities over inequalities and hunger. States that were bound to the interdependence of global finances and institutions found that they did not possess independent structures capable of handling social tensions. They were unable to

---

[32] These figures and those that follow are taken from the UN, *The Millennium Development Goals Report*, 2010, found at http://www.un.org.

optimize how their own resources could be used to solve their societal ills, as some rich countries were able to.

Despite the laudable efforts of the United Nations and significant economic growth since World War II, the world is left with an outstanding moral problem – why is the gap between rich and poor so large, and what should be done to reduce it?[33] Globalization has improved the overall world economy, but while it has challenged the role of the state, nothing has replaced it in terms of creating social harmony and meeting public needs. Inequalities between and within states remain and are increasing, and it has been left to local and regional political leaders (who are sometimes corrupt) to solve the resultant conflicts. Perhaps the argument should not be over the past effects of globalization but rather over how much it should be allowed to transform the world in the future.

[33] Jeffery Sachs, *The End of Poverty: How We Can Make It Happen in Our Lifetime* (New York: Penguin, 2005).

Select bibliography

Acemoglu, Daron, and James A. Robinson, *Why Nations Fail: The Origin of Power, Prosperity and Poverty* (London: Profite, 2012).

Bhagwati, Jagdish, *In Defense of Globalization* (Oxford: Oxford University Press, 2007).

Collier, Paul, *The Bottom Billion* (New York: Oxford, 2008).

De Soto, Hernando, *The Mystery of Capital: Why Capitalism Triumphs in the West and Fails Elsewhere* (New York: Basic Book, 2001).

Diamond, Jared, *Collapse: How Societies Choose to Fail or Succeed*, rev. ed. (New York: Penguin, 2011).

Diamond, Jared, *Guns, Germs, and Steel* (New York: Norton, 1997).

Easterley, William, *The White Man's Burden: Why the West's Efforts to Aid the Rest Have Done So Much Ill and So Little Good* (New York: Penguin, 2007).

Edkins, J., *Poststructuralism and International Relations* (Boulder, CO: Lynne Rienner, 2000).

Galbraith, James K., *Inequality and Instability: A Study of the World Economy Just Before the Great Crisis* (Oxford: Oxford University Press, 2012).

Krishna, Sankaran, *Globalization and Postcolonialism: Hegemony and Resistance in the Twenty-First Century* (Lanham, MD: Rowman & Littlefield, 2009).

Rapley, J., *Understanding Development* (Boulder, CO: Lynne Rienner, 1996).

Reuveny, Rafael, and Williams R. Thompson, eds., *North and South in the World Political Economy* (Malden, MA: Blackwell, 2008).

Rodrik, Dani, *One Economics, Many Recipes: Globalization, Institutions and Economic Growth* (Princeton, NJ: Princeton University Press, 2007).

Sachs, Jeffery, *The End of Poverty: How We Can Make It Happen in Our Lifetime* (New York: Penguin, 2005).

Sen, Amartya, *Poverty and Famines* (Oxford, UK: Clarendon Press, 1981).

Sharma, Shalendra D., *China and India in the Age of Globalization* (Cambridge: Cambridge University Press, 2009).

Singer, Peter, *One World: The Ethics of Globalization* (New Haven, CT: Yale University Press, 2002).

Stiglitz, Joseph E., *Globalization and Its Discontents* (New York: Norton, 2002).

Stiglitz, Joseph E., *Making Globalization Work* (New York: Norton, 2006).

Stiglitz, Joseph E., and Gerald Meier, *Frontiers in Development Economics* (Oxford: Oxford University Press, 2000).

Thomas, C., *Global Governance, Development and Human Security* (London: Pluto, 2000).

Part V Global challenges and prospects

Double, double, toil and trouble. ... [T]hings don't change, they just get more so. ... Blood will have blood.

– SHAKEPEARE'S *MACBETH*

The first four parts of this book examined the degree to which globalization is fostering an interconnected world and how new security and economic issues impact on today's global problems. In Part V we highlight major problems of the 21st century that require the attention of the world community – issues that are "intermestic" in nature and cannot be solved by single states, no matter how powerful. Understanding the interconnectedness and multiplicity of these issues and what can be done about them requires knowledge of governments and international relations. The list is indicative of the problems facing world leaders, and readers are encouraged to research and explore the quest for policy answers on these and other topics.

Chapter 14 addresses human rights. The events of September 11, 2001, sounded the alarm on international terrorism, led to quagmires in Iraq and Afghanistan, and foreshadowed tumultuous and violent change in the Middle East and North Africa. It has become increasingly important to reassess and respond to the new security issues around the world. How can states and international agencies react effectively to threats arising from ethnic hatred, religious bigotry, and failing states generally? Should states interfere in other states when human rights are under attack? Chapter 14 highlights these and many other human rights concerns, such as genocide and children in armed conflict.

Chapter 15 focuses on difficult issues that pertain to the global environment, including climate change, energy resources, population, and health. The degradation of the earth's atmosphere, air, soil, and water makes it urgent to find clean alternatives for the world's energy needs. Demographic trends, including population increase, aging, and migration, as well as health issues, are interrelated and vital to human well-being.

The book concludes with a short chapter on crises, ethics, and global politics, a theme that brings together the elements discussed throughout the book. How, it asks, will leaders manage modern crises of natural disasters, civil wars, pandemics, and other human-made problems, and how will they make the ethical trade-offs necessary to create a better world for everyone?

Human rights abuses are as old as history, but this is perhaps the first era that has demonstrated widespread global concern about them. Modern communication systems such as television, radio, and the Internet thrust human tragedies before us on a daily basis and convince people not only that something *should* be done about them but also that something *can* be done about them. There is no denying that human rights abuses abound, and there are many examples in which they have gone unpunished, but at the same time, there is increased global awareness of the issues, and even some progress has been made.

Global issues concerning human rights entail core values and call individuals and governments to examine their perspectives on the value of life. When antiapartheid and black leader Nelson Mandela was released from prison after twenty-seven years and became president of South Africa in 1994, we all extolled the virtues of human will and dignity in world politics. In that case, international economic sanctions and a strong determination to be free of white rule won out over Afrikaner prejudice and authoritarian rule. When Aung San Suu Kyi was allowed to leave house arrest after seven years, and contest the 2012 election in 2012, we all hoped for the best for her and Myanmar. Her struggle for freedom was highlighted by her claim that, "I'm not free until the people are free." Bigger-than-life actors on the world stage, like Nelson Mandela and Aung San Suu Kyi, draw attention to human rights and the importance of ethics in politics, and they illustrate how contrasting viewpoints about the proper role of states in the lives of their peoples are important factors in global politics.

Readers may begin with strong feelings about which human rights are inviolable, but this is in fact an exceedingly complex issue. In this chapter we explore the many meanings of human rights and the various debates over their interpretation and importance. Why is it so difficult to agree on what basic human rights should be accepted globally? We discuss the role of international law and human rights regimes as well as the governmental, intergovernmental, and nongovernmental institutions that monitor and attempt to enforce standards of human rights around the world. Should governments or the UN act against countries that commit blatant human rights violations? We apply established principles of human rights to recent cases of ethnic group persecution, genocide, and the abuses of women and children and then conclude with a section on the concept of human security and how its various facets intersect with issues about human rights. The latter sections stress the connections among the various theories of international relations and global politics.

Human rights: Definitions and debates

A human right is defined in standard dictionaries as just and fair treatment, but in reality the idea is much more complex and contentious. The belief that humans possess certain rights may conflict with the sovereignty and indivisibility of states, as it implies that humans may have claims against being abused by their own governments. The history of the concept of human rights derives from religion, legal philosophy, Western constitutional developments, and modern international law.

Many civilizations have claimed belief in the intrinsic worth and value of human beings. Nearly every religion posits that humans should be accorded dignity and respect. Medieval Catholic theology provided many justifications for human rights that are still adhered to today in Western political and legal thought. Natural law and natural rights of individuals have been discussed by philosophers throughout the history of Western civilization – Aristotle, John Locke, and Immanuel Kant, among others, all claimed that humans have the right to life, liberty, property, and happiness. The vast majority of modern constitutions, such as the French Declaration of the Rights of Man and Citizens and the Bill of Rights in the United States Constitution, contain discussions of natural rights and the rights of liberty.

A normative consensus has grown over time about the inherent worth of humans, and this has led to a definition of human rights as the political and civil liberties recognized by the international community as inalienable for all individuals in all countries simply by virtue of their humanity. Of course, how to interpret and apply such concepts has always been difficult and controversial, as it addresses core values. In the past century there has been an immense proliferation of declarations about such rights but much less compliance with them.

The concept of human rights is based on the premise that all people, regardless of nationality, culture, religion, language, ethnicity, color, ability, and gender, should possess the same basic freedoms. Although there is general agreement about this in the abstract, quarrels constantly erupt over precisely what these rights entail and under which conditions they should be upheld. Because of such controversies, some observers interpret human rights broadly to include topics such as equality and freedom from want, while others take a narrower view that human rights should concern only legal rights and remedies. In other words, they disagree about whether rights should provide an *opportunity* to gain a particular benefit or a promise that a particular *outcome* will be achieved. Disputes over the implementation of the distinctions and implementation of these ideas have often caused violent conflict and even war.

On the whole, realists claim that state authorities or constitutions should determine which rights are important for their own people, without the interference of outside institutions such as the United Nations. Others, such as ethically minded liberals and constructivists, claim that this argument leads to an abandonment of moral responsibility. These arguments go unresolved because they entail the clash of several philosophical and political principles. They are Gordian knots, or intractable problems. We discuss three of them.

First, there is a debate over universal values versus cultural relativism. From one point of view, there are universal values such as freedom of speech, free assembly, free press, and freedom of religion that belong to all men and women. In this case, human rights are defined as inalienable or valid for all individuals in all countries and at all times simply by virtue of their humanity alone. An inalienable right cannot, therefore, be legitimately limited or taken away. The principle of human rights should be accepted by everyone, including all states, and should even be defended as "natural rights" that predate modern state institutions and law. This idea contrasts with cultural relativism, the idea that rights are culturally determined (i.e., not universal) and differ from one historical period to the next and from one social and state system to the next. Different peoples and cultures understand, accept, and defend different conceptions and ideas about rights, and, therefore, any attempt to impose universal cultural standards on the world is akin to cultural imperialism. Indeed, the leaders of some southern and developing countries argue that the imposition of Western ideas and actions based on universal rights is tantamount to neocolonialism and racism, as it is "interference in their internal affairs." Non-Western societies, for example, may emphasize group or family rights above those of individuals, especially if their land is overpopulated or in dire economic or environmental stress. Some countries based on strong religious foundations may even deny the legitimacy of universal rights – unless, of course, they are based on the codes of their own religions.

These competing traditions need to be understood and respected even if they fly in the face of Western principles concerning human rights. Indeed, the very idea of human rights can easily be challenged. There is, for example, no universal agreement on topics as fundamental as personal and political freedom. Take the issue of the right to life. Would a universal principle of the right to life mean that no government could use the death penalty? Several states in the United States do so as punishment for heinous crimes. Is this an injustice that violates human rights? If universal rights arguments were totally accepted, this practice would have to be eliminated, or the international community might have a right to interfere in the domestic affairs of any country in which capital punishment was legitimized. Would or should administrators of the death sentence be tried in the International Criminal Court? In a similar vein, some countries allow female genital mutilation to be performed legally. If this practice is against the universal rights of women, then should it have to be condemned and prevented by international organizations? Should enlightened states join in a military attack on any country that engages in this obviously deplorable practice?

Second, if we don't accept universal principles, then how can we defend declarations of the United Nations concerning human rights? (See Chapter 6.) If we do accept them, how can the principles be compatible with the concept of the legal sovereignty of all countries and their right to determine laws for their own people? Any enforcement of rights by an international organization would interfere with the primary role of the state. Since membership in the United Nations is based on the concept of sovereignty and the absolute principle of noninterference in the affairs of states, any action based on adherence to principles of universal rights would call for the UN to coerce or declare war on deviating members. This would not only be logically untenable; it would be practically impossible. Indeed, going to war to defend the principle of human rights would violate the human rights of the people of the state that was attacked. As well, the number of blatant human rights abuses would quickly exhaust Western appetite for intervention.

In short, one can make a case for either sovereignty or intervention. China and Russia, for example, refuse to discuss their human rights abuses, claiming that it would amount to Western interference in their domestic affairs. And although the United States engages relatively little in rights abuse, it refuses to sign many of the UN documents on the subject. It has not even ratified the UN Convention on the Rights of Children.

Every time the UN proposes action based on human rights violations, competing arguments about cultural relativism, sovereignty, and practicality are raised. The UN is not a world government; international law does not allow one state to attack another just because it does not accept the other's moral principles. Indeed, the UN spends much of its time debating and trying to reconcile these conflicting ideas. Yet sometimes the UN, a collection of states, or even individual states, do act to enforce human rights. The justification for action or intervention is sometimes made in terms of universal values and sometimes in terms of prudent fears that the conflict could spill across states borders. Even World War II was justified in terms of both defending national interests and borders and ending human rights violations against Jews and other minorities in Germany.

The application and enforcement of human rights is much weaker than declarations about it. The claims of the United States to be a leader defending human rights was seriously undermined by evidence that American military officers inflicted abuses on Muslims in the Abu Ghraib prison in Iraq and Guantánamo Bay prisons during the Iraq and Afghan wars. The disclosure that the CIA runs secret prisons in foreign lands and that prisoners have been extradited to countries where torture is acceptable have undercut the moral and ethical claims and tarnished the image of the American government throughout the world.

The third issue concerns which topics should come under the heading of human rights. The two concepts of liberty espoused by the philosopher Isaiah Berlin are often used to sort out the fundamental differences about human rights.[1] Berlin argued that rights are either negative or positive. Negative rights are those covered by freedom from the restraints of others, especially the government. They include rights such as free expression, assembly, press, religion, and travel, as well as the right to a fair trial. Positive rights, in contrast, are those that provide freedom to obtain something, such as the right to education, employment, welfare, hospital care, and an adequate standard of living. In other words, the latter include economic obligations on the part of governments rather than solely legal ones, emphasizing the minimum material conditions that everyone should in principle possess. Do individuals have a right to adequate housing and social security?

Many countries list human rights in their constitutions. The American Constitution is essentially about negative rights, since the Bill of Rights lists what the government cannot do to individuals. For example, the Constitution states that Congress cannot make laws "respecting an establishment of religion, or prohibiting the free exercise thereof; or abridging the freedom of speech, or of the press." But many constitutions also include concepts of positive rights. Canada's Constitution contains individual negative rights but also lists positive and collective rights. It says, for example, that there must be equality before and under the law "without discrimination based on race, national or ethnic origin, color, religion, sex, age or mental or physical disability."[2]

In recent years the United States and China have engaged in a broad debate over human rights. Every year the U.S. Department of State issues a statement condemning the lack of human rights, political freedoms, and imprisonment of dissidents in China and elsewhere. China then responds with an attack on poverty, incarceration rates, and capital punishment in the United States, as well as a litany of complaints about racism and violence and the fact that not all Americans have adequate food, clothing, and shelter. In other words, the United States uses negative rights as a weapon in the discourse, and China criticizes the American lack of positive rights. The United States condemns countries that do not provide individual and negative rights, while China lauds collective and positive rights. Both countries attack interference in their domestic affairs based on the other country's conceptions of human rights. One country stresses personal factors for causing success and hardship in life, and the other blames the political system itself. Both call each other hypocrites.

Should governments or the UN take action against countries because of human rights violations? The U.S. government, for example, has often threatened to revoke China's "most favored nation" trade status because of human rights violations, but it has never carried through with the threat. Even after the tragedy at Tiananmen Square in 1989 Chinese-American relations did not change (Figure 14.1). Should more have been done?

---

[1] Isaiah Berlin, *Two Concepts of Liberty* (Oxford, UK: Clarendon Press, 1966).

[2] Robert J. Jackson and Doreen Jackson, *Politics in Canada*, 8th ed. (Toronto: Pearson, 2011).

Figure 14.1 Should governments or the UN take action against countries that clearly violate their people's human rights, as China did when it brutally killed protesters in Tiananmen Square in 1989? Or would this be a ridiculous idea? *Source:* Press Association.

Close Up 14.1. **Should a Chinese dissident be awarded a Nobel prize?**

In December 2010, the Swedish Nobel Peace Prize was awarded to Liu Xiaobo, a Chinese dissident and human rights activist. Liu, a writer, professor, and literary critic, was the first Chinese person chosen for the award. Ninety-eight other individuals and twenty organizations had received the honor since its foundation in 1901. At the time of the award, Liu, along with forty-five other writers, was serving a sentence of eleven years in a Chinese prison for various subversion charges. As a long-standing critic of Chinese authorities, he had signed the Charter 08 declaration, which called for major reforms of Chinese political institutions. It was this pamphlet, among other activities, that landed him in jail for "inciting subversion of state power." But the Nobel committee said Liu deserved the prize because of his "long and non-violent struggle for fundamental human rights in China." The Chinese government condemned the award, did not attend the award ceremony, asked other countries to boycott it, and said that the Nobel committee "desecrated" the prize by giving it to Liu. In 2012, the Nobel Prize in Literature was awarded to another Chinese citizen, Mo Yan, but he was not a dissident, and the Chinese authorities welcomed this prize.

Should the Nobel committee award prizes to prisoners? Should the Chinese government have interfered in the award ceremonies of the Nobel Peace Prize? Is this a question of fundamental human rights or third-party intervention in China's domestic legal affairs?

International law, the United Nations, and human rights

Since its inception, the United Nations has increased its efforts to pass treaties, conventions, and covenants in the field of human rights. But it has been less insistent on monitoring violations, enforcing the rules, and prosecuting human perpetrators of human rights abuse. In other words, despite the growing rhetorical acceptance of the significance of human rights, there has been much less agreement on how and when the global community should intervene to enforce them. There has nonetheless been some action in this field. On occasion, some abuses of human rights have been judged so extreme that the world community simply agreed that something had to be done about them. The most pertinent examples, perhaps, have involved maiming and killing women, children, and ethnic groups – especially those that were labeled genocide (more about that later in this chapter).

Human rights issues are covered by international humanitarian law, international jurisprudence, and UN Security Council Resolutions. The United Nations Charter upholds the principle of human rights. Article 1 announces belief in "promoting and encouraging respect for human rights and for fundamental freedoms."[3] The 1948 United Nations Universal Declaration on Human Rights recognizes "the inherent dignity" and "equal and inalienable rights of all members of the human family" and declares this to be "the foundation of freedom, justice, and peace in the world." This declaration, drafted by the UN Commission on Human Rights, listed both negative and positive rights, but it was never put into treaty form and therefore never had the force of international law. It was, however, an inspiration for future legally binding treaties. In fact, that same year, the Convention on Genocide was adopted as a treaty – in other words, it was legally binding on the signatories.

In 1966, almost two decades later, the general principles of human rights were put in treaty form and became legally binding. The International Covenant on Civil and Political Rights and the International Covenant on Economic, Social, and Cultural Rights were adopted by the United Nations General Assembly and distributed as treaties. As of 2012, 167 countries had signed the former,

and 160 had signed the latter. Essentially, the International Covenant on Civil Rights concerns negative rights, and the International Covenant on Economic, Social, and Cultural Rights is committed to the positive rights of social justice – as in its claim that there should be "fair wages and equal remuneration for work of equal value" and that one has a right to "an adequate standard of living for himself and his family, including adequate food, clothing, and housing, and to the continuous improvement of condition." The United States, along with many other countries, did not ratify the latter treaty because it objected to its broad commitment to equality rights, as well as its implied loss of state sovereignty.[4]

These conventions, along with the core document on the Universal Declaration of Human Rights, form the human rights legal framework (see Table 14.1). It should be recalled that covenants, statutes, protocols, and conventions are legally binding on countries that ratify them. Simply signing a treaty means that the signatories agree with the ideas in the treaty, but they are not legally obliged to obey them. Declarations, principles, guidelines, and standard rules have no binding legal effect, but as the website of the United Nations Human Rights Council (UNHRC) put it, these tools also have "undeniable moral force" and "provide practical guidance."[5] At the rhetorical level, most states support human rights. By signing and ratifying such treaties, they are bound to respect the rights of their own citizens and to challenge states that do not. However, although there has been a very significant increase in awareness and monitoring of these rights, major and minor violations regularly continue to occur. Lack of equal protection rights is important but pales beside major violations such as prison abuse, torture, and genocide.

---

[3] http://www.un.org.

[4] Indeed, the United States has not ratified many other rights treaties, including the Conventions on the Elimination of Discrimination against Woman, the Rights of the Child, Migrant Workers, and Persons with Disabilities.

[5] http://www.ohchr.org.

Table 14.1 Significant international human rights treaties, conventions, and covenants, and the dates adopted

Universal Declaration of Human Rights, 1948

Convention on Genocide, 1948

Convention on the Prevention and Punishment of All Forms of Racial Discrimination, 1965

Covenant on Economic, Social, and Cultural Rights, 1966

Covenant on Civil and Political Rights, 1966

Convention on Elimination of Discrimination against Women, 1979

Convention against Torture and Other Cruel, Inhumane, or Degrading Treatment or Punishment, 1984

Convention on the Rights of the Child, 1984

Convention on Protection of Migrant Workers and Their Families, 1990

Convention for the Protection of All Persons from Enforced Disappearance, 2006

Convention on the Rights of Persons with Disabilities, 2006

Source: See the complete list of treaties, conventions, covenants, and protocols at the website for the UN Office of High Commissioner of Human Rights, at http://www.ohchr.org.

Human rights institutions: Monitoring

The field of human rights is supported by a significant regime, a complex set of relationships of laws, institutions, and norms of behavior. Until recently, the major UN institution for handling human rights cases was the Commission on Human Rights (UN-CHR), a fifty-three member panel of states backed up by an Office of the High Commissioner for Human Rights (OHCHR) to enhance its monitoring powers. The commission has encountered enormous political difficulties. In 2003, for example, it elected the military authoritarian state of Libya, led at the time by Muammar Gaddafi, to assume its presidency; and in 2004 it elected the Sudanese government to the commission's membership even though it was alleged to be carrying out genocide in Darfur at the

time. After considerable debate about such absurd and inappropriate appointments, the committee was replaced in 2005 by the Human Rights Council (UNHRC). This council of forty-seven states meets more regularly than the commission did, but it, too, has members who engage in domestic human rights abuses, as well as many members with an unsuppressed hatred for the state of Israel. Despite such controversies, President Barack Obama officially gave the go-ahead for the United States to take up membership in the council in 2012.

As we saw in Chapter 7, transnational advocacy institutions monitor the work of intergovernmental organizations (IGOs), especially in the field of human rights, drawing attention to issues and putting pressure on states to respond to violations. As examples, two nongovernmental agencies that vigorously pursue such concerns are Amnesty International, with headquarters in London, and Human Rights Watch, with its head offices in New York. Both provide ongoing analyses of human rights issues in all parts of the world and report annually on compliance with laws and norms. They are quick to name and shame governments and institutions that do not live up to the ideals of human rights' campaigners. Media journalists help spotlight the work of these types of IGOs and NGOs while doing investigative reporting on human rights issues; and in recent years, the Internet and social networking systems have added greatly to the persuasive power of these types of organizations.

Unfortunately, despite the existence of treaties and constant monitoring by the UN, IGOs, NGOs, and the media, human rights abuses continue unabated. Imprisonment, rape, torture, and murder of political dissidents are regularly reported. UN institutions are not always vigilant, and the governments of some countries sign human rights declarations but then neglect their implications. As we have noted, a ratified treaty is no guarantee that a state will be willing or able to enforce its provisions. Many Islamic countries, for example, have signed treaties that require them not to discriminate against women, but they do so anyway.

As we saw in Chapter 6, the UN sometimes sends peacekeeping or peace enforcement soldiers to areas plagued by human rights abuses. More often than not, however, it cannot get sufficient agreement among the great powers to allow the soldiers to act robustly, and the UN's own rules on the application of force are very restrictive. Groups of states and other actors sometimes then respond to the crises with or without UN support. When there is no agreement on military intervention, the UN may use soft power such as diplomacy or economic sanctions – including prohibitions on trade, investment, and aid – to induce a country to change. Often, however, such soft power does not work. While it was a successful strategy in ridding South Africa of apartheid, it has had little impact in stopping many countries from suppressing ethnic or religious minorities.

Policies such as economic embargoes can be counterproductive. While the purpose of an embargo may be to decrease the abuse of human rights, it may also increase hardship on the very people it is intended to aid while doing very little to discomfort the government oppressing them. The UN embargo on Iraq after the 1991 war over Kuwait is a case in point. In an effort to bring down the regime of Saddam Hussein and end cease-fire violations, a UN embargo that did considerable harm to the Iraqi population was put in place. There are estimates that as few as seventy-five thousand or as many as half a million children younger than five years of age died as a result of the embargo, but it was insignificant in terms of decreasing human rights abuses: Hussein remained in power and thumbed his nose at the sanctions. His regime remained stable and continued to flout world public opinion until it was toppled by a U.S.-led invasion in 2003 that proceeded without the UN's blessing.

Practically everyone agrees that something should be done by the world community when people's lives are at risk from starvation, persecution, or genocide. But apart from uttering rhetorical flashes of dismay and engaging in consciousness raising, what should be done? If diplomacy and sanctions do not work, how and when is military intervention acceptable, necessary, or practical? Can a just response include UN interference in the sovereignty of a member state? Is history a guide? In earlier chapters we found that some humanitarian interventions have been worthwhile while others have been failures. The actions of the UN in Timor-Leste and Cyprus are usually considered examples of good interventions, but not all observers would concur (Figure 14.2). Practically everyone agrees, however, that the operations in Congo, Rwanda, Somalia, and many others were disastrous (see Chapter 10).

Although some interpretations of international law make it legal to use force to protect people from severe attacks by the state on their human rights, many countries continue to defend the traditional right of states to operate free of foreign invention, regardless of human rights issues. It is important to remember that the United Nations and other intergovernmental organizations can act only on the authority that member states give them. This principle often seems to be forgotten in the emotion and moral trauma that prevail when people are suffering from the collapse of governmental authority, internal war, genocide, and natural disaster.

Human rights institutions: Enforcement and the International Criminal Court

Another human rights issue concerns pursuing and punishing human rights abusers. In line with the adoption of international treaties and the evolution of international humanitarian law, there has been considerable progress in setting up tribunals and courts to try violators of human rights in the 21st century. There have been ad hoc tribunals with varying names, mandates, and authorities, such as those in Cambodia, Lebanon, Rwanda, Sierra Leone, and the former Yugoslavia. These tribunals were set up with UN assistance to prosecute human rights violators and prevent them from using their state's sovereignty as an excuse to avoid trial and conviction. Some were successful and others failures, but they all provided international legitimacy to the

Figure 14.2 José Ramos-Horta was the exiled spokesman for the East Timorese resistance during the Indonesian occupation of East Timor from 1975 to 1999. After independence, he became prime minister and then president until 2012. The author and his wife interviewed Ramos-Horta in Dili just after independence.

idea of judicial hearings for abusers by making it possible to believe that international human rights violators can be successfully pursued. The 1999 trial of Serbian leader Slobodan Milošević was a significant case in point. He died before his sentencing, but the trial's professional and transparent legal approach convinced many people that such a process could work effectively and fairly, although arguably there still were many problems with these ad hoc tribunals, including their lack of permanency, limited timetable for completion of trials, and an uncomprehensive treatment of all war crimes. Most important, the most powerful states do not allow their leaders or even citizens to be called before such tribunals.

In 2002 a permanent court, the International Criminal Court (ICC) was set up to alleviate these deficiencies in ad hoc tribunals. As we saw in Chapter 6, in contrast to the International Court of Justice, the ICC can actually try cases against

individuals. The Treaty of Rome names four kinds of crimes that can come before the ICC – war crimes (crimes that international organizations and states define as illegal), genocide (killing people because of their race, ethnicity, or religion), crimes against humanity (enslavement, forcible transfer of people, and torture), and undefined aggression (postponed, pending an agreement on its definition). The ICC can try individuals from signatory states, and its jurisdiction extends to citizens of countries that have not signed the agreement if the crime occurs on the territory of a state that has signed the agreement. However, the ICC comes into play only if the national courts of the accused are unable or unwilling to act. The Security Council has the power to begin or halt ICC action. The court has issued warrants for alleged war crimes in Central African Republic, Democratic Republic of the Congo, Kenya, Libya, Sudan, and Uganda (see Chapter 6).

Human rights abuses

With an understanding of these philosophical issues and novel institutions, we are ready to examine specific examples and problems of human rights activities. There are many disadvantaged people and ethnic groups around the world who suffer maltreatment, human rights abuses, and even genocide. Since many countries contain minority ethnic groups with different languages, cultures, heritages, and especially social customs, from the majority population, it is easy to understand why prejudice and abuse continue. Several thousand nations are lodged inside only 193 states, and more than three hundred million indigenous people (divided into five thousand indigenous groups) live in seventy countries. Data show a consistent economic gap between these minorities and the majorities even in developed states. The most difficult circumstances are in the least developed countries (LDCs), where more than two billion people live on less than two dollars a day. Examples are abundant. Two-thirds of the world's indigenous people reside in China where they face structural disadvantages and poverty. In India 47 percent of the indigenous people who are included in the Scheduled Tribes live in abject poverty and face human rights abuses.

Another broad group that faces discrimination includes the 43.7 million people around the world displaced by conflict, persecution, and natural disasters (see Chapter 15). At the end of 2010, 27.5 million people had been uprooted from their homes but remained within their own state borders, and more than 16 million more had fled to live outside their own country, often confined to refugee camps. Some of these people are considered refugees, but others are not. Their circumstances are often the result, but also a possible cause, of future conflict. These people normally flee political persecution or violent conflict and then find that they are ill treated in the host country because of their racial, ethnic, or religious affiliations. Leaving one's country to seek economic opportunities is not normally considered a proper justification for refugee status. States are wary of assigning refugee status because international law implies that refugees must be accepted by the host country. There are very significant refugee problems today in the Great Lakes region of Africa, where ethnicity and religion distinguish and define people, and inside Israel, where Palestinians have been displaced by the Arab-Israeli wars. The "Arab Awakening" of 2011 created millions of refugees as Syrians flooded into Turkey and Libyans sought refuge in Tunisia, Europe, and elsewhere in North Africa (Figure 14.3. See also Chapter 10).

Figure 14.3 Refugee camps quickly formed in Tunisia in 2011 as refugees from the fighting in Libya sought shelter across the border. Tunisia, which had only recently thrown off its own authoritarian leaders, had to appeal for international assistance. *Source:* UN multimedia.

No countries are immune to charges of human rights abuses, not even the United States. The American response to the 9/11 terrorist attacks included serious human rights violations. The disgraceful abuse of prisoners in Abu Ghraib and Guantánamo prisons has been well documented by official reports and journalists' accounts (see Chapters 10 and 11). Amnesty International called the Guantánamo prison "the gulag of our times."[6] Official U.S. interrogation policy allowed extreme measures (called enhanced interrogation techniques) such as the use of so-called stress positions during interrogation procedures, threatening prisoners with dogs, yelling, loud music, light control, and isolation. Beyond these methods, proven wrongdoings included waterboarding, desecration of the Koran, and sexual and physical abuse.[7] Several soldiers were punished for mistreating detainees, but the problem does not appear to have been random but rather systemic – that is, it emerged from rules set down by higher authorities. Clearly, the prisoners were not accorded the rights expected under international treaties or constitutional principles.

In the next section we examine cases of genocide – the most egregious type of human rights abuse – and then focus on two specific groups that have been the target of gross human rights abuses, women and children. The chapter concludes with a discussion of whether human rights abuses should come under the general rubric of human security, and an evaluation of the principle that the United Nations has a duty to protect all people around the world.

Genocide

The term **genocide** was coined in the 1930s from the Greek word *genos* and the Latin root *cide* – it means "tribe killing" or "race killing." While the

term itself is fairly new, genocidal practices have gone on for thousands of years, simply undefined or under different names.[8] In 1948 the United Nations **Convention on the Punishment and Prevention of Genocide** adopted the following definitions of genocide:

Article II. In the present Convention, genocide means any of the following acts committed with intent to destroy, in whole or in part, a national, ethnical, racial, or religious group, as such:

(a) Killing members of the group;
(b) Causing serious bodily or mental harm to members of the group;
(c) Deliberately inflicting on the group conditions of life calculated to bring about its physical destruction in whole or in part;
(d) Imposing measures intended to prevent births within the group;
(e) Forcibly transferring children of the group to another group.

Five separate genocide-related crimes were listed under article 3 of the convention:

1. Genocide
2. Conspiracy to commit genocide
3. Direct and public incitement to commit genocide
4. Attempt to commit genocide
5. Complicity in genocide

In other words, genocide includes acts such as systematic extermination by killing, causing harm, or imposing intolerable conditions on members of specified national, ethnic, racial, or religious groups. The behavior is severely condemned by both governments and nongovernmental agencies, but while the parties to the convention agreed to commit resources to stop it, far too many examples of genocide have occurred without opposition since that

---

[6] *International Herald Tribune*, June 6, 2005.
[7] Robert J. Jackson and Philip Towle, *Temptations of Power: The United States in Global Politics since 9/11* (London: Palgrave, 2006).

[8] Raphael Lemkin, a Polish Jew who fled the German Nazis and lived in the United States, helped get the United States to ratify the Convention on Genocide in 1948. In 1941 he popularized the term in his book *Axis Rule in Occupied Europe* (Clark, NJ: Lawbook Exchange, Ltd., 2008).

Figure 14.4 This photo of human skulls represents Cambodians who were killed by the Khmer Rouge. Two million were killed by the government between 1975 and 1979. *Source:* Getty.

time. Inaction has been in part because the path of intervention is bumpy, expensive, and unappealing, but many also criticize the UN convention's definition of genocide as being too vague and therefore vulnerable to political abuse.

The killing of an estimated six million Jews as well as Gypsies (Roma), homosexuals, and other selected groups in Nazi Germany is an obvious example of genocide. More recently, in Cambodia (Kampuchea) between 1975 and 1979, the Khmer Rouge communist government, led by the notorious Pol Pot, killed approximately two million Cambodians (Figure 14.4). Other examples include the 1990–91 case of Iraq dropping poison gas on its own Kurdish citizens; "ethnic cleansing" from 1992 onward throughout the former Yugoslavia; and the 1998–99 Serbian violence against people of Albanian ethnicity in Kosovo. The 1994 slaughter of Tutsis by the Hutu in Rwanda and the massacres of blacks in northwestern Darfur, Sudan, by the government-sponsored Janjaweed militia are even more recent examples. See Table 14.2 for other important cases.

Of all the human rights abuses, genocide is perhaps the most heinous and the most in need of

Table 14.2 Major genocides since 1945

State	Genocide Victims	Dates
Soviet Union	Repatriated nationals and ethnic minorities	1943–47
China	Landlords	1950–51
Sudan	Southern nationals	1955–72
Sudan	Southern nationals	1983–98
Sudan	Darfur	2003–
Indonesia	Communists and ethnic Chinese	1965–66
China	Cultural revolution victims	1966–75
Uganda	Opponents of Idi Amin	1971–79
Pakistan	Bengali nationals	1971
Cambodia	Educated urbanites	1975–79
Afghanistan	Regime opponents	1978–89
Iraq	Kurds	1984–91
Bosnia, Croatia, and Kosovo	Muslims	1991–95
Burundi and Rwanda	Tutsi, Hutu	1993–98

response, but international institutions and states often use subterfuge to avoid responding to requests for action. Worried leaders often label situations "ethnic conflict" or "acts" of genocide, but rarely genocide, because according to the Convention on Genocide once the term *genocide* itself is adopted states are required to try to stop it and punish offenders.[9] Add to this the UN's vague definition, and it is not surprising that there is resistance to applying it. In spite of the convention, no international body acted to prevent the Khmer Rouge genocide in Cambodia in the mid-1970s or the genocide of Bangladeshis by Pakistan's army in 1971. The horrific events in Rwanda in 1994 were called only "acts" of genocide by the United States and therefore Americans did not have to support increases in UN military troops to suppress the killing.

Even when intervention has taken place, it is often criticized as too late. However, in some cases limited, even late, intervention has proved effective at reducing murder rates, as was the case in Rwanda in 1993–98, where the presence of 470 UN peacekeepers initially prevented thousands of deaths in only a few short months. Because of inadequate support from the UN, however, the peacekeepers could not complete their work, and many thousands of Tutsis and moderate Hutus eventually died in the genocide.

Ethnocentrism is the tendency to see one's own group as superior to other groups and to depict out-groups as less worthy of fair treatment. Seeking solidarity with one's own group seems natural, but as individuals do so, they tend to develop biases against other groups, sometimes even deep ones that cannot be altered by new facts or ideas. At the extreme, such views lead to killing members of the despised group. In- and out-groups may be defined by a combination of ethnicity, race, religion, and other characteristics, large or small, that distinguish them. The out-group may be misunderstood or ridiculed or viewed with disdain

as unworthy – even inhuman. Such discrimination has often led to ethnic cleansing, a form of genocide that seeks the removal or extermination of an ethnic group from a particular geographical area. This is particularly odious when carried out by governments through forced exile or even death by governmental decree.

While many people have been killed because they were members of groups, their deaths qualify under the convention as *genocidal* only if they died as a result of their membership in a particular group. Group delineation is fluid, as evidenced in Nazi Germany in the 1930s and 1940s. In that case, the in-group was the ideal Aryan race, as envisioned by Adolf Hitler, and the out-groups included Jews (an ethnic distinction), but also communists (a political group), Jehovah's Witnesses (a religious group), the handicapped (a medical group), and homosexuals, along with half a dozen other groupings.

Another unique feature of the UN's definition of genocide is that it includes more than killing, a conceptual stretch that perhaps enlarges its mandate to the point that on occasion it takes on more than it can realistically achieve. Diminishing a group's ability to survive can be accomplished in many ways, most of which also come under the UN convention. While systematic murder was the method of choice in Nazi Germany, rape and genital mutilation of women occurred just as often as death in the genocides of the former Yugoslavia and Rwanda in the 1990s. These acts of violence were intended to traumatize the victims and discourage or prevent them from giving birth in the future. The forced relocation in the 18th century of Native American children to boarding schools in the Americas and Australia could now be considered genocidal because it attempted to prevent the continuation of indigenous culture through their progeny.

Genocidal agents, the agent or agents committing the crime of genocide, can be classified in a number of ways. The state itself may be the agent of violence, as in Nazi-controlled Germany, with its decidedly industrialized approach to mass murder. However, genocide also may develop as the result

---

[9] See Samantha Power, *The Problem from Hell: America and the Age of Genocide* (New York: Basic Books, 2002).

of more direct involvement of the masses with particular ethnic groups, as was the case in the Hutu killings of Tutsis in Rwanda, which were carried out by militias, street boys, rag-pickers, and homeless unemployed, among others.

Women's rights

Slightly fewer than half of the world's seven billion people are female. While there have been major steps in empowering women and securing their basic human rights in recent years, there is still a long way to go before equality with males will be achieved universally. Progress has been uneven around the world.

This is not a new problem. Throughout history women have often been treated as inferior to men, and discrimination has been enforced by social customs and laws. As the bearers of children, endowed with less physical strength than men, women have generally accepted primary responsibility for children and the family. Until relatively recently, even in developed countries, women were barred from various forms of participation in society, such as owning property, holding public office, and voting. Today, Western women have come a long way in terms of acquiring equality of opportunity, but equality of outcome has been more difficult to achieve.

Until recently, there was little hard evidence to back up claims of women's global and relative deprivation because the statistics that were collected tended to ignore their contributions to the family and the economy. Even today, household work is not counted in economic statistics such as gross domestic product (GDP) – the leading indicator of economic well-being. Since 1991, however, the United Nations has released statistical portraits and analyses of the situation of women that provide comparative information on the condition of women around the world. Moreover, in the past two decades an unprecedented politicization of women has taken place in many parts of the world, and in many countries young women can aspire to political leadership and to prominence in law, medicine, education, business, and the sciences.

Clearly, gender disparities are deep and pervasive. Of course, they are just one of the many inequities that are transmitted across generations and constrain life chances and opportunities, but when gender and poverty coincide, it is clear that impoverished women are especially badly off. They are most likely to be unschooled, die in childbirth, have poor nutrition and less access to clean water, be less able to participate in society outside the home, and have relatively less control over their lives in the household and society. Many, but not all, of these women are from developing countries.

Female inequality

The unequal treatment of women is a human rights issue, included in the 1949 Universal Declaration of Human Rights and in the 1981 Convention on the Elimination of All Forms of Discrimination against Women. The latter convention and its protocols outlaw trafficking in women and makes discrimination against them illegal in private and public life. By 2012, 187 parties had ratified or acceded to the treaty, but many countries opted out of specific clauses, such as article 19, which mandates arbitration by the International Court of Justice in cases of female discrimination. Many states also added conditions, such as that they would accept the treaty as long as it did not conflict with Sharia law or other local religious codes. The United States is the only developed democracy that has neither ratified nor acceded to this convention. Since the treaty has no monitoring or enforcement provisions, it is not surprising that around the world many women and girls continue to be excluded from educational opportunities, denied the right to vote, and sometimes subject to extreme abuses such as violence, trafficking, and sexual slavery.

In many countries, both households and governments traditionally spend fewer resources to educate and train girls than boys.[10] This reduces the potential social, economic, and political contribution of

---

[10] Unless otherwise noted, the data in this chapter come from the *Human Development Report 2010* or *Human Development Report 2011*, which includes the latest comparable statistics.

women to society, and it leaves women at a disadvantage in making major life decisions. The place to start reengineering this inequality is in the schools, and it is working. Women have made significant progress toward equal education with men in recent years. The enrollment of girls in primary and secondary schools in developing countries is now comparable to that of boys. In 2008 there were ninety-six females for every hundred males at the primary level, and ninety-five females for every hundred males at the secondary level.

The UN's Millennium Goal of female equality can be achieved in many countries by 2015, but not everywhere (see Chapter 13). Parity will be particularly difficult to achieve in the primary schools of Oceania, sub-Saharan Africa, and western Asia. At the secondary levels, the countries with the most difficulty reaching the goals will be in sub-Saharan Africa, western Asia, and southern Asia. At the university and college (tertiary) level, female enrollment is also improving around the world. Overall enrollment showed there are about ninety-seven females for every hundred males in 2008. Women continue to be most represented in humanities and social sciences, but less so in sciences, technology, and engineering.

As women are being educated, they are increasingly obtaining a fairer share of paid employment. Around the world about 41 percent of women were gainfully employed in 2008. Typically, however, they do not obtain jobs that are as good or as well-paid as men do. The gender wage gap, though narrowing, remains wide; even in the thirty-three developed countries, women earned only 74 percent of men's income from 1998 to 2002. Besides education and employment, another route for women to improve their position in society is through political involvement. Routes to power in government decision making are traditionally through the civil service and political candidacy. Reliable statistics on women in bureaucratic careers are not generally available, but one pattern is clear: significant numbers of women work in the lower government echelons, and their representation dwindles rapidly as pay and status increase.

The share of women in national parliaments around the world reached an all-time high of 19 percent in 2010 (up from 11 percent in 1995). However, the Millennium Goal of parity by 2015 is very unlikely to be met. Progress is very uneven. Fifty-eight countries have 10 percent or fewer women in their legislatures, and nine chambers have none at all. It is even more rare for women to achieve high executive office. On average, women hold 18 percent of ministerial posts, and sixteen states have no female ministers at all. Around the world, females tend to be more successful in local than national elections, and they are increasingly active in the politics of their local communities in such areas as discrimination, poverty, health and environmental issues, violence against women, and peace movements.

In an attempt to measure the overall equality of women in the world, the authors of the 2010 *Human Development Report* (HDR) invented a new dimension – the Gender Inequality Index (GII).[11] This index measures gender disparities in three dimensions – reproductive health, empowerment, and labor-force participation. Five indicators were employed to construct the matrix, including labor-force participation, educational attainment (secondary level and above), parliamentary representation, adolescent fertility, and maternal mortality (Figure 14.5). The new research on 145 countries in 2011 showed that while women have made major strides, they are unlikely to achieve parity by 2015. Some of the results were startling in their simplicity. Failures in reproductive health, which includes adolescent childbearing and maternal mortality rates, were the largest single contributor to gender inequality around the world.

The 2012 GII showed marked differences in gender inequality around the world:

In Sub-Saharan Africa the biggest losses arise from gender disparities in education and from high maternal mortality and adolescent fertility rates. In South Asia women lag behind men in each dimension of the GII, most notably in education, national

[11] *Human Development Report 2010*, p. 91.

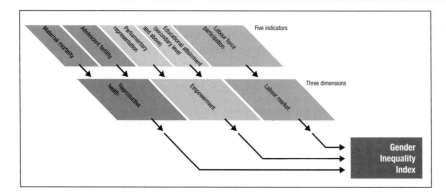

Figure 14.5 Components of the gender equality index. *Source:* United Nations Human Development Report 2010 (New York: UN Development Program, 2010), p. 91.

parliamentary representation and labour force participation. Women in Arab States are affected by unequal labour force participation (around half the globe average) and low educational attainment. All the low HDI countries have high gender inequality across multiple dimensions.[12]

Women and abuse

Unequal status and discrimination of women in LDCs lead to neglect and death. Girls in China no longer have their feet crushed by foot binding, but female infanticide there is not uncommon, and prenatal scans enable abortions of female fetuses in China, northern India, and elsewhere. Widows in India are still sometimes burned alive on the funeral pyres of their husbands.

Gendercide – the killing of a gender group – continues to be carried out through sex-selective abortions or female infanticide. Gendercide exists to uneven degrees on every continent. The causes include ancient customs and prejudices, a preference for small families, and modern technology. The result is that women are missing from the world in the millions, and it is not due to chance. If an ultrasound indicates that an unborn child is a girl and the parents prefer a boy, they could wait for the next child to arrive, but some choose an abortion, which allows them to get rid of the fetus and try again for a son. For those who oppose abortion in principle, this is mass murder, but for those who accept abortion, it is a tolerable practice. It is

common in India and China, especially among the wealthier and more educated, who can afford the tests and procedures. The less wealthy may resort to female infanticide after the birth. Of course, such practices distort natural demography. In India, an estimated six hundred thousand girls are missing every year because of sex selection.[13]

According to the 2010 Human Development Report the world sex ratio has reached 1.07.[14] This means that around the world there are 107 boys born for every 100 girls. This figure is not arrived at by chance; human choice is clearly involved. The preference for boys in China is instructive. Despite an official ban on prenatal sex determination and sex-selective abortions, special pension incentives for those with daughters, and the positive Care for Girls campaign, the sex ratio has reached 1.20. In Delhi, India, the figure reached 1.26 in 2009.

Human trafficking is defined as the acquisition of people by improper means such as force, fraud, or deception with the aim of exploiting them. Trafficking in persons, especially girls and women, is also a major human rights abuse issue.[15] The United Nations Convention on Transnational Organized Crime and its protocols on trafficking in persons, especially women and children, came into force in

---

[12] *Human Development Report 2012*, p. 61.

[13] "Gendercide in India," *The Economist*, April 9, 2011, p. 11.
[14] *Human Development Report 2010*, p. 76.
[15] E. Benjamin Skinner, "A World Enslaved," *Foreign Policy* (March–April 2008), pp. 62–7.

Figure 14.6 Many Muslim women are anxious to explain to their counterparts in the West why they want to conform to the tenets of Islam, including dress codes and societal and religious regulations that most Western women find restrictive and oppressive.

December 2003 and became the first legally binding instrument to deal with the practice. While 147 state parties have ratified the protocol as of 2012, many of them do not make adequate attempts to stop trafficking: many African countries, in particular, do not even have adequate, comprehensive laws on the subject.

Victims of trafficking can be men or women, boys or girls. Although data are difficult to confirm, it is basically agreed that around a million people, of whom about 80 percent are female, are trafficked every year. The exploitation can take many forms, including forced or bonded labor, domestic servitude, forced marriage, organ removal, exploitation of children through begging, forced work in the sex trade, and warfare. These forms of enslavement often, but not always, include the forced and illegal entry of persons into a state of which they are not a citizen.[16]

In some countries, especially theocracies like Iran today and Afghanistan under the Taliban, which

purport to encompass a complete religious way of life and system of government, women are subject to laws that profoundly restrict their freedom (Figure 14.6). In her examination of the complex world of women in Islamic countries, Geraldine Brooks pointed out that many customs attributed to Islam come from pre-Islamic customs and politics and from resistance to modernization.[17] The most notorious of these customs, the mutilation of female genitalia, seems to have originated in the Stone Age in central Africa. This is both an international health issue and a human rights issue. Today, it is practiced by specific groups across the Muslim world and, on rare occasion, even in North America. About two million adolescent and younger girls in much of central and North Africa are subject to **female genital mutilation** (FGM), or what is sometimes called female circumcision. The procedures, based on traditions, rites, and often very primitive methods, differ from country to country but include clitoridectomy (excision of the clitoris), which

---

[16] See United Nations Office on Drugs and Crime's *Global Report on Trafficking in Persons* (2009) and other details and explanations at http://www.unodc.org.

[17] Geraldine Brooks, *Nine Parts of Desire: The Hidden World of Islamic Women* (New York: Anchor Books, 1995).

Figure 14.7 Child labor is a serious problem in many developing countries. In this photo, children are working long hours in factories in Dhaka, Bangladesh. In 2010, the ILO estimated that 215 million children were engaged in labor that violates international standards. *Source:* Alamy.

deprives a girl of sexual sensation, and infibulations, the cutting away of all of a female's external genitalia and labia tissue.

Women and girls are particularly badly treated during wars, and this is one of the inadequately recognized aspects of warfare. Women are often captured by soldiers and used as servants. Violence, rape, impregnation, and sexual slavery are regular occurrences. Women may also be conscripted as combat soldiers along with boys and girls.

Children's rights

Several treaties govern the international treatment of children. The 1989 United Nations Convention on the Rights of the Child defines a child as a person younger than the age of eighteen, unless the laws of a particular country set the age for legal adulthood lower. According to this convention, children are born with fundamental freedoms and the inherent rights of all human beings. There also are two optional protocols: one on the sale of children, child prostitution, and child pornography and a second on the involvement of children in armed conflict. Both were completed in 2000. Participating governments must report to the UN concerning children's rights in their country, and many of them have enacted legislation, created

mechanisms, and put in place a range of measures to ensure the protection and realization of the rights of children.

The convention has been ratified by 193 countries – more than any other human rights treaty – including every member of the United Nations except the United States and Somalia. Officially, children deserve the same fundamental rights as everyone else, but unfortunately the convention and the protocols have had only a modest impact on reducing global child abuse. While almost every country of the world has ratified the convention, more than one-third of all children continue to live in countries that have not agreed to some parts of it. Many countries object to article 182, concerning the worst forms of child labor, and article 138 on minimum age requirements (Figure 14.7).

Given the various objections, it is not surprising that child labor is a prevalent human rights abuse. As of 2010 there were an estimated 215 million children doing labor that violates international standards.[18] They are held in bonded labor,

---

[18] See *Facts on Child Labour 2010*, at http://www.ilo.org. Katherine Boo's book based on her research of a Mumbai slum provides a fascinating glimpse into the topic of child labor. See Katherine Boo, *Behind the Beautiful Forevers: Life, Death, and Hope in a Mumbai Undercity* (New York: Random House, 2012).

slavery, or conditions similar to slavery. They are either too young to work and should be in school or they are working in improper conditions. Many are internationally trafficked for prostitution or involved in armed conflict. Many are forced to work in the drug trade, pornography, and other illicit activities.

As well as the United Nations Convention on the Rights of the Child and its protocols, the Rome Statute, which created the International Criminal Court, is the most obvious source of rules for the enforcement of children's rights. Act 8, section b, line 26 of the Rome Statute reads that "conscripting or enlisting children under the age of fifteen years into the national armed forced or using them to participate actively in hostilities" is a crime against humanity. Critical Case Study 14.1 illustrates the gravity of the issues in states like Democratic Republic of the Congo.

Critical Case Study 14.1 **Children and refugees in the Democratic Republic of the Congo**

The Democratic Republic of the Congo (DRC), formerly Zaire, is a highly populous state, with well more than seventy million inhabitants (Figure 14.8). It is located in central Africa and is the third-largest territory on the continent. Despite being blessed with abundant natural resources, it is one of the poorest countries in the world, placing last on the 2011 Human Development Index. The DRC has often been at war and is perpetually afflicted with widespread corruption and massive violations of human rights. The wars have been extraordinarily complex with large numbers of rebel groups fighting each other across borders and often changing sides. In recent years the country has faced a humanitarian catastrophe, with countless killings, rapes, and the use of child soldiers.

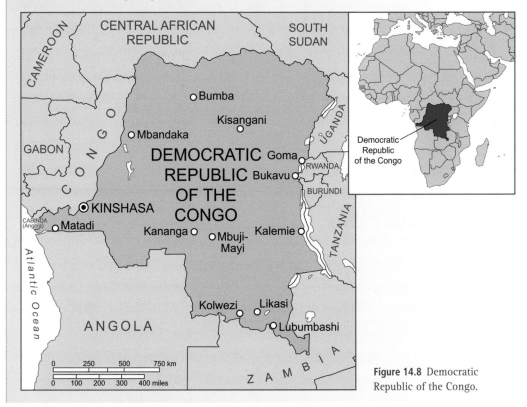

Figure 14.8 Democratic Republic of the Congo.

During the Cold War, Zaire, under Joseph Mobutu, was an ally of the West. Violence intensified throughout the region after the civil war in Rwanda in 1994. Rwandan Hutu rebels known as Interahamwe fled to the DRC, fearing reprisals for their part in the mass killing of Rwandan Tutsis. In 1997 Rwanda invaded Zaire to capture dissident Hutu militias, helping the anti-Mobutu rebels capture the capital Kinshasa and put Laurent Kabila in office as president. In 1998, the Interahamwe joined forces with the Zairian army to launch an offensive against the Congolese Tutsis in the eastern part of the country. A five-year conflict developed between government forces supported by Angola, Namibia, and Zimbabwe, and rebels from Uganda and Rwanda.

This so-called Second Congo War (some have even called it Africa's World War) ended in 1999 with the Lusaka Ceasefire Agreement signed by the DRC and the five regional states. The United Nations sent in a mission (UN Organization Mission in the DRC, or MONUC, later renamed MONUSCO) to help administer the cease-fire, demobilization, and supervise elections. This mission was, and is, the largest and most complex electoral-assistance mission the UN has ever undertaken. MONUSCO has more than twenty-two thousand uniformed military and police as well as civilian specialists in such areas as human rights, humanitarian affairs, child protection, political affairs, and medical support.

From 1998 to 2004, approximately 3.8 million people died either as a result of the crisis or because of disease and malnutrition. All parties in the conflict recruited, abducted, and used child soldiers. Children made up an estimated 40 percent of the members of some armed groups, with at least thirty thousand taking an active part in direct combat and thousands more, mostly girls, used for other services. The DRC had earlier ratified a number of international treaties that should have protected the rights of children. In 2001, for example, it signed on to UN Security Council Resolution 1341, which called for "an end to the recruitment of child soldiers to ensure their ... demobilisation, return and rehabilitation." During the war, these commitments proved little more than public relations exercises. Many child soldiers were killed in the war, and others were unable to return to their families because they had no immediate family left or their families would not accept them. Some families discouraged their children from returning home to protect them from being harmed by members of the community who blamed them for killing and other bad deeds.

Despite the end of the war, a new constitution and the relatively lawful 2006 election of Joseph Kabila as president of the DRC, instability and violence continued, especially in eastern areas with Ugandan rebels, Rwandan rebels in the Kivus, and other ethnic violence in the northwest over economic issues. Some estimates and reports place the number of people dying there as high as forty-five thousand per month, and the total war-related deaths at 5.4 million since 1998 – making the war the deadliest conflict since World War II. Rapes have been estimated as high as two hundred thousand and the number of child soldiers is in the thousands.[19]

Several citizens of the DRC and neighboring countries have been sanctioned by the United Nations and put on trial by the International Criminal Court (see Chapter 6). Is this the appropriate forum for handling such war crimes and crimes against humanity? Will elections in the country matter, or is the DRC such a failed state that nothing can be done to solve its difficulties short of making it into a UN mandate?

---

[19] See reports of the International Rescue Committee at http://www.rescue.org.

Children and armed conflict

A review of the literature on children and war yields some expected but also surprising findings about how children are affected by war and how they participate in armed conflicts. In 2009 the United Nations estimated that over the past decade two million children were killed in armed conflict and three times as many more were seriously injured or permanently disabled. Yet the recruitment and use of children in armed conflict is prohibited by international humanitarian law, international human rights law, labor laws, and most state criminal laws. These instruments – in particular article 77(2) of the Additional Protocol 1 of the Geneva Conventions – incontrovertibly prohibit recruiting or using children younger than the age of fifteen as soldiers. The Rome Statute of the International Criminal Court also classifies any conscription or enlistment of children younger than fifteen as a war crime.

Most specifically, the 2002 Optional Protocol on the Involvement of Children in Armed Conflict has been ratified by 140 countries.[20] It requires states to set eighteen as the minimum age for compulsory recruitment and fifteen years for volunteer enlisting in the military. It then prohibits signatories to the agreement from using children between fifteen and eighteen directly in hostilities. Recruitment of children between fifteen and eighteen is further complicated, because the protocol absolutely prohibits nonstate armed groups or rebel organizations from recruiting or using any children younger than eighteen. There are other legal prohibitions on using child soldiers younger than eighteen. The International Labor Organization Convention 182 declares that the use of children younger than eighteen is "one of the worst forms of child labor," and the African Charter on the Rights and Welfare of the Child prohibits "recruitment and direct participation in

hostilities of any person under the age of eighteen years."[21]

Despite these prohibitions, children are often taken into armed groups for use as combatants, servants, or sex workers. In militias and guerilla units, children may help sustain the organizations over the long term, and some even eventually become leaders. When pregnancies occur among the sex workers, resulting fetuses are often aborted, but when they are not, the babies still may face rejection from one or both parents or even their society. War can also directly threaten the security of children by exacerbating poverty in their area, perhaps forcing them eventually to relocate to refugee camps or internally displaced persons (IDP) camps.

In postconflict situations there is a fundamental need to develop the institutions and processes of a viable state to help the population return to normalcy. There are currently about twenty-six million people displaced by humanitarian crises, about half of whom are children. The UN and other agencies, therefore, guide the children, like they do adults, through a process of disarmament, demobilization, and reintegration (DDR). *Disarmament* requires participants to hand in their weapons as the first step for gaining access to UN programs. Participants are then *demobilized* to a DDR center, which is a kind of interim care center for those who have left armed groups. *Reintegration* is perhaps the most complex process for children. It involves effective reconciliation, reconstruction, and sometimes repatriation, as well as reeducation, because the children need to learn new skills, find employment, and function in the new state with or without their former families. The worst off may die, be injured, or develop mental illnesses. The impact on children who participate in civil wars is profound, and

---

[20] In Paris at a 2007 meeting, representatives of signatories agreed on the principles and guidelines about how to handle children associated with armed forces or groups.

[21] Office of the SRSG on "The Six Grave Violations against Children during Armed Conflict," http://www.un.org/children/conflict.

often engenders a web of ethical and legal implications.[22]

Children can learn about violence and warfare from direct experience in zones of conflict but also vicariously from parents, schools, media, fiction, and films. They do not have to be involved in battles, bombings, rapes, or refugee camps to suffer from war. Children may learn pro- or antiwar values and develop prejudice or empathy for people of other cultures or groups based on the messages about war that they receive from their parents, peers, and the media. Exposure to images and characterizations of the enemy can affect children's perceptions of people and places they may never meet or visit.

Research shows that political attitudes are absorbed from the media and surrounding culture at a very young age. How firmly they are embedded in children's minds and how damaging vicarious experiences are at different ages is less well understood.[23] Even the way children of different ages and circumstances learn about conflict and how they react to it are not clear. Carl Dodge has pointed out that while it is true that children in Africa "grow up" sooner than their Western contemporaries (in terms of contributing to the family work and income), it is not at all clear that they achieve enough maturity to handle the stress of war.[24] Empirical evidence has left experts deeply divided about how both direct and indirect experience of violence affects different age groups. Some claim that the most severe impact of direct conflict occurs between the ages of eight and puberty. Others believe that there is no age at which trauma does not have serious psychological impacts on children. Certainly, since professional soldiers (who experience combat and later reintegrate into society) routinely testify that no veteran ever truly leaves behind the trauma of war, it is hard to believe that children exposed to similar horrors are not permanently scarred by it.

This specific point reflects a more general argument about child resilience. Some scholars claim that children are more resilient than pessimists fear and may even be stimulated and advantaged by violence; others argue that adults have traditionally downplayed the negative psychological impact of violence on children. It is also clear that conflict affects individuals in different ways and that different cultures and families encourage varying responses.[25] There is also general agreement in the literature that panic may spread from parents to children, that children who are separated from their parents are particularly vulnerable, and that children may be less affected by violence when they are not personally targeted. However, experts remain divided about what type of child suffers most from violence – some arguing that it is the introverted, withdrawn child who is most seriously affected – but the topic is still not settled. One study of ten- and eleven-year-old children in Israel found, perhaps counterintuitively, that those with the highest stress levels in peacetime suffered the least when war broke out.[26]

Child soldiers

Throughout history children have been used in active military combat as **child soldiers** (Figure 14.9). There are many historical examples. Boys

---

[22] There is an extensive literature in this field. See, for example, Ilene Cohn and Guy S. Goodwin-Gill, *Child Soldiers: The Role of Children in Armed Conflict* (Oxford: Oxford University Press, 1994); Ed Cairns, *Children and Political Violence* (Hoboken, NJ: Wiley-Blackwell, 1996); G. Machel, *The Impact of War on Children* (London: Hurst, 2001); Michael Wessells, *Child Soldiers: From Violence to Protection* (Boston: Harvard University Press, 2007).

[23] Amiram Raviv et al., *How Children Understand War and Peace* (San Francisco: Jossey-Bass, 1999); Dafna Lemish, *Children and Media in Times of Conflict and War* (New York: Hampton Press, 2007).

[24] C. P. Dodge, "Health Implications of War in Uganda and Sudan," *Social Sciences and Medicine* 3, no. 6 (1990), pp. 691–8.

[25] Ibid.

[26] E. Cairns, C. McClenahan, and A. Hoskins, "The Impact of Political Violence on Children's Ideas about Peace: Evidence from Northern Ireland," in *Research on Children and Peace*, ed. S. Hagglund, I. Hakvoort, and L. Oppenheimer (Gothenburg: Department of Education, 1996), p. 38.

Figure 14.9 The Little Insurgent Monument, featuring a young armed child in an oversized helmet, honors the role played by children in the uprising to free Warsaw from Nazi Germany. Children were vital to the resistance. *Source:* Shutterstock.

were heroes in the U.S. Civil War and some fought valiantly in both World War I and World War II.[27] Children were also used as mass murderers by the Khmer Rouge in Cambodia and elsewhere.

While there are obvious practical difficulties in collecting reliable data, there are an estimated 250,000 to 300,000 child soldiers today. Girls represent about 40 percent of them.[28] The

United Nations has identified more than a dozen government and armed groups that have used child soldiers in active conflict for more than a decade. As General Romeo Dallaire puts it, children are "a weapon of choice for commanders."[29] Although they are young and small, they can easily handle the light small arms that are readily available. Today, their supply is almost limitless, renewable, cheap, expendable, and useful because they are vulnerable and easily manipulated. This is particularly the case in the developing world, where there are a large number of children who grow up in poverty, with little health care or sanitation, limited access to education, and low survival rates.

Most but not all child soldiers are found in nonstate groups. Their recruitment is sometime voluntary, sometimes forced – often a bit of each. Voluntary recruitment is not unusual in poorer developing countries, where it may offer advantages such as protection, shelter, food, and even comradeship. But children may also be forced to join illegal armed groups who abuse, torture, and rape them. In recent years, children under have been forcibly recruited from schools in Afghanistan, Central Africa, Burma, El Salvador, Ethiopia, Mozambique, and elsewhere.

The United Nations responds to children in armed conflict in several ways, searching for practical solutions to implement international treaties and UN Security Council resolutions. First, an appointed Special Representative of the Secretary General (SPSG) has responsibility for managing the Security Council's framework for monitoring and reporting on child abuse in conflict situations. The SPSG gathers evidence of grave violations against children in six areas:

1. Killing or maiming of children
2. Recruitment or use of child soldiers
3. Rape and other forms of sexual violence against children
4. Abduction of children

[27] David Rosen, *Armies of the Young: Child Soldiers in War and Terrorism* (New Brunswick, NJ: Rutgers University Press, 2005), p. 4.

[28] Romeo Dallaire, *They Fight Like Soldiers, They Die Like Children* (London: Hutchinson, 2010), p. 129.

[29] Ibid., p. 12.

Table 14.3 Monitoring and reporting mechanism for child soldiers

Stage 1	Stage 2	Stage 3	Stage 4	Stage 5	Stage 6
Armed force or group recruits and uses child soldiers	UN country team receives information that an armed force or group recruits and uses child soldiers	UN country team and MRM task forces "verify" the information that the armed force or group recruits and uses child soldiers (if UN has access to the conflict affected areas)	UN country team recommends to the secretary-general that he list the armed force or group in the annexes of the secretary-general's annual report	OSRG lists the armed group or force in the annexes of the secretary-general's annual report	Consequences: Naming? Shaming? Sanctions? ICC?

Source: Adapted from Watchlist, *Monitoring and Reporting Mechanism on Children and Armed Conflict*, January 2008.

5. Attacks against schools or hospitals
6. Denial of humanitarian access to children

Second, the Security Council established the Working Group on Children and Armed Conflict (one member from each country in the Security Council) and a monitoring and reporting mechanism (MRM) "to systematically monitor, document, and report on heinous abuses of the rights of children in situations of armed conflict."[30] The process for listing armed forces and groups in violation of children's rights is summarized in Table 14.3.

Considerable media attention is given to large scale UN efforts to obtain cease-fires and permanent peace agreements in places where children are violated, but some lesser-known actions of the secretary-general's staff go almost unmentioned. Groups, parties, or individuals may be "shamed" by being "named" in the secretary-general's annual report, and more rarely, they may be sanctioned by the Security Council. There are many examples. The Revolutionary Armed Forces of Colombia (FARC) has recruited children as young as seven and forced them into conflict. The Islamist armed group

Al-Shabaab in Somalia targets children as young as ten for forced recruitment. In mid-2010 the Security Council declared its readiness to impose targeted sanctions against persistent violators, including asset freezing, arms embargoes, and travel restrictions. Later that year, the UN Security Council imposed targeted measures including travel bans and asset freezes for grave violations against Congolese children, including recruitment and use of child soldiers, killing and maiming of children, sexual violations, and denial of humanitarian access. The Office of the SRSG used this occasion to warn those who offend international laws against children that they should "work with us to get off the list or face sanctions" or even be judged and sentenced in the International Criminal Court (discussed in Chapter 6).[31]

Several NGOs are involved in issues related to children and war. In fact, the International Convention on Children is the only treaty that specifically calls for work to be carried out by NGOs. Watchlist on Children and Armed Conflict, for example, is a network of international nongovernmental

[30] UN Security Council Resolution 1616, expanded by UN Security Council Resolution 1882 in 1999.

[31] Children and Armed Conflict, press release, December 2, 2010, http://www.un.org/children/conflict/english/pr/2010-12-02249.html.

organizations that cooperates with the United Nations' attempts to end violations against children. It works under UN Security Council resolutions and is led by a steering committee of NGOs. Other NGOs working in this area include Save the Children, World Vision, Coalition to Stop the Use of Child Soldiers, Human Rights Watch, Amnesty International, the Red Cross, and Invisible Children, which achieved notoriety in 2012 (see Close Up 14.2).

Close Up 14.2 Joseph Kony videos and invisible children

Invisible Children is a controversial American NGO working in Africa. It is a small activist documentary filmmaking organization from California that tries to raise awareness of the criminal activities of Joseph Kony in Central Africa. Kony, leader of the Lord's Resistance Army (LRA), is alleged to have abducted thirty thousand children and to have used them as soldiers and slaves.

The group began to be noticed when it made a film documentary about children in Uganda who were surviving in their relationship with the LRA. In it, the filmmakers described how the conflict began and how the LRA used children for their war efforts. In the first stages the movement was led by Alice Lakwena, who claimed she had been told by God to overthrow the Ugandan government. After Lakwena was exiled, Joseph Kony, claiming to be Alice's cousin, continued the movement. Kony combined religion and ethnic hatred in his messages. Today the LRA consists of about 150–200 core militants, with perhaps 200 more abducted children and adults. Sick of war, few adult Ugandans joined his effort, so Kony began recruiting children by preaching a brutally distorted version of Christianity. The primary target for the LRA was young children, often between the ages of five and twelve, because

they were more capable of sneaking into schools and abducting even more children.

To avoid being captured by the LRA, thousands of children began to "night commute" to public places such as bus stops and hospitals, where they were less likely to be captured than in their own homes. Invisible Children promoted a "national night commute day" in April 2006, calling for children to walk from their homes to the downtown of their city and sleep there with large groups of other people. The film closes with the statistic that (at that time) every three months 640 children were killed, 2,000 abducted, and 800,000 displaced in Uganda.

The emotional appeal of Invisible Children was augmented by an explosive video in 2012 that shows one of the leaders of Invisible Children telling his young son about Kony's criminal behavior. Within a few days of its release, the video was being viewed on social media around the world. International celebrities publicized the video and its contents, and within a short time *Kony 2012* had been viewed more than forty-five million times and Twitter users had mentioned it more than a million times. The viral nature of the video demonstrates the new power of social media on international communication (Chapter 7).

The video was soon attacked by some experts as the "work of an outsider," as "overly dramatic," and based on "faulty information about Kony and his whereabouts." Some said that it even "shocked other humanitarian groups in Central Africa who were trying to do something concrete about Kony." Regardless of such criticisms, *Kony 2012* shone an international spotlight on a major case of unsettled international crime.

Years of documented evidence show that Kony needs to be stopped from plundering and using children as war soldiers and sex slaves, and some steps are being taken to do so. He has been indicted by the International Criminal Court (see Chapter 6). The Ugandan army (whose own human rights record is checkered) leads an effort to apprehend Kony. In May 2012, President Barack Obama signed into law the Lord's Resistance Army Disarmament and Northern Uganda Recovering Act, which commits the United States to help bring an end to the brutality of the LRA. Obama sent one hundred troops to Central Africa to train Uganda's government soldiers in their quest to capture Kony. They have still not been successful. More could be done with the help of the UN, African Union, and the United States. In particular, the Central African Republic, Democratic Republic of the Congo, and Sudan need to be forced to eliminate LRA safe havens.

Are such videos appropriate tools to try to prevent crimes against humanity? Do they do more harm than good? How do they illustrate the changing nature of international communications and perhaps even global politics?

Conclusion: Human security and responsibility to protect

This chapter has examined issues of human rights – including genocide and abuse of women and children – that concern human, but not state, security. We have seen that these types of issues may demand policy trade-offs between country and individual security. In many cases, such as in Bosnia, Darfur, Libya, Rwanda, and Somalia, the UN Security Council explicitly linked its justification for military action with human rights violations. In these cases the council clearly paid more attention to human than state security, as their actions interfered in sovereignty and governments' right to control their own people.

Human security is defined as the security of people, including their safety, well-being, and the protection of their human rights. It means putting the welfare of people ahead of, or making it as important as, state security.[32] It is about ensuring the security of individuals and their communities based on the principle that individuals need to be protected as much as their states and borders. It stresses ethical or moral principles about the worth of all people as opposed to the abstract idea of the importance of the state and its institutions. Focusing exclusively on state security and protection from foreign enemies diverts concern from the mass of humanity or marginalized people. Human security, therefore, is widely used to describe the broad complex of threats associated with civil war, genocide, and displacement of populations. The list of threats that come under this rubric is very elastic – perhaps

---

[32] This distinction is adapted from the Human Security Centre, *Mini Atlas of Human Security* (Washington, DC: World Bank, 2008).

too much so. The *broad* concept of human security encompasses everything from genocide to poverty; the *narrow* conception focuses only on issues of violence – such as wars and terrorism.

The broad concept was first used by the United Nations in the 1994 *Human Development Report*, which stressed the importance of freedom from want as much as freedom from fear. The authors asserted that security traditionally has "been interpreted narrowly: as security of territory from external aggression, or as protection of national interests in foreign policy or as global security from nuclear holocaust. It has been related more to nation-states than people."[33] The broad use of the term, in contrast, includes food security, adequate shelter, security from poverty, and even threats to human dignity. It is based on the notion that hunger, disease, and natural disasters may kill more people than wars and terrorism. At its very broadest, the term therefore includes protecting individuals from any threat – including human rights abuses and even social and environmental dangers.

As the world's states and peoples become more interrelated by globalization, the overlap between narrow human security issues such as organized crime, child labor, human trafficking, drugs, cross-border violence, refugees, and failed states becomes ever more complex and daunting. Since all humans should be protected from harm, then states or international institutions may need to intervene in the internal affairs of states – in other words, impinge on their sovereignty. This broadest use of the term *human security* was incorporated in the report by the UN High-Level Panel on Threats, Challenges and Change, called *In Larger Freedom*.[34]

In 1999 and 2000, the UN secretary-general raised the issue of what the UN should do to avoid future incidents of social violence, genocide, and ethnic cleansing such as had occurred in Bosnia, Kosovo, Rwanda, and Somalia. The International Commission on Intervention and State Sovereignty (ICISS) was set up by the Canadian government to inquire into the situation. In its report, *The Responsibility to Protect (R2P)*, the commission adopted the principle that sovereign states have a responsibility to protect their own citizens, but when they are unwilling or unable to do so the United Nations should act. In such cases, the principle of non-interference in the sovereign right of states would have to yield to the international responsibility to protect the people concerned. The report concluded that if military intervention for human rights was to be entertained, there would need to be consistent, credible, and enforceable standards to guide international action.[35]

The report placed the primary responsibility for protection of people with individual states, but it contended that if people were being harmed and their state would not or could act, then the international community had responsibility to do

---

[33] UN Development Program, *Human Development Report 1994* (New York: Oxford University Press, 1994).

[34] United Nations, *In Larger Freedom: Towards Development, Security and Human Rights for All*, Report of the UN Secretary General, 2005.

[35] United Nations, *The Responsibility to Protect* (New York: United Nations, 2001).

so. It said that the international community cannot stand aside from its responsibility to protect people threatened by genocide, ethnic cleansing, and other massive violations of human rights.

In 2005, world leaders agreed to implement R2P on a case-by-case basis through the Security Council and based on the charter. But of course, any policy might be nothing but a pretext for military action by one group of countries against another. (Did the invasion of Iraq by American and allied forces in March 2003 count as humanitarian intervention?) The authors of the report also alleged that the United Nations had responsibility to prevent problems from arising by addressing the root causes of internal conflict and helping to rebuild societies after civil conflict. These are heavy ethical responsibilities that could end up creating a slippery slope for justifying foreign intervention.

Not only practitioners but also scholars have linked state and human security together as distinct ways of thinking about security. Realists assign paramount importance to state security, and the liberal wing of international relations theory has broadened the concept to include many aspects of human rights. But can one type of security actually be achieved without the other? If borders are not protected, will this not have an effect on individuals within the state? Of course it will! If plagues and diseases are allowed to spread across a state's borders, will it not affect the security of the state? Of course it will! The distinction between the two types of security may be false, especially in an interdependent world. State security and human security are complementary and mutually reinforcing and might mean the same thing.

Some writers take the view that realists, liberals, and constructivists approach these issues differently, but while it may be accurate that realists focus more on national interests, liberals more on individuals and values, and constructivists more on the construction of norms, all three come together regarding the importance of security. The weighting may differ from scholar to scholar and approach to approach, but most theorists take both types of ideas into consideration in their research. Until we achieve an inclusive and democratic form of global governance, this dilemma will remain, and perfection is a long way from being achieved.

Select bibliography

Baum, Steven K., *The Psychology of Genocide: Perpetrators, Bystanders, and Rescuers* (New York: Cambridge University Press, 2008).

Brysk, Alison, *Global Good Samaritans: Human Rights as Foreign Policy* (Oxford: Oxford University Press, 2009).

_____, *Global Good Samaritans: Human Rights as Foreign Policy* (Oxford: Oxford University Press, 2009).

Chirot, Daniel, *Why Not Kill Them All? The Logic and Prevention of Mass Political Murder* (Princeton, NJ: Princeton University Press, 2006).

Dallaire, Romeo, *They Fight Like Soldiers, They Die Like Children* (London: Hutchinson, 2010).

Donnelly, Jack, *International Human Rights* (New York: Westview, 2006).

Dunne, T., and Wheeler, N. J., eds., *Human Rights in Global Politics* (Cambridge: Cambridge University Press, 1999).

Falk, Richard, *Achieving Human Rights* (London: Routledge, 2008).

Jones, Adam, *Genocide: A Comprehensive Introduction* (London: Routledge, 2007).

Kiernan, Ben, *Blood and Soil: A World History of Genocide and Extermination from Sparta to Darfur* (New Haven, CT: Yale University Press, 2007).

Mahoney, Jack, *The Challenge of Human Rights: Origin, Development and Significance* (New York: Wiley, 2006).

Midlarsky, Manus I., *The Killing Trap: Genocide in the Twentieth Century* (Cambridge: Cambridge University Press, 2005).

Peterson, V. Spike, and Anne Sisson Runyan, *Global Gender Issues in the New Millennium*, 3rd ed. (Boulder, CO: Westview, 2009).

Power, Samantha, *A Problem from Hell: America and the Age of Genocide* (New York: Harper Perennial, 2003).

Rosen, David, *Armies of the Young: Child Soldiers in War and Terrorism* (New Brunswick, NJ: Rutgers University Press, 2005).

Singer, P., *Children at War* (New York: Pantheon Books, 2005).

Slaughter, Anne-Marie, *A New World Order* (Princeton, NJ: Princeton University Press, 2004).

U.S. State Department, *Human Rights Report*, http://www.state.gov.

Wessells, M., *Child Soldiers: From Violence to Protection* (Cambridge, MA: Harvard University Press, 2006).

15 Global threats

Environment, energy, demography, and health

We have examined global interactions in terms of history, politics, economics, conflicts, and human rights. Beyond these vital topics, and arguably just as significant globally, are the environment we all share, patterns of population growth and aging, and diseases and health issues that know no borders. Clean air, water, and fertile land for growing food are basic requirements for healthy and vibrant life, but there is a growing mismatch between fulfilling these escalating needs of the world's burgeoning population and our methods of achieving economic progress.

This chapter examines areas in which there are pressing threats to our shared globe: the environment, demographic change, and health. Our first topic, the environment, is extremely complex (Box 15.1). Climate change in particular has become a serious and controversial issue. Energy supply is critical for the global economy, but greenhouse gases emitted from fossil fuels and ozone-depleting chemicals contribute significantly to global warming and atmospheric degradation. We examine these perplexing environmental and energy issues as two sides of the same coin. We then consider alternative energy sources and other important environmental issues including water, agriculture, and biodiversity that also have global impacts.

Demographic issues underlie and interact with environmental problems today, so our second topic is population trends. Uneven population growth and distribution combined with factors such as aging and international migration have significant implications for the global environment, economic progress, and security. The third and final section of the chapter focuses on world health issues – topics including child and maternal health, contagious diseases, HIV/AIDS, and pandemics. Increasingly, global health is being viewed as an economic development issue and also as a human rights and security issue.[1]

Many observers believe that the global environment, demographic trends, and health issues are more serious than war and terrorism today because their effects are broader and perhaps irreversible. The speed of globalization and the new human security concerns of statesmen, NGOs, and international institutions all impact on these complex issues. Despite their importance, progress in meeting these challenges has been painfully slow. Is it too slow to ward off disastrous consequences for the world's next generations?

---

[1] United Nations, *Millennium Development Goals Report, 2010* (New York: United Nations). Data from this and the 2011 report are used throughout the chapter.

The environment: Scope and definitions

"Stop the plunder or Man will need two planets to survive by 2030" – this alarming newspaper headline was based on a 2010 scientific report that concluded that people are using the world's natural resources at 1.5 times the rate that they can be replaced.[2] It was a dramatic warning that Earth is under serious stress because of rapid and unsustainable use of its finite resources. Critics retorted that such claims are exaggerated because history shows that when a resource becomes scarce, its price rises, thus providing an incentive for research and development of new technologies that can resolve the problem. For example, if gasoline becomes too expensive, a substitute will be found; if food becomes scarce, new high-yield crops will be developed; and so on. In other words, economic or market forces will resolve the issue over time. However, most scientists also argue that if humans do not stop polluting the atmosphere, climate change will have catastrophic repercussions for millions of people. Already, they say, natural disasters tied to climate change kill about three hundred thousand people a year.[3] Critics again claim this to be an exaggeration and say that if global warming is indeed taking place, it is part of a natural, long-term cycle.

Environmental issues are grave, emotional, and highly political. Some scientists and engineers do not agree that drastic actions on global warming are needed.[4] Moderates warn about pollution, waste, and environmental degradation. Radicals go much further, rejecting capitalism and economic growth on the assumption that they inherently lead to environmental decay. Both groups accept that without wiser use of finite resources, economic growth and prosperity cannot be assured for future generations, and many advocate a global approach that aims to achieve a new lifestyle based on conservation. However, this goal is pitted against the world's increasingly desperate competition for scarce resources.

The planet's carrying capacity – its ability to support and sustain life – is at the heart of global environmental issues. This point can be illustrated by the tragedy of the commons, an influential theory put forward by the ecologist Garrett Hardin.[5] In villages and towns common or public land is invariably overgrazed and exhausted by individuals who use it extensively but do not properly care for it because it is not exclusively theirs. In other words, short-term, individual interests prevail over common concerns and issues. Domestically, only governments can solve such problems, but at the global level the decisions (or nondecisions) of single states or large international business corporations may negatively affect the benefits for all others. Selfish interests and negligence prevail when people have higher regard for their own immediate gain than for the greater public good. Thus, they treat the global commons in a way that spreads negative consequences for everyone – polluting communal air and water, creating environmental and health damages, and endangering species through such activities as overfishing.[6] The environment, therefore, needs to be seen as a public good, or a collective good, shared by all people around the world. It includes air, water, public lands, and other benefits that markets cannot or will not supply. Government action is needed, but without a global government or international regimes to enforce rules, negative activities are extremely difficult to counter. Good intentions are simply not enough!

Sustainable development is an approach to economic development that seeks to reconcile economic growth with environmental protection,

---

[2] Zoological Society of London and WWF, *Living Planet Report*, as reported in *The Times*, October 14, 2010, p. 25. Reports available at wwf.panda.org/about_ourearth/all_publications/living_planet

[3] "Climate Change Responsible for 300,000 Deaths a Year," *Global Humanitarian Forum*, http://ghfgeneva.org/NewsViewer/tabid/383/vw/1/ItemID/6/Devault.aspx.

[4] See, for example, Robert B. Laughlin, *Powering the Future* (New York: Basic Books, 2011).

[5] Garrett Hardin, "The Tragedy of the Commons," *Science* 162 (1968), pp. 1243–8.

[6] See Will Steger and Jon Bowermaster, *Saving the Earth: A Citizen's Guide to Environmental Action* (New York: Alfred A. Knopf, 1990).

Box 5.1 **Our complex environment**

A Climate Change

History of Policy Progress on Climate Change

Contemporary Approaches to Climate Change

B Energy Resources

Non renewable	*Renewable*
coal	nuclear power
petroleum	wind
natural gas	solar
shale gas	biofuels
and oil	

C Other Environmental Issues with Global Impact

Forests
Water (potable, oceans)
Agricultural land and food
Biodiversity

---

so that development can proceed while the world's resources are maintained, not damaged or used up so that following generations will not have access to them. This approach was introduced and popularized in the 1987 *Brundtland Report*, which alerted the world to the urgency of the deteriorating planet and was taken up by institutions such as the United Nations and the World Bank.[7] The report is the basis of much of the limited progress that has been made to date. Its approach was furthered by an American professor, Elinor Ostrom, who won a Nobel Prize in Economics in 2009 (the only female political scientist to have done so) for her research suggesting that people can cooperatively manage such common

resources as fisheries without relying on governments. She found that when communities share a common interest in preservation, they often succeed by establishing rules, and then effectively shaming or honoring members based on their behavior. At the same time, however, widespread sustainability cannot be realized without significant changes in current environmental policies, including in the fields of global warming, energy supply, and non-renewable resources.

Climate change: An intractable issue?

Climate change refers to extended alteration in the world's climate by natural causes, human activities, or some combination of the two.[8] It is commonly classed as an environmental problem, but is unlike forms of pollution that can be addressed by state regulations. Climate change is more difficult because it requires interstate cooperation and a "fundamental transformation in the most important part of our economies, shifting away from fossil fuels and on to something else."[9]

Almost all experts agree that global warming, a long, slow rise in the average world temperature, is currently taking place at an alarming speed, and that to a high degree, it is caused by human activity.[10] Natural factors cannot explain the dramatic acceleration, but human factors can. The greenhouse effect, in which the burning of fossil fuels acts like a blanket on Earth's atmosphere, trapping solar energy that would otherwise escape into space, makes temperatures rise and affects both weather and climate. It is caused by mankind's release

---

[7] *Our Common Future*, Report of the Brundtland Commission (Oxford: Oxford University Press, 1987).

[8] The Council of Foreign Relations has an online section "Crisis Guide: Climate Change" that offers an interactive database of climate change commentary, background, and analysis. See http://www.cfr.org/climate-change/crisis-guide-climate-change/p17088.

[9] Bill McKibben, "Think Again: Climate Change," *Foreign Policy* 88, no. 1 (January–February 2009), p. 36.

[10] A 2009 study showed that only 11 percent of published scientists and 1 percent of published climatologists in the United States disagreed with the idea that climate change is human induced. David McCandless and Helen Lawson Williams, "Climate Change: A Consensus among Scientists?," http://informationisbeautiful.net.

of pollutants – including carbon dioxide (CO_2), chlorofluorocarbons (CFCs), and methane – into the atmosphere (see Close Up 15.1). Carbon dioxide constitutes more than 75 percent of these greenhouse gas emissions, and about 80 percent of carbon dioxide comes from generating energy.[11] The gas acts like a greenhouse, trapping heat, hence the term *greenhouse gas*. Emissions of artificial gases including hydrofluorocarbons and perfluorocarbons are comparatively low, but they are even more powerful greenhouse gases, with much higher atmospheric lifetimes and high global warming potential.

Close Up 15.1 Ozone and the greenhouse effect

The ozone layer forms a protective layer in the upper atmosphere of Earth that shields the planet from the sun's harmful impact on living organisms. In the mid-1980s, scientists discovered that this thin layer encircling the stratosphere was being destroyed by the emission of chlorofluorocarbon (CFC) gases and bromine from halogens into the atmosphere. In the stratosphere, ozone has a cooling effect, which is lessened when the ozone layer thins or develops holes. Lower, in the troposphere, however, it is a powerful greenhouse gas. As the ozone layer is depleted, more ultraviolet light is able to reach Earth, causing serious health problems such as increased incidence of skin cancer, eye cataracts, and damage to immune systems, and endangering marine life. In 1987 in response to these concerns, the developed democracies signed and later amended the **Montreal Protocol on Substances That Deplete the Ozone Layer**, which froze and began to decrease the use of CFCs and halogen production.[12]

Significant amounts of ozone-depleting chemicals were phased out under the protocol. However, ozone damage is very slow to heal, and scientists predict that although good progress is being made in phasing out ozone-depleting substances, it will take decades for holes in the layer to mend. A large hole over Antarctica and severe depletion over the North Pole show little immediate sign of recovery, and scientists have estimated that the ozone hole over the South Pole will not heal until about 2065.[13]

Although there is little doubt that global warming is taking place, there is controversy among scientists over the speed of change and whether temperature increases will continue. The world's "normal" temperature has fluctuated very slowly in cycles over hundreds of years, but averages out at about 57.2°F (14°C). However, since the 1980s, temperature rises have accelerated, and Earth has been warming faster than at any point in the previous two thousand years.[14] From 1990 to 2006, its surface temperature increased approximately 1.2 to 1.4°F.[15]

Even that seemingly small change is having significant ramifications. The UN Intergovernmental Panel on Climate Change (IPCC), which has input from more than two thousand of the world's leading scientists, analyzed overall warming and patterns of change over different geographical regions and seasonal variations. They confirmed "a discernible human effect on global climate" and forecast an increase of 10.6°F (5.9°C) by the end of the 21st century if nothing is done about greenhouse gas

---

[11] World Bank, *World Development Indicators, 2010.* (Washington, DC: World Bank, 2010), p. 149.

[12] *The Millennium Development Goals Report, 2010*, p. 54.

[13] *Associated Press*, December 6, 2006. See also Science at NASA at: Science.NASA.Gov.

[14] Cited by Ross Garnaut, climate change adviser to the Australian government, quoted in *Australian*, March 11, 2011, pp. 1–2. See also Dinyar Godrej, *The No-Nonsense Guide to Climate Change* (London: New Internationalist, 2002), p. 12.

[15] U.S. Environmental Protection Agency, "Climate Change: Basic Information," http://www.epa.gov.

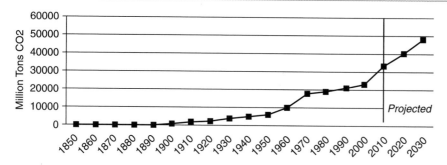

Figure 15.1 Global carbon dioxide emissions (1850–2030). *Sources: Global Issues* (Washington, DC: CQ Press, 2010), p. 417; Pew Center on Global Climate Change, "Climate Change 101: International Action," various dates; Carbon Dioxide Information Analysis Center updates these figures regularly. See website, http://cdiac.ornl.gov/trends/trends.htmpmis/ Derlim 2009 Z010 estimates.html.

emissions.[16] If the warming cannot be kept nearer to 3.6°F (2°C) over preindustrial levels, these experts predict that climate change will have dire environmental and even geopolitical effects.

Rising temperatures already are disrupting the ocean current system, damaging marine ecosystems and threatening coastal areas. The Gulf Stream flows from the Gulf of Mexico across the Atlantic, past the British Isles and Iceland. Its flow keeps the climate of Northern Europe much warmer than other regions of a similar latitude. Once they reach the Arctic, these waters sink and then flow back around the planet in a complex pattern, keeping world climate patterns relatively predictable. Even minor changes in the ocean's temperature or salinity due to freshwater runoff could disrupt this pattern and induce unusual and disruptive climate changes in its path. Glaciers that once reflected 80 percent of incoming solar radiation back into space are melting fast, and the water that replaces them absorbs the radiation instead. Huge amounts of methane that were trapped below the ice are escaping into the atmosphere, and it is an even more potent greenhouse gas than CO_2.

Human-generated global warming is directly related to carbon emissions, which have been rising since the beginning of the Industrial Revolution about 150 years ago but surged dramatically in the second half of the 20th century. Scientists have reached a general consensus that global greenhouse gas emissions need to peak and begin to decline by 2015 in order to reach the goal of reducing them to about 50 percent of their 1990 levels by 2050, and keep global warming below 3.6°F. This is necessary, they say, to avoid more dangerous and catastrophic climate change.[17] The world produced more than 33,000 million tons (33 gigatons) of CO_2 in 2010. Scientists are working to confirm how much warming a doubling of atmospheric carbon dioxide will actually produce. (If current trends continue, fifty-six gigatons could be produced in 2020. See Figure 15.1.)

Climate change policy pits poorer developing countries against their richer developed counterparts, which are largely responsible for the current buildup of CO_2 in the atmosphere. The prosperity of the West is based on industrialization, which has been achieved through burning fossil fuels. Carbon dioxide and other pollutants are released as by-products of burning the key fossil fuels – coal, oil, and natural gas. In 2010, 92 percent of CO_2 came from fossil fuels and cement manufacture (see Figure 15.2).

[16] Jessica Seddon Wallack and Veerabhadran Ramanathan, "The Other Climate Changers," *Foreign Affairs* 88, no. 5 (October 2009), p. 106.

[17] World Bank, *World Development Indicators*, 2010 (Washington, DC: World Bank), p. 149. Also see United Nations, *Fact Sheet: Stepping Up International Action on Climate Change: The Road to Copenhagen* (New York: UN Framework Convention on Climate Change, 2009); *World Development Report 2010: Development and Climate Change* (Washington, DC: World Bank, 2009).

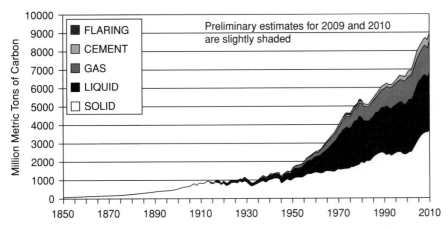

Figure 15.2 Estimates of global carbon emissions from fossil-fuel combustion and cement manufacture. Preliminary 2009 and 2010 global fossil fuel emissions estimates. *Source*: T. A. Boden and T. J. Blasing, "Record High 2010 Global Carbon Dioxide Emissions from Fossil-Fuel Combustion and Cement Manufacture," http://cdiac.ornl.gov/trends/emis/perlim_2009_2010_estimates.html. *Note*: Units are oxidized carbon, not CO_2. To convert, multiply by 3.67. For regular updates see http://cdiac.ornl.gov/trends/trends.htm.

Historically, LDCs have emitted less than a quarter of the CO_2 per capita of than developed economies, but as these poorer countries industrialize, their total emissions are growing about twice as fast. Energy use has been increasing rapidly particularly in China and India. In fact, China became the largest emitter of CO_2 in 2006, moving ahead of the United States (see Table 15.1). The world's top six total carbon dioxide emitters are China, the United States, India, Russia, Japan, and Germany. The United States and China together account for about 40 percent of the world's human-made CO_2 emissions.

Despite considerable evidence about humankind's role in global warming, a vociferous debate is ongoing, led by environmentalists on one side and industrial interest groups, labor unions, and their supporters on the other. When former U.S. vice president Al Gore addressed the harsh consequences of global warming directly in a controversial movie documentary and book, critics claimed that his argument was based on emotion and was little more than clever political advocacy.[18] Supporters argued that it was the content itself that was emotional

because it accurately portrayed a looming environmental disaster.[19]

Humans contribute to climate change in many ways. We turn next to a discussion of contemporary policy efforts to deal with this global problem.

History of policy progress on climate change

Since climate change has been widely recognized by policy makers for more than a decade, why isn't more being done about it? There are several reasons. First and foremost is the financial issue. The short-term costs are extremely high and immediate, while the benefits are less predictable and will come only over the long term. For centuries, gas and coal have been relatively cheap and easy to access, and alternative sources of energy such as nuclear or renewable energy are not economically competitive with gas or coal without considerable government support. As well, the costs of combating global warming would fall unevenly, so that a few states and companies would have to pay much more than others, creating massive political maneuvering and obstructive interest-group involvement. Since developed countries are responsible for most of the

[18] Al Gore, *An Inconvenient Truth: The Planetary Emergency of Global Warming* (New York: Rodale, 2006); Al Gore, *Earth in the Balance* (New York: Houghton Mifflin Harcourt, 2000).

[19] For example, Bjorn Lomborg, *The Skeptical Environmentalist: Measuring the Real State of the World* (Cambridge: Cambridge University Press, 1998).

Table 15.1 **National total fossil-fuel CO_2 emissions compared to per capita fossil-fuel CO_2 emission rates by country or territory: top 10 countries**

Total emission ranking, by country, 2010	Per capita emission ranking by country, 2009
1. China	1. Qatar
2. United States	2. Trinidad and Tobago
3. India	3. Kuwait
4. Russia	4. Brunei
5. Japan	5. United Arab Emirates
6. Germany	6. Aruba
7. Iran	7. Bahrain
8. South Korea	8. Luxembourg
9. Canada	9. Australia
10. Saudi Arabia	10. United States

Source: Tom Boden, Gregg Marland, and Bob Andres, Carbon Dioxide Information Analysis Center, Oak Ridge National Laboratory, doi 10.3334 /CDIAC/00001_V2011, http://cdiac.ornl.gov/trends/emis/top2008.cap and http://cdiac.ornl.gov/trends/emis/tre_tp20.html. Per capita emissions found at World Data Bank http://databank.worldbank.org/data/views/reports/tableview.asp.

environmental damage, poorer countries object to being held back or having to contribute to cleaning up the mess they did not cause. Yet the longer they do not contribute to the cleanup, the more they become part of the cause.

Second, among the developed countries, the United States has a unique position. While it has only about 4 percent of the world's population, it is responsible for nearly a quarter of the world's greenhouse gas emissions. Yet the population is rigidly divided about how serious global warming actually is. In 2009, President Obama committed his country to reduce its CO_2 emissions to 17 percent below 2005 levels by 2020, but Congress refused to pass the legislation. Democrats were divided on the plan, and Republicans refused even to acknowledge the existence of global warming. House Speaker John Boehner claimed, "The idea that carbon dioxide is ... harmful to our environment is almost comical," and Representative John Shimkus dismissed the dangers of climate change by quoting Genesis 9:22: "As long as the earth endures, seedtime and harvest, cold and heat, summer and winter, day and night will never cease."[20] Public opinion in the United States reflects these divisions.

The public, particularly in the United States, is currently skeptical because the impact of global warming is still distant and appears to be happening "elsewhere." Environmental issues consistently rate near the bottom of public concerns, and many people show deep ignorance and indifference to the topic. In Europe, the environment generally attracts more concern.[21] This may reflect a cultural distinction between the two countries, with Americans being much more individualistic, whereas Europeans are more collectivist in their orientations.[22] Values take a long time to change – it took hundreds of years, for example, to end slavery, in which moral and economic interests were involved.

Third, policy elites often engage in hyperbole and create fear with exaggerated claims. The science of climate change is still not completely understood, and this creates mixed messages. Some scientists act as advocates for interest groups or exaggerate their data to garner public support rather than maintaining objectivity. Conversely, many climate-change skeptics are connected to groups backed by the oil, gas, and coal industries, which are using stalling tactics. All these factors build resistance in the public, creating boredom and disbelief. The media do

[20] Both quoted in *The New Yorker*, November 22, 2010, p. 53.
[21] In 2008, 62 percent of Europeans saw climate as the world's gravest problem. In 2009, during the recession, that dropped to 50 percent. In 2011 about half of Europe's electricity comes from fossil fuels. *The Economist*, March 12, 2011, p. 56.
[22] *The Economist*, December 5, 2009, p. 15.

not do justice to such complex issues, often passing along simplistic and confused messages.

Global summits and climate change Because the responsibility for the global commons is diffuse, many individuals, groups, states, and institutions are involved in climate change issues. For more than two decades the UN has initiated global summits on the subject in an attempt to secure a binding agreement on curbing greenhouse gases. From the beginning, states disagreed on how to split the burden of emission cuts.

At the 1997 Kyoto conference, the richest countries signed a modest, tentative agreement to cut greenhouse gas emissions by at least 5 percent below their 1990 levels by 2012. While the global South received preferential treatment with lower levels of cuts per capita, many LDCs refused to sign the accord, arguing that today's problems are essentially due to the excesses of the rich world. Their leaders maintained that cutting emissions would reduce their economic growth. China and India refused even to debate the issue. Yet despite their low emissions per person, these countries have large and rapidly growing total CO_2 emissions.

Later, in Bonn, Germany, a revised Kyoto Protocol required thirty-seven major industrialized countries to slash carbon emissions to 5 percent below 1990 levels by 2012 and to adopt a "cap-and-trade" system that would allow countries to buy and sell emission credits from other countries. The treaty adopted compromises to allow some countries, like Russia, to offset their emission reduction targets with carbon sinks, or areas of water, forests, and farmland that absorb carbon through photosynthesis. India and China signed but were not required to comply with the protocol.

By October 2006, it was agreed that the Kyoto Protocol would be made legally binding. However, neither the Australian nor the U.S. governments ratified the accord, and other countries soon began to have second thoughts. In 2009, world leaders gathered in Copenhagen to replace the protocol, which was set to expire in 2012. The meeting ended in chaos, with the wealthiest countries insisting on deep and verifiable cuts in emissions from major emerging countries like China and India. The poorest countries demanded that the wealthiest ones do more to reduce their own pollution and more to help them adapt. It did not help, of course, that the Copenhagen meeting was held after the onset of the global economic crisis (discussed in Chapter 12). Japan, Canada, and Russia announced in 2010 that they would not sign up to a second commitment period.

Why did agreement for the Kyoto accords evaporate? Basically, when the Kyoto Protocol was agreed to in 1997, the industrialized world was emitting far more CO_2 than the combined developing world. By 2010, the industrialized world and developing country emissions were almost equal, and by 2030 the developing world is projected to be far ahead of the industrialized world in emission production. This change in emissions patterns undermines the idea agreed to at Kyoto that parties should protect the climate system in accordance with their "common" but "differentiated" responsibilities. Many industrialized countries no longer believe that the industrialized countries should shoulder the burden while the developing world is required to do nothing.

In the end, the Copenhagen Accord codified only the commitments of individual states to act on their own to tackle global warming. The United States, for example, pledged a total carbon reduction of 17 percent by 2020. China said it would cut CO_2 emissions by 40–45 percent per unit of gross domestic product (GDP) below 2005 levels by 2020. That would allow emissions to rise, but at a slower rate than before. The agreement also provides a system for monitoring and reporting progress toward those goals. However, the United Nations Environment Program (UNEP) calculated that even if the individual promises were carried out in full, they would still leave a massive gigaton "gap" to reach what is needed.[23] Perhaps the most concrete agreement to come out of Copenhagen

---

[23] United Nations, *The Emissions Gap Report*, http://www.unep.org/publications/ebooks/emissionsgapreport.

was the Reducing Emissions from Deforestation and Forest Degradation agreement to compensate countries for preserving their forests.

The next meeting in Cancún a year later produced a minimal agreement that was well short of a global treaty, with legally binding targets to limit climate change. As *The Economist* put it, the UN climate process did quite well in Cancún, but the climate not so well.[24] Rich countries agreed to consider an extension of the Kyoto Protocol, and for the first time poorer countries agreed to sign up to emission cuts. The forum also produced a series of key decisions on setting up a "green fund" to help poor countries cope with climate change. Richer countries pledged to transfer US$100 billion a year to help developing countries pay for emissions cuts and climate adaptation by 2020. At the meeting in Durban, South Africa, in 2011, it was announced that global emissions of carbon dioxide from fossil-fuel burning had jumped by the largest amount on record, 5.9 percent, in 2010. The parties agreed to work toward a new protocol that would require action from all parties, not just the rich countries (as in the Kyoto agreement). The agreement is to be concluded by 2015 and enter into force in 2020.

The failure to reach a new agreement to replace the Kyoto Protocol reflects the fact that many countries still do not view a strong global climate treaty as central to their national interests.[25] Short-term prospects for such a treaty are poor, so some states continue to move forward on their own policies to reduce carbon emissions and greenhouse gases and to pursue funding of green technology. In 2012, for example, six countries – the United States, Canada, Bangladesh, Ghana, Mexico, and Sweden – agreed on an initiative to cut the production of methane, soot (known as black carbon), and hydrofluorocarbons. The idea is to achieve relatively quick, measurable reductions in emissions without waiting

[24] *The Economist*, December 18, 2010, p. 122.
[25] Bernice Lee, "Beyond Doom and Gloom," Chatham House, *World Today* (August–September 2010), p. 33.

for politicians to act or the UN to produce a global agreement on carbon monoxide.

Contemporary approaches on climate change

There are three main approaches to reducing carbon dioxide emissions: emissions trading schemes, carbon tax, and subsidies. Emissions trading schemes (ETS), called carbon-trading or cap-and-trade schemes, reduce carbon emissions by making it expensive to emit greenhouse gases. Under an emissions-trading scheme, a government sets an overall cap on the amount of pollution specific companies can emit. The government then either sells or gives out permits, each representing a ton of carbon dioxide. If companies emit too much, they can buy or otherwise acquire more permits; if they emit less, they can sell their permits through brokers or in organized local or global markets. In theory, the amount of emissions would decline over time, and as the price of emitting carbon went up, companies would devote more of their own research budgets to finding new energy sources. However, in 2010, Congress blocked cap-and-trade legislation in the United States. Just over thirty countries are operating emissions trading schemes in 2013, all in Europe except for New Zealand. The problem is that if states do not act in concert, they risk hurting their industries and exporting jobs. Raising the cost of dirty energy such as coal is unpopular, especially during a weak economy.

An alternative scheme to reduce the use of fossil fuels is a **carbon tax** – taxing companies on the carbon they emit. The point of a carbon tax is to reduce the use of fossil fuels by making them more expensive. When Australia, the leading CO_2-emitting state per capita, adopted a tax on carbon fuels in 2011, it was very unpopular. Many Australians feared that acting alone to adopt a tax on carbon would hurt their economy without improving the world environment. Without international agreement, industries might simply leave their country for areas where they would not be taxed.

Many countries resist any such limitation on their carbon emission, but as of 2011, fifteen countries impose taxes on carbon fuels. (In Canada, carbon taxes are imposed by three provinces, Alberta, British Columbia, and Québec.)

In short, although scientists agree that human carbon emissions pose serious risks for disruptive climate change in this century, there is no prospect for a global agreement to meet the challenge. Many states therefore are providing subsidies – financing research in an attempt to find new breakthrough technologies that can compete with coal and oil. This can involve underwriting the cost of purchasing alternatives with tax credits or rebates or by governments investing in alternative clean energy technologies. China, for example, is investing more in alternative energy technology than any other country. In 2013, it had three of the top-ten solar companies in the world and the largest wind market.[26] Overall, investments in clean energy and efficiency are continuing to rise and undoubtedly will increase as states recognize that it is in their national interests to accelerate the phase-out of oil.

Natural resources, energy, and security

Energy supply is at the heart of the global economy and climate warming. The main sources of energy worldwide are oil, natural gas, coal, hydroelectric, nuclear, and geothermal (e.g., wind, solar, wood). Between 80 percent and 90 percent of energy requirements are met by fossil fuels – coal, natural gas, and petroleum. Since economies rely on energy for industry, motorized transport, and a great many other uses, economic modernization and energy consumption go hand in hand. World energy consumption has increased about 2 percent a year since 1970. The International Energy Agency

forecasts that under current conditions, there will be a 40 percent increase in energy demand by 2030.[27] People in high-income economies use about twelve times more energy, on average, than their low-income counterparts.[28]

Natural resources fuel industrial growth and economic well-being. Nonrenewable resources are limited in supply and can be a powerful political tool for states, sometimes leading to violent conflicts. Figure 15.3 shows estimates of the number of years that some key minerals will be available at current production rates. These resources can make a country rich, as oil did for Norway, or ruin it, as diamonds did in Sierra Leone.[29] Renewable resources are relatively abundant and considerably more climate and politically friendly. Energy security, meaning both adequate supply and ensured energy delivery, is a priority for governments. Since energy supply is often based on waning resources and can be a political tool, governments try to avoid relying too much on any one source. Supply becomes more competitive as demand increases, which raises anxieties about interruptions and delays. Delivery of energy becomes increasingly complex as sources of supply change or are depleted. Oil, natural gas, coal, uranium, and electricity pass along fragile networks of pipelines, transmission lines, and maritime routes that are vulnerable to accidents, sabotage, ransom, and theft. Increasingly, the supply routes originate in or pass through areas of instability and conflict. Some critics see oil as a target because it symbolizes for them the imperialist agenda of the global North.

As the 21st century began, world petroleum consumption and demand were rising, while the output of many oil fields was about to decline. Prices were high. In 1990, producers in the global North, including the United States, Canada, the North Sea

[26] "China Leading Global Race to Make Clean Energy," *The New York Times*, January 31, 2010, p. A1.

[27] Antony Froggatt, "Frontier Energy," Chatham House, *World Today* (August–September 2010), p. 36.

[28] *World Development Indicators, 2010*, p. 181.

[29] See Paul Collier, *The Plundered Planet: Why We Must – and How We Can – Manage Nature for Global Prosperity* (Oxford: Oxford University Press, 2010).

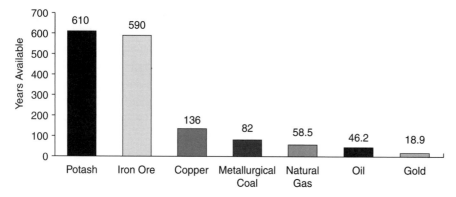

Figure 15.3 Estimates of number of years key minerals will be available. *Note*: Years of minerals in reserve, at current production rates. These are estimates by mining companies of available minerals from selected basins. New mining techniques, deeper drilling, and mining in new areas such as the Arctic and Mongolia are expected to increase these reserves. *Source*: John W. Miller, "Under Earth: Rocks or a Hard Place," *Wall Street Journal*, June 5, 2012, p. B1.

states, Russia, and a few others, had provided about 39 percent of the world output, but by 2030, their combined share was projected to plummet to about 26 percent with the difference to be made up by new discoveries in places like the Arctic and oil-rich areas in the global South.[30] However, many oil reserves in the South are in politically unstable and/or nondemocratic regions like the Central Asian states, Iran, Iraq, Kuwait, Libya, Nigeria, Saudi Arabia, the United Arab Emirates, and Venezuela.[31] Pressures mounted to drill in areas that had previously been out of bounds. By 2013, a third option had changed this situation dramatically. Fossil fuel technology had made remarkable advances, and shale gas and oil were fast becoming the revolutionary fuels of the future, promising to change the world's energy map.

Fossil fuels: Coal, petroleum, and natural gas

Coal was the first major source of energy for industry. It was plentiful and cheap, but it was also dirty and difficult to transport. The largest coal reserves are in Australia, China, India, and Russia, but it is

mined in more than a hundred countries.[32] Rising demand means that coal is now being transported over long distances rather than being burned near where it is mined, and as a result, prices are rising. Today, developed countries are closing or limiting the construction of coal-fired power plants because of concerns about pollution and global warming. Consequently, coal consumption in the United States and Europe is generally down. However, in Asia, particularly in China, coal use is rapidly expanding for industrial development. China is by far the world's largest coal producer, but it can meet less than half its needs from its own mines. It uses coal for most of its energy needs, and in 2009, it went from being a coal exporter to a leading purchaser.[33] Other top coal importers are Japan, India, and South Korea.

The environmental problems created by coal are well documented. When it is mined, burned, or processed to produce liquid fuel, coal generates pollution through waste products, contaminating land, water, and air, and creating acid rain, or acidic precipitation that damages forests, water quality, and soil far from its source. In Wales, horrific

[30] United States Department of Energy, 2006: 87, p. 155.
[31] See John Deutch and James R. Schlesinger *National Security Consequences of U.S. Oil Dependency* (New York: Council on Foreign Relations, Independent Task Force Report No. 58, 2006).

[32] Froggatt, "Frontier Energy."
[33] Elisabeth Rosenthal, "The West's Love-Hate Relationship with Coal," *International Herald Tribune*, November 22, 2010, p. 1.

memories are still vivid of the day in 1966 when a slag heap began to move, flowing over a primary school and killing almost all of the mining village's young children. Besides contaminating land, coal is the largest contributor to human-made CO_2 in the atmosphere. Efforts to create clean coal technology focus mainly on trying to reduce the emission of harmful pollutants or on trying to capture and store CO_2 emissions deep underground. The results are still far from clear or clean.

The massive increase in coal use in China since 2009 has created a nightmare for developed countries, because their own companies are unwilling to close mines and forego the massive profits they hope to reap by selling to China, as well as Japan and South Korea. The reality is that coal is king in the developing world. Coal-fired power generation is increasing in Asia, and any drop in coal use in the West in the coming years will be more than offset by increased use in Asia. Profits and jobs are a powerful enticement to mine. In British Columbia, Canada, for example, Vancouver has become a major location for loading and exporting coal.

The conflict between environmental and trade concerns is growing, particularly in Australia, Canada, and the United States. Environmental laws currently in practice often make it difficult to build new coal-fired plants but do not restrict coal mining. This is partly because emission accounting standards are based on where a fuel is burned, not where it is mined. Coal mining also remains a dangerous occupation, with many mines flouting safety standards. By the 20th century coal had been replaced for many purposes by petroleum and natural gas.

Petroleum is plentiful, burns cleaner, causes less pollution than coal, and appeared to be the perfect fuel for the growth of developed economies. Increasingly in the 20th century and rapidly in the 21st century it became the most vital resource in the industrial world. Developing countries began to follow that model to economic progress, thus increasing demand. The United States is the world's largest consumer of petroleum, and it is estimated that in the first quarter of the 21st century consumption there will grow by about a third. China, as an emerging economy, is expected to increase its use by nearly 300 percent.[34] Petroleum became so tied to economic growth that it is a major political asset for states that have it and a serious vulnerability for those that do not. States are willing go to almost any length to protect their supply. Its production and distribution are highly politicized and rife with conflict.

The world has proven oil reserves of about 1.3 trillion barrels, which are located in specific geologic regions. About ninety countries have at least some oil. The Middle East and Africa have proven reserves of about 66 percent of the total, of which approximately 20 percent is in Saudi Arabia and 11 percent in Iraq.[35] Canada has about 13 percent, and Venezuela and Russia follow, but these figures are constantly shifting. Estimates for Russia's percentage vary, and new prospects, particularly in Siberia, suggest that it may have 6 percent or more of the world's total. Russia also has the world's largest natural gas reserves and the second-largest coal reserves.

As demand for oil increased, many experts as early as the 1970s theorized that global production was close to its peak and soon would begin to decline. Global peak oil refers to the point in time when the maximum rate of global petroleum extraction is reached. After that point, the rate of production is said to be in irreversible decline. Global petroleum extraction, when plotted on a bell curve, indicates that oil supply eventually reaches a peak when oil is 50 percent depleted[36] (Figure 15.4). At that theoretical point, production begins to fall and costs go up.[37] However, the concern generated by the peak

---

[34] Energy Information Administration, *International Energy Outlook 2004*, http://www.epa.gov.

[35] From BP, cited in *The Economist*, July 25, 2009.

[36] M. King Hubbert, "Oil the Dwindling Treasure," *National Geographic* (June 1974).

[37] One expert opinion is that at the rate at which it is currently being extracted, oil reserves are decreasing by 4 percent annually (and gas, at 5 percent). Froggatt, "Frontier Energy," p. 36. Daniel Yergin argues that predictions of the end of oil have so far been wrong and will continue to be wrong. Daniel Yergin, *The Quest: Energy Security and the Remaking of the Modern World* (New York: Penguin, 2011).

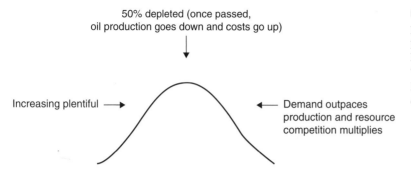

50% depleted (once passed,
oil production goes down and costs go up)

Increasing plentiful →

← Demand outpaces
production and resource
competition multiplies

Figure 15.4 Bell curve of global petroleum extraction. *Source*: The peak oil theory was devised by M. King Hubbert. See his article "Nuclear Energy and the Fossil Fuels, http://www.hubbertpeak. com/hubbert/1056/1956.pdf.

oil theory has been ameliorated by new discoveries of shale gas and oil since about 2010.

Global petroleum supply and price have fluctuated wildly since the mid-1970s. At that time, the major multinational oil corporations (called the Seven Sisters) had dominated the production and distribution of oil since the 1930s. They had unilaterally reduced the average price of crude oil in 1959–60 in response to a world glut in oil, severely undercutting the profits of the producing countries (Figure 15.5). The large Middle East and Venezuelan producers responded by forming the **Organization of Petroleum**

Exporting Countries (OPEC) and sought to assume control of the international oil market. Its formation and consolidation in the 1960s undercut the multinational corporations' domination. Over time, however, other producers came on-line, including Russia, Angola, Azerbaijan, Mexico, and Norway, which now share about 60 percent of the world's production but are not members of OPEC. Today, OPEC has twelve members that continue to produce about 40 percent of the world's oil.

Together, four oil shocks have affected the structure of the modern oil market and illustrate

Figure 15.5 Drilling for oil is taking place in increasingly difficult areas offshore. This is a large Pacific Ocean oil rig drilling platform off the southern coast of California. Such rigs have become a major concern of environmentalists in recent years because of the possibility of massive oil spills. *Source*: Photos.com.

the increasing "politicization" of oil." The first three were caused by threats to *supply* for countries that depended on oil for economic development. In the first, in 1974, oil prices rose dramatically and caused significant economic disruption, particularly in the United States. The price rises resulted from an oil embargo by the Arab members of OPEC against Western states that supported Israel in the Fourth Arab-Israeli War. In the second shock, political events in Iran in 1979 deepened the crisis for oil-consuming states. Islamic fundamentalists seized political power in oil-rich Iran, a member of OPEC. Panic set in as the price of a barrel of Gulf oil rose sharply, from about US$2 to $40 in less than a decade. The Iran-Iraq War in 1980 destabilized oil markets further, causing a 10 percent drop in world production. The third shock happened about a decade later, in 1991, when Saddam Hussein invaded Kuwait in the Gulf War, cutting production and burning oil fields when he retreated. Panic once again shook world markets.

The ongoing fourth oil shock began in the 21st century and resulted from increasing demand rather than from supply. As China and India have engaged in massive economic development, their need for petroleum products has surged. American dependency on oil has also increased. A new and competitive rush began to find new and reliable sources of supply. States are adapting their political allegiances and policies to secure what they need. China, for example, refused to censure Sudan over its policies in Darfur because it did not want to risk losing access to Sudanese oil. Russia cut off supplies to Ukraine when the Ukrainian government objected to price increases. Some critics claim that oil was behind the U.S.-led invasion of Iraq in 2003.

Panic occurs because oil supply is limited, and markets are subject to disruption by economic and political factors, as well as natural disasters like the massive spill following the breakdown of a British Petroleum well in the Gulf of Mexico in 2010. Higher prices mean that it is becoming more economically feasible to develop fuel from tar or oil sands (although extracting oil from oil sands produces four times as much CO_2 as conventional drilling, destroys forests, and pollutes regional water supplies) and from shale gas. Another response to the issues of scarcity and unstable supply has been to seek out new technologies to limit dependence on petroleum.

Natural gas is plentiful and highly efficient. It is the cleanest source of fuel from fossil, producing less greenhouse gas per unit of energy generated than oil and 50 percent less than coal, but it still contributes substantially to global emissions.[38] While relatively plentiful, it is not easy to transport or store. It is commercially produced in oil fields and natural gas fields and transported as liquefied natural gas (LNG) or liquefied petroleum gas (LPG). The largest proven reserves of natural gas are in Russia, Iran, Qatar, Saudi Arabia, and the United Arab Emirates. Natural gas is used for generating electric power, for powering domestic appliances, for transportation and aviation, and for fertilizer.

Over the past decade, new, *unconventional gas and oil* resources have been discovered in rocks – including tight gas, shale gas, tight oil, and coal-bed methane. These have become the hot, revolutionary fuels of the future and have expanded the regions of the world in which gas and oil can be produced. The United States in particular benefits from shale plays that are large and relatively shallow. Thanks to an accompanying revolution in fossil fuel technology, these resources now provide a fifth of the country's national energy needs, and they are projected by the IEA to become the largest single source of fuel in the U.S. energy market by 2030. The United States appears to have a hundred-year supply of natural gas. The potential extent of these unconventional gas reserves is huge, about five times greater than conventional natural gas.[39]

[38] For an assessment of whether natural gas could be the "new oil," see David Victor, Amy Myers Jaffe, and Mark Hayes, *Natural Gas and Geopolitics: From 1970 to 2040* (New York: Cambridge University Press, 2006).

[39] Paul Stevens, "Unconventional Gas," Chatham House, *World Today* (August–September 2010), p. 39.

However, it is not yet clear what the environmental costs of extracting it will be. It is extracted by a technique called hydraulic fracturing, which involves blasting water, sand, and chemicals deep into the earth to dislodge gas from the rock. Critics argue that it can pose threats to water quality and supply, landscape disfigurement, and underground leaks of chemicals and methane gas.

Alternative energy sources: Nuclear, wind, solar, biofuels

The world needs to severely reduce greenhouse gas emissions. Time is pressing. What can be done? There is no simple answer, but new energy technologies and delivery systems are required, and there has been a large increase in investment in both energy efficiency and renewable energy options in recent years.[40]

Electricity is vital for a good standard of living, but it is the source of even more emissions than oil. In 2009 the world's electricity generators emitted about nine billion tons of carbon dioxide of an industrial total of thirty billion tons (total emissions, including deforestation, were about fifty billion tons). Generating electricity using coal, gas, or oil significantly damages the environment. Coal releases the most carbon dioxide in the process, about twice as much as natural gas. Yet as we have seen, because coal is relatively cheap and available, sources of electricity generation have shifted since 1990, with developing economies relying increasingly on coal.

Nuclear power plants create electricity with less air pollution, but they have other problems. As of 2013, thirty-one countries had active nuclear power stations. There are 442 reactors worldwide producing about 14 percent of the world's electricity. The United States currently has the most plants: 104 plants produce 20 percent of the country's electricity, and there are plans to add 8 new reactors by 2020. France is next, with 58 plants. European countries altogether have 143 reactors

and another 8 under construction. Together, the OECD countries produce more than 80 percent of the world's nuclear electricity. But building new reactors has largely stagnated in the West because of the possibility of accidents and the high costs involved. In 2011, Germany announced it would totally phase out its nuclear power production. However, the number of plants continues to grow in Asia, where the International Atomic Energy Agency (IAEA) expects significant expansion by 2030. China has thirteen reactors and is building twenty-eight more; India has twenty and is planning dozens more. Indonesia, which is prone to major earthquakes, is planning to build four reactors in the coming fifteen years.

At one time it was expected that nuclear energy would dominate the generation of electric power. Indeed, countries like France and Japan, with few natural resources of their own, have come to rely on nuclear energy for much of their power. France now obtains nearly 80 percent of its electricity from nuclear energy and exports nuclear-generated power to Britain, Germany, Italy, and the Netherlands. But nuclear power plants are slow to build and notoriously expensive. They produce waste products, particularly radioactive waste, which comes in various levels of toxicity and can be very dangerous. Safe transportation and storage of nuclear waste are vital. High-level wastes need to be isolated for thousands of years until they no longer pose a hazard. The IAEA supervises waste management, but storage issues have never been satisfactorily resolved. Added to this is the difficulty of ensuring the security of the fuel at all stages.

Since nuclear power generation began in the 1950s, about twenty accidents worldwide have cost lives and/or large amounts of money. Three stand out, and in all of them human error was an issue. In 1979, a failure in the cooling system at the Three Mile Island reactor in Pennsylvania, United States, caused a partial meltdown. In 1986 a nuclear reactor exploded at Chernobyl, Russia, causing the reactor to spew out around a hundred times more radioactive material than the two atomic bombs

[40] Froggatt, "Frontier Energy," p. 37.

that destroyed Hiroshima and Nagasaki in 1945.[41] In 2011 the scenario was repeated when several of Japan's nuclear reactors at the Fukushima Daiichi power plant were damaged or destroyed following a massive earthquake and tsunami that left at least 25,600 dead or missing and 260,000 homeless. Radiation from at least one reactor leaked into the ocean, and the fertile land and fisheries around the plant will remain unsafe for years (see Chapter 16).[42]

Industry supporters argue that the reactors at Chernobyl and Fukushima were based on old technology, and lessons can be learned from those incidents to make reactors and waste storage safer. Shoddy safety standards and cover-ups can be addressed and overcome. Above all, advocates say, nuclear energy is the cleanest source of power available, and the number of deaths that have been caused by nuclear accidents is modest compared to deaths associated with coal-fired power.

Renewable energy options are becoming more abundant, but they are still expensive and very far from to replacing fossil fuels or nuclear energy on a large scale. Detractors often refer to them as hugely expensive "cottage industries." In the field of transportation, hybrid vehicles have been developed to run on a combination of gasoline and electric batteries. In industry, hydrogen fuel cells are being explored as replacement for the internal combustion engine. In agriculture, crops such as sugarcane, soybeans, and corn are being raised to develop biofuels. New sources of heat and energy are being sought through solar and wind power. In all areas, painstaking environmental reviews are being carried out and government incentives put in place for new technology research.

[41] A 2006 report by the Chernobyl Forum, a group that includes the UN, the International Atomic Energy Agency, and the World Health Organization, concluded that about 1,000 workers received high doses of radiation, of which 134 cases were acute, 28 died, 2 others died from injuries associated with the explosion, and 19 died during the following seven years, some not of radiation. There were no obvious spikes in rates of cancer or other illnesses, except for thyroid cancer, which caused about fifteen deaths.

[42] *The Economist*, March 26, 2011, pp. 29–30.

Solar power has shown promise and is being pursued in several different ways. Solar photovoltaic (PV) systems convert sunlight directly to electricity. A major drawback is that generation can happen only when sunlight is strong, for a short time each day. Solar power can be stored in batteries, which is relatively inefficient, or fed directly into a grid. Solar thermal plants work by intensely focusing sunlight to generate heat, which in turn can be used to power steam turbines. The thermal energy can be stored far more efficiently than electricity. However, solar-generated electricity is still four times more expensive than nuclear and more than five times as expensive as coal, so there is a long way to go to make it economically viable.

Wind energy is making headway in many regions such as Europe and China. Britain, for example, generated more energy from offshore wind turbines than any other country in 2010, with 268 wind farms. Critics claim that onshore farms are not very efficient, so the U.K. government is focusing more on offshore farms, even though they tend to be more expensive to build. However, wind is unreliable, hard to capture, and widely dispersed. It still produces less than 2 percent of the world's electricity. A major problem with both sun and wind energy sources has been the integration of grids and large-scale storage so that grid operators can keep power flowing reliably to users and save up energy for cloudy or windless days (Figure 15.6).

Biofuels include ethanol, produced from corn and sugarcane, and biodiesel from soybeans, palm oil, and rapeseed. Biofuels also have weaknesses. Their production on a global scale as alternative energy sources would divert land use from food supplies and thereby raise the price of food. It takes massive amounts of grain to make ethanol. The amount it takes to fill one SUV automobile tank with ethanol could feed a person for a year. As well, recent biofuels that require good agricultural land also require tractors, petroleum-based fertilizers, and distilleries that emit a lot of carbon, and combined this

Figure 15.6 Windmills stretch as far as the eye can see in the desert near Palm Springs, California, where they turn wind into electric power. California is a leading American state in introducing and enforcing environmental regulations.

may be worse than gasoline for global warming.[43] Critics argue that the money and energy going into biofuels should be stopped and the land turned back to food production.

The United States is the world's biggest ethanol producer, using about 40 percent of the country's corn crop. The American government subsidy is nearly US$6 billion annually for ethanol makers. Brazil leads in ethanol production from sugarcane. About half of all cars there run on ethanol.[44] But sugarcane production is taking land away from cattle ranchers, and they in turn are cutting down rain forests to make up for it. Indonesia has already destroyed much of its rainforest to grow palm oil for biodiesel, and in doing so it released so much carbon that it moved from the twenty-first carbon emitter to the third highest in just a few years. Other biofuels that are being examined include algae biomass, because photosynthetic algae can typically generate ten to twenty times more fuel per acre than agricultural commodities like corn. Since algae do not require arable land, they would not compete with food crops. They are also voracious consumers of carbon dioxide, and therefore have the potential to reduce greenhouse gas emissions. However, large-scale commercial development of this new technology is a long-term venture.

Renewable energy sources have to compete with readily available options such as coal, and now shale gas and oil, which are still abundant and relatively cheap. None is close to being able to solve the massive and growing greenhouse gas issue in any reasonable time frame. Table 15.2 shows some of the countries that have moved forward fastest in the renewable energy field. European countries currently have the most aggressive national policies in this respect, largely because most of them have little fossil fuel of their own, and the European Union has an emissions trading scheme that requires industry to pay for excessive carbon dioxide emissions.

Creating energy requires balancing supply, cost, and environmental damage. There is no easy answer for this since it is a matter of judging relative risk. The Intergovernmental Panel on Climate Change advised the UN in 2011 that renewable sources could deliver nearly 80 percent of the world's total energy by midcentury; however, a massive investment in research and technology would be required.

[43] Michael Grunwald, "Seven Myths about Alternative Energy," *Foreign Affairs* 88, no. 5 (September–October 2009), p. 131.

[44] *Wall Street Journal*, January 9, 2006.

Table 15.2 **Share of power fueled by renewable energy other than large hydropower, selected countries**

Country	Renewable energy as a percentage of total used
Iceland	29.8
Denmark	28.7
Portugal	21.6
New Zealand	13.7
Brazil	7.9
United States	4.3
India	3.6
Canada	3.3
China	3.1
Australia	2.8
Russia	0

Source: IHS Emerging Energy Research of Cambridge, Massachusetts, reported in *The New York Times*, September 30, 2010.

Currently, the percentage of the global energy supplied by alternative sources is negligible: geothermal, 0.1 percent; hydropower, 2.3 percent; biomass, 10.2 percent; wind, 0.2 percent; and solar, 0.1 percent.[45] Many argue that natural gas, which is relatively plentiful and less dirty than coal, is the best option in the short run.

Other environmental issues with global impact

There are a great many other serious global environmental issues, including the fragility of forests, water, land, agriculture, and biodiversity. (See Close Up 15.2 on biodiversity.) Problems associated with land and water became public issues in the West after Jacques Cousteau described in books and on film the wonders and degradation of the oceans, and when Rachel Carson wrote about the increasingly negative impact of chemicals, from both agriculture and industry, on the environment.[46] By the end of the 1980s, as the Cold War confrontation came to an end, pollution and other environmental concerns took on an even more alarming profile and became associated with questions of human survival. Environmental degradation began to be seen as a potential cause of human conflict and security. In 1994, Robert Kaplan published an influential and emotional essay in which he called the environment "the national-security issue of the early twenty-first century" and speculated that issues of deforestation, soil erosion, water depletion, air pollution, and rising sea levels would "prompt mass migrations and, in turn, incite group conflicts."[47]

Severe pollution of air, land, and water threaten human health in most areas of the world. New issues are regularly in the news. After the 2010 earthquake in Haiti, cholera swept the country. There were no sewage plants, and as the crisis unfolded, plastic bottles and bags, shredded clothing, shoes, animal carcasses, and globs of unidentifiable black muck choked the country's canals and ditches. Around the globe, plastic is a concern because different types of plastic take decades to centuries to biodegrade, and its consumption is expected to rise dramatically in coming years, particularly in developing countries. About 4.7 million tons of plastic reach the oceans every year.[48] Most of it is swept up by ocean currents and becomes tiny fragments that float on or near the ocean surface across thousands of square kilometers, prone to absorb chemical pollutants that may work their way into the food

[45] *The New York Times*, June 3, 2011, p. 1.

[46] Rachel Carson, *Silent Spring* (Boston: Houghton Mifflin, 1962); Jacques Cousteau, *The Ocean World* (New York: H. N. Abrams, 1979).
[47] Robert Kaplan, "The Coming Anarchy," *Atlantic Monthly* (February 1994), pp. 44–76.
[48] *International Herald Tribune*, May 23, 2011.

chain. Behind pollution of air, water, and land are two major contributors: the world's burgeoning population and the use of nonrenewable energy resources.

Forests

Forests are a natural resource that is vital to the issue of global warming. They both emit and absorb vast quantities of CO_2. Forests cover about 31 percent of the world's landmass, but this is a fraction of their original expanse. About half of Earth's original forest area has already been destroyed or badly damaged, particularly by logging, farming, and encroaching urban areas. Rising temperatures also have caused considerable loss due to fire and pests. Temperate boreal forests encircle the far Northern Hemisphere, mostly in Russia, Scandinavia, Finland, and Canada, but today, almost half the forest that remains is tropical, and nearly a third of it in Brazil. Congo and Indonesia have much of the rest, with smaller rain forests in places like Costa Rica, Gabon, and Guyana. Rain forests, both tropical and temperate, are particularly important for both biodiversity and global climate.

Although most rainforests belong to only a few states, their existence benefits the whole world. They are commercially important to the states that own them, but they present great environmental costs to the world when they are cut. Their value is immense. It is estimated that they absorb between 15 percent and 17 percent of the world's carbon dioxide emissions, "more than the share of all the world's ships, cars, trains and planes."[49] Forests are the cheapest large-scale carbon sequestration option available. According to *The Economist*, forests "actually eat the stuff."[50] Cutting them down not only reduces their ability to extract carbon dioxide from the air but also releases carbon dioxide that has been stored in the vegetation and soil. In other words, deforestation, like industrialization,

contributes very significantly to change in Earth's climatic conditions, thus compounding the problem caused by burning fossil fuels. But the destruction goes beyond that. As the forests disappear, so too does the source of about one-quarter of the world's natural medicines, as well as the habitats of about half the species of plants and animals in the world and the natural environment of many aboriginal peoples.

The focus of environmentalists and international agencies on the serious consequences of deforestation has brought some improvement. Tree planting has increased in China, North America, and Europe, and Brazil cut its deforestation rate dramatically in 2010. Much of the credit for this drop was given to an international effort known as Reducing Emissions from Deforestation and Forest Degradation (REDD), which pays people in developing countries not to cut trees. Half a dozen countries at the 2010 Copenhagen Conference promised $4.5 billion to start the program.[51] REDD's ability to act is limited by the amount of cash it can raise and by the fact that it can operate only in places that have relatively stable governments. Unfortunately, some of the most important forests are in places that are very badly governed and are the target of rapacious exploitation. It remains to be seen how effective REDD will be in the long term. After a promising year in 2010, deforestation in Brazil immediately soared again, largely because of changes that softened the government's strict forest code.[52]

Potable water

Since the world's population is increasing by more than eighty million people a year and is expected to continue growing until midcentury, the demand for

[49] "Special Report on Forests," *The Economist*, September 25, 2010, p. 3.
[50] Ibid., p. 16.

[51] The agreement was to provide $30 billion in aid between 2010 and 2012, and $100 billion annually beginning in 2020, to help poorer countries develop less polluting sources of energy, to preserve their forests, and to deal with global warming. In exchange, developing countries agreed in principle to a transparent system of reporting emissions.
[52] The changes were demanded by a powerful agricultural lobby that wanted to cash in on high world prices for soybeans, corn, and cattle.

water is increasing correspondingly. By 2025, "1.8 billion people will be living in countries or regions with absolute water scarcity, and two-thirds of the world's population could be living under conditions of water stress."[53] If water management does not improve, and climate change is allowed to progress along with rising consumption patterns, it will have serious repercussions for the entire globe. Developing countries that already suffer from growing populations, food distribution, and water-supply problems, particularly in Southeast Asia and sub-Saharan Africa, will be hardest hit. Intensive research in sustainability is needed to identify and remove inefficiencies and assign to water a market value to guide sustainable consumption decisions and policies. The challenge is immense: "If oil is the key geopolitical resource of today, water will be as important – if not more so – in the not-so-distant future."[54]

Water covers almost three-quarters of the earth's surface, but only a fraction of it is suitable for human consumption. About 1.1 billion people do not have access to clean water. Only about 3 percent of the world's water is potable, and supply is decreasing while demand is increasing. Humans consume only about one-tenth of the clean water that is used; most is used by agriculture (about two-thirds) and industry (about one-quarter). Although water is vital and cannot ultimately be replaced by other resources, it is becoming increasingly contaminated by agriculture, manufacturing, and mining wastes and by naturally occurring substances such as inorganic arsenic (a particular problem in Bangladesh and some other parts of South Asia). Most states, including China, decreased organic water pollutants in recent years, but they are still very high.[55] More than 75 percent of China's urban river water and 90 percent of its urban groundwater is contaminated. By 2025 it is estimated that water shortages will plague about two-thirds of the world's people.[56]

Not only is potable water scarce and not able to be replaced by any substitute, it is vital to food and energy production. Climate change combined with degradation of lakes and streams is producing life-threatening conditions in regions around the world and making water a key component of national security. In China, for example, in 2010 after a long drought in which the Mekong River had shrunk alarmingly, tensions rose as neighboring states suspected China of hoarding water behind dams it had built further upstream. New rains diverted the conflict, but the Asian Development Bank has warned that further such water shortages will threaten access to water and sanitation needs for millions of households and industries.[57]

Six of seven rivers that run through China and India begin in the Himalayan Tibetan Plateau and are affected by glacial melting caused by global warming. That water is needed by China, where nearly one-quarter of surface water is so polluted that it is unfit even for farming. But the glacier runoff is also vital to neighboring countries, including India and Pakistan. This has potential as a flash point for India-China relations.[58] Both countries are developing rapidly. Between them they house more than a third of the world's population, but they have less than 10 percent of the world's water. As their economies improve, their demand for meat, sugar, and wheat, which all require considerable water to produce, is growing even as their populations increase. China plans to build more dams on the Mekong and other rivers, which is raising concerns among its neighbors, including Vietnam, Thailand, Laos, and Cambodia.

There are, of course, a great many other places where water sources cross international boundaries. An amazing 90 percent of water resources pass through several sovereign states. The states furthest from the river sources are most vulnerable. India is planning more upstream dams and water diversion projects on the Indus River. Relations are already

[53] World Bank, *World Development Indicators, 2010*, p. 152.
[54] Erik R. Peterson and Rachel A. Posner, "The World's Water Challenge," *Current History* 109, no. 723 (January 2010), p. 31.
[55] *World Development Indicators, 2010*, p. 177.
[56] *International Herald Tribune*, October 12, 2010, p. 24.
[57] Asian Development Bank, *Water for All*, http://wwwadb.org/ sectors/water/overview.
[58] *Millennium Development Goals Report, 2010*, p. 58.

Figure 15.7 Life in Egypt has always revolved around the Nile, its main waterway. Early pharaohs introduced the system of canals that allowed their people to grow and transport food in the harsh desert landscape, and provide vital water for themselves and their animals. Today, however, as in many other countries, water is becoming a matter of contention as a lack of sources upstream is threatening supply.

tense with neighboring Pakistan, which will be directly affected. In the Middle East, Turkey has initiated massive upriver dam projects on the Euphrates, raising protests from Iraq and Syria, which are facing water crises brought on by consecutive years of drought. Iraq is completely dependent on water from the Euphrates and Tigris, which begin in Turkey, yet Turkey claims that the water is its natural resource, just as the oil is Iraq's. Water from the Nile is vital to Egypt but is threatened by developments upstream in Sudan and Ethiopia (Figure 15.7).

Also in the Middle East, Israeli authorities control access to scarce water from the Jordan River, exacerbating tensions with Palestinians. In Central Asia, since the breakup of the Soviet Union, Tajikistan and Kyrgyzstan control the water sources for more fertile areas downstream. In the United States the drying Colorado River is a matter of concern not only in Arizona, New Mexico, and California but also in Mexico. In all these cases freshwater is being lost through such activities as irrigation, draining of wetlands, pollution, and construction of dams, as well as climate change.

In recent years, some national governments have quietly been buying agricultural land in other countries so that they will have a future right to the water linked to it. South Korea, for example, has bought farms in Madagascar, China, Japan, Libya, and Egypt, and Persian Gulf countries have bought land in Laos, Cambodia, Burma, Mozambique, Uganda, Ethiopia, Brazil, Pakistan, Central Asia, and Russia.[59] About fifty million acres have been purchased or leased under such conditions in Africa and Asia.[60]

Oceans

Unlike forests, oceans are both commercially profitable and a part of the global commons. Commercial ocean fishing is a classic case of despoiling a shared resource. Overfishing is rampant. Cod stocks off of Newfoundland collapsed in the 1980s, for example, but fishers simply shifted their sourcing to other

---

[59] Peter Brabeck-Letmathe, "Water Is the New Gold," *Foreign Policy* 88, no. 2 (May–June, 2009), p. 93.
[60] Peterson and Posner, "The World's Water Challenge," p. 33.

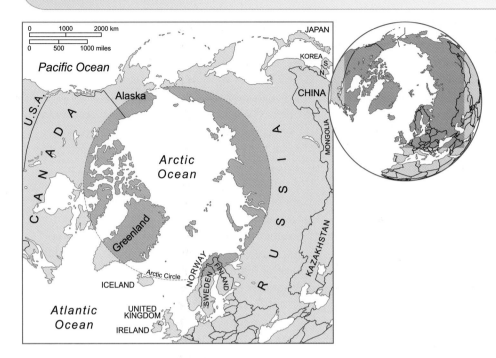

Figure 15.8 Global view of the Arctic. The rapid melting of summer sea-ice is making new shipping routes and access to underwater resources possible.

fish species, many of which are now endangered. About 28 percent of stocks worldwide are overexploited, depleted, or recovering. One-third of the world's seafood species are depleted, with the rest projected to go by midcentury.[61] On present trends of overfishing around the world, the oceans will be entirely denuded of wild fish within decades. Although there is clear evidence that fish stocks are desperately overfished, the demand for fish is rising. Governments are unwilling to damage their local industries and climate change is making the situation even worse because a warming ocean puts marine ecosystems under additional pressure.

Oceans are being undermined in another way. They serve as a "sink" because they absorb carbon dioxide, but when they get too much in a relatively short time, the result is acidification, a change in the chemical balance of the water that threatens the oceans' web of life. There is evidence that oceans may be turning acid far faster than at any time in the past million years. Increased acidity weakens the

shells of shellfish and the skeletal foundation of corals, the most diverse ecosystems on the planet, and contributes to extinctions of species. There is little sign of political will to slow or halt the process.

In the far north the polar ice cap is thinning and receding at an alarming rate, with implications for security as well as global warming. The process is giving rise to new shipping routes, new access to underwater resources, and a new source of potential conflicts and competition (Figure 15.8). The world's Arctic powers – the United States, Canada, Russia, Norway, and Denmark are studying how far their continental shelves – and by extension their resource rights – reach toward the North Pole. NATO, following realist assumptions, has examined the kinds of issues that could arise as a result of dependence on foreign sources of energy and is studying the effects of global warming in its long-term planning. The U.S. and U.K. militaries in particular are concerned that global warming will harm their critical overseas bases, which are vulnerable to rising seas and storms. Diego Garcia, an atoll in the Indian Ocean, is a logistics hub for American and British forces, for example, but it sits only a

---

[61] Food and Agriculture Organization, *State of World Aquaculture 2006* (FAO, 2006).

few feet above sea level. Melting ice in the Arctic will open a new shipping channel in the north that will have to be defended by the bordering states, and previously unattainable undersea resources are becoming yet another source of international claims and competition.

Agriculture and food

Only 29 percent of the planet is land, and almost half of that is covered with ice caps or is desert or wasteland, and about one-third is forest, marsh, or mountains. When urban areas are subtracted, only about 10 percent remains that can be used for agriculture, and even this is unevenly distributed among the world's states. There is little good, uncultivated land left. As well, desertification, the creation of deserts from combinations of overfarming, soil erosion, deforestation, and climate change, is making large portions of previously arable land useless for agriculture and wildlife habitats. Clearly, arable land is a precious resource that needs to be safeguarded for future generations.

Climate change is one of several factors affecting the world's food supply, including rising population, encroachment from urbanization, competition for land from biofuels, state bans on agricultural exports, export barriers to hold down food prices, environmental degradation, growing inequalities, and human migration. In late 2010 the UN warned that failure to make progress on climate change was putting at risk decades of progress in helping the world's poor.[62] Water for agriculture is a crucial problem. By 2030, it is estimated that farmers will need 45 percent more water than they have now, but they almost certainly will not be able to get it. Changes to diet and overall efficiency in irrigation are vital. It takes sixteen thousand liters of water to produce just over two pounds of beef, about eight times more than to produce two pounds of wheat.[63] As the climate warms, it will provide some small

beneficial impacts on crop yields in mid- to high-latitude regions, but it will have negative impacts in low-latitude regions, where there is already evidence of water scarcity, encroaching deserts, changing distribution of plants, plant diseases, and pests.[64] One expert claims that "water scarcity in China and India could cut wheat and rice production in these countries by thirty to fifty percent by 2050."[65]

Climate change impacts on agriculture, but the reverse is also true. Agriculture accounts for about 70 percent of global water withdrawals.[66] Agriculture also produces greenhouse gas emissions, primarily nitrous oxide and methane. Inefficient use of fertilizers increases nitrogen loss into the atmosphere through runoff and leaching from soil erosion. The trend to industrial farming makes food cheaper but destroys the natural carbon cycle that can exist in smaller operations, creating more pollution and CO_2.

As we saw in Chapter 13, it is a UN Millennium Development Goal to eradicate extreme poverty and hunger. Given the pace of population growth, however, food production will have to be augmented by an estimated 70 percent by 2050 to be sufficient. Global food production is rising, and according to the UN Food and Agriculture Organization (FAO), the world already produces enough calories for about four times the current world population and more than twice the minimum nutritional needs by some measures.[67] But malnourishment in many geographical areas is severe. Most people get enough calories, but many, even in developed countries, still suffer huge nutritional deficiencies that cause such problems as anemia, blindness, obesity, and

[62] United Nations, *Human Development Report, 2010* (New York: Oxford University Press, 2010).

[63] The diet issue is well argued in Michael Pollan, *The Omnivore's Dilemma* (New York: Penguin, 2006).

[64] This section is based on a study of four hundred world experts at the World Bank and the Food and Agriculture Organization. *Agriculture at a Crossroads* (Washington, DC: International Assessment of Agricultural Knowledge, Science, and Technology Development, 2008), http://www.agassessment.org.

[65] Roger Thurow, "The Fertile Continent, Africa, Agriculture's Final Frontier," *Foreign Affairs* 89, no. 4 (November–December 2010), pp. 102–10.

[66] *World Development Indicators, 2010*, p. 173.

[67] See "How Much Is Enough?" *The Economist*, February 26, 2011.

learning problems in children. The four nutrients that are in chronically short supply in poorer countries are vitamin A, iodine, iron, and zinc. As food prices rise, families switch from fresh produce to cheaper nutrient-poor staples that maximize calories, not nutrients.

In 1981 Nobel Prize-winning economist Amartya Sen wrote that the main reason for famines is not a shortage of basic food but rather factors such as wages, distribution, and even democracy.[68] There is a severe mismatch between food production and markets in large part because of the subsidies that protect the agricultural industry in many countries, making it cheaper for some developing countries to buy crops from Europe or America than to grow their own. Distribution of food is inadequate, and progress in this area requires new technologies, preservation, and distribution techniques and new, drought-tolerant crops. Agricultural sustainability is an important goal for preserving fertile land, and much needs to be done to educate farmers in sustainable methods. In some cases, food aid can actually undermine local agriculture by making it cheaper to eat foreign produce.

Demand for food is soaring in pace with population increase and the emergence of new, large markets. The combination of increased demand and shrinking supply is driving the price of food sharply higher around the world with potentially dangerous consequences. As George Marshall stated after World War II, "Hunger and insecurity are the worst enemies of peace."[69] A global index of food prices produced by the UN Food and Agriculture Organization shows that world prices began to rise alarmingly in 2010. Higher food prices are particularly devastating for people in developing countries, with potential for riots, panic buying, emergency price controls, and social unrest. Food prices were

a major factor in the revolutions during the "Arab Awakening" of 2011.[70]

There are two clashing views about how to proceed in agriculture reform. One is concerned mainly with feeding the world's growing population. It strongly supports genetic plant research into new seeds that can be substituted for those currently in use, modern industrial farming, and better food processing in poor countries. The other group is more concerned with the food issues of richer countries. It is hostile to the modern food business, especially industrial farming, and is concerned with issues such as animal welfare, human obesity, and genetic engineering of plants. It supports traditional and organic farming. The two groups vociferously debate the pros and cons of genetic modification, or putting a gene from one species of plant into another species that would not naturally interbreed with it. The first group dismisses the concerns of the second as a luxury of the rich. "Traditional and organic farming could feed Europeans and Americans well," they observe. "It cannot feed the world."[71] Roger Thurow for one concludes that developing countries must be helped to grow more of their own food – "the continent that has been fed by the world's food aid must now help feed the world."[72]

Close Up 15.2 Biodiversity: Why is it important and why is it so hard to protect?

Earth's renewable resources are being seriously depleted. Vegetation, oceans, forests, animals, and birds are under assault. Aridity, forest fires, and deforestation are a constant threat, and many plant and animal species are becoming extinct. When humans change the

[68] Amartya Sen, *Poverty and Famines* (Oxford: Oxford University Press, 1981).
[69] George Marshall, 1947, quoted in *The Economist*, February 16, 2011, p. 16.
[70] Catherine Bertinni and Dan Glickman, "Bringing Agriculture Back to US Foreign Policy," *Foreign Affairs* 88, no. 2 (June 2009), pp. 93–105.
[71] "The 9 Billion People Question," *The Economist*, February 16, 2011.
[72] Thurow, "The Fertile Continent," p. 110.

environment, they often eliminate species that play vital protective roles. On the east coast of the United States, for example, economic development chased away predators such as foxes, wolves, and owls. White mice increased, and with them the larval ticks that spread Lyme disease among humans also proliferated.

Biodiversity refers to the great diversity of plant and animal species that make up the earth's ecosystems, defined in terms of variability in genes, species, and ecosystems.[73] It underpins a wide range of ecosystem processes on which people rely for their livelihoods and even survival. There is increasing awareness of the threats to biodiversity, but efforts to improve the situation are having little impact. The loss of plant and animal species is unrelenting.[74] More than 20 percent of 5,487 known mammals are threatened with extinction – mainly due to destruction of habitat, climate, and other changes. Of the 5 percent of plant species have even been evaluated, and "70 percent of these are threatened with extinction."[75]

There is a large element of human responsibility in this destruction. Whales and fish are a good example. Many species of whales are harvested to the point that they are critically endangered. The International Whaling Commission imposed a moratorium on commercial whaling in 1986, but more than forty-one thousand whales were killed in the next decade and a half. Japan, the Soviet Union, Norway, and Iceland, which objected to the moratorium,

killed about half of them for commercial profit. At least thirteen thousand more were destroyed for "scientific research." Aboriginal whale hunting took the rest.

Fish also are overexploited. A 2010 UK report studied eight thousand populations of 2,500 species and related them to studies of changes in land use and water consumption in all parts of the world. The authors found that species in temperate regions were doing well, because of improvements in conservation and pollution control. However, the situation has seriously deteriorated in tropical regions, with freshwater tropical species showing the greatest decline.[76]

Although the need for solutions is evident, it has been difficult to reach international agreement. In 1992, the **Convention on Biological Diversity** (CBD) was established at the Rio Earth Summit, and today has 193 members who attend twice-yearly meetings. The United States did not ratify the convention, however, and is not a member, as it fears that its patent rights in biotechnology might be limited.[77] The forum has contributed to limited successes in halting deforestation in the Amazon and promotes financial models for conservation. It also is working to prevent damage by genetically modified organisms, to develop a strategy for plant conservation, and to increase the area of protected nature reserves. International regimes to protect whales and dolphins have had less impact, largely because participation is voluntary and agreements are not binding. The conflicting goals and interests of environmentalists, individual states, and free-trade advocates make progress difficult and slow.

Are governments doing enough in this field? What would you propose?

[73] See Timothy M. Swanson, ed., *The Economics and Ecology of Biodiversity Decline: The Forces Driving Global Change* (Cambridge: Cambridge University Press, 1998).
[74] Wild Earth Guardians and the Center for Biological Diversity are strong advocacy groups that have filed more than one hundred lawsuits against the U.S. Interior Department concerning threats to about a thousand species since 2007. *The New York Times*, April 21, 2011, p. A3.
[75] *World Development Indicators, 2010*, p. 169.
[76] Zoological Society of London and WWF, *Living Planet Report*, p. 25.
[77] "Convention on Biological Diversity," *The Economist*, October 23, 2010, p. 18.

Global demographic issues

Demography, the study of population changes, their sources, and impact, reveals the human dimension of global politics. Population issues underlie many contemporary problems and environmental issues, including global warming. Simply put, people are the key resource, but the more of them the earth must sustain, the greater the pressures on the environment and society. Thomas Malthus warned as early as 1798 that population growth would outstrip the world's food supply one day.[78] His pessimism was still being echoed in the 1970s by influential voices, including Paul Ehrlich and the Club of Rome,[79] but although these pessimists recognized that wars, famine, and moral restraint would limit population growth, they missed key contrasting trends – mainly that technological changes would lead to dramatically increased food production that would relieve the urgency of the situation.

The 20th century had unprecedented population growth. Humankind almost quadrupled between 1900 and 2000, from about 1.6 billion people to around 6.1 billion.[80] This growth was largely due to advances in health care that more than doubled global life expectancy at birth. However, the peak of population growth was in the late 1960s, when the total was rising by almost 2 percent a year. Early in the 1970s fertility rates started dropping, and since then the population growth rate has fallen. The world population is still growing, and reached more than seven billion in 2011, but rather than increasing indefinitely, it is forecast to level off by the mid-21st century. The reasons for this change are changing fertility rates and rising prosperity.

Fertility rate refers to the average number of children a woman is likely to have during her childbearing years. The rate of population replacement – a sufficient increase for the number of global inhabitants to remain stable – is 2.1 births per female. In 2010 the global average fertility rate was 2.3. By about 2020, it is expected to dip below the global replacement rate of 2.1 for the first time. Although projections are uncertain, the earth's population is conservatively expected to peak at around nine billion by 2050. Although developing countries are lowering their fertility rates quickly, they already account for more than four-fifths of the world's population, and they will continue to produce most of the population rise (Figure 15.9). The population of developed countries will peak in 2020, and then, without immigrants, shrink over the following three decades. The number of people in the world will continue to rise even when fertility rates are falling, because in some places high fertility in earlier generations produced greater numbers of women of childbearing years, so more children will be born, even though each mother is having fewer children.

In most relatively wealthy industrialized capitalist countries, and in the region that constitutes the former Soviet Union and Eastern Europe, fertility rates have already fallen well below replacement levels.[81] Without immigration, these populations will shrink over time. The United States is a demographic exception – it is set to grow by 20 percent, from 310 million to 374 million, between 2010 and 2030. Until the 1990s, few developing countries had low fertility rates or rising incomes. By 2011, however, there will be dozens of developing countries in which family size is shrinking, including emerging giants such as Brazil, most of China, and parts of India.[82] Family

---

[78] Thomas Malthus, *Essay on the Principle of Population* (London: J. Johnson, 1798).

[79] Paul Ehrlich, *The Population Bomb* (New York: Buccaneer Books, 1968).

[80] Nicholas Eberstadt, "The Demographic Future: What Population Growth – and Decline – Means for the Global Economy," *Foreign Affairs* 88, no. 4 (November–December 2010), pp. 54–64.

[81] The fertility rate in the United States was 2.06 in 2011. The population grew 9.7 percent to 309 million in the decade leading up to 2011. Ethnic minorities accounted for 92 percent of growth.

[82] See "Falling Fertility," *The Economist*, October 31, 2009, pp. 15, 29–30.

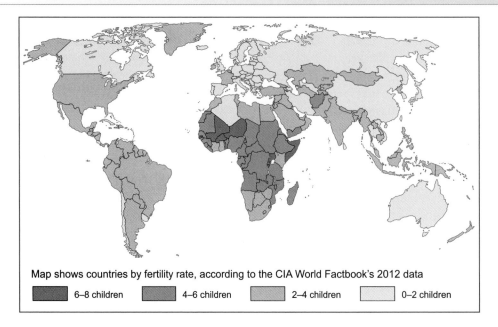

Map shows countries by fertility rate, according to the CIA World Factbook's 2012 data

■ 6–8 children	■ 4–6 children	■ 2–4 children	■ 0–2 children

Figure 15.9 Fertility by region.

size is falling as education and wealth improve. The speed with which fertility has fallen in these countries has been astonishing.

Are there already too many people for the world's fragile ecosystems to sustain? With the population growing, will demand on natural resources continue to increase? Already water tables are falling, glaciers are melting, soil is eroding, fish stocks are vanishing, and about one billion people go hungry every day. If, by 2050, there are two billion more mouths to feed, mostly in poor countries, how will the world cope? Aging and shifting populations complicate the matter.

Aging

The world is facing an old-age crisis. Aging has come in combination with fertility decline and a global increase in life expectancy. In 2010, humanity was evenly divided between those under and older than twenty-eight years of age. By mid-century, that median age will have risen to forty. The number of people older than sixty-five years of age is currently about 6 percent of the world total. It is expected to rise to 8.4 percent by 2015. However, the richest countries are aging most rapidly. Eighteen percent of their citizens will be older than sixty-five years of age at that time – a much higher proportion than in the developing countries. While the world faces an old-age crisis, much of the developing world is addressing a youth bulge. Their high youth populations are posing serious challenges to political stability. Rapid population growth and child-heavy populations go together, and this widens disparities of wealth among states because it drags down income per person. It becomes cyclical, so that states that do not have adequate incomes have greater population growth. When political systems in Egypt, Libya, Tunisia, and elsewhere in the Middle East and North Africa in 2011–12 could not provide employment and hope for a decent future for millions of young people, their frustration and despair helped trigger protests that toppled governments.

The challenge of how to deal with this demographic change is pressing. Aging populations affect workforce productivity, business psychology, and even capital flows. Countries with older populations are losing work to younger ones. A young labor force attracts global business and investors because costs are lower. This is currently the case in Latin America and Asia and particularly India. But the issue is circular. Younger workforces attract global investors and jobs, but as those young workers become urbanized and educated they have smaller families and the workforce ages. They get better health care and live longer. In other words, as Ted C. Fishman argues, globalization speeds up aging and aging speeds up globalization.[83]

The costs of keeping an aging population healthy and out of poverty is very high compared to a younger one. In developed countries, workforces are small and wages high. Older workers have particular skills, but they tend to be less educated and less healthy than younger ones. Employers are burdened with ever-expensive insurance to cover their aging workforces, and taxes are raised to pay for age-related public spending like pensions and health care. The rapid growth in pension expenditures in some European countries is a major factor in the debt crisis that rocked the euro zone from 2011 to 2012 and afterward. How can states enable seniors to maintain a decent standard of living without imposing crushing financial burdens on smaller, younger workforces? Governments are scrambling to prepare for the shift, but few are doing very well. According to a Global Aging Preparedness Index (GAP), which applies two separate subindexes – fiscal sustainability and income adequacy – in twenty selected countries, few countries score well on both indices.[84] All are struggling to maintain economic growth in

difficult economic times, and helping seniors is far down their list of priorities.

China is currently profiting from its population demographics. To achieve prosperity, it has encouraged hundreds of millions of young people to move into the cities and work in factories.[85] But China has entered what is being called the "4-2-1 problem," or one child having to care for two parents and four grandparents. By 2015, as wealthier Chinese workers have smaller families, the working population (younger than the age of sixty-five) will begin to shrink, and the number older than sixty-five will rapidly rise. The change will bring an abrupt end to China's cheap-labor manufacturing. With current trends, China will be older than the United States within a generation.[86] Chinese leaders express fear that the country will grow old before it grows rich, so it scrimps on providing pensions and health care, and supports jobs with short tenure and negligible benefits.

The fact that developing countries are growing more populous and younger while developed countries are getting less populous and older (with fewer consumers and workers) has huge implications for economic growth, the environment, and international security. The proportion of global GDP produced by Europe, the United States, and Canada dropped to 47 percent for the first time in 2003, and it is projected to fall much further by midcentury. There has already been a shift in economic activity from West to East. Not since 1800 has a majority of the world's economic growth occurred outside of Europe, the United States, and Canada. Never have so many people in those regions been older than

[83] Ted C. Fishman, "Graying Nations, Shifting Powers," *International Herald Tribune*, October 16–17, p. 10.

[84] According to the study by Richard Jackson, Neil Howe, and Keisuke Nakashima for the Center for Strategic and International Studies, two countries that were notable for their success in both areas were Australia and Chile. http://csis.org/publication/global-aging-preparedness-index.

[85] Foxconn, for example, is a giant Taiwan-based electronics manufacturer that builds components for Apple, Dell, and Hewlett-Packard. It has nearly 920,00 workers, nearly all of whom are younger than twenty-five, and it is still growing. Fishman, "Graying Nations, Shifting Power," p. 10. Also see Ted Fishman, *Shock of Gray: The Aging of the World's Population and How It Pits Young against Old, Child against Parent, Worker against Boss, Company against Rival, and Nation against Nation* (New York: Simon & Schuster, 2010).

[86] Richard Jackson, director of the Global Aging Initiative at the Center for Strategic and International Studies in Washington, referenced in Fishman, "Graying Nations, Shifting Powers."

Table 15.3 **Estimated percentage of population older than age sixty in selected countries, 2010 and 2050**

Country	2010	2050
Japan	30.5	41.5
France	23.0	30.5
United States	18.4	26.6
China	12.3	33.9
India	7.6	17.2

Source: Compiled from country profiles by the UN Department of Economic and Social Affairs, Population Division, World Population Prospects (medium fertility assumption), the 2010 revision. http://esa.un.org/unpd/wpp/unpp/Pa.

sixty years old. And never have low-income countries' populations been so young and urbanized.[87] Rapid urbanization in developing countries may be destabilizing, as countries with large, relatively young urban populations are especially prone to civil and political unrest. Some of them are ideal places for international terrorist networks to recruit followers and hide their networks. Demographic changes have also added to the pressure to restructure various global institutions such as the G8 into the G20 so that they include the world's fastest-growing and most economically dynamic countries.

Population shifts, refugees, and displaced people

Migration patterns reflect the inequality and volatility in the world.[88] Within states, migration from rural areas to cities is reaching record highs, with political and economic implications that are proving to have global significance. Half the world's population is now urban, and that will rise to 60 percent by 2030. About half the world's most *global cities* are in Asia.[89] These cities have influence over what happens beyond their borders, including integration with global markets, culture, and innovation. Some interpret the Asian migration from farms to cities as another indication that more "global clout" will move from West to East.[90] But the potential for growth in suffering is also growing on an epic scale, with the population of poor cities rising at the rate of sixty million people a year.

International population movements have increased dramatically in recent decades. In 2010 there were more than 43 million displaced persons and disaster victims around the world, of whom about 15.4 million were refugees.[91] People move across borders for many reasons: to flee poverty, persecution, and wars; to flee natural disasters; and to join extended families or study abroad. Most voluntary migration World War II has been for convenience. Movement has been from developing to developed countries, which has been economically beneficial to both recipient states and countries of origin, with low-cost labor benefiting the former and remittances that migrants send home benefiting the latter. Since 1996 remittances have been worth more than overseas development aid. In 2001, remittances to poor countries totaled US$372 billion. Most refugee migration in the same period has been within the developing world itself and has been to neighboring countries. Refugees fall into several categories, but they are all people who have sought refuge outside their own country – many from failed states (mostly in Africa and the Middle

---

[87] Jack A. Goldstone, "The New Population Bomb: The Four Megatrends That Will Change the World," *Foreign Affairs* 89, no. 1 (January–February 2010), p. 43.

[88] See Stephen Castles and Mark J. Miller, *The Age of Migration: International Population Movements in the Modern World*, 4th ed. (New York: Guilford Press, 2008).

[89] The 2010 Global Cities Index is a collaboration among *Foreign Policy*, the management consulting firm A. T. Kearney, and the Chicago Council on Global Affairs. Five of the world's ten most global cities were found to be in Asia and the Pacific: Tokyo, Hong Kong, Singapore, Sydney, and Seoul. Three – New York, Chicago, and Los Angeles – were in the United States. Only two, London and Paris, are in Europe.

[90] "The Global Cities Index," *Foreign Policy* (September–October 2010), p. 124.

[91] António Guterres, UN High Commissioner for Refugees, speaking to the Security Council, New York, January 8, 2009, said there were ninety million refugees that year. http://www.unhcr.org/admin/ADMIN/496625484.html.

East) whose governments cannot provide law and order (see Chapters 10 and 14).

The UN Convention on the Status of Refugees has been the basic underpinning of refugee law since 1951. Under the Refugee Convention (amended in 1967), a refugee is an individual who has a "well-founded fear of being persecuted for reasons of race, religion, nationality, membership of a particular social group or political opinions and has crossed borders." A person must meet the refugee standard before being granted asylum. Some refugees settle more or less permanently in another country on an informal basis, like the 1.1 million Afghans living outside formal refugee camps in Pakistan. Internally displaced people (IDPs), in contrast, are not technically refugees. They, too, have been forced from their homes, and for similar reasons, but they remain within their country's borders. Many of the world's nearly 26.5 million IDPs (as of 2013) receive no aid and live in desperate conditions without reliable access to food or clean water. Such conflict-caused displacements rose dramatically in the first decade of the 21st century.

The Refugee Convention therefore does not apply to the vast majority of individuals who are forced to flee their homes. The IDPs do not have legal protection because they have not crossed international borders. Neither do those who cross borders to escape natural disasters.[92] Some argue that the convention should be amended to cover all categories of refugees, but others claim that the treaty is already being misused by poor people who are merely seeking a better life. Some think that reopening the convention would cause countries to try to protect their borders rather than the refugees, and they do not want to lower current refugee protection standards. Richer countries are also accused of deflecting the refugee burden onto poor countries, which respond by turning away people who are legitimately refugees.

Migration can be expected to rise. A UN study calculated that in 2008 about twenty million people were displaced by climate change.[93] If global warming predictions are accurate, hundreds of millions of people may have to relocate. Rising sea levels threaten every continent.[94] Research indicates that the eco-migration "hot spots" will be river systems in Asia, dry parts of Africa, the interior and coast of Mexico and the Caribbean, and low islands in the Indian and Pacific Oceans.[95] Drought is also a prime mover of populations. In 2011 drought in the Horn of Africa created a massive famine and migrating population from Somalia to neighboring countries.

Famine is defined in technical terms as a condition in which 30 percent of children are severely malnourished, 20 percent of the population has no food, and deaths are at least two per ten thousand adults or four per ten thousand children every day. Under this definition, the UN estimates the number of people in Somalia subject to famine to be about 10.8 million.[96] As migrants and refugees increase, developed countries will find it much harder to isolate themselves from the deprivation and instability of the developing world (Figure 15.10).

Richer countries are often wary of accepting international migrants or refugees because they may establish ethnic minority diasporas that have an enduring effect on receiving countries. Despite the evident economic advantages that immigrants provide to aging populations, they can also threaten social cohesion and stability, particularly in times of economic difficulty, if they are seen as an economic burden and strain on the host population. Official government policies in support of "multiculturalism" often draw complaints from host populations

[92] Convention and Protocol Relating to the Status of Refugees, UN High Commissioner for Refugees, http://www.unhcr.org/protect/PROTECTION/3b66c2aa10.pdf.

[93] "Monitoring Disaster Displacement in the Context of Climate Change," UN Office for the Coordination of Humanitarian Affairs and Internal Displacement Monitoring Center, September 2009, p. 12.

[94] The Association of Small Island States (AOSIS) consists of forty-three island states that are at acute risk from climate change. They want developed countries to fund a new insurance scheme that would pay compensation for catastrophic loss to small states because of climate-related events.

[95] *The Economist*, June 27, 2009, p. 67.

[96] *The Economist*, July 30, 2011, p. 46.

Figure 15.10 In 2011, drought in the Horn of Africa created massive famine and migrating populations. If global warming predictions prove correct, droughts such as this will increase. *Source:* Corbis.

that their jobs and way of life are threatened when immigrants do not adapt to their new situation. Xenophobic backlashes against immigrants are common. In 2011 a young Norwegian bombed government buildings in Oslo and massacred at least seventy-six youth at a Labor Party summer camp. Before doing so he had posted a manifesto on the Internet depicting himself as a "Crusader" who would redeem Europe from invasion by Muslim hordes. He pled guilty and continued his "campaign" in the trials that followed in court.

Global health issues

Disease, like war, has been present since the dawn of humans. People's health is directly influenced by the environment in which they live. Clean water and basic sanitation are essential to prevent the transmission of life-threatening diseases that can spread quickly across land and oceans. Pollution is a cause of many serious illnesses. Violent conflict also kills and injures civilians, destroys infrastructure, and breaks down health systems. Global health issues involve circumstances and diseases that cause mass human suffering and death.

It was not until after World War II that health came to be widely viewed as a human right and international cooperation began to take place, particularly in combating communicable diseases. Later, in the post-Cold War shift away from military threats, health began to be regarded as a more diffuse threat that could affect security both at home and abroad, as well as international stability and economic growth. At the time, new infectious diseases were emerging, along with new strains of diseases resistant to existing drugs. HIV/AIDS was reaching pandemic proportions and was beginning to be viewed as a threat to national security and international stability.

Bioterrorism, or the use of biological weapons for purposes of terrorism, was also being raised as a threat. All of these developments were viewed as having potential to cause social disruption and state instability. Bioterrorism was particularly threatening. The Biological and Toxin Weapons Convention had addressed this issue as early as 1972. However, after the September 11, 2001, attacks in the United States, anthrax spores were found in American mail, and this focused attention anew on the possibility of a major terrorist attack using biological or chemical weapons. Public health and national security became firmly linked. In 2002 the U.S. Public Health Security and Bioterrorism Bill formally placed health in the purview of homeland security, and other countries followed the lead. The World Health Organization (WHO) advocated strengthened global surveillance measures, and the Global Outbreak Alert and Response Network were set up.

As significant as they are, these three issues – infectious diseases, HIV/AIDS, and bioterrorism – are only a small fraction of the health issues of the world. They focus very much on Western concerns and do not reflect the overall state of world health or the right of people from developing countries to the levels of health care in the West. The latter were recognized by the United Nations in the Millennium Development Goals (MDGs; see Chapter 13), as several of the objectives relate directly to health issues:

- Reduce child mortality by two-thirds between 1990 and 2015
- Improve maternal health by reducing maternal mortality by three-quarters between 1990 and 2015
- Encourage advances in reducing malnourishment
- Provide proper sanitation and clean water access to half of people in need by 2015, including half of those facing malnutrition
- Halt or reverse the spread of HIV/AIDS, malaria, and other diseases

Child and maternal health

Child and maternal health reflect the degree of development and social and economic well-being of a society. Many countries have made large gains in life expectancy in recent decades: a baby born almost anywhere today has a better chance to have a long life than at any time in history. However, that progress is very uneven. Less than 1 percent of child deaths occur in developed countries. Developing countries too have made absolute progress, but "huge health gaps remain, with eight times more infant deaths per 1,000 live births in developing countries than in developed countries."[97] A large part of progress in LDCs has been due to routine immunization against measles, but that success will be short lived if the international community cannot

[97] United Nations, *Human Development Report, 2010*, p. 32.

assure that measles-control activities continue (Figure 15.11). However, there are still countries with unacceptably high levels of child mortality in which little or no progress is being made. These are mostly in sub-Saharan Africa, where pneumonia, diarrhea, malaria, and HIV/AIDS account for nearly half of related child deaths.

The second Millennium Development Goal, improving maternal health, is also showing some progress. Maternal mortality refers to death resulting from complications of pregnancy or childbirth, most of which can be avoided. International agencies have accelerated provisions of maternal and productive health services to women in developing countries in all regions. Some countries have achieved significant declines in maternal mortality. However, the overall decline is still well short of the 5.5 percent annual decline needed to meet the MDG target. Maternal deaths are particularly numerous in South Asia and sub-Saharan Africa, where skilled care is often unavailable. More women are receiving prenatal care, but there are significant discrepancies in this practice between the wealthiest and poorest households even within developed countries. Poverty and lack of education correlate with high adolescent birth rates, which are particularly high in rural areas. Facilitating access to modern contraceptives for women who desire them could improve maternal health and reduce maternal deaths, but progress in expanding the use of contraceptives has slowed, and use is lowest in sub-Saharan Africa and Oceania, where they are needed most. Financial resources for family planning have not kept pace with demand there.

Clean water, sanitation, and malnutrition

Diseases caused by lack of clean water are estimated to contribute to at least 3.4 million deaths a year. Malnutrition is linked to low income and food scarcity. It causes sickness for approximately 850 million people a year, and most of these cases are associated with unclean water and inadequate sanitation. The UN made it a key Millennium Development Goal to provide proper sanitation and clean water access

Figure 15.11 The millennium development goals of the United Nations include efforts to reduce child mortality. Here, children receive immunization and health checkups at a clinic in Ethiopia. *Source:* Corbis.

to half of people in need by 2015, including half of people facing malnutrition. Sanitation is closely related to the issue of clean water. Unfortunately, it is generally a relatively low priority for domestic budgets. In low-human-development countries, 65 percent of people lack access to improved sanitation.[98] The practice of open defecation, particularly high among the rural poor and urban slum dwellers, is the most serious cause, because it enables transmission of diseases with symptoms such as diarrhea that are often lethal for children or lead to stunting and malnutrition. Slum improvements are not keeping pace with the number of slum dwellers, which is still growing in the developing world, particularly in conflict-affected countries. The only bright news is that the overall proportion of the urban population living in slums in the developing world is declining.

Local or small economies are unable to achieve economic progress and advance when workers are chronically too ill to work and participate in society. Poverty is both a source and an outcome of disease. People in extreme poverty are often unable to take

steps to prevent the further spread of disease – such as good nutrition or building water or sanitation infrastructure (see Chapter 13). Data from the MDG preliminary study show "encouraging advances in reducing the rate of malnourishment. But the absolute number of malnourished people – defined by minimal energy consumption – hardly budged from 850 million since 1980."[99] Diarrhea-related deaths among children have declined tremendously as a result of availability of oral rehydration salts. It has been estimated that basic health services cost about $40 per person per year. About one-third of the world's population cannot afford that, and the funds have to come from international organizations.

Contagious diseases

From the days of early traders, explorers, and colonists, people carried diseases such as smallpox, measles, and tuberculosis to foreign populations. Diseases that were originally European or Asian in origin killed great numbers of indigenous peoples as explorations and colonization proceeded. The wider the expanses that people traveled, the further

[98] United Nations, *Human Development Report, 2011* (New York: Palgrave Macmillan, 2011), p. 53.

[99] United Nations, *Human Development Report, 2010*, p. 35.

more deadly diseases such as smallpox, cholera, and malaria spread.

Vaccinations limited many of these early diseases in the 20th century after political leaders recognized the need for international cooperation in global health issues. International agreements developed acceptable procedures to prevent the spread of contagious and infection diseases. Conditions of quarantine were established. Progress was made in preventing the spread of diseases such as yellow fever and plague. In 1948, the UN set up the WHO as a specialized agency to deal with the eradication of malaria and smallpox. Considerable progress was made in developed areas. Advances were much slower in developing countries such as Pakistan, India, and much of Africa. In the global North people live longer and about four times fewer die of communicable diseases than in the global South.

Smallpox, which originated more than three thousand years ago in Egypt or India, killed more than three hundred million people in the 20th century alone, including many native inhabitants of the Americas. It was finally eradicated in 1977, thanks to a persistent campaign by the WHO. The last known case was in Somalia. Polio also has been brought under control thanks to immunization, although there was a resurgence in some areas of Africa and India in 2003, when religious authorities halted vaccinations there. Today, malaria is primarily a disease of developing countries, killing about two million people a year. It has been singled out as a target of the MDGs, and significant progress is being made through such simple measures as increasing global production and distribution of mosquito nets, improving access to antimalarial drugs, and increasing international funding for malaria control. Preliminary data from the UN reports show that more than a third of the 108 countries in which malaria exists documented a 50 percent reduction in malaria cases from 2000 to 2008.

Tuberculosis is a major cause of adult deaths from a single infectious agent in developing countries. It is the second leading killer after HIV/AIDS.

Its incidence fell to 139 cases per 100,000 in 2008, after peaking in 2004 at 143 in 100,000. Prevalence rates have fallen in all regions except in countries of the Commonwealth of Independent States in Central Asia. If current trends continue, the MDG target of reversing and halting the global incidence of tuberculosis will be reached, but global health experts are concerned because about 450,000 new cases of multiresistant tuberculosis are still appearing each year. The misuse or overuse of drugs along with the presence of counterfeit and substandard drugs have caused resistance to penicillin and other antibiotics to become costly and dangerous. Resistant "superbugs" such as methicillin-resistant staphylococcus aureus (MRSA) threaten lives, especially of children, the elderly, cancer patients, and the chronically ill, and the problem is growing. Gonorrhea is on the growing roster of diseases that are less susceptible to antibiotics. Use of antibiotics to fatten livestock and prevent infections from sweeping through crowded pens of animals is being questioned because it weakens the drugs' usefulness against diseases that plague people, but little concrete has yet been done to resolve this issue.

Tobacco does not cause infectious diseases, but it is worth noting because it is known to cause heart and other vascular diseases and cancers of the lungs and other organs. Developed countries have greatly restricted its use, so many tobacco companies have moved their operations to developing countries, where the potential for profits is huge. Since there is a long delay between starting to smoke and the onset of disease, the health impact of smoking is expected to rise dramatically in the next few decades in the developing world. The Framework Convention of Tobacco Control came into force in 2005, and parties to the agreement have agreed to take steps such as raising taxes on cigarettes and banning advertising, but the conflict with the tobacco industry and their partners is intense and ongoing.

HIV/AIDS

Another Millennium Development Goal is to halt and reverse the spread of HIV/AIDS. Acquired immune-deficiency syndrome (AIDS) is a virus that has become so widespread and dangerous that it rates alongside environmental and population issues as of immediate worldwide concern. The virus crossed from chimpanzees into humans when bush-meat hunters butchered them for human consumption. Human immune-deficiency virus (HIV) is the precursor and cause of AIDS. It damages the key cells of a body's immune system and makes it extremely vulnerable to normally preventable infections. HIV is transmitted by an exchange of bodily fluids through sexual contact, blood transfusion, shared intravenous needles, or open sores. Mothers can also transmit it to their unborn children. The highest rates of AIDS are found among drug abusers and people who do not practice safe sex (i.e., using a fluid barrier such as a condom).

HIV/AIDS is not only a medical and humanitarian issue but also an economic one, as people in their primary productive years are often rendered incapable of work. The UN Security Council identified the AIDS virus as a threat to global security some thirty years ago. By the end of 2000, more than twenty-seven million people were living with HIV, and only about two hundred thousand were receiving treatment. The rate of infections among UN peacekeepers was up to five times that of the general population. That year, the UN Security Council (Resolution 1308) identified HIV/AIDS as a security issue that poses a risk to stability, militaries, and peacekeepers.

Over the following decade dramatic progress was made in both treatment and funding. By 2008, 33.4 million people were living with HIV, but the number of new infections had dropped from a peak of 3.5 million in 1996 to 2.7 million.[100] The rate of infection is much higher in some parts of the world, especially in Africa. For example, 60 percent of all HIV infections are found in sub-Saharan Africa, and one-quarter of the people in Zimbabwe and Botswana are known to be infected. Globally, the spread of HIV infections appears to have peaked

in 1996 and stabilized in most regions, with more people surviving longer. It nonetheless remains the world's leading infectious killer.

Many intergovernmental organizations have entered the fight against AIDS. The WHO created AIDS programs as early as 1986 and has been active ever since, setting standards for levels of care and drug treatments. In 1996 the Joint UN Program on HIV/AIDS (UNAIDS) was established and began to coordinate projects among agencies such as the WHO, the World Bank, the UN International Children's Emergency Fund (UNICEF), and the UN Development Program, as well as with NGOs such as Cooperative for Assistance and Relief Everywhere (CARE) and Médecins sans Frontières, and with corporations such as multinational pharmaceutical companies and state governments. The UN also began calling a global AIDS conference every two years, and individual states have educated and distributed condoms and eventually facilitated drug distribution. Some countries, like Brazil and Uganda, moved quickly, while others such as South Africa, India, and China moved much more slowly, thus allowing the situation to deteriorate. It is difficult for the international community to intervene in AIDS issues if state governments are not in agreement.

As new antiretroviral drugs came on the market, their expense initially placed them out of reach of many people, particularly in developing countries. Near the turn of the 20th century pharmaceutical companies in India and Brazil began manufacturing inexpensive generics, and this triggered international disputes over intellectual property violations. NGOs led public campaigns against pharmaceutical companies, and in the end, the companies lowered prices in the developing world. In 2010, UNAIDS, the UN body charged with combating the epidemic, reported that the rate of new infections is falling fastest in many of the heaviest-infected countries in sub-Saharan Africa and South and Southeast Asia. The new drugs are making it harder for those who are infected to pass on the disease. What might slow down progress, once again, is funding. Currently, about $17 billion a year is being spent, but more

[100] *Millennium Development Goals Report*, 2010.

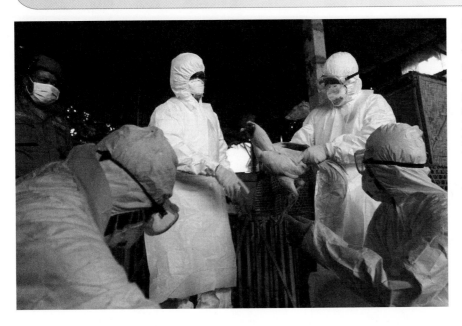

Figure 15.12 Avian flu (H5N1) is an influenza virus that requires constant international vigilance because of the possibility it will mutate and allow human to human transmission. Pandemics are high on the international crisis agenda. *Source:* Press Association.

like $25 billion is calculated to be needed to be fully effective.[101]

Pandemics: Death and international involvement

The most serious diseases for global health today are those that create pandemics. A pandemic is an epidemic of an infectious disease that spreads through human populations across a wide region, or even around the world. Microbes that present a risk of widespread disease usually emerge from animals – that is, they are zoonotic, transmitted from animals such as lice, rats, and monkeys to humans (plague and malaria, for example). Emerging diseases have become more numerous because humans are increasingly encroaching into wildlife habitats.

There have been a great many pandemics throughout history. Some of the earliest included various forms of the plague, including the bubonic plague (541–750 CE), which spread from Egypt to Europe, and the bubonic plague, which moved from Asia to Europe in the 14th century, and again from China to all inhabited continents in the mid-19th century. It is estimated that more than two hundred million people died worldwide in these pandemics.

There also were eight pandemics of cholera between 1816 and 2002, and several of influenza. The first recorded influenza pandemic was in 1580, and since then, Asiatic flu, Spanish flu, Avian flu, and Hong Kong flu have killed millions of people (Figure 15.12).[102]

The ability of diseases to cause pandemics varies because some require close personal contact, while others spread easily and quickly without human contact. Nobody can yet predict the ways in which a new virus will mutate or how virulent it may become, and this makes it difficult for health officials to give advice or make emergency plans. Viruses under surveillance today include bird flu (H5N1), mad cow disease, viral hemorrhagic fevers such as Ebola virus (a hemorrhagic fever), West Nile virus (a mosquito-borne illness from Africa spread in North America by birds), and the highly

[101] See "HIV's Slow Retreat," *The Economist*, November 27, 2010.

[102] Influenza viruses are grouped as A, B, or C. Influenza A and B viruses are of particular concern for human health. They are able to cause annual winter epidemics of varying scale and severity. Influenza A and B viruses alter gradually through a process of random mutation every few years, and when they do, this can result in a significant epidemic. Influenza A may also change abruptly, thus leading to a new subtype and causing a pandemic. Only influenza A has the ability to cause a pandemic.

contagious pneumonia called severe acute respiratory syndrome (or SARS). The growing incidence of such diseases is frightening and requires continuous international cooperation and action.

Abundant and fast modern means of transportation of tourists and businesspeople, human migrations, and refugees have made the spread of disease much quicker and harder to control than previously.

Close Up 15.3 **Pandemic pandemonium? Avian influenza timeline (H5N1)**

2004: Avian influenza virus is detected in birds in Vietnam, increasing fears of new variant strains of the virus that might be highly contagious and lethal in humans and able to cause a global influenza pandemic.

2005: Scientists urgently call on states to prepare for a global influenza pandemic that could strike as much as 20 percent of the world's population.

2005: Cases of the avian flu H5N1 are identified in Turkey, then Romania and Greece, with a direct relationship to viruses found in Russia, Mongolia, and China. More possible cases were found in Bulgaria, Croatia, and the United Kingdom.

2007: Numerous confirmed cases of H5N1 are identified across Europe, but relatively few people (about 330) died as a result of it. New outbreaks of the virus are closely monitored.

In the final analysis, avian flu was not categorized as a "pandemic," because the virus did not cause sustained human-to-human transmission. Cases so far have been transmitted from bird to human rather than proven human-to-human transmission. The threat of a mutation is ongoing. The new strain of bird flu that emerged in China in 2013 (H7N9) is considered one of the most lethal flu viruses to date.

Table 15.4 Influenza pandemics since 1900

1918	Spanish flu, a deadly strain of H1N1 virus infected 20–40 percent of the world population; 50 million died.
1957/58	Asian flu, H2N2, started in China and within six months spanned the globe; deaths exceeded 1 million.
1968/69	Hong Kong flu, H3N2, introduced in United States by troops returning from Vietnam; spread to Europe; 33,800 died.
2009/10	Swine flu, AH1N1, a new strain of H1N1 virus that caused the 1918 pandemic; began in Mexico and spread worldwide; about 8,870–18,300 died.

Source: U.S. Department of Health and Human Services, http://www.flu.gov/pandemichistory/index.html; WHO Disease Outbreak News, May 14, 2010.

In 2003 SARS was stopped only by rapid actions taken by the WHO, which slowed its transmission and broke the chain of infections. The scenario of avian influenza illustrates the need for constant international vigilance (see Close Up 15.3).

Many organizations, including the WHO, and individual countries are working to stop pandemics in their early stages. The Global Viral Forecasting Initiative is an organization that has recently set up virus monitoring stations in China, Laos, Madagascar, Malaysia, and the Democratic Republic of the Congo in an effort to capture viruses when they enter human populations.[103] More broadly, international regulations have been put in place to ensure the quality of pharmaceuticals and to reduce unhealthy practices such as diluting baby formula with impure water or using tobacco. The World Bank is the largest multilateral financier of health programs in developing countries. Besides UN organizations that work on global health issues, there also is considerable cooperation between major research institutes such as the U.S. Center

---

[103] Nathan Wolfe, "How to Prevent a Pandemic," *The New York Times*, April 30, 2009, p. A25.

for Disease Control and Prevention and the Pasteur Institute in France. Organizations such as the Bill and Melinda Gates Foundation donate billions of dollars to projects such as childhood immunization and better health-delivery systems. About $22 billion annually is devoted to international development assistance for health from various agencies. India receives the most external health funding, with about $1.6 billion from the World Bank and another $500 million annually from the Global Fund to Fight AIDS, Tuberculosis, and Malaria. This financial assistance is not without its critics. Some observers complain that budgetary priorities in India are misaligned. While collecting international financing for aid, India spent $40 billion on defense during the same period. This is not an aberration but a regular occurrence. China, the tenth-largest recipient of external health funding, officially spent $143 billion on defense in 2010. It also spent about $46 billion staging the 2008 Olympic Games and the 2009 Shanghai Expo. In 2011, the Global Fund – founded in 2002 as a pool for public and private donations and currently funding 150 countries – held back payments of an AIDS grant to China because of its mismanagement and the fact that it did not allow grassroots organizations to participate. Officials claimed that China was using the funds in other sectors and for "hard power."[104]

[104] *International Herald Tribune*, May 2–22, 2011, p. 5.

Conclusion: Thinking about global threats and solutions

Environmental, demographic, and health issues are all affected by globalization and the new human security issues. The world is becoming smaller as people travel more and are more interrelated and in closer communication. Population shifts and demographic changes are significant factors in global economics, migration, and politics. Diseases know no borders. A crisis in one country often affects other states and global institutions.

Our shared environment is deteriorating. The global commons – the air, land, water, and oceans that sustain life – are threatened by neglect and lack of a co-ordinated global vision and action. In seeking solutions, realists emphasize state security. They tend to base their arguments on concepts such as the state, power, sovereignty, and the balance of power among countries and to place environmental issues in the broad context of security. Liberals, with their view of an interdependent international system and a variety of international actors, are relatively optimistic as to the ability of international cooperation to solve natural resource and climate change issues. Constructivists share the idea of the need for international cooperation in the environment field. They focus on how political and scientific elites define the issues and how beliefs about them become embedded in normative systems. They are particularly interested in how environmental issues challenge state sovereignty. When radicals fit environmental arguments into the context of their theories, they argue that the developing countries, and poorer groups in the developed countries, are paying for the environmental misdeeds of the wealthy. For them, carbon reduction, for example, is about slowing capitalism and enabling less developed countries to catch up. Like adherents of other theoretical perspectives, most agree that scarcity of resources such as water or oil can lead to violence and war.

Conflicts over energy, water, land, climate change, and other environmental issues are topics of growing concern in global studies because of their propensity to contribute to violent conflicts, especially between developed and developing countries and among developing countries. Imagine, for example, a future scenario in which Pakistan, India, and China (all nuclear powers) are in conflict over shared but dwindling water, arable land, refugees, and fishing rights.

Global health initiatives are currently fragmented, uncoordinated, and inefficient. They are arranged around specific diseases. To reach the MDGs, some observers suggest a more integrated approach that focuses on health as a basic human right. National and international health funding and activities would be shifted "in the direction of basic survival needs, a traditional public health strategy essential to maintaining and restoring human capability and functioning."[105] Areas of activities would include sanitation and sewage, pest control, clean air, potable water, diet and nutrition, and tobacco and alcohol reduction. Not all health-care initiatives are expensive, and much can be done with little funding.

Since virtually everyone agrees that good health and curtailing the spread of disease are desirable, liberals, realists, constructivists, and radicals are in relative agreement on these issues. All would support international cooperation and sharing of information and advice. Disagreements may emerge when considering how to approach the issue and which institutions should handle it. Realists stress the responsibility of individual states in health issues, particularly when state security is threatened. Liberals focus initially on international responsibility and cooperation, and they seek the participation of state, substate, or nongovernmental organizations as needed. Radicals fit health issues into their wider framework of economic disparities between the developed and developing worlds, casting blame on capitalists and multinational corporations that they portray as more concerned with profits than humane objectives.

More generally, however, collective action requires international institutions to solve threats that arise in the global environment, population, and health. International agencies and individuals try to fill the void, but they are often too fragmented, uncoordinated, and inefficient. Globalization and the new security concerns are magnifying and highlighting the issues, but the will to solve them remains fitful and uninspiring.

---

[105] Devi Sridhar and Lawrence Gostin, "Millennium Development Goals: Health," Chatham House, *World Today* (August–September 2010), p. 28.

Select bibliography

Chatham House, *Public Opinion and Climate Change* (London: Chatham House, 2011).

Collier, Paul, *The Plundered Planet: How to Reconcile Prosperity with Nature* (London: Allen Lane, 2010).

Deffeyes, Kenneth S., *Hubbert's Peak: The Impending World Oil Shortage* (Princeton, NJ: Princeton University Press, 2001).

Diamond, Jared, *Collapse: How Societies Choose to Fail or Succeed* (New York: Penguin, 2005).

Fishman, Ted C., *Shock of Gray: The Aging of the World's Population and How It Pits Young against Old, Child against Parent, Worker against Boss, Company against Rival, and Nation against Nation* (New York: Simon & Schuster, 2010).

Friedman, Thomas L., *Hot, Flat and Crowded: Why the World Needs a Green Revolution – and How We Can Renew Our Global Future* (New York: Penguin, 2009).

Jacobs, Michael, *The Green Economy: Environment, Sustainable Development and the Politics of the Future* (London: Pluto Press, 1992).

Kalicki, Jan H., and David L. Goldwyn, eds., *Energy Security* (Washington, DC: Woodrow Wilson Center Press, 2005).

Klare, Michael T., *Blood and Oil: The Dangers and Consequences of America's Growing Dependency on Imported Petroleum* (New York: Metropolitan Books, 2004).

Lee, Kelley, *Globalization and Health* (Basingstoke, UK: Palgrave Macmillan, 2003).

O'Neill, Brian, F. Landis MacKellar, and Wolf Lutz, *Population and Climate Change* (Cambridge, Cambridge University Press, 2001).

Sandalow, David, *Freedom from Oil: How the Next President Can End the United States' Oil Addiction* (New York: McGraw-Hill, 2008).

Smith, Laurence C. *The New North, Our World in 2050* (New York: Dutton, 2010).

Solomon, Stephen, *Water: The Epic Struggle for Wealth, Power and Civilization* (New York: HarperCollins, 2010).

Stern, Nicholas, *The Global Deal: Climate Change and the Creation of a New Era of Progress and Prosperity* (New York: Public Affairs, 2009).

United Nations, *Human Development Report 2011* (New York: Oxford University Press, 2011).

Yergin, Daniel, *The Prize: The Epic Quest for Oil, Money and Power* (New York: Simon & Schuster, 2008).
The Quest: Energy, Security, and the Remaking of the Modern World (New York: Penguin Press, 2011).

Crises and ethics in global politics

Global politics is replete with crises. As we conclude our survey, it is clear that understanding and debating this theme is an essential part of our study of international relations. In Chapter 1, we introduced globalization and the new security issues and factors that drive modern world politics and showed how they affect governments. In the next 14 chapters we analyzed how individuals, states, and international organizations cope with these factors.

Myriad unexpected, horrific events occur intermittently around the world, creating crises that quickly move to the top of global policy agendas. They regularly force politicians and decision makers to appraise and judge which principles should guide their responses and to grapple with difficult conceptual, ethical, and policy issues.

Crises and contingencies

As we witnessed in the first fifteen chapters of this book, dangerous events are ubiquitous; we truly live in a world of risk. We see this in daily news reports, where various types of crises make up the bulk of daily headlines. At the individual level, the crises range from the tragic to the absurd, as almost any event can be a crisis for someone. At the state level, crises arise continually in the form of natural disasters, such as floods, hurricanes, and earthquakes, as well as human-made disasters such as mining accidents and even nuclear accidents. At the global level, crises also are perpetual, ranging from saber rattling among states to shared issues such as health pandemics and internal and interstate war. Television and the Internet relay a constant stream of horrifying pictures about massacres, earthquakes, hurricanes, and famines. The pool of events is seemingly endless. Indeed, a startling phenomenon of modern global politics is how many contemporary crises span state

borders and sometimes even continents. It is the complexity and multiplicity of such crises that is the greatest challenge.

The speed of globalization has given rise to novel crises based on the interconnectedness of the world and its growing reliance on new technologies. A good example is the 1984 chemical spill at an American-owned plant in Bhopal, India, which killed three thousand people immediately and thousands more later from toxic gases. A plant owned by citizens of one country killed citizens of another. Compound crises such as the 2011 earthquake, tsunami, and nuclear power explosion in Japan include a combination of financial, environmental, health, and ethical issues (Figure 16.1). Future transnational crises undoubtedly will include ecological destruction and mass migration, events that will have serious implications for international health, economic, and social well-being. New security issues often help create their own unique crisis atmosphere. The mere threat of a terrorist event on

Figure 16.1 In 2011, a massive earthquake hit the east coast of Japan followed by a giant tsunami. The combined effects severely damaged Fukushima's nuclear reactors, causing a massive crisis, and complete towns and villages were washed out to sea. *Source:* Alamy.

the tenth anniversary of 9/11 put U.S. officials into high response mode, warning Americans to be on the watch for an attack – which never occurred.

Cynics may caution that including so many types of events in our analysis we are trying to understand the "impossible." But a comprehensive approach is required to respond satisfactorily to contemporary crises. A modest portrayal of global politics, however, needs to project the fact that even though knowledge about the world is increasing, there may be no ideal solutions to many global problems. In this chapter we use a broad-brush approach to generalize about the detailed crises of global politics that inevitably create what U.S. philosopher and psychologist William James called "bloomin' buzzin' confusion."[1] Nuclear war and disaster management have been studied for generations, but today international terrorism, global health pandemics, earthquakes, floods, hurricanes, volcanic eruptions, and even wildfires are among the crises to be understood and managed across state borders. Globalization and the new security issues ensure that new waves of crises will be inter-

national in scope, and mass media will transmit and fan emotions about them around the world.

In the new landscape of shared crises and contingencies, the sometimes-naive public expects leaders to be able to handle all the old and new transnational issues with near perfection. But while governments can improve their responses, they cannot be prepared for all eventualities in advance. All countries are to some extent vulnerable to random disasters, hazards, and human-made calamities.[2] Governments must learn to prioritize crises and determine what political, organizational, and financial capital they can and should spend preparing to manage them. Not all risks can be eliminated without doing more harm than good. Terrorism has had great saliency in political circles since 9/11, but it is neither rare nor likely to disappear. Like the seasonal flu, it can never be wiped out completely. Perhaps new strains of terrorism can be kept in check by careful preparation and monitoring, but there will always be dissatisfied and dangerous people, and terrorism

[1] *The Economist*, January 3, 2009.

[2] Uncertainty presents the challenges of dealing with unforeseen threats and yet still solving problems. See G. Bammer and Michael Smithson, eds., *Uncertainty and Risk: Multidisciplinary Perspectives* (London: Earthscan, 2008).

is merely one of many ways those people can vent their frustrations in free and open societies.

The situation is analogous to an old Russian joke about the difference between an optimist and a pessimist: The optimist says, "Things are so bad, they couldn't possibly be worse." The pessimist says, "No. They could be worse."

Definitions of crises

Policy makers need theories with which to assess crises, but their efforts quickly give way to details of circumstance, stress, and trauma that make particular events appear unique and incomparable. Yet if one is going to learn from the unpleasant, unscheduled events that are called crises in politics and international relations, then some order must be imposed on them. The Concise Oxford Dictionary defines crises as "turning-points" or "times of danger or suspense in politics." The root is the Greek word *krisis*, which encompasses multiple ideas, such as separation, distinguishing, decision, choice, judgment, and dispute. It refers to crucial or decisive periods or unstable situations. In politics, a crisis is often seen as a situation that can either quickly improve or take a dramatic turn for the worse. However, the universe of crises is not limited, and there is no definition that meets the philosopher's condition of "if, and only if," so that one can know exactly what exactly is and is not a crisis.

Clearly, a crisis is difficult to define. A sociologist may call a crisis "a large and unfavorable change in the inputs of some social system."[3] Disaster experts may call it "an event, concentrated in time and space, in which a society or a relatively self-sufficient sub-division of society undergoes severe danger and incurs such losses to its members and physical appurtenances that the social structure is disrupted and the fulfillment of all or some of the essential functions of society is not provided."[4] The classic definition in international relations has

been that of C. F. Hermann, who describes a crisis as a situation "that (1) threatens the high-priority goals of the decision-making unit; (2) restricts the amount of time available before the situation is transformed; and (3) surprises the members of the decision-making unit when it occurs."[5]

Some contemporary international relations writers have reduced the definition of crises so that it applies only to situations that may lead to war. They regard a crisis as something to be managed in order to avoid warfare. For them, a crisis is "a situation in which the threat of escalation to warfare is high and the time available for making decisions and reaching compromised solutions in negotiations is compressed."[6] World Wars I and II are often used as examples of wars that could perhaps have been avoided with better crisis management. The Cuban Missile Crisis is depicted as a success from such a crisis management perspective, as war was avoided. Unfortunately, this definition of crisis is not adequate for studies of modern global politics, as the word *crisis* would not be applicable to such events as climate change, genocide, or even terrorism.

What do crises have in common? To reduce the number of crises in global politics to a manageable level, perhaps Kenneth Hewitt's 1983 classic requirement of "un-ness" is useful. In his approach, crises are unscheduled, unexpected, unplanned, unpleasant, and sometimes unimaginable and unmanageable.[7] Another similar approach is that of Paul C. Nutt, who declared that crisis management is about making tough decisions during periods of uncertainties, ambiguities, and risks.[8] Neither of these approaches restricts the subject to warfare.

A crisis also always includes a subjective element – an event is not a crisis unless it is labeled as

[3] A. H. Barton, *Social Organization under Stress: A Sociological Review of Disaster Studies* (Washington, DC: NAS-NRC, 1963).

[4] C. E. Fritz, "Disaster," in *Contemporary Social Problems*, ed. R. K. Merton and R. Nesbit (New York: Harcourt, Brace and World, 1971).

[5] Charles Hermann, *Crises in Foreign Policy* (Indianapolis, IN: Bobbs-Merrill, 1969), p. 29.

[6] Charles W. Kegley and Shannon L. Blanton, *World Politics: Trend and Transformation* (Boston: Wadsworth, 2010–11), p. 346.

[7] Kenneth Hewitt, ed., *Interpretations of Calamity: From the Viewpoint of Human Ecology* (London: Allen & Unwin, 1983), p. 10.

[8] Paul C. Nutt, *Making Tough Decisions: Tactics for Improving Managerial Decision-Making* (London: Jossey-Bass, 1989).

one. If no alarm is raised about a threat to some core values or vital parts of a political system, there is no political crisis. This is a major reason that ideas of rationality and efficiency may be overdone in discussions of crisis management.[9] Crises also ebb and flow in significance. Events interpreted as crises at one time may become less urgent another day, perhaps even becoming routine in another location or time period. At one time airplane hijacking was considered a crisis in the Western world, then the topic slipped away from the public agenda for some time, only to reemerge with the horrific events of 9/11. Moreover, what is seen as a crisis by some people may prove an opportunity for others. A city blackout may be a crisis for ordinary people but an opportunity for criminals. It may even be seen by clever police officers as an opportunity for professional advancement. The compound Chinese word for crisis may be helpful here, as *wei-chi* indicates that a crisis always includes both dangers and opportunities.

This definitional problem is the fundamental reason why measurement of the degree or level of a crisis situation is impossible, perhaps even meaningless. Different situations invoke different definitions and perceptions of the same set of events. In that sense social constructivism adds to our understanding of the various interpretations of crises, while perhaps narrow realism may not. The relative urgency and importance of competing demands about crises requires an understanding of societal and state norms and rules.

The literature on crises in global politics includes the three traditional ideas of threat, uncertainty, and urgency of response.[10]

1. Threat: The event or situation must threaten an important subject for which governments take some responsibility.[11] In practical terms this means external challenges to sovereignty and national interests, such as war or breakdown of law and order and extreme loss of life or property. The threat of death, damage, and destruction from war; from natural disasters such as earthquakes, floods, hurricanes, and fires; and from human-made disasters such as climate change and nuclear explosions are clearly crises as far as politicians, senior policy makers, and the public are concerned.

2. Uncertainty: Crises emerge from unusual events for which governments take some responsibility. The trigger to a crisis may be relatively unexpected. The Japanese attack on Pearl Harbor in World War II and the 9/11 attacks on New York and Washington, DC, are examples. There were clues that Japan might retaliate against U.S. foreign policy because of energy issues, but few thought this would lead to a full-scale attack on Pearl Harbor. Similarly, there were consistent warnings from al-Qaeda that it would punish the United States for involvement in Middle East affairs, but few anticipated the 2001 attack. Sometimes efforts to solve such uncertainties increase the danger. For example, see Close Up 16.1.

3. Urgency of response: A crisis offers what policy makers consider a limited amount of time to respond. However, the time for decision making cannot be taken as an absolute, and crises are usually depicted as a process rather than a single static event and reaction. President George W. Bush may have reacted too slowly to Hurricane Katrina, but that cannot be said about his reaction to 9/11, however much one may disagree with his strategy in each case. The element of surprise is included in most crises, but its inclusion as part of the definitional requirements presents difficulties. In recent years, practitioners and scholars have begun to call even well-known or unsurprising situations crises. Chapters 12 and 13 described, for example, long, drawn-out

[9] Deborah Stone, *Policy Paradox: The Art of Political Decision-Making* (New York: Norton, 2002).

[10] Uri Rosenthal, M. T. Charles, and P. 'T Hart, eds., *Coping with Crises: The Management of Disasters, Riots and Terrorism* (Springfield IL: Charles C. Thomas, 1989).

[11] Of course, in reality many organizations besides governments are involved in crisis handling. Sometimes the state causes the crisis in the first place. But this chapter is concerned only with the role of states and intergovernmental organizations in handling crises in global politics. International corporations and NGOs play important roles in international crises too.

financial crises and their impacts on the global economy. Chapter 14 dealt with enduring social crises, such as the abuse of women, use of child soldiers, and genocide, while Chapter 15 examined slow-moving or creeping crises, such as climate change, desertification, and deforestation.

Sorting out such definitional issues about crises is bound to be political and controversial. Molding and exploiting crisis language is a large part of the rhetoric of domestic and international politics. Indeed, crisis hype has become a big business – see the labeling and framing issues discussed later in this chapter. Disasters, emergencies, and crises can be used by government officials or opposition members to strengthen and defend their policy positions. In democratic countries this is part of the drama of politics, used to win public acceptance and perhaps votes. Definition and molding of language to frame issues is indeed part of "blame management" in the political battlefront.[12]

Close Up 16.1 **Complex emergency in Haiti**

Haiti is one of the poorest, least developed countries in the world. Its island landscape, barren and eroded because of deforestation and poor farming techniques, provides its people with a woefully inadequate domestic food supply and a vulnerability to hurricanes and other natural disasters (Figure 16.2). The country has a long history of corruption and political instability, and in recent decades it has alternated between civilian and military regimes. The United Nations has spent about US$5 billion on peacekeeping operations to maintain stability there since the United Nations Stabilization Mission in Haiti (MINUSTAH) was established in 2004.

In January 2010 an earthquake shook the densely populated capital of Port-au-Prince,

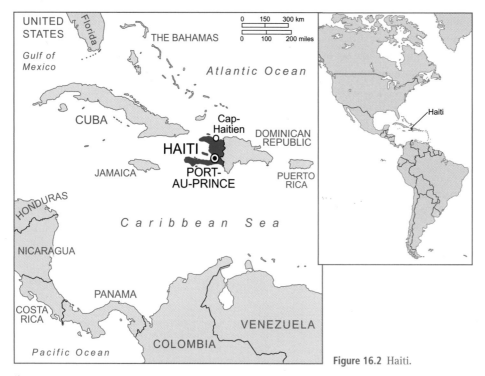

Figure 16.2 Haiti.

---

[12] James A. Robinson's distinction of the "most crisis-like situations" has not resolved this issue, as no empirical cutoff points have yet been determined that can delineate which events are the most crisis-like. James A. Robinson, "The Concept of Crisis in Decision-Making," in *Readings in the International Political System*, ed. N. Rosenbaum (Englewood Cliffs, NJ: Prentice Hall, 1970).

flattening its poorly constructed buildings and shanties. About 250,000 people died, including 96 UN peacekeepers. The government was overwhelmed. International aid flowed in, and the UN force was augmented to 9,000 peacekeepers to support reconstruction and stability. By that spring, however, there had been little progress in reconstruction, crime was rampant, and in the overflowing refugee camps Haitians were raising bitter complaints about the politically connected leaders who were benefiting from the reconstruction projects. There were also numerous Hatian accusations of rape and sexual assault by peacekeepers. The only thing that seemed to have worked was that in spite of a chronic lack of access to clean water and sanitation, disease had not broken out over the hot summer.

In October 2010, however, while a huge international mobilization was still dealing with the effects of the earthquake, cholera broke out in the country. The Haitian government, UN agencies, and the humanitarian community struggled to coordinate a response, building treatment centers and providing water-purification materials and public information. Despite these efforts, the disease spread wildly, killing more than 7,050 Haitians and sickening more than 531,000. It erupted into the world's largest cholera epidemic.

Epidemiological and genome studies indicated that UN peacekeepers almost certainly ignited the epidemic, but the UN was not willing to acknowledge that responsability. Evidence pointed to a UN contingent from Nepal for contaminating the river tributary beside its base in Mirebalais through a faulty sanitation system that poured into the water that Haitians used to drink, bathe, and do laundry. Haphazard piping at the base also showed "significant potential for cross-contamination" between showers and toilets.[13]

In this case, international assistance in a crisis situation actually caused a second disaster. UN aid to Haiti continues, but a cholera vaccination program has protected only a tiny fraction of the population. At the height of the crisis, many states pledged billions of dollars to the country, but much of it has not materialized. Three years after the earthquake and despite billions of dollars in reconstruction, adequate water and sanitation systems are still lacking. Meanwhile, studies indicate that the cholera is evolving into two strains, which suggests that it will be hard to eradicate and that people could get it a second time. Current projections indicate that 200,000 to 250,000 more people could succumb to the disease.

Substance of crises and crisis management

There is virtually a limitless supply of global situations that could cause massive social disruption, environmental degradation, and the collapse of states themselves. Widespread diseases and natural disasters all have the potential to cause, crises. Natural occurring crises such as earthquakes or human-inspired events are always possibilities for officials to have to contend with. Global economics, technology, weaponry, and communications are changing the nature of all crises, and globalization and the new security challenge mean that crises often have no borders. Modern transportation, energy, financial, chemical, food, and even Internet networks are all vulnerable. The global crisis possibilities listed in Table 16.1 are only some of the cases discussed throughout this book.

When events such as these occur, governments rush into action. Paul 'T Hart and Karen Tindall summarize the policy makers responses to unexpected events with the following questions:

- How bad is the situation?
- How did this occur?

[13] *The New York Times*, editorial, April 3, 2012.

Table 16.1 **Global crisis nightmares**

1. Nuclear bomb detonation (Chapters 9, 10, 11)

2. Nuclear power plant explosion (Chapters 11, 15)

3. Radiological attack (Chapters 10, 11)

4. Traditional explosive attack or accident (Chapters 9, 10)

5. Natural disasters – earthquake, hurricane, flood (Chapter 15)

6. Biological attack or outbreak – anthrax attack, disease outbreak (e.g., flu, pneumatic plague, as well as food and mouth disease), food contamination and pandemics (Chapters 9, 11, 15)

7. Chemical attack or accident – blister agent, toxic industrial chemicals, nerve agent, chlorine tank explosion (Chapter 11)

8. Cyberattack – cyberterrorism, cybercrime, cyberwarfare (Chapters 7, 11)

9. Environmental catastrophes, including climate change (Chapter 15)

10. Natural resource depletion (Chapter 15)

11. Mass migrations (Chapters 10, 15)

12. Hazards in medical technology and genetic manipulation (Chapter 15)

13. Genocide (Chapter 14)

14. Famine (Chapters 14, 15)

15. Global poverty (Chapter 14)

16. Nuclear war (Chapters 4, 9)

17. Collapsing states and internal wars (Chapters 10, 11)

18. Financial and debt crises (Chapters 12, 13)

19. Children and women's abuse (Chapter 14)

- Who are what is to be held accountable for it?
- What, if any, changes to our current ideas, policies, and practices are required to deal with it?[14]

The answers to these questions will come in many forms, as a crisis may follow a fairly precise, orderly pattern that is logical and subject to routine management, or it may be unimaginable and seemingly unamenable to analysis or solution.[15] The former type is more prone to scientific analysis, but even the contingent or seemingly irrational crises can be studied and the findings made useful for future crisis management. Probably the most standard approach to managing crises is to examine them in four relatively discrete stages:

1. Mitigation and prevention
2. Preparation and planning
3. Response
4. Rehabilitation and recovery

If all crises were preventable, they would be prevented (or so the gullible imagine). If prevention could be perfected, all dams would be high enough and solid enough to prevent the worst cases of flooding. Nuclear reactors, aircraft, trains, and other forms of transportation would be totally invulnerable. Oil spills would never happen. Hazards and risks would be predicted, and crisis management organizations would create accident-free environments. But despite all efforts at mitigation and prevention, calamities continue to occur. Perfection can never be achieved. While the mitigation and prevention phase is crucial in crisis management, plans cannot be in place for every conceivable possibility, as this would require an infinite variety of responses – a practical impossibility.

In reality, plans are and must be made for the most predictable crises, and some of them are easier to predict than others. For example, detailed

---

[14] Paul 'T Hart and Karen Tindall, eds., *Framing the Global Economic Turndown: Crisis Rhetoric and the Politics of Recessions* (Canberra: Australian National University Press, 2009).

[15] Rosenthal, Charles, and 'T Hart, *Coping with Crises.*

plans may be drawn up for managing recurrent floods and hurricanes, but at this time less precision can be achieved about tsunamis or aberrant nuclear reactor breakdowns. This means that planners may devote more attention to some types of crises than others, stressing resilience, or the ability to recover after a crisis, rather than prevention. Stephen Flynn, for example, shows how the United States can both reduce its vulnerabilities and increase its capacity to respond to crises after they occur.[16]

Crisis managers try to include both worst-case and best-case scenarios in their calculations. This is a particularly difficult task when dealing with high-impact, low-probability events. Preparations to respond are based on past historical experiences and include both routine methods of response and elements of flexibility because of the contingent nature of events. The ability to cope or rebound from crises with sufficient resolve is the motto of most security institutions today. A good example of the stress on resilience is California's program National Earthquake Preparedness Month, which teaches the public what to do after an earthquake. Critical Case Study 16.1 illustrates the complex mix of prevention and resilience in the 2011 earthquake and tsunami in Japan and their inadequacies.

Critical Case Study 16.1 **Complex crisis: Earthquake, tsunami, and nuclear power in Japan**

On March 11, 2011, a massive earthquake in Japan moved its territory about 2.4 meters, shifting the Earth on its axis and shortening the length of a day by a tiny fraction. Parts of eastern Japan moved as much as 3.65 meters closer to North America, and downward about 60 centimeters. The giant quake was one of the world's largest ever, measuring 9.0 points on the Richter scale. It took place in the Pacific Ring of Fire, a volatile, horseshoe-shaped area of fault lines that runs forty thousand kilometers through New Zealand, Samoa, Philippines, Japan, across to Alaska and down the entire coast of North and South America, an active area of constantly shifting, interconnecting tectonic plates.

When the clash of tectonic plates severed the seafloor, it caused a rupture about five hundred kilometers long and an uplift that produced a giant tsunami (a series of long, high waves). A wave more than thirteen meters high hit the northeastern coast of Japan. The combined impact of the earthquake and tsunami was many times greater than the Japanese nuclear industry's crisis disaster plan had envisaged. The Fukushima nuclear power reactors, directly in the line of the tsunami, were inundated, and a nuclear catastrophe ensued. Hydrogen explosions and fires released radioactive material into the atmosphere. Fuel rods were exposed, releasing large amounts of radiation into the air and eventually the ocean.

The main damage to Japan came from the tsunami rather than the earthquake. Human error was involved. Fukushima was a relatively old facility, and the generators had been installed at sea level. Once they were flooded, it was not possible to keep water circulating to cool the rods, and workers had

---

[16] According to Stephen Flynn, this concept of resilience came from Yossi Sheffi, a professor of engineering, who wanted to depict how material can "recover its original shape following a deformation." For an excellent overview of this topic, see Stephen Flynn, *The Edge of Disaster* (New York: Random House, 2007), p. xxi. Another exponent of this concept is David Ormand in the United Kingdom. See his volume *Securing the State* (New York: Columbia University Press, 2010).

to use improvised pumps and seawater to try to keep them cool enough. But there were many other crisis management failures, including the proximity of four reactors built so close together that a fire or explosion in one affected the others.

The nuclear industry in Japan is run by a large, private company (Tokyo Electric Power Co., or TEPCO), not the government. After the event, its leaders were severely criticized for many things: not adequately preparing for a worst-case scenario, a culture of collusion that put a higher priority on promoting nuclear energy than on protecting public safety (Japan's regulators are not nuclear specialists – they rely for expertise on the companies they monitor), lack of transparency, mismanagement, and lying about the severity of the problem. The public was given little information about contamination levels, and the lack of reliable information fed fear at home and abroad. Roads were gridlocked, railway stations and airports jammed, and evacuation centers quickly overcrowded. Radiation seeped into the food supply. Tap water turned up low amounts of radioactive iodine as far away as Tokyo. There was a run on iodine tablets. Uncertainty over the extent of nuclear fallout caused panic selling in global stock markets.

To try to manage the crisis, the Japanese government set a twenty-kilometer exclusion zone around the nuclear complex and then extended it to include a no-fly zone. International experts speculated that this action was not enough, and they complained that Japan was underplaying the severity of the contamination and not providing information to outside nuclear regulators. It took months for the government to admit that villages outside a thirty-kilometer radius had also been affected. About nine months after the event, it was revealed that one reactor core had likely burned through its containment chamber, then bored more than two meters into the concrete base of the containment vessel. This was much closer to a catastrophic meltdown than previously indicated.

The confusion greatly hampered rescue efforts for victims of the earthquake and tsunami. Food and drinking water were scarce, and emergency aid could not get through to where it was needed. In the end, more than ten thousand people died in the event, and much valuable agricultural land was contaminated. However, as in the Chernobyl and Three Mile Island nuclear crises, only a small handful of deaths were directly attributable to the nuclear accident. The fear factor damaged public faith in the nuclear industry not just in Japan but in countries around the world. Japan opened itself to international scrutiny, hoping to regain public trust, and most of the country's reactors were taken off-line. Investigations have concluded that new reactors could have withstood even this rare earthquake and tsunami disaster and can be made even safer in the future. A 2012 report concluded that TEPCO had avoided implementing some safety measures for the nuclear plant through fear of spurring lawsuits, protest, or plant closure. It also said TEPCO's accident response plan was poor, and employee training on how to respond to an accident was inadequate.[17]

The cleanup effort is ongoing. The government has proposed three years to clean up the melted fuel in Fukushima Daiichi's damaged reactors, but experts warn that it may take much longer. Radiated water was still leaking into the ocean in late 2012, and a pool "brimming with used fuel rods and filled with vast quantities of radioactive cesium still sits on the top floor of a heavily damaged reactor building, covered only with plastic."[18] The government has said that the cleanup needs to include the removal of

[17] *The Wall Street Journal*, Oct. 13–14, 2012, p. A6.
[18] *The New York Times*, May 27, 2012, p. 9.

about 2,419 square kilometers of contaminated soil, the pressure hosing of houses in urban areas, and removal of all dead leaves from forests that were radiated. So far nobody knows where the contaminated material will be dumped. Much more is to be learned about steps that should be taken in handling a crisis of this type and magnitude.

Regulators in other countries are taking low-probability, high-consequence events like this one under consideration in their own countries. In the United States, for example, ninety-six reactors have been built in the central and eastern parts of the country but only eight in the West, which is more geologically active. However, new research has revealed that nearly 3,300 earthquakes have taken place in the central and eastern United States since 1568, which makes the risk for all these reactors much higher than previously anticipated.[19]

Could the crisis in Japan have been better handled? Can governments adequately prepare for every type of crisis having to do with earthquakes, hurricanes, floods, and nuclear reactors, or is that just a pipe dream?

Dynamics of crises

The timing and sequence of government or international response to a crisis are vital. While the context and nature of a crisis are unique to some extent, all crises share similar properties. All of them alter the status quo or normal circumstances to some extent. Some are more predictable than others. States and international organizations are continually monitoring, evaluating, and forecasting situations that may break from the routine and become a crisis. Conceptually, such information can provide simple forewarning (as in preparing for an "overdue" earthquake in California) or more detailed forecasts that include projections of time, frequency, location, scope, intensity, and duration of the predicted event (as in "a hurricane will arrive at New York on Saturday, August 27, 2013, with wind force of a hundred miles an hour that will last thirteen minutes"). The choice of how to respond will normally prove easier the more precise the prediction is.[20]

Perfect prediction of crises is not possible, and yet planning for them is essential. This is partially why crisis management analysts often prefer the word "risk" for events rather than "threat" as the former seems to describe degrees of possibility and therefore predictability. However, although plans cannot be drawn up for every conceivable future event, the most likely occurrences do need to be identified, and on the whole, the greater the degree of predictability of a crisis, the greater is the chance that it will be resolved satisfactorily. Planning for crises and contingencies is important, and it is not surprising that governments and international institutions prepare different scenarios as the cornerstone of their crisis management strategies. Unfortunately, since prediction of crises is an unpredictable art, forecasting is always inexact and plans for them are also questionable.

In theory, predictions are fine, as long as they are not applied to the future or are not remembered when events prove them faulty! Here are a few notorious but not-so-enlightening predictions that have been made by top professionals in their field:

- Heavier than air flying machines are impossible.
- There is not the slightest indication that nuclear energy will ever be attainable.

[19] "New Risks at Nuclear Plants," *The Wall Street Journal*, February 1, 2012, A3.

[20] E. L. Quarantelli, "The Future Is Not the Past Repeated: Projecting Disasters in the 21st Century from Current Trends," *Journal of Contingencies and Crisis Management* 4, no. 4 (1996), pp. 228–40.

- There is a world market for about five computers.
- Stock prices have reached what looks like a permanently high plateau (just before the stock market crash of 1928).

Much that is unpredictable and unpredicted can and will happen, and governments and other organizations must be prepared for all eventualities.

Politicians, state officials, and publics need to be able to distinguish among the number, variety, and magnitude of crises and to recognize the gap between naive idealism and practically possible responses to these events. Of course, top government decision makers include people who understand the need to reconcile the myriad contradictions found in politics, diplomacy, and war, but when an event happens suddenly and by chance, even the most experienced policy maker has difficulty judging its importance and formulating possible responses. The simple rule for success in these situations is not to restrict the opportunities for success but also not to underestimate the difficulties. Denial is not a long-term strategy.

Crises and government decision making

Once the label "crisis" is assigned to a situation, the event is immediately placed on the agenda of political controversy. But how does this occur? Assigning the label to an event or a series of events can be very problematic as the desks of senior bureaucrats and politicians are always cluttered with issues seeking that designation. Once the value of crisis is assigned, however, governments, political leaders, and other elites automatically become involved, but this does not mean that they will know what to do. Management theorists have summarized the leadership predicament as falling under one of three sets of conditions:

1. Certainty: "Alternatives in the choice to be made are known and each alternative is known invariably to lead to a specific outcome."[21]

2. Risk: The alternatives are known, and each alternative leads to one of a set of possible specific outcomes, each outcome occurring with a known probability.
3. Uncertainty: The probabilities of specific outcomes are unknown or perhaps not even meaningful.

Of course, leaders are likely to prefer the conditions of certainty, but the very nature of crises makes it much more likely that decisions will take place in the conditions of uncertainty or risk. Once the crisis label is designated, government resources will be assessed. In relatively routine policy-making situations, availability of resources such as manpower and finances is likely to be one of the predominant variables determining the policy outcome, but a surprising, perhaps counterintuitive, conclusion of crisis research is that a government's standard arguments about limited resources is often conveniently forgotten when the "crisis" label is assigned to an event. This is particularly the case in wars and rebellions, but it is also true of decisions regarding other types of crises.

Many sections of this book have assumed that states and international institutions are composed of a single hierarchy. Of course, this is not accurate, as demonstrated in the section on decision making in Chapter 4. States and international organizations have complex internal processes with many subunits, and they may or may not be arranged in a workable, hierarchic form. In a crisis situation, therefore, a number of actors and institutions may get involved – perhaps too many to be effective. Interdepartmental conflict and rivalries may prevent coherent action, and on occasion subunits may even act against overall government goals. The Cuban Missile Crisis is often cited as proof of this thesis.[22] After Russian missiles were deployed on Cuban soil, President John F. Kennedy, the White House, the Pentagon, and the State

---

[21] These classic definitions are from D. W. Taylor, "Decision Making and Problem Solving," in *Handbook of Organizations*, ed. J. G. March (Chicago: Rand McNally, 1955), p. 50.

[22] G. T. Allison, *Essence of Decision: Explaining the Cuban Missile Crisis* (Boston: Little, Brown, 1971).

Department prepared for a war over Cuba but simultaneously attempted to manage the crisis without war. They proved successful, but Graham Allison's classic study found that the overall decision resulted from a complex set of choices by major players, results of minor games among officials, and even foul-ups (see Chapter 3).[23]

At the onset of a crisis, decision makers base their actions on relatively simplified models of reality and change, seeking the most obvious solutions in an attempt to produce the conditions of certainty. Short-term answers rather than long-term planning tend to be paramount, and alternative or radical policies for handling the issue are usually given short shrift. Leaders are likely to choose the first alternative that seems reasonable rather than continuing to search for a perfect solution. This is called satisficing. Policy making tends to be incremental (step by step) and in line with what is normally acceptable in similar circumstances. Transformational change is rare, as government policy tends to develop through slow, disjointed incremental steps. As issues escalate, lines of command are usually shortened to exclude those who may wish to subvert the decisions of top leaders, and as a crisis is seen as a serious turning point in politics, leaders and officials are affected by psychosocial factors and perhaps stress and suspicion (see Chapter 4).[24]

Governments attempt to assure the public that the event or situation is being handled well. Public opinion is important. Symbolic outputs such as positive statements and robust commitments may be as important as those that require funding, extensive personnel, or materials. Some type of coercive force – military, police, and administrative authorities – is also likely to be employed when an event is termed a crisis and therefore deemed important to decision makers. Of course, as we saw in Critical Case Study 16.1, the details of each

crisis are highly contingent on contextual factors. Moreover, since there is assumed to be urgency in a crisis, routine policy making (e.g., legislation, regulations, government expenditures) is likely to be shunted aside during the resolution of the crisis.[25] After the crisis is over, governments will always prepare postincident analysis, create new plans, and categorize what they think they have learned from the events. Almost always, officials conclude that there was insufficient planning and that important factors were neglected or that information deficiencies were too great to avert the crisis. The U.S. presidential commission with which we began this book was set up just after 9/11. It reported its findings on prevention of mass destruction, proliferation, and terrorism in 2008, but most of its recommendations have still not been implemented as of 2013.

Media and crises

When a government attempts to respond to a crisis, it automatically will be involved in public relations. If the crisis is depicted as an "institutionalized drama," as crises tend to be in democracies, then information processing and media management will be crucial to government officials. The current 24/7, nonstop, in-your-face media makes the detachment required for handling crises difficult, if not impossible. As the cliché goes, if CNN defines a situation as a crisis, it becomes one. Labeling or framing and masking are important, if controversial, parts of government-media relations.

Framing and labelling refer to the language used to describe a situation or event. We have seen that if an event is named as a crisis, then a government will have to resolve it in those terms. The U.S.-led attacks after 9/11 were defended as part of a "global war on terrorism," and President George W. Bush used this language to describe

23 Ibid.
24 R. Wohlstetter, *Pearl Harbour: Warning and Decision* (Stanford, CA: Stanford University Press, 1962).
25 See Robert Jackson, "Crisis Management and Policy-Making: An Exploration of Theory and Research," in *The Dynamics of Public Policy*, ed. Richard Rose (London: Sage, 1976).

his government's response to the situation. It was difficult for President Obama to shift this language without losing political support. In other words, the idea of a global war on terrorism was wonderful for rhetorical purposes to rally people, but it soon became a kind of straitjacket on U.S. policy. The concept "axis of evil" had the same effect on government–media relations. Masking refers to leaders' efforts to dampen down expectations about what can be done about a crisis. If 9/11 had been described as a criminal act and the legal response called for punishment for those who perpetrated or planned the attacks, then U.S. foreign policy would have differed substantially. Masking is sometimes called "lying" by the press and public, but in their response to changing circumstances, politicians are often caught between uttering "clichés" and "dissembling."

The "mediaization" of political events means that journalists compete over the speed and breadth of their news and announcements. Satellite communications have shrunk geographical space and reduced the time required for the flow of information. The twenty-four-hour news programs on cable television and social networks on the Internet have turned news into a quick, selective, undisciplined affair. The rush of journalists to cover the events in Egypt, Libya, Mali, Syria, Tunisia, and Yemen in 2011–13, for example, contrasts sharply with their much slower response and limited attention to violence in Côte d'Ivoire and Sudan and famine in Somalia. The media help define a situation. Sometimes they sensationalize it, and at other times they ignore it altogether. They pay particular attention to the emotional aspects of crises and much less attention to the actual administration of complex emergencies, a strategy that may generate greater profits for their companies and raise the profile of a particular event but one that does not lead to better-informed citizens.

The media play a vital role, but they are not strong on analysis and criticism. Not everything that appears obvious is true, and not everything that is true is obvious, but sometimes it seems that the world of the "commentariat" does not understand that principle. Perhaps we should all bear in mind the skeptical view expressed by T. S. Eliot in his poem "The Hollow Men":

> Between the idea
> And the reality
> Between the motion
> And the act
> Falls the Shadow.

Ethics in global politics

Ethics provides criteria for evaluating right and wrong in the actions of individuals and states in global affairs.[26] It guides the search for fairness, justice, and the proper allocation of rewards for virtue and punishment of vice. In Chapter 3 we studied the theories or conceptual lenses used to examine global politics and found that they often involve fundamental questions about the role of ethics in government affairs. Theorists differ over the importance of ethics in global politics. Some believe that international politics should be informed by liberal and constructivist ideas about values. Others do not. Some theorists think that international relations is beyond questions of ethics, while others believe that ethical considerations should be primary.

Perhaps the distinction between realists and liberals on this topic has had the most visibility in the discipline. The clearest arguments have often been articulated on questions of violence and war. Liberals, feminists, and constructivists write the most often about the importance of ethics and morality in informing their research and conclusions. Their shared belief, for example, that civil liberties

---

[26] Philosophers and theologians have long sought to formulate theories that would provide principles for resolving moral dilemmas. This is not the place to resolve the problem of determining how to achieve ethical rules, especially on a global scale. For a difficult but comprehensive view of moral theory, see Derek Parfit, *On What Matters*, vols. 1–2 (Oxford: Oxford University Press, 2011).

and peaceful methods of conflict resolution can be enhanced by ethical positions seems to contrast with the realist and Marxist notion that power is the fundamental concept in understanding international relations. When Immanuel Kant's ideas are contrasted with those of Niccolò Machiavelli on these topics, ethics is clearly the subject that separates them the most.

But scholarship in the field is much more nuanced than this simple comparison suggests. Realists do, of course, believe that national interests will and should be put ahead of ethics in determining foreign and defense policy, but even they understand that ethics may actually be a force in the development of what is seen considered as the national interest. The theologian Reinhold Niebuhr combined ethics and power in the famous expression that politics is about "moral man and immoral society."[27] Moreover, as we have seen throughout this text, globalization and the new security dilemmas have meant that states are not able to handle many of their problems in isolation from the rest of the world. Borders, oceans, and armies can no longer provide total security. As the world becomes ever more connected, a multilateral approach is necessary to handle the growing torrent of transnational issues and interconnected dangers. There is a need for cooperation and belief in a collective effort based on the idea of sharing and caring for a global commons. Multilateralism is required in crisis management, and this idea itself is based on an acceptance of common values and a belief that much of humanity faces the same types of issues. In fact, the very idea of narrow, selfish, national interests is being questioned in the 21st century.

The most significant distinction in ethics in international relations today is between those who believe the world cannot, and should not, act until there is a global government with perfect solutions to global issues and pragmatists who believe that leaders can and should proceed step by step long before a unified and unanimous view of ethics in global politics is achieved. In a world of 193 states, ten thousand nations, and more than seven billion people, achieving a consensus with one vision and specific shared values is bound to prove difficult if not impossible.

Perhaps the issue can be illustrated by contrasting the works of two scholars, philosopher John Rawls and economist Amartya Sen. Rawls's most famous book, *A Theory of Justice*, claims that it is possible to secure perfect agreement on what constitutes a just society, but that to do so requires putting in place *just* institutions and rules.[28] While Rawls wrote other books that added the need for overlapping consensus to the argument, his main claim was that just social outcomes require perfect institutions. Amartya Sen's book *The Idea of Justice* is a trenchant criticism of this idea.[29] Not only does Sen not accept that just institutions will produce social justice; he contends that we can agree that some outcomes are better than others, even without perfect institutions. Since perfect agreement is impossible to obtain, we should act without it on the basis of our knowledge of problems in the world and how they can be resolved. In fact, Sen believes that trying to reach agreement on what would be perfect institutions would actually prevent action. By applying reason, while acknowledging the turmoil of human life and experiences, Sen believes that we can identify clear social injustices today without waiting for a perfectly fair society to be organized. Since injustices can be identified, we should opt for policy changes that will eliminate them now. If we name the worst injustices (which we can find in documents like the *UN Human Development Report* and elsewhere), we can decide how to act appropriately.

In many theories of international relations the same division appears. Some scholars search for perfection in their theories, even though this search

---

27 Reinhold Niebuhr, *Mortal Man and Immoral Society: A Study of Ethics and Politics* (New York: Scribner, 1932).

28 John Rawls, *A Theory of Justice* (Boston: Harvard University Press, 2005). Also see his effort at reasoning about global issues in John Rawls, *The Law of Peoples* (Boston: Harvard University Press, 2001).

29 Amartya Sen, *The Idea of Justice* (Boston: Harvard University Press, 2009).

Figure 16.3 Can the world ever achieve the nirvana that Pablo Picasso evokes in this painting? The title, *War and Peace*, indicates that peace is a dream but war and crises are always with us. *Source:* DACS & AKG.

for the perfect hinders the search for the good. If there can never be a perfect theory on which all will agree, would we not be wise to concentrate on whichever part of each theory helps us understand a segment of reality better and which can help point out the injustices that could be prevented today? Many, if not all, international crises could and should be observed and managed through Sen's practical and sensible approach, and in Chapter 3

and elsewhere we have made the case for an eclectic approach to problem solving. If we are to keep alive man's greatest creations in liberty and justice, passing them from generation to generation, we are going to have to approach theory with modesty and an abiding concern to solve problems and crises throughout the 21st century. It is unlikely that a single theory of the polity or international relations will ever be accepted across the entire globe.

Figure 16.3 (*continued*)

Crises and change

Change is one of the certainties of life, and many crises concern political change. Everything about history is dynamic. States emerge, stabilize, and decay. Empires rise and fall. Civilizations and war and peace come and go (Figure 16.3). Global history tends to focus on the stability and instability of states and the security of citizens within them. The search to understand how political order and change take place in and between states has been traced through 2,500 years of political thought. During that period, some philosophers have believed that nothing ever really changes, whereas others have proffered that states develop by evolution or by distinct stages. These two issues of change and decay are persistent themes of Western thought and political science.

In the fifth century BCE, the Greek philosopher Heraclitus observed, "You can never step in the same river twice"; in other words, all things are in constant flux. On the other side of the coin, Aristotle (384–322 BCE) examined the reasons for stability along with the characteristics of "good" government in the Greek city-states. He described development in terms of the laws of birth, growth, maturity, and decay. For him, states developed in a manner fairly similar to the life stages of individuals.

Crises are critical times of change. Hazards, disasters, diseases, and wars are constants. They may mark periods of transition between one political system and another or between one social system and another. They trigger uncertainty, threat, and urgency of response, which may result in progress or decay. Crises are a permanent feature of human organization and are increasingly global in scope. Solving them requires ethical, creative and global leadership.

Select bibliography

Bammer, G., and Michael Smithson, eds., *Uncertainty and Risk: Multidisciplinary Perspectives* (London: Earthscan, 2008).

Boin, A., Paul 'T Hart, P. Stern, and B. Sundelius, *The Politics of Crisis Management: Public Leadership under Pressure* (Cambridge: Cambridge University Press, 2005).

Bovens, M., and 'T Hart, P., *Understanding Policy Fiascos* (New Brunswick, NJ: Transaction, 1966).

Canes-Wrone, B., *Who Leads Whom? Presidents, Policy, and the Public* (Chicago: University of Chicago Press, 2006).

Flynn, Stephen, *The Edge of Disaster* (New York: Random House, 2007).

Ormand, David, *Securing the State* (New York: Columbia University Press, 2010).

Geuss, Raymond, *Philosophy and Real Politics* (Princeton, NJ: Princeton University Press, 2008).

Rawls, John, *A Theory of Justice* (Boston: Harvard University Press, 2005).

Rosenthal, Uri, M. T. Charles, and 'T Hart, P., eds., *Coping with Crises: The Management of Disasters, Riots and Terrorism* (Springfield IL: Charles C. Thomas, 1989).

Sen, Amartya, *The Idea of Justice* (Boston: Harvard University Press, 2009).

Sil, Rudra, and Peter Joachim Katzenstein, *Beyond Paradigms: Analytic Eclecticism in the Study of World Politics* (New York: Palgrave, 2011).

Glossary

9/11 – the September 11, 2001 terrorist attacks on the United States in New York and Washington.

Absolute advantage – when a company or country could produce every good more efficiently than every other company or country.

Acid rain – precipitation made acidic through contact with sulfur dioxide and nitrogen oxides so that it damages forests, water quality, and soil.

Acquired immune-deficiency syndrome (AIDS) – a widespread and dangerous virus that in the 1980s became a medical, humanitarian, and economic issue of worldwide concern. Dramatic progress has been made since then in both treatment and funding, but infection is still high in some parts of the world.

Affective bias – refers to feelings of liking or disliking someone or something. These affective components drive the way information is perceived about events and outcomes, and how people view outcomes as good or bad.

Afghanistan Compact – an agreement that established the legitimacy of the interim government and paved the way for Hamid Karzai to take office as president of Afghanistan.

Al Jazeera – an Arab-based news network available since 2006, with twenty-four-hour English-language broadcasts, and among the top two hundred most visited Internet sites worldwide.

Alliance – a coalition of two or more states that combine their military capabilities to increase mutual security – not a collective security organization.

Al-Qaeda in the Arabian Peninsula (AQAP) – a terrorist group with headquarters in Yemen and linked to the international group al-Qaeda.

American Revolution (1776) – the American rebellion in which thirteen colonies in North America joined to break free from the British Empire. During this war for independence (1775–83), Congress issued the Declaration of Independence, rejecting the monarchy and proclaiming the new United States of America.

American Service Members Protection Act – a law that prohibits American cooperation with the International Criminal Court.

Anarchy – absence of political authority or government. A condition in which states are subject to few, if any, overarching institutions to regulate their conduct in the international sphere.

Andean Community – a trade group that includes Colombia, Ecuador, Peru, and Venezuela.

Anti-Ballistic Missile (ABM) Treaty – a treaty that limited the deployment of antiballistic missile systems to two sites each in the Soviet Union (Russia) and the United States. The United States withdrew from the ABM treaty in 2001, but the Russians still operate an antimissile defense system outside Moscow.

Antipersonnel Landmines Treaty (APLT) – a 1999 agreement that bans the use, production, stockpiling, and sale of antipersonnel land mines.

Antiterrorism Assistance Program (ATA) – provides partner countries with the training, equipment, and technology to find and arrest terrorists.

Appeasement – making concessions to another state in the hope of avoiding war or additional demands; most infamously associated with British Prime Minister Neville Chamberlain's acquiescence to Hitler's aggression in Austria and Czechoslovakia.

Arms control – bilateral or multilateral agreements for reducing the growth and proliferation of arms, and restricting the manufacture or deployment of weapons systems.

Arms race – a competitive buildup of weapons and military forces between and among states in a search for security.

Article 5 of the NATO Charter – allows the invocation of the mutual defense principle, which calls on all NATO members to come to the aid of any member attacked by another state.

Asia-Pacific Economic Cooperation (APEC) – a trade bloc of twenty-one members, including the most powerful

Pacific countries – China, Japan, Russia, and the United States.

Association of Southeast Asian Nations (ASEAN) – a trade bloc that includes Brunei, Cambodia, Indonesia, Laos, Malaysia, Myanmar, the Philippines, and Vietnam.

Asymmetrical warfare – armed conflict between belligerents of unequal strength in which the weaker party attempts to neutralize its opponent's advantages by exploiting its weaknesses.

Atomic bomb – nuclear weapons dropped on Hiroshima and Nagasaki in Japan, in August 1945, killing thousands of people.

Balance of payments – the flow of money into and out of a country through trade and investment, which creates either a surplus or a deficit.

Balance of power – a relatively equal distribution of power among states that is sufficient to maintain peace and security among rivals.

Balance of trade – the value of a country's exports relative to its imports.

Bargaining model of war – posits that decisions to go to war are part of a process between adversaries to settle disputes and disagreements over items of value such as territory or resources.

Behavioral approach – the methodology of striving to use scientific methods such as measurement, data, and evidence to explain or predict political phenomena by discovering uniformities in political behavior.

Beijing Consensus – a term applied to China's economic approach, which combines state capitalism with political authoritarianism or communism.

Biological terrorism – the deliberate dispersal of pathogens through food, air, water, or living organisms to cause disease and death.

Bioterrorism – the use of biological weapons for purposes of terrorism.

Bipolarity – a situation in which states coalesce around two poles of attraction; for example, two states and their allies share power on the international stage and compete with rival poles of attraction. Describes the global order dominated by the United States and the Soviet Union until the latter fell apart.

Bipolar balance of power – two rival superpowers dominate allied states as they pursue their military, economic, political, and ideological goals.

Blogs – online diaries that people use to spread information and ideas.

Bretton Woods – a 1944 agreement by allied states to create a credible international economic order, including a monetary system based on the U.S. dollar being tied to the value of gold, and other countries' currencies being linked to the dollar. It led to a series of cooperative economic institutions and arrangements dedicated to lowering barriers to international trade and investment.

Buddha – a sixth-century Nepalese aristocrat whose philosophical ideas spread from northern India to Tibet, China, Southeast Asia, and Japan.

Byzantine Empire – a Christian empire based in Constantinople, now Istanbul, Turkey.

Cap-and-trade (carbon trading) – a scheme to reduce carbon emissions by making it expensive to emit greenhouse gases, in which government sets an overall cap on the amount of pollution specific companies can emit, and then either sells or gives out permits, each representing a ton of carbon dioxide that companies can buy or sell. In theory, emissions should decline over time.

Capitalism – an economic system based on the private control of business and minimal governmental regulation of the private sector; human labor and its products are bought and sold in a market.

Carbon sinks – areas of water, forests, and farmland that absorb carbon through photosynthesis.

Carbon tax – a tax that countries may impose on carbon fuels to reduce the use of fossil fuels.

Carrying capacity – the maximum number of humans that can be supported in a given territory; it refers to the planet's ability to support and sustain life.

Caste system – a hereditary system delineated in terms of certain occupations, rules of marriage, and rules of interaction with other castes dating back to the origins of Hinduism more than two thousand years ago.

Certainty – in management theory refers to situations in which alternatives for a decision are known, and each alternative is known to lead invariably to a specific outcome.

Chapter VI of the UN Charter – the "pacific settlement of disputes" clause allows the Security Council to act when international peace is threatened.

Chapter VII of the UN Charter – allows the Security Council to enforce its decisions by imposing embargoes and sanctions or by taking collective military action.

Chemical weapons – includes agents such as mustard gas and nerve gas that can cause mass casualties.

Chicken – a game-theoretical scenario that applies to confrontational crisis situations.

China's first industrial miracle – began about 600 BC and culminated during the Sung dynasty; achievements included textile manufacturing, water-powered spinning machines for hemp and silk, iron and steel production, and smelting to produce cast iron.

Christianity – a religion based on the doctrines of Jesus Christ and his apostles.

Citizens – individuals, not subjects, with the status to be able to participate and be represented in a state, and with rights such as life, liberty, and property.

Civil wars – internal wars fought between rivals for control of individual states or regions within states.

Classical realism – a theory that explains relations between states and justifies their foreign policies. In its classical form, it begins with the assumptions that individuals are primarily selfish and power seeking, and that states act in their own national interest.

Climate change – extended alteration in the world's climate by natural causes, human activities, or some combination of the two.

Cognitive bias – refers to limitations of the human brain in making choices caused by perceptual distortion and illogical interpretations. These biases come from many causes and processes, such as hindsight, framing an issue too narrowly, or a tendency to search for or interpret information in a way that confirms one's preconceptions and self-serving analyses.

Cold War (1949–89) – the world-wide rivalry between the United States and the Soviet Union, and their competing alliances of the North Atlantic Treaty Organization and the Warsaw Treaty Organization (WTO).

Collective hegemony – shared responsibility of great or major powers to maintain stability in international affairs.

Collective security – a belief that organizations of states can enforce international law by taking collective action to stop a country if it commits aggression against another state; that is, aggression by any state will be met by the collective response of the others. Each state accepts that the security of one member is the concern of all.

Colonialism – the rule of a region or area by an external sovereign power.

Common Agriculture Policy (CAP) – A policy that subsidizes all EU farmers so they are brought up to the level of farmers from the states with the highest domestic subsidies. It came into effect in the EU in 1962.

Common market – a free-trade arrangement with a customs union and common policies on capital, labor, and the movement of goods and services.

Comparative advantage – the idea in liberal economics that since businesses and states differ in their ability to produce goods, it is better for each to produce the goods that it can make most efficiently and acquire other goods from elsewhere.

Compellence – using or threatening force to get an adversary to do something against its will or desire.

Comprador **class** – a term used to depict indigenous people who are "bought" by former colonizers and become part of the exploitation carried out in the postcolonial period.

Comprehensive Nuclear Test-Ban Treaty (CTBT) – a 1996 treaty that bans the testing of all nuclear weapons and provides a world monitoring system.

Concert of Europe – the pledge of the five dominant European powers – Austria, Britain, France, Prussia, and Russia – to cooperate to maintain peace and stability on the continent, 1815–1914.

Conditionality – refers to conditions on loans from the International Monetary Fund that require aid recipients to fix the conditions and practices that led to the need for the loan in the first place.

Confucianism – a philosophy that originated in China; the teachings of Confucius became orthodox doctrine and dominated Chinese ethical and political thought, especially in the north, until roughly the 20th century.

Congress of Vienna – established peace in 1815 after Napoleon's forces were crushed at the Battle of Waterloo.

Connally Amendment – an American amendment to the optional clause that declares that the jurisdiction of the International Court of Justice will apply only "as determined by the United States."

Conscription – forced enlistment in the military.

Consequentialism – an approach to evaluating ethical choices on the basis of the results of the action taken.

Containment – a strategy to prevent an opponent state from using military force to alter the balance of power or increase its sphere of power. First espoused by an American diplomat, George Kennan, in 1947.

Convention on Cluster Munitions (CCM) – a 2008 agreement signed by most countries of the world but, by 2013, ratified only by seventy; it prohibits the use, production, stockpiling, and transfer of cluster munitions.

Convention on Genocide – a 1948 UN convention adopted as a treaty and legally binding on all signatories.

Convention on the Elimination of all Forms of Discrimination against Women – a 1981 convention that, through its protocols, outlaws trafficking in women and makes discrimination against them illegal in private and public life.

Convention on the Rights of the Child – a 1984 UN convention that defines a child as a person younger than the age of eighteen, unless the laws of a particular country set the age for legal adulthood lower.

Convention on Transnational Organized Crime – a 2003 UN convention that, along with its protocols on trafficking in persons, was the first legally binding instrument to deal with organized crime.

Conventional weapons – a term used to describe traditional weapons such as pistols, rifles, artillery, and tanks.

Council of Ministers – ministers from each member state of the EU representing particular policy fields.

Counterinsurgency – when the government and/or foreign power opposes irregular guerilla attacks by insurgents with overt and covert measures.

Counter-Terrorism Committee – established by the United Nations after 9/11 to help member states combat terrorism.

Coup d'état – a domestic military strike against the government.

Crimes against humanity – defined in the Treaty of Rome as crimes that can come before the International Criminal Court; includes enslavement, forcible transfer of people, and torture.

Critical theory – focuses on how existing political relationships can be changed so that people can be freed from social, economic, or political constraints.

Crusades – journeys organized by the papacy in the 11th century in an attempt to wrest the Holy Land from Islam.

Cultural relativism – the idea that rights are culturally determined, not universal, and that they differ from one social and state system to the next and from one historical period to the next.

Customary international law – implicit rules of behavior and conduct based on usage or practice; rules that are binding on states with or without explicit consent.

Customs union – an agreement in which countries adopt a free-trade zone between the participating countries and a common external tariff for imports from the outside world.

Cyberspace – a term used to describe the global electronic web of people, ideas, and interactions on the Internet, to a large extent uncontrolled by states and borders.

Cyberterrorism – attacks on a state's telecommunications and computer networks, to destroy technological systems vital to economic and defense institutions.

Cyberwarfare – warfare based on cyberweapons that attack vital government infrastructures in energy, nuclear, transportation, banking, and commerce as well as military and government targets.

De facto state recognition – a state's recognition that another state is an independent governing entity, on the basis of practical or pragmatic considerations.

Defensive realists – realists who argue that because states achieve security by maintaining their position in the international system they constantly will try to maintain an appropriate or adequate degre of power in relation to other states.

De jure state recognition – a state's recognition that another state is an independent governing entity, on the basis of formal legal recognition and involving the concept of legitimacy.

Defensive war – a war to protect a state's territory, government, and people.

Deficit – at the state level, a situation that arises when more money flows out of a country than into it, and the country has a deficit in its balance of payments.

Democracy – a political system that reconciles competing interests with competitive elections.

Democratic peace theory – a theory that holds that wars do not develop between or among democratic states. Advocates argue that the mere existence of democracy promotes peace and reduces the possibility of war; a hotly contested idea.

Department of Homeland Security (DHS) – a department of the U.S. government responsible for securing American borders and protecting ports from illegal immigration, security risks, drug smuggling, and human trafficking.

Dependency school – a branch of global politics that blames the plight of developing countries (especially the least developed countries), on their being incorporated into the global, capitalist economy during periods of colonization and subsequent neocolonialism.

Dependency theory – a theory based on the premise that less developed countries are exploited by global capitalism.

Deterrence – preventive strategies for the avoidance of war as a result of each side threatening a great-enough response that an initial strike would be irrational or counterproductive.

Development – The processes or political steps required to increase a state's capacity to meet its people's basic human requirements and raise its standard of living. A broad term used to distinguish among countries that have or have not achieved high development levels or as the "process" by which states evolve to higher levels of economic and political success.

Diplomacy – the art of conducting official relations among countries.

Diplomatic immunity – the protection of ambassadors and diplomatic staff from the laws of host countries.

Dispute Settlement Panels (DSPs) – panels set up by the World Trade Organization or NAFTA and composed of experts to hear trade disputes among members, and having the power to demand the end of discriminatory practices and to authorize retaliatory sanctions on violators.

Divided societies – societies in which ethnic or religious groups or nations are not satisfied with the states in which they reside or where religious groups harbor long-standing quarrels and hatreds about the leadership of their countries and would prefer to exist in a new state.

Divine Right of Kings – the concept underpinning centralized power of sovereign monarchs in the Middle Ages, who ruled as the personification of law and by the grace of God.

Doha Round – the ninth, continuing round of the World Trade Organization discussions on trade and development.

Durand Line – the unverified border between Afghanistan and Pakistan.

Economic and monetary union – a treaty with free trade, a customs union, a common market, and a common currency.

Economic globalization – the global integration of goods, services, capital, and markets; accepted as a fundamental shift in social organization.

Economic nationalism – a state-centered philosophy of economic and government relations that dominated economic thought from the development of the Westphalian state system until the pre–World War II period. See *mercantilism*.

Economic summits – meetings of some of the largest economic powers that have taken place annually since 1975.

Emancipation – a highly contested concept in international relations that is usually associated with an idealistic belief in the positive transformation of the world.

Emissions-trading scheme (ETS) – a system that allows countries to buy and sell emission credits from other countries.

Empire – a single political unit that rules other groups and states directly or through intermediaries.

Empirical theory – deals with the observable world and how it can be understood scientifically.

Energy security – refers to an adequate supply and ensured delivery of energy.

English School of international relations – a form of liberal interpretation holding that the globe may consist of separate states but that those states exist in much more than pure anarchy.

Epistemology – the study of knowledge and justified beliefs that examines questions such as: What are the necessary and sufficient conditions of knowledge? What are its sources? What is its structure, and what are its limits?

Espionage – spying.

Ethics – Ideas that provide criteria for evaluating right and wrong in the actions of individuals and states in global affairs. They guide the search for fairness, justice, and the proper allocation of rewards for virtue and punishment of vice.

Ethnic cleansing – a form of genocide that seeks to remove or exterminate an ethnic group from a particular geographical area.

Ethnic groups – groups based on family, blood relatives, distant ancestors, or some form of kinship such as clans or tribes.

Ethnicity – a primarily subjective characteristic of "sameness" shared by groups of people with similar ancestral customs, language, dialect, and/or cultural heritage, and sometimes distinct racial characteristics.

Ethnocentrism – the tendency to see one's own group, nation, or state, as superior to other groups and to depict out-groups as less worthy of fair treatment.

Euro – the common currency of participating members of the European Union (seventeen states as of 2013).

Euro-Atlantic Partnership Council (EAPC) – a forum for forty-six countries of diverse backgrounds and security traditions to cooperate on security issues in Europe.

European Central Bank (ECB) – in 1999 the ECB replaced domestic central banks and most members of the European Union adopted a single currency, the euro.

European Coal and Steel Community (ECSC) – a 1952 agreement among Belgium, France, Italy, Luxembourg, the Netherlands, and West Germany to create sectoral free trade in coal, iron, and steel.

European Commission – the permanent bureaucracy of some twenty-five thousand Eurocrats that initiates, administers, and oversees EU legislation and policies and is led by twenty-seven commissioners, one from each member state.

European Council – consists of the political heads of each EU member state and sets the broad agenda for the EU.

European Court of Human Rights (ECHR) – a European court that dominates in the area of human rights abuse.

European Court of Justice (ECJ) – a court that imposes law on citizens inside all states of the European Union. Its regional power has vastly increased over time.

European Parliament – a body of 754 members of Parliament as of 2012, directly elected by voters in each country for a five year term; in certain fields it shares legislation determination with the Council of Ministers.

European Stability Mechanism (ESM) – a 2012 permanent reserve plan that was to follow the European Financial Stability Facility. Almost all EU countries agreed to adopt a "fiscal compact" that would commit them to keeping their budget deficits to less than 3 percent of gross domestic product.

European Union – created by the Maastricht Treaty in 1992 from the European Economic Community with three pillars of supranational institutions and European citizenship. All nontariff barriers to the movement of goods, services, capital, and persons were removed, and foreign policy cooperation was established as a goal.

Exceptionalism – the belief that one's state is better than other states or has a unique historical mission to fulfill.

Exchange rate – the value of a country's currency compared to that of others.

Failed states – countries that have disintegrated to a point at which the government has collapsed and the country has fallen into civil war or states without a functioning government or a government unable to control the instruments of coercive force such as military, police, and a criminal justice system.

Failing states – countries close to disintegration because their governments have lost (or never had) adequate authority over their peoples and territories.

Famine – as officially defined by the UN, a situation in which 30 percent of children are severely malnourished, 20 percent of the population has no food, and deaths are at least two per ten thousand adults or four per ten thousand children every day.

Fanaticism – excess of loyalty to a cause and the willingness to risk anything for it, including death.

Federal Reserve (the Fed) – the U.S. central bank institution responsible for controlling inflation and maintaining employment and growth while supporting the government's broader objectives.

Federal state – a state with at least two levels of government but which integrates all aspects of economics inside the composite state so that the country functions as a single unit.

Female genital mutilation (FGM) – clitoridectomy (excision of the clitoris), which deprives a girl of sexual sensation, and infibulations (the cutting away of all of a female's external genitalia and labia tissue).

Feudalism – a medieval European political system with a hierarchically organized system of rights and obligations, based on a "chain of being," with God and monarchs at the top and commoners as serfs or pawns at the bottom.

First world – a defunct category of states that included those that were considered both politically and economically developed.

Fixed exchange rates – international currency rates that are set at a fixed value.

Floating exchange rates – currencies that change value in relation to the value of one another.

Foreign direct investment (FDI) – international investment that includes buying ownership or partial ownership of foreign companies or real estate.

Foreign Intelligence Surveillance Act (FISA) – established under the administration of President Jimmy Carter to allow the United States federal government to use electronic methods in the surveillance of citizens and resident aliens alleged to be acting on behalf of foreign governments.

Foreign policy – government decisions that have external ramifications, including diplomatic and military relations among countries.

Foreign portfolio investment (FPI) – international investment that includes shares in stocks and bonds in foreign countries.

Foreign trade – the export and import of goods and services or the exchange of commodities among states.

Framing and labelling – the language used to describe a situation or event; for example, if an event is framed as a "crisis," then the government has to resolve it in those terms.

Free market – a market in which the distribution and costs of goods and services are determined by supply and demand, not by governments.

Free trade – an agreement or treaty in which two or more countries substantially eliminate trade barriers.

Free Trade Area of the Americas (FTAA) – a proposed free-trade area that would have created the world's largest free-trade area, including the entire Western Hemisphere.

Free-trade zone – an area with few barriers to the movement of goods, services, capital, and sometimes labor.

French Revolution (1789) – a revolution that led to the overthrow of the most powerful monarchy of Europe; the rallying cry was "Liberty, equality, and fraternity!"

Game theory – the use of games of logic and mathematics to predict bargaining outcomes; an approach to the analysis of making rational decisions on the basis of how players in a game react to different types of situations.

Gender Inequality Index (GII) – a new dimension for measuring the overall equality of women in the world adopted by the authors of the 2010 *Human Development Report* (HDR).

General Agreement on Tariffs and Trade (GATT) – established following the meeting at Bretton Woods, as both a treaty and an institution. As a treaty, it set out a code of rules for conducting trade in order to promote free trade. As an institution in Geneva, it provided a forum for discussion of trade problems and negotiating solutions. In 1995 GATT became the World Trade Organization.

General Assembly – consists of all member states of the United Nations and basically a deliberating body whose decisions are not legally binding on states.

Genocide – defined in the Treaty of Rome as crimes such as systematic extermination by killing, causing harm, or imposing intolerable conditions on members of specified national, ethnic, racial, or religious groups.

Geopolitics – refers to the role that territory, resources, and location play in global politics.

Global Aging Preparedness (GAP) Index – part of a study that applies two separate subindexes, fiscal sustainability and income adequacy, to twenty selected countries to compare how they maintain economic growth and the ability to help seniors without imposing crushing financial burdens on a smaller, younger workforce.

Global civil society – a sphere or community of people, events, organizations, networks, and their norms and ethical behavior that includes the family, the state, and the market, and that operates beyond states in the transnational arena and outside government control.

Global peak oil – refers to the theoretical point in time when the maximum rate of global petroleum extraction is reached; after that point, the rate of production would enter irreversible decline.

Global politics – the patterns of international beliefs and behavior that help define and condition states and other actors; interests and power transcend states.

Global structure – describes the defining characteristics that shape the actions of actors such as states, intergovernmental organizations, and other institutions in the global system.

Global system – the broadest network of relations among states, intergovernmental organizations, and the activities of citizens and nonstate actors; consists of parts but is also more than the sum of its parts.

Global Terrorism Database (GTD) – the most comprehensive unclassified database of terrorist attacks held by the U.S. government.

Global Viral Forecasting Initiative – an organization that runs virus-monitoring stations in China, Laos, Madagascar, Malaysia, and Democratic Republic of the Congo in an effort to locate viruses when they enter human populations.

Global war on terror – an extremely broad goal based on the U.S. declaration after 9/11 "to answer these attacks and rid the world of evil." For the Bush administration, it justified the ensuing wars in Afghanistan and Iraq.

Global warming – a long, slow rise in the average world temperature, which is currently taking place at an alarming speed and to a high degree is caused by human activity.

Globalization – the integration of states and people through increasing contact, communication, and trade that binds the world together.

Gold standard – the exchange of gold and silver among countries as forms of payment for goods and services, which makes the metals the equivalent of an international currency.

Government bargaining or bureaucratic model – a decision-making model that assumes that decisions result from constant bargaining among various government actors and organizations that are likely to hold different views about the goals and utility of each course of action.

Great Game – the competition between Victorian Britain and tsarist Russia over power and influence in Central Asia, and especially over the routes to India, during the 18th and 19th centuries.

Great powers – the most powerful countries in the world economically and militarily at any particular time. Often interchanged with the concept major powers.

Greenhouse effect – a phenomenon in which the burning of fossil fuels acts like a blanket on the earth's atmosphere, trapping solar energy that would otherwise escape into space, making temperatures rise, and affecting both weather and climate.

Gross domestic product (GDP) – a measure of the total goods and services of a state.

Gross world product (GWP) – the total value of goods and services produced in the world.

Groups of 5, 7, 8, and 20 (known as G5, G7, G8, and G20) – annual forums of political leaders with consultations on a wide range of economic and political issues and efforts at collaboration on global economic problems.

Group of 77 (G77) – during the 1970s a coalition of developing countries that brought demands to the UN and receive considerable support for a new international economic order. Sometimes referred to as "the global South."

Groupthink – the tendency for members of a group to disregard contradictory information and to go along with, rather than stand up to, popular decisions.

Hard currency – money that can readily be converted to the value of the major currencies.

Hegemon – a single state that, while not holding absolute power, remains far more powerful than all other countries and can therefore dominate the patterns of world politics and create rules for others to follow.

Hegemony – the power or predominance of one state over others. Hegemonic stability theory refers to the controversial idea that global dominance by a single great power is a necessary condition for a stable global order.

Hinduism – an ancient religion from the Indian subcontinent based on Brahmanism.

Holy Roman Empire – an empire (essentially located in Central Europe) less powerful and less centralized than the earlier Roman Empire. It was created in the 8th century by the pope, with Charlemagne as its first emperor.

Human Development Index (HDI) – a UN comparative measure that combines three basic capabilities for people – to live a long and healthy life, to be educated, and enjoy a decent standard of living.

Human immune-deficiency virus (HIV) – the precursor to and cause of AIDS. It damages the key cells of a body's immune system and makes it extremely vulnerable to normally preventable infections. It is transmitted by an exchange of bodily fluids through sexual contact, blood transfusion, shared intravenous needles, or open sores.

Human Rights Council (UNHRC) – a UN council of forty-seven states that handles human rights cases.

Human security – the security of people, including their safety, well-being, and protection of their human rights. The term expands the concept of security so that the list of possible reasons for UN intervention includes civil war and human rights issues, as well as economic, health, and environmental problems.

Human trafficking – the trade in people by illegal means such as force, fraud, or deception with the aim of exploiting them.

Humanitarian intervention – the use of UN peacekeepers to protect people from violations of human rights, disintegrating order, lack of food and medicines, and mass murder or genocide.

Hypernationalism – the point at which nationalism becomes virulent, divisive, and threatening.

Hypothesis – a statement or generalization presented in tentative and conjectural terms.

Idealism – the notion that ideas have significant effects on events in international relations and that ideas can change; often depicted as utopian by realists and others.

Identification – the way individuals empathize with the economic and political conditions that affect others.

Identity group – a group of people who share a characteristic or characteristics that define them and set them apart from others.

Ideology – an organized set of ideas and values that purport to explain and evaluate social conditions and propose guidelines for action.

Imperial overstretch – a term coined by Paul Kennedy to explain the rise and fall of great powers.

Imperialism – a situation in which one country controls another country or territory against its interests or desires; imperialism provides hierarchy and subordination in global relations.

Incrementalist model – a decision-making model that assumes that most problems are complex and inter-related, and that since political decision makers operate in a climate of uncertainty and limited resources, they tend to proceed one step at a time, or incrementally, in their approach to problems.

Industrial Revolution – the transformation from an agricultural to an industrial economy that took place in the later part of the 17th-century in Britain.

Inequality-Adjusted Human Development Index (IHDI) – a measure of the average level of human development that takes inequality into account.

Institutions – the persistent sets of rules and practices that prescribe roles, constrain activities, and shape the expectation of actors; institutions include organizations, bureaucratic agencies, treaties and agreements, and informal practices accepted as binding.

Insurgencies – engagement by relatively small rebel forces in low-level asymmetrical warfare against state authorities and their more powerful militaries.

Inter-American Convention on Transparency in Conventional Weapons Acquisitions – a convention that requires member states of the Organization of American States to report on the export and imports of all weapons.

Intergovernmental organizations (IGOs) – international organizations based on state membership that contribute to cooperative international activities and help resolve disputes.

Intergovernmental Panel on Climate Change (IPCC) – a UN panel with input from more than two thousand of the world's leading scientists, set up to analyze overall warming and patterns of change over different geographical regions and seasonal variations.

Intergovernmentalists – those who argue that the states of the EU have not ceded any final authority to the EU.

Intermediate-Range Nuclear Forces (INF) Agreement (1987) – the most comprehensive of the strategic arms reduction treaties, covering missiles that travel 500–5,500 kilometers. NATO and the former Warsaw Pact member states agreed to eliminate all land-based INFs in their arsenals. Intermediate-range weapon – a weapon, such as a cruise missile, that travels between 500 and 5,500 kilometers.

Intermestic – issues that are simultaneously domestic and transnational or global.

Internally displaced people (IDPs) – people who have been forced from their homes for reasons similar to refugees but who remain within their own country's borders. They may receive no aid and often live in inadequate conditions.

International Atomic Energy Agency (IAEA) – part of the UN system and responsible for monitoring nuclear facilities to prevent noncompliance with the NPT treaty. The IAEA has a duty to report violations of the treaty.

International Commission on Intervention and State Sovereignty (ICISS) – established by the UN and the Canadian government to inquire into future situations of social violence, genocide, and ethnic cleansing, as had occurred in Bosnia, Kosovo, Rwanda, and Somalia.

International Court of Justice (ICJ) – the primary judicial organ of the United Nations, in The Hague, Netherlands, sometimes incorrectly referred to as the "World Court."

International Covenant on Civil and Political Rights (ICCPR) – a 1966 UN covenant on negative rights adopted as a treaty and legally binding on the signatories.

International Covenant on Economic, Social, and Cultural Rights – a 1966 UN covenant on positive rights adopted as a treaty and legally binding on signatories.

International Criminal Court (ICC) – a permanent court set up in The Hague in 2002 to alleviate deficiencies in the use of ad hoc tribunals. It deals with four types of international criminality.

International Implementation Force (IFOR) – NATO's first ground-force operation, used to help implement the Dayton Peace Accord for the former Yugoslavia, later called the Stabilization Force (SFOR).

International law – the binding rules of conduct among states.

International Monetary Fund (IMF) – an institution set up following the Bretton Woods summit along with the World Bank and the General Agreement on Tariffs and Trade (GATT) to make rules, settle disputes, and punish wrongdoers in the global economy.

International norms – expectations about global relations and their appropriateness, which can develop over time and be manifest in cooperative behavior that is regarded as mutually beneficial.

International organized crime (IOC) – includes activities such as trafficking in people, narcotics, small arms, and nuclear material; the smuggling of illegal aliens; and money laundering.

International political economy (IPE) – an academic field of study that examines the complex interrelationships of politics and economics.

International regimes – networks of norms, rules, and decision-making processes that act as guides to states and decision makers in solving common problems.

International relations – the traditional study of the relations among states.

International Security Assistance Force (ISAF) – the combined members of NATO and other military allies in Afghanistan.

International Stabilization Force in Afghanistan (ISAF) – the 2006 NATO mission in Afghanistan, the first mission outside the Euro-Atlantic region.

International wars – large scale and geographically dispersed wars, such as World War I and World War II.

Iron Curtain – the name given by Winston Churchill to the division of Europe between the forces of democracy and communism.

Islam – a religion founded by Muhammad (570–632 CE). Apart from spiritual guidance, it provides a comprehensive system of law and instructions for good government.

Isolationism – a policy of remaining apart from other states to avoid entanglement in their political affairs.

Jewish homeland – the state of Israel, which was created in 1948.

Jihad and McWorld – terminology used by Benjamin R. Barber in which jihad refers to the forces of self-righteous, fanatical devotees of religious, ethnic, national, or political groups and *McWorld* refers to the forces of greed and capitalism.

Jurisprudence – legal philosophy or the science and philosophy of human law.

Kyoto Protocol – an agreement that followed from the 1997 Kyoto conference in which thirty-seven major industrialized countries agreed to slash carbon emissions to 5 percent below 1990 levels by 2012 and to adopt a cap-and-trade system that would allow countries to buy and sell emission credits from or to other countries.

Laissez-faire – the policy that there should be minimum intervention by government in economic affairs so that competition and markets are free to act efficiently in the distribution of goods.

Law – a body of enacted or customary rules recognized by a state as legally binding.

League of Nations – an international institution set up after World War I to provide collective security and prevent war. The U.S. Senate blocked American membership in the organization. The League failed in its primary task of preventing war.

Legalism – the concept that individuals possess certain individual rights and can only be deprived of those rights only by due process.

Legitimacy – a requirement that those who govern should possess the consent of the governed.

Less Developed Countries (LDC) or Lowest Least Developed Countries (LLDC) – terminology used to categorize states at the bottom of the economic ladder; includes countries characterized by extreme poverty.

Levels of analysis – international relations framework used to explain events by examining individuals, states, and the international system as separate actors.

Liberal institutionalism – an idea based on the belief that reason and ethics can lead to international organizations and laws that can bring about orderly, cooperative and just international relations.

Liberalism – the view that human nature is basically good; holds that people and states are capable of improving their moral and material conditions, thus making societal progress possible.

Limited disarmament – a policy of reducing or destroying weapons or other means of attack, including weapons of mass destruction (WMDs).

Limited war – a regional war involving fewer great powers than world wars and entailing less destruction; generally fought for restricted goals, such as preventing an enemy from taking over new territory.

Lisbon Treaty – a proposal by the EU to strengthen economic and political integration but diluting some of the provisions of an earlier proposed constitution that had failed to gain acceptance; passed in 2009.

Long-cycle theory – a theory of history that argues that empires always fail because of a war that shatters one equilibrium and imposes another with a new unrivaled power. In time, this cycle repeats itself. Contrasts with power-cycle theory.

Maastricht Treaty (1992) – a treaty that created a framework for the further "deepening" of European integration by creating not only the European Community but also the European Union.

Market – a place at which people sell and purchase goods and services; also refers to terms on which the exchange of commodities for goods or for money takes place or how much to pay or charge for what one buys or sells.

Marshall Plan – a plan for the United States to come to the aid of Japan and the European economies crippled financially from World War II, providing them with billions of dollars and assistance to rebuild their countries.

Masking – leaders' efforts to dampen expectations about what can be done about a crisis; sometimes called "lying" by the press and public.

Mediterranean Dialogue – developed by NATO to enhance its geographical reach.

Mercantilism – a state-centered economic philosophy in which the government regulates its country's commercial interests and trade by encouraging exports and discouraging imports to increase the country's financial wealth and power.

Mercenaries – civilians who fight wars for personal, usually financial, gain.

Merchandise trade – the import and export of tangible items, such as primary goods, raw materials, and manufactured goods.

Methodology – the manner of gathering, measuring, and explaining information.

Middle powers – countries that are not great or major powers but have significance in a geographical region outside their own borders or locality.

Military Review Tribunals – U.S. military institutions set up to determine the status of prisoners who were considered "unlawful enemy combatants."

Mirror image – the tendency of individuals or groups to see in opponents the opposite characterizations of those they see in themselves, or when the sides in a political contest see themselves in a positive light as friendly and compromising, but cast their adversaries in a negative light as bad, aggressive, or untrustworthy.

Mixed polarity – the global system in a state of multipolarity, accompanied by the increasing significance of intergovernmental and nonstate actors.

Model – a normative ideal that all should seek to emulate, or a simplified version of reality that is designed to show how various components or parts fit together as a whole.

Modern state system – ushered in by the Treaty of Westphalia (1648), states were no longer subject to higher religious authority but were sovereign entities with defined rights and obligations.

Monotheism – belief in one God.

Moral hazard – an economic term used to depict the tendency to take undue risks because the costs are not borne by the party taking the risk.

Most favored nation – a concept that requires states to treat all members of GATT the same as they treat their most favored trading partners.

Movement – a collective or group that is ideologically inspired, usually idealistic, action oriented, and that aims at social change.

Mukhabarat – an intelligence service, with a coterie of informers, that bolsters an authoritarian ruler, mainly in Middle East and North African states.

Multi-Dimensional Poverty Index (MDPI) – a UN measure designed to complement money-based income studies that examines the number of deprived people and the intensity of their deprivation in terms of health, education, and standard of living.

Multi-Lateral Debt Relief Initiative (MDRI) – a program intended to assist the 2015 UN Millennium Development Goals endeavor by ensuring that no poor country is burdened with a debt it cannot manage, thus allowing 100 percent debt relief on eligible debts for some countries.

Multilateralism – cooperation among countries or international institutions to manage shared problems through collective action.

Multinational corporations (MNCs) – also called transnational corporations (TNCs); businesses that extend across state borders, with subsidiaries (wholly or substantially owned companies) and employees in one or more other states.

Multipolar – the distribution of power into three or more poles of attraction, with most states allied with one of the great or major powers.

Mutual assured destruction (MAD) – a strategic doctrine that calls nuclear deterrence theory a "game of Chicken" because any miscalculation or irrational act could result in human annihilation.

Nation – a cultural entity, a sense of social belonging, and ultimate loyalty based on a feeling of commonality. A nation may possess, or aspire to, autonomy, self-government, or independent statehood.

National Counterterrorism Center (NCTC) – a center under the auspices of the U.S. State Department that collects, analyzes, and shares relevant information and consolidates terrorist watch lists from the various agencies.

National Cybersecurity Center (NCSC) – a U.S. center to combat cyberterrorism, located in the Department of Homeland Security.

National identity – the creation or belief in a wide sense of familiarity and belonging through emotional attachment to geographical features of a territory; common experiences that promote pride; a common language; shared history, values, traditions, and customs; and perhaps even a common literature or sport.

National interest – the most important interests and goals of a state, namely the protection and security of its territory and sovereignty; often seen as selfish aspirations.

Nationalism – the collective action of a politically conscious ethnic group (or nation) in pursuit of increased territorial autonomy, sovereignty, or simply prominence. It embodies the idea that the nation is the primary unit of political allegiance and that boundaries of nations and states should coincide.

Nation-state – a problematic concept that implies that each state consists of only one nation.

Natural law – a body of principles for human behavior ordained by God or nature.

Necessary cause – a cause that is required but not sufficient in itself to determine a particular effect or condition. See *sufficient cause.*

Negative rights – freedom from the restraint of others, including the government; negative rights typically include free expression, assembly, press, and religion, and the right to a fair trial.

Neocolonialism – a situation in which colonizers may not actually govern newly independent states but indirectly control them through the actions of intermediaries.

Neoconservatives – a school of thought in the U.S. Republican Party that stresses an aggressive ideological and political agenda.

Neoliberalism – a modern school of liberalism that accepts some of the assumptions of realism, in particular the role of states in an anarchical framework, but retains liberalism as a philosophy with its stress on cooperation and peace through collective action.

Neo-Marxist approach – a radical political economy approach to public policy.

Neorealism – a revision of realism that discards the classical notion that human nature is inherently pessimistic and posits that the anarchical structure of the international system is the most important factor influencing the states within it. Also known as structural realism.

New security dilemma – the idea that an increase in a country's military strength may not provide a corresponding increase in its security because states are open to globalization forces, international terrorism, and transnational challenges.

New security issues – issues of how states and societies may be adversely affected by nonstate actors and the changing characteristics of global affairs.

New Strategic Arms Reduction Treaty (New START) – a ten-year agreement signed in 2010 that commits Russia and the United States to cut their nuclear warheads to the lowest level in half a century, adding a new monitoring regime and agreeing that within the following seven years they would reduce their strategic warheads to 1,550 from 2,200 and their launchers or delivery vehicles to 700 from 1,600.

New world order – a hypothetical new system of international relations built on the principle of collective values and security perhaps embodied in a world government.

Newly industrializing countries (NICs) – states such as South Korea, Singapore, Taiwan, and Hong Kong – sometimes called Asian tigers – that became prosperous as a result of their ability to produce and export manufactured goods to the developed world.

Nice Treaty – a 2003 treaty that instituted various reforms in the European Commission and European Council, such as expanding the use of majority voting.

No first use – the military doctrine that a nuclear state will not be the first one to use its strategic nuclear weapons.

Nonaligned Movement (NAM) – a group of newly independent countries that wished to advance the interests of the global South eventually growing to more than one hundred states that wished to escape from the clutches of the Soviet Union and the bloc of Western capitalist countries led by the United States.

Nonalignment – a policy of neutrality or not joining one of the great power military blocs.

Noncombatants – innocent bystanders in violent conflict.

Nongovernmental organizations (NGOs) – private organizations that carry out activities across state borders and take part in global activities such as transnational advocacy campaigns. Example: International Red Cross.

Nonproliferation of Nuclear Weapons Treaty (NPT) – a 1968 treaty that prohibits the sale, acquisition, and production of nuclear weapons to countries that are not already in the nuclear "club."

Nonrenewable resources – natural resources that are finite and limited in supply.

Nontariff barriers – the government imposition on incoming goods of special rules on health, security, and other items to discourage imports.

Norms – shared expectations about what behavior is considered proper.

Normative theory – theories that involve value judgments about the correct ethical or moral goals and behavior in politics.

North American Free Trade Agreement (NAFTA) – a free-trade bloc that includes Canada, Mexico, and the United States.

North Atlantic Treaty Organization (NATO) – an alliance established at the end of World War II to bind democratic states together in opposition to the threat of communist expansion.

Nuclear deterrence – the ability of each superpower to persuade others not to attack it by threatening retaliation with nuclear weapons.

Nuclear Suppliers Group (NSG) – the forty-six-state organization that sets rules for world nuclear trade

Offensive realism – a view that the degree of uncertainty about how states will act in the international arena compels states to maximize their power capabilities. States are seen as security maximizers.

Offensive war – a war to gain control of another country's territory or other advantages.

Official development assistance (ODA) – foreign aid, bilateral or multilateral.

Offshoring – the setting up by a corporation of production in a foreign country to employ cheaper labor or escape regulatory rules.

Old security issues – traditional state security and how states maintain their vitality in global politics.

Operation Enduring Freedom – the exclusive U.S. command in Afghanistan, not under NATO, allowing for other U.S. antiterrorist policies in the region.

Operation Iraqi Freedom (OIF) – a 2003 attack on Iraq launched by the United States and its "coalition of the willing" without UN agreement.

Optional clause – article 36 of the International Court of Justice Charter, which allows states to choose, or not choose, to accept its compulsory jurisdiction.

Optional Protocol on the Involvement of Children in Armed Conflict – a 2002 UN protocol ratified by 140 countries that requires states to set eighteen years as the minimum age for compulsory recruitment and fifteen years for volunteer enlisting in the military; it prohibits signatories from using children between the ages of fifteen and eighteen directly in hostilities.

Organization for Economic Cooperation and Development (OECD) – created in 1961 by the United States, Canada, and Western European countries to discuss economic issues, collect data, carry out studies, and provide economic and technical advice.

Organization of Petroleum Exporting Countries (OPEC) – an organization formed by large Middle East and Venezuelan producers in the 1960s in an effort to gain control of the international oil market; OPEC countries continue to produce about 40 percent of the world's oil.

Organization of the Islamic Conference (OIC) – an organization of fifty-seven states on four continents that aims to enhance the collective voice of the Muslim world.

Organizational process model – a decision-making model that describes how leaders make decisions, with the assumption that decision makers rely on standardized responses or operating codes to reach their policy conclusions.

Outsourcing – the contracting of services of one corporation by another, which thereby moves jobs out of the company and perhaps even the state.

Ozone layer – a protective layer in Earth's upper atmosphere that shields the planet from the sun's harmful impact on living organisms.

Pacifists – those who defend the view that all violence and war is morally wrong.

Pacta sunt servanda – the principle in international law that requires that states should observe treaties to which they are parties.

Pandemic – an epidemic of an infectious disease that spreads through human populations across a wide region or even around the world.

Partnership for Peace – a partnership developed by NATO to include Russia and former members of the Warsaw Pact in discussions about peace and security.

Patriot Act – U.S. legislation rushed through Congress after 9/11 to provide extensive tools for tracking down and prosecuting terrorists by increasing the government's capacities for law enforcement and intelligence collection.

Peace enforcement – the term used for UN military intervention in an armed conflict without the approval of the participants in the conflict.

Peace of Paris (1919) – a meeting of victorious powers after World War I that determined the peace terms for the defeated countries. The treaties reset the map of Europe and imposed stiff and controversial financial penalties on Germany. It also confirmed many of Japan's territorial gains and gave it mandates to German colonies in the Pacific.

Peace operation – encompasses both UN peacekeeping and peace enforcement activities.

Peacekeeping – a broad term used to describe the efforts of the UN, in situations in which the parties to the conflict agree to ask for UN help in violent conflicts such as civil wars or ethnic conflict, with the goal of limiting harm to noncombatants and preventing possible escalation to a larger war.

Podcasts – a type of digital media file that individuals can make with audio and visual images and then make them available for download.

Polarity – a term that characterizes a situation in which dominant states attract or repel other countries into their orbit of diplomatic power to varying degrees by their economic, military, and diplomatic capabilities. The degree to which the global system has poles or centers of power.

Political bias – the deliberate manipulation of the context and presentation of news so as to favor certain political interests over others.

Political economy – theories about the relationships between government and economics.

Political modernization – a branch of global politics that concentrates on a state's development in terms of its internal economic changes over time.

Political participation – the means by which groups and individuals participate in the political process.

Popular sovereignty – the concept that people are not serfs or subjects but citizens with rights who have a stake in their state.

Positive rights – legal rights or entitlements owed to individuals or groups by the government, such as the right to education, employment, welfare, hospital care, and an adequate standard of living.

Positivism – the belief that the accumulation of knowledge requires similarities in methodologies, that there is a stark distinction between normative and empirical research, and that there are observable regularities in the social and political worlds that can be understood by such methods.

Postbehavioralism – a modified approach that argues for both scientific and traditional approaches in the discipline.

Postmodernist approach – based on philosophical deconstructionism and the premise that comprehensive and satisfactory descriptions and explanations about politics are impossible and should be replaced by efforts to uncover the hidden motives of practitioners.

Poverty Reduction and Growth Facility (PRGF) – a program of the International Monetary Fund devoted to the very poorest of countries that provides loans at extremely low rates.

Power – the ability to influence and/or coerce others to accept certain objectives or behave in a particular manner through means ranging from influence to coercion.

Power configuration – the overall pattern of power and influence among states.

Power-cycle theory – the idea that a single dynamic of structural change contours the power cycles of all great powers. All such states reach an upper limit and decline as smaller states sustain higher growth rates. All great powers eventually fail, therefore, but collapse into a major war is not predetermined. Contrasts with long-cycle theory.

Preemptive war – a military strike to forestall an imminent enemy attack.

Preferential trade agreement – free trade that is accomplished by reducing trade barriers sector by sector. Sectoral free trade.

Preventive war – a war undertaken to stop a long-term increase in the power of a potential enemy and thus prevent a future attack.

Principle of reciprocity – the principle that states conform to international law most of the time because they want other states to do the same.

Prisoner's Dilemma – a conflict game used by international relations experts to show that rational players (individuals or states) can choose policy options that lead to outcomes such that all players are worse off than they would be with a different set of choices.

Prisoner of war (POW) – a military prisoner who falls under the Geneva Conventions and is sent home at the end of war.

Private international law – covers the routine activities of states and nonstate actors in fields such as international commerce, communications, and travel.

Propaganda – deliberate distortion of the truth to achieve political objectives.

Proportionality principle – comes from the just war theory; the violence employed in a war should be only to the degree necessary to attain the war's goals.

Protectionist measures – measures to prohibit or restrict foreign imports.

Protestant Reformation – a 16th-century movement aided by Martin Luther that undermined the authority of the Roman Catholic Church.

Public (collective) good – a good shared by all people such as air, water, public lands, and other benefits that markets cannot or will not supply.

Public choice approach – the study of economic nonmarket decision making, or more broadly, the application of traditional economics to political science.

Public international law – regulation of the relations among states and intergovernmental agencies such as the United Nations.

Purchasing-power parity (PPP) – an adjusted measurement that includes as a factor how much a country can actually purchase with its money.

Quad – the powers that dominate the decision making of the World Trade Organization: the United States, Japan, European Union, and Canada.

Quantitative easing (QE) – a central bank's purchase of large amounts of government and corporate debt, paid for with money the bank creates itself, which is released it onto the wider economy. It is intended to slash interest rates and stimulate consumption.

Race – an arbitrary social category consisting of people who share inherited physical characteristics such as skin color and facial features.

Racial discrimination – the imposition of handicaps, barriers, or different treatment on individuals solely because of their race.

Radical Islamic jihadists – those Islamists who are prepared to use violence and kill, justifying it by the Koran.

Rational actor model – a decision-making model that describes the elements or stages in the decision-making process by assuming that the government will attempt to maximize its strategic goals and objectives by analyzing the costs and benefits of all alternatives.

Rational choice – an approach in decision-making theory used to examine definitions of situations, weighing of goals, consideration of alternatives, and the selection of policies most likely to achieve those goals.

Realist theory – a theory based on the idea that global politics is essentially anarchic and that self-interested states struggle among themselves for power, with each state pursuing its own national interests.

Reducing Emissions from Deforestation and Forest Degradation (REDD) – an international agreement, agreed to by half a dozen countries at the 2010 Copenhagen Conference on the environment, to pay people in developing countries not to cut down trees.

Refugee – an individual who has a well-founded fear of being persecuted for reasons of race, religion, nationality, membership of a particular social group or political opinions, and has crossed borders.

Refugee migration – migration across borders occurs when people of one state seek refuge outside their country because their governments cannot provide law and order.

Regime – a term that refers to implicit or agreed-on rules, norms, and procedures for managing shared problems that emerge from high levels of state cooperation.

Regional international system – a set of interrelated states connected to form a whole in a particular geographical area.

Religion – an organized, institutionalized system of beliefs based on the superior authority of a supernatural being, or beings, the purpose of which is to instruct the faithful in morally responsible behavior.

Religious fundamentalists – those who believe in the literal truth of a holy text or texts that justify actions as God's will.

Renaissance – a European period of revival of art and letters under the influence of classical Greek models in the 14th to 16th centuries.

Rendition – sending noncitizen presumed combatants to other countries for interrogation and imprisonment.

Renewable resources – natural resources that are relatively abundant and not limited; that are renewed through natural processes.

Resilience – the ability to recover after a crisis.

Responsibility to protect (R2P) – a principle agreed to by UN leaders that holds that when a sovereign state fails to prevent atrocities to its own people, foreign governments led by the United Nations have the right to intervene and stop them.

Retribution-revenge cycle – when the actions of each side in a conflict are fueled by escalating demands for vengeance against the other.

Revolution in military technology (RMT) – new weapons able to hit targets with a very high degree of accuracy and reliability, such as precision-guided bombs and missiles controlled by lasers, satellites, and other guidance mechanisms.

Risk – in management theory, situations in which the alternative choices are known and each one leads to a particular "set" of possible outcomes, and each outcome occurs with a known probability.

Rule of law – an understanding that the citizen, no matter what his or her transgression, should not be denied due process of law.

Russian Revolution (1917) – Russian Bolsheviks fomented a civil war between communists and anticommunists. Radical communists under Vladimir Lenin seized power.

Safe havens – ungoverned, undergoverned, or ill-governed areas in which terrorists are able to organize, plan, and raise funds in relative security, allowing them to plan acts of terrorism.

Satisficing – the tendency of groups to seek conformity and solidarity and search for a solution that is simply "OK" rather than the most effective solution possible.

Satrapies – geographical divisions of large domains or empires, as in the Persian Empire.

Schengen Agreement – an agreement that allows people admitted to one EU state to move to the territory of "some" other EU member states without internal border controls.

Scientific theory – involves three elements: generalizations, new observations, and testability.

Second world – a defunct category of states that included those that were communist with neither a competitive party system nor a free market.

Second-strike capability – a situation in which one side must be able to withstand a first attack by weapons of mass destruction and still be able to retaliate at a level unacceptable to the aggressor. If both adversaries possess a second-strike capacity neither side could win a nuclear war, so mutual deterrence is achieved.

Secretary-general of the UN – chosen by the Security Council and approved by the General Assembly for a five-year renewable position.

Security and Prosperity Partnership (SPP) – an initiative signed in 2005 including Canada, Mexico, and the United States, aimed at deepening the integration of the three countries.

Security Council – a body of the UN set up to reflect political and military realities, with the primary responsibility of acting on questions of peace and security. There are five permanent members – Britain, China, France, Russia, and the United States – and ten temporary members elected for two-year terms by the General Assembly.

Security dilemma – the situation in which each state faces the dilemma of whether to increase military strength and provoke others or not to arm and leave itself vulnerable to attack. As states increase their security, it frightens others, thus encouraging them to strengthen their own militaries and security apparatuses and creating a cyclical dilemma.

Security – a primary function of the state, to defend its territory and people from physical violence or the threat of it.

Self-determination – the liberal view that people should be allowed to control their own affairs and be able to escape domination by others.

Separatist movements – ethno-national or ethno-regional movements that seek to form their own states.

Serfs – persons attached to the soil as the property of a ruler.

Services – intangible things, such as education, medical services, and transportation, which are sold and purchased in the marketplace.

Shanghai Cooperation Agreement (SCO) – a 2002 agreement that combines China, Russia, Kazakhstan, Kyrgyzstan, Uzbekistan, and Tajikistan into a Central Asian security organization.

Sharia law – Islamic law.

Shia – a branch of Islam that believes that the successor, or leader, of the Muslim religion must be a direct descendant of Muhammad.

Short-range weapon – a tactical weapon that travels only short distances, usually less than five hundred kilometers.

Single European Act (SEA) – an act signed by twelve European states in 1986 to remove the last impediments to the integration of Western Europe into a single economic market.

Slaves – persons who are the legal property of another and are bound to obedience.

Smart bombs – bombs that can penetrate bunkers and caves and detonate explosives at a precise moment underground.

Smart power – political strategies that consist of creating the right balance among military, economic, and soft power approaches to foreign policy.

Social constructivism – an offshoot of postmodernism that encompasses many, but not all, of its criticisms. As a theory it concentrates on the role of norms and values in understanding human organization and behavior. States are not determined by a realist anarchy but by the ways states socially construct and understand other states and their behavior.

Social identity – identity characteristics that have gained prominence in international relations theory in recent years, the main components of which are ethnicity, nationalism, and religion.

Social networking – communication between people online using new technology, such as Twitter and Facebook.

Soft currency – a situation in which a country's currency cannot be readily converted to the value of other currencies, as when a country suffers a major devaluation, caused, for example, by a high inflation rate.

Soft power – the means or attributes a state uses to ensure that it gets what it wants without resorting to coercion.

Southern Common Market (MERCOSUR) – established in 1995 as the largest trading bloc in South America. Its full members include Argentina, Brazil, Paraguay, and Uruguay. There are five associate members that do not enjoy full voting rights or complete access to the markets of the full members.

Sovereign wealth funds (SWFs) – state-owned pools of money that the state can invest strategically for political purposes.

Sovereignty – the legal doctrine that states possess supreme authority and share characteristics such as territory, authority, and recognition. It conveys a sense of legitimacy, and describes and justifies the notion that states should not intervene in the internal affairs of other states.

Special drawing rights (SDRs) – the International Monetary Fund finances its operations with money received from member countries and interest from its loans. The fund's unit of account is called special drawing rights, a virtual currency whose value is based on an average value or market basket of several currencies, including the U.S. dollar, the euro, the British pound, and the Japanese yen.

Special representative of the secretary-general (SRSG) – an appointed position of the United Nations with responsibility for managing part of the UN's mandate. An example would be the SRSG who is responsible for monitoring and reporting on child abuse in conflict situations.

Sphere of influence – a region of the world dominated by a great power.

Stag hunt – a game-theoretical scenario used in international relations to illustrate problems of coordination and trust.

State – a form of political organization in which governmental institutions are capable of maintaining order and implementing rules or laws (through coercion if necessary) over a given population and within a given territory. In everyday language, *state* is synonymous with *country*. States have three components – territory, population, and government.

State capitalism – an approach in which the state itself rather than private enterprise plays the prominent role in the economy; the approach of some of the most important states in the global economy, especially China. It is not a complete theory of the global economy but a belief in the power of the market combined with authoritarian rule.

State sovereignty – a number of characteristics, such as territory, authority and recognition, which convey a sense of legitimacy and describe and justify the notion that states should not intervene in the internal affairs of other states.

State terrorism – violence carried out by governments or clandestine operatives working for governments against other states or their citizens.

Statecraft – the art of managing state affairs by strategizing, negotiating, and bargaining with other states.

Strategic Arms Limitation Talks (SALT) – talks between the United States and Soviet Union to reduce their stockpiles of strategic missiles.

Strategic Arms Reduction Treaty 1 (START 1) – the first agreement by the USSR and the United States to make major cuts in long-range nuclear weapons; the treaty froze the total number of fixed land-based ICBMs SLSMs and bombers and reduced the possibility that one side could attack and win a nuclear war.

Strategic Arms Reduction Treaty 2 (START 2) – after the Soviet Union fell apart, this agreement between Russia and the United States called for bans on multiple-warhead, land-based missiles. The treaty was ratified by the United States in 1996 and Russia in 2000, but it never entered into force because of disagreements over the U.S. withdrawal from the ABM Treaty.

Strategic Defense Initiative (SDI) – a policy designed to establish a high-technology shield to defend American territory against incoming missiles to complement its deterrence strategy. An effort to deploy an antiballistic missile system using space-based lasers that could destroy enemy nuclear missiles.

Strategic Offensive Reduction Treaty (SORT) – a 2002 treaty in which the United States and Russia agreed to reduce warheads to about 2,200 each by 2012; ratified in 2003 but superseded by the fact that the earlier START I agreement came up for renewal.

Strategic weapon – weapons that travel over large distances to strike an enemy, such as intercontinental ballistic missiles (ICBMs) or submarine-launched ballistic missiles (SLBMs) or long-range bombers.

Strategy – plans dictated by an overall goal.

Strong currency – a currency that has relative strength over others.

Structural adjustment policies – policies of the International Monetary Fund that typically require a country to enact harsh economic reforms to eradicate the causes of its financial difficulties.

Structural realism – see neorealism.

Subsidy – a government's promotion of its own country's products and services by supporting them through financial subsidies to lower the costs of production.

Subversion – support for the rebellious activity of disaffected groups in foreign countries.

Sufficient cause – a cause that alone, without other contributing causes, can determine a particular effect or condition. See *necessary cause*.

Sunni – a branch of Islam that does not believe that the successor, or leader, of the Muslim religion must be a direct descendant of Muhammad.

Superpowers – contemporary concept for great powers, the United States and Russia.

Supranationalists – those who think that Europe should deepen its integration and head toward a type of federation similar to that of the United States and Canada.

Surplus – the situation in which more money flows into a country than out of it.

Sustainable development – an approach to economic development that seeks to reconcile economic growth with environmental protection, so that development can proceed while the world's resources are maintained, not damaged or used up, so that following generations will continue to have access to them.

Taliban – an Afghan Islamic and Pashtun tribal movement that originated in Pakistan during the Soviet occupation of the 1980s and today leads the opposition to the current Afghan government and the presence of foreign troops.

Tang dynasty (618–907 CE) – ruled for about three centuries, making China a massive, sophisticated empire.

Tariff – a type of tax on a foreign good or service that raises its cost and makes domestic equivalents cheaper and more acceptable to consumers.

Terrorism – the systemic use of violence or threat of violence against civilians and/or states to obtain political concessions from a designated enemy.

Theory – ways of making sense of events by explaining how or why they are interconnected, which means making an effort at generalization. A set of hypotheses that postulate relationships between variables or conditions that describe, explain, or predict phenomena.

Third world – a defunct category of states that included all the countries that remained outside the categories of "first world" and "second world." Basically the poorer and less developed countries.

Tigers of Tamil (LTTE) – an insurgent group in Sri Lanka that attempted for twenty-six years to establish a homeland (Eelam) in the north and east of the island.

Total War – when domestic populations are directly affected by the range of warfare; for example, when air power is used to bombard civilians.

Trade Policy Review Mechanism (TPRM) – a mechanism set up by the World Trade Organization to scrutinize trade practices.

Traditional peacekeeping – the actions of UN peacekeepers, at the behest of participants in a conflict, to maintain cease-fires and armistices; lightly armed UN soldiers, identified by their blue berets, act as buffers between militants.

Tragedy of the commons – a theory put forward by ecologist Garrett Hardin that holds that short-term, individual interests prevail over common concerns and issues.

Transnational advocacy groups (TANs) – social movements that include individuals or organizations that share the basic principles, normative objectives, information, and actions of the network and act across state borders.

Treaty – a legal contract and agreement between two or more state signatories.

Treaty of Amsterdam (1999) – a treaty that allows for the appointment of a president of the European Union and the appointment of a foreign policy envoy for the Common Foreign and Security Policy of the EU, indicating a desire to move forward in unified conflict prevention and crisis management.

Treaty of Rome – a 1957 agreement by the six ECSC members to establish the European Economic Community, with internal free trade and a customs union.

Treaty of Versailles (June 1919) – the treaty that ended World War I (1914–19).

Treaty of Westphalia (1648) – ended the Thirty Years' War in Europe, brought the final break between church and secular authorities, and began the modern state system.

Treaty on Conventional Armed Forces in Europe (1990) – signed between NATO and the Warsaw Pact, sharply reduced conventional force levels in Europe, limiting each alliance to equal inventories in five areas.

Triple Alliance (1882) – a military pledge by Germany, Austria-Hungary, and Italy to come to one another's aid if one was attacked by a great power.

Triple Entente – a 1907 pledge by Britain, France, and Russia to counter the Triple Alliance.

UN Register of Conventional Arms (1991) – a mechanism that requires states to list all major weapons exported or imported.

UN Secretariat – a permanent body of several thousand international civil servants.

Uncertainty – in management theory, situations in which the probabilities of specific outcomes are unknown or perhaps not even meaningful.

Unilateralism – one state acting alone, without other countries or international institutions, and having the ability to prevail in the strategy.

Unipolarity – when the international system has only one dominant state; in contrast to bipolarity or multipolarity.

Unitary state – a state with a single government over the entire territory.

United Nations – an international institution created in 1945 to provide stability and institutionalize global collective security; unlike the League of Nations, which preceded it, the United States became a member of the United Nations.

Universal Declaration of Human Rights – a 1948 declaration that recognizes "the inherent dignity" and "equal and inalienable rights of all members of the human family" and declares this to be "the foundation of freedom, justice, and peace in the world."

Universal values – values such as free speech, assembly, press, and religion that are defined as human rights belonging to all people.

Unlawful enemy combatants – individuals who are not military personnel fighting on behalf of a state but rogue terrorists (or freedom fighters, from their perspective).

Uruguay Round – the last completed round of GATT discussions, which lasted from 1986 to 1994. It made several breakthroughs, solving difficulties in the service sector and on intellectual copyright for patents and licenses.

Variable – a changeable phenomena such as a feature of a social situation or political institution that may appear in different degrees or forms in various situations and institutions.

Very high development – a measure used in UN Human Development Reports to refer to a country with a high per capita gross national product (GNP).

Veto – the ability to block a decision; for example, the five permanent member states of the UN Security Council have a veto over all Security Council decisions.

Voluntary migration – migration across state borders for convenience and choice.

War – clashes between organized military forces between two or more states.

War crime – defined in the Treaty of Rome as a crime that can come before the International Criminal Court; a crime that international organizations and states define as illegal.

Warsaw Treaty Organization – an organization formed in 1955 by the Soviet Union and its Eastern European allies (known as the Warsaw Pact or WTO); an alliance to counter NATO.

Washington Consensus – a term invented in 1989 by John Williamson to express a philosophy or set of ideas emphasizing that free trade enhances global development.

Wassenaar Export-Control Treaty (1995) – a treaty that monitors the transfer of some weapons technology.

Watchlist on Children and Armed Conflict – a network of international nongovernmental organizations that cooperates with the United Nations' attempts to end violations against children.

Weak currency – a currency that is relatively weak compared to others.

Weapon of mass destruction (WMD) – nuclear, chemical, biological, or radiological armaments that have become part of the arsenal of warfare. The purpose of WMDs is to produce massive carnage without discriminating between military and civilian targets. They can be small and easy to transport, and they are not necessarily prohibitively expensive.

WikiLeaks – an international, online, nonprofit organization that published private, secret, and classified government documents from anonymous sources and whistle-blowers.

Wikipedia – a free encyclopedia on the Internet for which articles are written, edited, and regulated almost entirely by unpaid volunteers.

World Bank – an institution set up following Bretton Woods along with the International Monetary Fund (IMF) and the General Agreement on Tariffs and Trade (GATT) to make rules, settle disputes, and punish wrongdoers in the global economy. Its initial purpose was to aid the reconstruction of Europe after World War II, but over time it has shifted its work to development goals.

World Health Organization (WHO) – a specialized agency set up by the UN in 1948 to monitor and respond to issues of global health such as malaria and smallpox.

World Trade Organization (WTO) – developed from GATT in 1995, with authority to administer multilateral trade agreements; today its membership comprises almost all countries of the world.

World war (or general war) – a war that involves a number of great powers, massive destruction of combatant and civilian lives and property, and extensive objectives such as destroying enemies or installing favorable governments.

World-system approach – a radical approach that regards the entire globe as one capitalist world economy with all the attributes of a single economy.

Yalta (February 1945) – after World War II Europe's borders (especially Germany's) were established at Yalta by Churchill, Stalin, and Roosevelt.

Zero-sum game – a theoretical game situation in which a participant can win only if another loses.

Zoonotic – a disease that is transmitted to humans from animals such as lice, rats, monkeys, or birds.

Index